THE LETTERS OF ERNEST HEMINGWAY, VOLUME 1: 1907–1922

"The delight of these letters and the sheer quantity of useful editorial material . . . should entice even the most ardent Papa-reviler to delve into the spontaneous words of a creative genius."
Publishers Weekly, starred review

"The existence of some of these documents (predating Hemingway's fame) is close to a miracle, and the Letters is without question a spectacular scholarly achievement."
Arthur Phillips, *New York Times*

"A work of monumental authority, shrewd and sympathetic, which will be indispensable for anyone delving into Hemingway's childhood affections, adolescent bravura, and the hope, enthusiasm and disgust of his early manhood."
Spectator

"His letters burst off the page with all his swaggering vigour, brio, brilliance, wit and rage, uncensored and unrestrained."
Sarah Churchwell, *Guardian*

"[Hemingway's] letters were never intended for publication, and they are surprising . . . Behind the hard-living, hard-loving, tough-guy literary persona we find a loyal son pouring his heart out to his family, an infatuated lover, an adoring husband, and a highly committed friend."
Robert McCrum, *Guardian*

"Hemingway admirers, scholars, and students will find the book essential. The letters fill in abundant biographical and intellectual details, and readers will revel in the young man's exuberant wordplay, private language, and slang."
Booklist

"Magnificently edited . . . [this volume] is a work of true literary scholarship . . . what makes this first volume more than a mere collection of juvenilia is that here is all the evidence of the writer – and the man – that he was to become."
Literary Review

"The collected Hemingway letters will be enthusiastically welcomed by the scholarly world as well as the legion of Hemingway enthusiasts around the world. He is not only one of the most important twentieth-century writers in the world, but a fascinating and frank letter writer. This collection will be an invaluable addition to the world of letters."
Noel Riley Fitch

"By any measure it's a Very Big Deal."
Roger Cox, *Scotsman*

"And so begins the ambitious – and highly anticipated – publication of The Letters of Ernest Hemingway, a vast collection that proves to be both a revealing autobiography and the passkey to his literary works."
A. Scott Berg

"To know what Ernest Hemingway was really like, don't read biographies of him. Read his letters."
Chronicle of Higher Education

THE LETTERS OF ERNEST HEMINGWAY, VOLUME 2: 1923–1925

"This essential volume, beautifully presented and annotated with tremendous care and extraordinary attention to detail, offers readers a Hemingway who is both familiar and new."
Times Literary Supplement

"With more than 6,000 letters accounted for so far, the project to publish Ernest Hemingway's correspondence may yet reveal the fullest picture of the twentieth-century icon that we've ever had. The second volume includes merely 242 letters, a majority published for the first time . . . readers can watch Hemingway invent the foundation of his legacy in bullrings, bars, and his writing solitude."
Booklist

"It would be hard to find a more crucial three year period in a writer's life."
Independent on Sunday

"This second volume of The Letters of Ernest Hemingway documents the years in which he became himself . . . His style is at once close to and yet unutterably distant from that of his fiction."
Michael Gorra, *New York Times*, Editor's Choice

"The volume itself is beautifully designed and skillfully edited . . . As a book, it is perfect."
Los Angeles Review of Books

"Never is Hemingway more fascinating or in flux than in these letters from his Paris years, that dark and dazzling confluence of literary ascendancy and personal maelstrom. Bravo to Sandra Spanier for giving us this dazzling gem of literary scholarship, and the young Hemingway in his own words—unvarnished, wickedly funny, mercilessly human."
Paula McLain, author of *The Paris Wife*

THE LETTERS OF ERNEST HEMINGWAY, VOLUME 3: 1926–1929

"The publication of Ernest Hemingway's complete correspondence is shaping up to be an astonishing scholarly achievement…. Meticulously edited, with shrewd introductory summaries and footnotes tracking down every reference, the series brings into sharp focus this contradictory, alternately smart and stupid, blustering, fragile man who was also a giant of modern literature."
– Phillip Lopate, *Times Literary Supplement*

"Reading Hemingway's letters is to go back in time by stepping into the fascinating world of a revolutionary wordsmith; a voyage through decades to the very moments when literature was taking a sudden bend in the road; a shift that was being steered by the father of modern literature. Indeed, the value of these letters cannot be overstated."
– Nick Mafi, *Esquire*

"This monumental publishing project… has reached the pivotal chronological moment in the late 1920s when Hemingway emerges as an astounding new voice in American literature…. Scholars will be deeply absorbed; general readers will find enjoyment and enlightenment."
– Steve Paul, *Booklist*

"*Volume Three*'s letters are an invaluable record of Hemingway as a professional author…another stellar contribution to a series of grand scope and vision, executed with rigorous professionalism, and resulting in a deeply satisfying volume for the reader and an unsurpassable resource for the scholar."
– James McNamara, *Australian Book Review*

"The newly published third volume of his complete letters gives a more nuanced picture of his life before nostalgia set everything in aspic. Away from the chisel work of his early fiction … the letters show Hemingway at play in figurative language, humour, meandering sentences and desultory subjects."
– Naomi Wood, *Literary Review*

"meticulously edited"
–Nicolaus Mills, *Daily Beast*

"The letters are profane, witty, gossipy, literary, emotional, and insightful...
Hemingway's boozing, boasting, and bullying have been well-documented elsewhere, but his body of work, and his letters here, illustrate what a truly great
writer he was."
– Paul Davis, *Philadelphia Inquirer*

"The correspondence reveals Hemingway as a ravenous reader and gossip, gob-
bling up books, short stories and newspapers—as well as the latest rumors... His
letters are speckled with slang, unorthodox spelling and punctuation, and creative
stabs at French, Spanish and German."
– Brenda Cronin, *Wall Street Journal*

"These correspondences, which are being published in up to 17 volumes, already
show that Hemingway was a disciplined and painstaking artist who relied on
mentors as he struggled to perfect his craft. He was also chatty and gossipy with
friends, a man whose epistolary persona differs in many respects from the laconic
speaking styles of his fictional protagonists."
– Tony Evans, *Idaho Mountain Express*

"What's most enjoyable is how lacking in self-consciousness Papa could be; he
didn't yet realise people would be keeping his bits of paper. Or he simply didn't
care, so one sees the brilliance and offensiveness all at once."
– *The Tablet*

"Like the first two installments, *Volume 3*... is expertly collected and annotated.
The quality of the ancillary details on each page is... unmatched by other letters-
compilations of famous writers—a testament to the passion, skill, and dedication
of the editorial team. The collection is a great achievement and a superb resource
for scholars of Hemingway's work and American literatures more generally."
– Jeffrey Herlihy-Mera, *Hemingway Review*

"... the range of correspondents and subject matter is extraordinary... This
volume is painstakingly yet unobtrusively annotated. Endnotes after each letter
explain obscurities with a sensitive anticipation of the reader's questions.... The
editors are scrupulous in their attention to detail..."
– Byron Landry, *Hopkins Review*

"It's difficult to overestimate the effect of this project.... It's clear that the publication of these letters is already stimulating scholars to revise prior judgments
and incorporate insights from them into new projects."
– Peter Coveney, *Firsts: The Book Collector's Magazine*

THE LETTERS OF
ERNEST HEMINGWAY
VOLUME 4
1929–1931

The Letters of Ernest Hemingway, Volume 4, spanning April 1929 through 1931, featuring many previously unpublished letters, records the establishment of Ernest Hemingway as an author of international renown following the publication of *A Farewell to Arms*. Breaking new artistic ground in 1930, Hemingway embarks upon his first and greatest non-fiction work, his treatise on bullfighting, *Death in the Afternoon*. Hemingway, now a professional writer, demonstrates a growing awareness of the literary marketplace, successfully negotiating with publishers and agents and responding to fan mail. In private we see Hemingway's generosity as he provides for his family, offers support to friends and colleagues, orchestrates fishing and hunting expeditions, and sees the birth of his third son. Despite suffering injuries to his writing arm in a car accident in November 1930, Hemingway writes and dictates an avalanche of letters that record in colorful and eloquent prose the eventful life and achievements of an enormous personality.

THE

CAMBRIDGE EDITION OF

THE LETTERS OF
ERNEST HEMINGWAY

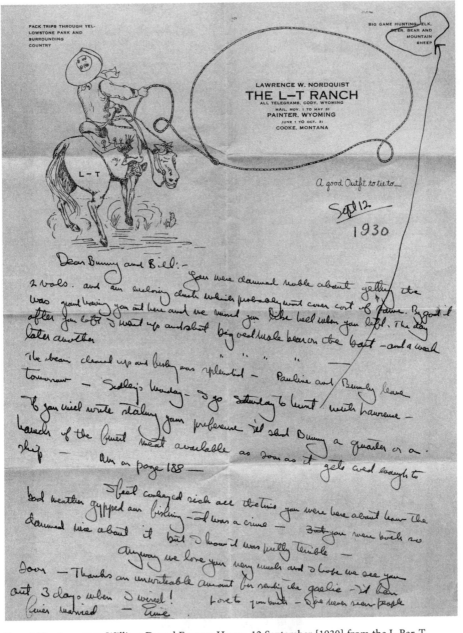

Ernest Hemingway to William D. and Frances Horne, 12 September [1930] from the L-Bar-T Ranch, Wyoming. The Newberry Library, Chicago, MMS Horne-Hemingway.

THE LETTERS OF
ERNEST HEMINGWAY

VOLUME 4
1929–1931

EDITED BY

Sandra Spanier
Miriam B. Mandel

VOLUME ASSOCIATE EDITORS

J. Gerald Kennedy
Rena Sanderson
Albert J. DeFazio III

CAMBRIDGE
UNIVERSITY PRESS

CAMBRIDGE
UNIVERSITY PRESS

University Printing House, Cambridge CB2 8BS, United Kingdom

One Liberty Plaza, 20th Floor, New York, NY 10006, USA

477 Williamstown Road, Port Melbourne, VIC 3207, Australia

314–321, 3rd Floor, Plot 3, Splendor Forum, Jasola District Centre, New Delhi – 110025, India

79 Anson Road, #06–04/06, Singapore 079906

Cambridge University Press is part of the University of Cambridge.

It furthers the University's mission by disseminating knowledge in the pursuit of education, learning, and research at the highest international levels of excellence.

www.cambridge.org
Information on this title: www.cambridge.org/9780521897365
DOI: 10.1017/9781139051361

First published 2018

Printed in the United States of America by Sheridan Books, Inc.

A catalogue record for this publication is available from the British Library.

ISBN 978-0-521-89736-5 Hardback

CONTENTS

PLATES

The plates are located between pages 228 and 229.

These illustrations appear courtesy of the following:
    Hemingway Collection, John F. Kennedy Presidential Library, 5–6, 10, 17, 24, 27–29, and with courtesy of Karin Peirce, 2; Bruce Family Archives, courtesy of Benjamin C. Bruce, 15, 18–20, 25–26, 31; Manuscripts Division, Department of Rare Books and Special Collections, Princeton University Library, 1, 14; Irvin Department of Rare Books and Special Collections, University of South Carolina, 11, 13; Louis Henry and Marguerite Cohn Collection, University of Delaware Library, 22–23; Fitzgerald Smith Papers, Archives and Special Collections, Vassar College Libraries, 4; Albert and Shirley Small Special Collections Library, University of Virginia, courtesy of Lucy Dos Passos Coggins and the Estate of John Dos Passos, 8; Beinecke Special Collections, Yale University Library and the Estate of Honoria Murphy Donnelly/Licensed by VAGA, New York, NY, 12; Hemingway-Pfeiffer Museum and Educational Center, 16; Wyoming State Archives, 21; Paul Quintanilla Collection, 30.

MAPS

GENERAL EDITOR'S INTRODUCTION

Sandra Spanier

PARIS, Nov. 18–Perhaps one in a thousand comes out of the sordid crucible of the Latin Quarter to contemporary literary fame. This percentage of achievement makes the bestseller "arrival" of Ernest Hemingway of Oak Park, Ill., a fitting subject of attention.

Hemingway really deserves oodles of attention. He coolly saturated himself with the night life of Montparnasse and then wrote "The Sun Also Rises," after which he made a mental cutback to his soldier life on the Italian front, and wrote "A Farewell to Arms."

New York Evening Post, 18 November 1929[1]

Hemingway's latest novel, released in New York by Scribner's on 27 September 1929, was an immediate critical and commercial success. In one of the earliest reviews, published just nine days later, James Aswell wrote: "I have finished 'A Farewell to Arms,' and am still a little breathless, as people often are after a major event in their lives. If before I die I have three more literary experiences as sharp and exciting and terrible as the one I have just been through, I shall know it has been a good world."[2]

By the time Aswell's letter enclosing the review reached Hemingway in Paris, *A Farewell to Arms* had already soared to the top of the bestseller lists. On 21 October 1929, Hemingway wrote to thank him (crossing out a mild profanity in the opening line): "Dear Mr. Aswell:– Your review just came and what the hell can I say—except that if the book made you feel like writing a review like that I'm a lucky bastard to have written the book." In a postscript he added, "This is a lousy letter but by Christ the review made fine reading for me."[3] To Maxwell Perkins, his editor at Scribner's, Hemingway wrote on 17 November, "In spite of having written the bloody book and having worked over it so much that I am completely unable to read it when I read this review I wanted to go right out and buy one—"

As volume 4 of *The Letters of Ernest Hemingway* opens in April 1929, the author is aboard the S.S. *Yorck* bound for France, returning to live in Paris after spending the past year in the United States. He is accompanied by his wife Pauline, their eight-month-old son Patrick, Hemingway's six-year-old son "Bumby" from his first marriage to Hadley Richardson, and his younger sister Madelaine, nicknamed "Sunny." Within weeks the first of ten serial installments of "The eagerly awaited New Novel" will appear in the May issue of *Scribner's*

Magazine.[4] After the book is published in September, he will begin filling sixty-seven scrapbook pages with clippings of reviews (now preserved among Hemingway's papers at the John F. Kennedy Presidential Museum and Library in Boston). Over the next two years, *A Farewell to Arms* will be adapted for the Broadway stage, appear in German and French translations, be dramatized in German for a run in Berlin, and the rights sold to the movies for $80,000.

The volume ends in December 1931, as Hemingway and his family, including a newborn son, have just taken up residence in an old Spanish-colonial-style house with iron railings and balconies, across from the lighthouse in Key West. "Mr. Hemingway, author of international fame, with his wife and two sons, Patrick and Gregory, are occupying the home recently purchased by him," the local newspaper, the *Key West Citizen*, reports on the front page with civic pride.[5] The Hemingway house at 907 Whitehead Street will quickly become a Key West landmark and remains a magnet for tourists and aficionados to this day.[6]

In the span of the thirty-two months covered in this volume, Hemingway makes four transatlantic crossings. He follows the bullfights across Spain, returning to Pamplona during the annual Fiesta of San Fermín in the summers of 1929 and 1931, all the while gathering material for his long-planned treatise on bullfighting. He travels to Berlin and to the Swiss Alps, rounds up friends for winter fishing expeditions to the Dry Tortugas in the Gulf of Mexico, and rounds up more friends for fishing and hunting in the mountains of Wyoming and Montana. Periodically he retreats to work alone in Hendaye or Madrid, or at the L-Bar-T Ranch near Cody, Wyoming, then rejoins family and friends for another round of camaraderie—all the while reporting in his letters the page counts of his work in progress. As Hemingway biographer Michael S. Reynolds astutely observes, "His contemplative and his active life are jammed together so tightly that only minutes separate them."[7]

In terms of Hemingway's creative output, the period of this volume is bounded by the completion and final revisions of *A Farewell to Arms* (with forty-seven surviving draft endings produced in the process—different ones appearing in the final *Scribner's Magazine* installment and in the published book) and completion of the first draft of his book on bullfighting, to be published in 1932 as *Death in the Afternoon.*

In between, he returns to the scene of his own beginnings as a writer, contributing an introduction for the translated memoirs of Alice Prin, the woman known as "Kiki of Montparnasse"—famed habitué of Left Bank cafés, model and muse for photographer Man Ray. Like Hemingway's own first two books, *Kiki's Memoirs* (1930) is a slim, limited-edition volume published by a small avant-garde press in Paris. Hemingway's other publications during this period include the 1930 Scribner's edition of his 1925 story collection *In Our*

Time, a bullfight article for *Fortune* magazine, and two short stories—"Wine of Wyoming" appearing in *Scribner's Magazine* and "The Sea Change" in the little magazine *This Quarter*.

In an automobile accident in Montana on 1 November 1930 (Hemingway at the wheel and John Dos Passos in the passenger seat), Hemingway's arm is badly broken, and subsequent surgeries and complications keep him hospitalized in Billings for seven weeks. After slowly and painfully regaining use of his right arm—his writing arm—he is finally able to resume work and finish the first draft of *Death in the Afternoon* by early December 1931.

Of the 430 items of correspondence included in Volume 4, about 85 percent are previously unpublished. Whereas each of the first two volumes (spanning 1907–1922 and 1923–1925, respectively) represents some sixty correspondents, and Volume 3 (1926–April 1929) represents ninety-nine, the letters in this volume are directed to 125 recipients.

As in the previous volume, Maxwell Perkins continues to be far and away Hemingway's most frequent correspondent, the recipient of eighty-seven letters (more than two-thirds of them previously unpublished). As testimony to their deepening friendship, Volume 4 includes twenty-three letters to Archibald MacLeish, compared to a total of nine letters to MacLeish in Volume 3. Perhaps surprisingly, the third most frequent correspondent represented in this volume is Hemingway's mother. Grace Hall Hemingway is the recipient of twenty letters over this period, during which Ernest and Pauline established a trust fund to provide financial security for her and his younger siblings following the suicide of his father, Dr. Clarence E. Hemingway, in December 1928.

Next in succession of frequent correspondents are the artists Waldo Peirce (eighteen letters) and Henry Strater (seventeen letters). Each painted an iconic oil portrait of Hemingway begun while visiting him in Key West, Peirce in 1929 and Strater in 1930. Milford Baker, a fellow veteran of the American Red Cross Ambulance Service in Italy during World War I, received fourteen letters from Hemingway—all written in 1930. After reencountering each other by chance in the elevator of the Abercrombie & Fitch sporting goods store in New York City, the two carried on an active correspondence. While Hemingway obligingly autographed books for Baker, Baker advised him on the best firearms and ammunition for hunting in the American West and on an anticipated African safari. Baker kept carbons of all his letters as well as Hemingway's responses, and the complete exchange—preserved at Princeton University Library—is a fascinating and detailed record of Hemingway's education as a big game hunter.

Other frequent correspondents of this time include Guy Hickok, Paris-based correspondent for the *Brooklyn Daily Eagle* (recipient of thirteen letters in this volume), followed by Hemingway's in-laws, Mary and Paul Pfeiffer (eleven and nine letters, respectively, some addressed jointly); bibliographer Louis Henry Cohn (ten letters); and F. Scott Fitzgerald tied with Kansas City obstetrician Don Carlos Guffey (nine each, with those to Dr. Guffey mainly written in the form of substantive inscriptions in first editions of Hemingway's books, relating their composition history).

The letters trace the ebb and flow of Hemingway's friendships and measure the increasing number and importance of his business associations. The diminishing number of surviving letters to F. Scott Fitzgerald is telling. Only nine are included in this volume, down from thirteen in the span of the previous volume, when their friendship was in full flower. The fact that Hemingway wrote seven of these nine letters to Fitzgerald between July and December 1929 and only one letter each year in 1930 and 1931 reflects the growing strain and distance between them that Scott Donaldson details in his Introduction to this volume.

Even more dramatic is the falling off in correspondence with Ezra Pound, arguably Hemingway's most important early champion and mentor, who helped pave his path to prominence among the Left Bank literati after the two met in Paris in 1922. Pound was the recipient of thirty-five letters in Volume 2, eighteen in Volume 3, and only four in Volume 4 (one of them a picture postcard from Havana).

Those new to the roster of correspondents in Volume 4 include a number of professional associates: Hemingway's French translator, Maurice-Edgar Coindreau; his German publisher, Ernst Rowohlt; Laurence Stallings, who wrote the 1930 Broadway adaptation of *A Farewell to Arms*; attorney Maurice Speiser; bibliographer Louis Henry Cohn, whose proposed project Hemingway initially resisted but ultimately supported; and Caresse Crosby, who with her husband Harry Crosby founded the Black Sun Press in Paris. After Harry's sensational murder-suicide with a mistress in 1929, Caresse carried on the work of the press and launched her own Crosby Continental Editions of inexpensive paperback avant-garde works, persuading Hemingway to let her publish *The Torrents of Spring* as the first volume in the series in 1932.

Hemingway's growing celebrity is marked by the number of recipients to whom he wrote only a single located letter—seventy-nine, or more than half the recipients represented in this volume—as he replied to fan mail, answered queries, and responded to requests for autographs. Many of these brief correspondences go well beyond the perfunctory. On 9 December 1931, Hemingway responded cooperatively to a questionnaire from Philadelphia endocrinologist Israel Bram, who had written to dozens of persons listed in *Who's Who of America* asking about their sleep habits. We learn that Hemingway never worked at night "because of difficulty of getting to sleep afterwards" and that "Brandy keeps me awake— rarely drink after eating at night except continuing beer and wine drunk with meal—" Prompted by the doctor's request for "personal or abstract" comments about sleep and dreams, Hemingway responded, "Enjoy sleep and dreams very much— Have gone with very little sleep for long periods due pain of wounds, infections, broken bones etc—very hard on nerves— Have often heard clock strike every hour and half hour from midnight to daylight—would like to sleep 9 hrs. every night—"

Only a handful of correspondents are represented in all four volumes of the edition published to date. They are his mother and siblings; Isabelle Simmons Godolphin, the girl next door as he was growing up in Oak Park; Dorothy Connable, whose family employed Hemingway as a live-in companion to her brother in their Toronto home in 1920; and Ezra Pound.

Of course, the number of located surviving letters is not a reliable indication of the importance or magnitude of a correspondence. People have to keep their mail, and we have to find it. From incoming letters that Hemingway saved and from his comments in letters to others, we know of letters he wrote that either do not survive or remain unlocated. We know, for example, that he corresponded regularly with Pauline's Uncle Gus Pfeiffer, a supporter of Hemingway's work and generous benefactor to them both. The Kennedy Library holds sixteen letters from Gus to Hemingway during the period of this volume, yet only three items from Hemingway to Gus have been located, two of them cable drafts that Hemingway kept.

Unfortunately (if understandably, from the recipients' perspective), the vast majority of Hemingway's letters to his first two wives, Hadley and Pauline, do not survive. Hadley burned most of his letters after he fell in love with their close friend Pauline and the marriage collapsed. Most of his letters to Pauline were destroyed after her death in 1951, in compliance with her stated wishes. This volume contains only one letter from Ernest to Hadley and two to Pauline. Yet the Hemingway Collection at the Kennedy Library contains fourteen incoming letters from Hadley written during the period of this volume, and twenty-six from Pauline.

Their surviving letters to him afford tantalizing glimpses into these relationships at this time. As might be expected, Hadley's letters frequently concern their son, Bumby—his tonsillectomy, his school report card, her wish that he not be raised as a Roman Catholic by Ernest and Pauline (despite her earlier consenting to their request to do so). But Hadley's letters to Ernest also testify to the enduring warmth between them. She signs off affectionately with variants on his old nicknames for her—Kat, Catherine Cat, Hadlein, and Haddlekat. In a letter postmarked from Paris on 27 April 1931, she seeks his "advice & opinion as a friend on Paul's and my situation," referring to journalist Paul Mowrer, whom she would marry in 1933: " Will you let me talk & you listen, and then if you'll talk I'll listen. Maybe you can help clarify things for me." Although we do not know what Hemingway said in return, we do know he responded: the back of the envelope bears the notation in his hand, "Answered May 28th."[8]

After Ernest and Pauline sailed separately from Key West to Europe in the spring of 1931, Pauline arrived in Paris to find letters from him waiting for her at the Guaranty Trust Company, which they used as their Paris mailing address. Again, the surviving incoming correspondence hints at the quantity and quality of his lost letters to her. "That was the loveliest collection of letters at the bank—13 of them and each more lovely than all the rest. Full of love and full of meat—the ideal combination," she wrote to him in Madrid on 30 May. "I came home and read and read and got more excited every minute and you are certainly the finest husband a woman ever had." Looking forward to joining him in Spain, she added, "Only a week now, and thanks for the enchanting beautiful letters & I'm going to cover them with gold stars and keep them forever" (JFK).

Hemingway loved getting letters. "Write me all the dope," he urged friends repeatedly, supplying his travel itineraries and the varying addresses where mail would reach him along the way. As he was following the bullfights in Spain in the summer of 1929, he wrote to Waldo Peirce from Valencia on 28 July to say that he and Pauline would be spending August at the Hotel Suizo in Santiago de Compostela: "Write me there. It is always fun to get letters but in Spain or in the country it is damned fine excitement."

Patrick Hemingway, the author's surviving son, has observed that his father tailored his letters to each of his correspondents as part of their continuing conversation, carrying on "a sort of going dialog with them about the things they had mutually in common."[9] To F. Scott Fitzgerald, who had been struggling for four years to complete his next novel after the success of *The Great Gatsby*, Hemingway ended his letter of 23 July 1929 by commiserating about the difficulty of writing: "Wish the hell I could work—will try again now," signing off, "Your afft. friend— / E. Cantwork Hemingstein." In a postscript he added, "This Couldn't be a duller letter but want to hear how you are and hope your work and everything goes well—"

The letters are laced with apologies for the quality or infrequency of his correspondence "Excuse this lousy letter" (to Waldo Peirce, 6 April [1930]); "Excuse this punk letter" (to his World War I comrade Bill Horne, 1 June [1930]). In a "Dear Family" letter to his mother and younger siblings, he wrote in August 1930, "Excuse brevity of letter and lack of general correspondence but when working cant write letters— Had to write so many this winter that ruined my work— Am sticking to work for a while—"

In Hemingway's hierarchy of priorities, letter writing clearly took a distant second place to his professional writing. "This is a lousy letter and I wish it could be a good one," he told Max Perkins on 31 July 1929. "Started a story day before yesterday and went pretty well then and yesterday. Am playing truant to be writing a letter now—" After the frustrating delay in his work on *Death in the Afternoon* as he regained the use of his broken right arm, he told Henry Strater around 1 May 1931, "for Christ sake forgive me either not writing or writing such a foul scrawl as this because until I get this book done I am unfit for human consumption—"

The letters vividly evoke the immediate circumstances of their composition. In a letter to Perkins of 20 November 1929, Hemingway explained his use of stationery embossed with the letterhead "Writing Room / Guaranty Trust Company of New York / 4 Place de la Concorde / Paris." Penning a letter on ten sheets measuring 5 ½ by 8 ¼-inches, he commented, "(This paper is too small to write on— They are doing some fumigating to the house and am turned out)." To his inlaws, Paul and Mary Pfeiffer, he wrote on 23 April 1930 with the expensive fountain pen they had given him for Christmas, "This is the great pen and if I'd had anything worthy of being written by it this letter would not have been so long delayed."

In several erratically spaced typewritten letters written between October and December 1931, Hemingway complained about the machine he was using (a gift from the manufacturer): "This bitch of a typewriter is a R emington noiseless presented by the company and it skips letters and makes typeing bloody impossible," he told Eric Knight around 19 October 1931.

Hemingway's commentary on his immediate surroundings—including the weather—adds to the conversational quality of his letters. "I've been lousy about writing because when get through work am too pooped— Then it's been hot too—really hot—42° and one day 46° in shade— Try that on your fahrenheit thermometer—" he wrote to Archibald MacLeish from San Sebastian on 29 June 1931. MacLeish was "a smart fellow" to be at Conway, Massachusetts, "working in the cool." "This is a punk letter Archie— There is something about writing becoming not a physically painful but merely an uncomfortable act that buggers up the writing of letters— If you were here I would tell you a lot of funny things but it is too damned physically uncomfortable to start writeing anything— This no complaint—just an explanantion—"

During the weeks Hemingway was confined to St. Vincent's Hospital in Billings with his arm immobilized, his only means of corresponding was by dictating letters to the ever-patient Pauline. Three are typewritten on "X-Ray Department" forms. In the 23 November 1930 letter to Bill Horne, she typed "Pauline P. Hemingway" in the space designated "Interne Attending." Hemingway did not take naturally or well to dictation.

"It is lousy to have my one writing tool, my right arm, busted in the way that it is," he told Max Perkins on 17 November: "as you see from this letter, I can't relie on dictating, but that's all I can do now, as I am still in bed in the same position that they put me in two weeks ago, and cannot move from side to side." He couldn't resist a bad pun in his 22 November letter to MacLeish, saying, "if this is the worst letter you ever got, it's because Mussolini is the dictator, not old Pappy." He continued to be amused by the double entendre, telling Guy Hickok in a letter of 5 December, "In case this letter should not seem sweet in tone, it is because it's being dictated. Pen pencil, or glass in hand I am the sweetest tempered of mortals (Mrs. Hemingway may refuse to type this). But dictating that old Primo de Rivera strain comes up."

Regaining the full use of his "writing tool" came slowly, and Hemingway's frustration with the physical impediments to his writing is a continuing refrain in his letters in early 1931. "Am typeing this with one hand and it goes damned slowly. By the time you get something to say and have it ½ typed have forgotten the rest of it," he told Waldo Peirce on 17 January. "Write me kid and dont pay any attention to what a bum letter I write because this method is just about as slow as building with blocks."

Hemingway's correspondence takes a variety of forms. During his summer 1929 travels through Spain, Hemingway wrote from his Valencia hotel to Guy Hickok in Paris that he had received five letters from Hickok and apologized, "I would try and do better but lack of typewriter makes punk letters" [c. 30 July 1929]. Writing a month later from Santiago de Compostela, he struck a similar note in a letter to Evan Shipman on 24 August: "It is hell for me to write a letter without the typewriter so please forgive this—" Obviously intended as an excuse for not writing more often, it is an odd comment nevertheless. Of the 430 items of correspondence in this volume, 290 of them, more than two-thirds, are handwritten letters. Only thirty-six are letters typewritten by Hemingway himself. The volume also contains twenty-one dictated letters, four postcards, forty sent cables, ten cable drafts, and ten transcriptions of letters made by biographer Carlos Baker and preserved in his files at Princeton University Library.

Hemingway said he never wanted his letters to be published and in 1958 typed out a directive to his executors to that effect. During his lifetime he had, in fact, consented to publication of a handful of his letters. He wrote others expressly for publication, including letters to the editor, public petitions, book jacket blurbs, and a few commercial endorsements (including for Ballantine's Ale and Parker Pens).[10] After his death in 1961, a trickle of additional letters appeared in print, and scholars began to call for publication of his letters to satisfy the "demand for literary history."[11] Finally, Hemingway's fourth wife and widow, Mary

Hemingway, in consultation with publisher Charles Scribner, Jr., and her attorney Alfred Rice, determined that the time had come to authorize publication of a volume of his letters. They chose as its editor Carlos Baker, the Princeton professor who had written the 1969 authorized biography, *Hemingway: A Life Story*. Baker's edition of *Selected Letters, 1917–1961* was published by Scribner's in 1981, encompassing 581 letters. Since then, a few other clusters of Hemingway's correspondence have been published, including letters he exchanged with Maxwell Perkins, his sister Marcelline, Sara and Gerald Murphy, and A. E. Hotchner.[12]

When the Cambridge Edition of *The Letters of Ernest Hemingway* was launched in 2011 with the publication of the first volume, only about 15 percent of Hemingway's some 6,000 known surviving letters were previously published. The project was authorized by the Ernest Hemingway Foundation and the Hemingway Foreign Rights Trust, holders, respectively, of the U.S. and international copyrights to the letters.

It is the express wish of Patrick Hemingway that this be as complete a collection of his father's letters as possible, rather than a selected edition. "I felt that if they were going to publish his letters at all, there shouldn't be any picking and choosing, that you either got the whole picture of him as a correspondent, as a letter writer, or nothing at all," he said.[13] Of his father's directive that his letters not be published, Patrick has said, "I find that puzzling. He surely was pretty savvy about these things. I mean the sign that you're destroying your letters is that you're destroying them." Beyond their obvious biographical interest, Hemingway's letters constitute a primary record of the history of his times. Likening his father's letters to the seventeenth-century diary of Samuel Pepys, who witnessed and wrote of the plague and the Great Fire of London, Patrick noted that Hemingway's letters "are a portrait of the first half of the twentieth century."[14]

The Cambridge Edition aims to be as comprehensive as possible, affording readers ready access to the entire body of Hemingway's located surviving letters, those previously published as well as those appearing here in print for the first time. The letters are presented complete and unabridged, arranged in chronological order of their composition. Although we do not publish the letters that Hemingway received, they inform our editorial comments on his outgoing letters.

Fortunately for posterity, Hemingway was a packrat. Like many writers, he saved drafts, manuscripts, and galley proofs of his published work, manuscripts of work in progress, and occasional carbon copies of business letters. But over the years he also preserved drafts and false starts of letters, letters he wrote but decided not to mail (sometimes scrawling "Unsent" across a dated envelope), and outtakes from letters that he scissored off or tore away before sending.

We define "letters" broadly to include postcards, cables, identifiable drafts and fragments, letters Hemingway wrote for publication, and those he thought better of sending but nevertheless saved. As a rule we do not include book inscriptions, except those the editors consider substantive or of particular interest. Volume 4 includes fifteen inscriptions that the editors feel meet those criteria.

Letters are transcribed whole and uncut whenever possible. However, when they are known only through facsimiles or extracts appearing in auction catalogs or dealer listings, or through published quotations, we present whatever portions are available, citing their source. While they are no substitute for the original documents, such extracts can serve as place markers in the sequence of letters until such time as complete originals may become available.

Because Hemingway did not routinely keep copies of his letters and because they are so widely dispersed, simply locating the letters has been a massive undertaking. It helps that Hemingway was famous enough at an early enough age that many of his correspondents beyond his family saved his letters. Furthermore, many recipients of his letters were sufficiently well known themselves that their own correspondence has been preserved in archival collections, with Hemingway's letters among their papers. His letters to Maxwell Perkins, F. Scott and Zelda Fitzgerald, Henry Strater, and others survive at the Princeton University Library; those to Archibald MacLeish at the Library of Congress; and letters to Waldo Peirce, along with photographs and scrapbooks, at Colby College. The Pennsylvania State University Special Collections Library holds a collection of more than one hundred previously inaccessible family letters acquired in 2008 from Hemingway's nephew Ernest Hemingway Mainland, son of Hemingway's sister Sunny. He also donated a trove of other family materials, including several volumes of scrapbooks that Grace Hemingway compiled for Sunny (as she did for each of her six children) and an ancient suitcase filled with newspaper clippings, sheet music, event programs, and other mementos of life in the Hemingway household.

To date we have gathered copies of letters from some 250 sources in the United States and around the globe. These include more than seventy libraries and institutional archives. The world's largest repository of Hemingway papers, the John F. Kennedy Library in Boston, has donated copies of all outgoing letters in its collection (some 2,500 letters). The edition has benefited from the generosity and interest of scores of scholars, archivists, aficionados, book and autograph specialists, collectors, and Hemingway correspondents and their descendants, including members of the author's extended family, who have provided valuable information or shared copies of letters.

As an important part of our editorial process, our transcriptions, initially made from photocopies or scans provided by institutional repositories and private owners, have been meticulously compared against the original documents on site visits whenever possible. For the most part only one authorial copy of each letter exists; thus we have faced few problematic issues of textual history and textual variants. When such issues do arise, they are addressed in the notes that follow each letter.

Since the Hemingway Letters Project was initiated in 2002 to produce this edition, I have learned that it is almost impossible to overestimate public interest in Hemingway and the broad appeal of his work. Dozens of people from around the world have contacted us to share information or copies of letters, and new letters continue to surface.

Based on the estimated number of letters we expected to find, we initially planned a twelve-volume edition. We now project the complete edition to run to at least seventeen volumes to hold the nearly three million words Hemingway wrote in letters, along with our own introductory materials, annotations to the letters, chronologies, maps, and other editorial apparatus. The final volume will feature a section of "Additional Letters," for those that come to light after publication of the volumes in which they would have appeared chronologically.

Hemingway's letters present more editorial challenges than some might expect from a writer so renowned for simplicity. In transcribing Hemingway's letters, we generally leave it to readers to experience Hemingway's language on their own as he wrote it, without editorial intervention or attempts at explication. We have preserved exactly Hemingway's idiosyncrasies of spelling, punctuation, syntax, and style, including his well-known habit of retaining the silent "e" in such word forms as "writeing" or "sizeable." To silently correct Hemingway's spelling and punctuation or to regularize capitalization in the letters would strip them of their personality and present a falsely tidy view of the letters his correspondents received. Such cleaning up also would render meaningless his own spontaneous metacommentary on the imperfections of his letters or his likely misspellings.

Typing a letter to Megan Laird on 1 January 1931, two months after his automobile accident, he began, "This is being written with the left hand, the right arm being at present and for some months to come, useless, so with your permission I'll let the caps go and you will not mind spelling etc." Despite his ardent admiration for MacLeish's long poem *Conquistador*, Hemingway was hesitant to write a blurb for it, explaining in a 10 April 1931 letter to Laurence Stallings his fear that "every little constipated dioehreic (mis-spelled) enemy I had would be transferred to him and that his poem was too damned good to need anything said on the jacket anyway."

Yet even as we attempt to preserve the idiosyncratic flavors of Hemingway's letters, we strive to make them as accessible and readable as possible. We have regularized the placement of such elements as dateline, inside address, salutation, closing, signature, and postscripts. We also normalize Hemingway's often erratic spacing and paragraph indention. No published transcription of a typed or handwritten letter can ever fully capture its actual appearance on the page. This is not a facsimile edition, and for those wishing to study in depth the physical characteristics of a letter, no printed rendition can substitute for an examination of the original.

In endnotes following individual letters we supply necessary contextual information, reasoning for conjectured dates, translations of foreign words and passages, and first-mention identifications of people in each volume. A more detailed description of our editorial practices and procedures appears in the Note on the Text in this volume. Our overarching aim is to produce an edition that is at once satisfying to the scholar and inviting to the general reader.

This project has benefitted tremendously from the support and interest of Patrick Hemingway, who has been unfailingly generous in supplying information, answering questions, and sharing anecdotes that only he can tell. One nagging question in our work on this volume concerned the name of Patrick's French nanny, who is variously referenced in Hemingway biographies as Henrietta or Henriette. Hemingway mentions her by name nineteen times in this volume's letters, and his handwriting is sometimes ambiguous. Biographer Michael Reynolds, apparently drawing upon a ship passenger list, gives her name as "Henrietta Lechuer."[15] But our editorial policies call for verifying all details with at least two reliable sources whenever possible. In April 2016, during what has become a delightful tradition of meeting for breakfast in Boston the morning after the annual PEN/Hemingway Award ceremonies at the Kennedy Library, I asked Patrick if he remembered his French nurse. "Henriette Lechner," he immediately replied (pronouncing her first name in the French manner). When I showed him a copy of the January 1930 passenger manifest of *La Bourdonnais* with her named spelled "Lechuer," he examined it closely, but posed the sensible question, "Why would I remember it another way?" The spelling on the ship passenger list was a typographical error. Once we knew the correct spelling of her name, we finally were able to locate more information about her by searching databases of historical records. Patrick also recalled staying with Henriette and her husband in Bordeaux when he was about six years old. "According to my dad, I would never have my heart broken by a woman because she did it first," he laughed. "She was the master of pommes frites."[16]

Conjecturing dates for undated letters is akin to putting together a jigsaw puzzle—trying to match up circumstances, stationery, the weight or length of a fish caught, Hemingway's word count of works in progress. Sometimes, particularly before or after his travels, or while he was staying at the Wyoming ranch with once a week mail service, Hemingway would write letters in clusters—

sometimes as many as five or six in a single day. The challenge then—even assuming the letters bear the day's date—is to determine the best sequence in which to present them in the absence of any internal clues (such as "I just finished writing to Archie"). We were fortunate to be able to call upon Valerie Hemingway, who worked as the author's secretary during the last two years of his life (later marrying his son Gregory) and knows better than anyone his habits of correspondence. Although Hemingway's correspondents of 1959–1960 were different from those of 1929–1931, Valerie outlined his approach to letter writing:

> He always started with business, Max Perkins (Harry Brague in my day), Charlie Scribner, Alfred Rice, and any other business, agents, foreign publishers, translators, etc. including Hotchner if they were discussing business. Then Carlos Baker, his chosen official biographer, if there was something to report or if Carlos had written to him. He followed this with close friends such as Buck Lanham, Harvey Breit, Lillian Ross, Bernard Berenson, Ezra Pound, Lenny Lyons and many, many more. Finally he wrote to the family, mostly to his sons, particularly to Patrick. In many of these cases as you will find out, he wrote virtually the same news with slight variations depending upon the recipient. Any unsolicited queries, requests for autographs etc. were considered after that.[17]

We have followed these general principles in arranging same-day letters in this volume: business first, then letters to close friends, letters to family, and finally, his more perfunctory responses to requests and queries.

Two months after the publication of Hemingway's 1929 novel, John Dos Passos wrote in a review for the *New Masses*:

> Hemingway's *A Farewell to Arms* is the best written book that has seen the light in America for many a long day. I don't mean the tasty college composition course sort of thing that our critics seem to consider good writing. I mean writing that is terse and economical, in which each sentence and each phrase bears its maximum load of meaning, sense impressions, emotion. The book is a firstrate piece of craftsmanship by a man who knows his job. It gives you the sort of pleasure line by line that you get from handling a piece of wellfinished carpenter's work.[18]

The contrast between the unhoned prose of Hemingway's letters and the meticulous craftsmanship of his published work could not be starker. The letters give a different kind of pleasure.

"Never for gods sake use or turn over to the advt. dept. anything I say in a letter—" Hemingway implored Max Perkins in late August 1929. Hemingway's letters are hasty, spontaneous, unfiltered, and unpolished. Cleaning them up for consumption was not where he chose to invest his efforts. He was certainly not writing them for posterity.

Writing to Perkins from the L-Bar-T Ranch in Wyoming on 30 September 1930, Hemingway acknowledged the freestyle nature of his correspondence: "My God Max I seem to write you the lousiest letters— But if I rewrite this and make it as decent as I wish it would sound it will take all tomorrow and the last mail for a week goes at breakfast—"

Each of Hemingway's letters captures the events and moods of a particular day and hour. Taken together they chart the arc of an epic life story and record an unedited running history of his eventful times. It is exactly in their lack of polish that the letters add texture, depth, and nuance to our understanding of their iconic author.

NOTES

1 Raymond G. Carroll, "Paris, the Real, As Seen Today / Hemingway Gives up Old Life With Literary Success," *New York Evening Post*, 18 November 1929, 6.

2 James Aswell, "Critic Lavishes Praise on New Hemingway Novel," *Richmond Times-Dispatch* Sunday Supplement, 6 October 1929, 3; reproduced in Robert W. Trogdon, ed., *Ernest Hemingway: A Literary Reference* (New York: Carroll & Graf, 1999), 106–7.

3 Unless otherwise cited, all letters quoted here are included in this volume.

4 Scribner's advertisement in *Publishers Weekly*, 20 April 1929, 1883.

5 "To 'Love at First Sight' For Key West, Ernest Hemingway Attributes His Coming Here," *Key West Citizen*, 23 December 1931, 1. As an indication of the mythos already surrounding the author, at least three 1931 articles in the *Key West Citizen* refer to the Hemingways' Paris residence as a "chateau" near Paris ("Hemingway Glad To Be Here Again," 15 January 1931, 1; "Hemingway Deed To Residence In This City Filed," 30 April 1931, 5; "Personal Mention," 18 May 1931, 4).

6 For a full account of the history of the house, Patrick Hemingway's memories of living there, and a debunking of some of the manufactured mythologies surrounding it, see Carol Hemingway, "907 Whitehead Street," *Hemingway Review* 23, no. 1 (Fall 2003): 8–23.

7 Michael S. Reynolds, *Hemingway: The 1930s* (New York: W. W. Norton, 1997), 48.

8 Hadley Hemingway to Ernest Hemingway, [April 1931], postmarked Paris, 27 April 1931 (JFK). A key to Abbreviations and Short Titles used in this volume follows the Note on the Text. Hadley mailed the letter to Ernest at his Key West address, but it arrived after he had left for Europe and was forwarded from Key West to his Paris bank.

9 Patrick Hemingway, interview with Sandra Spanier, Bozeman, Montana, 8 June 2011.

10 The history of publication of Hemingway's letters is discussed in more detail in the "General Editor's Introduction to the Edition" in *The Letters of Ernest Hemingway*, Volume 1 (2011), in the "General Editor's Introduction" to Volume 2 (2013) and Volume 3 (2015), and in my "Letters" chapter of *Ernest Hemingway in Context*, ed. Debra A. Moddelmog and Suzanne del Gizzo (Cambridge: Cambridge University Press, 2013), 33–42. Letters he wrote for publication during his lifetime are collected in Matthew J. Bruccoli and Judith S. Baughman, eds., *Hemingway and the Mechanism of Fame: Statements, Public Letters, Introductions, Forewords, Prefaces, Blurbs, Reviews, and Endorsements* (Columbia: University of South Carolina Press, 2006).

11 E. R. Hagemann, "Preliminary Report on the State of Ernest Hemingway's Correspondence," *Literary Research Newsletter* 3, no. 4 (1978): 163–72.

12 Matthew J. Bruccoli, ed., with Robert W. Trogdon, *The Only Thing That Counts: The Ernest Hemingway–Maxwell Perkins Correspondence* (New York: Scribner's, 1996); Marcelline Hemingway Sanford, *At the Hemingways: With Fifty Years of Correspondence Between Ernest and Marcelline Hemingway* (Moscow: University of Idaho Press, 1999); Linda

Patterson Miller, ed., *Letters from the Lost Generation: Gerald and Sara Murphy and Friends,* expanded edn. (Gainesville: University Press of Florida, 2002); and Albert J. DeFazio III, ed., *Dear Papa, Dear Hotch: The Correspondence of Ernest Hemingway and A. E. Hotchner* (Columbia: University of Missouri Press, 2005).

13 Patrick Hemingway, interview with Sandra Spanier, Bozeman, Montana, 8 June 2011.

14 Patrick Hemingway, interview with Sandra Spanier, Boston, Massachusetts, 20 April 2015.

15 Reynolds, *Hemingway: The 1930s,* 37.

16 Patrick Hemingway, interview with Sandra Spanier, Boston, Massachusetts, 11 April 2016.

17 Valerie Hemingway, email correspondence with Miriam B. Mandel and Sandra Spanier, 31 August 2016.

18 John Dos Passos, review of *A Farewell to Arms, New Masses* (1 December 1929), 16; reprinted in Robert W. Trogdon, ed., *Ernest Hemingway: A Literary Reference* (New York: Carroll & Graf, 1999), 107–8.

ACKNOWLEDGMENTS

The Cambridge Edition of *The Letters of Ernest Hemingway* owes its existence to the authorization and kind cooperation of the Ernest Hemingway Foundation and the Hemingway Foreign Rights Trust, which hold, respectively, the U.S. and international copyrights to the letters. It was Patrick Hemingway who originally conceived of a complete scholarly edition of his father's letters, and he has been most supportive of this effort, meeting with the general editor on several occasions and generously answering questions, identifying references, and sharing his unique knowledge and insights. Patrick and Carol Hemingway were particularly gracious in welcoming the general editor to visit them in Bozeman, Montana, bearing a fat stack of letters marked with queries. For their roles in securing permissions, we extend special thanks to Michael Katakis, representative of the Trust, and to Kirk Curnutt, permissions officer for the Foundation.

From the start the Hemingway Letters Project has benefited immensely from the sound guidance and strong support of our Editorial Advisory Board, whose members have given tirelessly of their time and expertise. Headed by Linda Patterson Miller, the advisors include Jackson R. Bryer, Scott Donaldson, Debra Moddelmog, and James L. W. West III. They deserve special recognition for their exceptional commitment and active involvement, including advising in the establishment of editorial policies and reading the manuscript of this volume at several stages. The edition is much the stronger for their contributions. We are most grateful, too, to J. Gerald Kennedy and Rodger L. Tarr, who have brought to bear their deep knowledge and meticulous attention to detail and have made vital contributions in advisory roles as well.

The Hemingway Letters Project has been supported in part by Scholarly Editions grants from the National Endowment for the Humanities. We are honored to have been designated a *We, the People* project, "a special recognition by the NEH for model projects that advance the study, teaching, and understanding of American history and culture." (Any views, findings, or conclusions expressed in this publication do not necessarily represent these of the National Endowment for the Humanities.)

We deeply appreciate the generosity of those organizations and endowments that have supported the Project through grants and gifts: AT&T Mobility, the Heinz Endowments, the Michigan Hemingway Society, the Dr. Bernard S. and Ann Re Oldsey Endowment for the Study of American Literature in the College of the Liberal Arts at The Pennsylvania State University, and the Xerox Corporation, which has contributed copying, printing, faxing, and scanning equipment as well as a DocuShare database management system that has been customized for our needs.

We are grateful, too, to individual donors, including Ralph and Alex Barrocas, Linda Messer Ganz, Eric V. Gearhart, Walter Goldstein, Gary Gray and Kathleen O'Toole, Harold Hein, Bill and Honey Jaffe, Lewis Katz, Ira B. Kristel, Mary Ann O'Brian Malkin, Randall Miller, Barbara Palmer, Graham B. Spanier, David A. Westover III, and Mark Weyermuller.

For fellowships and grants to support travel to archives and other research activities by Project scholars, we also wish to thank the Bibliographical Society (U.K.), the Bibliographical Society of America, and the John F. Kennedy Presidential Library. We are grateful to the Idaho Humanities Council for its support for the work of Rena Sanderson. A generous grant from the National Endowment for the Humanities enabled Miriam B. Mandel to conduct extensive on-site taurine and historical research in Spain.

The Pennsylvania State University has provided indispensable institutional support and an ideal home for the Project from its inception in 2002. We particularly wish to thank the following, in addition to those named in earlier volumes: Dean Susan Welch, College of the Liberal Arts; Dean Barbara Dewey and Dean Emerita Nancy Eaton, University Libraries; Nicholas P. Jones and Neil Sharkey, Offices of the Provost and of the Vice President for Research; Mark Morrisson, head of the Department of English; and Michael Bérubé, director of the Institute for the Arts and Humanities. Rodney Erickson strongly supported the project from the beginning, and for that we are most appreciative. We also wish to thank Rodney Kirsch, senior vice president emeritus for Development and Alumni Relations, Beth Colledge, and John Dietz; Ron Huss and the Intellectual Property division of the Office of Technology Management; in the College of the Liberal Arts, Associate Dean Eric Silver, Senior Adviser to the Dean Raymond E. Lombra, Chris Hort, Mary Kay Hort, Mark Luellen, and Chris Woods; in the Department of English, graduate studies director Debra Hawhee, internship coordinator Elizabeth Jenkins, Kim Keller, and the staff; cartographer Erin Greb and the Peter R. Gould Center for Geography Education and Outreach; and in Liberal Arts Information Technology, director Veronica Longenecker, Art Fogleman, Jeff Foltz, Shane Freehauf, Marc Kepler, Michael Renne, Ian Spears,

John Taylor, and Morgan Wellman. In Israel, computer expert Uri Hubara provided additional technical support and advice to Miriam B. Mandel.

In addition to those named on the title page of this volume, we owe special thanks to Hemingway Letters Project editorial team members Mark Cirino and Robert W. Trogdon, and to Stacey Guill, Hilary K. Justice, Verna Kale, Ellen Andrews Knodt, and LaVerne Maginnis for their various contributions, including perfecting transcriptions of letters against original documents.

We are indebted to the dozens of libraries, museums, and institutional archives that have supplied copies of letters in their collections and assisted in research for the edition.

The John F. Kennedy Presidential Library, the world's largest repository of Hemingway papers, has been particularly generous in its support of the Project, donating copies of its entire holdings of some 2,500 outgoing letters and other materials, providing images for illustrations free of charge, and responding tirelessly to our requests and queries. Special thanks are due to Acting Director James Roth, Director of Archives Karen Adler Abramson; former Library Director Thomas J. Putnam; former Hemingway Collection curator Susan Wrynn; Hemingway Program specialist Hilary K. Justice; in Reference, Stacey Chandler, Christina Fitzpatrick, Elyse Fox, Kelly Francis, and interns Corbin Apkin, Dana Bronson, David Castillo, Samuel Smallidge, and Marti Verso-Smallidge; and in Audio-Visual Archives, Maryrose Grossman, Laurie Austin, Connor Anderson, Aubrey Butts, Milo Carpenter, and Jacqueline Gertner.

Princeton University Library holds important collections of Hemingway correspondence, accounting for some 40 percent of the letters in this volume, and we are most grateful for its ongoing support and assistance. In particular we wish to thank Stephen Ferguson, Acting Associate University Librarian for Rare Books and Special Collections; Don C. Skemer, Curator of Manuscripts; Chloe Pfendler, Curatorial Assistant for Manuscripts; Gabriel Swift, Head of Public Services and Reference Librarian for Special Collections; AnnaLee Pauls, Special Collections Reference Assistant; Sandra Bossert and Brianna Cregle, Special Collections Assistants; and Squirrel Walsh, Special Collections Imaging Services Coordinator.

We also gratefully acknowledge the outstanding support of the Pennsylvania State University Libraries, with special thanks to Athena Jackson, Head of Special Collections, and her predecessor, William L. Joyce; Sandra Stelts, Curator of Rare Books and Manuscripts; and William S. Brockman, Paterno Family Librarian for Literature. Jeff Friday and Linda Klimczyk in the Department for Information Technologies have provided indispensable technical and database management support. We also wish to thank Timothy R. Babcock, Sandy Confer, Barbara Coopey, Ann Passmore, Albert Rozo, and Meredith Weber.

For supplying copies of letters in their collections and granting permission for their publication in Volume 4 of *The Letters of Ernest Hemingway*, we acknowledge the following additional libraries and archives, with special thanks to the individuals named here: Colby College Special Collections—Patricia Burdick and Erin Rhodes; College of Physicians of Philadelphia—Beth Lander and Chrissie Perella; Columbia University, Rare Book & Manuscript Library—Karla Nielsen; Cornell University, Kroch Library, Division of Rare and Manuscript Collections; Detroit Public Library, Burton Historical Collection—Dawn Eurich; Deutsches Literaturarchiv Marbach—Mirko Nottscheid; Historical Society of Oak Park and River Forest—Frank Lipo; Indiana University, The Lilly Library—Zachary Downey and David K. Frasier; Karpeles Manuscript Library; Key West Art and Historical Society—Cori Convertito; Knox College Library, Special Collections and Archives—Mary McAndrew; Library of Congress; Mills College; Missouri History Museum Library and Research Center, Archives Department—Dennis Northcott; Newberry Library, Chicago—Martha Briggs; New York Public Library, Manuscripts and Archives Division, Berg Collection of English and American Literature—Isaac Gewirtz; Northwestern State University of Louisiana—Mary Linn Wernet; Oak Park Public Library; Smith College, Neilson Library—Barbara Blumenthal; Southern Illinois University, Morris Library, Special Collections Research Center—Pam Hackbart-Dean and Aaron Michael Lisec; Stanford University Libraries, Special Collections and University Archives—Tim Noakes; University of California, Berkeley, the Bancroft Library—Shannon Supple, Allen Arthur, Kathi Neal, Kate Tasker, Kai Tomeo; University of Delaware Library—Timothy Murray, head of Special Collections, Alexander Johnston, Valerie Stenner, and Anita Wellner; University of Maryland Libraries, Special Collections—Beth Alvarez and Amber Kohl; University of Missouri—Kansas City; The State University of New York, University at Buffalo, The Poetry Collection of the University Libraries—James Maynard; University of Pennsylvania Libraries, Kislak Center for Special Collections, Rare Books & Manuscripts—Mitch Fraas; University of Reading Library, Archives of Jonathan Cape Ltd.—David Plant; University of South Carolina Library—Elizabeth Sudduth, director of the Irvin Department of Rare Books and Special Collections, Mary Anyomi, Kate Foster Boyd, Jessica Dowd Crouch, Laura D. Marion, Kate Moore, and Paul Schultz; University of Texas at Austin, Harry Ransom Center—Rick Watson; University of Tulsa, McFarlin Library, Department of Special Collections—Marc Carlson; University of Virginia Library, Albert and Shirley Small Special Collections—Nicole Bouché, director, Mary Schwartzburg, curator, Margaret Downs Hrabe and Regina Rush, reference coordinators; Wake Forest University, Z. Smith Reynolds Library—Rebecca Petersen May; Yale University, Beinecke Rare Book and Manuscript Library—

Nancy Kuhl, curator of the Collection of American Literature, Anne Marie Menta and Phoenix Alexander, and for assistance to Miriam B. Mandel during her 2013 visit, Melissa Barton, Moira Fitzgerald, John M. Monahan, Karen Nangle, Adrienne Leigh Sharpe, Dolores Colon, and Sara Azam.

The many additional libraries and archives whose contributions of materials and assistance pertain primarily to later volumes of the edition will be acknowledged there.

We are extremely grateful as well to these individuals who have provided letters or other materials appearing in or pertaining to Volume 4: Benjamin C. Bruce, Herbert S. Channick, Lucy Dos Passos Coggin, Alessandra Comini, Roger DiSilvestro, Robert K. Elder, Virginia Fritch (trustee of the Jean M. Breeden estate), David Mason, David Meeker, Paul Quintanilla, James Sanford, Stanley L. Weinberg family (courtesy of Irene, Ellen, and Sue Weinberg), and Mel Yoken.

The following also provided assistance or materials useful in the preparation of Volume 4: Grolier Club—Meghan Constantinou and Barbara Bieck; John Simon Guggenheim Memorial Foundation—Mary Kiffer; Morgan Library and Museum—Declan Kiely; Pfeiffer University—Jonathan Hutchinson; and Traverse Area District Library—Amy Barritt. For help with historical maps, we thank Mark Fritch and Kellyn Younggren of the University of Montana Library and Ben DiBase, Florida Historical Society.

We also thank the following for sharing copies of letters and other materials pertaining to other volumes in the edition: Anne Fadiman, Betsy Riggs-Fermano, Tom Fuller, Michael Halpern, Jobst Knigge, Maurice F. and Marcia Neville, Piero Ambogio Pozzi, Filippo di Robilant, Daniel Robinson, John E. Sanford, Nicolas Sarkozy, Charles Scribner III, and Wolfgang Stock. We are grateful, too, to Douglas LaPrade together with José Belmonte Serrano, Liborio Ruiz Molina, and the Fundación José Luis Castillo Puche. Representatives of Hemingway's European publishers have also been most helpful: Gallimard—Alban Cerisier, Eric Legendre, and Jean Mattern; Mondadori Foundation; and Rowohlt Verlag—Thomas Überhoff. We remain grateful to those named in previous volumes and to the donors of letters who wish to remain anonymous.

The following manuscript specialists and dealers have been most helpful: in addition to those named in previous volumes, James E. Arsenault; Bart Auerbach; B & B Rare Books; David and Natalie Bauman and Eric Pedersen, Bauman Rare Books; James Cummins; Thomas A. Goldwasser; Glenn Horowitz Bookseller, Inc.; Selby Kiffer, Sotheby's New York; Stuart Lutz; Jeffrey H. Marks; David Mason and Debra Dearlove, David Mason Books, Toronto; Peter L. Stern; and Claudia Strauss-Schulson, Schulson Autographs; University Archives; Hugo Wetscherek and Martin Peche, Antiquarian Inlibris. David Meeker of Nick Adams Rare Books in Sacramento, California, deserves special thanks for inviting the general editor to come view his extensive Hemingway collection and, along with Stephanie Meeker, for being so hospitable during her visit.

In order to inform our annotations and ensure accuracy in the transcriptions of letters that Hemingway wrote from a range of locales, addressing an array of specialized topics, and employing other languages, we have called upon the particular expertise of a number of willing volunteers. We especially wish to thank the following people for their assistance relative to Volume 4.

Brewster Chamberlin has served generously and tirelessly as Our Man in Key West and, with Lynn-Marie Smith, was a most gracious host to the general editor. We are also grateful to Cori Convertito, Michael Curry, Bill Geiser, Tom Hambright, Art Noble, and Wendy Tucker for sharing their knowledge about Hemingway's Key West connections.

Ruth Hawkins and Adam Long of the Hemingway-Pfeiffer Museum and Educational Center have been unfailingly helpful in matters concerning Pauline Pfeiffer, her family, and Hemingway's time in Piggott, Arkansas. Steve Paul has been, as always, generous with his knowledge of Hemingway's Kansas City connections. Members of the Ernest Hemingway Foundation of Oak Park have continued to be most supportive: Barbara Ballinger, John W. Berry, Virginia Cassin, Kurt and Mary Jane Neumann, and Alison Sansone. Channy Lyons and Wendy Greenhouse provided valuable information about Grace Hall Hemingway as an artist.

Susan Beegel has been our expert consultant regarding Hemingway's fishing and all marine matters. Silvio Calabi has provided important information and insight about firearms, fishing boats, trap shooting, elk bugling, and more. Sara Kosiba has been a fount of information about John Herrmann and Josephine Herbst. Paul Preston has kindly shared his expertise and provided materials concerning the history of the Second Spanish Republic.

We also thank James Byrne and Janice F. Byrne for their careful research about Dorothy Fauntleroy; Michael Culver for sharing his knowledge and unpublished manuscript, "Sparring in the Dark: The Art and Life of Henry Strater"; Ethan Mannon for information on Louis Bromfield; Laura Reiner of Wellesley College for information on alumna Dorothy Connable; and Raymond Wemmlinger, Librarian of The Player's Club, for information on Hemingway's membership.

We are most grateful, too, to those who shared their language skills and local knowledge. For French language and Parisian references, Kathryn Grossman, Monique Jutrin, and Julia Kelsey. For German language and references to Germany, Switzerland, and Austria, Thomas Austenfeld, Thomas Beebee, Gail and Stan Galbraith, and Rena Sanderson. For Hemingway's Italian, Mark Cirino and Sherry Roush. For Spanish language questions, Hjalmar L. Flax, Miriam B. Mandel, Pablo Pésaj Adí, and Enric Sullà. For details about Pamplona, Emilio Goicochea Zubelzu, Maria Goicochea, and José Mari Marco, with thanks to Gary Gray.

For assisting the Project in various other ways, we also wish to thank Elizabeth Barker, Danny Bennett, Suzanne Clark, Donald Daiker, Michael Federspiel, Cheryl Glenn, John Harwood, Hilary Hemingway, John Hemingway, Mina Hemingway, Sean and Colette Hemingway, Valerie Hemingway, Gary Scharnhorst, Gail Sinclair, Sarah Allen Wilson, and Hidso Yanagisawa, as well as those named in previous volumes.

An important benefit for this edition has been the preservation of Hemingway's letters and other documents at Finca Vigía, his longtime Cuban home; the 2009 and 2013 opening of these materials to researchers by both the Museo Hemingway in Cuba and the Kennedy Library in Boston; and the continuation of the preservation efforts. For their parts in this endeavor, the following deserve recognition: in Cuba, Gladys Collazo Usallán, President, Consejo Nacional de Patrimonio Cultural (National Council of Cultural Patrimony); Gladys Rodríguez Ferrero, Ana Cristina Parera, Ada Rosa Alfonso Rosales, Isabel Ferreiro Garit, Néstor Álvarez Garciaga, and the staff of the Museo Hemingway; in the United States, Congressman Jim McGovern, Jenny and Frank Phillips, Bob Vila, Mary-Jo Adams, Thomas D. Herman, Deborah Harding, Vicki Huddleston, Consuelo Isaacson, Joel Schwartz, and the Finca Vigía Foundation. For enhancing our understanding of Hemingway's life in Cuba we also are grateful to Ana Elena de Arazoza, Enrique Cirules, Esperanza García Fernández, Oscar Blas Fernández, Raúl and Rita Villarreal, and René Villarreal.

The Hemingway Letters Project has been most fortunate to have the benefit of the skills, professionalism, and dedication of project assistant editors Jeanne Alexander and Bryan Grove and project assistants David Eggert and Linnet Brooks. For their substantial contributions as postdoctoral research associates, we also thank Bethany Ober Mannon and Krista Quesenberry.

Those who have served as graduate research assistants at Penn State also deserve much appreciation for their many valuable contributions. They include Jace Gatzemeyer, Michael Hart, Juliette Hawkins, Michelle Huang, Leslie Joblin, Justin Mellette, and Sean Weidman, in addition to those named in previous volumes. We appreciate, too, the fine work of these undergraduate and postbaccalaureate assistants at the Project center involved in this volume: Coral Flanagan, Julia Kelsey, Luiza Lodder, Benjamin Rowles, Erin Servey, and Adam Virzi.

We are most grateful to our publisher, Cambridge University Press, for its commitment to producing this comprehensive scholarly edition. We wish to express our particular thanks for the vision and support of publisher Linda Bree and the expert assistance of Tim Mason. It has been a great pleasure to work on publication of this volume with Thomas D. Willshire and Diana Risetto in the New York office, and Victoria Parrin, Hilary Hammond, Amy Watson, and Chris Burrows in the United Kingdom. For his cover design, we warmly thank Chip Kidd.

Finally, we are deeply grateful for the interest and support of other colleagues, family members, and friends too numerous to name, but who, we trust, know of our appreciation. The editors wish to express special appreciation to the following: Miriam B. Mandel to Jessica and Naomi Mandel, Pablo Pésaj Adí, her women's groups, and Franz Schubert. Sandra Spanier to Graham, Brian, and Hadley Spanier, and to her parents, Richard and Maxine Whipple. The list of those to whom we owe thanks inevitably will grow much longer as publication of the edition proceeds, and we will continue to acknowledge our accumulating debts of gratitude in subsequent volumes.

NOTE ON THE TEXT

RULES OF TRANSCRIPTION

As a rule, the text is transcribed exactly as it appears in Hemingway's hand or typewriting, in order to preserve the flavor of the letter—whether casual, hurried, harried, inventive, or playful (as when he writes "goils" instead of "girls," refers to his cats as "kotsies," remarks "we cant stahnd it," or exclaims "Goturletter thanks!"). When his handwriting is ambiguous, we have given him the benefit of the doubt and transcribed words and punctuation in their correct form.

Special challenges of transcription are treated as follows:

Spelling
- When a typed character is incomplete, distorted, or visible only as an impression on the paper (whether due to a weak keystroke, type in need of cleaning, or a worn-out ink ribbon) but nevertheless is discernible (as ultimately determined in the field checking of the original document), the intended character is supplied without editorial comment.
- When a blank space suggests that an intended letter in a word is missing but no physical trace of a keystroke exists on the manuscript page, or when Hemingway types a word off the edge of the paper, the conjectured missing letter or portion of the word is supplied in square brackets: e.g., "the[y] are trying," or "meningiti[s] epidemic."
- Similarly, when a word is incomplete due to an obvious oversight or a slip of the pen, and the editors deem it advisable for clarity's sake, we supply missing letters in square brackets: e.g., "I[t] makes no difference."
- Because typewriter keyboards varied over time and from one country to another and did not always include a key for every character Hemingway wished to write, he necessarily improvised: e.g., for the numeral one he often typed a capital letter "I," and for an exclamation point, he would backspace to type a single quotation mark above a period. We have not attempted to

reproduce those improvisations or conventions of the day but have silently supplied characters that Hemingway would have typed himself had his keyboard allowed.

- We have not attempted to reproduce in print the appearance of mechanical malfunctions. For example, when jammed typewriter keys cause two letters to appear superimposed in a single letter space, such errors are silently corrected, the letters transcribed without comment in the sequence that makes sense.

Capitalization

As a rule, Hemingway's usage is preserved exactly. However, while his handwriting is generally open and legible, his uppercase and lowercase letters are sometimes indistinguishable (the letters "a" and "g," for example, almost always take the form of the lowercase, with capital letters often differentiated only by their size relative to other letters). In ambiguous cases, we have silently followed correct usage in the context of the sentence.

Punctuation

Whether Hemingway is writing by hand or on a typewriter, there is no apparent pattern to his use or omission of apostrophes, and in handwritten letters he frequently marks the end of a sentence with a dash rather than a period. Hemingway's often erratic punctuation—or lack thereof—has been strictly preserved, except in the following instances:

- In handwritten letters Hemingway sometimes marked the end of a declarative sentence with a small "x" (likely a carryover from his early habits as a newspaper reporter), a wavy flourish, or another mark difficult to render in print. Rather than attempting to reproduce these markings, we have normalized them without comment as periods.
- Hemingway sometimes wrote parentheses as vertical or slanted lines; these have been normalized as curved parentheses.
- Hemingway often neglected to put a period at the end of a paragraph's last sentence (as indicated by indentation of the following line) or at the end of a sentence enclosed in parentheses. Other sentences simply run together. To routinely insert ending punctuation for the sake of grammatical correctness would alter the letters' pace and tone: masking Hemingway's carelessness or breathlessness, erasing both the inadvertent charm of some childhood letters and his intentional wordplay, and imposing an arbitrary logic or false clarity on some ambiguously worded passages. Generally we do not supply missing full stops, except when the editors deem it necessary for clarity or when

Hemingway's intention seems obvious: e.g., as indicated by extra spacing after a word and capitalization of the following word to mark the beginning of a new sentence. In such cases, we supply a period within square brackets.

- Whenever the editors have supplied punctuation for clarity's sake, those punctuation marks are enclosed within square brackets: e.g., as when Hemingway neglected to use commas to separate proper names in a list.

Cancellations and corrections

Hemingway rarely bothered to erase errors or false starts in his letters, typically canceling or correcting written material either by drawing a line through it or typing over it. Usually his intent is clear, and we have not reproduced every cancellation and correction. However, when deleted or altered material is legible and the editors deem it of significance or interest, a cancellation or correction may be retained in place, with a line drawn through the text that Hemingway canceled, as the reader would have encountered it in the letter.

When he typed over his misstrikes with more forceful keystrokes so that his intended phrasing appears in darker type, we present only his corrected version. When he canceled words and phrases by backspacing and typing over them (usually with strings of the letter "x"), he occasionally missed a letter at the beginning or end of the canceled material; we do not reproduce stray characters that he obviously intended to cancel. Nor do we transcribe stray characters and false starts that he simply neglected to cancel: e.g., a portion of a word typed off the right margin of the page, followed by the complete word on the following line.

Interlineations, marginalia, and other markings

Hemingway's insertions, whether they appear as interlineations or marginalia, have been transferred into the text at a point that, in the editors' judgment, most accurately reflects his intended placement. However, when the insertion would render a sentence or passage ungrammatical or confusing if simply transcribed at the indicated point without comment, we enclose the inserted material within square brackets and provide a brief editorial explanation in italics: e.g., [*EH insertion:*]. When the intended position of any material is questionable or an insertion merits editorial comment, the situation is addressed in a bracketed in-text notation or in an endnote.

When Hemingway's markings indicate that the order of letters, words, or phrases should be transposed, we have done so without comment. When he uses ditto marks to indicate repetition of a word or phrase appearing on a previous line of the original text, we have supplied the word or phrase within square brackets at the indicated place: e.g., "Did you write the Steins? [*Ditto marks*: Did you write the] Ford Maddox Fords."

Whenever possible, Hemingway's occasional sketches or drawings are reproduced as they appear in the text of the letter. Otherwise, brief descriptions are provided in square brackets where such graphic elements appear in the text: e.g., [*Drawing of a sleeping cat*], and any commentary that the editors deem necessary is supplied in a note.

Other markings in the text that are difficult to render in print, such as stray doodles, demarcation lines underneath the letter date or return address, or flourishes following his signature, are not noted unless the editors deem them to be of particular interest. We do not transcribe Hemingway's page numbering.

Indentation and spacing

In both handwritten and typewritten letters, Hemingway's indications of paragraph breaks are irregular or non-existent. Sometimes, instead of indenting, he signaled a paragraph break by starting a new page, leaving a gap between lines, or ending the previous sentence in midline. The editors have indicated new paragraphs by regular indentation of the first line.

In typewritten letters, Hemingway's spacing is erratic. Frequently he hit the space bar both before and after punctuation marks or several times between words, and extraneous blank spaces occasionally appear in the middle of a word. The spacing around punctuation marks and between words has been normalized, and extraneous blank spaces appearing within words have been silently eliminated.

However, when Hemingway ran words together with no space between, they are transcribed exactly as they appear, as it is often impossible to determine whether he did this accidentally or intentionally for effect. Run-together words also may indicate a mood of haste or excitement that would be lost to readers if conventional spacing were editorially inserted.

Compound words

Transcriptions follow Hemingway's treatment of compound words exactly, with no attempt made to impose consistency or to correct or standardize hyphenation or spacing: e.g., there is no apparent pattern to his usage of such compounds as "good-bye," "goodbye," and "good bye," or "someone" vs. "some one."

In handwritten letters, Hemingway's "y" is often followed by a space that might or might not mark a gap between words: e.g., it is sometimes difficult to tell if he intended to write "anyway" or "any way." When Hemingway's handwriting is ambiguous, we transcribe the word as it would be used correctly in that sentence.

Underlined words
Words underlined by Hemingway are underlined in the transcriptions; the double, triple, and quadruple underlining he occasionally employed also is indicated in order to capture his emphasis or exuberance.

Missing portions of text
Square brackets are used to indicate illegible, damaged, or missing text at the point of occurrence, with a description of the manuscript's condition in italics: e.g., [*illegible*], [*MS torn*], [*MS razor-cut by censor*]. Any conjectured reconstruction of missing text is supplied in roman type within square brackets.

Date and place of writing
The date and place of origin (often a specific return address) as supplied by Hemingway in the text of his letters are transcribed exactly as he wrote them; however, we have standardized the line placement of these elements so they appear flush to the right margin. The use of letterhead is indicated in the source note following the complete text of a letter, and letterhead address information also is recorded there rather than transcribed as part of the text of the letter.

Valediction and signature
Hemingway's valediction and signature are transcribed as he wrote them, whether on one line or two, but their position on the page is standardized so that they appear flush to the right margin.

Postscripts
Regardless of where a postscript appears in the manuscript (in a margin, at the top or bottom of a letter, or on the back of a letter's final page), it is generally transcribed as a new paragraph following the signature, reflecting the probable order of composition. Occasionally the position of a postscript is described in a square-bracketed editorial note: e.g. [*on envelope verso:*].

Joint letters
Letters that Hemingway wrote with another person or to which he adds a postscript are presented in their entirety so as to preserve the context of his portion, with the point at which one writer takes over from another indicated in brackets: e.g., [*EH writes:*] or [*Pauline writes:*]. Where one writer inserts a brief

remark into the text of another, the point of interjection as well as the remark itself are indicated in brackets: e.g., [*EH interjects*: I doubt this.].

Foreign languages

Any portion of a letter written in a language other than English is transcribed exactly as Hemingway wrote it, with no attempt to correct errors or to supply any missing diacritical marks.

When a word, phrase, sentence, or passage within a letter is in a foreign language, a translation is supplied in a note preceded, when deemed necessary for clarity, by the correct spelling or diacritical form of a word. Translations are not supplied for words or phrases presumably familiar to most readers: e.g., *adios, au revoir*. When Hemingway wrote an entire letter in another language, the transcription of the original text is followed by an English translation in square brackets.

We do not attempt in our translations to replicate Hemingway's foreign-language grammatical errors: e.g., in conjugation of verbs and in gender agreement of nouns and adjectives. Rather, we provide a translation that conveys the sense of the message, while briefly noting the presence and nature of such errors. Similarly, we do not attempt to replicate the exact syntax and mechanics (e.g., capitalization and punctuation) of Hemingway's use of a foreign language, but rather aim in our English translation to convey the style and tone of his usage, whether formal or colloquial.

EDITORIAL APPARATUS

Heading

Each letter is preceded by a heading indicating the recipient and date of the letter, with any portion supplied by the editors enclosed in square brackets.

Source note

A bibliographical note immediately following each letter provides information about the source text upon which the transcription is based, including the location and form of the original letter. Abbreviations used are described in the list of Abbreviations and Short Titles in the front matter of each volume. Information appears in this order:

(1) Symbols indicate the location and form of the original letter. For example, "JFK, TLS" indicates a typed letter signed that is located in the collections of the John F. Kennedy Library. When the original letter cannot be located and the transcription derives from another source (e.g., a photocopy, a recipient's

transcription, a secretary's transcription of dictation, an auction catalog, or another publication), that source is indicated. When Hemingway closed a letter with a "mark" instead of writing his name (as when he drew a beer stein to signify his nickname "Stein," short for "Hemingstein"), we have considered the letter to be signed, describing it, for example, as "TLS" rather than "TL."

(2) The use of letterhead stationery is noted and the address information supplied. Additional letterhead elements tangential to the study of Hemingway (e.g., an advertising slogan, description of a hotel's facilities, proprietor's name, phone number) are not generally recorded. However, in the rare cases when Hemingway provides commentary on these elements, the situation is described in a note. If the text is from a picture postcard, a brief description is provided: e.g., A Postcard S, verso: Sun Valley Lodge, Idaho.

(3) Surviving postmark information is supplied. When a postmark stamp is incomplete or illegible, portions of place names or dates supplied by the editors are enclosed in square brackets: e.g., SAN SEBA[STIAN]. When the original letter cannot be consulted and postmark information derives from another source (e.g., a description in an auction catalog), we enclose that information in square brackets.

Endnotes

Annotations appear as endnotes following each letter. In notes Ernest Hemingway is referred to as EH. Initials are not used for any other persons, but editors frequently use the short names that Hemingway would have used: e.g., Hadley for his first wife, Elizabeth Hadley Richardson Hemingway; or Buck Lanham for his friend General Charles T. Lanham. Recipients of letters included in a given volume are identified in the Roster of Correspondents in the back matter of that volume. Other people are identified in endnotes at first mention. Square-bracketed information (such as a last name) has occasionally been inserted into the text of a letter to briefly identify a person without adding to the number of endnotes. There necessarily may be some duplication and cross-referencing as we aim to make the volumes useful to readers, not all of whom will read the letters strictly chronologically within a given volume or across the edition.

In determining which references merit annotation, we have been mindful of the international audience for the edition and, in consultation with the publisher, have provided notes for some references likely to be familiar to U.S. readers: e.g., Karo syrup, Old Faithful geyser. We do not generally attempt to explicate Hemingway's inventive expressions, private slang, and other wordplay, leaving it to readers to experience and interpret his language as he wrote it.

The editors have made every effort to identify Hemingway's references to people, places, events, publications, and artistic works. However, the identities of some are inevitably lost to history. When a note is not provided at the first mention of a reference, the reader can assume that it remains unidentified.

SANDRA SPANIER

ABBREVIATIONS AND SHORT TITLES

LOC	Library of Congress; Washington, D.C.
Mason	David Mason Books; Toronto, Canada
MHM	Archives Department, Missouri History Museum Library and Research Center; St. Louis, Missouri
Mills	F. W. Olin Library, Mills College; Oakland, California
Newberry	The Newberry Library; Chicago, Illinois
NWSU	Cammie G. Henry Research Center, Watson Memorial Library, Northwestern State University of Louisiana; Natchitoches, Louisiana
NYPL–Berg	The Berg Collection of English and American Literature, New York Public Library, Astor, Lenox, and Tilden foundations; New York, New York
OPPL	Oak Park Public Library; Oak Park, Illinois
Penn	University of Pennsylvania; Philadelphia, Pennsylvania
PSU	Rare Books and Manuscripts, Special Collections Library, Pennsylvania State University Libraries; University Park, Pennsylvania
PUL	Department of Rare Books and Special Collections, Princeton University Library; Princeton, New Jersey
James Sanford	James Sanford Collection
SIU	Special Collections Research Center, Morris Library, Southern Illinois University; Carbondale, Illinois
Smith	Mortimer Rare Book Room, Neilson Library, Smith College; Northampton, Massachusetts
Stanford	Department of Special Collections and University Archives, Stanford University Libraries; Stanford, California
SUNYB	The Poetry Collection of the University Libraries, University at Buffalo, State University of New York; Buffalo, New York
Syracuse	Special Collections Research Center, Syracuse University Libraries; Syracuse, New York
UCalB	Bancroft Library, University of California, Berkeley; Berkeley, California
UDel	Special Collections, University of Delaware Library; Newark, Delaware
UMD	Special Collections, University of Maryland Libraries; College Park, Maryland
UMKC	LaBudde Special Collections, Miller Nichols Library, University of Missouri–Kansas City; Kansas City, Missouri
URead	Archives of Jonathan Cape Ltd., Special Collections, University of Reading Library; Reading, Berkshire, United Kingdom

USCar	Irvin Department of Rare Books and Special Collections, Ernest F. Hollings Special Collections Library, University of South Carolina; Columbia, South Carolina
UT	Harry Ransom Center, University of Texas at Austin; Austin, Texas
UTulsa	Special Collections and University Archives, McFarlin Library, University of Tulsa; Tulsa, Oklahoma
UVA	Albert and Shirley Small Special Collections Library, University of Virginia; Charlottesville, Virginia
Wake Forest	Z. Smith Reynolds Library, Wake Forest University; Winston-Salem, North Carolina
Weinberg	Stanley L. Weinberg Family Collection
Yale	Yale Collection of American Literature, Beinecke Rare Book and Manuscript Library, Yale University; New Haven, Connecticut
Yoken	Mel Yoken Collection

FORMS OF CORRESPONDENCE

The following abbreviations are used in combination to describe the form of the original source text (e.g., ALS for autograph letter signed, TLS for typed letter signed, ACD for autograph cable draft, TLcc for typed letter carbon copy, phJFK for a photocopy at the John F. Kennedy Library):

A	Autograph
C	Cable
cc	Carbon copy
D	Draft
Frag	Fragment
L	Letter
N	Note
ph	Photocopy
S	Signed
T	Typed

Other Abbreviations

b.	born
c.	circa
d.	died
m.	married
n.d.	no date
n.p.	no pagination

PUBLISHED WORKS

Works by Ernest Hemingway

The following abbreviations and short titles for Hemingway's works are employed throughout the edition; not all of them appear in the present volume. First U.S. editions are cited, unless otherwise noted.

ARIT	*Across the River and into the Trees.* New York: Scribner's, 1950.
BL	*By-line: Ernest Hemingway; Selected Articles and Dispatches of Four Decades.* Edited by William White. New York: Scribner's, 1967.
CSS	*The Complete Short Stories of Ernest Hemingway: The Finca Vigía Edition.* New York: Scribner's, 1987.
DLT	*Dateline: Toronto; The Complete "Toronto Star" Dispatches, 1920–1924.* Edited by William White. New York: Scribner's, 1985.
DIA	*Death in the Afternoon.* New York: Scribner's, 1932.
DS	*The Dangerous Summer.* New York: Scribner's, 1985.
FC	*The Fifth Column and the First Forty-nine Stories.* New York: Scribner's, 1938.
FTA	*A Farewell to Arms.* New York: Scribner's, 1929.
FTA–HLE	*A Farewell to Arms: The Hemingway Library Edition.* Foreword by Patrick Hemingway. Edited with an Introduction by Seán Hemingway. New York: Scribner's, 2012.
FWBT	*For Whom the Bell Tolls.* New York: Scribner's, 1940.
GOE	*The Garden of Eden.* New York: Scribner's, 1986.
GHOA	*Green Hills of Africa.* New York: Scribner's, 1935.
GHOA–HLE	*Green Hills of Africa: The Hemingway Library Edition.* Foreword by Patrick Hemingway. Edited with an Introduction by Seán Hemingway. Scribner's, 2015.
iot	*in our time.* Paris: Three Mountains Press, 1924.
IOT	*In Our Time.* New York: Boni & Liveright, 1925. Rev. edn., New York: Scribner's, 1930.
IIS	*Islands in the Stream.* New York: Scribner's, 1970.
Letters vol. 1	*The Letters of Ernest Hemingway: Volume 1 (1907–1922).* Edited by Sandra Spanier and Robert W. Trogdon. New York: Cambridge University Press, 2011.
Letters vol. 2	*The Letters of Ernest Hemingway: Volume 2 (1923–1925).* Edited by Sandra Spanier, Albert J. DeFazio III, and Robert W. Trogdon. New York: Cambridge University Press, 2013.

Letters vol. 3	*The Letters of Ernest Hemingway: Volume 3 (1926–1929)*. Edited by Rena Sanderson, Sandra Spanier, and Robert W. Trogdon. New York: Cambridge University Press, 2015.
MAW	*Men at War*. New York: Crown Publishers, 1942.
MF	*A Moveable Feast*. New York: Scribner's, 1964.
MF-RE	*A Moveable Feast: The Restored Edition*. Foreword by Patrick Hemingway. Edited with an Introduction by Seán Hemingway. New York: Scribner's, 2009.
MWW	*Men Without Women*. New York: Scribner's, 1927.
NAS	*The Nick Adams Stories*. New York: Scribner's, 1972.
OMS	*The Old Man and the Sea*. New York: Scribner's, 1952.
Poems	*Complete Poems*. Edited with an Introduction and Notes by Nicholas Gerogiannis. Rev. edn. Lincoln: University of Nebraska Press, 1992.
SAR	*The Sun Also Rises*. New York: Scribner's, 1926.
SAR-HLE	*The Sun Also Rises: The Hemingway Library Edition*. Foreword by Patrick Hemingway. Edited with an Introduction by Seán Hemingway. New York: Scribner's, 2014.
SL	*Ernest Hemingway: Selected Letters, 1917–1961*. Edited by Carlos Baker. New York: Scribner's, 1981.
SS	*The Short Stories of Ernest Hemingway*. New York: Scribner's, 1954.
TAFL	*True at First Light*. Edited by Patrick Hemingway. New York: Scribner's, 1999.
THHN	*To Have and Have Not*. New York: Scribner's, 1937.
TOS	*The Torrents of Spring*. New York: Scribner's, 1926.
TOTTC	*The Only Thing That Counts: The Ernest Hemingway–Maxwell Perkins Correspondence, 1925–1947*. Edited by Matthew J. Bruccoli with Robert W. Trogdon. New York: Scribner's, 1996.
TSTP	*Three Stories and Ten Poems*. Paris: Contact Editions, 1923.
UK	*Under Kilimanjaro*. Edited by Robert W. Lewis and Robert E. Fleming. Kent, Ohio: Kent State University Press, 2005.
WTN	*Winner Take Nothing*. New York: Scribner's, 1933.

Selected reference works cited in this volume

Baedeker's *Paris*	Baedeker, Karl. *Paris and its Environs with Routes from London to Paris: Handbook for Travellers*. Lepzig: Karl Baedeker, 1924.

Baker *Life*	Baker, Carlos. *Ernest Hemingway: A Life Story.* New York: Scribner's, 1969.
Brasch and Sigman	Brasch, James D. and Joseph Sigman. *Hemingway's Library: A Composite Record.* New York: Garland, 1981. Electronic edition, Boston: John F. Kennedy Library, 2000.
Bruccoli and Baughman *Mechanism*	Bruccoli, Matthew J., and Judith S. Baughman, eds. *Hemingway and the Mechanism of Fame: Statements, Public Letters, Introductions, Forewords, Prefaces, Blurbs, Reviews, and Endorsements.* Columbia: University of South Carolina Press, 2006.
Bruccoli and Clark *Auction*	Bruccoli, Matthew J. and C. E. Frazer Clark, Jr., eds. *Hemingway at Auction, 1930–1973.* Detroit: Gale Research, 1973.
Bruccoli *As Ever*	Bruccoli, Matthew J., ed. *As Ever, Scott—Fitz: Letters between F. Scott Fitzgerald and His Literary Agent, Harold Ober 1929–1940.* Philadelphia: J. B. Lippincott Company, 1972.
Bruccoli *Fitz–Hem*	Bruccoli, Matthew J. *Fitzgerald and Hemingway: A Dangerous Friendship.* Paperback edition with appendices. New York: Carroll & Graf, 1995.
Bruccoli *Sons*	Bruccoli, Matthew J., ed. *The Sons of Maxwell Perkins: Letters of F. Scott Fitzgerald, Ernest Hemingway, Thomas Wolfe, and their Editor.* Columbia: University of South Carolina Press, 2004.
Cabot	Cabot, Maud. *Maud's Journey: A Life from Art.* Berkeley, California: New Earth Publications, 1995.
Calabi, Helsey, and Sanger	Calabi, Silvio, Steve Helsey, and Roger Sanger. *Hemingway's Guns: The Sporting Arms of Ernest Hemingway.* Lanham, Maryland: Lyons Press, 2016.
Calabi "Safari"	Calabi, Silvio. "Ernest Hemingway on Safari." In Miriam B. Mandel, ed., *Hemingway and Africa.* Rochester, New York: Camden House, 2011: 85–121.
Callaghan	Callaghan, Morley. *That Summer in Paris: Memories of Tangled Friendships with Hemingway, Fitzgerald, and Some Others.* New York: Coward-McCann, 1963.
Chamberlin	Chamberlin, Brewster. *The Hemingway Log: A Chronology of his Life and Times.* Lawrence: University Press of Kansas, 2015.

Cohn   Cohn, Louis Henry. *A Bibliography of the Works of Ernest Hemingway*. New York: Random House for the House of Books, 1931.

Crosby   Crosby, Caresse. *The Passionate Years*. London: Alvin Redman Limited, 1955.

Donaldson *Force*   Donaldson, Scott. *By Force of Will: The Life and Art of Ernest Hemingway*. New York: Penguin Books, 1977.

Donaldson *MacLeish*   Donaldson, Scott. *Archibald MacLeish: An American Life*. Boston: Houghton Mifflin, 1992.

Elder, Vetch, and Cirino   Elder, Robert K., Aaron Vetch, and Mark Cirino. *Hidden Hemingway: Inside the Ernest Hemingway Archives of Oak Park*. Kent, Ohio: Kent State University Press, 2016.

Grissom   Grissom, C. Edgar. *Ernest Hemingway: A Descriptive Bibliography*. New Castle, Delaware: Oak Knoll Press, 2011.

Hanneman   Hanneman, Audre. *Ernest Hemingway: A Comprehensive Bibliography*. Princeton, New Jersey: Princeton University Press, 1967.

Hanneman *Supplement*   Hanneman, Audre. *Supplement to Ernest Hemingway: A Comprehensive Bibliography*. Princeton, New Jersey: Princeton University Press, 1975.

Hawkins   Hawkins, Ruth. *Unbelievable Happiness and Final Sorrow: The Hemingway–Pfeiffer Marriage*. Fayetteville: University of Arkansas Press, 2012.

Kuehl and Bryer   Kuehl, John and Jackson Bryer, eds. *Dear Scott/Dear Max: The Fitzgerald–Perkins Correspondence*. New York: Scribner's, 1971.

Ledig-Rowohlt   Ledig-Rowohlt, Heinrich Maria. *Meeting Two American Giants*. Germany: Clausen & Bosse, Leck/Schleswig, 1962.

Long   Long, Ray, ed. *20 Best Short Stories in Ray Long's 20 Years as an Editor*. New York: Ray Long & Richard R. Smith, 1932.

Mandel *HDIA*   Mandel, Miriam B. *Hemingway's Death in the Afternoon: The Complete Annotations*. Lanham, Maryland: Scarecrow Press, 2002.

L. Miller	Miller, Linda Patterson, ed. *Letters from the Lost Generation: Gerald and Sara Murphy and Friends.* Expanded edition. Gainesville: University Press of Florida, 2002.
M. Miller	Miller, Madelaine Hemingway. *Ernie: Hemingway's Sister "Sunny" Remembers.* New York: Crown Publishers, 1975.
Norman	Norman, Charles. *Ezra Pound.* New York: The Macmillan Company, 1960.
Reynolds *1930s*	Reynolds, Michael S. *Hemingway: The 1930s.* New York: W. W. Norton, 1997.
Reynolds *Reading*	Reynolds, Michael S. *Hemingway's Reading, 1901–1940: An Inventory.* Princeton, New Jersey: Princeton University Press, 1981.
Sanford	Sanford, Marcelline Hemingway. *At the Hemingways: A Family Portrait.* Boston: Little, Brown, 1962. Centennial edition, *At the Hemingways: With Fifty Years of Correspondence Between Ernest and Marcelline Hemingway.* Moscow: University of Idaho Press, 1999. Citations are to the expanded 1999 edition.
Smith	Smith, Paul. *A Reader's Guide to the Short Stories of Ernest Hemingway.* Boston: G. K. Hall, 1989.
Trogdon *Racket*	Trogdon, Robert W. *The Lousy Racket: Hemingway, Scribner's, and the Business of Literature.* Kent, Ohio: Kent State University Press, 2007.
Trogdon *Reference*	Trogdon, Robert W., ed. *Ernest Hemingway: A Literary Reference.* New York: Carroll & Graf, 1999.

INTRODUCTION TO
THE VOLUME

Scott Donaldson
College of William and Mary

The three previous volumes of Hemingway's letters cover his adolescence, growing up in Oak Park and northern Michigan, his early newspaper work in Kansas City and Toronto, his wounding in World War I, his marriage to Hadley Richardson and their years together in Paris, the birth of their son Bumby, his discovery of bullfighting in Spain, his work as a foreign correspondent, his connections to such guiding literary figures as Ezra Pound and Gertrude Stein, his first publications in little magazines and limited editions succeeded by major books *In Our Time* (1925), *The Sun Also Rises* (1926), and *Men Without Women* (1927), his divorce from Hadley to marry Pauline Pfeiffer, his return to the United States and the fishing (off Key West) and hunting (out West) that he always valued, the birth of his son Patrick and suicide of his father, and the completion of his second novel *A Farewell to Arms*.

Volume 4 contains his correspondence from April 1929 through the end of 1931. During this period Hemingway established himself as a major writer with a growing awareness of the literary marketplace, continued his outdoor adventures, with the aid of Pauline's Uncle Gus set up a trust fund to support his family in Oak Park, suffered a painful broken bone in his arm that delayed completing *Death in the Afternoon*, and saw the birth of his third son Gregory.

BRINGING OUT 'A FAREWELL TO ARMS'

"I'm a Professional Writer now," Ernest Hemingway wrote to Maxwell Perkins at Scribner's on 3 October 1929, a week after publication of *A Farewell to Arms*. "Than which," he added, "there isn't anything lower."[1] The book was to become a bestseller and establish Hemingway as a leading figure in the literary world, but at the time he wasn't particularly proud of it. In his view, he had knuckled under to his publisher by deleting the irreverent cuss words that were common parlance for his military characters. The dispute over this issue dominated much of the communication between Hemingway and his editor during the spring and summer of 1929, after Ernest and Pauline, accompanied by their infant son Patrick, came back to Paris in April to resume their life as expatriates.

He'd worked "like a convict" on the novel for a year, he wrote Thornton Wilder on 26 May 1929, and in several places: Paris, Key West, Arkansas, Kansas City, Wyoming, and back in Key West again. He felt elated when it was finished, followed by a bout of depression and a troubling period when he couldn't get any fiction down on paper.

As a professional writer, Hemingway accepted an offer of $16,000—a lot of money in those days and far more than he had earned from previous books, to serialize the book in six installments of *Scribner's Magazine*. Though he didn't like it, Hemingway understood that the magazine serial would have to cut certain words to avoid scandalizing its genteel readership. But he stoutly resisted similar changes in the book itself.

In two letters written to Perkins on the same day, 7 June 1929, Hemingway pleaded his case. His publishers objected most of all to three words regularly uttered by soldiers in wartime: specifically *shit, balls,* and the "Supreme insult" *cocksucker.* These words were to be found in Shakespeare, Hemingway maintained, and also in Erich Maria Remarque's *All Quiet on the Western Front,* a popular German war novel then available in translation in England and about to be published in the United States.

To sum up his argument, Hemingway wrote that if "a word <u>can</u> be printed and is needed in the text it is a <u>weakening</u> to omit it. If it <u>cannot</u> be printed without the book being suppressed all right." He didn't want to make trouble, Ernest added. He only wanted all they could "possibly get" in the fight for full use of the language. He never used a word if he could avoid it, he pointed out. Then if Perkins decided that it was "unpublishable really unpublishable I suppose I must leave it blank—But I want the blanks to indicate what the word is."[2]

Two weeks later the issue became further complicated when the Boston police chief banned the sale of the June issue of *Scribner's* on the grounds that the serial of *A Farewell to Arms,* with its love affair unsanctified by marriage, was salacious. This was hardly a surprise inasmuch as the Boston censors had banned *The Sun Also Rises* on similar grounds three years earlier. But the stakes were higher this time. His publishers had not only invested in a serialization of Hemingway's novel, but were planning to promote the book vigorously when it came out in late September.

At first, Hemingway did not take the ban very seriously. Boston was manifestly the nation's capital for book censorship, and something of a laughing stock for its recent suppression of books by prominent authors—among them, H. G. Wells, Conrad Aiken, John Dos Passos, Sherwood Anderson, Sinclair Lewis, and Theodore Dreiser, in addition to Hemingway.

Perkins, however, was not amused. The incident, he wrote to Hemingway on 12 July 1929, guaranteed that the book itself would be "scrutinized from a prejudiced standpoint" when it came out and therefore the three words they had talked so much about "could not be printed, or plainly indicated." He was particularly worried that the federal authorities might be stirred up. Both United States Customs and the Post Office had recently been busy suppressing books. Customs ruled against admitting the unexpurgated British edition of *All Quiet on the Western Front*, and Little, Brown was forced to bring out a sanitized version of that novel. Even more to be feared was a refusal by the Post Office to mail copies of books they regarded as obscene. "[I]f the post office should object," Perkins pointed out, "we would be in Dutch."[3]

"Max sounded scared," Hemingway wrote to Fitzgerald on 23 July 1929, and if Scribner's decided to "lay off the book I'll be out of luck." Fitzgerald had more or less orchestrated the 1925–1926 maneuvers that enabled Hemingway to break his contract with Boni & Liveright and sign on—like Fitzgerald himself—with Scribner's and with Perkins as editor. And at this time Ernest continued to consult Scott, the more experienced writer three years older than himself, on professional matters.

On 26 July 1929, Hemingway capitulated on the three words that most bothered Perkins and the conservative firm he worked for. "I understand your viewpoint about the words you cannot print," he wrote Perkins. "If you cannot print them—and I never expected you could print the one word (C—K—)—then you cannot and that lets me out." Accordingly, the words *shit*, *fuck*, and *cocksucker* were represented by blanks in *A Farewell to Arms* and at Ernest's suggestion *scrotum* was substituted for *balls*.

This dirty language was hardly the only thing about the novel that invited censorship. There remained the love affair between the unmarried Frederic Henry and Catherine Barkley, for example. A few reviewers focused on that matter, titling their comments under "Naughty Ernest" and "What is Dirt?" Veteran writer Owen Wister, a friend of Perkins, objected to the frank use of obstetrical details in describing Catherine's death during childbirth. And Italians and Italian Americans were offended by the book's graphic depiction of the catastrophic defeat at Caporetto and the defections and desertions of the troops during the disorganized retreat afterwards. Hemingway, anticipating the problem, wrote a disclaimer that appeared in *Scribner's Magazine*, to the effect that the story was fictional, not autobiographical, and no more intended as a criticism of Italy or Italians than *Two Gentlemen of Verona*.

The publicity generated by the ban in Boston and by Scribner's itself undoubtedly stimulated sales. *A Farewell to Arms* was published in a first printing of 31,050 copies, more than five times as many as the 6,000 initial run of *The Sun Also Rises* three years earlier. Most reviews were highly favorable, and the book quickly shot up the bestseller list. The Boston censors took no action. Neither did the Post Office. Only in Italy was the book banned. Hemingway was pleased by the sales, but continued to regret backtracking on his conviction that fictional soldiers could only emerge as authentic on the page if they spoke like real ones.

THE PROFESSIONAL AT WORK

The Hemingways spent most of July and August 1929 in Spain. Ernest and Pauline were happy traveling together, leaving Patrick in the care of a French nanny. After attending the fiesta at Pamplona, they visited artist Joan Miró at his home in Tarragona, the site of the famous painting *La Ferme* (*The Farm*) that Ernest had purchased in 1925 as a birthday gift for his wife Hadley. Then they followed the bullfight season in Valencia and Madrid and in August sojourned to Santiago de Compostela in Galicia.

In Madrid, Hemingway saw and was impressed by Sidney Franklin, the bullfighter from Brooklyn whose exploits were making news in the press. Hemingway was asked by his close friend Guy Hickok, the *Brooklyn Daily Eagle*'s European correspondent, to interview Franklin. This was not a simple matter, now that Hemingway was becoming a well-known author. He could write something for the *Eagle*, he replied to Hickok on 30 July 1929, but not under his own name. "You see," he explained, "I could sell an interview with [Franklin] . . . for a thousand seeds [dollars] I think and if we did it signed for nothing wd just poop that away."

A few months later Archibald MacLeish, then working for *Fortune* magazine, invited him to write an article on bullfighting as an industry. He could do "a hell of a good" piece with lots of data and the "inside stuff" he'd acquired as an *aficionado*, Hemingway answered on 15 December 1929. But he'd want $2,500— or $2,000 at least—for a 5,000–6,000-word article, the same price, he maintained, that a long story of his would command in the marketplace. This was an exaggeration, and it didn't persuade the magazine. *Fortune* offered $1,000 for 2,500 words, and Hemingway took it, without enthusiasm. "It's a romance of business magazine," he told Perkins, but there wasn't any romance in his article, which was "written in journalese full of statistics." Still, though he was keeping his article "as dull as possible," he realized that "[e]very aspect" he touched on could eventually "make a long chapter in a book." In fact, the project helped pave the way for what would become *Death in the Afternoon* (1932).

As his correspondence with Hickok and MacLeish indicated, Hemingway was becoming savvy about money matters by the fall of 1929. At the beginning of his literary career, he pursued any and all avenues—little magazines, private presses, limited editions—leading to publication of his work. Though he was paid little or nothing, the important thing was to get his stories into print where they could be noticed. But after bringing out four books—*In Our Time* (1925) with Boni & Liveright, and *The Torrents of Spring, The Sun Also Rises* (both 1926), and *Men Without Women* (1927) with Scribner's— and with the success of *A Farewell to Arms* virtually assured, he took an increasingly aggressive stance about payment for his work.

He secured an advance of $6,000 on *Farewell* from Scribner's, and as the book boomed, renegotiated his contract to a higher royalty rate—20 percent—for sales beyond 25,000. "You and Mr. Scribner are both damned fine about it," he wrote to Perkins on 4 January 1930.

The firm had every reason to be supportive of its author, who at age thirty had emerged as a major literary property. Within three months after *A Farewell to Arms* came out—partly because of false rumors that he was unhappy with Scribner's—he was approached by Harper's, Coward-McCann, and Knopf about switching publishers. Hemingway loyally let Perkins know about these overtures, each time declaring that he had no intention whatsoever of leaving Scribner's.

He was somewhat uncomfortable in his double role as dedicated artist and hard-headed businessman. But he felt it was incumbent on him to earn as much as possible to support Pauline and Patrick, contribute to Bumby's welfare, and— above all—provide financial assistance to his family in Oak Park. As he told Perkins on 26 July 1929, now that he had "all these bloody people" to take care of and couldn't write more than one book every two years, he had to make all the money he legitimately could.[4] The suicide of Dr. Clarence E. Hemingway in December 1928 had left the family in dire straits. He had sunk most of his resources into basically worthless Florida real estate, and as the eldest male child, Ernest considered himself responsible for providing his mother and younger siblings with enough income to live on.

Throughout 1929 Ernest sent his mother Grace monthly checks for $100 and assured her that he would be able to do so indefinitely. Sometimes the correspondence between the two grew contentious. The son distributed advice as well as funds, and the mother wanted things done her own way. But these disputes faded away when, in April 1930, he was able to establish a $50,000 trust fund to guarantee his family long-term support.

Hemingway supplied $20,000 toward that fund from the royalties of *A Farewell to Arms*, and the other $30,000 came from Pauline's wealthy and generous Uncle Gus (Gustavus Adolphus) Pfeiffer. Gus doted on Pauline, admired Ernest, and was determined to assist them whenever he could. He provided them with a new Ford Model A in 1928 when they came to America, and shipped them a new Ford

Cabriolet in 1929 after they arrived in Europe. Later he paid for their house in Key West and for an African safari. Ernest dedicated *A Farewell to Arms* to G. A. Pfeiffer, explaining to Max Perkins on 26 July 1929 that there could hardly be "a less graceful name nor a much better man."

The success of his novel brought Hemingway a great deal of attention, not all of it welcome. Ironically, for a man who would become the most famous writer of the twentieth century, he took a hard line against personal publicity. In a letter of 12 October 1929 he cautioned his mother against submitting to any interviews about him. "Don't ever give out <u>anything</u>. Just say your sorry but you can't." Scribner's had the same instructions, he wrote, adding, "If I'm to write at <u>all</u> I have to keep my private life out of it."

Even for Dorothy Parker's laudatory piece about him—"The Artist's Reward," in the 30 November 1929 *New Yorker*—Hemingway refused to supply personal information. And Max Perkins earned his gratitude by purchasing half a dozen letters Hemingway had sent to Ernest Walsh, editor of the little magazine *This Quarter*, in 1925 and 1926. "It certainly is a crappy business to find your own personal letters up for sale," Hemingway wrote to Perkins (c. 24 April 1930). There were some he'd written to girls he'd be prepared to pay a good price for.

Hemingway was incensed when Grosset & Dunlap included "biographical <u>crap</u>" on the back wrapper of its inexpensive edition of *The Sun Also Rises*. He wrote to Perkins on 31 July 1930 to instruct the firm to remove that material at once, warning particularly against any references to his war service and marital status.

Then there was the matter of dealing with letters from readers who praised *A Farewell to Arms*. He faithfully replied to these communications from fans in brief notes, thanking them for liking his work and bothering to tell him so. The trouble was that each response cost him a significant chunk of time and 1.50 francs in postage. How was he supposed to manage that? he asked English writer Hugh Walpole on 10 December 1929. *The Sun Also Rises* had elicited only a few letters from elderly ladies offering to make a home for him despite his (or Jake Barnes's) unfortunate disability and from drunks who claimed to have met him in one watering hole or another; his 1927 book of stories, *Men Without Women*, generated almost no letters at all. But it was different with *A Farewell to Arms*. What was he to do when he really started to get letters?

A few of the letters came from aspiring young writers seeking advice. Early in October 1929 he told younger sister Carol to try to "write straight English," never using slang—"swell," for example—except in dialogue. She'd need a lot of luck to make money as a writer, he warned another young woman on 30 November 1929. "If you want to make a living writing I would say it was easier to make it any other way," he said. But if she wanted to write anyway, "the only thing is to write and no one can help you."

Some correspondents sent stories of their own for comments, and Hemingway sometimes supplied them. Of a promising story from George Albee, for example, Ernest observed on 7 May 1931 that he didn't quite believe that the protagonist would have killed himself at the end. "You see in all writing when you first start to do it you, writing, get a terrific kick and the reader" did not. Only later, and there was no short cut, could "you learn to give it all to the reader."

Much of the incoming mail involved professional matters. Magazine editors inquired if he had anything to send them. No, he told *Pagany* and *Hound & Horn*, he had nothing new to submit. He wasn't getting much down on paper during late 1929 and early 1930. Besides, he'd promised Ray Long at *Cosmopolitan* first crack at commercially viable long stories, and *Scribner's Magazine* remained a reliable place for his shorter pieces.

There were also letters from book collectors eager to acquire copies of his writings. The prices for his early limited edition publications in Paris were rapidly accelerating. In June 1930 a copy of *in our time* (1924) fetched $160 and one of *Three Stories and Ten Poems* (1923) $150 on the open market. Hemingway himself only had one copy of *Three Stories* and none at all of *in our time*. He arranged to send *Three Stories* to Dr. Don Carlos Guffey in Kansas City, an avid collector as well as the obstetrician who supervised both of Pauline's difficult deliveries.

Hemingway cooperated fully with Captain Louis Henry Cohn of New York, who was preparing the first bibliography of his work by tracking down stories and poems in little magazines that were hard to find or no longer in existence. In several long letters Hemingway supplied Cohn with lively anecdotes about the circumstances of these publications. He refused, however, to be of any assistance when it came to his newspaper articles. These pieces, he insisted in a letter dated 24 June 1930, were written to be timely and not permanent, and bore no relation to his "signed and published writing in books and magazines." It was "a hell of a trick on a man . . . to dig [them] up" and confuse them with his real work.

THE FITZGERALD RELATIONSHIP

Hemingway's most interesting letters concerning a literary figure during the 1929–1931 period were those to or about Scott Fitzgerald. In 1929, Fitzgerald was not quite halfway through his nine-year struggle to complete *Tender Is the Night*, the novel he began shortly after *The Great Gatsby* and that was to go through substantial changes in plot and characters before finally being published in 1934. From the beginning, though, Fitzgerald had been promising Perkins that the book was all but finished and that he would deliver it to Scribner's for the spring list, or the fall list, or in any case very soon, and then missing the deadlines.

Worried about the delays and aware that the Fitzgeralds were in Paris in the spring of 1929, Perkins apparently asked Hemingway to keep him informed about Scott's health and welfare. "Got in last night, so haven't seen Scott yet," Hemingway wrote to their editor on c. 23 April 1929, the day after arriving in Paris. "They said at the bank that he was in town—I'll see him soon and let you know." When he had located Fitzgerald, he reported to Perkins that Scott was doing well and working on his writing: a report that may have been motivated more by the writers' friendship than by entire fidelity to the facts.

Their relationship was at least slightly compromised one spring afternoon in the basement gymnasium of the American Club, where Hemingway and the Canadian novelist Morley Callaghan—recently moved to Paris—occasionally boxed with each other. Though smaller than Hemingway and not in particularly good shape, Callaghan was a very good boxer who knew his way around the ring.

On the day in question, Hemingway indulged in an extravagant luncheon with Scott and John Peale Bishop, eating lobster thermidor and drinking white burgundy, and was ill prepared for the bout with Callaghan. Enlisted to serve as timekeeper, Fitzgerald unfortunately froze and let the round overrun as Callaghan kept landing punches. When Scott finally called time, Hemingway wrote to Perkins on 28 August 1929, "I was pooped as could be and thought I had never known such a long round." Afterwards Fitzgerald said he "was very sorry and ashamed and would I forgive him."

The symbiosis between them as professionals was also undergoing a shift. Hemingway continued to rely on Fitzgerald for counsel on financial issues, but in a letter of 13 September 1929 he assumed the role of authority, imploring the older writer to finish his stalled novel. Fitzgerald might no longer have "the bloom" of his earlier career, he acknowledged, but that was no reason to despair. "You lose everything that is fresh and everything that is easy and it always seems as though you could <u>never</u> write." But Scott had more métier now and knew more, and when he got "flashes of the old juice" he could write better than ever. And, Hemingway added, Fitzgerald should stop turning out high-priced stories for the *Saturday Evening Post* and concentrate on the novel instead. "You have more stuff than anyone and you care more about it and for Christ sake just keep on and go through with it now and dont please write anything else until it's finished. It will be damned good—"

In mid-November Fitzgerald warned Hemingway that sales of *A Farewell to Arms* were liable to fall in the wake of the stock market crash. To forestall that happening, Fitzgerald recommended promoting the book as a love story and not just another story of war. This led Hemingway to compose a long letter to Perkins on 19 November 1929 with two specific and widely different suggestions: either prepare an ad "hammer"ing away that *Farewell* was "A Great MODERN Love STORY" or simply run James Aswell's rave review in the *Richmond Times-Dispatch* in its entirety. A month later, Hemingway apologized for his advertising advice. That was Scribner's job, not his, and he wouldn't have done it but for Fitzgerald seeming "so alarmed." He was "damned fond of Scott and would do anything for him," he wrote Perkins on 15 December 1929, "but he's been a little trying lately."

As—for example—at a gathering Gertrude Stein organized at 27, rue de Fleurus, specifically asking Hemingway in advance to bring Fitzgerald along as the one writer with the most talent. At the soirée itself, Stein was praising "her head off" to Hemingway about Fitzgerald when Scott came over to join them. She started to repeat her praise and then, "to spare [Scott] blushes and not be rude to [Ernest]" commented that the two writers had contrasting "flames."

Fitzgerald took that remark as a veiled attack, feeling sure that Stein meant to deprecate his work vis-à-vis Hemingway's. Writing to Scott c. 28 November 1929, the highly competitive Ernest maintained that it made no sense to worry about which of them was better. They'd started "along entirely separate lines and as writers ha[d] nothing in common except the desire to write well." So why talk about superiority? They were "all in the same boat," after all.

Toward the end of 1929 the unhappy spring boxing workout with Morley Callaghan came back to roil their friendship. The trouble started when Hemingway read in Isabel Paterson's 24 November *New York Herald Tribune* column that he had insulted Callaghan, who challenged him and knocked him cold. This was a blatant falsehood. As Ernest wrote to Max Perkins in high dudgeon in a letter of c. 8–10 December 1929, Callaghan had indeed hit him "whenever he wanted" on the day when he "was tight and could hardly see," but he was certainly not knocked out.

Callaghan promptly denied this rumored yarn, but Paterson—one of the few critics to review *Farewell* unfavorably—did not print this retraction until 8 December. In the meantime, still feeling guilty about his errant timekeeping, Fitzgerald cabled Callaghan demanding a correction. This angered Callaghan, who chastised Fitzgerald in response. On c. 12 December 1929, Hemingway wrote to Scott that he knew he had not "let the round go on deliberately" and not to trouble himself about it.

The Hemingway–Fitzgerald friendship was fractured but not entirely shattered by this series of events. Back from overseas and hearing the sad news of Zelda Fitzgerald's psychological breakdown and hospitalization in Switzerland, on 24 July 1930 Hemingway asked Perkins to send Fitzgerald his love. On 12 August he went further. "Please let me know ... anything you think of that I can do [for Scott]," he wrote to Perkins. "I'd go over [to Europe] if you think it would do any good."

THE ARTIST AS OUTDOORSMAN

By early 1930 the Hemingways were back in Key West, with Ernest eager to resume the fishing trips that meant so much to him and his friends. "Key West is a hell of a fine place don't you think," he wrote to the painter Waldo Peirce on 29 August 1929. "We want to get a shack there and one in Wyoming and live between the two." Peirce had come down from Maine the previous year to pursue the "monsters" of the deep, but was living overseas and unable to repeat his visit in the winter of 1930.

Too bad, but Hemingway had other candidates for journeys to the ideal fishing waters of the Dry Tortugas and the Marquesas. In a series of letters written in February 1930, Ernest rounded up companions for these outings, including Archie MacLeish, Mike Strater, and Max Perkins. Perkins caught a record fifty-eight-pound kingfish during his visit.

Other overtures went out to John Dos Passos and Bill Horne, who'd served with him in Italy—both of them recently and happily married. Dos Passos had married Kate Smith, one of Hemingway's closest friends up in Michigan. Dos and Kate came to Key West in April. And in August, Bill and Bunny Horne joined the Hemingways in Wyoming for trout fishing and game hunting. He'd never "seen people finer married," Hemingway wrote to them on 12 September 1930.

He wasn't getting much writing done during 1930, but had a plenitude of professional matters to attend to. To an unusual degree, Hemingway himself—not his agent Paul Reynolds, and not his editor Perkins—handled negotiations for translations of his work, *A Farewell to Arms* in particular. He drove a hard bargain with the German publisher, chose among three potential Spanish offers, and settled on the expert Maurice-Edgar Coindreau to translate his novel into French.

The Reynolds agency, he believed, did a poor job of selling the theatrical rights to *Farewell*. Neither the play written by Laurence Stallings (it flopped on Broadway in mid-1930) nor the movie rights based on that play brought in the funds he'd hoped for. After he learned that Harold Ober—Fitzgerald's agent as well—had left the Reynolds firm, Hemingway switched representation to lawyer Mo Speiser.

He was spending most of his time pursuing the outdoor life in 1930, and—as he wrote to Waldo Peirce on 1 June 1930—the "book racket" was "just about belly up" with publishers unable to move volumes even at $1 prices. Nonetheless, Hemingway understood that he had to keep writing. It was his occupation, and his calling. He contemplated writing a play before deciding on bullfighting as the subject for his next book. In late July, when he was staying at the Lawrence Nordquist ranch in Wyoming, he was humming along on *Death in the Afternoon* at 700 to 1,200 words a day, and planned to stay out West until he finished it.

The other literary venture in summer and fall of 1930 had to do with Scribner's bringing out a new edition of *In Our Time*, the first book of stories published by Boni & Liveright in 1925. In an exchange of correspondence with Max Perkins, Hemingway lobbied for an introduction by Edmund Wilson, resisted any wholesale revisions that would make it seem as if this were a new book and not a reissue, and worried over possible libel suits inasmuch as several of the stories were based on actual events and real people. Scribner's published it on 24 October, with a legal disclaimer stating that both the characters and their names were fictitious.

It was not all work in Wyoming: far from it. Just as he had in Key West, Hemingway sang the praises of the place in letters to potential outdoor companions. Best trout fishing in the world, he declared, and he could guarantee shots at mountain sheep, elk, deer, and bear once the hunting season opened on 15 September. Equipped with a new Springfield rifle recommended by gun expert Milford Baker, he himself brought down a bear that had been attacking the livestock, a bull elk, and a ram sighted high above the timber line.

Hemingway corresponded intensively with Baker in preparation for the ultimate hunting trip he was planning for the following year: a three-month African safari, with three fellow outdoorsmen. "How would you like to go to Africa to hunt and see the country?" he wrote to Archie MacLeish in early to mid-August 1930. Mike Strater and Charles Thompson were coming along, with the magnanimous Uncle Gus financing everything. They'd leave around the end of May 1931 and spend three months in the bush.

The safari plan had to be delayed when Hemingway suffered two injuries out West. The first, and less damaging, occurred when his horse bolted through the timber and he was cut up pretty badly: legs, arms, and a face wound requiring stitches from mouth to chin. The second and more serious injury resulted from an automobile crash. On the evening of 1 November, Ernest was driving with John Dos Passos on the second day of a cross-country trip from Wyoming to Key West. As they approached Billings, Montana just after sundown, one of the cars going in the opposite direction pulled out of line to pass, forcing Hemingway's car off the road and into a deep ditch.

Dos Passos was unhurt, and aside from having its doors sprung and scratches from the rocks the car itself weathered the accident. Hemingway, as always prone to wounds, broke his right arm badly. The arm was broken between the elbow and the shoulder, with the sharp bone churning up the flesh. A couple of attempts to set it failed, so finally the doctor operated, notching the bone, boring a hole through one side, and then tying it together with kangaroo tendons. Making light of the matter, Hemingway proposed that Scribner's might secure more money by insuring him against accident and disease than by publishing his books. Since he'd been under contract with the publisher, he'd had anthrax, cut his right eyeball, suffered congestion of the kidney, cut his index finger, gashed his forehead, torn open his cheek, run a branch through his leg, "and now," as he wrote to Perkins on 17 November 1930, "this arm."

He was less breezy about the fracture in a letter to Mike Strater, also in mid-November 1930. The doctor said he'd have to stay in the hospital for a month, confined to one position while waiting for the nerve to regenerate, and in more or less constant pain. "Don't let anybody ever mix you up in this broken bone racket because it hurts like hell all the time," he told Strater. These letters were dictated to Pauline, who had hurried back from Piggott to care for Ernest during his long period of recuperation. MacLeish, at the time one of Hemingway's closest friends, made the long trip from Conway, Massachusetts, to visit him in the hospital. "You know . . . how much it meant to us your coming out there," Ernest wrote him on 28 December 1930.

With his right arm immobilized, Hemingway could not write at all for several months. Finishing *Death in the Afternoon* was thus delayed, and he had to put aside for the time being the experiences in the Billings hospital that he eventually chronicled in "The Gambler, the Nun, and the Radio." Not until 16 February 1931 could he announce to Evan Shipman, "First writing with right hand! Still very difficult."

The safari was also postponed. As Hemingway wrote to MacLeish around 4 December 1930, "I can't tell you how terribly I feel about putting the trip on the bum." But he had no choice. The doctors were talking six months before the nerve could heal. They'd have to wait until 1932, he told Mike Strater, and in letters to MacLeish the departure date changed from June to September of that year. As it happened, neither Strater nor MacLeish made the journey. It was not until the end of 1933 that the Hemingways—Ernest and Pauline—and their Key West neighbor Charles Thompson went on safari in Africa.

HEMINGWAY AS AUTHORITY

The Hemingways spent the winter and most of spring 1931 in Key West while Ernest's right arm was healing. Max Perkins came down once again for a fishing trip to the Dry Tortugas that included John Herrmann and—as skipper-cook—Berge Saunders. Hemingway had only two new stories to offer *Scribner's Magazine* at that time: the rather grisly "A Natural History of the Dead" and the controversial "A Sea Change," an explicit foray into the realm of lesbianism. He was able to work steadily on *Death in the Afternoon*, though, and assured Perkins that he would finish the book after a summer visit to Spain to obtain photographs and bring his account up to date.

Family matters were being settled that spring as well. Pauline was pregnant with a second child, with delivery expected in November. The Hemingways planned to spend the interim period in Paris—which while not as wonderful as it once was yet still, as he wrote to MacLeish on 12 October 1930, was "the only city in the world to live in"—and in Spain. When they returned, it would be to inhabit an old stone house at 907 Whitehead Street in Key West that Uncle Gus had bought for them: their first permanent home in the United States.

A good many of Ernest's letters in 1930 through 1931 demonstrated his propensity to adopt an air of authority. As an autodidact who'd never been to college, he set himself the task of achieving expertise on any number of subjects. He was a quick learner who knew a lot of things and was eager to dispense his knowledge. Bullfighting was but one of the fields of study in which he felt qualified to instruct others, and just as he expounded on tauromachy in *Death in the Afternoon*, he discoursed on a number of other subjects in his correspondence.

Noteworthy among these were his evaluations of other writers. In a letter to Ezra Pound of 28 February 1930, he traced a downward arc of Gertrude Stein's career. She had started out well, as in the Melanctha section of *Three Lives* (1909) and the first part of *The Making of Americans*. Next, when this work failed to achieve general acceptance, she lapsed into a period of near automatic writing, cranking out copy "without corrections." But Stein needed to get this less worthy material "approved and accepted and accoladed," which led her to a "pretty awful" third "period of trying to get into the Academy."

In similar fashion, Hemingway divided the fiction of Ford Madox Ford into categories. Ford was interested in locating an American publisher for his writing, and on 28 September 1930, at Ford's request, Ernest wrote to Max Perkins about him. Ford goes "about like this," he said: (1) good book, (2) regular megalomania, (3) poor work, (4) success "pee-ed away," (5) discredited, (6) depression, (7) megalomania diminishes, (8) gets down to work, (9) good book again. Ford "might be due" for that next good book, he told Perkins, "anyway it's up to you."

Hemingway railed against Sinclair Lewis winning the 1930 Nobel Prize in Literature. He'd been "damned happy" to see previous Nobel awards go to Thomas Mann and William Butler Yeats, but it was "a filthy business" for Lewis to be chosen over Ezra Pound or James Joyce, he wrote to Guy Hickok on 5 December 1930.

Hemingway had become aware of William Faulkner as a rival fiction writer—often, he thought, a very good one, if sometimes "unnecessary." But the man whose life and work he particularly admired in 1930–1931 was his friend Archibald MacLeish. He tried to add MacLeish to Perkins's cadre of authors at Scribner's. "You couldn't get a better name, a better writer, or a better guy for your list . . . and his future is ahead of him instead of behind him," he assured Perkins on 28 December 1930. (Perkins and MacLeish explored the possibility, but in the end Archie decided to stick with Houghton Mifflin as his publisher.)

Ernest rarely wrote blurbs for fellow writers—he had no facility for doing so—but composed endorsements both for John Herrmann in late 1930 and for MacLeish's Pulitzer prizewinning *Conquistador* on 23 December 1931. As a friend, he felt awkward about praising MacLeish's work, Hemingway admitted, "but even those who do not like him nor what he writes must see by now that he is a great poet."

In the longest letter of this volume, dated 1 January 1931 and running to fourteen pages, Hemingway expounded on various alcoholic beverages for the benefit of his brother-in-law Karl Pfeiffer, who was about to leave on a trip to Europe. Much of his advice dealt with French wines. In this letter Hemingway expressed his admiration for the "continental" attitude toward consumption of alcohol. An aperitif before a meal, wine or beer during it, and possibly a liqueur afterwards could give you "a sense of well being and a pleasant feeling," he observed. And unlike in the United States—and particularly in the teetotalling household where he had been brought up—it was not regarded "as immoral to drink."

It was early May 1931 before the Hemingways traveled to Europe on separate ships. Pauline, Patrick, and Patrick's nurse-governess sailed from New York to France, while Ernest went directly to Spain, then in the throes of revolution. The bullfight season was about to begin, but in the meantime Hemingway immersed himself in the political situation. By way of personal observation, conversations with Spaniards and with newsmen, and considerable reading, he arrived at conclusions that he duly dispensed in his letters. On politics as on drinking or bullfights or a number of other subjects, he played the role of expert.

After six weeks in Spain, Hemingway summed up his judgments in a 26 June 1931 letter to John Dos Passos. He felt sure that the Republicans would win the election two days later. But they were so divided into factions—"Red White and Black Republicans"—that it would be difficult for them to govern the country. Besides, the various regions had different priorities.

He'd been following the Spanish situation as closely as if he were "working for a paper," he wrote to Max Perkins on 1 August 1931, and wished there was a market for what he'd learned. Instead, he buckled down to prepare a glossary of bullfight terminology and write two final chapters for *Death in the Afternoon*. Ernest's time alone in Madrid had ended when Pauline came down from Paris in mid-June and they went together to visit Patrick and Bumby at Hendaye, where Pauline remained while Ernest attended the fiesta at Pamplona. This time, seven-year-old Bumby went with him and had a wonderful time.

The principal family event of the year was the birth of Gregory Hancock Hemingway on 12 November. On 15 July 1931 Ernest asked Guy Hickok about the possibility of a delivery in Paris. A Caesarian might be necessary, he pointed out, and they knew that Dr. Guffey in Kansas City could perform that operation. Who was the best doctor in Paris? The best hospital? Did Hickok think it would be "gambling" for Pauline to have the baby in Paris?

In the end Pauline and Ernest decided on Kansas City, and the birth turned out to be as difficult as they feared. Pauline's pains started about 6 p.m. on 11 November, "armistice night," and twelve hours of heavy labor failed to move the child at all. Dr. Guffey, who wanted to avoid a Caesarian if possible, then performed the operation "<u>very</u> well." Pauline suffered terribly, Ernest wrote to her parents later that day, and it took nearly twenty minutes to get the baby to breathe, but both mother and son Gregory, nearly nine pounds and physically perfect, were doing well.

The Hemingways returned to their new home in Key West a week before Christmas. The furniture Pauline had shipped from Paris was on hand, but plumbers and carpenters were still at work while Ernest typed all day on the bullfight manuscript. It would be finished by the end of the year, he promised Perkins.

By that time, Ernest Hemingway had become an experienced professional writer, sensitive to the complications of the literary marketplace and wary of the costs of his growing fame. At only thirty-two, he was the father of three sons and the principal provider for his mother and two youngest siblings. He was happily married to a wife who cared deeply about him, and they had just moved into a home of their own.

Despite injuries and other setbacks, he continued to revel in the outdoor life of fishing and hunting. These pleasures, shared with male companions, were balanced by a devotion to his craft and a rigorous work ethic. He had established himself as the kind of writer, with the kind of recognition, he had only dreamed of in his youth.

NOTES

1 Unless otherwise cited, all letters quoted are included in this volume.
2 The blanks used in the novel, as published, did not indicate which words had been omitted. For full discussion of this issue, see Scott Donaldson, "Censorship and *A Farewell to Arms*," *Studies in American Fiction* 19 (Spring 1991): 85–93.
3 Maxwell Perkins to EH, 12 July 1929 (PUL; *TOTTC*, 108).
4 The American literary marketplace was not organized during this period to generate continuing income after first publication of a book. Book clubs were just getting started. Paperbacks did not arrive until 1939. Drama and film rights were rare windfalls, hardly to be counted upon.

VOLUME 4 (1929–1931) CHRONOLOGY

5 April 1929	EH, Pauline, son Patrick, along with EH's son from his first marriage to Hadley, John (nicknamed "Bumby") and EH's sister Madelaine (nicknamed "Sunny") sail from Havana to Boulogne aboard the *Yorck*.
21 April 1929	Hemingways arrive at Boulogne, take a train to Paris, and arrive the next day at their apartment, 6, rue Férou. Sunny will stay in a nearby pension. Bumby returns to Hadley, who lives in an apartment at 98, boulevard Auguste-Blanqui.
May 1929	EH's poem "Valentine for a Mr. Lee Wilson Dodd and Any of His Friends who Want it" appears in the final issue of Margaret Anderson and Jane Heap's *Little Review*.
early May 1929	The first of six installments of *A Farewell to Arms* appears in *Scribner's Magazine*. EH is at Hendaye Plage, staying as usual at the Barron family's Ondarraitz Hotel, as he continues revising the novel's ending and page proofs for later installments. Sunny remains in Paris; Pauline is diagnosed with exhaustion and a sinus infection, Patrick with the flu. EH is back in Paris by 10 May.
18 May 1929	The Hemingways share a turbulent dinner at the Paris apartment of F. Scott and Zelda Fitzgerald.
June 1929	EH boxes several times with Morley Callaghan in Paris, including the infamous match refereed by Fitzgerald, who gets distracted and lets the round run for too long, to EH's disadvantage.

7 June 1929	EH protests Scribner's decision to excise from the book version of *A Farewell to Arms* "certain" words they deem censorable.
19 June 1929	The June issue of *Scribner's Magazine*, which appeared on newsstands on 25 May and contained the second installment of *A Farewell to Arms*, is banned by Boston's Superintendent of Police.
c. 1–2 July 1929	EH drives to Spain in the new Ford Cabriolet, a gift that Pauline's uncle, Gus Pfeiffer had shipped to them in Paris. He is accompanied by Guy Hickok and Jinny Pfeiffer.
6–14 July 1929	EH and companions, including Hickok, Jinny Pfeiffer, and Patrick Morgan, stay at the Hotel Quintana in Pamplona for the annual Fiesta of San Fermín. Pauline travels from Paris to join EH in Spain c. 12 July.
18 July 1929	EH and Pauline are visiting Joan and Pilar Miró, in Montroig, Tarragona province.
21 July 1929	EH and Pauline are staying at the Hotel Regina in Valencia, where they celebrate their birthdays (on 21 and 22 July) and attend the city's annual taurine fiesta.
26 July 1929	EH unwillingly accedes to the excision of three words and the replacement of another in the book version of *A Farewell to Arms*.
3 August 1929	EH and Pauline begin the drive to Santiago de Compostela, where they will stay at the Hotel Suizo until the end of the month.
13 August 1929	Sunny sails for home aboard *Nieuw Amsterdam*.
16 August 1929	Maxwell Perkins sends proofs of Scribner's book edition of *A Farewell to Arms* to EH's British publisher, Jonathan Cape, with blanks to represent three excised words and with pages containing the words in case Cape decides to include them.
31 August 1929	EH and Pauline begin the drive from Santiago to Madrid by way of Orense, Benavente, León, and Palencia, where they experience extreme heat and

see two bullfights on 1 and 2 September. While in Madrid, they meet Sidney Franklin, the bullfighter from Brooklyn, New York, and EH's passport, *carte d'identité*, and automobile documents are stolen by a pickpocket but later returned.

6 September 1929	In Madrid, EH buys a copy of an etching from Goya's series *Los Disastres de la Guerra* (*The Disasters of War*), executed between 1810 and 1820, and a catalog of Goya's works.
12 September 1929	EH and Pauline leave Madrid for Hendaye Plage, where they again stay at the Barron family's Ondarraitz Hotel.
16 September 1929	At a bookstore in San Sebastian, EH purchases three works by Goya (etchings and lithographs).
18–20 September 1929	EH and Pauline drive back to Paris.
25 September 1929	Date of the Scribner's contract for *A Farewell to Arms*, probably signed in Key West in March 1930 but backdated to precede the novel's publication date. The contract stipulates that the first $20,000 of royalties be set aside in a separate account which, with additional contributions by Pauline and her uncle Gus Pfeiffer, would become a trust fund for EH's mother and younger siblings.
26 September 1929	EH, with Morley and Loretto Callaghan, tours Versailles and Chartres.
27 September 1929	*A Farewell to Arms* is published in New York to rave reviews and within two weeks appears on the bestseller lists.
3 October 1929	EH, not having received copies of his book, buys two at a Paris bookshop. He complains to Perkins about the cover design.
4–22 October 1929	Fearing further cuts, EH rejects an offer from Current News Features (Washington D.C.) for newspaper syndication of *A Farewell to Arms*. EH and Perkins revise royalty rates and discuss dramatization rights for *A Farewell to Arms*; Perkins recommends retaining literary agent Paul R. Reynolds.

5–6 October 1929	EH, Pauline, and Harry and Caresse Crosby visit the restaurants and racetracks of Paris.
8 October 1929	*A Farewell to Arms* has sold 24,500 copies, the sales rising to 33,000 by 22 October.
24 October 1929	On "Black Thursday" a record 12.9 million shares are traded on the U.S. Stock Exchange. The panic selling continues and on "Black Tuesday" (29 October 1929) the stock market collapses, marking the beginning of the Great Depression.
25 October 1929	Heeding Perkins's recommendation, EH accepts the Modern Library offer to publish a 50,000-copy edition of *The Sun Also Rises* and rejects Coward-McCann's offer of a $25,000 advance for his next book.
November 1929	EH begins a bullfight article commissioned by Archibald MacLeish for *Fortune* magazine.
10 November 1929	EH travels to Berlin with Guy Hickok and Gus Pfeiffer, arriving on Monday, 11 November.
11 November 1929	Perkins cables that *A Farewell to Arms* has sold 43,000 copies, the number growing to 45,000 by the next day.
11–15 November 1929	While in Berlin EH meets Pfeiffer relatives and negotiates the German serialization rights to *A Farewell to Arms* with publisher Rowohlt Verlag. On 15 November he makes a partial payment on Paul Klee's painting *Monument in Arbeit* (*Monument Under Construction*, 1929) at Alfred Flectheim's Berlin gallery, with the concluding payment to Flectheim's Galerie Simon in Paris following on 18 November.
16 November 1929	EH arrives back in Paris.
24 November 1929	In her weekly column for *New York Herald Tribune Books*, Isabel Paterson reports that Morley Callaghan had knocked out EH in a June boxing match in Paris.
27 November 1929	EH, Fitzgerald, Allen Tate, and Caroline Gordon meet at Gertrude Stein's home in Paris.

late November 1929	Dorothy Parker's profile of EH, "The Artist's Reward," is published in the *New Yorker* (30 November 1929). EH reacts angrily to Robert Herrick's negative review of *A Farewell to Arms* ("What is Dirt?") published in the November issue of *Bookman*.
7 December 1929	Sales of *A Farewell to Arms* reach 57,000.
8 December 1929	Callaghan's correction of Isabel Patterson's report is published in *New York Herald Tribune Books*. He denies that he knocked out EH during a boxing match.
9 December 1929	EH and Pauline dine with Fitzgerald, who reports that Robert McAlmon has been spreading rumors around New York that EH was gay, Pauline a lesbian, and that EH had physically abused Hadley while she was pregnant with Bumby.
10 December 1929	In New York City, Harry Crosby shoots and kills his lover, Boston socialite Josephine Rotch Bigelow, and himself in a suicide pact.
20–31 December 1929	The Hemingways are at the Palace Hotel in Montana-Vermala, Switzerland, to spend Christmas with the Murphys, whose son Patrick is being treated for tuberculosis at a sanatorium. Other friends gather to lend their support around this time as well, including the Fitzgeralds, John and Kate Dos Passos, Donald Ogden and Beatrice Stewart, and Dorothy Parker.
c. 31 December 1929	EH, Pauline, and Patrick return to Paris. EH has finished an article on bullfighting for *Fortune* magazine.
late December 1929–early January 1930	EH writes an introduction to *Kiki's Memoirs*, Samuel Putnam's translation of the memoirs of French model Alice Prin, who was known as "Kiki of Montparnasse." EH's introduction is published as a pamphlet in New York by Edward Titus in an edition of twenty-five copies in order to secure copyright before it is included in the book published in Paris in June 1930.

10 January 1930	The Hemingways and Patrick's French nanny, Henriette Lechner, sail from Bordeaux aboard *La Bourdonnais*, stopping at Vigo and Halifax en route to New York; the family's Ford Cabriolet is in the hold of the ship.
25 January 1930	*La Bourdonnais* docks in New York, where EH meets with Perkins and Henry (Mike) Strater, visits Ada MacLeish in hospital, and makes arrangements for the Grace Hemingway trust fund.
27 January 1930	The Hemingways depart from New York on *La Bourdonnais*, arriving in Havana on 31 January.
February 1930	EH begins writing *Death in the Afternoon*. Mike Strater arrives in Key West and begins his third portrait of EH. John Herrmann and Josephine Herbst are in Key West, where they will stay until April.
2 February 1930	After a one-day stopover in Havana, the Hemingways arrive in Key West, where they have rented a house at 1301 Whitehead Street and a four-horsepower boat.
7 February 1930	EH signs a release permitting Fox Film Corporation to use the title *Men Without Women* for a film unrelated to the stories in EH's 1927 collection of that name; EH is paid $500.
10 February 1930	EH asks Milford Baker, a fellow American Red Cross ambulance driver in Italy during WWI, for advice on rifles and other hunting equipment for a planned safari to Africa the following year, to be financed by Gus Pfeiffer.
16 February 1930	EH hooks, fights, and shoots a 205-pound, 8-foot long mackerel shark whose photograph and jaw-bone he will send to Ezra Pound in late February.
18 February 1930	Details of the $50,000 trust fund for Grace Hall Hemingway are finalized, with EH and Pauline as trustees.
22 February 1930	The Modern Library pays $3,000 to republish *The Sun Also Rises*, with royalties assigned to Hadley.

late February 1930	Waldo Peirce's pregnant girlfriend Alzira Boehm arrives in Key West, where she will stay while Peirce is in Paris negotiating his divorce from Ivy Troutman.
March 1930	"Bullfighting, Sport and Industry" is published in *Fortune* magazine.
17 March 1930	Perkins arrives in Key West for a fishing vacation. He hand-delivers a letter from Louis Henry Cohn, who is interested in preparing an annotated bibliography of EH's work.
18 March–5 April 1930	EH, Perkins, Mike Strater, John Herrmann, Archibald MacLeish, and Berge Saunders sail from Key West to Cape Sable, Florida, but the mosquitoes drive them away and they continue to the Marquesas and Dry Tortugas. Stranded in the Dry Tortugas by a storm c. 26 March, they are rescued on 30 March by the large yacht *Caroline*, which returns them to Key West when the storm is over.
April 1930	The trust fund that EH and Pauline have established for Grace Hemingway goes into effect.
8 April 1930	Perkins reports that letters EH had written to Ernest Walsh in the mid-1920s had been offered for sale in London and were purchased by Scribner's Rare Books Department to get them off the market. He offers to send the letters to EH.
c. 13 April 1930	John and Kate Dos Passos arrive in Key West.
15 April 1930	EH, Pauline, John Dos Passos, and Pat Morgan embark on a fishing cruise to the Dry Tortugas.
c. 22 April 1930	The boat pump breaks down as the fishing party is returning from the Dry Tortugas to Key West, forcing them to spend the night at anchor. The next morning EH brings Pauline and Dos Passos back to Key West in an outboard motor boat.
24 April 1930	EH agrees to Cohn's proposed bibliography of his works.

early May 1930	EH requires six stitches on his right forefinger, injured during a workout with a punching bag. The finger will be stiff and painful for all of May.
8 May 1930	First serial installment of the German translation of *A Farewell to Arms* appears as *Schluss Damit. Adieu Krieg!* in *Frankfurter Zeitung*, with the final installment appearing on 16 July 1930.
20 May 1930	Alzira Boehm and her two sisters leave Key West; she will join Waldo Peirce in Paris.
June 1930	*Kiki's Memoirs*, with an introduction by EH, is published in Paris by Edward Titus's Black Manikin Press.
7 June 1930	Pauline, Patrick, and Henriette leave Key West by train, bound for Piggott, Arkansas.
c. 12 June 1930	EH has received and is pleased with the customized Springfield rifle that Milford Baker assisted him in purchasing.
14 June 1930	EH leaves Key West for New York, to meet Bumby and Jinny, who are due to arrive from Paris aboard the *Lafayette* on 23 June. In New York EH discusses the publication of *In Our Time* with Perkins and lunches with Milford Baker. EH stays at the Brevoort Hotel.
21 June 1930	The *Lafayette* arrives two days earlier than expected.
24 June 1930	EH writes to Cohn, declining to provide an introduction or epilogue to the bibliography but returning the completed questionnaire Cohn had sent him in May.
25 June 1930	EH and Bumby travel by train to Cincinnati, where they will pick up the Ford roadster, shipped from Key West, for the drive to Piggott.
2–14 July 1930	EH, Pauline, and Bumby drive from Piggott to the Nordquists' L-Bar-T Ranch in Wyoming, where EH will stay through October. Patrick and Jinny remain in Piggott.
24 July 1930	EH has written 700–1,000 words of *Death in the Afternoon* since arriving at the L-Bar-T Ranch.

31 July 1930	EH objects to biographical material published on the dust jacket of the Grosset & Dunlap edition of *The Sun Also Rises*. By 6 August, the jackets will have been removed and destroyed.
August 1930	"Wine of Wyoming" is published in the August issue of *Scribner's Magazine*. EH works on revising "Up in Michigan" for the Scribner's edition of *In Our Time*.
8 August 1930	Bill and Frances (Bunny) Horne arrive in Wyoming for a two-week visit.
22 August 1930	EH's horse bolts during a bear hunt and EH suffers cuts to face, legs and arms. His face requires several stitches. He resumes the hunt the following evening and kills a bear.
30 August 1930	EH kills a second male bear.
13 September 1930	EH writes a new will before going to the mountains for a two-week hunting trip. Pauline and Bumby depart by train for Piggott. There they will pick up Henriette, who will sail with Bumby from New York to France and remain there with her family for five months.
mid- to late September 1930	*A Farewell to Arms* is published in French and German translations.
22 September 1930	The Laurence Stallings stage adaptation of *A Farewell to Arms* opens at the National Theatre in New York; it will close on 11 October.
2 October 1930	EH is on page 205 of *Death in the Afternoon*. He acknowledges receipt of a new Mannlicher rifle, ordered for him by Milford Baker.
21 October 1930	Dos Passos arrives in Wyoming for a ten-day hunting trip.
24 October 1930	The Scribner's edition of *In Our Time* appears with an introduction by Edmund Wilson. "Up in Michigan" is not included in the volume.
31 October 1930	EH, Dos Passos, and cowboy Floyd Allington leave Cooke City in EH's car, bound for Billings,

	Montana; they camp out that night in Yellowstone National Park.
1 November 1930	In a road car accident near Billings shortly after sundown, EH's right arm is broken about three inches above the elbow. He is taken to St. Vincent's Hospital. Dos Passos cables Pauline in Piggott on 2 November and she leaves the next day for Billings, arriving on 4 November.
5 November 1930	Sinclair Lewis is awarded the Nobel Prize in Literature.
6 November 1930	After two attempts at setting the broken arm, Dr. Louis Allard operates, notches the bone, and uses kangaroo tendons to hold it. EH's nurses and fellow patients will become prototypes for characters in EH's story "The Gambler, The Nun, and the Radio."
15 November 1930	Paramount acquires the movie rights to *A Farewell to Arms* for $80,000, of which EH will receive $24,000.
1 December 1930	EH is allowed to sit up for the first time since the surgery. He is still in great pain.
c. 6–7 December 1930	Infection has set in where the broken bone in EH's arm had lacerated muscles and flesh. EH has fever and difficulties urinating.
c. early to mid-December 1930	MacLeish travels to Billings to visit EH in hospital.
21 December 1930	EH is released from hospital. He and Pauline travel by train to St. Louis, where Paul Pfeiffer meets them and drives them to Piggott, arriving on 24 December. EH is running a fever.
early January 1931	The Hemingways, accompanied by Jinny Pfeiffer, return to Key West and move into a rented house at 1425 Pearl Street. Their car, repaired in Montana and driven to Key West by Nordquist ranch hand Chub Weaver, has already arrived.
c. 26–27 January 1931	Grace Hemingway visits Key West, staying at the Casa Marina resort.

31 January–1 February 1931	EH and Pauline host a fishing trip to the Dry Tortugas for Lawrence and Olive Nordquist, John Herrmann, Chub Weaver, and Leonard Outhwaite.
27 February–c. 12 March 1931	EH and Pauline host another fishing expedition to the Dry Tortugas. The party includes Uncle Gus and Aunt Louise Pfeiffer, Carol Hemingway, Jinny Pfeiffer, John Herrmann and Josie Herbst, Lawrence and Olive Nordquist, Chub Weaver, and William and Elaine Sidley, whom EH met at the L-Bar-T Ranch. Stormbound in the Dry Tortugas, they return later than expected.
26 March–10 April 1931	EH, Pauline, Max Perkins, John Herrmann, Berge Saunders, Chub Weaver, and Pat and Maud Morgan go fishing in the Dry Tortugas. Perkins is obliged to return before the others and is back in New York c. 3 April. On 2 April, Saunders and Herrmann return to Key West to fetch supplies, and Perkins departs for New York. On 7 April, Herrmann and Saunders, delayed by mechanical problems, rejoin EH and the others in the Dry Tortugas.
c. 11–12 April 1931	EH has started to write with his right hand again.
29 April 1931	With the financial assistance of Uncle Gus, EH and Pauline purchase a house at 907 Whitehead Street. EH resumes writing *Death in the Afternoon*.
2 May 1931	EH leaves Key West for Havana.
4 May 1931	EH sails for Spain from Havana on the *Volendam*.
15 May 1931	EH debarks in Vigo and takes the train to Madrid to work on *Death in the Afternoon*. The city's San Isidro festival presents daily bullfights on 15, 16, and 17 May.
16–28 May 1931	Pauline, Patrick, and Henriette leave Key West for New York, from whence they sail for France aboard the *President Harding* on 20 May. Landing in Cherbourg on 28 May, they take a train to Paris, where Pauline begins packing their

	belongings in the apartment on rue Férou for shipping to Key West. Henriette and Patrick travel to Bordeaux and Hendaye Plage.
early June 1931	On a brief visit to Paris, EH sees Sylvia Beach, Adrienne Monnier, Hadley, and Bumby. By mid-June EH and Pauline have returned to Madrid, where they stay at the Hotel Biarritz and renew their acquaintance with Sidney Franklin.
4–5 July 1931	EH and Pauline go to Hendaye to see Patrick and Bumby, who has recovered from his tonsillectomy in Paris of c. 30 June.
6–14 July 1931	EH and Bumby are in Pamplona with Sidney Franklin for the annual Fiesta of San Fermín.
15 July 1931	EH and Pauline are at the Barrons' hotel in Hendaye "for a little while seeing the kids." EH writes to Guy Hickok that Pauline is pregnant.
9 August 1931	EH and Pauline are staying at the Hotel Avenida in San Sebastian, where they see a bullfight in the company of Caresse Crosby and Jacques Porel.
14–18 August 1931	The Hemingways are in Hendaye, where EH meets with attorney Maurice Speiser. They also visit San Sebastian, where the annual taurine festival takes place 15–17 August.
19–end August 1931	EH, Pauline, Bumby, and Patrick travel to Madrid, where they stay at the Hotel Biarritz.
1 September 1931	*Kat*, a dramatization of *A Farewell to Arms*, opens in Berlin at the Deutsches Theater.
c. 6 September 1931	Pauline leaves Madrid for Paris. EH remains in Madrid to work on the "Explanatory Glossary" of *Death in the Afternoon*.
14 September 1931	EH cables Perkins from Paris to say that he has finished work on the illustrations for *Death in the Afternoon*. He has had serious eye trouble since mid-August.
23 September 1931	EH, Pauline, Patrick, and Gabrielle sail for New York on the *Île de France* and arrive on 29

September. Among the belongings they are shipping home is a recently acquired painting by Juan Gris, *Man with a Guitar*. Fellow passengers include Jane and Grant Mason and Don and Beatrice Stewart.

late September–early October 1931	Gabrielle and Patrick travel to Piggott while EH and Pauline remain in New York. EH delivers photographs for *Death in the Afternoon* to Perkins and meets with Louis Henry Cohn and Eric Knight. EH and Pauline visit the MacLeishes in Conway, Massachusetts. EH, MacLeish, and Waldo Peirce attend a Harvard football game in Cambridge, Massachusetts.
12 October 1931	EH and Pauline travel by train through Philadelphia and St. Louis on their way to Kansas City, Missouri, for the birth of their second child. Arriving on 15 October, they stay with relatives Ruth and Malcolm Lowry at 6435 Indian Lane before moving to the Riviera Apartments at 229 Ward Parkway around 9 November.
12 November 1931	Gregory Hancock Hemingway is born by Caesarian section at Research Hospital. Pauline is attended by Dr. Don Carlos Guffey, who also delivered Patrick.
late November–early December 1931	EH finishes the first draft of *Death in the Afternoon*.
December 1931	"The Sea Change" is published in *This Quarter*.
1 December 1931	While Pauline and Gregory remain in hospital, EH travels to Piggott for a week of quail hunting with Pauline's brother, Karl Pfeiffer.
8 December 1931	Pauline is discharged from hospital; EH joins her at their rented apartment in Kansas City for a few days before they begin the journey to Key West with their newborn son.
14 December 1931	EH, Pauline, and Gregory leave Kansas City by train for the three-day trip to Key West, picking up Patrick and Gabrielle en route in Jonesboro, Arkansas.

19 December 1931	The Hemingway family takes up residence in their new home at 907 Whitehead Street, Key West, which is being remodeled.
25 December 1931	Patrick sprays his baby brother with mosquito powder. Carol Hemingway is in Key West to celebrate Christmas with EH's family.

MAPS

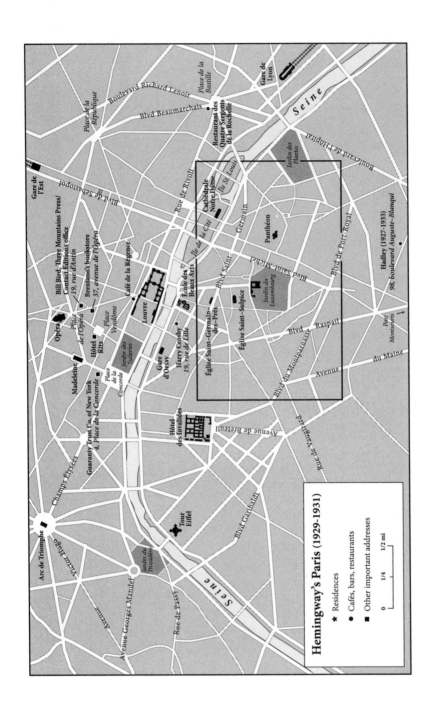

Hemingway's Paris (1929–1931)

★ Residences
● Cafés, bars, restaurants
■ Other important addresses

0   1/4   1/2 mi

Seine

Gare de Lyon

Place de la Bastille

Boulevard Richard Lenoir

Place de la République

Blvd Beaumarchais

Restaurant des Quatre Sergents de la Rochelle

Jardin des Plantes

Boulevard de l'Hôpital

Gare de l'Est

Rue de Rivoli

Cathédrale Notre-Dame

Île St Louis

Blvd de Sébastopol

Germain

Panthéon

Blvd de Port-Royal

Hadley (1927–1933)
98, boulevard Auguste-Blanqui

Bill Bird, Three Mountains Press/
Contact Editions office
19, rue d'Arün

Brentano's bookstore
37, avenue de l'Opéra

Café de la Régence

École des Beaux Arts

Blvd Saint-Michel

Blvd Saint

Jardin du Luxembourg

Opéra

Place de l'Opéra

Place Vendôme

Louvre

Harry Crosby ★
19, rue de Lille

Église Saint-Germain-des-Prés

Église Saint-Sulpice

Blvd Raspail

Parc Montsouris

Hôtel Ritz

Madeleine

Place de la Concorde

Jardin des Tuileries

Gare d'Orsay

Blvd du Montparnasse

Avenue du Maine

Guaranty Trust Co. of New York
4, Place de la Concorde

Champs Élysées

Hôtel des Invalides

Avenue de Breteuil

Rue de Vaugirard

Arc de Triomphe

Victor Hugo

Avenue Georges Mandel

Jardin du Trocadéro

Rue de Passy

Tour Eiffel

Blvd Garibaldi

Seine

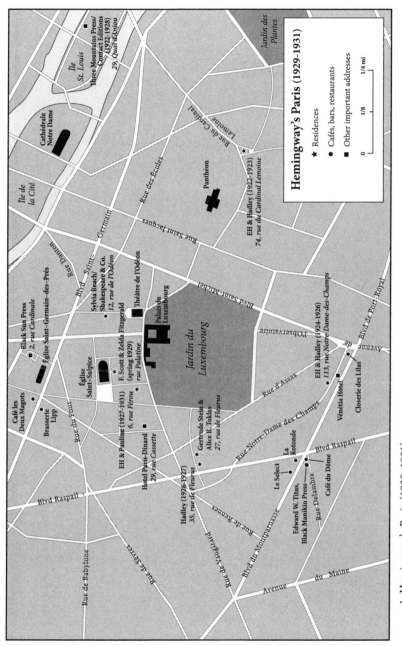

Three Mountains Press/
Contact Editions
(1922-1928)
29, Quai d'Anjou

Jardin des
Plantes

Île
St. Louis

Cathédrale
Notre Dame

Île de
la Cité

Rue du Cardinal
Lemoine

Panthéon

EH & Hadley (1922-1923)
74, rue du Cardinal Lemoine

Rue des Écoles

Rue Saint-Jacques

Germain

Hemingway's Paris (1929-1931)

★ Residences
● Cafés, bars, restaurants
■ Other important addresses

0   1/8   1/4 mi

Rue Denfert

Blvd   Saint-Germain-des-Prés

Sylvia Beach/
Shakespeare & Co.
12, rue de l'Odéon

Théâtre de l'Odéon

Palais du
Luxembourg

Blvd Saint-Michel

Black Sun Press
2, rue Cardinale

Église Saint-Germain-des-Prés

F. Scott & Zelda Fitzgerald
(spring 1929)
rue Palatine

Église
Saint-Sulpice

Jardin du
Luxembourg

l'Observatoire

EH & Hadley (1924-1926)
113, rue Notre-Dame-des-Champs

Avenue de

Blvd de Port-Royal

Café les
Deux Magots

Brasserie
Lipp

Rue du Four

EH & Pauline (1927-1931)
6, rue Férou

Gertrude Stein &
Alice B. Toklas
27, rue de Fleurus

Rue d'Assas

Venetia Hotel

Closerie des Lilas

Hotel Paris-Dinard
29, rue Cassette

Rue-Notre-Dame des-Champs

Blvd Raspail

Hadley (1926-1927)
35, rue de Fleurus

Rue de Rennes

La
Rotonde

Le Select

Blvd Raspail

Café du Dôme

Blvd Raspail

Rue de Sèvres

Rue de Babylone

Rue de Vaugirard

Blvd du Montparnasse

Edward W. Titus,
Black Manikin Press

Rue Delambre

Avenue   du   Maine

1 Hemingway's Paris (1929-1931)

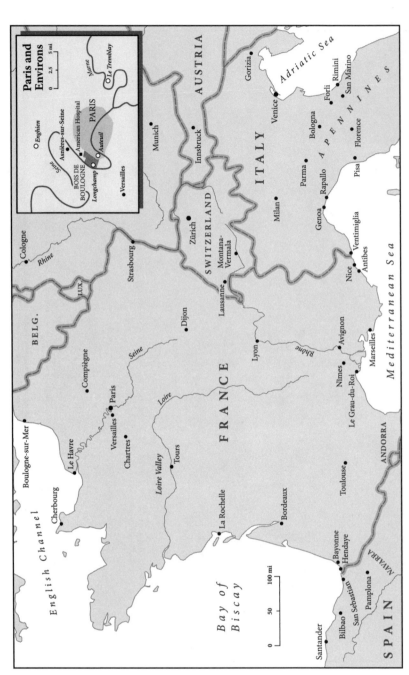

2 France and Switzerland

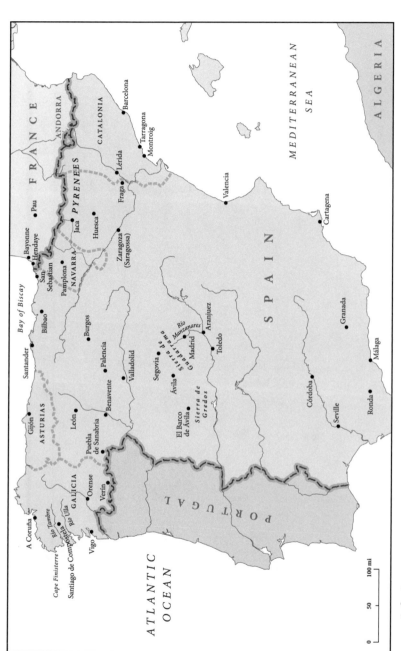

3 Spain

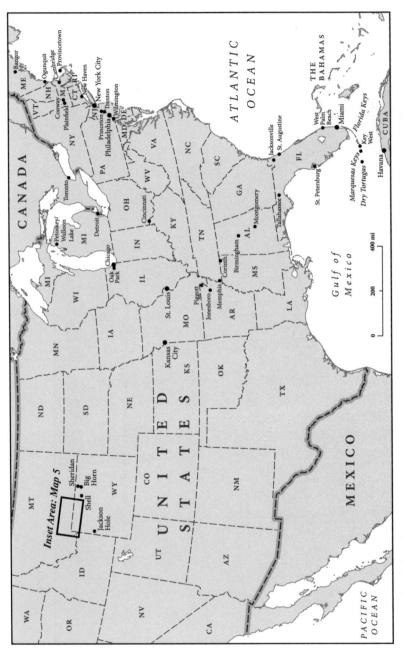

4 North America

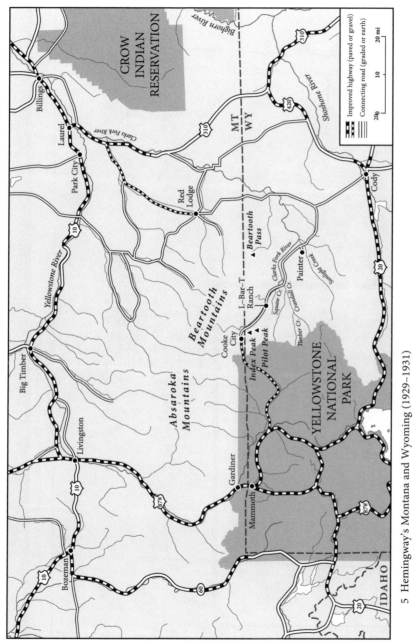

5 Hemingway's Montana and Wyoming (1929–1931)

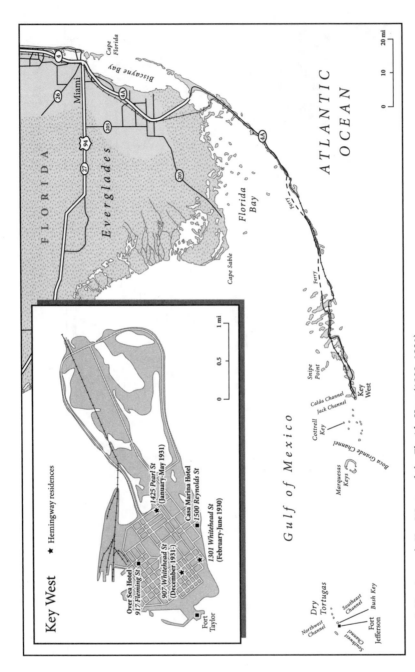

6 Hemingway's Key West and the Florida Keys (1929–1931)

THE LETTERS
April 1929–1931

To Henry Strater and Lansing Holden, Jr., [c. 7–20 April 1929]

Dear Mike—

Enclosed is a letter to Denny Holden and wife that I should have written long ago. How are you Kid?

[*Enclosed letter:*]

Dear Denny—

Ive never written to thank you for the Scotch the 300 yds of No 15 and the picture—you and Edith certainly made bums out of us attempting to act as hosts. We missed you badly after you went that night[1]

Once we got into March we got plenty of tarpon—8 in two nights at Marquesas—9 in two nights the next time—Biggest 107—next 97—Nothing else over 65— We took a trip to Tortugas and had damn good fun—[2]

Sailed on this boat April 5 for Vigo-Coruña—Gijon and Boulogne—[3] Have been asleep all afternoon and this letter shows it— But it was fine to meet you both and I hope we'll fish and drink together again some time soon— Bra had two bottles of Sea gin for you that he was all broken up you never called for—[4]

We drank it however—

Best always

Hem.

JFK, AN with enclosed ALS; letterhead: Norddeutscher Lloyd Bremen / An Bord des D. „Yorck"

EH wrote this cover note and letter on separate sheets of the same letterhead stationery. They are enclosed in a single envelope addressed to "Henry H. Strater Esq. / Players Club / Gramercy Park / New York City / Estados Unidos." The envelope bears neither a postage stamp nor a postmark and may not have been sent (see EH to Strater, 21 July [1929]).

1 Lansing (Denny) and Edith Holden (née Gillingham, 1896–1970), along with Henry (Mike) and Maggie Strater (née Margaret Yarnall Conner, 1895–1971), had visited EH and Pauline in Key West c. 4–22 February 1929. No. 15 refers to fifteen-thread fishing line with a test or breaking strength of 45 pounds, light tackle appropriate for marlin, tuna, sharks, and kingfish.

2 In a letter to Maxwell Perkins of [30 March 1929], EH had described the catch of eight tarpon, including one weighing 107 pounds, while fishing off Marquesas Keys about 25 miles west of Key West (*Letters* vol. 3, 554). EH and a group of companions made a fishing trip to the Dry Tortugas, another cluster of small islands in the Gulf of Mexico about 70 miles west of Key West, c. 19–25 March 1929.

3 EH was returning to live in Paris after spending the past year in the United States. He had sailed from Havana aboard the *Yorck*, a passenger liner of the North German Lloyd (Norddeutscher

Lloyd) shipping company, accompanied by his wife Pauline (née Pauline Marie Pfeiffer, 1895–1951), their son Patrick (b. 1928), his sister Madelaine Hemingway (nicknamed "Sunny," 1904–1995), and his son John Hadley Nicanor Hemingway (nicknamed "Bumby," 1923–2000) from his marriage to his first wife, Hadley (née Elizabeth Hadley Richardson, 1891–1979).

4 Edward "Bra" Saunders (1876–1949), a Key West charter boat captain and fishing guide. In a January 1929 letter to Waldo Peirce, EH reported that Saunders had salvaged 45 bottles of gin from a "rumboat from Bahamas" that ran aground in shallow waters near Key West— likely the "Sea gin" he refers to here (*Letters* vol. 3, 500).

To Charles and Lorine Thompson, 21 April [1929]

April 21

Dear Charles and Lorine:

Outside the English Channel is acting like No-Man's Land—[1] Bumby and Pat are fine but Pauline's still sick— The grippe is better though— We land at Boulogne tonight and if we have luck will get the 9 o'clock train to Paris

Spain was fine. The weather was warm and we had a fine afternoon in Vigo— The next morning we were at Coruña and then all the next day along the coast of Spain— Snow still on the tops of the mountains—went ashore at Gijon at night and wandered around the town—then pulled out and across the Bay of Biscay and this morning in the English Channel with a norther blowing and a gray mist—

Won $20 in the pool yesterday— It's [*illegible*] They've just posted the days now and we are still 89 miles from Boulogne— That means we may get there by 7 o'clock and there should be a 9 oclock train to Paris—

Someone has written in pencil on the inside of our wardrobe— The Germans is a wonderful people but this boat is terrible!

Anyway we're off it tonight—

Best to you both—
Ernest.

Pauline is sending Mrs. Gallagher 5$^{\underline{00}}$ to replace broken glasses— If she hadnt been sick she would have looked after that at the time— Thanks so much for sending the guns— The Tuna had left Vigo they pulled out in January and won't be back until August— They migrate like Kingfish— How big are your Tarpon now?— Does Waldo still hold the record?[2]

You'd need all your thin blood for how cold it is outside now. They took the temperature of the water just now— It was 7.5°— In the Gulf it was 20°

Centigrade— It takes a better man than Pappa to figure those into Fahrenheit— But 20 is HOT and 7.5 is DAMN COLD— I wish I were back thinning my blood— Just won [20 ?] in the pool— [*illegible line*]

RR Auction online catalog, Boston, 17 June 2015, Lot 645 (illustrated), ALS; letterhead: Norddeutscher Lloyd Bremen / An Bord des D. „Yorck"

On the envelope flap EH wrote, "Ernest Hemingway / Guaranty Trust of N.Y. / 1, rue des Italiens / Paris – France."

1 Probably a reference to the area in the Gulf of Mexico that EH and his fishing companions called "No man's land," which he described in a January 1929 letter as a "2hrs/ and 45 minutes run beyond Marquesas" (*Letters* vol. 3, 506–7).
2 American painter Waldo Peirce (1884–1970) had visited EH in Key West and joined him on fishing expeditions in 1928 and 1929. In a letter of [30 March 1929] to Maxwell Perkins, EH reported, "We got 8 tarpon the last two nights at Marquesas– Waldo got one of 107 pounds" (*Letters* vol. 3, 554).

To Grace Hall Hemingway, [22 April 1929]

[*Madelaine Hemingway writes:*]
Dear Mother:

We have already been to one port—Vigo, Spain. We all went ashore and had a big time with the language. Ernie being the only one of the crowd we've accumulated here on this boat, that speaks spanish, we all clung to him with all we had. He ordered the food and ran the party in general. I acquired a beautiful white mantilla— Perhaps to be used in a wedding! Never know.

Will write more later it seems I must join a game of dominoes.—

The letters I intended to send at Vigo will get there faster by waiting to mail them in France so I held them over for that.

Last night we got off at Gijon, Spain and hired a car to take us up to town we only had one hour ashore but we had fun walking up & down the main street where they were having "fiesta." I'm a nervous wreck but soon I will be alone and able to get some rest. I sent a wire from this boat to Miriam's boat but have had no answer from her.[1]

It will be heaven to get away from all the responsibilities—

Pauline has been in bed almost all the time. And [to] slave for an unappreciative audience is no fun.[2]

Our boat is getting in to Bolougne too late to catch the train to Paris so that means one more night.

Soon I'll be able to write cheerful letters—but God knows there's no cheer in my heart now nor has there been for many moons.

I hope I won't be an old woman when I get back. Anyway Miriam will put me on my feet.

I must stop now for everything is getting wild again— Love to all you men.

Sunny.

[EH writes on envelope flap:]

Rec'd your letter— Sunny fine—well installed and waiting Miriam— Thanks for property list—[3] best love E.

JFK, ANS on envelope of ALS by Madelaine Hemingway; letterhead: Norddeutscher Lloyd Bremen / An Bord des D. „Yorck"; postmark: [Paris] / [R. DE V]AUGIRARD, [*illegible*] / 22 – 4

EH's sister Sunny apparently completed her letter by 21 April, when the *Yorck* docked at Boulogne. EH likely wrote the note to their mother on the envelope flap the next day, after arriving at the apartment at 6, rue Férou in Paris and reading his mail. On the envelope front he wrote: "via Paqueboat / 'Homeric' / partant Cherbourg 24 Avril" (directing that the letter be carried on the *Homeric*, sailing from Cherbourg on 24 April).

1 Miriam A. Rickards (1906–1969), Sunny's friend from Oak Park, with whom she planned to tour Europe. On leave from her studies at Grinnell College, Miriam had sailed from New York aboard the *De Grasse*, a passenger and cargo liner of the Compagnie Générale Transatlantique (French Line), which was scheduled to dock at Le Havre on 25 April 1929 but arrived one day early.
2 Sunny, who had stayed with EH and Pauline in Key West to help with childcare and typing the manuscript of *FTA*, shared lower-deck quarters with Patrick and Bumby and was largely responsible for them during the voyage. She would recall that Pauline "took to her bed" almost immediately after boarding the ship, yet "Somehow after the children were asleep at night, Pauline revived to enjoy life aboard" (M. Miller, 118).
3 EH had arranged lodging for Sunny in a pension at 3, rue de Fleurus. In her letter to EH of 7 April 1929, Grace Hall Hemingway enclosed a listing of the family's Florida real estate holdings, as he had requested (*Letters* vol. 3, 555). The failed investments included properties in St. Petersburg, Gulfport, and Clearwater (JFK).

To Maxwell Perkins, [23 April 1929]

Dear Max—

We're back in Paris. [*EH insertion*: Got in last night so] Havent seen Scott yet[.] They said at the bank he was in town— I'll see him soon and let you know—[1]

Have meant to send the contract but havent yet—never been anyone around to witness it—[2] Pauline has been <u>very</u> sick with the Flu— Baby has picked it up now— Bumby well however—

Am looking for another installment anytime— I wonder if you would have them send me a check for the 5000 still due on the serial— If it's not inconvenient—[3] I may need to draw the same as an advance on the book— Please tell me if that's all right— Things going badly more or less with the family— ~~Am [illegible] that have to pay more in taxes etc. [illegible] property [illegible]~~ —[4]

Planned to work immediately on arriving here but everybody sick and the man who owns this place is selling it and we'll probably be kicked out— Was met with that news— I have 2 good stories to write— Suppose must reconcile to losing it—wanted it for a pied a terre for the rest of my life if possible.[5]

I don't know if Waldo showed you a portrait he did of me looking like somewhere between Balzac and Backhouse— His idea was it would be good to reproduce or use— But perhaps it wouldnt— I should think not except to use it alongside of some tough snap shot to contrast two versions of same pan ie. face)—otherwise in this age of psychoanalysis people would say (seeing you avoiding the barber) that you were going this—or going that— (a beard or any hirsute irregularity always an object of suspicion) when all you do is avoid the barber a certain length of time— I dont want to lose my faithful public through the use of Waldo's picture—[6]

I miss America and am homesick as hell— That's the best state to write well in— There's no such thing as <u>A</u>merica with a big A as in Waldo Frank— Thats all horseshit—[7] Nearly all generalities are (including this one I suppose)— A book of generalities is pretty awful— I mean the parts of America that I love— And of course it is always 20–1 that when you come back they will be ruined—

But we'll fish together again— With Waldo and Charles and Burge—[8] If I ever get any money I'll get a boat and have Burge run it— It would be cheaper for a whole winter—

Best to you and from Pauline—

Ernest

PUL, ALS

The conjectured letter date is based on EH's return to Paris on 22 April 1929.

1 In his 18 April 1929 letter to EH, Perkins inquired about their mutual friend and Scribner's author F. Scott Fitzgerald (1896–1940), saying, "He will come out all right if things do not pile up on him too much, but I was worried about him" (PUL).

2 Perkins enclosed a contract for *FTA* with his letter to EH of 14 March 1929 (JFK), offering the standard royalty rate of 15% on all copies sold—the same terms that governed EH's first two Scribner's publications, *TOS* and *SAR*. EH would return the *FTA* contract with his letter to Perkins of 7 June, but after the book was published on 27 September and quickly became a bestseller, he would renegotiate the terms and a second, more favorable contract would supersede the original.

3 Scribner's paid a record $16,000 for the serial rights to *FTA*, publishing it in six installments in *Scribner's Magazine* from May to October 1929.

4 The sentence is heavily canceled in pencil. After the 6 December 1928 suicide of his father, Clarence Edmonds Hemingway (b. 1871), EH assumed responsibility for the family's shaky financial situation. In her recent letter of 7 April 1929, Grace Hall Hemingway had updated EH on the details of the family's nearly worthless Florida real estate holdings (JFK).

5 Since 1 April 1927 (shortly before their marriage on 10 May), EH and Pauline had leased the apartment at 6, rue Férou, from René Pottier (1897–1968), French writer, painter, and member of the Academy of Colonial Sciences. They maintained the lease on the Paris apartment throughout the year they lived in the United States (April 1928 to April 1929), and they would keep it until they moved back to Key West in September 1931.

6 During his recent visit to Key West, Waldo Peirce (1884–1970) had painted an oil portrait of EH, signing it "For Ernest (alias Kid Balzac) Key West first April/29 – WP." The portrait of a mustached EH wearing a loose, open-necked white shirt, his dark hair covering his ears, bears a striking resemblance to a well-known daguerreotype of French realist writer Honoré de Balzac (1799–1850) by French photographer Louis-Auguste Bisson. Peirce's portrait is reproduced in the plate section of this volume. "Backhouse" is a slang term for an outhouse or privy; EH may also be punning on "Bacchus," the Roman god of wine.

7 Waldo Frank (1889–1967), American novelist, magazine editor, social historian, and cultural critic who urged writers to develop a uniquely American art free of European influence. His best-known books include *Our America* (New York: Boni & Liveright, 1919) and *The Re-Discovery of America: An Introduction to a Philosophy of American Life* (New York: Scribner's, 1929), which was serialized in *New Republic* in 1927. In a letter to Owen Wister of 11 March 1929, EH had expressed irritation with *The Re-Discovery of America*, which linked EH's work with that of Sherwood Anderson and was critical of both (*Letters* vol. 3, 546, 548).

8 Birchland "Berge" Saunders (1897–1970), a Key West fishing guide and half-brother to Bra Saunders. Although EH consistently refers to him as "Burge," Birchland himself spelled it "Berge" (in a letter to EH of 6 September 1929, Bruce; also noted in Chamberlin, 97).

To Alfred Dashiell, [c. April 1929]

The author wishes to state that this book is fiction, that although it is written in the first person it is not autobiographical and that it is no more intended as a picture or criticism of Italy or Italians than was Two Gentlemen of Verona. [*On verso*:]

I want this to go somewhere— I imagine in the back of the magazine under the personal column.

PUL, AL

The May 1929 issue of *Scribner's Magazine* featured the first installment of *FTA*, with EH's statement appearing verbatim in the back section of the magazine, titled "Behind the Scenes: Biographical Notes on Contributors to this Number." EH's statement also appeared in news announcements of the novel's forthcoming serial publication (including the *Cincinnati Enquirer*, 27 April 1929, 8).

To John Dos Passos, [c. late April 1929]

Dear Dos—

Thanks ever so much for the jack—it came in handy as hell—[1] Sunny smashed the car etc. Flaming childhood.[2]

[W]e had a swell time all right— Forget [*page torn away; missing text*] Tortugas expenses unless you get a big [*page torn away*] We caught 8 at [*page torn away*] got weighed 107— [*page torn away*] has [*page torn away*] [*Fragment continues on verso:*]

[O]ur address 6 rue Férou

Paris VI.

or care Guaranty Trust Co of NY

1, rue des Italiens

Will send this to Harper's—[3] The address I [*page torn away*] down that night I lost [*page torn away*] Ad [*page torn away*]

UVA, ALFrag

This fragment is written on both sides of a page that has been torn diagonally, the lower portion of which is missing.

1 EH apparently had loaned money to Dos Passos so he could join EH and others on the March fishing trip to the Dry Tortugas. In an undated note to EH, Dos Passos had written that he was coming to Key West, adding, "Hope to have jack enough for trip to Marquesas and Tortugas" (JFK). Dos Passos had recently lost most of his investments in the production of his play *Airways, Inc.*, staged 19 February–17 March 1929 by the New Playwrights of New York during the theater's final season.

2 EH's sister was involved in a collision while driving EH's Model A Ford—a wedding gift from Pauline's uncle Gus Pfeiffer (1872–1953), delivered to the couple shortly after their arrival in Key West in April 1928. The accident occurred when Sunny detoured to see a Key West cigar factory ablaze—probably the Ruy Lopez Cigar Factory, destroyed by fire on 27 March 1929. (For Sunny's account of the incident, see M. Miller, 116–17.)

3 The New York firm of Harper & Brothers had been Dos Passos's publisher since 1925, when it brought out his novel *Manhattan Transfer*. In 1930 they would publish *The 42nd Parallel*, the first novel in his *U.S.A.* trilogy.

To Grace Hall Hemingway, 10 May 1929

May 10—1929

Dear Mother:—

Enclosed please find check for 100 for month of May—also June July and August which you can cash as they come due.[1]

Hope everything is going well. Sunny and Miriam are off next week on their Grand Tour.[2]

Pauline has been sick for about 6 weeks— Flu and finally sinus— Pat not too well— Bumby very well—

I am working very very hard— Have had no time to write—

Best to you all—

Ernie

IndU, ALS; postmark: PARIS 110 / R. DE RENNES, 11 / MAI / 20 [H] 15

1 Starting in March 1929, when he received $6,000 of the $16,000 Scribner's would pay for the serialization of *FTA*, EH sent Grace monthly $100 checks, adding occasional checks to cover unanticipated expenses. The envelope accompanying this letter bears the note "Important Checks / 1929" in Grace's hand.

2 Sunny and Miriam Rickards would tour France, Italy, and Switzerland for about a month, their trip arranged by the Thomas Cook & Son travel agency.

To Owen Wister, 12 May [1929]

May 12

Dear O.W.:—

I was more pleased than I can tell you that you spoke well of the book. It's splendid too that you are coming over— We will be in Paris until July 1, anyway. I hope you really like the damned book.[1] I've read it and re-read it so many times and been over and over it until I cant tell a thing about it.

Paris seems a fairly nasty place— They are Americanizing it as fast as possible[.] You see I was never expatriated for any other reason than economical—and naturally like whatever place I live in—live in it long enough and love it— Then when they change it hate it. But this place is very changed and I cant live in town—not even this town— Am working so this is only a note to say how glad we will be to see you—

Yours always

Ernest Hemingway.

Thanks ever so much for Judge Holmes letter— I was terribly sorry to hear that his wife had died[2] I didn't answer the letter because everyone has been sick— Pauline 5 weeks in bed with flu— The baby ill etc. Have been trying to write and no go. Everything starting to go well now.

LOC, ALS

1 In a letter to Maxwell Perkins of 30 April 1929, Wister wrote that he had finished reading *FTA* "last night," expressing admiration and offering to write a blurb for the book, although he worried whether the final scene "may not be too outspoken in its medical details" (PUL). In a letter to Perkins of 6 May, Wister wrote that after finishing the novel, "I pondered a while and after a day or so wrote E. H. enthusiastically; then I lightly touched on that last terrible scene" (PUL). Here EH is apparently responding to that letter from Wister, which remains unlocated. For details of the EH–Wister–Perkins correspondence concerning *FTA*, see Alan Price, "'I'm Not an Old Fogey and You're Not a Young Ass': Owen Wister and Ernest Hemingway," *Hemingway Review* 9, no. 1 (Fall 1989): 82–90.

2 American jurist Oliver Wendell Holmes, Jr. (1841–1935; Associate Justice on the U.S. Supreme Court, 1902–1932). His wife of nearly fifty-seven years, Fanny Bowditch Dixwell Holmes (1840–1929), had died on 30 April. In his letter of 27 February 1929, Wister had offered to show EH "the whole of Judge Holmes' letter about The Sun Also Rises," but in a letter dated 8 March 1929 he apologized, writing "I can't find Judge Holmes's letter, the one I quoted the sentence from to you at the ranch: 'He is an artist. Let him survive'" (JFK). Presumably Wister had found it and enclosed it in the letter that EH is responding to here.

To Maxwell Perkins, 13 May 1929

GB 205 0 PARIS 13 0930

MAXWELL PERKINS CHARLES SCRIBNERS SONS NEWYORK

ACCEPT MONES TRY FOR ROYALTY THANKS HEMINGWAB[1]

597 FIFTH AVE

PUL, Cable; French Telegraph Cable Company destination receipt stamp: May 13 1929

1 On 10 May 1929, Perkins wired EH to say that he had received an offer of $1,000 for rights to base a three-act play on EH's story "The Killers," with literary agent Eric Pinker (1891–1973) to get 10%; Perkins asked if he should try "for small royalty on possible movie of the play" (PUL). Upon receipt of EH's cabled approval, Perkins accepted Pinker's offer, requesting 10% of the profits if there should be a movie, and clarifying that EH "is parting with no rights to the story itself, that the actual dialogue is not to be used, nor the title" (PUL). The first dramatization of "The Killers" for stage or screen would be the 1946 Universal Studios film adapted by Anthony Veiller, directed by Robert Siodmak, and starring Burt Lancaster, Ava Gardner, and Edmond O'Brien.

To Jonathan Cape, [c. mid-May 1929]

Dear Cape:

Thanks very much for sending the contract. It all seems satisfactory except that I am afraid I must get £200 pounds advance on the novel— £100 is all right on the short stories. I remember you offered £150 on the short stories and being sure they would not sell I said £100 was enough. I know of course that my stuff has not sold as yet in England but I am equally sure that it will sooner or later and will make plenty of money for whoever has it. As I said when we talked I prefer to stay with you This is a long novel that I've worked a year and a half on plus another six months going over proof and I do not think £200 is an exaggerated advance to ask.

[*Remainder of letter as quoted in the catalog description:*]

If you know any way that this £200 can be kept from being reduced to £160 by income tax I would be glad to know it. I paid some $500 tax in the states and have just been billed for $100 more tax by the French and as I have a wife, two children, my mother, two sisters, and a brother at school dependent on me I do not think cheerfully of the idea of paying an additional $200 in tax in England when I have no earned income but only advances which I owe to your goodself. If you choose to make the advance £200 I will write that in ink in place of £150 in the contract, initial it and sign it. If you don't it is quite all right and will return the contract blank . . . [1]

Ernest Hemingway

Christie's catalog, New York, 19 May 2000, Lot 286 (partially illustrated), ALS

This incomplete transcription is derived from a facsimile of the letter's first page and from text quoted in the auction catalog description. The date of this letter is conjectured relative to the final signed contract governing Jonathan Cape's publication of the English edition of *FTA*, dated 31 May 1929. The terms of that contract reflect EH's wish, expressed in this letter, to receive an advance of £200 rather than the £150 Cape had offered. This item seems to be an unsent or retained draft of a letter that EH sent to Cape when he returned the original contract on which he had written in and initialed the higher advance figure.

1 EH's contract with Cape for the English edition of his short-story collection *Men Without Women* (published 20 April 1928) specified an advance of £100. His advance for *In Our Time*, his first story collection published by Cape (on 23 September 1926), had been only £25 (URead).

To Robert Bridges, 18 May [1929]

May 18

Dear Mr. Bridges:—

I am returning the proof with the exception of Galley 19— I have been rewriting the last 3 paragraphs for ten days and hope I now have it almost right—will mail it on the fast boat leaving May 23 due New York May 29— There is not more than 150-or 200 words difference in the length—shorter I believe.[1]

With best wishes
Ernest Hemingway.

PUL, ALS

The letter bears the handwritten notation by Bridges: "Recd / May 29 / RB."

1 EH drafted some forty-seven different endings to *FTA*. The published ending of the *Scribner's Magazine* serial differs from that of the published book, although in every version, the character Catherine Barkley dies. These alternate draft endings, which survive at JFK, are discussed and reproduced in the 2012 Hemingway Library Edition of the novel, edited by Seán Hemingway (*FTA–HLE*, xvii–xviii, 303–22).

To Thornton Wilder, 26[–27] May [1929]

May 26—

Dear Thornton,

Damned good to hear from you and pleased to see that as a move toward higher things they illustrated the personal piece about old Hem in Scribners with a photo of you and the late Wm. L. Phelps.[1] I'm awfully glad if you like the book but hate to have you read it in chunks and possibly bowdlerized.[2] It will be out in the fall and I'll send you one then. [*EH autograph insertion*: The best part isnt for about 2 or 3 more installments. I'll want to know how you like the Italians in it. I hope the hell you will really like it.] It would be fine to see you. We'll be back in the fall probably though not in N.Y.. [*EH autograph insertion*: Now we probably wont— Plans changed—will go Spain all summer then ski and go to Key West and Mexico in Spring.] Maybe we could get together somewhere Christ I can't write a letter but I wish we could talk. [*EH autograph insertion*: Let's see each other somewhere inside of next 6 mo. All of us guys shouldnt be so far apart that we never meet I only get rid of shit by talking it]

The ex-pupil was fine. We took him out to lunch and tried to ease his hangover and later he sent a christmas card. Send along any ex-pupils you want. Am always at your service.

I won't send you any former pupils on acct of having none but take it out in telling people how I am a great friend of yours which has won me the respect of many a citizen. Were in America about 14 months and at no time encountered anyone who had read anything of mine but by judicious use of your name acquired quite a reputation as a literary gent.

All I did was work like a convict on this book for a year—[*EH autograph insertion*: Wrote it everywhere—Paris—Key West—Arkansas—K.C. Wyoming—back in Key West— Drove 17,000 miles in a new Ford.] then laid off and fished and shot and took grand trips with Pauline and Dos and old Waldo Pierce. Now can't write a damned thing. It always seems like that— either working and not speaking to anyone and afraid each day you will get out of it and living like a damned monk for it—then a fine time after it's done then hellish depression until you get into it again. My father went in for shooting himself and leaving a family and etc. on my handsto support. With this serialize they'll support for quite a while. ~~and then I can always remind them that they~~ If you ever hear I'm dead don't believe a word of it as will turn up in blackface having changed name or something to get rid of economic pressure. [*EH autograph insertion*: (All this in pencil written next day[.] Feel fine now and as though I could write! Hesitating to put it to the proof however.)]

Paris is going to pot. Seems awfully lousy. More traffic than N.Y.. Everybody has too much money and it's expensive as hell and after where we've been and what seen and how felt this last year there's no damn fun in drinking at a cafe with a lot of hard faced lesbians (converted ones not even real ones) and all the little fairies when you-ve been out day after day on the carribean in a small boat with people you like and black as a nigger from the sun and never any shoes nor any underwear and champagne in the water butt covered over with a chunk of ice and a wet sack—dove for the champagne out on the reef where a rum boat went aground—flying fish instead of fairies—and with only so long to live why come back to cafes and all the little snivelling shit of literary politics.

What the hell does success get you? [*EH autograph insertion*: (Money of course but I ~~always~~ dont get that)] All it gets is that people treat you snottily because they think you must have a swelled head. That's the lousiest thing of all. I may quit the whole business and buy a boat with what dough I can get together and shove off. Then have a book every five years or ten years or whenever ~~you~~ have one not write them because they bring some bloody pressure on you[3]

On the other hand pressure may make more and as good. But I doubt it. Have always had plenty of pressure to write without it having to be economic.

How are you anyway. Write me how everything goes. I'm not as gloomy as this sounds. Damned fit in reality—only in the wrong place— Would like to be off the coast of Mexico opposite Lower California someplace— Would you like to go on a tough trip sometime before we are both too old? I have a couple of fine ones figured out.

You're a hell of a good writer—better even than they think and <u>Don't Let Them Hurry You</u>.

Best luck always—
Ernest

Yale, TL/ALS

1 Along with the first serial installment of *FTA*, the May 1929 issue of *Scribner's Magazine* featured an extensive profile of EH and his work in the "Behind the Scenes" section. However, the illustration accompanying the article was a large photograph of Wilder with William Lyon Phelps (1865–1943), American writer and professor of English at Yale University whose column, "As I Like It," appeared regularly in *Scribner's Magazine*. "The late Wm.L.Phelps" is likely EH's joking reference to the February 1928 column in which Phelps praised Wilder's second novel, *The Bridge of San Luis Rey* (1927), but devoted more space and

enthusiasm to eulogizing American golfer Walter J. Travis (1862–1927), whose full-page photograph, captioned "The Late Walter J. Travis," was the column's sole illustration.

2 EH had strongly objected when *Scribner's Magazine* editor in chief Robert Bridges made cuts and replaced certain words with blanks in the serial installments of *FTA*. EH expressed his concern and displeasure in several letters to Perkins in February and March 1929 and one to Bridges (*Letters* vol. 3, 527–28, 535–36, 549–50, 551). Perkins had reassured EH that "There is, and was, and never will be, any idea of change without your approval" (15 March 1929, PUL; *TOTTC*, 96).

3 The remainder of the letter is handwritten.

To Madelaine Hemingway, 1 June 1929

148 PARIS 54220 24 1 1205=

GREETINGS SENDING MANY LETTERS LUCERNE MARCE HAS NEW BABY JIMMY GOOD LUCA TO YOU AND MIRIAM STEEN=[1]

PSU, Cable; destination receipt stamp: 1 GIU. 1929; postmark: UFF TELEGRAF^CO. PRINC[:] FIRENZE / EDIZIONE, 106.29

1 James Sterling Sanford was born on 27 May 1929 in Detroit, Michigan, the second child of EH's older sister, Marcelline (1898–1963), and Sterling Skillman Sanford (1893–1990). EH's sister Sunny was then travelling through Europe with her friend Miriam Rickards. "Steen" derives from EH's high school nickname, "Hemingstein."

To Madelaine Hemingway, 2 June [1929]

—June 2—

Dear Nunbones—

Here's everything received up to date. No word from Miriam's money unless it's in these wires. Got them at the hotel after youall had left Florence— That was last address you gave before Lucerne— I wired you to Florence—[1]

Hope youve had fine weather and a good trip—

Everybody's well here— Mother writes Leicester[2] to be operated on for appendicitice and tonsils—to cure his run downess— Tonsils sounds all right but why appendix— Doctors love to operate—

Best to Miriam and yourself—

Yrs. always

Steen

PSU, ALS

1 In her letter to EH of 18 May 1929 Sunny reported that she and Miriam Rickards had traveled from Paris to Avignon and Monte Carlo, and noted their next stops: Naples (25–29 May), Florence (29 May–2 June), and Lucerne (7–9 June) (JFK).
2 Leicester Hemingway (1915–1982), youngest of Clarence and Grace Hall Hemingway's six children and EH's only brother.

To Grace Hall Hemingway, [c. 3 June 1929]

Dear Mother:—

Rec'd yesterday your letter of May 19.[1] It is a shame about Leicester— I hope by now he is fine. If you have confidence in the doctors you name I suppose it is all right— Removing diseased tonsils is doubtless necessary but I believe a great many appendixes are taken out needlessly. Anyway give Leicester my best and I hope he will have no needless suffering and be well soon.

I'm sorry that my method of sending checks to you is unsatisfactory. On May 10th I wrote and mailed you 4 checks dated May—June—July and August. You say "this way I dont know when or where it is coming from." It is coming (when) each month—(where) it is coming from my bank account.

During the month of April I drew 5 checks—(1) $678.^{93} to you (2) $380^{00} to Sunny (salary) (3) $28^{00} Doctor Bill (4) $100^{00} to Sunny To help on her trip (5) $260.^{00} for Pauline's and my own expenses. A 7th check for $100^{00} went to Hadley.

You write that you wish the money sent in a lump sum so the interest will not be wasted. I shouldnt think you would consider it wasted because it remains in my bank account and is paid to me. You see we need a certain amount of money too to live on. I have no complaint but do not think it is being completely wasted here.

Have heard from Sunny from Nice and Rome. She was due at Florence the other day and have written her at Lucerne forwarding letters received from O.P.

Glad to hear Uncle is well.[2] I do hope Leicester is better. If we could have known what was going to happen it would have been much better to have had him in Florida rather than Sunny. She could have stayed in O.P. and collected her money that way we could have had someone to do the things she did for Pat for about $7^{00} or $8^{00} a week without any of the complications of relationship and Leicester could have had the winter there. I am sure Sunny would have been happier in O.P. and Leicester would have been better off in Florida. I thought of bringing him down but Sunny with that admirable unselfishness so characteristic of Hemingways said she would leave if he came down—

If I would have had any sense I would have taken her up— She was the greatest disappointment I have ever had— Dirty slovenly sullen completely self centered and without any manners or any interest in anything except boy running and petting—completely selfish and with an utter disregard for anyone elses property—

JFK, AL

The letter is unsigned and perhaps unsent. The conjectured letter date is based on EH's reference in the preceding letter to Sunny, dated 2 June [1929], and to their mother's letter about Leicester's surgery, which he says here he received "yesterday."

1   Grace's letter of 19 May 1929 remains unlocated.
2   EH's great-uncle Benjamin Tyley Hancock (1848–1933), the brother of EH's maternal grandmother, Caroline Hancock Hall (1843–1895). He had lived with the Hemingways in Oak Park when the children were young.

To Maxwell Perkins, 7 June 1929

June 7 1929

Dear Max:—

I got the proofs—two days ago— They were held up at the Customs because the notation "Proofs For Correction"—was made in such small type—without capitals—on the label that the Customs People did not notice it— I cleared them at the Customs and was on them all day yesterday and today—[1]

I am sorry to have made you so much trouble having the corrections made on the original galleys copied.

I find many more suggested—some of them very good. Others bad. When it makes no difference I am glad always to make it conventional as to punctuation

About the words— I have made a notation at the side about the bed pan— Originally I had about 2,000 words of that aspect of hospital life— It really dominates it— I cut it all out with the exception of the one reference to the bed pan.[2]

It is the same with other words.

You say they have not been in print before—one may not have—but the others are all in Shakespeare—

But more recently you will find them in a book called All Quiet on The Western Front which Scott gave me and which has sold in the 100s of thousand copies in Germany and is around 50,000 copies in England with the word shit, fart etc. never dragged in for coloring but only used a few times for the thousands of times they are omitted.[3] Please read the statement on page 15 of that book.[4]

The trouble is Max that before my book will be out there will be this All Quiet on The Western Front book and possibly at the same time the Second volumne of the man who wrote Sergeant Grischa—who knows his eggs also—and I hate to kill the value of mine by emasculating it.[5] When I looked up in the Quiet on W.F. book to find the words to show you I had a very hard time finding them. They dont stand out.

There has always been first rate writing and then American writing—(genteel writing)

No one that has read the Mss. has been shocked by <u>words</u> The words do not stand out unless you put a ring around them

There is no good my pleading the case in a letter. You know my view point on it. What would have happened if they had cut the Sun Also? It would have flopped as a book and I would have written no more for you.

[*EH marginal insertion*: But you should not go backwards. If a word <u>can</u> be printed and is needed in the text it is a <u>weakening</u> to omit it. If it <u>cannot</u> be printed without the book being suppressed, all right.]

The first place you say you think a word must go is in galley 13—

I can consider you leaving that a blank—but in galley 51 where the same word is used by Piani if that is cut out it is pretty ruinous— I don't consent and it's done over my head.

In galley 57 a word is used that is used again at the top of galley 60.

If you think this word will cause the suppression of the book make it C —— S ——— R.[6]

You see I have kept out all the words that are the constant vocabulary—but have given the sense of them by using once -twice or three times the real words. Using then only the most classic words.

You know what General Cambronne said at the battle of Waterloo instead of "The Old Guard Dies but Never Surrenders!" He said <u>Merde</u> when they called on him to surrender.[7]

In a purely conversational way in a latin language in an argument one man says to another "Cagar su madre!"[8]

You see there is nothing wrong with any of the words I have used except the last—the one of galley 57—which is used an an expression of Supreme insult and contempt— The others are common enough and I dare say will all be in print in U.S.A. before the year is out.

It's unsatisfactory to write this and I hope you dont think I am getting snooty about it. I wish we could talk and you could tell me just how far you <u>can</u> go and what the danger is— [*EH marginal insertion*: I do not want to make trouble— But want everything that can be had without trouble.]
I thought you said that if I accepted certain blanks etc in the serialization the book would be published as it was. I see in the 2nd installment cuts made without my knowlege but am of course in their hands.

Anyway am working all the time on this proof and will get it back to you as soon as possible— By a boat the first of the week.

I hope you got the signed sheets OK. I mailed them about a week ago.[9] Am enclosing the contract.

Yours always
Ernest Hemingway—

P.S.

About the place in galley 38 where F.H. is talking to the hospital matron— I don't know what to do— It is supposed to be the deliberate insult and routing of a person through the use of direct language that she expected by her sex and position never to be exposed to— The final forced conflict between someone from the front and someone of the genteel base. Is the word so impossible of printing?

If it is the incident is killed It was the one word I remember we omitted from the Sun. Maybe if it had been printed then we'd know now if it was printable.

If you decide that it is unprintable how about—

b —— ls [10]

I think that's the only solution.

I suppose on galley 57

C —— S —— RS and C —— KS —— R

galley 60.

will do for the other too.

Certainly those letters cannot corrupt anyone who has not heard or does not know the word. There's no proof it isnt cocksure

PUL, ALS

1 In a letter of 24 May 1929 Perkins told EH that he was about to send the book proof for *FTA*, on which he had made a "few slight comments." In his letter he offered "one or two more serious ideas" for revision, including referring to the War at the end of the novel and "reducing the physical detail" of Catherine's pain in labor (PUL).

2 In the margin of galley 23 Perkins wrote: "I should think this unpleasant implement might be omitted." EH responded on the same page: "On the other hand this instrument dominates hospital life— I have only mentioned it once— I believe I mentioned it to give the natural and unembarrassed attitude of the nurse toward all the natural functions. The first and biggest impression one who has never been in a hospital receives E.H." (JFK). The bed pan reference would appear unaltered in the published book (Chapter 13).

3 *All Quiet on the Western Front*, bestselling WWI novel by German novelist Erich Maria Remarque (1898–1970), was serialized in the November and December 1928 issues of *Vossische Zeitung* and published in January 1929 as *Im Westen nichts Neues* (Berlin: Propyläen). Within three months 500,000 copies in the original German were sold and fourteen translations appeared, including an English translation by A. W. Wheen published in March in London (Putnam) and in June in Boston (Little, Brown). The American Book-of-the-Month Club, which planned to offer the novel as its June selection, requested that it be expurgated to avoid censorship problems; it was nonetheless banned in Boston on obscenity grounds.

4 EH probably refers to the passage on page 15 of the British edition, part of a longer segment that was cut from the U.S. edition, describing experienced soldiers' lack of inhibition about bodily functions: "The soldier is on friendlier terms than other men with his stomach and intestines. Three-quarters of his vocabulary is derived from these regions, and they give an intimate flavour to expressions of his greatest joy as well as of his deepest indignation. It is impossible to express oneself in any other way so clearly and pithily. Our families and our teachers will be shocked when we go home, but here it is the universal language."

5 German author Arnold Zweig (1887–1968) served in the army during 1915–1918. His first novel, *Der Streit um den Sergeanten Grischa* (1927), enjoyed immediate popular and critical success; the English translation by Eric Sutton was published in 1928 as *The Case of Sergeant Grischa* (New York: Viking). In this antiwar novel, the Russian prisoner of war Grischa is executed as a spy by his German captors even though they know he is an innocent victim of mistaken identity. Zweig's next novel would be *Junge Frau von 1914* (1931; translated by Sutton as *Young Woman of 1914*, 1932). The books became part of a six-novel cycle published between 1927 and 1957, known collectively as "Der grosse Krieg der weissen Männer" ("The Great War of the White Men").

6 The word "shit" in galleys 13 and 51 of *FTA* would be replaced by a long dash in the published book, as were "cocksuckers" and "cocksucker" in galleys 57 and 60.

7 Pierre Jacques Étienne, Viscount Cambronne (1770–1842), French general. The French *merde* (shit) has come to be known as the *mot de Cambronne*. EH would employ this anecdote in his essay "Defense of Dirty Words: A Cuban Letter" in the September 1934 issue of *Esquire*.

8 *Cagar su madre*: literally, "Shit your mother" (Spanish). EH may mean to say *Me cago en su madre*: I shit on your mother.

9 In his letter to EH of 2 May 1929 Perkins explained that he was sending 575 copies of pages for EH to sign for insertion into the 510 hand-numbered volumes of the limited edition of *FTA* that would be published simultaneously with the first edition (PUL). In a 12 June letter, Perkins would report that "The four packages of sheets for the limited came safely" (PUL).

10 "Balls" in galley 38 would be replaced by "scrotum" in Chapter 22 of the published novel: when Miss Van Campen accuses Frederic Henry of trying to avoid returning to the front by drinking excessively to induce jaundice, he retorts by asking if she had ever known a man to disable himself by kicking himself in the scrotum. Acceding to Perkins's concerns about censorship, EH had agreed to change "Tell him that bulls have no balls" to "Tell him that bulls have no horns" in the first edition of *SAR* (Chapter 16). EH's original wording would be restored in the 1954 edition and subsequent editions (Trogdon *Racket*, 41).

To Maxwell Perkins, 7 June [1929]

June 7 1929

Dear Max:—

I've just finished a labored letter on the word business and yours of May 29th has just come.

Please dont feel badly about the Wister thing. Your cable explained it— It's nothing— But dont think I blame you either. I havent thought of it since the cable came.

And I do hope your troubles whatever they are clear up the way mine have. Pauline is fine— We wont be coming back until Spring— Pat is well again— I was damned near bughouse from worrying about Pauline or I wouldnt have blown up so about what I mistook for Wister's interference. Please take care of yourself and Dont worry about anything. I feel frightfully to have made you more worry and trouble.[1]

Please believe that I understand and appreciate both your and Wister's suggestions and was a fool to blow up. And for God's sake, not to mention your author's, dont worry and do take care of yourself because soon you'll have the cursed hay fever anyway and thats enough of a hell for any man without anything else.

I hate to add any worry to you with my attitude on the publishable or unpublishable word business— But that is only official worry remember—

You know what I want— All we can possibly get. It's a fight with me for the return to the full use of the language and what we accomplish in that direction may be of more value in the end than anything I write. I never use a word if I can avoid it—but if I must have it I know it— Then if you decide it is unpublishable really unpublishable I suppose I must leave it blank— But I want the blanks to indicate what the word is.

It's been fine outside all day but I've been with the proofs— Now there is a big storm coming up— Dark sky and every one shutting windows— Couldnt you come to Spain in Aug. or Sept. No hay fever— We could go in the car and fish. Boats run from N.Y to Coruña— We'll be at Santiago de Campostella— There will be no hay fever on the boat— We'll meet you with the car at Coruña— Would it do any good for me to refuse to publish the book unless you came over to straighten it out?

Ernest.

PUL, ALS

1 In his letter to Perkins of 30 April 1929, Wister expressed his reservations about the last scenes of *FTA*, finding the details "so terrible and painful that I personally shrank from them as I read" (PUL). Both Wister and Perkins apparently expressed their concerns in letters to EH (though Wister's remains unlocated), and EH responded angrily to what he saw as a concerted effort to interfere in his work. On 29 May Perkins cabled EH, "Wister suggestions were made only to you and not over your head stop He asked me if you would mind and I said no stop I am wholly to blame stop Terribly sorry" (PUL). No additional letter from Perkins to EH dated 29 May 1929 has been located. In a letter dated 31 May, Perkins further apologized for "having got Wister in so wrong with you" (PUL).

To Gustavus A. Pfeiffer, [c. 7 June 1929]

Quickpill.
Newyork.

GAP ship cabriolet on degrasse in my name to asnieres will pay here stop if any complications or too expensive wire and will buy roadster here stop thanks your generous offer pauline well now no need return before middle spring Ernest

Quickpill
Newyork

Gap ship cabriolet on degrasse to asniers in my name will pay here stop if complications wire and will buy roadster here stop pauline well now no need return before middle spring thanks your generous offer Ernest

JFK, TCD with typewritten signature

These two cable drafts are typewritten in sequence on a single page. "Quickpill, New York" was the cable address for the William R. Warner pharmaceutical manufacturing company, owned by the Pfeiffers. EH refers to Pauline's Uncle Gus by his initials (GAP). In his letter to EH of 28 February 1929, Gus had enclosed a check to pay for a new car (JFK). EH is requesting transatlantic shipment of a Ford Cabriolet aboard the *De Grasse* to Asnières-sur-Seine, a river port suburb of Paris about 5 miles northwest of the city center. Pauline was recovering from persistent sinus trouble that had required treatments by a specialist at the American Hospital in Paris.

To Owen Wister, [15 June 1929]

Saturday 5 pm

Dear O.W.

I just missed you at the house. We sent you a telegram to the Minnewaska this noon.[1] Could you lunch with us tomorrow Sunday at 12:30— Make it one if that is any better for you. We will expect you from 12:30 on[.] I feel awfully badly to have missed you this afternoon. Hope the crossing was good. We have a dinner engagement tonight.

Yours always
Ernest Hemingway.

LOC, ALS; letterhead: FÉLIX HOTEL / 26 – Rue Molière – 26 / Paris (1ER ARR^{T})

1 EH's telegram remains unlocated. The *Minnewaska*, of the American Atlantic Transport Line, sailed from New York on 8 June and landed at Cherbourg on Saturday, 15 June. Both the letter and the envelope bear the letterhead of Wister's hotel, which suggests that EH went to the hotel, did not find Wister, and left him this undated note.

To Mary Pfeiffer, [c. mid-June 1929]

Dear Mother Pfeiffer;

Three letters from you this morning—all fine ones including the boat letter to the Yorck. What the Spanish on it said was that we were unknown at the General Delivery in Havana. Which seems reasonable but unrelated to the boat.[1]

Glad to hear about another relative; especially one so well informed as J.C.K.[2] If she wants any more uptodate bits to broadcast we might tell her that Pauline is still sick—about 8 weeks now. That Patrick caught it from her. That we were met by the news that we would probably have to give up our apartment in December and that we must allow people to visit it any time after 10 a.m. and 2 p.m. in the meantime, that her distinguished relative Mr. Hemingstein cannot write at all—.

It's really much better than that though because Pauline is over the actual flu and has an excellent doctor that operated on her sinus and is draining and curing it. But she hasn't much strength or resistance and picks up a fresh cold the minute that she's over one. Pat is much better. Jinny is well—have not seen her for about a week as she has been driving in the country and around with Delight and Garfield each day.[3] They are splendid, healthy, happy, comfortable, solid and very good company.

I'm worried about Pauline and it is such hard luck for her to be sick— She's never had anything really the matter with her before and so doesn't realize that she must rest and get strong or there is no end to it— Just getting up and thinking you are well and then relapse after relapse. I'd hoped to be able to get her off to the south somewhere to get strong again but that would mean Jinny staying her in the apartment with Patrick—he has a good nurse that does everything very well but someone has to take the responsibility. But with Clara arriving this next week thst's impossible to ask.

Jinny is a fine girl she and Catherine lived in the apartment here before we came and had everything running beautifully and we can't inflict our troubles on her.[4] Jinny has made some good friends of her own age and I have been lining up the finest I can find for her to meet and I know sooner or later she would hit it off with someone but Clara will kill all that in a week. She conducts this constant propaganda against Pauline and me and especially against marriage and all men.[5] She did her absolute level best to break Jinny away from Pauline and succeeded for a long time. I taxed her with it finally and she said she was justified because we "used" Jinny i.e. Jinny had helped Pauline get the apartment in shape and to get married and was happy at having done it but Clara went out for convincing her she was abused. Jinny has been a godsend in helping us out several times as she helped Karl and Mathilda but I would much rather never have any help from her or even not see her and know she was healthy and happily married thsn anything in the world.[6] But marriage is one thing that Clara is determined shall never happen. I got in awfully worng by opposing Clara last time andI don't know how to act this time. The simplest way would be to shoot her. But like all simple things it is very difficult.

So suppose will have to put up with the compliments to the face and sneers behind the back and the insidious nasty propaganda and watching her turn Jinny from a girl of twenty six or whatever it is to an old maid of forty before our eyes. But on the other hand may kill her. If I can't write might as well go back to my older profession only employing it to some good purpose instead of the extermination of Austrians—all of whom had more right to live than I did.

JFK, TL

1 Mary Pfeiffer had written to "My dear Children" in a letter of 30 March sent to their ship, the *Yorck*, but returned to sender (PUL); to EH in a letter of 4 May asking him to "translate the senseless phrases" on the envelope, hoping they might explain why the March letter was returned (JFK); and to Pauline in a letter of 5 June 1929, expressing worry about her health (PUL).
2 Surviving letters from Mary Pfeiffer do not illuminate EH's reference to "J.C.K." In her 30 March letter, Mrs. Pfeiffer had enclosed a letter from Pauline's sister, Virginia Pfeiffer, nicknamed "Jinny" (1902–1973), written from Naples; EH may be referring to news in Jinny's letter, which remains unlocated.
3 Benetta Delight Ward Merner (1885–1958) and her husband Garfield David Merner (1883–1972). Garfield was a nephew of Annie Merner Pfeiffer (1860–1946), wife of Henry Pfeiffer (1857–1939), the eldest of Pauline and Jinny's paternal uncles.
4 Katherine Coffin (1903–1977), Pauline and Jinny's first cousin on their mother's side, had taken leave from her job as a high school teacher in Carroll, Iowa, to travel in Europe from January through April 1929. She arrived back in New York on 3 May 1929, aboard the *Aquitania*.
5 Clara Rogers Dunn (1890–1979) and Pauline had become friends while attending the University of Missouri and had traveled to Europe together in 1922. During the summer of 1927, while EH and Pauline were on their honeymoon, Clara and Jinny also became close friends. Clara would marry John Zeleny, a physicist at Yale, in 1938. In Chapter 10 of *GHOA*, the narrator remarks, "I hate Clara Dunn."
6 Pauline and Jinny's brother Karl Gustavus Pfeiffer (1900–1981) and Matilda C. Schmidt (1904–2002) were married on 9 December 1922.

To Waldo Peirce, [23] June [1929]

Sunday June ?
Grand SteepleChase day.[1]

Dear Waldo:

Damned sorry to hear about your father and all the trouble with your leg. Hope you are both o.k. now.[2] Haven't heard a thing since leaving america except the one letter from you and one from Charles [Thompson]. Felt like hell getting back here—just like jail after the damned fine year we had. Now going to Pamplona the first of July in another Ford furnished by Uncle Gus. Damned nice of him.

By the way I never got an answer to my letter to Fred Parke about mounting the sunfish. It was shipped to him at Long Key[3] and in the letter I asked him to send me the bill and send the fish to G. A. Pfeiffer — The Homestead — Westport — Connecticut.[4] But never heard anything. I figured perhaps he was like many good men a non-answerer of letters. But having heard nothing since I'm pretty worried. Would you go around and see him and ask about the sunfish? I want the bill sent to me and will send him a check. It was to be mounted on a plain walnut board I think.

About the films. Don't send any over. We'll be seeing each other soon I hope to God and will see them then. If you have a copy of the roll we took on the trip where Uncle Gus caught the Sunfish and Tarpon and would send them to him at that address I know he would be cockeyed pleased. He's been so damned good to us that I would like to do anything possible for him. I know damned well he would get us a boat next time and that is what we really need. With a boat there is then no worry about the daily expense or shortening of trips on a money basis or dependence on the vagaries of the marine hardware trade or the influx of tourists. With a boat we could get Burge to run it and go on cruises when we felt like it and bottom fish when we pleased without always the thought we had to be getting out twenty five seeds worth per day. I think it will make a hell of a lot of difference. I know Uncle Gus would stake us to one.

If you look up those films send him the one or two rolls—probably its one— of that Marquesas trip we took with him and Barnett.[5]

Did you really kill a rattle snake,? Where was it?[6]

Write me all the dope. We went to see Ivy and because I didn't know you and she were divorcing I guess she thought I was some sort of 3rd class Machiavelli. We met Chantal and a damn fine woman too.[7] She asked my advice about going to America. I told her I thought she would have a grand time with you at Key West and would be fine. [*EH typewritten insertion*: Or anywhere else except Bangor unless Ivy was along too which would make

27

Bangor possible also.] She asked about going to be with you alone at Bangor and I said I thought it would be a bad play. That the annoyance of irregularity of position in a town where everybody knew you and your family would be more trouble than fun. Hope the hell I gave the right answers. I did not have any dope from you to go on and so gave the answers I thought would make the least trouble. Had and haven't any intention of giving anybody advice or for gods sake not interfering in your show or plans. She came and the first time we met her asked for advice about U.S. and had no dope from you to go on somhad to put out only what I could figure myself. Probably said the wrong thing. But if you want me to advise any wife wench woman or child tell me what you want and I will advise them in that direction.

We go to Pamplona the first or so and hope if where Pat is parked works out well to stay through September[8]—bumming around and fishing in Galici[a] and the Asturias etc.

What about Dos? I've written him a couple of times but no word. We'll be back at Key West next March or so and then out west all summer with any luck and shoot at Piggott in the fall and then go down to the keys. Pauline's father—abetted by Uncle Gus—has purchased 43,000 more acres of land.[9] I don't know whether that is much land in yr. part of the country but it seems a great deal of land in Paris.

Write me the dope. I'll be glad to pay for getting the films made to send to Uncle Gus. Pauline sends her love. She was sick as hell but is o.k. again. Pat fine too. Bumby auch.[10]

Wish you were going to Spain. Yours always

Ernest.

Colby, TL with typewritten signature

1 The Grand Steeple-Chase de Paris is run annually on penultimate Sunday in June at the Hippodrome d'Auteuil, built in 1873 at the edge of the Bois de Boulogne. The race marks the beginning of the last week of the Paris season, which culminates with the Grand Prix, run at Longchamps the last Sunday in June. In 1929, the Grand Steeple-Chase was run on 23 June.
2 In a letter to EH of 17 June, Peirce had reported that his father, Mellen Chamberlain Peirce (c. 1847–1936), had almost died of pneumonia and that Waldo himself was suffering from an infected arm and leg (JFK).

3 During the fishing expedition of c. 19–25 March 1929, Gus Pfeiffer caught a large sunfish. Fred C. N. Parke (1881–1968), noted taxidermist based in Bangor, Maine, had agents throughout the United States, including at the Long Key Fishing Club. The exclusive saltwater fishing resort was established in 1906 by Henry Flagler (1830–1913), owner of the Florida East Coast Railway and its Over Sea Railroad extension that connected Key West and the Florida mainland. In his 10 July 1923 reply to this letter, Peirce would report, "Saw Fred Parke— Fish isn't yet but about to be stuffed with pine & sent as you wish to Uncle Gus—& you get the bill" (JFK).

4 Gus and his wife, Louise Foote Pfeiffer (1872–1948) had established a large family compound of more than twenty homes in Aspetuck, Connecticut, near Westport. Family and friends were invited for holidays, weekends, or longer vacations; some of the houses were occupied year-round. Gus and Louise's own residence there was called the Homestead.

5 Lawrence "Larry" Barnett (1901–1964), from Winnetka, Illinois, had served with EH in Section 4 of the American Red Cross Ambulance Service in Italy during WWI.

6 In his 10 July reply, Peirce would describe his encounter with a snake coiled near the shore ("blown off his course I suppose"), which he shot and killed.

7 Peirce was estranged from his second wife, American actress and painter Ivy Troutman (1883–1979), whom he had married in 1920. She was living in Paris, where their divorce would become final on 10 October 1930. In his 10 July letter, Peirce would describe Chantal as "a good sturdy Normand & a hustler" and "a hard worker" for whom he had "no carnal aptitude." No further information identifying Chantal has been located.

8 Patrick had been left in the care of his recently hired French nanny, Henriette Lechner (b. c. 1895), and her family in Bordeaux (Hawkins, 112).

9 On 1 May 1929, the Piggott Land Company, in which Gus and Paul Pfeiffer each owned a 49.5% interest, purchased 46,340 acres in Clay County, Arkansas, from the Great Western Land Company for $24,725.00 (Sherry Laymon, *Pfeiffer Country* [Little Rock, Arkansas: Butler Center for Arkansas Studies, 2009], 82, 86).

10 *Auch*: also (German).

To Owen Wister, [23 June 1929]

Sunday Morning

Dear O.W.

It was great to see you and I hope you have a pleasant trip and that every thing goes well with your health and the work.[1]

This morning I woke about 3 o'clock with a dreadful feeling of having talked I I me me all evening ~~where~~ I would much rather have heard you on anything you would speak about and I feel I lost a great deal through the overuse of my mouth and I hope you will put it down to being tired or some cause like that.

Already this letter is full of the detestable pronoun— Just after having told Bumby that it was a word he could dispense with for a week—it is bad to find it here after having talked so damned much about myself last night.

We started to talk about Kipling but instantly were away from Kipling and I was on what I thought about him. For all of which I, damn that word, have the remorse this morning.[2]

Yours always

Ernest Hemingway.

LOC, ALS; postmark: PARIS – 25 / RUE DANTON, 11$\frac{30}{}$ / 24 · VI / 1929

1 EH addressed this letter to the Hotel Felix, 26 rue Moliére; it was forwarded to "Bretagne et Queens Hotel, Vichy Allier," apparently Wister's next stop. A spa and resort town, Vichy is in Allier, a department in the Auvergne region.
2 English novelist and 1907 Nobel Laureate Rudyard Kipling (1865–1936) had discussed EH's work with Wister, who relayed the conversation to EH in a letter of 8 March 1929. According to Wister, Kipling dismissed *SAR* as "smut" but praised "The Killers," ultimately telling Wister, "If you vouch for him, I'll believe in him" (JFK). In his reply to Wister dated 11 March 1929, EH said of Kipling, "I have great respect for him as a writer and none for his opinion" (*Letters* vol. 3, 540, 547).

To Maxwell Perkins, [23] June [1929]

Sunday June 24[1]

Dear Max—

Thanks for your letter about the literary guilds etc. I think you have exactly the right dope and that there is no reason to submit. [2] Also received the magazine publicity and one batch of magazine galleys. I hate awfully to have put you to so much trouble.

Am returning the galleys I hope this Tuesday on the Homeric. That should land them in N.Y. about the 2nd of July.[3]

Have worked over and over and have a new and I think much better ending. We leave for Spain July 2nd. Will keep you informed of an address. For Cabling purposes will be at the Hotel Quintana—Pamplona—Spain from July 6 to 14.[4] Will let the bank have my address all the time. We'll settle down in Santiago in August.

Owen Wister was here and we saw him twice and enjoyed it greatly. He agreed there was no change to be made in the last chapter and has read this ending and likes it very much he says. His last words were last night— Don't touch a thing! He is nice and damned kind and generous and I was certainly the last of the wahoos to get angry and write as I did to you. I wish you would destroy the letter. No one knows about it except ourselves and that would wipe it out perhaps and make me feel not quite so lousy about having exploded in such a foul way. The strain of going over and over and living through a thing each time trying to make it better and for two months getting nowhere coupled with other things may have had something to do with me misuderstanding it so completely. But without alibis I wish you would destroy the letter.[5]

Now must go to church at noon mass and then to Auteuil to try and get a winner in the Grand Steeplechase. A damned fine race. Wish you could see it. Jock Whitney's horse Easter Hero is running. The course is not as difficult as the Grand National but bad enough and fine to watch.[6] Scott is working hard he says. I have seen Morely Callaghan several times and boxed with him five times I think. He has not the apperance but is an <u>excellent</u> boxer.[7] I have been working hard over the book but have made almost no changes. Write them out, try and better it and then come back to the way it is. Will be awfully glad to see the last of it.

Some one clabled that the June number was banned in Boston.[8] Wister was here at dinner and I told him that and he seemed to think it meant nothing. I hope it causes you no annoyance.

Yours always Ernest
excuse typographical mistakes.

PUL, TL with typewritten signature

1 EH's mention of attending the annual Grand Steeple-Chase that day identifies the date as Sunday, 23 June 1929.

2 In his letter of 16 April 1929, Perkins had suggested submitting *FTA* to "the Book-of-the-Month Club, or the Literary Guild, or both" (PUL), but by 12 June he had changed his mind, writing to EH that although such clubs guaranteed a sizable audience, they generally offered books at reduced prices, and "an established writer" like EH could attract a large readership and higher income without their help. In addition, Perkins wrote, they would probably request the omission of certain words and passages (PUL).

3 The *Homeric*, a White Star Line luxury steamship in service on transatlantic routes 1914–1936, would leave Cherbourg on Tuesday, 25 June and arrive in New York on Tuesday, 2 July 1929.

4 The Hotel Quintana, centrally located on the Plaza del Castillo, was the model for the Hotel Montoya in *SAR*; its owner and manager, Juan (Juanito) Quintana Urra (c. 1891–1974) appears in the novel as the character Montoya. Frequented by bullfighters, bull breeders, and taurine critics, the Hotel Quintana became EH's hotel of choice in Pamplona, and Quintana a lifelong friend. Quintana would lose the hotel during the Spanish Civil War.

5 Perkins presumably carried out EH's request; EH's angry letter to Perkins (who had agreed with Wister's objections to the hospital scene at the end of *FTA*) does not survive in the archives of Charles Scribner's Sons at PUL. EH had apologized for his outburst in his letter to Perkins of 7 June [1929].

6 John Hay ("Jock") Whitney (1904–1982), whose wealthy family were prominent in the world of thoroughbred racing, acquired Easter Hero (foaled 1920) in 1928. On 22 March 1929, despite running much of the race on a broken shoe, the horse came in a close second at the British Grand National, held at the Aintree racecourse near Liverpool. He was the only cross-Channel entry in the 1929 Grand Steeple-Chase de Paris, where he was injured on the second water jump and, though heavily backed, failed to finish.

7 Canadian expatriate writer Morley Callaghan (1903–1990), whom EH had met in 1923 when both were working for the *Toronto Daily Star* and whose efforts at fiction EH had encouraged.

8 On 20 June 1929 Michael H. Crowley, superintendent of the Boston Police Department, banned the June issue of *Scribner's Magazine* on the grounds that portions of the second installment of *FTA* were deemed salacious. The cable EH refers to remains unlocated.

To Grace Hall Hemingway, 24 June 1929

6 rue Férou

Paris—France

June 24, 1929.

Dear Mother—

I am enclosing the checks for September and October so that there will be no possible slip-up on your receiving them.

I hope Leicester is feeling much better now. Poor kid he had a tough time certainly. A good summer out of doors if you <u>make</u> him eat and not accept excuses ought to fix him up. Wrote him we would pay his fare I.E. rr. ticket— Pullman and food enroute to the coast to help out on the Honolulu thing— It is splendid that he can go there.[1] Have been going over the check book and checking my accounts and find that in April Drew 678\frac{93}{}$ to G.H.H. 28\frac{00}{}$ in Doctor Bill at Key West— $480 to Madelaine H. and 260\frac{00}{}$ for myself and family for Expenses. Only mention that en re you wrote asking me to send you the $100 a month I promised in a lump sum for a year or two years so interest would not be wasted. But I figure it's not being wasted if it goes to the support of my own family

If this present book will have a big sale everything will be very simple. Otherwise it wont be so simple But I will manage in any event. I told you I had that 100 a month for you for 2 years and you have no cause to worry about it.

Everyone is well here now and I hope you are all well too and have a fine summer at Windemere.

Am finishing the work on the proofs of the book today and hope to send it off tomorrow. I have been working on it now since last January—Jan 1928 that is—18 months.

I know it probably seems I have favoured Sunny rather than the other children but you must remember that the obligation I undertook toward Sunny was before there was any tragedy and I had figured that as my entire contribution to the family for that year. I planned to do something for each of the kids in turn. But plans were smashed in the general emergency. I feel bound, however, naturally, to go through with what I had promised Sunny.

Would have cabled Marceline at the time Sterling wired about her child but did not have her address. Pauline is sending a present to the child.

I hope Leicester is well and that you all have a fine summer.

Yours always—

Ernie

IndU, ALS; postmark: PARIS / R. DE VAUGIRARD, 15 45 / 25–6 / 29

1 In a letter of 24 May 1929, EH's mother wrote that her sister-in-law and EH's paternal aunt, Grace Adelaide Hemingway Livingston (1881–1959), had invited Leicester to her home in Honolulu, Hawaii, to recover from his tonsillectomy and appendectomy and to attend high school there for one year. Aunt Grace had offered to cover Leicester's expenses, though his mother would have to pay for his travel as far as Los Angeles (JFK). A teacher of children's literature, Aunt Grace had lived in her parents' Oak Park home and cared for them until their deaths. When she married Chester Gilbert Livingston (1880–1961) in 1927, she moved to his home in Honolulu.

To William Lengel, 24 June [1929]

June 24

Dear Lengel:

When you were in Paris I was down in Spain. Thanks ever so much for your letter but really I wasn't upset by the Herald interview. I wondered why you thought I was going gaga and tried to take stock to see if I was but if you didn't say it—all the better.[1]

Am damn near gaga as a matter of fact from working over and over this book but have shipped the proofs off today— We go down to Spain to stay through September next week and will try and write some good stories and send them to

Ray Long. If you dont hear from me it means I havent anything any good yet.[2] Will be back in Florida by the time the tarpon start.

We were on a Cruise to Dry Tortugas and around when Ray Long was in Miami Beach. I felt awfully badly to miss him and went up to the awful Sharky Stribling thing especially to see him but the 3 drunks I was with made it impossible.[3]

I will send you anything I write that's any good. and Thanks again for your letter.

Yours always

Ernest Hemingway.

6 rue Férou

Paris VI

Profiles in History catalog, Calabasas, California, 19 December 2013, Lot 90 (illustrated), ALS

1 According to the auction catalog description of this letter, "Hemingway heard that Lengel recently gave an interview to the *Miami Herald* in which he called the author 'crazy.'" Both Lengel's letter and the interview remain unlocated.
2 Ray Long (1878–1935) was vice president and editor in chief of Hearst's International Magazine Company and editor of *Cosmopolitan* magazine from 1919 to 1931. In 1927 while an editor at *Cosmopolitan*, Lengel had tried to persuade Long to publish EH's "Fifty Grand." Despite his efforts, *Cosmopolitan*, along with *Collier's Weekly, Liberty*, the *Saturday Evening Post*, and *Scribner's Magazine*, rejected the story, which finally appeared in *Atlantic Monthly* in July 1927 and in *MWW* that October.
3 In the elimination fight at Miami's Flamingo Park on 27 February 1929, American heavyweight boxer Jack Sharkey (né Joseph Paul Zukauskas, 1902–1994) defeated William Lawrence "Young" Stribling, Jr. (1904–1933) in a lackluster bout that was settled by decision. The fight was promoted by Jack Dempsey, and the notorious American gangster Al Capone was in attendance despite his having been subpoenaed earlier the same day for possible violation of the Prohibition Act. Waldo Peirce attended the fight with EH; they had been fishing that day with Charles Thompson and Bra Saunders, who may also have accompanied them to the fight.

To Richard Johns, 24 June [1929]

12 rue de L'odeon

Paris VI

June 24

Dear Mr. Johns:

I'm awfully sorry that I havent a thing now to send. Have been working on a novel for 18 months and havent written any stories.

Thank you for asking me to contribute.[1]

Yours very truly

Ernest Hemingway.

UDel, ALS

On the verso of the sheet is the circled page number 3 and the cancelled sentence: "Make connections that day." EH was apparently reusing a sheet of stationery.

1 In the late 1920s, Richard Johns launched *Pagany*, a literary quarterly dedicated to promoting American writing. None of EH's work would appear in the magazine, which was published in twelve numbers between January 1930 and February 1933. Johns's letter of invitation remains unlocated.

To Otto Dempewolf, 24 June [1929]

June 24

Dear Mr. Demperwolf:

I'd be delighted to autograph your copy of The Sun Also Rises but it might be difficult for you just now as we leave for Spain on a trip next week to be gone through September. The Spanish postal service is, to put it very mildly, lousy.

Maybe you would send it to me about the 1st of Oct. to this address.

12 rue de L'odeon

Paris VI[1]

And I will autograph it and return it promptly—

Yours very truly

Ernest Hemingway.

Stanford, ALS; postmark: PARIS 110 / R. DE RENNES, 25 / JUIN / 20 H 15

In addition to the notation "1929" on the envelope in an unknown hand, the year of the letter is confirmed by the year the postage stamp was issued. The French 50 centime blue stamp commemorated the five hundredth anniversary of the 1429 battle in which Joan of Arc led the French troops to victory in Orleans.

1 The address of Sylvia Beach's bookstore and lending library, Shakespeare and Company, which EH and other expatriates sometimes used as a mailing address.

To [Unknown], [c. 6–14 July 1929]

Muy Senor Mio:—

Sabe yo que hablo muy malo el castellano en Espanol y sin duda escribo peor. Ayer noche ha dijado a vd. que ha perdido mia Senora. Es verdad. Pero no ha perdido por muerte pero por divorcio y divorcio pidido para ella por mi culpa.

Como usted ha conocido la Senora Hadley es necessario que digo eso. Tengo por ella como siempre respecto y admiraceon total toda qu ha pasado es de mi culpa. Quanda ha visto usted hace dos anos no puede hablar de eso hora tampoco y no hablara. Pero si vamos encontramos en Valencia no quiero que existe un situacion equivocado o falso.

Hora soy casado hace casi dos anos y venga mia esposa di Paris al terminar los San Fermines primeras corridas aqui y marchamos junto a Valencia y despues a Galicia. Lo Siento Mucho molestar a usted con detalles cosas como esos y

Hora es acaba

Ha escrito por poner fin

no es necessario contestar a esta carta.

[*Translation follows:*]

My dear Sir:

I know that I speak Spanish very badly and undoubtedly write it worse.[1] Last night I told you that I had lost my wife. It is true. But I have lost her not through death but through divorce and a divorce requested by her through my fault.

As you have known Mrs. Hadley, it is necessary that I say this. I have for her as always total respect and admiration. All that has happened is my fault. When I saw you two years ago I couldn't speak of this, not now either and I will not speak. But if we are going to meet in Valencia I don't want there to be a mistaken or false situation.

Now I am married almost two years and my wife is coming from Paris upon conclusion of the San Fermines first bull fights here and we will go together to Valencia and then to Galicia. I'm very sorry to bother you with details things like these and

Now it is finished

I have written to put an end

it is not necessary to answer this letter.

JFK, ALD; letterhead: Hotel Quintana / Pamplona

This apparently abandoned and unsent draft addresses an unidentified Spanish follower of the bulls whom EH and Hadley had known in Pamplona. The conjectured letter date is based on the letterhead of the Pamplona hotel where EH stayed during the Fiesta of San Fermín (held annually on 6–14 July), on EH and the intended recipient's having spoken the previous night in Pamplona, and on EH's statement that he had been married to his second wife for "almost" two years now. (EH and Pauline were married in May 1927, but he attended the 1927 *sanfermines* without her.) EH and Hadley were last in Pamplona together in July 1926, with Pauline among their companions. In a letter postmarked from Paris on 5 July 1929 and addressed to EH at the Hotel Quintana, Pamplona, Pauline wrote, "How was the trip?" and asked if Jinny [Pfeiffer] and Guy [Hickok] were "funny." (JFK). In a second letter, written "Sunday" [7 July], Pauline looked forward to joining EH in five more nights (JFK).

1 EH's Spanish is error-ridden.

To Charles Thompson, 14 July [1929]

July 14

Dear Charles—

We're at Pamplona where the bulls chase the citizens through the streets. Think of you both often. The rods came fine. Thanks ever so much.[1] Pauline and I go from here to Valencia in new Ford. Hot as Marquesas. Bull fights have been Lousy. All except one Kid. Felix Rodrigues.[2] Have been swimming all the time. Write me all the dope. Best to Lorine—[3]

Yours always—

Ernest.

Profiles in History catalog, Calabasas, California, 19 December 2013, Lot 91 (illustrated), A Postcard S; verso: photograph of men scrambling over a street barrier during the running of the bulls in Pamplona

EH addressed the postcard to "Mr. Charles Thompson / (The Marine Hardware King) / Key West Hardware Co. / Facing Thompson Fish Co. / Key West / Florida / Estados Unidos." Charles managed the Thompson family's marine hardware and tackle shop. The family's Key West holdings also included a fleet of fishing boats and a fish-processing company.

1 In his 26 July 1929 reply Thompson would apologize, "Sorry that I sent your rods after you didn't want them, but they were ship[p]ed before your letter came" (JFK). That letter from EH remains unlocated.

2 Spanish bullfighter Félix Rodríguez Ruiz (1905–1943) performed in sixty-five bullfights during 1929, including those held in Pamplona on 9, 10, and 14 July.

3 Thompson's newsy response of 26 July was forwarded from Paris to the Hotel Suizo, Santiago de Compostela. The envelope bears EH's handwritten notation that he answered it on 20 August 1929, but that letter remains unlocated.

To Edward Saunders, 14 July [1929]

Dear Bra: This town is carried away with bulls. Think of you whenever I'm drunk and plenty of times sober. We're all well and having a fine time. Best regards to your family and take care of yourself! Best luck always, your friend Ernest Hemingway

PUL, Typewritten transcription of EH postcard

This transcription of EH's postcard is reproduced here verbatim from the Carlos Baker Collection (CO365) at PUL. The transcription bears the typewritten notation "EH to Capt. Eddie Saunders. Postcard from Pamplona, dated 14 July, with year unclear." EH was in Pamplona for the *sanfermines* in 1929, missed 1930, and returned in 1931 with Bumby. The year [1929] is conjectured on the basis of the postcard's similarity in content and wording to others he wrote that summer.

To Thornton Wilder,18 July [1929]

July 18—
Montroig (Prov. Tarragona)

Dear Thornt—

Damned good to hear from you. Any communication from the Dean of American letters is always welcome. You old Colony haunter![1] I hope you're fine. We are down here visiting (what a thing that is to do) Joan Miro—he lives here[.] It's a lovely country— Tarragona is a fine town if you ever want a quiet nice one on a hill above the sea with good swimming and a cool breeze every day and night and pleasant people.[2] You probably know all the history of it but if you dont it has a swell history

That damned book [*FTA*] reads like tripe in the magazine—

I couldnt read it[.] They've cut the guts out of it—but I hope you'll like it when it is all in one piece.

Dont let the lightning hit me yet because it wd. be too late or too early— am fine now and know that the only way could take death now [*EH insertion*: without getting angry.] would be when am too worn out and tired for it to make any difference[.] Would like to live to be an old old man and see it all go to hell (very good for the writing business) ~~Hope that wont be for [*illegible*].~~ Feel too damned good today. Might even write again sometime.

We'll be back in U.S. in Spring for a year or more— Hows to come down to Key West then— Can fix you up a lecture date if you have to ease your stern and rockbound conscience— We're going to get a boat—cant promise any thunderbolts—but a good Norther could do the business and still give you time to get into a state of grace—

This is a lousy letter—

Address Hotel Suizo

    Santiago de Campostella

    Spain

Until Aug 15—[3]

    Guaranty Trust Co. of N.Y.

    4 Place de la Concorde

    Paris

will always forward.

Glad youre going to be in Chicago— Fine town— Shitty University but maybe your friend will fix it up.[4]

I'll have to go to Chicago, and we'll go out and get drunk.

Yours always Ernest.

Yale, ALS; postmark: CAM[*illegible*] / [TA]RRA[GONA], 20. JUL [2]9

EH addressed the envelope to "Thornton Wilder Esq. / (Ye Dean of American Letters) / Lake Sunapee Summer School / Blodgett's Landing / N. Hampshire / Estados Unidos." In the upper left corner, he wrote, "From Ye Dean's Boyhood Friend. / Ernest Hemingway / Santiago de Campostella / Spain." In the 1920s Wilder taught for several summers at the Lake Sunapee Summer School, a tutoring camp for boys.

1 Wilder was a frequent resident at the MacDowell Colony, an artists' colony founded in 1907 by American composer Edward MacDowell (1860–1908) and his wife, pianist Marian Griswold Nevins MacDowell (1857–1956), at their farm in Peterborough, New Hampshire. Wilder's first residency was for the summer of 1924. During his 1926 residency he worked on *The Bridge of San Luis Rey* (1927), and in 1929 he returned to work on *The Woman of Andros* (1930). During his 1937 residency, he would write the Pulitzer Prize-winning drama *Our Town* (1938).

2 Joan Miró (1893–1983), Spanish (Catalan) Surrealist painter whose large oil painting *La Ferme* (*The Farm*, 1921–1922) EH had bought in Paris in 1925. In Chapter 20 of *DIA* EH would recall visiting Miró.

3 EH drew a large circle around this line and the address above. The Hotel Suizo in Santiago de Compostela had occupied a modernist four-story building on the Avenue Cardinal Payá 18, near the Plaza de Mazarelos, since 1904.

4 Robert Maynard Hutchins (1899–1977), a classmate of Wilder's at Yale, had assumed the presidency of the University of Chicago on 1 July. During his tenure (1929–1951), he would institute the study of the Great Books and discourage nonacademic pursuits such as football. He would soon appoint Wilder to teach literary classics, creative writing, and comparative literature at the university (1930–1936).

To Archibald MacLeish, 18 July [1929]

Montroig (Prov. Tarragona)

July 18

[*EH marginal note*: Visiting Miro here—]

Dear Orchie:—

For Chrise sake Mac dont drop any more rocks on yr. hands. Heave them at Kerstein.[1] He says I'm a shit too and imitate <u>Callyghan!</u>[2]

Got your letter at Pamplona.[3] Fine town. I intend to write about it sometime or at least attempt to put it in a book. There was, however, a good deal of drinking going on and so, eventually, we left.

I'm glad as hell you liked the start of the book[4]—if it seems to go shitty later on dont despair because that is emasculation by the magazine authorities—a tiny operation with a great effect. I think you'll like it as a book. If it is still emasculated as a book— They are scared now on acct the Boston Business—[5] We'll have the Mss. bound and give you that.

I am holding out for all the words and everything so will probably end up in the Poorhouse. Let us hope the Poorhouse will prove to be your Turkeyhouse.[6]

It is swell to hear from you, you ignorant rock dropping bastard, so why not write to Hotel Suizo—Santiago de Campostella—Spain—

The bloody book starts to be readable again in about the August No. I hope— I dont think there is much there for the literary gents on the magazine to cut. So if you think you cant write me because it seems so rotten read the Aug. one and we'll be all right again. I hope anyway write even if it's rotten. I'm all through with it now.

Give our love to Ada Aida and yr. esteemed children.[7] When do we shoot some more ghost partridges?[8] I cant go with Gerald on acct. of proofs.[9] We'll be in U.S. in March. Everybody fine.

Best love—Pappy.

LOC, ALS; postmark: [*illegible*] / [TARRAGONA], 20. JUL 29

1 In his letter to EH of [24 June 1929], MacLeish explained that he had spent two weeks building a dam at his farm in Conway, Massachusetts, and had dropped rocks on both hands, making it "agony to push this pen" (JFK). Lincoln Edward Kirstein (1907–1996), as editor of *Hound & Horn: A Harvard Miscellany*, had included in the January–March 1929 issue a review by R. P. Blackmur that dismissed MacLeish's recent book, *The Hamlet of A. MacLeish* (Boston and New York: Houghton Mifflin, 1928), as derivative and lifeless ("Am Not Prince Hamlet Nor Was Meant to Be," 167–69).

2 Kirstein (in a review of Ezra Pound's *Exile*) had compared Callaghan's "concise, depressing stories" to those by EH, calling the writers "two of a kind." Kirstein continued, "This manner of writing can have only a limited sustaining effect—for its background and irony are too easily duplicated to maintain a necessary novelty" (*Hound & Horn*, December 1927, 383).

3 MacLeish's letter, addressed to EH at 6, rue Férou, Paris, had been forwarded to the Hotel Quintana, Pamplona.

4 In his letter MacLeish praised the opening segments of *FTA* serialized in *Scribner's Magazine*, saying, "your book starts like Tolstoy—it starts slow + deep + real the way Tolstoy starts—it is like the beginning of a year not the beginning of a book—(+ the first chapter is a magnificent poem)."

5 Reference to the Boston banning of the June issue of *Scribner's Magazine*, containing the second installment of *FTA*.

6 Facing economic difficulties, the MacLeishes began raising cows, sheep, and turkeys on their Cricket Hill Farm. They advertised "Cricket Hill turkeys, raised on crickets and milk" to their friends in New York and earned $300 to $400 per delivery trip to the city. EH addresses MacLeish as "The Laird of Turkpen" on this letter's envelope.

7 Ada Taylor Hitchcock (1892–1984) and Archibald MacLeish had married in 1916 and from 1923 to 1928 lived in Paris, where they met EH. Ada was a trained and accomplished singer, hence EH's pun on her name and the 1871 opera *Aida* by Giuseppe Verdi. The MacLeishes had three living children: Archibald (1917–1977), whose name was changed in 1919 to Kenneth (Kenny) in memory of his paternal uncle killed in the war; Mary Hillard,

nicknamed "Mimi" (1922–2012); and Peter (1928–2015), who would be renamed William Hitchcock in the late 1930s. Their second son, Brewster Hickok MacLeish, was born in January 1921 and died six months later.

8 Baker's explication of this reference in the letter reads: "'Partridges that weren't there—but Ernest shot a double' (MacLeish to Carlos Baker, 2 April 1980)" (*SL*, 300).

9 American artist and expatriate Gerald Murphy (1888–1964). In spring 1929 Murphy, a sailing enthusiast, had invited EH to join him on the two-week Course-Croisière from Cannes to Barcelona (L. Miller, 43). MacLeish had closed his 24 June letter saying he hoped EH would join Murphy "with yacht-yacht in Mederraneannersee."

To Henry Strater, 21 July [1929]

Valencia

July 21

(Hem's birthday)

Dear Mike—

Hope to hell you get a big tuna with or without harpoon gun. We'll be back in March to go to Key West.[1]

I wrote you a letter and 1 to Denny Holden to forward. Still in Paris from lack of address.[2]

Hope you have a swell Baby—this includes Maggie.[3]

I still feel lousy about the black eye you gave me.[4]

Will you write what luck you have to Hotel Suizo

Santiago de Compostella

Spain

Christ I hope you nail one of those big bastards. Besure and let plenty of line run.

Let me know how you are. If there is any way of telling Denny Holden I wrote him a letter thanking him like hell for the fine whisky w'd appreciate it. Can still taste your 3000 dollars worth of champagne.

You and your wife Maggie are a swell guy—2 swell guys—

Well love from us merchants—

Hem.

Every sort of luck.

[*On verso of envelope:*]

Pauline just got fine letter from Maggie. Santiago address good until end of August. Hang onto Harpoon gun—we'll get some porpoises yet—use up shells and harpoons however. Throw gun after them if any need. Hem.

PUL, ALS; postmark: ALCANCE NORTE / VALENCIA, 22. JUL. 29

1 In a letter of 26 June 1929, written from Ogunquit, Maine, Strater thanked EH for sending him a harpoon gun, adding that he had "trolled for tuna but is too early yet" (JFK). Strater would give back the harpoon gun when EH returned to Key West in early February 1930.
2 EH likely refers to his note to Strater with a letter enclosed for Holden [c. 7–20 April 1929], written during EH's return voyage to France aboard the *Yorck*. In his 26 June letter, Strater had reported: "Saw Denny at reunion at Princeton. A really A-1 person. He is designing the new Washington D.C. airport."
3 Maggie was then pregnant with the couple's third child, Michael Henry Strater (1929–1984), born in New York on 9 December.
4 From the time they met in Paris in late 1922, EH and Strater often boxed together.

To Nino Frank, 22 July 1929

Hotel Regina
Valencia
Spain
July 22 1929

Dear Mr. Frank:—

The reason I did not answer your very kind letter was because I was waiting for the translation of the two stories Mr. Joyce spoke about to be completed.[1]

When the first was completed I was not at all satisfied with it and did not feel I could send them to you.

These two stories were from the book—Men Without Women— If you like I can have this book sent to you; marking the stories which have never been published in French and you can choose whichever one you wish.[2]

Or if you would prefer an extract from my new book—A Farewell to Arms— which is to be published this fall in October in America I can send you one.

There are extracts which would be complete in themselves—and might do better even than the stories.

If you care to write me here at Valencia we will be here until August 3—at the Hotel Regina—

After that we will be at the Hotel Suizo

     Santiago de Campostella

     Spain

until the middle of August.

I regret greatly to have caused you any annoyance or delay [and] hope you will pardon me and consider me completely at your service.

Yours very truly,

Ernest Hemingway.

UTulsa, ALS

1 EH is responding to a 19 June 1929 letter from Frank, editor of the Paris-based magazine *Bifur* (1929–1931), which published translations of contemporary international authors. James Joyce (1882–1941) had told Frank that EH might contribute an unpublished story for the next number (JFK). "Les Collines Sont Comme des Elephants Blancs" ("Hills Like White Elephants"), translated by Alice Turpin, would appear in the third issue (30 September 1929).

2 Two stories included in *MWW* had already appeared in French translation: "The Undefeated" ("L'Invincible," translated by Georges Duplaix, *Navire D'Argent*, March 1926) and "Fifty Grand" ("Cinquante Mille Dollars," translated by Duplaix under the pseudonym Ott de Weymer, *La Nouvelle Revue Française*, 1 August 1927).

To F. Scott Fitzgerald, [23 July 1929]

[*Top portion of paper is torn off diagonally, resulting in missing text on both sides of the page*]

We had a fi[*missing text*] down here [*missing text*] Tarrogona. Am trying to write today and cant [*missing text*] this letter or the Pyramids.

Had a letter from Max dated June 20 enclosing a clipping about seizing the June issue of Scribzenoff's Family Monthly in Boston— The Herald Tribune protested editorially against it saying they could find nothing obscene or lascivious and thanking the Police for calling their attention to it.[1] Max sounded scared. If they get scared now and instead of using that publicity try and lay off the book I'll be out of luck. Havent asked for an advance so far. I know I should because in the end it is more difficult to lay off a book if they have money tied up in it already. Max is such a damned fine fellow that I hate to act as I know I should act. Not that I think that they would lay off but there is always a [*missing text*] 100 to 1 [*missing text*] It's awfully hot here and am at [*missing text*] read all the papers. No news; except China that I don't understand. [*EH insertion*: wish I did. ~~because~~][2] Lost your address. So will send this through the bank. 11 bull fights start day after tomorrow.[3]

If you see Benchley's Parkers—or Murphys give them our love—[4]

Have heard nothing from anybody— Everybody well— Wish the hell I could work—will try again now—

Best to Zelda—[5]

Your affct. friend—

E. Cantwork Hemingstein.

This couldnt be a duller letter but want to hear how you are and hope your work and everything goes well—

Address Hotel Regina

    Valencia

    Spain

until Aug 3—then

    Hotel Suizo

    Santiago de Compostella

    Spain—

PUL, ALSFrag

The conjectured letter date is based on EH's remark that "bullfights start day after tomorrow." In "Dates of Bullfights" (*DIA*), EH notes that the Valencia fiesta opens with a bullfight on 25 July, St. James's Day, in honor of St. James (Santiago), the patron saint of Spain.

1 A clipping from the 21 June 1929 *New York Times* that survives in the Scribner's Archives at PUL is headed "Boston Police Bar Scribner's Magazine / Superintendent Acts on Objections to Ernest Hemingway's Serial, 'Farewell to Arms,' Special to The New York Times, Boston, Mass., June 20." The article noted that as the June issue had been on sale since 25 May, the banning "was similar to locking the stable door after the horse had been stolen." An editorial in the 22 June 1929 *New York Herald Tribune* stated, "Until Chief Crowley acted, many readers had doubtless missed Mr. Hemingway's powerful story, and they will be grateful to the chief for calling attention to it" ("Thanks to Chief Crowley," 12). No letter from Perkins to EH dated 20 June 1929 has been located; however, EH may be mistaken about that date, as these articles were published after that.

2 In mid-July China reported Russian aggression along the Sino-Soviet border in Manchuria. Russia claimed control over the Chinese Eastern Railway as well as of Yinlong Island, and China prepared for war. The Sino-Soviet conflict would continue into December 1929, with the Chinese suffering heavy casualties and loss of territory along the border.

3 The 1929 bullfighting posters for the annual Valencia feria advertised eleven bullfights from Thursday, 25 July, through Sunday, 4 August.

4 EH refers to American humorist Robert Charles (Bob) Benchley (1889–1945) and his wife, Gertrude Darling (1889–1980). Benchley was a founding member of the Algonquin Round Table along with Dorothy Parker (née Rothschild, 1893–1967), American poet, fiction writer, and columnist. Parker had divorced her husband, Wall Street broker Edwin Pond Parker II (1893–1933), in 1928. Gerald Murphy and his wife, Sara (née Wiborg, 1883–1975), were mutual friends of EH and Fitzgerald.

5 Fitzgerald and Zelda Sayre (1900–1948) met in 1918 while he was stationed at an Army training camp in Montgomery, Alabama, and were married in New York City in 1920.

To Maxwell Perkins, 26 July [1929]

Hotel Regina
Valencia—Spain
July 26

Dear Max:—

Pauline brought your letter of June 24 enclosing the two clippings from the Herald Tribune and today your letter of July 12 arrived.[1]

Have not yet received the wire about the page proof— It will probably arrive in a day or so and there may be other letters between those dates.[2] A weeks mail was held until we knew our address here.

We'll be here until Aug 3— Then to Santiago de Campostello—|address

Hotel Suizo
Santiago de Campostella
Spain.

Until the 20th of August at least if you want to wire me directly about anything. However on leaving here I will give the Guaranty Trust the Santiago address so there will be no delay.

As I understand it from your last letter the book is being published as it appears in the last galleys I sent you except that "the three words we have talked so much about can not be printed nor clearly indicated."[3]

I take it this means the word b——— as spoken to Miss Van Campen will be left blank. The other two words must be the word s——— spoken by Piani where the drivers are talking before leaving Goritzia on the retreat and the word   spoken by Piani when Aymo is shot by the Italian rear guard and the same word spoken by the Lieutenant Henry when arrested by the battle police after crossing the Tagliamento. I take it these words are to be blank.

I understand your position I.E. Scribners' position. The Boston thing was to be expected. I do not see how it could be expected not to be banned in Boston when the Sun Also was.

As for the Remorque book— That seems to me to be completely the fault of its publishers and the Book Club.[4]

It's publishers altered the English text to please the Book Club— There is not 1 chance in 1000 of it being banned or barred had it appeared complete at first as it did in England because no words stood out and the sincerity of the book carried it. The English edition being seized as it comes to America is completely legal even if there were no changes in text. When a book is sold to two different publishers in different countries each one should be protected.

I regret very much the Boston incident but feel it was to be expected. The book—if <u>any</u> of it were allowed to remain—could not pass the Boston Standard of censorship.

The lousiness of the publishers and the book club have created the other situation about the Remorque book. This setting a precedent shoves everything back again.

I understand your viewpoint about the words you cannot print— If you cannot print them—and I never expected you could print the one word (C—S—)—then you cannot and that lets me out.

About the page proof— I do not want to delay the book in any way. If the only deletions are the ones you have mentioned I.E. marked yourself with pencil on the galley I returned and about which we had correspondence—if you prefer and if it will cause delay there is no need to send me the page proof. If there are any other changes I'd better see the proof.

———

What are you doing about the statement I wrote in which it was stated that there were no living people nor any actual units or organizations mentioned in the book? If it could be put in inconspicuously enough it would avoid any aspirant characters writing you.[5]

The dedication stands to G. A. PFEIFFER. There couldnt be a less graceful name nor a much better man. I would use the full name but it happens to be Gustavus Adolphus.

There was one other thing too—

What about the signed Limited edition— What does it sell for and what is the royalty to be?[6] I do not know what is custumary and leave it to you. I should think that unless the paper, printing, binding etc. are on a very elaborate scale that a large part of the justification of the price would be that it was limited in No. and signed— Therefore unless there is a great deal more expense; if the limited edition is printed from the same plates it might have a greater royalty. I know that royalty is a very delicate matter and if I shouldnt be right in this please dont be offended.

I would like to stop writing to you as the official representative of the Great Organization and ask you personally what about the advance business. You know I do not want any money I do not earn and prefer to have it paid after it is earned. Now that I have all these bloody people to support and cant write more than a book every 2 years I have to make all I legitimately can. Especially I have to have money ahead in the bank to see them through at least a year at a time. The best way is to get a good advance[.] But I dont want to become unpopular or to get in wrong with you or Scribners.[7]

Especially not with you. I'm afraid I said something in one of the letters about the word business that offended you. But if I did it was not intentional and I hope I didn't. I write the damned letters when I'm pooped from working over the proofs and if I'm ever rude forgive me.

Am feeling badly now from trying every day to write stories and not being able to write a damned bit and so as always—this seems like my last book— Wister is a sweet old bird— What a skunk I was to write cursing him out to you— You did destroy the letter didnt you?[8]

Wonderful bullfight yesterday[9]—but better fun to fight with a tarpon than to see anyone fight anything else[.] You feel better afterwards anyway.

Pauline and the children are well. I will send you some pictures when I get back to Paris. Will get a bunch taken for the publicity dept.

I'd rather, I think, they did not use the Balzac portrait of Waldos—[10]

As for any bloody senseless statements I make in letters about how I try to write (See July issue of magazine)— Please dont let them fall into anybody elses hands.

As old Foch said about conversation)— "It is unfair to quote a man in conversation. We all say foolish things. The only things I stand by are those I have written and read the proof on"[11]

———

It is now 10 oclock of the same day after dinner and another bull fight— Not such a good one this time—[12]

But do not you get in opposition to me now; ie—you = "we" and me = the author who does not understand the risks of using words. Because we both run risks[.] It is only that where the writer risks hundreds the publisher risks thousands— But it all comes from the writer who doesn't write until he has at least risked that. We all lose in the end. That is the one thing we can be sure of. You'll be dead and I will be dead and that is all we can be completely sure of. This, of course, all seems nonsense but it is really true— And when you write your guts out (and your life out) and you do not write easily it is bad to see a few organized ignorant Irish co-religionists try to sabotage it aided by a few extra dollar seeking book organizations that have given a great blow to all good writing or anyway attempts at good writing. There is damned little good writing and the way things are going there will be less.

I'm sick of all of it. Of course I have nothing to complain of. You have been swell (what a lousy word to mean so much) consistently. But I am sick of writing; of the disaster of a family debacle; of the shit-i-ness of critics— (Harry Hansen IE. Naughty Ernest in the World which Wister just sent me)[13] of damned near everything but Pauline and to get back to Key West and Wyoming— Paris has been—nasty enough.

This letter is enough and too much. But don't confuse me with this un-understanding user of obsolete anglo-Saxon words you consider your adversary as an officer of Scribners but rather, (if only in P.S.es) as your fellow absinthe drinker, tarpon seeker and non discusser of advertising (tho probably have discussed much worse in this letter)

Anyway

Yours always

Ernest.

What about saying—(kicked in the <u>scrotum</u>) in conversation with
Miss Van Campen

Remember last time balls was changed to Horns—[14]

isnt that O.K?

PUL, ALS

1 EH seemingly refers to Perkins's letter of 27 June 1929 (PUL); if Perkins sent another letter dated 24 June, it remains unlocated. EH apparently refers to the *New York Herald Tribune* editorial regarding the Boston banning of the June *Scribner's Magazine* issue containing the second installment of *FTA* ("Thanks to Chief Crowley," 22 June 1929, 12). In his 12 July 1929 letter, Perkins wrote that Scribner's had considered but decided against "taking the Boston ban to court." Perkins acknowledged receiving the galleys EH had returned, but because sending page proofs to Spain could delay publication, he suggested that EH skip this step, as "everything seemed right and plain with the proof" (PUL).

2 In his 12 July letter, Perkins quoted the text of the wire he sent: "Galleys received stop Will not send you page proof unless you send word but will supply Cape. stop. Writing."

3 In his 12 July letter, Perkins wrote that Scribner's had concluded that when *FTA* appeared in book form, it would be "scrutinized from a prejudiced standpoint" and therefore "the three words we have talked so much about, could not be printed, or plainly indicated."

4 In his 27 June letter, Perkins wrote that the American edition of Remarque's *All Quiet on the Western Front*, which was also banned in Boston on the grounds of obscenity, was "very badly cut here."

5 The statement that EH sent to Alfred Dashiell [c. April 1929] appeared in the "Behind the Scenes" section of the May 1929 issue of *Scribner's Magazine* together with the first installment of the novel.

6 In a letter of 14 August 1929, Perkins would respond that the limited edition would run to "500 copies at $10.00 each, and you are to receive full royalty, i.e., $1.50. That would mean $750.00 there" (PUL).

7 In his 14 August letter, Perkins would reply, "We would readily send you five thousand at any time, or more" but warned (citing Fitzgerald as an example) that it can be discouraging to an author "to see his book doing very well, and then to find on the next royalty report that he gets nothing from it, or very little, because of a large advance."

8 See EH to Perkins, [23] June [1929]. Perkins apparently complied with EH's request to destroy his angry letter.

9 On 25 July 1929 the festive opening bullfight of Valencia's fiesta featured eight Villamarta bulls and four matadors: Valencia II (né Victoriano Roger Serrano, 1898–1936), Marcial Lalanda del Pino (1903–1990), and Niño de la Palma (né Cayetano Ordóñez Aguilera, 1904–1961)—all renowned matadors whom EH had already seen often—plus the young Enrique Torres Herrero (1908–1980).

10 In his 12 July letter, Perkins reported he had recently seen Peirce, who "promised me that he would go right back to Maine and send down the portrait." Heeding EH's objection, Scribner's would primarily use photographs of EH taken in Paris in spring 1928 by Helen Pierce Breaker (1890–1936) in its promotion of *FTA*. The new photographs EH promised seem not to have materialized.

11 Ferdinand Foch (1851–1929), French general who led the Allied offensive that resulted in
    Germany's defeat in WWI. Foch was known to be laconic and reserved, but two books
    published in 1929 purported to record his conversations: Raymond Récouly's *Foch:
    My Conversations with the Marshal* (New York: Appleton) and Charles Bugnet's *En
    Écoutant le Maréchal Foch 1921–1929* (Paris: B. Grasset), translated as *Foch Speaks*
    (New York: Dial) and, in the British edition, as *Foch Talks* (London: V. Gollancz). EH
    owned Bugnet's book in the French edition (Brasch and Sigman, item 941; begining with
    the present volume of the *Letters*, citations from this source are indicated by item number
    rather than page number, as page numbers vary between the 1981 print edition and the
    2000 electronic edition published online by the John F. Kennedy Library.)
12 The Valencia bullfight of 26 July featured the customary six bulls (from the Concha
    y Sierra ranch) and three matadors: Marcial Lalanda, Vicente Barrera Cambra
    (1908–1956), and Julián Sacristán Fuentes (1912–1966), who was promoted to full *mata-
    dor de toros* by Lalanda on that afternoon.
13 Harry Hansen (1884–1977), American literary critic and author of "The First Reader"
    column in the *New York World*. His 26 June 1929 column, about the Boston ban of
    the June *Scribner's Magazine* containing the second installment of *FTA*, was subtitled
    "Naughty Ernest." Perkins had enclosed a clipping of the column with his 27 June letter
    but had cut off the offending heading. EH also spoke of the Hansen column in the
    following letter to Wister, also dated 26 July.
14 Perkins accepted this revision (*FTA*, Chapter 22). Before *SAR* was published in 1926, EH
    had reluctantly agreed to change the sentence "Tell him bulls have no balls" to "Tell him
    bulls have no horns."

To Owen Wister, 26 July [1929]

July 26

Dear O.W.

I was damned glad to get your letter. Your advise is always good and I will
take all I can of it. You must see, having gone through it, that much of the
plain speech is from being unable to do it any other way. It is hard as hell for
me to write—really— You have <u>always</u> had much greater talent [*EH insertion*:
I will try hard to give the effect. (Will you quote me the passage? (in your own
work.)] The other (plain speech) is where it seems it must be and that I must
stay with. All we can do to restore the old language—as it is spoken it should
be written or it dies—is to the good— What if you become an outlaw—? I'm
afraid we are anyway. We should be maybe. Perhaps not. But really you write

for a sort of hidden | legal metre (100 metre centimetres) | somewhere within yourself—

without pleasure in trying to attain it but only a sense that you must.[1] And it is an added pleasure if one can please yourself, too IE. O.W.

You see too, I know, not like that Harry Hansen, how damned much I try always to do the thing by 3 cushion shots rather than by words or direct statement. But maybe we must have the direct statement too.[2] It was good in the old days and our life now is very like those days— Especially 1914–1921—and much now in various places— Taste is all that can guide you— Except that I am very grateful when you tell me things—

You are a better writer than Merimee if you do not mind me saying it. Having read both the gents without benefit of instruction. But the French being more literary than Nosotros always speak so skillfully of themselves— where we apologise they imortalize. (misspelled probably)[3]

We came here via Pamplona, Jaca, Huesca, Fraga, Lerida, Tarrogona (a lovely place) A good bull fight yesterday—bad one today— The horses wear mattresses on their stomachs now—[4] Here at Hotel Regina until Aug 3— Then at Hotel Suizo (Santiago de Campostella) until end of Aug. I wish we were to see you again. I have written to send you the Torrents of Spring— It seemed funny once. Maybe it will get a dispensation and seem funny to you.

Have been trying to write stories or a story rather and can't a damn bit. This time next year we'll be in Wyoming. Pauline sends her best greetings—

I am always yours—(and thank you very much for the dope)

Ernest Hemingway—

LOC, ALS

1 The letter from Wister to which EH is responding remains unlocated. Between 1796 and 1797, marble carvings showing the recently established length of a "legal meter" were installed at sixteen sites throughout Paris for public use in standardizing measurements in commerce. One of these carvings survives in its original location under the arcade at 36, rue Vaugirard, across from the Palais du Luxembourg and close to EH's residence on rue Férou.

2 In his 26 June 1929 *New York World* column (subtitled "Naughty Ernest"), Hansen wrote of *FTA*, "Now it is wholly unnecessary for an author to deal constantly with sex relations in order to appear sophisticated" and further complained about "all the Hemingway tricks of style which he has made his own, especially that of the reiterated word and the lack of punctuation which go contrary to all rules of grammar" (15). EH alludes to the precision of three-cushion billiards, in which the cue ball must hit the first object ball and make three distinct cushion contacts before hitting the second object ball.

3 In the preface to his story collection *Members of the Family* (1911), Wister acknowledged the influence of French author Prosper Mérimée (1803–1870), whose novella *Carmen* (1845–1846) inspired Georges Bizet's 1875 opera. *Nosotros*: we (Spanish).

4 The *peto*, a padded carapace to protect the picador's horse from the bull's horns, was used for the first time in 1927, made mandatory in Spain in 1928 (Article 85 of the *Reglamento taurino*, or official bullfight code), and written into the code itself in 1930 (Mandel *HDIA*, 340).

To Grace Hall Hemingway and Family, 27 July [1929]

July 27

Valencia (Spain)

Dear Mother and all:—

I was glad to get your letter and hear you are all up at Windemere and Sunny arrived O.K.

Do not worry about money at all. I can send the checks <u>indefinitely</u> and the florida taxes cant be as much this year. Have plenty of money to pay them. I'll be back in US. in the Spring and will try to sell some of the Florida lots then. This time of year there is nothing to be done. I will have them looked up and everything possible done as soon as winter starts. In the meantime <u>Dont Worry</u>.[1]

If I have some luck with my book everything will be <u>easy</u>— Even without any luck it is all <u>possible</u>—not possible but certain—

Virginia Hemingway arrived in Paris after I left for Spain so I missed her. Wrote to her hotel but havent heard.[2] Ask Les to write me how his pistol shoots. Tell him to clean it <u>Every Day</u>—at least wipe it out with oil because such small bores need attention—only shoot 22 long rifle Kleanbore ammunition— Hollow points for game—[3]

Everyone well— Best to you All— Have a fine time on all your birthdays— Especially you Carol—you the 19th—me the 21st and Pauline the 22nd.— When does Leicester go to Hawaii?— Best to you Nunbones![4]

Love

Ernie

Address—Hotel Suizo

Santiago de Campostella

Spain

during August.

PSU, ALS; postmark: VALENCIA, 27 JUL 29 81; forwarding postmark:
PETOSKEY / MICH., AUG 9 / 7 AM / 1929

1 Clarence Hemingway, on the advice of his brother George Roy Hemingway (1876–1953), an Oak Park real estate agent, bought several lots in Florida between 1924 and 1927, mortgaging the Oak Park home to finance these speculative investments. After the real estate bubble burst in 1926, he disregarded George's advice to sell some of the properties, which were losing value but still taxable. Because Clarence had forgotten to pay the first installment the previous year, the 1929 taxes were double the amount, with a penalty besides.
2 EH's cousin Virginia Hemingway (1903–1975), daughter of George and Anna Ratcliff Hemingway (1875–1957). EH's letter to her remains unlocated.
3 In her 11 August 1929 reply, Grace would write that Leicester "is very happy with the Colt pistol and takes the utmost care of it" (JFK). Kleanbore: a brand of ammunition sold by the Remington Arms Company. Hollow point bullets are designed to expand on impact.
4 In her 11 August letter, Grace wrote that Leicester would leave Petoskey "two weeks from today," arrive in Los Angeles on the 26th, and sail for Hawaii on the 27th. Nunbones: another nickname for EH's sister Sunny.

To Waldo Peirce, [28] July [1929]

Valencia

July 29[1]

Dear Waldo:—

Your letter was damned welcome. Hot here and the daily papers a great event. I was damned surprized to hear about Dos and Kate. Hadnt heard from either since Key West until a letter from Dos a little while ago. Kate is a hell of a swell girl and she couldnt marry a better guy than Dos— What is her address? Tell me and I'll write her so. Not that my nuptial blessing would be worth very much.[2]

Had a fine time at Pamplona—we wrote you a card. Have been trying to write some stories and cant get going.

Pauline and all are fine.

You eat too much in Spain and here in the South no exercise. It's better than Paris a damned sight but I wish we were in Wyoming and will be next summer. You're lucky to have a good place in Maine. I felt the same way about Michigan but the Lumber Barons cut off all the timber and that dried up the streams and motor roads did the rest.[3]

Pat Morgan was at Pamplona and damned good kid too.[4]

We go from here to
> Hotel Suizo
> Santiago de Campostella
> Spain

for August. Write me there. It is always fun to get letters but in Spain or in the country it is damned fine excitement.

They have 11 successive bull fights here— First two were good— Last two lousy— (4 run off so far) Tomorrow should be good—Muruves[.] Marcial Lalanda very good this year[5] We're going to pass up the 11th one next Sunday to head for Santiago— Have a Ford Cabriolet— Courtesy of Uncle Gus— Thanks for sending him the films—only ones to send are the one or ones of him and us at Marquesas. He's been damned good to me. That was funny about the Snake. I knew I did well never to enter the water![6] Wish we had that water to swim in now— It was wonderful at Tortugas— That's a fine place— Remember that early morning Punch and the stench Bra's sea garden put out coming back!

Would like to have a week or ten days there with our own boat—plenty of Food and time to loaf.

Sorry your money's in bad shape. Hope it all straightens out. If we get a boat that will cut out the major item of expense at Key West—we'll take some fine trips. You have to be in Europe to appreciate that life. Im bloody sick of doctors.

You ought to come out west some time too. Damned good trout fishing— wading clear gravel streams—no brush and in August no flies or gnats— we'll take a trip out there.

Write to Santiago— Pauline sends her love— I'm sorry if you cared about Kate. I hope the hell she does marry though. She'd make a good wife. You're responsible for it if she does. The break to Key West was what got her away from those bastards at Provincetown.[7]

> Yours always
> Ernest

LOC, ALS

1 EH evidently misdated this letter. He mentions having seen the fourth bullfight of the feria (held 28 July 1929), and the Murube bulls he anticipated seeing "tomorrow" were featured on the 29th.

2 Katharine Foster (Kate) Smith (1894–1947), EH's longtime friend, had met Dos Passos when both were visiting EH and Pauline in Key West in April 1928. They would marry on 19 August 1929 in Ellsworth, Maine. In his letter to EH of 10 July 1929, Peirce reported that Kate had told him "she might marry Dos—on the strength of blessing from Papa Ernesto Primo" (JFK).

3 In his letter Peirce described a 300-mile trip through northern Maine and into Quebec that included driving "on private lumber baron's road."

4 American abstract painter Patrick Morgan (1904–1982), son of wealthy financier James Hewitt Morgan. Educated at Harvard, Morgan moved to Paris in the late 1920s, where he and EH met.

5 After a lackluster 1928 season, Lalanda was one of the most successful matadors in 1929, with eighty-five corridas, including four in Valencia (on 25, 26, 30, and 31 July), and consistently fine reviews.

6 In his letter Peirce described an incident with a snake "coiled about 8 inches from shore" that he shot at and eventually "punctured [on] the 103 or 104th shot," gaffed, and skinned.

7 Peirce had been visiting Key West in April 1928 at the same time as Kate, her brother Bill (William B. Smith, Jr., 1895–1972), and Dos Passos, and it was Peirce who accompanied Kate to Key West in March 1929 when she and Dos Passos met again. In his letter, Peirce confessed to EH that he had "woed her a bit meself." In the 1920s, Kate and Bill shared a house with friends at 571 Commercial Street, Provincetown, Massachusetts. EH may refer more generally to Provincetown as a haven for artists and writers and the home of the Provincetown Players theater company.

To Guy Hickok, 30 July [1929]

July 30

Dear ~~Max~~: (Started to write Max Perkins) Gros:—[1]

Didnt you go to San Sebastien? It seems Franklin was very good there. Carried out on the shoulders again.

There is no official notice that he will be here yet. So I cant promise to interview him for you— Will write something for you if I meet him but not under my name.

You see I could sell an interview with him by me for a thousand seeds I think and if we did it [*EH insertion*: signed] for nothing wd just poop that away. But as you know I'll be damned glad to write anything for you to use yourself.[2]

All the correspondents who were at San Sebastien and saw him praised him greatly— Corinto y Oro in La Voz of Madrid etc. Those who were not there—Heraldo de Madrid put in their telegraphed accounts (picked up from the agencies) that he was grotesque. Evidently he hasnt come through with the shakedown anymore than yr friend MacDonald.[3] The Valencia papers either said he was ridiculous or did not mention him. Everybody that saw him said he was damned good.

We've had a fine trip. Hot as hell now.

Address Hotel Regina
    Valencia—Spain
until Aug 3— Then
    Hotel Suizo
    Santiago de [Compostela]
    Spain

I am trying to write and can't a damn bit—
We certainly had a fine time at Pamplona—
Pauline sends her love to you and yr. family—

Yrs Always
Ernest

Have had no word from anyone—

phPUL, ALS

1 *Gros*: fat (French); EH's nickname for Hickok.
2 Sidney Franklin (né Frumpkin, c. 1903–1976), American bullfighter from Brooklyn whose Spanish debut in June 1929 Hickok had covered for the *Brooklyn Daily Eagle*. In a letter from Paris postmarked 13 July 1929, Hickok asked if EH would interview Franklin for the *Eagle*, either under EH's own name or Hickok's, although Hickok could not pay for the piece (JFK). If EH ever wrote such a piece, it has not been identified. EH would write admiringly of Franklin in *DIA*, devoting an appendix to "A Short Estimate of the American, Sidney Franklin, as a Matador."
3 On 21 July 1929 Franklin had performed in San Sebastian in a program featuring not only an American bullfighter but also Mexican bulls—novelties that drew media attention. Maximiliano Clavo Santos (1879–1955), one of the most prominent bullfight critics in Spain, wrote under the pseudonym "Corinto y Oro" (Bordeaux and Gold) for the Madrid newspaper *La Voz* (1920–1939). *La Voz* and *El Heraldo de Madrid* (1890–1938), like other major newspapers, employed professional taurine reporters. EH may refer to J. Carlisle MacDonald (1894–1974), American journalist who covered the Paris Peace Conference in 1919 and was a Paris-based correspondent for the *New York Herald Tribune* and the *New York Times* through the 1920s.

To Guy Hickok, [c. 30 July 1929]

Monday or Tuesday
(<u>Tuesday</u> by God!!)

Dear Gros—

Five letters from you Gros and I would try and do better but lack of typewriter makes punk letters.[1]

I will watch Frumkun like a Hawk and if he is killed— Made a matador or anything else will try and make the earliest Eagle with it. He was a success in Madrid as I wrote you. Yesterday (Sunday) he didnt torear. But he isnt doing with little bulls— Novilleros also have to take the bulls that are too <u>Big</u> for the matadors of alternative. In Madrid he had two very big ones.[2] Now as to Pauline she has not yet become a blond of any sort so don't let that worry you. That is the sort of thing we would only do when Drunk and since seeing you have not been really drunk yet.[3]

Jinny is a fine girl. She is at Hotel Barron—Hendaye Plage[4] as far as I know since she and Sylvia [Beach] due to Vaulty Dransmission of my Delagram sent all my mail, checks—telegrams to Lista de Correos <u>Palencia</u>—Where I have wired Sunday to get them and maybe someday will.

The reason I have only 1 girl on these trips Gros Hickock is because that way safety lies— Then no matter how many people fall for her they are all protected—including her. I am just kidding you Gros— But, now, seriously I doubt if any man who has kissed Felix Rodriguez should go out with a member of my family without the Corresponding Wasserman test.[5]

No Jinny is a swell girl and you are an even better guy and we all had a fine time and I wish the hell you were here— You never said anything that wasnt O.K. We would have driven up to Madrid to see Sidney— It meant driving all night and I said to Pauline I wished the hell you were here and we would do it. But we didnt but are going to leave here Sat. morning and hope to see Sydney in Madrid Sunday— Dont know yet. If we do I'll do the stuff for you—

Had something else to tell you and cant remember it. Oh yes. Hang onto the book Mss. I'm glad as hell you liked it.[6] It ought to be better than the others. I hope to God so anyway. Write to—Hotel Suizo

Santiago de Campostella

Spain—

Hope we'll be there by August 6 or 7—

Pauline sends her love to you and Mary.[7] Glad you finally saw yourself in that bathing suit—[8]

Best always—

Ernest.

If you see Ezra give him my best and tell him to write me to Santiago—

phPUL, ALS; letterhead: Regina Hotel / VALENCIA

The conjectured letter date is based on EH's receipt of Hickok's letters (the latest dated 27 July), his use of Valencia hotel letterhead, his comment that it is Tuesday, which was 30 July, and his departure from Valencia on 3 August 1929.

1 Hickok's surviving letters to EH of July 1929 include an account of his meeting with Ezra Pound and Jinny Pfeiffer, his admiration for *FTA*, and his frustration with EH's apparently not receiving his mail ([13 July], 23, 26, 27 July, and n.d., JFK).

2 *Torear*: to fight the bull (Spanish). *Novillero*: one who fights *novillos*, younger and lighter bulls, or bulls which are "defective" and therefore unfit for the higher-ranking matador. Bulls could also be deemed unfit for matadors if their size or age exceeded legal limits. *Matador de alternativa*: a bullfighter who has been promoted from the rank of novillero to the rank of matador. If the promotion was granted outside of Madrid, it is repeated, or confirmed, when the matador first performs in that city's bullring.

3 In his letters of 23 and 26 July, Hickok wondered if Pauline were a "streaked blonde" or "a blonde"—perhaps responding to an unlocated letter from EH or Pauline.

4 In his 23 July letter Hickok praised Jinny's beauty, writing, "I'll bet a bull I don't get her out of my head inside a year." The Ondarraitz Hotel in Hendaye Plage was owned and operated by R. Barron.

5 Rodríguez had contracted syphilis in the winter of 1927–1928, causing him to cancel seventy bullfighting engagements in 1928. The Wassermann test, developed in 1906 by German bacteriologist August von Wassermann (1866–1925), was used to detect syphilis.

6 In his letters of 26 and 27 July Hickok wrote that he had picked up the manuscript of *FTA* from Sylvia Beach in Paris on 25 July, stayed up all night reading, and finished it the next day. "It is a Hell of a fine book, a grand and noble book, a swell and superb book, a magnif book, an elegnt book," he wrote on 27 July: "a goddam, goddam, double double goddam, good book."

7 Guy Hickok and Mary Elizabeth Chandler (1892–1983) had married in 1914.

8 In his 23 July letter Hickok called himself "a fat forty-one year old" who "almost fainted" when he saw himself in a bathing suit.

To Maxwell Perkins, 31 July [1929]

July 31

Dear Max:—

Your letter of June 27 just came. It was with all the bunch of mail that had been held for me and then sent on registered and I was damned glad to get it.

Harry Hansen has been consistently against the stuff—fundamentally inside himself—while feeling that he had to praise it too. Although with him it's mostly dumbness—not being a gent—he fears always that something may offend and that he must be the first to denounce. He's really almost the dumbest of the critics— He says "it is amazing that so simple a story can become so interesting!" Then to say that the talk with the priest about "sex aberrations"! may be highly objectionable. When did that occurr? As always he is not worth noticing— He's always a fool but manages to get in something damageing like "Naughty Ernest!"[1]

Yeah I suppose I felt like Naughty Ernest writing that book.

You cut off the "Naughty Ernest" so that I wouldnt get in a rage but Owen Wister sent it to me. He's always fine though. He has me all mixed up now with Henry James but he doesnt always know whether it is me that is Henry James or whether it is he that is H.J. Sometimes one sometimes the other.[2] If you want my honest to God opinion:—neither of us is Henry James! However we must keep that from Wister. He is damned nice though and if I could act on <u>all</u> his advice at once I would not only make hundreds of thousands of dollars but also be qreater than Tolstoi, Dostoevski, Fitzgerald (F. Scott), Dickens, James (Henry and William) and Tarkington.[3]

Vive Dashiell! That was a statement to ring men's hearts.[4] It could not have been more moving if SS. Van Dine had been attacked![5] (am feeling good this morning so do not show these irreligious sentiments to anyone.) No; seriously it was fine.

I will pay for any subscriptions Mr. Bridges loses up to 100—not counting any that are discontinued after the October number.[6]

Really though— Im not sore any more because it's over—but they did cut a big chunk of Rinaldi's conversation with F. Henry in the field hospital and a couple of other places. I don't mention this except that you ask me what did I think was changed. If I had the magazine here could show you but it is of no importance now.

Molly Colum is a fine woman. I wish I could have seen the letter[7]

This is a lousy letter and I wish it could be a good one.

I'm dreadfully sorry your daughter was ill and I know how terribly tragic the damned exams can be. People suffer in the world pretty much altogether in the measure of responsibility they bring to it—and exams coming at the time of life when things are most tragic are a terrible business anyway— I know how you worried— But you mustnt worry or put yourself too much in the place of your children (It's enough to go through that once yourself) because we, being older and with more perspective, ought to put that

perspective (which is all $\left\{ \begin{matrix} \text{we} \\ \text{you} \end{matrix} \right.$ learn) at the service of any younger ones—

which of course is exactly what you did when you told her you didnt give a damn about the exams.[8] Asthma and hay fever are so damned bad though. I hope she's all right now. And I hope too you're not having too bad a time with the hay fever.

Pauline is fine. I'll be glad to get away from here into the North. Started a story day before yesterday and went pretty well then and yesterday. Am playing truant to be writing a letter now—

My bank in N.Y. now has the name of

City Bank Farmer's Trust Company

That's a really beautiful name!

I think Harry Hansen's column did more harm than the Boston Suppression. But you have to remember that no one has yet the part of the book that will make it I.E. the retreat etc. And god knows nobody is going to suppress a book that ends with that last chapter as some of the work of Naughty Ernest whose mind is often on sex.

Had Molly Colum read the whole book or only the magazine part? I think it must be hard to read as a serial. Can't read it myself. On the other hand Rupert Hughes, the Hearst people write me, cant wait for the next issue. Vive Rupert Hughes.[9]

I ought to try and write now. Pauline has gone out to wander in the town so I can have the room—but I dread to start. We will come over in the Spring—March maybe—to go to Key West— If there are any warrants out for me will not come through N.Y. Have written Scott but havent heard from him. Long letter from Waldo. In case you wonder who G.A. Pfeiffer is—he is an Uncle of Paulines who came over to Paris when her family felt pretty badly hearing that she was, after 14 years in the convent, to marry a citizen who had been married before, hailed as a drunk and a man of bad associates by the critics, etc. Uncle Gus made no inquiries about me at all. Pauline brought him one evening to the dreadful dump where I was living, he only stayed about ten minutes because he did not want to disturb my work (sic) and cabled the family about 500 words to say that Pauline could marry no better and finer Citizen and the family instead of worrying should be proud and happy.[10] So I owe him a couple of books on that anyway. He sent copies of The Sun Also and Men without to all members of the family to prove what a fine citizen I was and I believe has sent them all Subscriptions to the magazine which may account for some of the cancellations. Wonderful bull fight yesterday.[11] We ought to swim now but I'm going to try and write.

Best always
Ernest.

PUL, ALS

1 In his 27 June 1929 letter, Perkins wrote of Hansen's column on *FTA* ("Naughty Ernest," *New York World*, 26 June 1929, 15) that it "is all on our side;—but I don't like it" (PUL).
2 After their first meeting in Wyoming in August 1928, Wister wrote to EH, "Not since I last talked with Henry James at Rye in 1914 have I opened up at such a rate" (13 September 1928, JFK). In a letter of 27 February 1929, Wister wrote, "I lament so grievously that I'm to have no chance to talk to you as Henry James used to talk to me" (JFK).
3 EH names Russian writers Leo Tolstoy (né Lev Nikolaevich Tolstoy, 1828–1910) and Fyodor Dostoevsky (1821–1881); American novelist Henry James (1843–1916) and his brother, William James (1842–1910), psychologist and philosopher; and Booth Tarkington (1869–1946), American regionalist author whose novels included *The Magnificent Ambersons* (1918, Pulitzer Prize 1919) and *Alice Adams* (1921, Pulitzer Prize 1922).
4 The 21 June 1929 *New York Times* published a statement issued by Charles Scribner's Sons that declared: "Mr. Hemingway is one of the finest and most highly regarded of the modern writers. The ban on the sale of the magazine in Boston is an evidence of the improper use of censorship which bases its objections upon certain passages without

taking into account the effect and purpose of the story as a whole" ("Boston Police Ban Scribner's Magazine," 2).

5 S. S. Van Dine, pen name of Willard Huntington Wright (1888–1939), American mystery writer best known for his character Philo Vance, an erudite detective who first appeared in *The Benson Murder Case* (1926). Wright, who was also under the guidance of Perkins at Scribner's, had gained success as a popular fiction writer with subsequent mystery novels published in 1927, 1928, and 1929.

6 In his letter Perkins wrote that *Scribner's Magazine* "lost eight or ten subscribers or so and had a few stupid and violent kicks;—and many people who truly admired the story said they were astonished to see such things in print." The October issue of the magazine would carry the last installment of *FTA*.

7 Pen name of Mary Catherine Gunning Maguire Colum (1884–1957), Irish American writer and critic who was a frequent contributor to *Scribner's Magazine*. Perkins had written, "Molly Colum wrote a fine indignant letter to the Times about the Boston act." Molly and her husband, Padraic Colum (né Patrick Collumb, 1881–1972), Irish poet, dramatist, and playwright, were neighbors and friends of Max Perkins.

8 Bertha Perkins (1911–2005), the eldest of Perkins's five daughters, suffered from recurrent eye problems that required visits to an eye specialist in Washington, D.C. She attended high school at Miss Chapin's School for Girls in New York City.

9 Rupert Hughes (1872–1956), American novelist, historian, playwright, and film director. Author of a three-volume biographical work on George Washington (1926, 1927, 1930), Hughes also published a novel a year in the 1920s and was a frequent contributor to literary magazines, publishing a series of short stories in *Hearst's Magazine*.

10 Pauline had spent twelve years under the tutelage of Roman Catholic nuns at the Academy of the Visitation in St. Louis, graduating in 1913. Gus Pfeiffer first met EH when EH was living in Gerald Murphy's studio at 69, rue Froidevaux, where he had moved in August 1926 after separating from Hadley.

11 On Tuesday, 30 July, the sixth bullfight of the feria in Valencia featured Marcial Lalanda, Félix Rodríguez, and Enrique Torres.

To Manuel Caberas, 8 August 1929

Hotel Suizo
Santiago de Campostella
8 de Agosto 1929—

Senor Don Manuel Caberas
Distrito Forestal de Pontevedra—Coruña.
Pontevedra

Muy Senor Mio:—

En el verano de 1927 estaba en La Coruña con mi senora y ha pedido dos licencias de pecsca al el ingeniero Jefe del Serviscio piscicola por pecar a truchas con cana y moscas. Ud. los ha enviado a mi los dos licencias que estuvieron de 7ª clase—4 pesetas—no 426 y 427 en titulo de Dⁿᵃ Pauline Hemingway—transiente profession—laborer—~~fecha de Pontevedra 11 de agosto~~ y D. Ernest Hemingway—transiente—profesion Escritor ~~y con caduca~~ 12 clase numero 4975—esta numero de cedula correspondiente al numero del visa de la Consuldo de Espana a Paris—a precio de 14 pesetas. Esta Ano tengo el visa 1199[.] Bueno un ano de fecha Paris 29 de Abril 1929.

Estamos en Santiago de Campostella Este ano ~~veraniento~~ por el mes de Agosto y como tenemos gran aficion a la pesca por truchas (¡Aun quando, como el otro ano encontramos poco!) pide de ud. el ~~gran~~ favor de degarse de expedia[rn]os otro dos licencias por los gasto de que adjunto remito un billete de 25 pesetas.

Perdoneme ~~los defectos y~~ el poca abilidad de escribir en Espanol de esta carta y con el mayor respecto y consideracion su affmo. S.S.

Q.B.S.M.[1]

Ernest Hemingway

Hotel Suizo

Santiago de Campostella

[*Translation follows*:]

My dear Sir:—

In the summer of 1927 I was in La Coruña with my wife and requested two fishing licenses from the engineer Chief of Fishing Service to fish for trout with rod and flies. You sent me the two licenses which were 7th class—4 pesetas—number 426 and 427 in the name of Mrs. Pauline Hemingway—tourist[—] profession—laborer ~~dated Pontevedra 11 August~~ and Mr. Ernest Hemingway—tourist—profession Writer ~~and with expiration~~ 12 class number 4975—this document number corresponding to the number of the visa of the Consulate of Spain in Paris—at a price of 14 pesetas. This year I have a visa 1199. Good for one year from the date Paris 29 April 1929.

We are in Santiago de Compostela this year ~~summering~~ for the month of August and as we are great devotees of trout fishing (even when, like that other year, we find few!) we ask you the ~~great~~ favor of issuing us another two licenses for which I enclose a 25 peseta note to cover the cost.

Pardon ~~the defects and~~ my poor skill in writing Spanish in this letter and with the utmost respect and consideration your faithful servant,

Ernest Hemingway
Hotel Suizo
Santiago de Campostella

JFK, ALS

1 *Su afmo. S. S. Q. B. S. M.*, abbreviation for *Su afectísimo seguro servidor que besa su mano*: Your most devoted faithful servant who kisses your hand, an antiquated formal valediction used in Spanish correspondence.

To Sylvia Beach, 18 August [1929]

Aug 18
Hotel Suizo
Santiago de Campostella
Spain.

Dear Sylvia:—

The illustrious LLona has written that he is getting up some sort of an anthology and that he wants or has gotten Maurois (André) to write a piece about me and needs The Sun Also Rises and Men Without Womens to send to La Mauroise.[1]

Would you cause to be sent to Victor LLona at

"Les Glycines) (a pretty name!)

Marlotte

(S et M.)

a copy of each of those oeuvrogeries and charge them to me. This I will pay for as soon as I get back.[2]

The whole thing sounds like another ghastly plot by these unfortunate creatures but anyway I will send them to LLona and hope they get to Mauroise.[3]

I'm awfully sorry I bothered you for so long with my mail— I thought the bloody bank was holding it—

Am trying to work— Write stories but they dont turn out— Work like hell too.

Will be here 10 days more if there is anything to forward.

I wrote Jolas a nice letter and he wrote a nice one back so we are all old buddies again[4]

Pauline sends her love— Our best to Adrienne—[5]

The water is so low from drouth that the fishing isnt worth a hoot—

Oh yes—

Could you send a copy of The Torrent of Springs to

    Owen Wister Esq.

    c/o Morgan and Co Bank.

    Place Vendome—

Paris— I will pay you big for this too— The reason I dont send money is because we are without it—going to Coruna to get some soon.

I hope you have ze good vacation Madame—[6]

This is the Royaume de Pinchazos—we've had 10 in 7 days—
The Gallegos strew the roads with nails to bastardize the motor citizens—[7]
Really they do! Pat is fine they write—.

Best love and I hope you are both well—

Ernest Hemingstein

If you send me The Mountain Tavern by Liam O'Flaherty I'll pay for that too.[8] By now I owe you tousands.

Maybe we all better go in another business. I think literature is on the bum. Dont tell Anybody.

PUL, ALS; postmark: SANTIAGO / CORUNA, 19 AGO29

1 Victor Llona (1886–1953), Peruvian novelist, critic, and translator. In a letter to EH of 6 August 1929 Llona asked if he might translate and publish one of EH's stories (either "Ten Indians" or "Now I lay me down" [*sic*]) in an anthology of American writers he was compiling (JFK). Llona's translation of "Now I Lay Me" ("Je Vous Salue Marie") would appear in the first number of *Revue Européenne* (1 January 1930). It would be republished in Llona's anthology *Les Romanciers Américains* (Paris: Denoël et Steele, 1931) along with an introductory piece by French novelist André Maurois (né Émile Salomon Wilhelm Herzog, 1885–1967). The same piece by Maurois, translated into English by Florence Llona and titled "Ernest Hemingway," would first appear in *This Quarter* vol. 2, no. 2 (October–December 1929). *La Mauroise*: the wife of Maurois.

2 In his letter to EH of 10 August 1929, Llona gave his own address in the village of Marlotte, about 45 miles southeast of Paris in the department of Seine-et-Marne, saying he would forward the books to Maurois, who was then in England (JFK). *Les Glycines*: the wisteria (French).

3 EH may be referring to Llona's French translation of *The Great Gatsby* (*Gatsby le Magnifique*, 1926), produced at Fitzgerald's expense, which sold poorly and received little attention. In a 12 February 1929 letter to Beach, EH mocked "that big monument of business acumen Victor Llona—and to hell with him, too" (*Letters* vol. 3, 524).

4 Eugene Jolas (1894–1952), American journalist, co-founder (with Elliot Paul [1891–1958]) and editor of the experimental little magazine *transition* (1927–1938). EH's "Hills Like White Elephants" was the opening piece of the August 1927 number. EH's correspondence with Jolas remains unlocated.

5 Adrienne Monnier (1892–1955), Beach's close friend and longtime domestic partner, who in 1915 had founded the bookshop La Maison des Amis des Livres on rue de l'Odéon, across the street from Shakespeare and Company.

6 Beach and Monnier regularly vacationed in Les Déserts in the French Alps, often staying at a farm owned by Monnier's cousins.

7 *Royaume*: kingdom (French); *pinchazos*: punctures, flat tires (Spanish); *Gallegos*: Galicians, from the Spanish province of Galicia (Spanish).

8 *The Mountain Tavern and Other Stories* (London: Cape, 1929) by Liam O'Flaherty (1896–1984), Irish political activist, WWI veteran, and author of short stories, novels, and autobiographies.

To Paul and Mary Pfeiffer, [22 August 1929]

Santiago de Campostella

Dear Folks:

Pauline has written you all the news. She is fine and well now and quite husky. We have had a card from Jinny from Bavaria where she said she hoped to meet Uncle Gus but as we have had a letter from Uncle Gus via the Graf Zepplin from New York that seems doubtful.

The Graf Z. is due to leave today from Tokio— I hope by the time you get this they will be back at Frederickshaven without having any bad luck.[1]

It will make a quick way for people to travel who want to say they have been around the world. They will be exposed to none of the annoyance of Foreign Parts.

I hope you are having good weather still and the prospects are still fine. This is supposed to be the rainy-est part of Europe but it hasn't rained since we've been here. Streams dried down to rivulets.

We went swimming near Cape Finisterre day before yesterday in the coldest water I've ever been in. The engine of the car runs beautifully but the body shakes to pieces. The body doesn't seem nearly as well made as last years. The Ford organization here has 3 Salesmen and no mechanic. The idea seems to be sell sell sell and to —— with them afterwards[.] Going along the road whenever we hear a strange noise we stop and get out to pick up the important part that has fallen loose. However I dont let anybody else criticize it. ~~Wont stand~~

Most of the roads in Spain are excellent. Some of the through roads are wide concrete room for 4 cars abreast—you dont see many cars. Others are good gravel. The roads here in Galicia (which were good) are cut up by the heavy busses. There is no R.R. and many heavy bus lines and they go fast and pull the road up by the roots. No matter how much they are taxed they cannot pay for the damage they do. All out from Barcelona they have good Ford organization. They sell more than any other car because there are so many hills and mountains. The French cars cant compete with them on that account.

In the official garage here where they sent us from the hotel we had 7 punctures in 6 days— I picked up myself over 20 nails scattered around in the courtyard. They were doing a good business at 50 cents a puncture— I collected all the nails all over the garage and told them I would have them all arrested. Going to get a picture taken of the nails on a white paper. There are enough to start a blacksmith shop.

Found a good garage about a mile from here but I'd be glad to walk there backwards to avoid punctures— Altogether we had 9 in a week. Two one night coming home after dark. The only way you can avoid them on the road is to go directly in the tracks of another car. All nails. For three thousand kilometers over all the rest of Spain we only had one.

Of course it's the bad roads—cut up by the busses—that shake the body so—you see I cant let even myself attack it.

Pat's nurse writes that he is fine and healthy and strong.

Hope you can read this writing—even though it doesn't say anything.

Since Snowden started to speak up the French have stopped hating us a little and gone back to their good old hate for the English.[2]

It would be some compensation to me if I had a little of this money that all Americans are supposed to have made out of the allies. They hate you just the same so it would be better to have some of it at least.

What is Hoover doing for you so far? Has the farm board guaranteed cost production? Let me know when it does as am anxious to start farming again!![3]

I dont remember the Clarkes— But I've been away so much that doesn't mean anything. Was the cousin's name Hines or Hemingway? It might have been one of my Uncle Frank Hines daughters.[4]

It will be fine to see the new Cash Bottoms land. The highways sound fine. That is awfully pretty country toward Corning.[5]

Have you followed the Chinese-Russian business.[6] Think the government may be getting ready to recognize the Russian Govt. The Russians have stopped supporting the U.S. Communist party and I imagine that was one of the conditions of recognition.[7] It's a big market for farm machinery and plenty of other things that Canada and England would like to have.

The British are in a bad way. Their markets going everywhere. Twenty dollars in the hundred income tax alone—on the smallest income. The Germans and French are taking the Transatlantic passenger trade away from[8]

Now they are going to start a line building race with Germany with public subsidy to give employment to the shipyard workers that will be out of work if they start scrapping navy program. Hope they will. I'd like to see enough liners to have a Transatlantic rate war.[9] But if they keep making money on stocks in U.S. there will be plenty of people to travel on them.

Europe more Americanized everyday. Coca-Cola sold all over Spain.[10] Chewing gum too. These just symptoms.

Well this is too long now.

Love to you from us all—
Ernest.

Wrote this to thank you for the birth Day present and haven't done it. Thanks very much! E.H.

PUL, ALS; postmark: SANTIAGO / (60), 22 AGO 29. 7 T

1 *Graf Zeppelin* LZ 127, the hydrogen-filled, passenger-carrying airship, named after its developer, Count Ferdinand Graf von Zeppelin (1838–1917), and launched in July 1928. On 7 August 1929, it embarked upon a highly publicized journey around the world that included a transpacific leg from Tokyo to Los Angeles (23 to 26 August). The airship would land safely at its home base in Friedrichshafen, Germany, on 4 September.

2 Philip Snowden (1864–1937), Chancellor of the Exchequer (1929–1931) under the Labour government of British Prime Minister Ramsay MacDonald. At the first Hague Conference (6–31 August 1929), convened to discuss the U.S. proposal for war reparations payments, Snowden argued that France and Italy were receiving too large a share and insisted on a plan more favorable to Britain—a condition eventually adopted at the expense of France and Italy.

3 In a letter of 10 July 1929 Paul Pfeiffer wrote, "Well we now have a Farm Bill and Board of 12—eventually think they will be of some value to the growers— ... We do not want excessive prices but we do think that as govt protects practically every other industry—we are entitled to guaranteed cost production—" (JFK). U.S. President Herbert Hoover (1874–1964) had been inaugurated on 4 March 1929. In mid-June he called a special session of Congress and supported the passage of the Agricultural Marketing Act, which established the Federal Farm Board, a government agency that worked to stabilize agricultural prices.

4 Paul wrote that he and Mary expected to have a picnic with "Clarks folks" from Iowa who had a contract for enlarging the Pfeiffers' ditches, saying that "his Bro Mike Clark" had married a cousin of EH's and asking if EH knew her. The Pfeiffers and Clarks had been business associates since the 1890s, when Gus and Paul Pfeiffer employed G. N. Clark in their drugstore in Parkersburg, Iowa; after Paul left the business in 1895, Gus and Clark became partners, renaming the drugstore G. A. Pfeiffer and Company (Hawkins, 12–13). EH's uncle Frank Bristow Hines (1859–1933), past president of the Southern Collegiate Institute in Albion, Illinois; Congregationalist minister and farmer in southern Illinois. When he married EH's paternal aunt Anginette Blanche (Nettie) Hemingway (1868–1945) in Oak Park in 1897, he was a widower with three daughters: Laura, Marion, and Margarette. Frank and Nettie Hines had four children: Frank Bristow, Jr. (1901–1968), Anginette (1903–1966, who would marry Arthur Hatch in 1931), Adelaide (1906–1994, who would marry R. M. Van Matre in 1935), and Anson Hemingway (1910–1963). The cousin of EH's that Paul Pfeiffer refers to remains unidentified.

5 In her letter of 4 May 1929 Mary mentioned that they had recently purchased "several thousand more acres of land" that included a fishing resort, presumably along the Cache River (JFK). In his 10 July letter, Paul wrote that they had driven on the new hard-surfaced state highway between Piggott and Corning (about 17 miles to the west) that went through "our Cache bottom lands."

6 The Sino-Soviet conflict, involving Russian control of the Chinese Eastern Railway as well as the seizure of Yinlong Island, had begun in July 1929, and by mid-August armed forces of both countries were massing along the Manchurian border, with newspapers reporting that a clash was imminent ("Major Clash Nears as Chinese Advance; Harbin Threatened / Russians Seen as Determined to Use Force in Effort to Make China Yield," *New York Times*, 23 August 1929, 1). The conflict would end on 22 December in a decisive victory for the Soviet Union.

7 Early in May 1929 Joseph Stalin (1879–1953) called leaders in the American Communist Party (CP/USA), including its general secretary, Jay Lovestone (1897–1990), to Moscow, where he denounced the argument for "American exceptionalism," a claim that the increasing strength of American capitalism made the United States resistant to Communist revolution. On 14 May at a meeting of the Communist International (Comintern), Stalin denounced the "factionalism" and insubordination of the CP/USA and demanded the removal of its leaders. Stalin's orders reached the United States on 4 July, whereupon the CP/USA ousted Lovestone and his associates in order to retain the support of the Comintern.

8 EH left this sentence unfinished when he began writing on a new page.

9 In April 1929 the British Cunard Line announced plans to construct two "monster liners" and the British White Star Line planned a "Super-Olympic" liner to compete with Germany for the high-speed transatlantic passenger service ("British Plan Two 1,000-Foot Atlantic Liners To Answer German Challenge for Supremacy," *New York Times*, 24 April 1929, 1). In July, both the British and U.S. governments announced substantive cutbacks to their naval programs ("Hoover Halts Plan for Three Cruisers, Acts Immediately in Response to MacDonald Announcement of British Navy Cuts," *New York Times*, 25 July 1929, 1). These good-faith gestures paved the way for the London Naval Conference on disarmament (21 January–22 April 1930), during which the United States, Great Britain, Japan, France, and Italy would establish limits on their respective navies.

10 By early 1929 Coca Cola was sold in seventy-eight countries. A company publication proclaimed, "Coca-Cola is now found within the bull fight arenas of sunny Spain and Mexico, at the Olympic Games Stadium below the Eiffel Tower above 'Gay Paree,' on the holy pagoda in distant Burma, and beside the Coliseum of historic Rome" (quoted in Mark Pendergrast, *For God, Country, and Coca-Cola* [New York: Collier, 1993], 173).

To Evan Shipman, 24 August [1929]

Santiago de Campostella

Spain.

Hotel Suizo

Aug 24

Dear Evan:—

We visited Joan at the Ferme— He has a lovely place there[.] His mother is very nice.[1] He says that marriage he was going through perparations for before would have been a great mistake. It was called off just as the gong was about to ring. Now he is going to marry a fine girl this fall. From Palma de Mallorca. We saw her pictures and she looks lovely. He is very excited about it.[2]

It is hell for me to write a letter without the typewriter so please forgive this—

I'll subscribe to the horse paper as soon as we get to Paris but that wont be until the end of Sep. I know how you feel to be deprived of the dope.[3]

Dont mourn Paris too much. It is Awful. Terrible. Everybody lousy with money rich. Streets as full of cars as N.Y. All cafés enlarged with crowds of thousands on the terraces. Expensive as hell. Everything gone to hell. All Europe being Americanized so fast you cant watch it.

Santiago here with Streets all torn up like N.Y. Building a R.R. here along the best trout stream[.][4] All fish dynamited. Takes years to make a big trout—dynamite him in a minute.

I went to races, Enghein, Tremblay, Longchamps and Auteuil—went behind 4 straight times[.] Then got a winner at Longchamps that pulled me even—went down again— Pulled even the last two times at Auteuil and quit a few 100 out finally. It costs 100 francs to get into the pesage (sic) at Enghein with Pauline.[5] Money is nothing any more and is harder than ever to get.

André left ~~Whatsername~~ Odette finally. He has a girl and is somewhere in the south. I didnt see him. Tried to but he was gone.[6] All the little [pricks] that couldnt write straight are all writing like Joyce now in his last manner.

I have received my first mash note from a Fairy. He is through at Wisconsin and going to Harvard and says he is going to be my dearest friend whether I want it or not.

I would like to lay a bet against it.

Dont start worrying about life now. When you should have worried I couldnt get you to and I'll be damned if I'm going to have you worrying now.

It is Christ awful work to write. I've failed at it every day for damn near a month now. You will be a great writer and so will Papa but we will have to work our asses off to do it. It's just bite on the nail all the time

We'll be back in Dec. or in March. If you arent in Paris by then come down to Florida. Saw Harold a couple of times. He looked pretty good. Is the veritable Pickem. He's run out of fiancees and gives himself entirely to the horses.[7]

I will go around to Kahnweilers and see about your book.[8]

Hart Crane, they tell me, is rich and a fairy. I hope he's a good poet too but it seems too much to ask.[9]

I'll get the La France Chevaline off as soon as we get back.

I cant read my damn book as a serial but hope it will be all right as a book. Reads terribly in the magazine. They cut it too—

Pauline sends her love. Bumby and Pat are both well. Hadley too.

Nobody in Paris to talk too. Dont know much gossip.

Nancy Cunard is reported finally broken off with Aragon. She has a press.[10] So have the Crosbys—The Crosbys.[11] Kay Boyle who is now with

Laurence Vail—Jolas, various other citizens all signed a manifesto about The Word![12]

I thought the Word was God—or anyway merde at least if it wasnt capitalized.

Dont worry about money as long as you <u>eat regularly</u>. Really that's all a citizen needs unless he wants to get married or something like that— I know you will write a fine book— It is the only thing I look forward to reading.

Writing is on the bum— The German book— All Quiet etc. is <u>no advance</u> over Le Feu[13] and other bum war books— Just a little— It is good though where the guy goes home on leave and they buy him beers etc. All that killing Frenchmen in nomansland is whoopee— Maybe not but it stinks a little to me.

Terrible discipline [if? of?] prose is right—

If Paris seems any better this Fall I'll write you—but I <u>hated</u> it this Spring— First time I ever have. Maybe I'm going to die or something and see too clearly—or more probably am going to live and talk too much.

Please write me again. I get worried when I dont hear from you so long— Take care of yourself for god's sake— I wish we could come up to Plainfield this fall—[14] Why dont you see Archie [MacLeish]? He lives at Conway— Mass. Would be glad to see you I know.

I wish I knew more news—

Best to you always—

Hem

Channick, ALS; postmark: HOTEL SUIZO / SANTIAGO, 24 / AGO / 29

1 The country house of Joan Miró's family, outside Montroig del Camp (Tarragona), was the subject of *La Ferme*, the painting EH had purchased in 1925 as a birthday present for Hadley after vying with Shipman for the right to buy it. Miró's mother was Dolores Ferrà Oromí, daughter of a cabinetmaker from Palma de Mallorca. EH and Hadley had planned to visit Miró in July 1926 but cancelled the visit after Miró's father died suddenly.

2 Miró would marry Pilar Juncosa (1904–1995), a distant cousin, on 12 October 1929. The woman he nearly married remains unidentified.

3 In a letter to EH of 20 June 1929 Shipman expressed his worries about money, his difficulties with his writing, and his homesickness for Paris. He asked EH for information about mutual friends and for a three-month subscription to *La France Chevaline*, a Parisian horse-racing publication for which he did not have an address (JFK). In May 1929, the title of the publication became *Le Trotteur*.

4 An ambitious project of Spanish dictator Miguel Primo de Rivera (1870–1930) during his rule (1923–1930) was construction of a national railway system, begun in 1926.

5 *Pesage*: the weighing room or paddock of an equestrian racetrack (French).

6 French surrealist painter André Masson (1896–1987) met and married Odette Cabalé in 1920; they divorced in late 1929. EH had met Masson in Paris in the early 1920s; he and Hadley acquired Masson's triptych, *The Forest* (1922–1923) as well as *The Throw of the Dice* (1922). EH and Pauline would purchase two more Massons in 1931: *Animaux tués* and *La petite mare*.

7 Harold Edmund Stearns (1891–1943), expatriate American journalist, writer, and editor. From 1925 to 1930, he wrote a racing column for the European edition of the *Chicago Tribune* (generally known as the Paris *Tribune*) under the byline Peter Pickem.

8 Daniel-Henry Kahnweiler (1884–1979), German-born Paris-based publisher, art historian, collector, and dealer, owner of the Galerie Simon. He was an early supporter of Pablo Picasso (1881–1973) and other Cubist painters, as well as of André Masson and the Surrealist group. In his letter of 20 June, Shipman expressed concern about a book manuscript he had left with Kahnweiler, wondering what Kahnweiler intended to do with it, and telling EH there were poems in it that Shipman did not want published.

9 Hart Crane (1899–1932), son of a successful Ohio candy maker, was a gay American poet whose work Shipman admired. Crane had published a poetry collection, *White Buildings* (1926), and several individual poems that would be included in his best-known work, *The Bridge* (1930). Shipman had read that Crane was in Paris and suggested in his letter that EH look him up.

10 The troubled relationship between Nancy Clara Cunard (1896–1965), English shipping heiress, poet, social activist, and patron of the arts, and French surrealist poet Louis Aragon (1897–1982) ended after she entered a relationship with married African American jazz musician and composer Henry Crowder (1890–1955), whom she had met in 1928. That year she purchased the Three Mountains Press, which she renamed Hours Press (1928–1931), and moved it to Normandy. The Hours Press would publish her pamphlet, *Black Man and White Ladyship: An Anniversary* in 1931. Her relationship with Crowder, which caused her to be disinherited, would last until 1935.

11 Expatriate American poet Harry Crosby (1898–1929) and his wife, Caresse (née Mary Phelps Jacob, 1892–1970), had launched their Black Sun Press in Paris in 1925.

12 American writer Kay Boyle (1902–1992) and American artist and writer Laurence Vail (1891–1968) met in Paris in December 1928 and would marry in 1932. The June 1929 edition of *transition* carried a twelve-point "Proclamation" calling for the "Revolution of the Word," signed by Boyle, Vail, the magazine's editor Eugene Jolas, Hart Crane, and the Crosbys, among others. It declared that "The revolution in the English language is an accomplished fact" and concluded, "The plain reader be damned."

13 *Le Feu* (Paris: Flammarion, 1916) by French novelist Henri Barbusse (1873–1935), which won the prestigious Prix Goncourt (1916) and was published in English translation as *Under Fire* (1917), gained prominence as one of the premier works of antiwar fiction. In *FTA*, Count Greffi recommends *Le Feu* to Frederic Henry (Chapter 35). EH would praise the novel in his "Introduction" to *Men at War* (1942).

14 EH addressed the letter to Shipman at Brook Place, Plainfield, New Hampshire, the home Shipman's parents had bought in 1903. The letter was forwarded to "Marletotz / Keswick / Virginia."

To Charles Brackett, 24 August [1929]

Hotel Suizo
Santiago de Campostella
Aug 24

Dear Brackett—

Now I suppose I'll have to face being called by Scribners A Brackett Without Pity— But it is Christ irritating to have a book reviewed on the blurb— Especially one of Liveright's blurbs—or any blurb— They are always bloody fools[1]

How would it be to send the book? We're away from home Six weeks more and if you sent it to the Guaranty Trust in Paris they would forward it and it would be damned welcome— We came here to fish and there has been a drought that has dried the streams down to rocks and weeds—have worked like a bastard all day for 4 trout— So use some of that compassion and send the book— I'm awfully sorry they annoyed you with the name name shit. When will we meet?

Yours always
Ernest Hemingway

JFK, ALS

1 Published in July, Brackett's novel *American Colony* (New York: Liveright) was loosely based on the escapades of artistic expatriates on the French Riviera, where Brackett and his family had been guests of Gerald and Sara Murphy in the late 1920s. In a letter to EH of 6 August [1929], Brackett disclaimed any responsibility for "the assininity of putting 'Brackett is a compassionate Hemingway'" on the book jacket (JFK). Boni & Liveright, the firm founded in 1917 by Horace B. Liveright (1886–1933) and Albert Boni (1892–1981), had published EH's first American book, *IOT* (1925), but rejected his second submission, *TOS*, thus freeing him from his contract with them and allowing him to move to Scribner's. Liveright's use of other writers' names and endorsements on the jacket and in the advertising for *IOT* had irritated EH.

To Maxwell Perkins, 28 August [1929]

Aug 28

Dear Max—

Excuse the beautiful edging on the paper—It's Paulines. I got your two letters of Aug 14 yesterday— Im awfully glad you had such a good summer.[1]

You can certainly get drunk on Port and it is bad afterwards too— Those famous 3 and 4 bottle men were living all the time in the open air—hunting, shooting, always on a horse—[2] In That life as in skiing or fishing you can drink any amount—

Am cheerful again—have written 3 pieces—have some more in my head— Going to go over them and copy off in Paris[.][3] We leave here day after tomorrow—for Madrid— want to see Sidney Franklin of Brooklyn— They say he's good—

Be back in Paris Oct 1— Maybe before—

Glad Meyer likes the book—[4] I hope to God it's better than The Sun— The comparative that way doesnt bother me—

Did I ever write you about seeing Morley Callaghan in Paris—several times—he was working hard— You would not believe it to look at him but he is a <u>very</u> good boxer— I boxed with him 3 or 4 times— One time I had a date to box with him at 5 pm— lunched with Scott and John Bishop at Pruniers—at[e] Homard Thermidor[5]—all sorts of stuff—drunk several bottles of white burgundy— Knew I would be asleep by 5— So went around with Scott to get Morley to box right away— I couldnt see him hardly—had a couple of whiskeys enroute— Scott was to keep time and we were to box 1 minutes rounds with 2 minute rests on acct. of my condition— I knew I could go a minute at a time and went fast and used all my wind—then Morley commenced to pop me and cut my mouth, mushed up my face in general— I was pooped as could be and thought I had never known such a long round but couldn't ask about it or Morley would think I was quitting— Finally Scott called time— Said he was very sorry and ashamed and would I forgive him— He had let the round go three minutes and 45 seconds—so interested to see if I was going to hit the floor!

We boxed 5 more rounds and I finally fought myself out of the alcohol and went all right— Can still feel with my tongue the big scar on my lower lip— He is fast, knows a lot and is a pleasure to box with— He cant hit hard—if he could he would have killed me— I slipped and went down once and lit on my arm and put my left shoulder out in that first round and it pulled a tendon so that it was pretty sore afterwards and did not get a chance to box again before we left. Morley had been boxing nearly every day in Toronto for a year. He is fat and looks in bad shape but is really darned good. [6]

What reminded me of this was how you could get rid of alcohol by exercise— After 5 rounds—during which I took a bad beating in the first—I was going well—judgement of distance good—in really good shape and out pointing (or holding my own) with someone who had been beating me all over the place to sweat it out of me

PUL, AL

1 EH's letter is written on gray stationery with a darker gray-and-white border. Only one letter from Perkins dated 14 August 1929 has been located—a brief letter promising a longer one later that evening. In it he responded to three questions EH asked in his letter of 26 July, saying that the royalty for the *FTA* limited edition of 500 copies would be $75, that EH could have an advance whenever he asked, and that "scrotum" could be used instead of "b___". He added, "I did destroy the letter immediately as you said to," referring to EH's request of [23] June [1929] to destroy EH's angry letter complaining about Wister (PUL).
2 According to a nineteenth-century history of drinking lore, "The usual allowance for a moderate man at dinner seems to have been two bottles of port. Men were known as two-bottle men, three- and four-bottle men, and even in some instances six-bottle men" (John Bickerdyke, *The Curiosities of Ale and Beer: An Entertaining History* [London: Swan Sonnenschein, 1889; reprinted London: Spring Books, 1965], 292).
3 EH may have completed early or preliminary drafts of "Wine of Wyoming," "A Natural History of the Dead," and "After the Storm," none of which would be published before 1930 (Smith, 218, 232, 240).
4 Wallace M. Meyer (1892–1985) had managed Scribner's advertising campaign for *SAR* and *FTA*. In his letter of 12 July 1929, Perkins told EH that Meyer was reading proofs of *FTA* and "thinks it magnificent" (PUL).
5 American poet John Peale Bishop (1892–1944) and Fitzgerald had become friends while students at Princeton. Prunier's, established in 1872 and named in the 1924 Baedeker guide to Paris among "Restaurants of the Highest Class," was noted for its fish, oysters, and caviar (Baedeker's *Paris*, 15). *Homard*: lobster (French); EH refers to a classic French dish of lobster in cream sauce.
6 This is EH's first, most detailed, and most charitable account of the infamous June 1929 boxing match that would eventually end his friendship with Callaghan and strain his friendship with Fitzgerald. In his Paris memoirs Callaghan recalls tension between EH and Fitzgerald, with EH accusing Fitzgerald of intentionally letting the fight go overtime (see Callaghan, 213–16).

To Maxwell Perkins, [c. late August 1929]

Have an idea for the next book— Maybe it is punk—but started to write some things about fishing—hunting—about Bull fights and bull fighters— About

eating and drinking— About different places—mostly things and places—
Not so much people—though I know some funny ones about people—
Several about fishing—. If there were enough of these and they were good
enough they might make a book—[1] Started to write because my Goddamned
imagination wasn't functioning—still tired maybe—and still I know a lot of
things— Thought it's better to write than constipate trying to write
masterpieces— When I'm writing then I can write stories too— But when
cant write then cant write anything— Maybe if I got some ahead the
Magazine might publish some— They are quiet and not awfully exciting—
More like that Big Two Hearted River story-—only not so long— Might be
good for the magazines— Somewhere between Essays and Remeniscences—
The two worst qualifications I could find— What do you think?— I dont
want to have any correspondance with Dr. Bridges about them yet—-want to
write a bunch first— Will divide them into three kinds—quiet ones—Funny
ones—immoral ones— He can have the quiet ones— Will help the magazine
as much as that piece by Doc Phelps about how awful we pornographers are.
Who are the other pornographers? What was funniest was where he said
about the <u>healthy</u> public interest in <u>murder</u> stories [war] and stories of <u>Crime</u>.
I thought there were 10 Commandments and adultry was only the 7<u>th</u>![2]

But am <u>going to write</u>— I think that's Scott's trouble with his novel—among
other things of course more complicated— But he thought he <u>had</u> to write
a masterpiece to follow The Gatsby—as good as Seldes etc. said he was—and to
consciously write such a thing that had to be <u>great</u> just constipated him—[3]

Then too you have to use up your material—you never use <u>Anything</u> you
save— I thought I'd used up everything in In Our Time— Should always
write as though you were going to die at the end of the book— (This doesnt
seem to go with what's before but it's a good idea too!) Never for gods sake
use or turn over to the advt. dept. anything I say in a letter—

I think I could write some pretty good things—about Key West—Here—
Paris—Constantinople— Try to have more than meets the eye and the old
iceberg stuff[4]—but no more stories than that Che Ti Dice La Patria thing—[5]
What do you think? You'll say fine whether you think so or not because that
is what you have to do with these bloody Authors— But I could write some
pretty good ones I think— Did you ever read Far Away and Long Ago— by

W.H. Hudson— Like that only not so good— That's a swell book—[6] Swell is a dreadful word— When I hear somebody say it that thinks I would like to hear it—Jews usually—my stomach turns over— These wont be anything like Sherwood Anderson in Vanity Fair—[7]

Yours always
Ernest—

I'll write when I want the advance—[8]

PUL, ALFragS

The conjectured date of this letter fragment (the pages numbered 5 and 6 in EH's hand) is based on EH's references to the column by William Lyon Phelps that appeared in the August 1929 issue of *Scribner's Magazine* and to a letter from Perkins dated 14 August 1929 (PUL).

1 EH's next book would be *Death in the Afternoon* (1932).
2 William Lyon Phelps, in his "As I Like It" column in the August 1929 issue of *Scribner's Magazine*, lamented the vulgarity of much contemporary fiction and claimed, "many serious-minded folks are turning to read with relief and enjoyment detective stories." Asking rhetorically why "stories of murder and policemen" were so popular, he answered, "Because these books are interesting tales and free from the sultriness of sex" (119–20). In his nine-page article, Phelps reviewed a number of books but did not mention EH or *FTA*.
3 Reviewing *The Great Gatsby* in the *Dial*, critic Gilbert Seldes (1893–1970) proclaimed that Fitzgerald "has mastered his talents and gone soaring in a beautiful flight, leaving behind him everything dubious and tricky in his earlier work, and leaving even farther behind all the men of his own generation and most of his elders" (August 1925, 162).
4 EH would famously define his "iceberg principle" in *DIA*: "If a writer of prose knows enough about what he is writing about he may omit things that he knows and the reader, if the writer is writing truly enough, will have a feeling of those things as strongly as though the writer had stated them. The dignity of movement of an ice-berg is due to only one-eighth of it being above water" (Chapter 16). EH had first written about the submerged portion of an iceberg in "The Ice-Berg Patrol," a brief piece published in the *Co-operative Commonwealth* (1 October 1921). Both Hadley and Pauline referred to the iceberg principle in letters to EH, suggesting he had discussed his ideas with them (Hadley to EH, 10 August 1921, JFK; Pauline to EH, 27 November 1926, JFK).
5 EH's "Che Ti Dice la Patria?" first appeared as "Italy, 1927" in the May 1927 *New Republic* before its publication in *MWW* that October. EH's story, drawn from his March 1927 trip to Italy with Guy Hickok, exposes the deteriorating conditions of everyday life under the dictatorship of Benito Mussolini (1883–1945), who founded the Italian Fascist Party in 1919, became prime minister in 1922, and ruled as dictator from 1925 to 1943.
6 William Henry Hudson (1841–1922), English naturalist and novelist born in Argentina to American parents, described his childhood in *Far Away and Long Ago: A History of My Early Life* (London: J. M. Dent & Sons, 1918). EH wrote in his own copy of the book, "Hudson writes the best of anyone" (Reynolds *Reading*, 139), and in a February 1935 essay in *Esquire* magazine, he would include it in a list of seventeen recommended books a writer should have read ("Monologue to the Maestro: A High Seas Letter" in *BL*, 217).

7 Sherwood Anderson (1876–1941), author of *Winesburg, Ohio* (1919), was a frequent contributor to the monthly magazine *Vanity Fair* beginning in the early 1920s. By 1928 his
"Small Town Notes" were a regular feature, examining the "drabness" of small towns and
their inhabitants' "little subterfuges to get through life" ("Small Town Notes," *Vanity Fair*,
1 June 1928, 58).
8 In his letter of 14 August 1929 Perkins had offered EH an advance of $5,000 "at any time, or
more."

To Waldo Peirce, 29 August [1929]

Santiago Aug 29

Dear Waldo—

Lousy trout fishing this summer—a bloody drought for the whole
summer streams dried down to their beds—boulders and weeds usually on
the bottom on the top. Work like a bastard for 8— Kill yourself and wife for
10— Trout are damned good fun though— Pop way out of water for a dry
fly floating down—

We leave here day after tomorrow for Palencia—couple of corridas there
on Sunday— Mon— Sept. 1–2— Then Madrid for a week. Sara and Gerald
Murphy may be coming down— Then work home to Paris—maybe stop at
Cap D'Antibes if all the Dolly Sistaires gone.[1]

Glad to hear from Reneé that you are a regular looking fellow— Tell her
to go easy on motorcars though.[2]

You must miss the beard though as a blind to trap unwary golfers with—
It will grow again anyway— Shaving is a hell of a job. Good to do for a while
then you appreciate the beard again.[3] I weigh 87½ kil to 88½— Went to 92
at Valencia with no exercise except eating 8 or ten course meals— Got down
again now— Pauline's fine and in good shape— Bumby in Brittany—Cote
du Nord— Pat near Compeigne—[4] Both fine—

We'll be in Paris by the end of Sept.

What about Fred Parke and the Sunfish? I wish you could stir him to
crash through— In return for us giving him that Sunfish Uncle Gus has
already given us this car and offered to buy us a house and I would like to
come through with the Sunfish! Let me know about it will you?

If there is anything you want stuffed in Paris will be glad to do it— That
leads to you for dirty joking but still holds— Have no pep to write— We'll

come over either in Nov. or March— Depends on if we get evicted out of apt.

Hope my book sells— Have only about a thousand bucks in bank and checks written against it to the family will clean it by Oct 1— Have lived here on 4 bucks a day between us— 1 Buck a day for Spending money between us— Damn good value too—get a can of aceitunas rellanos—[5] Bottle of Cinzano and bottle of Manzanilla and have Gay Café life in our room— It is good to have wine at 150 pesetas a bottle instead of 2 dollars in Key West—or was it more? 3½ maybe— But no tarpon—yellowtail or snappers— Key West is a hell of a fine place dont you think? We want to get a shack there and one in Wyoming and live between the two— Paris is damned expensive now—as much as N.Y. I think— We went broke there in no time—

Will be glad to see it though—go out to Enghein and Auteiul and see Harold Pickem Stearns— Fall is damn nice in Paris— We'll see you there— This is a punk letter— Give my best to Reneé—

Yours always
Ernesto El Shito

Pauline sends her love—

[*On verso in lower right quadrant of folded letter:*]
Ever read Jew Süss[6]
<u>Exciting</u> lot of tripe.

Colby, ALS

1 Yansci (Jenny) Deutsch (1892—1941) and Roszika (Rosie) Deutsch (1892–1970), identical twins born in Budapest who after immigrating to the United States at the age of twelve became successful vaudeville dancers known as the Dollies or the Dolly Sisters. At the age of eighteen, they performed in the Ziegfeld Follies and soon became international stars. They announced their retirement in 1927. Rosie spent the summer of 1929 at Cap d'Antibes, hobnobbing with other celebrities, creating headlines, and gambling compulsively.
2 Renée, Peirce's nickname for Ada Rainey (1909–1969), who occasionally worked as a cook in the Peirce household and was also employed by Waldo's father. In a 10 July letter to EH, Peirce had reported, "Renèe took a boy friends car out alone & tipt over in it—& got pretty well banged up" (JFK).
3 Renée had added a postscript to Peirce's 12 August 1929 letter to EH, announcing that Peirce had shaved off his beard. Peirce sketched a multi-chin self-portrait captioned "new nude mug with alcoholic dewlaps" (JFK).

4 As in previous summers, Bumby was staying in Brittany with his longtime caregiver Marie Rohrbach, a native of Mur-de-Bretagne. Patrick was in the care of his French nurse, Henriette Lechner. The town of Compiègne is located about 50 miles northeast of Paris.
5 *Aceitunas rellenas*: stuffed olives, often with anchovies (Spanish).
6 *Jud Süß* (1925), historical novel by German-born novelist and playwright Lion Feuchtwanger (1884–1958), translated into English as *Jew Süss* (London: Martin Secker, 1926). The novel recounts the life of Joseph Süß-Oppenheimer (1698–1738), a successful Jewish financier who in 1732 became financial advisor to Prince Carl Alexander (1684–1737). Falsely accused and convicted of financial misdeeds, Süss refused to save himself by converting to Christianity and was publicly executed. The novel, a critical and popular success, would be translated into more than twenty languages and adapted as a play (1929), an English movie (1939), and a Nazi propaganda film (1940).

To F. Scott Fitzgerald, 4 September 1929

Madrid—Sept. 4
1929

Dear Scott— About that "nervous bitterness." You remember my blowing up about the people coming in to look at the Apt while I was working (I paid 3000 dollars on a promise to have it permanently and considered it our home) but you seem to have damned well forgot my coming around the next day to tell you that I thought Ruth Goldbeck Vallambrosa was a fine girl, had always admired her and told you for Gods sake never to let her know that I had cursed about the apt. She did not know I was sore and the only way she would ever find out would be through you.[1]

You said you understood perfectly and for me not to worry you would never mention it to her.

I'm damned glad you are going well. There is very small chance of our coming to the Riviera[.] There was some talk of Gerald and Sara coming here and we going back with them but a wire from Gerald yesterday says Sara has had to go to the mountains with Patrick and a letter following.[2] Havent got the letter yet but believe their Spanish trip off. Would have been damned glad to see them. Havent spoken English to anyone since left Pamplona the 12th July except with Pauline. Havent even heard it.

If they arent coming we will probably go North and see Bumby and Pat Bumby having good fishing in Brittany he writes.

I cant tell you how glad I am you are getting the book done.[3] Fashionable thing is to deprecate all work and think the only thing is to go to pot gracefully and Expensively but the poor bastards doing this—giving up their writing etc. to compete with people who can do nothing and do nothing but go to pot

Cant finish that Jeremiad without mentioning great friends and contemporaries— It sounds pretty bad anyway— Cant write that sort of tripe without a typewriter!

Of course all this may be premature and you may not be finishing your book but only putting me on the list of friends who receive the more glowing reports—

But I hope to god it's true. As far as I read it was better than anything I ever read except the best of Gatsby. You know what part that is.

The good parts of a book may be only something a writer is lucky enough to overhear or it may be the wreck of his whole damn life—and one is as good as the other

You could write such a damn fine book— What held you up and constipated you more than anything was that review of Seldes's in the Dial.[4] After that you became self conscious about it and knew you must write a masterpiece. Nobody but Fairies can write Maspertieces or Masterpieces consciously— Anybody else can only write as well as they can going on the system that if this one when it's done isn't a masterpiece maybe the next one will be. You'd have written two damned good books by now if it hadnt been for that Seldes review.

Of course there are other complications God knows but they are self made. They're not something that's done to you. Like using the juice to write for the Post and trying to write masterpieces with the dregs.[5] But now if your using the juice and are desperate enough so you know you have to write one Seldes or no Seldes you will write a damned fine book.

This should be enough from Jeremiah Hemingstein the great Jewish Prophet

If you want some news Dos is married.[6] And if you write a good and unsuperior letter with nothing about my nervous bitterness I'll write and tell you who he's married and all the dope.

On re-reading your letter I find it Is not Snooty at all. And old HEm wrong again.[7]

Evidently a prey to his nervous bitterness! (This not sarcastic) But if I dont send this will never send any so throw out the N.B. in it (Son of a bitch if I have that!) and write care the Guaranty when your not too tired from work. I know how damned pooping it is and I'm gladder than I can ever let you know that it is going finely— Yours always affectionately

Ernest—

Best to Zelda and Scotty from us.

Are you going to Stay down in Cannes? How long. Might come down later when you get the book done—

Max is fine. He'd never let anybody down and I never worry about him.

PUL, ALS

1 Ruth de Vallombrosa (1900–1992), widow of American painter Walter Dean Goldbeck (1882–1925); in January 1928, she married Count Paul de Manca de Mores de Vallombrosa (1890–1950). EH is responding to Fitzgerald's letter of 23 August 1929 in which he reported, "Now—Ruth Goldbeck Voallammbbrrossa not only had no intention of throwing you out in any case, but has even promised on her own initiative to speak to whoever it is—she knows her—has the place. She is a fine woman, I think one of the most attractive in evidence at this moment in every sense, + is not deserving of that nervous bitterness" (JFK). EH and Pauline faced the prospect of losing their apartment on rue Férou, as they were subtenants of a man renting the building. Because that man was not renewing his lease, the owner had the right to evict all the occupants. The owner was looking for someone to rent the entire building at a much higher rate but had not yet found a tenant; if he did, EH and Pauline could rent from the new tenant, even at a higher price (Gus Pfeiffer to Louise Pfeiffer, 21 December 1929, HPMEC).

2 Scott, Zelda, and their daughter, Frances Scott ("Scottie") Fitzgerald (1921–1986), lived in a rented villa in Cannes from June to October 1929. Fitzgerald had written to EH, "Hope you'll be here in Sept for a week or so." Gerald and Sara Murphy's son Patrick Francis Murphy II (1920–1937) had been diagnosed with bronchitis and taken to Villard-de-Lans, in the mountains of southeastern France. By October he would be diagnosed with tuberculosis.

3 Fitzgerald had written, "I've been working like hell, better than for four years, and now am confident of getting old faithful off before the all-American teams are picked—hence the delay." His next novel, *Tender Is the Night*, would not be published until 1934.

4 EH refers to the laudatory review of *The Great Gatsby* by Gilbert Seldes, "Spring Flight" (*Dial*, August 1925).

5 The *Saturday Evening Post* paid Fitzgerald as much as $4,000 per story. In 1929, Fitzgerald earned some $27,000 from eight *Post* stories and $31.71 from book sales (Bruccoli *Fitz-Hem*, 138). That year, the average net income for a United States taxpayer was $6,132.22 (*Statistics of Income for 1929* [Washington D.C.: United States Government Printing Office, 1931], 4).

6 John Dos Passos and Kate Smith had married on 19 August 1929.

7 In a 9 September 1929 letter Fitzgerald would reply, "I'm glad you decided my letter wasn't snooty—it was merely hurried" (JFK).

To John Dos Passos, 4 September [1929]

Madrid.

Sept 4

Dear Dos—

Damned glad to hear you men are married. Best love from us to Kate. I'm happy as hell about it!

I wrote you just the other day from Santiago. Paulines is out in the town and as it is raining like hell probably getting wet. Not much news—
We came from Santiago to Orense and then down along the Portuguese Border—Verin and a swell town Puebla de Sanabria—(where got drunk) on to Benavente—up to Leon—(a lousy hole) along to Palencia—worst road in Spain 120 Kil of pot holes, dust, heat to crack your head open. Two <u>swell</u> bull fights in Palencia—[1] Me in bed between fights with a busted gut—get up for the bull festival then back to bed— Then here by way of Valladolid and the Guadarramas— Damned nice—

Well it's fine to hear you citizens are married. Let us know where to send 30 or 40 thousand seeds worth of presents—

We're going to come back to U.S. in December or March— Europe is the tripe. I'll bet yr. first Vol is damn good— Trilogies are undoubtedly the thing— Look at the Father, Son and Holy Ghost— Nothings gone much bigger than that—[2]

I wish the hell we could go to the Sailfish side of Mexico on a trip—
We could live on game, fish and what tomatoes you brought along— I'd be glad to go anywhere for months on onions alone if we had enough onions and salt— We could take enough stuff though— Lets go winter after next?

The Stewarts were ruined by Don getting that 25 thousand contract and meeting the Whitneys—[3]

Am relying on you to avoid that— Sign nothing. Shoot as soon as you the whites of a Whitney's eye—[4]

Bishop was ruined by Mrs. Bishop's income.[5] Keep money away from Katey.

Eternal youth has sunk the Fitzes— Get old Passos— Age up Kate—

Old Hem ruined by his father shooting himself. Keep guns away from Katherine's old man—

It certainly will be fine to see you guys— I wish we could shoot you a bottle of absinthe—

Well this letter is tripe—

Yrs always—

Hem

Pauline sends her love— She's writing too

UVA, ALS

1 The 1 September bullfight featured as senior matador Nicanor Villalta Serris (1897–1980)—after whom EH and Hadley had named their son John Hadley Nicanor Hemingway—along with Antonio Posada Carnerero (1905–1986) and Félix Rodríguez. On 2 September, EH saw Marcial Lalanda del Pino, Félix Rodríguez, and Vicente Barrera Cambra. EH had mentioned Lalanda and Villalta in *SAR* and would discuss all of these bullfighters, except Posada, in *DIA*.

2 In his 22 August 1929 letter, Dos Passos told EH he was trying to finish his novel *The 42nd Parallel*, the first in a planned trilogy. "This trilogy stuff is the cats nuts to a writer because you can always think that if vol. 1 is shit vol. 2 will be swell," he wrote (JFK). *The 42nd Parallel* (1930) would be followed by *1919* (1932) and *The Big Money* (1936). The completed trilogy, whose working title had been "The New Century," would be published as *U.S.A.* in 1938.

3 When Donald Ogden Stewart's 1925 novel *The Crazy Fool* became a bestseller, he was contracted by a Hollywood studio to write the screenplay. Stewart (1894–1980) married Beatrice Ames (1902–1981) on 24 July 1926, and the couple settled in New York City in 1927. There they became close friends with Jock Whitney and other "wealthy 'socialites' who were eager to enjoy the exciting world of the speakeasies and the night clubs," as Stewart later recalled in his memoirs (*By a Stroke of Luck!* [New York: Two Continents Publishing Group, 1975], 159–60).

4 Colonel William Prescott (1726–1795), American Revolutionary War commander at the Battle of Bunker Hill on 17 June 1775, reputedly ordered his troops not to fire "until you see the whites of their eyes."

5 In 1922, John Peale Bishop married heiress Margaret Grosvenor Hutchins (1898–1974), daughter of banker and railroad magnate Robert Grosvenor Hutchins (1869–1949).

After his marriage Bishop quit as managing editor of *Vanity Fair* (1920–1922), and the couple traveled in Europe before settling in France, where they lived from 1926 to 1933.

To Charles Thompson, [c. 4 September 1929]

Madrid

Dear Charles:—

Pauline got a grand letter from Lorine telling about how you were again ruined by a lot of doctors. The full time Rod holding doctor sounds about the worst—although the citizen that laid down the rod when you went to gaff the tarpon wasn't bad—

We ought to have a rule that no one with any handle to their name should be allowed on board a boat except those legitimate Doctors Thompson, Pierce, Passos and Hemingway.

Got a letter from Dos yesterday that he and Kate were married! Dont you think that's fine?

Thats about all the news— We left Galicia and came here by way of Palencia. Saw two fine bull fights there. Had a letter from Bumby that he is catching lots of perch and nearly Catches pike! up in Brittany.

Heard from Waldo. He said he would winter in Key West—

I guess we'll be over either the end of December or early in March. Bumby and Pat both well. Sunny went back to U.S end of June—

Pauline is out on the town trying to get some old 2nd hand silver— We've never had any. She has gotten 12 forks but So far only two knives— We'll live in Key West and eat fish. When we get turtle steak will borrow knives from you Can eat birds with the fingers. I'll be glad to be back again.

Marlin (the gun not the sword fish makers) are getting out a lever action 410 ga. shot gun.—6 shot— It ought to be a good—handy gun—[1] We'll have plenty of guns though— That's all my estate will be— Pauline has a 28 ga. Double barrell I got her for her birthday and I will bring back the Browning 16 ga. Automatic—[2] That makes the 12–20-(2-410s) a 16 and a 28—

We ought to all go Duck shooting—Lorine and you and us— I'm awfully glad Kate and Dos are married— They ought to make a fine pair— Waldo likes all women until he marries them— And, as he says, he had nothing to offer Kate except Bigamy!

I suppose my book will be out in another month— Hope it will support all my numerous relatives offspring, furnish us transport and buy a boat too— Bought a Motor Boating here— The Banfield Sea Skiff is a fine practical looking boat for fishing and sleeps four comfortably— But the sad end of that story is that they want $7,150^{00} for it which lets Papa out.[3] It doesnt look as though there were enough room on the top deck to lie down and be sick either. That is a thing you have to have! Have you heard from Mike Strater if he has harpooned any Tuna?

Must stop this letter—

Yours always
Ernest

Best to Lorine—

Profound greetings to Rev. Dr. Bra [Saunders]—

USCar, ALS

1 The Marlin Firearms Company was established in 1870 in New Haven, Connecticut, by John M. Marlin (1836–1901). The company made a lever-action .410-bore shotgun in very limited numbers from 1929 to 1932, primarily to attract investors, who would receive one shotgun for every four shares of Marlin preferred stock they purchased.
2 EH owned a 16-gauge Browning A-5 shotgun, "the first commercially successful semi-automatic shotgun," patented in 1900 by Utah gunsmith John M. Browning (1855–1926) and manufactured in Belgium (Calabi, Helsley, and Sanger, 81–82, 93–95).
3 *Motor Boating* magazine was first published in New York in 1907. The Banfield Sea Skiff Works of Atlantic Highlands, New Jersey, manufactured a variety of models. EH may have seen an ad for the Banfield "32," with a 100 horsepower motor priced at $7,150 (*Yachting*, April 1929).

To Maxwell Perkins, 7 September 1929

MADRID SEPT 7 1929 NFT
LCD[1] PERKINS CHARLES SCRIBNERS SONS
NEWYORK (FIFTH AVE 48)

CHAPTER FORTY SHOULD READ QUOTES WE HAD A FINE LIFE STOP WE LIVED STOP THROUGH THE MONTHS OF JANUARY ETC.

AS IT APPEARED IN MAGAZINE WITH NOTHING BETWEEN
THOSE FIRST TWO SENTENCES STOP FIND TODAY PARAGRAPH
SUPPOSEDLY CROSSED OUT IN GALLEYS IN ENGLISH PAGE
PROOFS THIS WOULD RUIN BOOK HEMINGWAY THOMAS COOK
MADRID.

3P

PUL, Cable

An undated draft of this cable in EH's hand surviving at JFK reads as follows: "Chapter Forty should read quotes We had a fine life ~~period~~ stop we lived through the months of January ~~and~~ etc. Stop Should be Nothing between these two sentences find ~~extra~~ paragraph ~~inserted~~ omitted crossed out in galleys in English page proofs / Hemingway." Perkins's return cable dated 9 September confirmed that Chapter 40 would appear as EH requested (PUL).

1 "LC" is the designation of a reduced-rate deferred telegram, transmitted after more urgent full-rate telegrams. "LCD" denotes a deferred telegram sent in the language of the country of destination (as opposed to "LCO," language of the country of origin).

To Maxwell Perkins, 9 September [1929]

Madrid Sept 9

Dear Max—

Cabled you day before yesterday about the chapter 40 beginning— You remember there was a long piece in there (philosophizing) that I cut out.[1] Found part of it <u>in</u> in the English page proofs. They never sent me galley proofs— So was panic stricken that it might be in your page proofs too—

In a way it's a bad business not to see Page proofs— They are only seen in order to catch last minute mistakes that might be overlooked— I got the Mss to you by Feb of this year— But it may be O.K. Hope so.

If the whole long thing of philosophizing were in it would not be so bad— But just to have that first part— It would be fatal from my standpoint—

What did you do too about the note in the front? That in the English edition reads—"None of the characters in this book is a living person, nor are the units or military organizations mentioned actual units or organizations[.] E.H."[2]

That seems to cover the business of disclaiming any <u>autobiography</u> or slander of Army [*EH insertion*: Red X] etc.

89

Hope this is in somewhere—or the one I wrote for the serial— If its impossible to get, or isnt in, the book couldnt it go somewhere on the inside of the jacket?—

When is the book out? I suppose I was put out not getting page proofs as it is there that I check finally— But you know the exigencies of getting the book out and it may all turn out for the best.

Had my pocket picked here in Madrid getting on a crowded street car in the dark. Thief got away before could get him in jam. Lost passport—Carte d'Identité, all papers of the car etc. all taken. A bull fight critic that I know put in the paper that I was an illustrious escritor and greatly handicapped by these documents being taken and the pickpocket turned them in—[3] You can use this in the publicity notes!)[4] (He Put them (this not so hot for the notes!) in the mail box on a tramway along with the papers from the pocket books of 3 other gents Including a Lt. Col. of the Guardia Civil) Pickpockets here always return papers—one man told me he had his pocket picked twice in a month—pocket book taken— But all documents and papers returned through the mail.

Lost no money— Had money in an inner pocket— Damned nice of thief to return all the papers— No joke to be without passport—and all foreign papers—drivers license—permits etc. on Car.

—Send this in haste—

We leave here day after tomorrow— Pauline hasnt been so well last few days— Have been meeting Sidney Franklin—the Brooklyn matador—not bad—[5]

Yours always—

Ernest

Hope the letter in the magazine by Julian Capers is not forerunner of others. All it proved was that I perjured in regard to my age— Dont want to land in jail—wish <u>private life</u> could stay out— He's an awfully nice fellow of course.[6] Hope to be judged as <u>Writer</u> nothing else— Book fiction dont want to try to tie it up with fact. It's not Joan Lowell. It's fiction must stand as such— Dont want to lay ourselves open to someone proving it's not fact.[7]

PUL, ALS

1 F. Scott Fitzgerald had recommended deleting or trimming this section in which the protagonist Frederic Henry ponders religious belief and temporal happiness and reveals Catherine's impending death (Bruccoli *Fitz–Hem*, 115–18). EH retained only the opening sentence of the long passage: "We had a fine life." The excised material is included in *FTA–HLE* (301–02).

2 The disclaimer appeared on page 5 of the English edition, published 11 November 1929 by Jonathan Cape. Scribner's ran it only in the second and third printings of the U.S. edition (1 and 9 October). Grissom counters the claim in both Cohn's and Hanneman's bibliographies that the disclaimer appeared in the second printing only (109).

3 Although the critic remains unidentified, a likely candidate is Spanish journalist Rafael Hernández Ramírez (1889–1971), who wrote taurine criticism and reports for the Madrid dailies *ABC, La Libertad,* and *Informaciones*. Hernández, whom EH met in 1924, appears under his nom de plume, Rafael, in Chapter 16 of *SAR*. *Escritor*: writer (Spanish).

4 Perkins apparently shared EH's letter with Harry Hansen, who quoted the first four sentences of this paragraph in his 19 October 1929 column for the *New York World*, commenting, "In a few brief sentences Ernest Hemingway gives Maxwell Perkins, his friend and Scribner editor, the outlines of an episode which we may expect any day to develop into a Hemingway short story" ("The First Reader," 14).

5 EH refers to Franklin's Madrid debut as a *novillero* on 8 September 1929. Franklin would not be promoted to full *matador de toros* until 18 July 1945, his last appearance in the Spanish ring.

6 The September 1929 *Scribner's Magazine* included an admiring letter to the editor from Julian Capers, Jr., who had met EH on the staff of the *Kansas City Star*, where EH, then eighteen years old, had worked as a cub reporter from October 1917 to April 1918. Capers mentioned meeting EH during the war "when he was 17" and claimed that EH had "signed an affidavit that he could read, write and speak Italian and French fluently, whereas the fact was he knew no language but English." In a letter to EH of 16 October 1929 (JFK), Capers would enclose a copy of his signed review of *FTA*, "Love and War Are Basic Elements of New Hemingway Novel," in which he inaccurately claimed that EH "saw with his own eyes . . . the Caporetto debacle" (*Dallas Morning News*, 13 October 1929, Editorial, Book, and Amusement Section, 3).

7 American actress Joan Lowell (née Helen Wagner, 1900–1967) had published a memoir titled *The Cradle of the Deep* (1929) detailing her youth spent on the trading ship captained by her father. An enthusiastic review by Fanny Butcher (1888–1987) boosted its popularity ("Sea's Girl Child Tells Story of a Windjammer / Storms, Oaths, Floggings, and Cat Soup!," *Chicago Daily Tribune*, 9 March 1929, 13) and it was selected by the Book-of-the-Month Club as its March title. By early April, however, Lowell's childhood acquaintances challenged her story, and the ensuing controversy received national attention.

To William D. and Frances Horne, 9 September [1929]

Sept 9

Dearest Bunny and Horney:

Congratulations and Best love to you both. We both think it is grand you men are married and we hope we see you soon.

The wire came through garbled to Santiago and I couldnt know it was really you— It mentioned <u>Bill Wheaton</u>—[1] Didnt have Bunny's Address Couldnt be sure it was the Horned Article But compromised on wiring Bunny to 1100 and 1200 Lake Shore Drive—[2] Hope you got it— Anyway just got a note forwarded from Dort Fauntleroy in Paris giving the dope—[3] We backed Bunny marrying anybody she wanted but married to <u>Bill Horne</u> Yeah Citizens. When do we see you and where can we send Renoirs?

By God I am glad you two grand people are marrying each other— Dos Passos and Kate Smith are just married too.

Vive la Marriage—

Where are you now— I'll send this to the Horneds Employers—[4]

God bless you both— Pauline sends her best love—

Ernie

[*Pauline writes*:]

Horny, it's <u>wonderfull</u>.

Much love to you both. I'm writing to Bunny when I get back to Paris. I have a small first edition there for her shop.[5]

Pauline

PUL, ALS; postmark: [*illegible*] / MADRID, 10 SEP [*illegible*]

1 EH's old friend Bill Horne had married Frances (Bunny) Thorne in Chicago on 19 August 1929. The wire EH received at the Hotel Suizo, Santiago de Compostela, read "YOU TWO EL[E]CTED NONRESIDENT BEST MAN AND FLOWER GIRL FOR FUCTION TAKE PLACE AUGUST NINETEENTH LOVE AND KISSES— BUNNY AND BILL WHEATON" (JFK).

2 Frances Thorne's family lived in a luxurious apartment building at 1130 Lake Shore Drive in Chicago.

3 Dorothy Dort (1893–1992), daughter of Josiah Dallas Dort, founder and president of several manufacturing companies, including the Dort Motor Car Company. Dorothy married Gorton "Brick" Robinson Fauntleroy (1890–1962) in April 1917. Fauntleroy and Bill Horne had been friends and classmates at Princeton (class of 1913), and both joined the war effort. EH probably met Dorothy and Gorton through Bill Horne, with whom EH shared an apartment in Chicago in 1920.

4 Horne worked at a Chicago advertising firm. EH addressed the envelope to the couple "c/o Green, Fulton Cunningham Co. / Michigan Avenue (Near Bridge) / Chicago, Illinois / Estados Unidos" with the notation "Please Forward."

5 The 16 March 1929 *Publishers Weekly* reported: "Miss Frances Thorne of the Washington Book company has left for a tour of European countries to purchase rare and fine editions."

During her absence, the Washington Book Shop at 1012 Rush Street would "undergo several changes," including work by interior decorator Edgar Miller "to revamp the shop in the modern manner" (Milton Fairman, "Chicago Book News," 1410).

To F. Scott Fitzgerald, 13 September [1929]

Sept 13

Dear Scott—

That terrible mood of depression of whether it's any good or not is what is known as The Artist's Reward.[1]

I'll bet it's damned good—and when you get these crying drunks and start to tell them you have no friends for Christ sake amend it—it'll be sad enough—if you say no friends but Ernest the stinking serial king. You're not burned out and you know plenty to use— If you think your running out of dope count on old Hem— I'll tell you all I know—whom Slept with who and whom before or after whom was married— Anything you need to know—

Summer's a discourageing time to work— You dont feel death coming on the way it does in the fall when the boys really put pen to paper.

Everybody loses all the bloom—we're not peaches—that doesnt mean you get rotten— A gun is better worn and with bloom off— So is a saddle— People too by God. You lose everything that is fresh and everything that is easy and it always seems as though you could never write— But you have more métier and you know more and when you get flashes of the old juice you get more results with them—

Look how it is at the start— All juice and kick to the writer and cant convey anything to the reader— You use up the juice and the kick goes but you learn how to do it and the stuff when you are no longer young is better than the young stuff—

You just have to go on when it is worst and most hopeless— There is only one thing to do with a novel and that is go straight on through to the end of the damn thing. I wish there was some way that your economic existence would depend on this novel or on novels rather than the damned stories Because that is one thing that drives you and gives you an outlet and an excuse too— The damned stories—

Oh Hell. You have more stuff than anyone and you care more about it and for Christ sake just keep on and go through with it now and dont please write anything else until it's finished. It will be damned good—

(They never raise an old whore's price— She may know 850 positions— They cut her price all the same— So either you arent old or not a whore or both[2] The stories arent whoreing They're just bad judgement— You could have and can make enough to live on writing novels.

You damned fool. Go on and write the novel—

We drove here from Madrid in a day—Hendaye-Plage— Saw our noted contemporary L. Bromfield Going up to Paris— Have you heard from Max if the Farewell is out? Got a bunch of literary periodicals from Brommy— All full of great German War Books— It was funny how I couldnt get into All Quiet etc. but once in it it was damned good— Not so great as they think— But awfully good— L. Bromfield is writing a war book.[3] It's bad luck maybe that mine comes out now after all these and that have not had opportunity to profit by them in writing it— In about 2–3 years a man should be able to write a pretty good war book.

Old Dos married Kate Smith—she went to school (college)—(not convent) with Pauline— He met her down at Key West last winter— She's a damned nice girl—

We've had letters from Gerald and Sara. It's a damned shame about their Patrick being sick— I think he'll be all right—

Good day today—water nice to swim and the sun the last of summer—

If this is a dull shitty letter it is because I felt so bad that you were feeling low—am so damned fond of you and whenever you try to tell anybody anything about working or "life" it is always bloody platitudes—

Pauline sends her love to you, Zelda and Scotty—

Yours always—

Ernest—

PUL, ALS

1 In his letter to EH of 9 September 1929 Fitzgerald had written, "Just taken another chapter to the typists + its left me in a terrible mood of depression as to whether its any good or not" (PUL). Dorothy Parker would use EH's phrase, "The Artist's Reward," as the title of her profile of EH, explaining that she took it "unasked" from a letter EH wrote to Fitzgerald. She

quoted EH as follows: "'I am now,' he wrote, 'in the state of depression where you've gone over and over until you can't tell whether anything you've written is any good or not; this is called the Artist's Reward'" (*New Yorker*, 30 November 1929, 30).

2 Fitzgerald had written in his letter, "Here's a last flicker of the old cheap pride:—the Post now pay the old whore $4000. a screw. But now its because she's mastered the 40 positions—in her youth one was enough."

3 Louis Bromfield (1896–1956), American novelist and veteran of the U.S. Army Ambulance Service in WWI, had moved to France in 1925. Although WWI provides the background for some of Bromfield's writing, his characters are civilians; EH's reference to a "war book" is uncertain. The New York publishing house Frederick A. Stokes Company issued Bromfield's novels of the mid and late 1920s, including *Awake and Rehearse* (1929), *Twenty-Four Hours* (1930), and *Tabloid News* (1930).

To Paul Johnston, 14 September [1929]

Hotel Barron

Hendaye Plage

BP.

Sept 14—

Paul Johnson Esq.

Silvermine

Norwalk, Conn.

Dear Sir:—

Thank you for your letter of August 31 asking me to contribute to the collection you are preparing for Random House.[1]

I am afraid, as things stand now, I cannot afford to do this. I should for a story of the same length receive from $500 to $1500 from three different magazines which have asked me for stories under two thousand words and as the story would not be acceptable to them if it had been published anywhere else you see why I am afraid I must regretfully refuse your invitation.

Yours very truly

Ernest Hemingway.

P.S.

I assume that these pamphlets are being published [2]

JFK, ALS

1 In a letter of 31 August sent to EH in care of agent Paul Reynolds, Johnston invited EH to contribute a short story or literary essay to a collection of prose pamphlets to be published by Random House in a limited boxed edition of 875 copies (JFK). He enclosed a list of the ten contemporary American authors being invited. Johnston had offered $200 for a submission of at least 2,000 words.

2 Six pamphlets would appear in *Prose Quartos* (1930): "The Litter of the Rose Leaves" by Stephen Vincent Benét, "Fine Furniture" by Theodore Dreiser, "Feathers" by Carl Van Vechten, "Gehenna" by Conrad Aiken, "Tabloid News" by Louis Bromfield, and "The American County Fair" by Sherwood Anderson.

To Madelaine Hemingway, 14 and 15 September [1929]

Hendaye Plage—

Sept 14.

Dear Sun—

Suppose you're back in Oak Park now. Bill Smith wrote me he saw you and Carol this summer.[1] Kate and Dos were married in August. They are going to Mexico on their honeymoon as soon as his book is done— Waldo is still up in Maine.

Bumby and Pat are both well. We go to Paris next week. Have been working hard on some stories etc. Going to start another novel.

Did Les get off all right? I havent the date he was to leave at hand but had a good letter from him yesterday written from Walloon.[2]

Would you send me Ura's address? We never heard if Ura or Carol got the things Pauline sent. I've wanted to write Ura but havent her address. [3]

Glad you had a good trip over. Bill Spoke as though you were having a good summer.

Dont know whether you told the folks how badly you were treated and how disappointed etc. you were in Key West etc. Ura and Carol are the ones I care about and I thought if you had talked or written to them perhaps as I dont have any chance to see them and value their opinion of me I ought to write and give them the dope from my side. Have never let any member of the family know if I was even disappointed about you—much less criticism. I wish you would tell me, truly, if you have talked about your bad treatment, my unreasonableness etc to Mother, Carol or Ura— In our family not to make a defence or accuse someone is supposed to be a sign of guilt and as

I do care about what Ura and Carol think of us if you've put out anything I ought to let them hear the other side. Marce is out of my life— Les is too young for it to matter. But I do care about the others.

Of course you may not have talked or written— If so fine. But I'd like to know—[4]

I hope this book sells well— Finished the last batch of page proofs for England last week. That's how long it drags on—it should be out in U.S. soon.

Dont know whether we'll be back in Dec. or March. Depends on the apt. in Paris. How is Uncle Tyley? When you see him will you give him my love.

Best to you and all the family,

Ernie

Write to the Guaranty— Journey's End still running in Paris—[5]
P.S. Sept 15

Read this over and realize that even if you did talk about me, which probably you didn't, I wont do any defending. Life's too short. You were fine about Les and the car. Good girl.[6]

Hope you have the job you want. Sorry to hear Duke received the gate but that is your business of course[7]

PSU, ALS

1 In a letter of 28 July 1929 from Horton Bay, Michigan, Bill Smith reported, "Mingled with your kith, here. Sunny and Carol. A good pair" (JFK). Since 1899, members of the Hemingway family had vacationed at Windemere, their cottage on Walloon Lake in northern Michigan. Bill and Kate Smith had inherited a farmhouse and land in nearby Horton Bay, where they had spent summers in their youth, becoming close friends with EH.

2 According to the itinerary their mother described in her 11 August letter to EH, Leicester was to leave Petoskey, Michigan, on 25 August bound for Honolulu, where he would live for a year with their Aunt Grace (JFK). His letter to EH remains unlocated.

3 Sunny showed this letter to their sister Carol, who in a letter to EH of 26 September would apologize for not having written to thank Pauline (JFK). In her response of 30 October, Sunny supplied their sister Ursula's address: 1129 Xerxes Avenue South in Minneapolis, Minnesota (JFK).

4 In her 30 October letter, Sunny would respond: "Don't ever worry about me saying mean things about Steen you + Paulinos made it possible for me to have a wonderful trip + I'm not so low as to run down fellows who did as much for me as you did."

5 *Journey's End*, the drama by English playwright R. C. (Robert Cedric) Sherriff (1896–1975) about nine soldiers during the last days of WWI, premiered in London on 9 December 1928

and opened in New York City on 22 March 1929, where theater critic Arthur Pollock called it "the Best of War Plays" (*Brooklyn Daily Eagle*, 23 March 1929, 12). A production by the English Players opened in Paris at the Théâtre Albert Ier in June 1929. A French production, *Le Grand Voyage*, would open in Paris on 26 September at the Théâtre Edouard VII.

6 To his penciled letter, EH added this postscript in black ink after receiving a letter from Sunny on 15 September, as he notes in the following letter to her, written the same day in the same black ink. That letter from Sunny remains unlocated. As Grace Hall Hemingway would describe Leicester's car accident in a 25 October letter to EH, "He was driving at 15 miles an hour—and the girl dashed out in front of his car—with no warning" (JFK).

7 In her 11 August letter, Grace reported that Leicester would be "started off" on his train trip from Chicago to Los Angeles by Duke T. Hill, Jr. (1904–1972), an Oak Park acquaintance. She added, "Sunny has severed her engagement to Duke— It had to come— But I was very sorry, I'm so fond of Duke."

To Madelaine Hemingway, 15 September [1929]

Sept 15.

Dear N. Bones—

Thanks for the fine letter. I wrote you a punk one last night and then this morning got yours—

That was tough luck about Les and Charlevoix. Glad it was no worse— It was a shame you didnt have a lawyer to see the woman the first day and make a payment and get a receipt of release from any claim. Of course that's what you tried to do. (I'm not criticizing) You played it right but a lawyer would talk her on into it. They're supposed to stay until they do. Of course too they might jip you too. A lawyer that is. Unless you had one who was a friend. It was a lawyer put <u>her</u> up to getting the money. Glad it was no worse.

When I get to Paris will send you 100 seeds as my contribution. I hope you got a valid release from all claim. People have been sued for 5 or 10 thousand for less. You did finely.

About Duke—as I said last night it is you doing the marrying or not marrying and it is no good marrying anybody because he is so damned nice to the family.

Tell mother not to worry about money. I wrote her this but tell her again. If this book sells well and it might go big I'll be all jake. Have money on hand anyway, or coming due, to keep up the 100 seeds indefinitely and will be able to pay Florida taxes. Am going to have the Florida land looked up and valued and see what we can do with it. Of course the summer and fall are the worst time there so have laid off so far. Uncle George should take ~~over~~ off the mortgage on the house. I think that's the <u>least</u> he can do. After what he did to Dad. If he doesnt I'll see that he becomes so well known that no amount of Foreign Mission work will ever whitewash him.[1]

Im awfully sorry your cold in chest hung on so long and hope you get rid of it now— Dont get T.B. We'd have to shoot you if you did. You were very sporting about the Les woman running business and I appreciate it. Take good care and follow out the bronchial treatment.

We lived on 2 bucks a day apiece in Santiago with a seed a day between us spending money to save expenses so when you drive the old junk remember we're all in the same soup.

It's awfully fine of Aunt Grace to have Les out there—She's carried away with kids as it is—[2] It's pretty good that she that they all cursed out so was the only one to come through like a white woman—

Well this letter seems to be punk too— Tell Mother Louis Bromfield is here—we ate with them night before last—and he spoke about how charming she was.[3]

Have had a good offer for serial rights of my next book— But now to write it—and what about? I hope we can keep the Paris apt. It will be much less bother and worry— Jinny can live there and that handles the rent when we're away— Spent a couple of days with Sidney Franklin the American matador and got some good dope—

Had my pocket picked getting on a Street car in Madrid—got passport— all my french car papers, etc. Thief returned everything because there was no money. Not like America.

Hope everything goes finely with you and you all get on well.

Ask Carol if there's anything she would like from Paris—French Books or magazines.

Pauline sends her love—

Best always—

Steen

P.S. Dont think I'm writing this as a crab

<u>But</u> Dont <u>you</u> or <u>anybody else in the family</u> drive a car without liability insurance for damage to others. You must do this— Because what would

I do if I heard you had killed somebody and were sued for 25 or 50 thousand. You cant take such risks. I'll pay for the insurance but take it out now before you take the car out again. Maybe you have it. If so dont let anybody not of legal age drive. People who have accidents are liable to have plenty of them. There's no use to work to try and get things straightened out if it's all to be at the mercy of a single car accident. In a year Dad had one, Lester one and you one— Karl, Paulines brother, had a bad accident car completely destroyed. Anybody's liable to have them but you must be covered by Insurance against all damages to other people or their property![4]

PSU, ALS; postmark: HENDAYE PLAGE / B^{SES} PYRENNES, 13 * / 16 9 / 2[9]

1   EH's sister Marcelline recalled that in late 1929 Clarence Hemingway had asked his brother George, a real estate broker and bank director, for a loan to make payments on the Florida properties that were due by 10 December. George instead encouraged him to sell the lots and take the losses so as not to incur more debt (Sanford, 230–31). Clarence committed suicide on 6 December. George was a church deacon and prominent in civic affairs of Oak Park.
2   EH's paternal Aunt Grace had moved to Honolulu in 1927 after marrying Chester Gilbert Livingston, who had been left with four young children after his first wife died in 1924.
3   Having received a 1927 Pulitzer Prize for his novel *Early Autumn* (1926), Bromfield had embarked on a U.S. lecture tour upon the publication of his next novel, *A Good Woman* (1927). On 10 October 1927, he spoke to the Oak Park Nineteenth Century Club. In her 14 October 1927 letter to EH, Grace reported that when she introduced herself to Bromfield, he told her that EH was one of his best friends (JFK). Bromfield and his family had lived in France since 1925.
4   Marcelline recalled that during the fall of 1928, Clarence feared having an angina attack while driving and no longer allowed passengers in his car (Sanford, 229), but his accident remains undocumented. In a letter of 4 July 1929, Mary Pfeiffer had reported that Karl's "lovely new Packard was wrecked" but that no one was injured (PUL); in a 17 August letter she added that neither party had insurance to cover damages (PUL). In her 5 October 1929 letter to EH, Grace Hall Hemingway would respond, "Sunny is lots of help, running the old Ford (from Windemere) and doing errands—never fear, we have insurance on it fire theft— property + personal liability" (JFK).

To Virginia Pfeiffer, [c. 16 September 1929]

[*Pauline writes:*]
Dear Jinny—

We just got your letter, mentioning other communications to be had in Madrid and we have telegraphed for them. We weren't really worried about

Patrick, but wanted his diet changed as soon as possible. Thanks for this change. Crazy to see the pictures I know just how you felt about Dos.[1] I felt a little that way myself—but another fine man will come along. Cant think of anyone anyone knows who's in Paris now to come to see you. However, will be along ourselves next week. But dont think you have to go for our arrival. Stick around. We've been alone for so long we'd welcome a third party, esp. you. You can sleep in your bed (we can move Patrick in the Salon nights so he wont wake you) and there's lots of room for your things. And if you're going to Portugal why dont you just stick around till you go, for its hardly worth while getting a place for that long. And then you can come back to us while you look for domicile. Please do this. We both want you very much. You can be just as free, coming to as many meals as you want— all would be fine, have your own key, entertain your friends etc. And it's much cheaper. Ernest can work in his room, and we can go about getting that nightmare the fall wardrobe. I'm stript bare as a leaf. What about you?

The Barrons are crazy about you. Isn't he a darling?[2]

The weather is glorious here, sunny and warm, and we swim every morning, loaf afternoons and have a fine time. I'll let you know when we will arrive in Paris—probably Thursday or Friday. We have you a present. We wont give it to you if you go away. And you must eat with the new silver. Kisses to Patrick, souvenirs à Henriette (fine girl)[3] Ernest wants to add a few words.

Pauline

[EH writes:]

Dear Jin:—

It will be grand to see you. Plan to stay on in the house as long as you can and we will have fine meals with oyster cocktails and gibier.[4] I can work fine at the far end. It will be such luxury to have a table the feet go under and a chair to sit in. Did Pauline tell you about how they picked my pocket in Madrid and stole Passport, Carte D'Identité, cartes gris and verte, permis de conduire and everything but money and then returned it all?[5]

Met Sidney Franklin and bummed around with him for two days— Pauline's got fine old silver for the table

We wrote De la Penas but havent heard from them yet.[6]

Dont know who's in Paris for you to see— Pat went to U.S. maybe back by now— Gros has been at Geneva—maybe he's back— But Dont go riding with Miss Barbara Harrison—[7] Maybe she really did fly down into the bullring— We drove from Madrid to here in a day— Had lunch at Burgos—

Left at 9 am and got to San Sebastian at 7–500 some. Lovely road from Madrid out— Weather's been grand and hot on the beach Think maybe I have sun stroke if this letter sounds that way— I wish I knew citizens in Paris— We'll be there anyway in a couple of days— Souvenirs to Henriette— Have a lot to write when get to Paris— Funny things to tell you—too sunstruck to write a letter— You could have married Dos if you would have come to Key West last winter— It's in those hot climates that marriages are made—there and in heaven.

Yr affect Bro.
Ernest[8]

For Patrick

JFK, ALS

Internal evidence indicates that this joint letter was started by Pauline [c. 14 September 1929] and continued by EH [c. 16 September 1929].

1 The two known surviving letters of this period from Jinny [c. 5 and c. 22 August 1929] do not mention Patrick's diet, pictures, or Dos Passos (JFK). In the first of these, she mentions the possibility that some mail may have been lost.
2 The Barrons owned the Ondarraitz Hotel in Hendaye Plage, where Pauline and EH stayed in 1927 and 1929.
3 Henriette Lechner, Patrick's French nanny.
4 *Gibier*: game (French).
5 French documents: *carte d'identité*: identity card; *carte grise* and *carte verte*: gray and green cards, signifying automobile ownership and insurance, respectively; *permis de conduire*: driver's license.
6 Jinny's friend Alice Winthrop Goddard (b. 1898), a New York socialite, married Antonio González de la Pena in New York City on 28 October 1927.
7 After the fiesta in Pamplona that July, Jinny, Pat Morgan, and Guy Hickok returned to Paris together by train. Barbara Harrison (1904–1977), American heiress; she and American poet

and publisher Monroe Wheeler (1899–1988) would co-found the Harrison of Paris press, which operated from 1930 to 1934, publishing fine limited editions of works in English.
8 Following a family tradition from his own childhood, EH drew circles around two dots to signify "tooseys" or "toosies," Hemingway family slang for kisses.

To Maxwell Perkins, 27 September [1929]

September 27

Paris

Dear Max—

Thanks for the royalty reports and the check of September 12. When is the book supposed to be out?[1]

If it is not inconvenient could you let me have 6000 advance now sending it in two checks of 3000?

I drove Morley Callaghan and his wife out to Versailles and Chartres yesterday. The cathedral seemed like a pretty cold proposition after Santiago de Campostella. I know this is heresy.[2] It is lovely weather now. Callaghans are leaving for London today. Gerald Murphy and his wife arrived from Antibes with Dorothy Parker. They say Scott was working splendidly and was on the next to the last chapter of his novel.[3]

Have been working well ever since back a week ago. Have done two more stories. Have six now but between ourselves only two seem saleable.[4] But don't tell anyone—might be able to sell them all. Maybe the book is out by now. I am anxious to see what happens to it. How it goes is a damned serious matter.

We haven't heard yet if we can stay on in this aprtment. (Put 3000 dollars into fixing it and improvements on strength of supposedly valid lease.) If we are kicked out will store things and bring others over, probably landing in Cuba and Key West as before sometime in December. Otherwise may go to ski in January and come over in March.

Paris is fine now in the fall and a good place to work.[5]

My kid brother (14) has been shipped out to Hawaii— Had his appendix and tonsils out and seems to be healthier. He will stay a year with an aunt out there. The rest of the family are well. I have got something the matter with me that makes the fingers and thumb of my right hand swell up in the morning like little balloons— Am cutting out meat and drinking vichy—

Will send this off— Ill probably have heard from you about the book before you get this. Thanks for the cable about Chap 42—

Yours always

Ernest Hemingway

PUL, TL/ALS

1 In his letter of 12 September [1929], Perkins enclosed "a small cheque" for royalties for *MWW* as well as royalty reports on *SAR* and *TOS* (PUL). *FTA* was published on 27 September, the date of this letter.
2 Morley Callaghan married Loretto Dee (1901–1984) on 16 April 1929. Notre-Dame de Chartres, Gothic cathedral built between 1194 and 1260, renowned for its stained-glass windows. The Cathedral of Santiago de Compostela, a Romanesque cathedral built between 1060 and 1211, reportedly holds the remains of St. James and is the end point of the ancient pilgrimage route, the Camino de Santiago.
3 Fitzgerald's novel would be published by Scribner's in 1934 as *Tender Is the Night*.
4 In letters to Perkins of 31 July and 28 August, EH had mentioned working on stories but supplied no details. Likely candidates (according to their composition history) are "Wine of Wyoming" (October 1928–May 1930), "A Natural History of the Dead" (January 1929–August 1931), and "After the Storm" (April 1928–June 1932) (Smith, vi).
5 The remainder of the letter is handwritten.

To Maxwell Perkins, 27 September [1929]

September 27

Dear Max:

Robert McAlmon is leaving for New York tomorrow on the Berengeria and I asked him to look you up when he is there.[1] He can give you news of Scott, Sir Morely Callaghan, and myself. It is too late to get the letters in the boat mail tonight and I am going out to try and find him in the cafe and get him to mail the letters and perhaps mail this to you in N.Y. Pauline has one to her family and I have one to you that should have gone this afternoon.

I know from experience that it is hard to talk in the office and I wish you could go out to lunch with him and talk to him about his stuff. I asked him to see you before he saw anybody else in N.Y. You will find him damned intelligent to talk with whether you do any business or not. Though I would be awfully happy if you could!²

Yours always,

Ernest

PUL, TLS

1 Robert Menzies McAlmon (1895–1956), American expatriate writer and publisher, whose Contact Editions published EH's first book, *TSTP* (1923), as well as McAlmon's own poetry and fiction. The Cunard Line's *Berengaria* would depart from Southampton on 28 September and arrive in New York City on 4 October 1929.
2 In letters to EH of 7 and 8 October, Perkins would report that he and McAlmon planned to meet for dinner on 8 October (PUL). Perkins would find McAlmon's work unsuitable for publication by Scribner's.

To James Joyce, [c. late September 1929]

To Joyce with complete admiration and much affection

Ernest Hemingway.

(Excuse all the mis-spelled Italian words— They never sent me any page proofs—dashes the same)

E.H.

[*On the inside front cover facing EH's inscription, a small sticker placed upside down features a likeness of William Shakespeare and reads, "'SHAKESPEARE AND COMPANY' / Sylvia Beach / 12, rue de l'Odéon / Paris-VIᵉ." Below the sticker EH drew an arrow pointing to it and wrote the following comment:*]

Shakespeare upside down.

SUNYB, Inscription

EH wrote this inscription on the front free endpaper of a mass-printed first edition of *FTA* (Hanneman A8A). He wrote in the censored words to fill in the blanks on pages 35, 50, 204, 205, 209, 211, 221, 222, 228, and 238.

A FAREWELL TO ARMS 209

looked up. She looked perhaps a year younger. Aymo put his hand on the elder girl's thigh and she pushed it away. He laughed at her.

"Good man," he pointed at himself. "Good man," he pointed at me. "Don't you worry." The girl looked at him fiercely. The pair of them were like two wild birds.

"What does she ride with me for if she doesn't like me?" Aymo asked. "They got right up in the car the minute I motioned to them." He turned to the girl. "Don't worry," he said. "No danger of ⸺," using the vulgar word. "No place for ⸺." I could see she understood the word and that was all. Her eyes looked at him very scared. She pulled the shawl tight. "Car all full," Aymo said. "No danger of ⸺. No place for ⸺." Every time he said the word the girl stiffened a little. Then sitting stiffly and looking at him she began to cry. I saw her lips working and then tears came down her plump cheeks. Her sister, not looking up, took her hand and they sat there together. The older one, who had been so fierce, began to sob.

"I guess I scared her," Aymo said. "I didn't mean to scare her."

Bartolomeo brought out his knapsack and cut off two pieces of cheese. "Here," he said. "Stop crying."

The older girl shook her head and still cried, but the younger girl took the cheese and commenced to eat. After a while the younger girl gave her sister the second piece of cheese and they both ate. The older sister still sobbed a little.

"She'll be all right after a while," Aymo said.

An idea came to him. "Virgin?" he asked the girl next to him. She nodded her head vigorously. "Virgin too?" he pointed to the sister. Both the girls nod-

James Joyce's copy of *A Farewell to Arms* in which Hemingway filled in the blanks. The Poetry Collection of the University Libraries, University at Buffalo, The State University of New York.

To Guy Hickok, [c. late September 1929]

To Gros Hickock
   With much affection trusting him to fill in the blanks—

Ernest Hemingway.

Sotheby's catalog, New York, 11 June 2013, Lot 194 (illustrated), Inscription

The Sotheby's catalog description notes that EH inscribed a "first edition, first issue" copy of *FTA* to Hickok, to whom EH had given a copy of the manuscript of the novel, "one that certainly had the expletives that the publisher replaced with dashes intact." EH "did not replace the profanities for Guy as he did in the copy he presented to Joyce."

To Arthur Hawkins, [1 October 1929]

[*Excerpt as published in University Archives catalog:*]
"I cant [*sic*] very well make an appointment for a sketch as we wont [*sic*] be back here until December. But Scribner's have some pictures & I haven't any or would send some with this.[1] Will you give my best regards to Samuel Putnam.[2] Yours very truly, Ernest Hemingway."

University Archives online catalog, Westport, Connecticut, Stock Number 13675–001, LS

The sale listing indicates that this item was written from Paris on 1 October 1929 "To Arthur Hawkins, an artist, regarding a sketch for a book" and that it was "Accompanied by a sketch of Hemingway signed by Hawkins."

1 Hawkins's collection of drypoint caricatures of notable authors of the 1920s, including EH, would be displayed at the G.R.D. Gallery in New York City in October 1930.
2 Hawkins had illustrated the dust jacket for *François Rabelais, Man of the Renaissance* (1929) by American expatriate writer and translator Samuel Putnam (1892–1950).

To Maxwell Perkins, 3 October [1929]

October 3

Dear Max:—
   The books havent come. But I heard today they were on sale at Galignani's and went down and bought two.[1]

Your cable about the first reviews came (Thanks ever so much) and your letter about newspaper syndicating— I agree with you about the latter and would not want it unless (1) It would help in every way the book (2) It would bring ~~plenty of~~ in some respectable sum of money (over 1000 dollars) I believe it would hurt rather than help the book. I Don't want it.[2]

Anyhow I dont like it and wont sell to anybody to cut—

God knows it's cut enough.

About the Jacket— You must know best but it seems lousy to me— I'm no actress wanting the name in Big electric lights— But the name must have some value as a selling point and comparing it to the jackets of the Sun Also its a little over half as big type and about ⅓ as big as on Men Without Women— All I know about the effect of the jacket is that with the book in a pile on the counter with other books and me looking for it I could not find it and the clerk had to find it for me.

It looks as though the Jacket designer had been so wrapped up in that beautiful artistic effort on the front that she had tried to eliminate if possible the title and author's name so they wouldn't intrude on the conception of that nude figure with those horrible legs and those belly muscles like Wladek Zabyenko's who is labelled Cleon (a character in the book I presume or the spirit of no sex appeal) and the big shouldered lad with the prominent nipples who is holding the broken axle (signifying no doubt the defeat of The Horse Drawn Vehicle)[3]

A little more restraint by the artist would have left more room for the title— It has the same number of letters as the sun also rises—and there would have been room for the author to be referred to as the author of The Sun and Men Without—

You understand this is a layman's criticizm— The old Sun jacket that I didnt care for when I saw it—looks like a masterpiece now compared to this one of Mr. and Mrs. Cleon among the poinsettias or The tragedy of the Broken Axle. Really and truly if the book is banned anywhere I think it will be on account of that girl on the cover.

In the blurb—Caporetto is spelled with an A and Catherine Barklay as we finally agreed to spell her in the book is Katharine (as in Katharsis)[4]

What about the Signed ones?— How many of those do I get?[5]

Could you send me the proofs I corrected and sent back? If it's impossible I will write and try and get the other set of them from Cape. [*EH marginal insertion*: Although I hate to write them for favors because I think I am <u>through</u> with them I hope to God for good. I'm digusted with his yellow deletions. They cut sentences out without a word to me and only sent me page proofs and wrote me on the 18th when going to ~~England~~ America the 21st. of Sept.] What I want to do is to get them cut and bound up so I can have one copy of it as ~~I wrote it~~ it was before the blanks.

Thornton Wilder said for me to write you that if you got in any trouble about the book or if they attacked it he would be glad to write or wire anything to help.[6]

What I'm afraid of now that I've actually seen it is that in a little while it will all be over and ~~there wont be so many sold and the~~ when a respectable number are sold then it will be laid off being pushed and ~~then~~ not sell anymore and the book will be just the same only no one will ever buy it— I wont have another one for two years anyway

I always figured that if I could write good books they would always sell a certain amount if they were good and some day I could live on what they would all bring in honestly— But Scott tells me that is all bunk— That a book only sells for a short time and that afterwards it never sells and that it doesnt pay the publishers even to bother with it. So I guess it's all just a damned racket like all the rest of it and the way I feel tonight is to hell with all of it— All I got out of this book is disappointment— I couldn't pay any attention when my father died— Couldnt let myself feel <u>anything</u> because I would get out of the book and lose it— Of course the thing as a serial supports them all and the book is going to have to too— But I would rather write and then go over it and when I know it's right stick to it and publish it that way the way it was if it never sells a damned one— That's what I should have done— Instead of starting in on the polite Owen Wister compromise— The fact I do it on acct. of my family is no excuse and I know it— I'm a Professional Writer now— Than which there isn't anything lower— I never thought I'd be it (and I'm damned if I'm going to do it any more)— But if I can get one copy of it and I can see I got it set up the way it was (rather you set it up and deserve all credit) in type it will take some of the curse off it.

Dont think I'm sore at you— I'm not. You've <u>always</u> been grand to me. I just hate the whole damned thing. And the Jacket and blurb on Julian Greens book by Harpers made me want to vomit— They said he was to be compared to Balzac, Flaubert, Doestoevsky, Emily Bronte and Conrad— The one who compared him to Flaubert was Grant Overton who writes whole propaganda books for publishers— As much critical integrity as a crab between your dirty toes—[7]

A $10,000 prize given to 2 women and 2 Fairies— ~~all under~~ The last two under contract already—[8] How many books did Cumming's Enormous Room sell?[9] It's all a racket— Sometimes I wish to God you weren't my friend and instead I was with some firm I hated so I could put the screws on and rachet them from the other side.

This is a pretty letter all right— Did McAlmon come to see you? He's been unjustly treated— His Village was good enough to publish— But much of his stuff is terrible— His best stuff was a couple of stories of homosexuality in Berlin Underworld and quite unpublishable—also he's a damned gossip—[10] I swore to kill him once for a damned lying story he spread about me— (How I'd beaten Hadley while Bumby was being born!) But sometimes he's very intelligent and wish he could be published if only to take him out of the martyr class. But dont know what stuff he has with him and it may be terrible.

Anyway I'll end this before it goes on any further— It's been raining all day—raining outside now— Havent had a drink for a week—

Yours always
Ernest

JFK, ALS

The fact that this heavily revised original document is among EH's papers at JFK suggests it is an unsent draft of the more restrained and polished letter that EH wrote the next day and sent to Perkins.

1 In his letter of 23 September, Perkins told EH, "I am sending you the book today. It is to be published on the 27th" (PUL). Galignani's, at 224, rue de Rivoli, advertised itself as "The First English Bookshop Established on the Continent." It was founded in Paris in 1800 as an English language library by Italian publisher Giovanni Antonio Galignani (1752–1821).

2 Perkins wired EH on 28 September, "First reviews splendid Prospects bright" (PUL). In a letter of 18 September, Perkins reported that he had been approached by Current News Features, a Washington, D.C. subsidiary of the Consolidated Press Association, with an offer for newspaper syndication of *FTA*. Perkins advised that "The truth is you cannot tell what they would do with it: they feel perfectly free to cut anything they buy, to any extent." Although Perkins believed "no harm could come from the syndication," he felt that "whatever value there is in periodical publication has been got through Scribner's" (PUL).

3 American illustrator Cleo Theodora Damianakes (1895–1979) signed her dust jacket designs "Cleon" for *SAR* (1926) and *FTA* (1929), and for F. Scott Fitzgerald's *All the Sad Young Men* (1926). Her design for *FTA* featured a sleeping man and woman, both nearly nude, with the signature "Cleon" printed beneath the woman's bent legs. The jacket is reproduced in the plate section of this volume. Wladek Zbyszko (né Wladyslaw Cyganiewicz, 1891–1968), Polish-born American professional heavyweight wrestler who held world championship titles in 1917 and 1919. He and his brother headed a troupe of strongmen and wrestlers who toured internationally and gave exhibitions throughout the 1920s.

4 The blurb on the first edition dust jacket mentioned "the English nurse, Katharine Barclay" and "the terrible Caparetto retreat." The character in the novel is Catherine Barkley.

5 The limited edition of *FTA*, also issued on 27 September, consisted of 500 numbered and autographed boxed copies for sale and another ten for presentation (Hanneman A8b). In a letter of 4 October 1929, Perkins would write, "P.S. I have four copies of the limited edition, unnumbered, reserved for you" (PUL).

6 In a letter to Perkins of 2 November 1929 thanking him for sending a copy of the "handsome" *FTA*, Wilder would report that when he had recently dined with EH in Paris, "I intimated to Ernest that if the book caused a controversy etc. I should be glad to line myself with other and more authoritative names among its enthusiasts" (PUL).

7 Julian Green (1900–1998), French-born American author, was awarded the $10,000 Harper prize in August 1929 for *The Dark Journey* (New York: Harper & Brothers, 1929), published that March in French as *Léviathan* (Paris: Plon, 1929) under the name Julien Green. Grant Overton (1887–1930), American author, literary critic, and editor whose books included *Authors of the Day* (1924), *The Philosophy of Fiction* (1928), and *The American Novel* (1929). Overton, Carl Van Doren, and Ellen Glasgow were the judges who awarded the prize to Green.

8 In September 1923 Harper & Brothers established a monetary prize to be awarded in alternate years for the best novel submitted to the firm by an American author who had not published a novel before 1 January 1921. The first went to Margaret Wilson (1882–1973) for *The Able McLaughlins* (1923; Pulitzer Prize for Fiction, 1924), followed by Anne Parrish (1888–1957) for *The Perennial Bachelor* (1925), Glenway Wescott (1901–1987) for *The Grandmothers: A Family Portrait* (1927), and Julian Green. EH had earlier expressed resentment at the financial success of authors who did not have "wives and children to support" (*Letters* vol. 3, 388).

9 The first edition of the WWI novel *The Enormous Room* (New York: Boni & Liveright, 1922) by American poet E. E. (Edward Estlin) Cummings (1894–1962) sold 2,000 copies at $2.00 each; subsequent editions also had disappointing sales, with a total of 2,454 copies sold by the end of 1930 (Walker Gilmer, *Horace Liveright: Publisher of the Twenties* [New York: David Lewis, 1970], 245). In his own copy, EH wrote, "Best book published last year. One of the best written by an American" (Reynolds *Reading*, 114).

10 Perkins and McAlmon would meet for dinner on 8 October. McAlmon's own Contact Editions had printed his novel *Village: As It Happened Through a Fifteen Year Period* (1924) and *Distinguished Air (Grim Fairy Tales)* (1925), a collection of stories about three American homosexuals in Berlin. EH had enthusiastically praised *Village* in letters of 1924 and 1925 to McAlmon, Edward J. O'Brien, Sylvia Beach, and Ezra Pound (*Letters* vol. 2, 154, 223, 228–29, 395–96), but his feelings toward McAlmon had generally soured by the end of 1925. Perkins would agree with EH's evaluation of McAlmon's current work as unpublishable (Perkins to EH, 12 November 1929, PUL).

To Maxwell Perkins, 4 October 1929

October 4—1929

Dear Max:—

Thank you for the cable about the reviews and prospects.

I agree with your letter about newspaper syndicating— It can do <u>nothing</u> to help the book— So why do it? It has been serialized enough— The syndicating seems all just a part of the idea of killing a book off and getting it out of the way as soon as possible after publication— In any event I won't consent to any more cutting so that ought to handle it.

No books have arrived here as yet. About the signed copies. Are you sending my copies of that edition here or do you want me to give you the addresses they are to go to?

I bought two copies yesterday at Galignani's—one for Allen Tate—who was with me—[1]

In the blurb Caporetto is spelled Caparetto and Catherine Barklay is spelled Katharine. You will probably have corrected these already.

About the jacket; I think both the title of the book and the name of the author have been sacrificed to Mr. Miss or Mrs. Cleon's artistic (sic) conception. The type in size of the title and author's name—which must have some selling interest to the reader—are ⅓ smaller—than in The Sun and ½ as big as in Men Without Women. There are the same number of letters and spaces in A Farewell To Arms as there are in The Sun Also Rises— The Cleon drawing has a lousy and completely unattractive decadence [*EH insertion*: i.e. large, misplaced breasts etc.] about it which I think might be a challenge to anyone who was interested in suppressing the book.

Altho on the other hand it is probably very fine and supposedly classical and I a damned fool. But at least I cannot admire the awful legs on that woman or the gigantic belly muscles. I never liked the jacket on the Sun but side by side with this one The Sun jacket looks very fine now— So maybe this one is fine too—

If it is not too great trouble it would be a great favor to me if I could have the galleys back that I sent over corected. Want to get them cut up and bound to make a book of it to have one copy as it was before the blanks.

I wrote you last week—one letter about an advance and another about McAlmon— He was to mail them both aboard the Berengeria— If you did not get them would you let me know? McAlmon's Village should have been published I think. Other stuff of his is sometimes very bad. He has written several very good stories though. I did not see what he was bringing to you. He has a lot of intelligent information and much unbelievably untrue gossip. Just meeting him you should get the information I wish he had something as good as Village was so that it might be published. But it might have been something terrible.

I hope everything goes well— Thanks again for the cable

Yours always

Ernest

I'll be glad to see the reviews.

Oct 4—pm.

P.S.

Your letter of September 23 and the cable about re-orders and a fine press just came—[2] If the jacket is selling it must be good—already it does not look so bad. But for the future maybe no more Cleon.[3]

About the alibi note.[4] The reason I suggested it was that I wanted to avoid your having troubles [*EH insertion*: any possibility of troubles] caused by Italians— Caporetto has been abolished in Italy— It is not allowed to be referred to and is not mentioned in histories of the war—[5] I thought if anyone wanted to make trouble for the book it would be the Italians and a note of that sort would stop any possibility of their doing so at the source— It may be an exaggerated precaution—using so many Italian names there must be people with those names and I did not want the It. government suing in their name— Of course it is 10,000 to 1 against any possibility of any trouble— But as I read in the contract that I would be held responsable for any libel of any sort I thought it was my duty—like getting insurance altho not expecting to die. I put it in not because anyone was libelled or there being any even remote possibility of libel— But only as an alibi against anyone trying in bad faith to trump anything up—and you know that is completely improbable— So if you want to leave it out of other printings that is a matter for your judgement— It's out of my hands—[6] All I know is the book is fiction and I have not used the name of anyone I have ever known or seen— There was an American Red Cross hospital in Milan with a Superintendant named Miss K.C. DeLong. But as she did not land in Italy until 1918 and the hospital was not founded until June of that year and all the action in the hospital in the book takes place in 1917—specifically stated—at which time such a hospital did not exist— there is no possibility of any libel there.[7]

When I wrote The Sun I looked up in Debretts and Burke's Peerage to make sure there was no Lady Ashley— There was none— But as you wrote me a chorus girl who after the book was out became Lady Ashley after breaking up with her husband wanted to make trouble— But did not succeed.[8]

Naturally there must be Italians with all the names I have used— Under English law anyone whose name is used can sue for damages— I wrote the note in order to protect against any such monkey business— I said Living People because that is the formula they use—

Had better mail this off—

Thanks ever so much for the cables— I look forward to seeing the first clippings— Do you want any more pictures? Gerald Murphys say Scott is going finely.

Yours always
E.H.

PUL, ALS

The previous letter in this volume, located among EH's papers at JFK, appears to have been an unsent draft of this one, which survives in the Scribner's Archive at PUL.

1 American poet and critic Allen Tate (1899–1979), whose reviews of EH's work had been laudatory. Recently arrived in France, Tate was introduced to EH by Sylvia Beach. Both Tate and his wife, Caroline Gordon (1895–1981), would become Scribner's authors, she with her first novel, *Penhally* (1931), and he with *Poems, 1928–1931* (1932).

2 In his letter of 23 September 1929, Perkins gave the publication date of *FTA* as 27 September (PUL). On 3 October Perkins cabled: "Already getting reorders stop Very fine press" (PUL).

3 Perkins would respond to EH's complaints about the Cleon design in a letter of 15 October, writing, "I felt some anxiety about it on the grounds you gave, but I think we have safely passed that now, for good and all.— And the main thing about a jacket is that it should give a book <u>visibility</u>" (PUL). The dust jacket of Scribner's 1930 edition of *IOT* would be the last of EH's books to carry a Cleon design.

4 In his 9 September letter to Perkins, EH had quoted the disclaimer that appeared in the English edition of *FTA*: "None of the characters in this book is a living person, nor are the units or military organizations mentioned actual units or organizations— E. H."

5 Immediately following the catastrophic military defeat at Caporetto in November 1917, the Italian Ministry of the Interior created the Secretariat for Propaganda Abroad and the Press to monitor representations of the war. The exposé *Viva Caporetto* (1921) by Curzio Malaparte (né Kurt Erich Suckert, 1898–1957) was censored and suppressed when it first appeared and again when published in 1923 under the title *La Rivolta dei Santi Maledetti* (*The Revolt of the Damned Saints*). Under Mussolini, Italian censorship was expanded: a 1926 law allowed suppression of any publication "damaging to the prestige of the state or its authorities, or offensive to the national sentiment, to moral sense, and public decency." *FTA* was never published in Fascist Italy. Italy would ban the 1932 film version of the novel, and would not permit translation until 1945.

6 EH's contract with Scribner's for *FTA* stipulated that the author "and his legal representatives shall and will hold harmless the said PUBLISHERS from all suits, and all manner of claims and proceedings which may be taken on the ground that said work contains anything scandalous or libelous." The disclaimer would appear only in the second and third printings of the Scribner's edition (10,000 copies each, dated 1 and 9 October) (Grissom, 108).

7 Canadian-born nurse Katherine Capron DeLong (1868–1938) was in charge of the American Red Cross Hospital in Milan when EH arrived there in July 1918. She may have served as a model for the authoritarian Miss Van Campen in *FTA*.

8 *Debrett's Peerage and Baronetage*, reference publication founded in 1769 providing genealogical details of Britain's royal and titled families, first published by London bookseller John Debrett (1753–1822) in 1802. *Burke's Peerage*, genealogical and heraldic history first published in 1826 by John Burke (1789–1848). In a letter to EH of 24 May 1928, Perkins reported that Scribner's had recently been threatened with a lawsuit by a woman named Lady Ashley, who "considered the use of the name Lady Ashley for the heroine of 'The Sun Also' libelous" (PUL; see *Letters* vol. 3, 388–89 n. 1).

To Mr. Feldheym, 4 October 1929

Paris, October 4, 1929

Dear Mr. Feldheym:—

Thank you very much for your letter. I'm awfully sorry that I haven't any pictures—since this letter was interrupted Ive been looking around and cant find even a passport picture.

Anyway it was damned nice of you to write me that you like my writing— And I hope this letter will do for an autograph—

Yours very truly—
Ernest Hemingway

William Doyle Galleries catalog, New York, 5 May 1999, Lot 24 (illustrated), ALS

To Carol Hemingway, [c. early October 1929]

Dear Carol:—

Thanks for the letter. I'm glad you got the piece of underwear. Pauline sent it, not me. The only reason I asked was because thought it might have been lost or custom-confiscated. Your letter doesnt read much as I remember you.[1] Look, if you're trying to write I'd suggest that you avoid the sort of style employed by Sunny in conversation; ie. mis-used adjectives as ejaculations to cover a sort of mental ~~vacuity~~ vacancy. For instance I am guilty of using "swell" in writing. But only in dialogue; not as an adjective to replace the word you should use. Try and write straight English; never using slang except in Dialogue and then only when unavoidable. Because all slang goes sour in a short time. I only use swear words, for example, that have lasted at least a thousand years for fear of getting stuff that will be simply timely and then go sour.

I know letters are different form other writing— But this letter didn't sound like you very much. Plenty of times people who write the best write the very worst letters. It's almost a rule. I'm not criticizing your letter.

[*EH insertion with arrow pointing to the following paragraph*:

(This doesnt seem to be about anything in particular. Was thinking about certain things and this came in the head)]

The worst poverty anyone can have is a poverty of mental interests. Money does not remove it and it does you no good to travel because you take it with you wherever you go. And a person with no interests in their head cannot converse intelligently or even comfortably, and conversation is one of the greatest pleasures—because they only feel at home with people as mentally limited as they are.

When I saw you in Oak Park I thought you were a grand girl and would go a long way. And I hope to God you are not going to be corrupted by the cheapness, flipness, petting instead of love, complete self absorbtion and cheap, cheap, petting vacantness that has come to such a perfect flowering in Oak Park.[2]

It doesnt do any good to hope, of course, but you've come to the place where you will go one way or the other and I do hope you will go the one rather than the other.

"Dont listen to him. He's just preaching," I can hear.[3]

But anyway good luck to you. We may be back around Christmas—maybe see you somewhere around then.

Best love,
Ernie

JFK, ALS

The conjectured letter date is based on the contents and date of Carol's incoming letter of 26 September [1929] (JFK).

1 Carol's letter to EH of 26 September was dotted with such expressions as "gosh" and "plooey," and she apologized for not having thanked Pauline for the "swell teddy."

2 Then in her senior year at Oak Park and River Forest High School, Carol had written, "All my subjects are very dumb except zoology which is fun but quite smelly." She also remarked, "Most everybody I know is in college now but I've found a few good gents at school."

3 In a 4 November 1929 letter, Carol would respond, "I appreciated your letter, and don't think I thot it too preachy," adding, "I know I'm too slangy" (JFK).

To Maxwell Perkins, 5 October 1929

October 5 1929

Dear Max:—

Today various publishers have been here to see us. The first a Mr. Hamilton from Harper's London office had heard, he said, from Louis Bromfield that I was fed up with Scribners—Thoroughly fed up I believe.[1] I told him this was not true, that our relations had never been better and that I had complete confidence in you and hoped you had in me. So if you hear that damned lie dont let it worry you. The only possible basis I can imagine was my telling Bromfield I was sick of Cape! I have always been sick of Cape and was a fool not to have left long ago. However I didn't and it was my own bloody fault so must make the best of it.

Please dont repeat this to Bromfield or anyone as I do not want to make trouble. But untrue news travels fast and I did not want you to be worried.

I bought the Sept 27 Herald Tribune today and read Isabel Paterson's review.[2] Hope this is not the Splendid Press you have cabled about. You remember she is the one Mike Strater told us about who damned me personally and as a writer to him extensively some two or 3 years ago. You remember she reviewed the Sun by saying that a good reporter would have reported "No story" instead of writing the novel.[3] I have never seen her nor had any communication with her and would not like her to know that I ever saw her review. But the funny thing about being called a fakir and using tricks of rain etc. is that I'd never noticed until I read her review that there was rain in the last paragraph! I hope I'm not getting touchy but the thing did seem to have an animosity beyond regular Criticism and I know that Henry in the book was sorry about Catherine—not himself in that passage—so it didnt seem Self Pity—[4]

Why get angry— But the thing she really liked— The really fine original work by Will Cuppy helped draw the sting of being called a clever fakir etc. and certainly there must be attacks and it is better to have them by the Isabel Patersons.[5] Still when you write trying never ever to be anything but honest someone has their god damned nerve to call you a cheap fakir and try at the same time to give away all the story of your book and call you a clever faking something or other. A public performer automatically rates this but I hope

I will have a chance to do the young woman a good turn some day— But the best I can do to start is never let her know I've seen it—

This is no letter— Just a note so you wont worry about any gossip— I made it strong to Harpers and the other citizens— The man, Hamilton, was really a very nice fellow— They're always nice fellows—

Yours always

Ernest—

What was the first printing?

PUL, ALS

1 Hamish Hamilton (1900–1988), previously employed by Jonathan Cape, had been manager of Harper & Row's London office since 1926. He would establish his own publishing house in 1931.
2 Isabel Mary Paterson (neé Bowler, 1886–1961), Canadian journalist and novelist. In her review of *FTA* she deemed EH's writing formulaic: "His style and point of view are now sufficiently fixed as to be easily recognizable. He may refine them, but it is unlikely that he will make any violent departures. The public knows what to expect" ("Books and Other Things," *New York Herald Tribune*, 27 September 1929, 17).
3 Reviewing *SAR* in her "Turns With a Bookworm" column for *New York Herald Tribune Books*, Paterson wrote that she read the beginning of *SAR* "with pop-eyed amazement" but then "wondered if, after all, it was anything to write a novel about," adding that "a sagacious reporter of life, handed this theme as an assignment, would have replied, 'No story'" (24 October 1926, 27). A few weeks later she also wrote in reference to *SAR* that when EH "gets a story worthy of the style he may be surprised to find himself a best seller" (*New York Herald Tribune Books*, 21 November 1926, 27).
4 In a section of her review of *FTA* subtitled "The Universal Emotion of Self-Pity," Paterson wrote that "the trick of having Catherine 'Scotch and crazy'—the word the less hard-boiled writers use [*sic*] to use was 'fey'—so that she foresaw herself dead in the rain, and then in the last chapter she was dead and 'after awhile I went out and left the hospital and walked back to the hotel in the rain'—that is one of the best in the whole bag of fiction tricks. It always works" (17).
5 In the same column Paterson heaped praise upon *How to Be a Hermit or a Bachelor Keeps House* (New York: Horace Liveright, 1929) by American humorist and book reviewer William Jacob (Will) Cuppy (1884–1949), calling him "a really original writer" (17). Cuppy had dedicated the book to Paterson, his colleague at the *New York Herald Tribune*.

To Grace Hall Hemingway, 12 October [1929]

October 12

Dear Mother:—

Your cheerful letters have been very welcome. Glad Les is doing so well and hope Uncle Tyley will enjoy his trip.[1] I am enclosing the check for November. Have added an additional hundred—50 to use for Carol—clothes—and 50 to please send or turn over to Uncle Tyley with my love as a belated birthday present.[2]

We arrived too late last Spring to get your pictures in the Spring Salon and got back from Spain just too late for the Salon D'Automne— I figured we were in time but had the wrong dates. They will be sent to the Spring Salon, however, whether we are here to do it or not. That is the one that really counts anyway. Meantime you may tell people that your pictures have had much praise and most favourable criticism in Paris. When they are in the Salon I know they will receive even more. Hope you have good luck with them at home.[3]

I have not yet heard how the book is going but hear it has had very good reviews and Scribners cable "splendid press. prospects bright."[4]

Sorry about Leicester running into the girl and consequent hold up. Altho you were lucky to get off as lightly as that. The fact that he was under age to drive and evidently did not know how to drive anyway made it indefensible from a legal standpoint. I told Sunny I would send her one hundred of what she paid and enclose it with this.[5]

Bumby, Patrick and Pauline are all well. Hope you are all having a good fall.

If anyone ever wants to interview you about me please tell them that you know I dislike any personal publicity and have promised me not to even answer questions about me. Dont ever give out <u>anything</u>. Just say your sorry but you cant. Scribners have the same instructions. If I'm to write at <u>all</u> I have to keep my private life out.[6]

Well, good luck to you all, Love
Ernie

PSU, ALS; postmark: PARIS-[6] / R. DE VAUGIRARD, 16 30 / 12 – 10 / 29

1 In letters to EH of 24 September and 5 October 1929, Grace praised Leicester's school in Hawaii and said he was active in swimming, diving, surfing, and shooting. Grace also reported that her uncle, Benjamin Tyley Hancock, who had been suffering heart pain, had traveled to California to visit his sister and her family (JFK). Tyley's nephew, Clarence Roome (1879–1961), who had urged him to come, was a physician.
2 EH's monthly checks to Grace were in the amount of $100 with frequent gifts for birthdays or special events. Uncle Tyley's eighty-first birthday was on 28 February 1929.
3 In 1927 EH had described the competitive nature of the two major annual art exhibitions in Paris to Grace: the conservative spring Salon (established 1774) and the more progressive Salon d'Automne (Autumn Salon, formed in 1903). Nonetheless, he invited

her to send him canvases to present in a Parisian show (*Letters* vol. 3, 331–33). Grace mailed paintings to him in Key West in March, and in her letter of 5 October 1929, she wrote, "It would mean an awful lot to me if those pictures could get into the 'Salon' or other good show and possibly be purchased for a public building or good collection."

4 On 28 September Perkins cabled, "First reviews splendid Prospects bright" (PUL). In her 5 October letter, Grace said she had been reading *FTA* in *Scribner's Magazine*: "It is the best you have done yet and deserves the high praise it is receiving."

5 In her reply of 25 October 1929, Grace would defend Leicester as "a good driver and very careful," saying "He had a license to drive and we all trusted our lives to him all summer" (JFK). EH enclosed a $100 check to reimburse Sunny for the compensation paid to the girl, but Grace clarified that since she herself had paid the $200, Sunny endorsed the check to her mother.

6 In response to EH's increasing concern for privacy, Perkins assured him in a letter of 23 September 1929: "I understand the way you feel about publicity touching your private life, and no such publicity will be sent out by us" (PUL).

To Maxwell Perkins, 15 October 1929

34 PARIS 10

SCRIBNERS NY

NO LETTERS SINCE PUBICATION HOWS BOOK GOING[1]

  HEMINGWAY

C HAS SCRIBNERS SONS FIFTH AVE

PUL, Cable; French Telegraph Cable Company destination receipt stamp: OCT 15 1929

1 Perkins cabled his response immediately: "Sale at end of last week twenty-eight thousand copies. Have printed in all fifty thousand copies. Prospects excellent" (15 October 1929, PUL).

To Hugh Walpole, 16 October 1929

October 16 1929

Dear Walpole:—

Thanks ever so much for writing about the book. I havent heard from Scribners for about three weeks but I know you must have written them something damned good.[1]

You must be right about the dialogue [*EH insertion*: I'd have cut more] but I'd worked over it all so many times that I couldnt tell one sentence from another finally. I'm so glad you liked it.[2]

Why dont you come over to Paris this week end? We'd love to see you. The weather is lovely and I cant write a damn line. We could drive to Chartres in the car or anything you'd like. The country is still fine. Come to get here on Saturday.

Come here to the house and we'll find you a pub close by to sleep at. It would be grand to see you.— I cant write and you coming would be a wonderful excuse not to have to try to and I want very much to see you.

Later we'll be gone and in the States[.] We'll be in Key West which is a fine place but 48 hours by train from anywhere you'll lecture.[3]

Would you wire if you can come over? And please come. It's probably very rude to ask anyone to do anything on such short notice— But your letter just came— The middle of next week I'm going away shooting— In November maybe to Russia manuscript with a citizen that gives a free trip with wagon lits and wont have to write or "observe" anything—[4] Then we go to Key West— It would be grand if you could come sometime between Friday and next Wednesday— I'll send this airmail, will make no engagements and wait for a wire—[5]

Yours always

Ernest Hemingway

6 rue FÉROU

PARIS VI

(near St. Sulpice)

NYPL–Berg, ALS

1 Having read *FTA* in manuscript, Walpole lavishly praised the novel in a letter of 20 September 1929 to a Mr. Walsh at Scribner's, saying "I find it magnificent" (PUL). Walpole's praise was quoted in a *New York World* ad of 2 October 1929 and in other Scribner's advertisements for the novel.
2 EH may be referring to the letter from Walpole that he mentions but that remains unlocated.
3 Walpole's lecture tour would run from 7 January to 2 March 1930 and encompass several Canadian and U.S. cities.
4 EH would travel to Berlin with Gus Pfeiffer, 10–16 November, but would decline Gus's invitation to accompany him to Russia (see EH to Gus Pfeiffer, [c. late October 1929]). *Wagon-lit*: a railroad sleeping car (French).
5 At the bottom of the page, a notation in another hand reads: "Sorry impossible to come at present / writing / Hugh W."—apparently the text of Walpole's wired response to EH's invitation.

To Cyril Hume, 19 October 1929

[Excerpt as published in Christie's catalog:]
"Thank you so damned much for the letter. I can't tell you how fine it made me feel nor how happy that you liked the book. You were damned fine to write and I only wish you'd put some address on so I would know this would reach you. . . ."

Christie's catalog, New York, 14 May 1997, Lot 103, ALS

According to the catalog description, this letter is dated 19 October 1929 and signed "Ernest Hemingway." The one-page letter is "slightly wrinkled, with the original envelope, addressed by Hemingway (defective). Hemingway thanks Hume for his praise about (undoubtedly) A Farewell to Arms (which was published on 27 September)."

To Mrs. Jamar, 19 October 1929

Dear Mrs Jamar;

Thank you very much for your note. I am very pleased you liked the book and you were very good to write to tell me. I hope this signature will do for an autograph

Yours very truly
Ernest Hemingway.
Paris October 19—1929.

UMD, ALS

To Maxwell Perkins, 20–21 October 1929

October 20—1929

Dear Max:—

Your cable to the bank about the sales and the two letters came the first of this week. I've been waiting for the letter sent Oct 4 to answer— But nothing's come yet. Hope something hasn't gone wrong and the checks been stolen. If the letter of Oct 4 doesnt come by day after tomorrow I'll wire you to stop payment on the checks if there were any in it.[1]

It is grand that the book is going so well. Keep on printing them. This is our big shot and with the impetus it has now it ought to go on up and over 100,000. The English Book Society (Book of the Month Club) wanted it and agreed to take it if Cape would hold off publication until January—[2] This would have been a good thing—a citizen from them came over to ask me if I would agree to hold off and use my influence with Cape. Meantime Capes refused and put it up to them to take it November or nothing—which was impossible as they had books for Nov. and Dec.—and Capes told them it was me who wanted it published at once without ever consulting me. Makes just one more time of being gypped by them

It would have been a fine thing. But Capes preferred the immediate nickels to the ultimate dollars. And we all lose by it. It would have been fine to announce in Jan. that it was the book of the month in England. Thus speeding everything up after Christmas. But there will be other foreign stuff you can use.

Its going to be serialized in Germany. Was sold to Norway and am getting offers on it from other countries all the time If you want to use that in the advertiseing later on.[3]

Saw Mr. Aley the Colliers King at lunch on ~~Saturday~~ Friday.[4] Took Col. Charley Sweeney along and told him (the [*EH drew an arrow pointing to* "Colliers King" *in the previous sentence*]) that Charley was my manager.[5] We kept off business plied the representative and each other with drinks and signed nothing. He was a nice man[.] I know I can't go out to lunch with people and not agree to do things So am going to lunch with no one without Charley along to make sure that I dont get the signing jeebies. But all that lunching is an awful thing anyway. Have to do it once more on Monday with Wren Howard of Capes and then will never meet for business under pretense of social meeting again. (I hope!) That sounds like for God for Country and for Yale—[6] This is a punk letter.

The limited Edition looked very handsome. The long page is very good looking. Theyve done a fine job.[7]

Cant remember what else I had to write about. Patrick Bumby and Pauline are all fine. Bumby has gotten much taller and huskier.

What about Key West? If you came down in March we could go to Marquesas and Tortugas—

Monday

This is now the end of the typewritten letter—[8] They're both punk. Have had five letters from unknown citizens about the book. If I answer them all wont be able to write anything else. But most all have been swell letters by deeply moved citizens many of whom did not even give their addresses or say whether they were Mrs. or (Miss.) If you want a picture for the window why dont you get the portrait by Mike Strater?— He has it at his place I think—the original—and it would do him good to have it exhibited.[9] You have his address I think. Anyway he's in the telephone book. How was MacAlmon? Did he have many interesting new dirty theories and stories about any of us? Since he left I have heard he was putting out a fine one that, in Pauline, I had married a noted Lesbian! Whoopee![10] Christ I will be glad to get out of the city and to Key West and fishing again. Maybe we will leave to be in Piggott for Xmas. Thanks for the 3000 check. What is this Scribner Short Story book advertized? What story of mine are they using? Hope it's not a big one as no use killing the Men Without Women piecemeal. How are the profits on it split?[11] The first I heard about it was from Scott.

How does Waldo look without his beard?[12]

Well this letter should get off—

Best to you always—
Ernest.

PUL, ALS

1 This letter and the one that follows in this volume appear to have been folded and sent together. In the following letter, EH writes in reference to this one: "Am enclosing a very punk scrawl that I wrote yesterday before the two letters came" (Perkins's letters of 4 and 7 October, PUL). In letters to EH dated 7 and 14 October, Perkins sent two equal checks for the $6,000 advance that EH had requested in his 27 September letter to Perkins (PUL).

2 Jonathan Cape would publish the English edition of *FTA* on 11 November 1929. Inspired by the success of the American Book-of-the-Month Club founded in 1926, the English Book Society was established in 1928 with Hugh Walpole as the chairman of the selection committee. Instead of *FTA*, the society chose *Whiteoaks* (1929) by Canadian novelist

Mazo de la Roche as the selection for November 1929. Cape's partner, George Wren Howard (1893–1968), claimed in a letter to EH of 14 October 1929 that the society had agreed to consider *FTA* for November but then rejected it without offering an explanation. Howard thought the reason for the rejection was that the book would be "rather strong meat for some of their subscribers, and a comparatively new Society of this kind cannot afford to antagonise any of its supporters" (JFK).

3 The German serialization of *FTA* would appear in the *Frankfurter Zeitung* from 8 May to 16 July 1930 under the title *Schluss Damit. Adieu Krieg!* (*And Thus an End. Goodbye War!*) translated by Annemarie Horschitz (née Rosenthal, 1899–1970), who also translated *SAR* (*Fiesta*, 1928) and *Men Without Women* (*Männer*, 1929). The Norwegian edition, *Farvel til våpnene* (translated by Herman Wildenvey) would be published in Oslo by Gyldendal in 1930.

4 Maxwell Aley (1889–1953), American writer, editor and literary agent. In a letter to EH (8 or 15 October 1929), Hadley Hemingway had enclosed a letter she received from Aley, dated 6 October 1929, saying he would be coming to France and hoped to meet with EH about "the possibility of some work for Collier's Weekly" (JFK).

5 Charles Sweeny (1882–1963), American-born soldier of fortune who lived mainly in France. EH and Sweeny had met in Constantinople in 1922 when EH was covering the Greco-Turkish War for the *Toronto Star*, and the two became good friends. Sweeny would serve as a prototype for Colonel Richard Cantwell in *ARIT* and would be an honorary pallbearer at EH's funeral in 1961.

6 The final lines of the 1881 song "Bright College Years," the unofficial hymn of Yale University (lyrics by Yale graduate Henry Durand, 1861–1929), are "Oh, let us strive that ever we / May let these words our watch-cry be, / Where'er upon life's sea we sail: / For God, for Country and for Yale!"

7 The dimensions of the limited edition of *FTA* are $9\frac{1}{6}$ by $6\frac{1}{6}$ inches, larger than the first edition, which measures $7\frac{3}{8}$ by $5\frac{3}{16}$ inches (Hanneman A8a and A8b, 23–24).

8 This "Monday" portion of EH's handwritten letter is a continuation of his typewritten letter to Perkins (dated "Monday," [21] October [1929]) that follows in this volume.

9 Strater had painted two oil portraits of EH during the winter of 1922–1923, one in profile and one in full face; a woodcut of the full face portrait served as the frontispiece for *iot* (1924). Perkins finally chose a portrait of EH by Waldo Peirce, rather than Strater, to display in the window of Scribner's New York City book store at Fifth Avenue and 48th Street.

10 In his 7 October letter to EH, Perkins said he would be dining with McAlmon the next day. Perkins would report to EH in a letter of 25 October that he had had "a nice dinner with McAlmon," who had seemed "to be in rather a bad, envious state of mind, but I do think he has had mighty hard luck, considering what he has done in helping to bring other people forward, and it is not unnatural that he should be a little bitter about it" (PUL). Perkins was more forthcoming in a letter to Fitzgerald, dated 30 October: "Ernest simply hoped that we would be able to do something for McAlmon as publishers, and yet when we got out to dinner what does McAlmon do but start in to say mean things about Ernest (this is absolutely between you and me) both as a man and as a writer" (Kuehl and Bryer, 157–58).

11 The Scribner's collection *Present-Day American Stories*, published on 13 September 1929, included EH's "The Undefeated," the opening story of *MWW*. In his reply of 12 November, Perkins would explain that Scribner's expected the collection to be used as a textbook and therefore EH would receive an "educational royalty" of two cents. Perkins said he did not think sales of *MWW* would be affected (PUL).

12 In his 7 October letter Perkins had reported, "Waldo came in today without a beard."

To Maxwell Perkins, [21] October [1929]

Monday Oct. 22

Dear Max:

Your two letters of Oct 4 and 7 received yesterday.[1] Am cabling this morning about the dramatic rights business. Confirming my cable: The last letter I had from Reynolds gave their cable address as Carbonato and the members of the firm as Paul R. Reynolds and Harold Ober with a line and then Paul R. Reynolds Jr.[2] When I got a letter from Brady (the elder) asking for my terms to negotiate I wired Reynolds firm address to negotiate with Brady reserving movie rights negotiating these best terms possible. [*EH autograph insertion*: (Scott tells me now the movie rights are negotiated by the producer.)][3] I had no idea that Ober was not handling this as he had for Scott. It was because I knew they had handled this for Scott that I wired. Now Scott tells me that Ober has left, you confirm this, and that Mr. Reynolds has never handled the dramatic negotiations. So I wired as you will get today.[4] I think Mr. Reynolds will see what the situation is. I would do nothing to embarrass or make trouble for them but as I was given to believe that I was dealing with Ober I should deal with him or with some one as experienced and as good as you and Scott say he is.

Am enclosing a very punk scrawl that I wrote yesterday before the two letters came.[5] I would have answered the wire to say how splendid the sale news was but was broke.

Would you send one of the presentation copies to G. A. Pfeiffer Esq. 113 West 18th Street with the authors compliments. And one to Mr. and Mrs. William D. Horne Jr. — 25 East Cedar Street — Chicago. With the enclosed slightly dirty card.[6] It's one I fell overboard with at Key West. Where you will have to come this Spring if I have to make out it is to protect the interests of the firm. Everything up to 70,000 I'm going to fix up the family with and all over that we'll buy a boat with. So the sooner you get it past 70,000 copies the more comfortably we'll all sleep [*EH autograph insertion*: afloat!] Burge is going to run the boat.[7] Have fixed it up with him.

—Typewriter gone on the bum—

Scott says he has a contract whereby above certain large amounts of sales the royalty percentage rises. He told me what it was but I forget it. What about this? Do you want to make some increase over 50,000? over 75,000? and over 100,000? Will you let me know about this. The principal thing I want is for it to keep on going of course and am not avaricious. But have heard this is ~~customary~~ done so write to ask you.

E.H.

Thanks ever so much for seeing Reynolds—I hated to bother you.

PUL, TLS

1 EH misdated this letter, as Monday was the 21st of October. Certain post offices in Paris were open on Sunday, so he could have received mail "yesterday" (Baedeker's *Paris*, 28).

2 In his 4 October 1929 letter, Perkins wrote, "I don't know any book that ever got better reviews" and advised EH to postpone dramatic rights negotiations as the book's success would ensure better terms later on. Perkins said he would consult with Harold Ober (1881–1959), "who is Scott's agent, and was for years with Reynolds, and knows the game" (JFK). The Paul R. Reynolds literary agency was founded in 1893 by Paul Revere Reynolds (1864–1944); his son Paul Revere Reynolds, Jr. (1904–1988) joined the firm in 1926. Ober had been with the Reynolds firm since 1907, but left in September 1929 to establish his own agency.

3 William Aloysius Brady (1863–1950), San Francisco-born actor and theatrical producer who began his Broadway career in 1896. He had produced Owen Davis's stage play of *The Great Gatsby* in 1926. His son, William A. Brady, Jr. (1900–1935), was also a theatrical producer.

4 In letters to Perkins dated 12 and 30 August, Reynolds extended an offer to be relayed to EH (PUL). On 21 September Ober cabled Fitzgerald that he was opening his own offices, requesting "Please cable me authorization to continue [*as your agent*] Persuade Hemingway send stuff through you to me." Fitzgerald cabled back: "Following you naturally" (Bruccoli *As Ever*, 146–47). Ober would later explain in a letter to Fitzgerald that matters had become tense between him and the younger Reynolds ([October 1929], JFK).

5 EH apparently enclosed the preceding two-part letter that he began on 20 October (a Sunday) and finished "Monday" after writing this letter. The paper, ink, and fold lines in the two letters are identical.

6 In his 4 October letter, Perkins wrote that he had reserved four unnumbered copies of the limited edition of *FTA* that he would send with EH's compliments to whomever EH wished. The card is inscribed "With love to Bunny and Bill / Ernie" just above EH's engraved name, and the Hornes' Chicago address is handwritten on the back. The presentation copy of *FTA* was a wedding gift following the couple's marriage in August. The book and card are described in the Sotheby's catalog for the New York sale of 21 June 2007 (Lot 119).

7 The remainder of the letter is handwritten.

To Maxwell Perkins, [c. 21 October 1929]

NA462 CABLE=PARIS 77

LCD PERKINS (PERKINS% CHARLES SCRIBNERS SONS 5TH
AVE & 48TH ST)=

SCRIBNERS NEWYORK (NY)=

CABLED REYNOLDS FIRM ADDRESS NEGOCIATE DRAMATIC
RIGHTS UNDER IMPRESSION OBER STILL HANDLING THEM HIS
NAME APPEARING LETTER HEAD LAST COMMUNICATION
RECEIVED REYNOLDS STOP WISH TO ACT ACCORDING YOUR
LETTEROCTOBER FOURTH RECEIVED YESTERDAY DELAYING
NEGOCIATIONS IF BOOK STILL GOING BIG STOPPLEASE SEE
REYNOLDS EXPLAIN STOP HOLD UP NEGOCIATIONS UNLESS HE
HAS MAN AS EXPERIENCED=

[*On second page:*]

NA462 2/18=

AS OBER STOP IF ACCEPT COLLIERS OF COURSE WILL DO ALL
BUSINESS THROUGH REYNOLDS[1] WHATS SALE[2] THANKS ERNEST.

PUL, Cable

1 In a letter to EH of 30 August 1929, Paul Reynolds wrote that *Collier's* was offering $30,000 for the first American and Canadian serial rights to EH's next novel and would pay $2,500 per short story. Reynolds had written on letterhead stationery that included Harold Ober's name as well as his own (JFK).
2 Perkins would respond in a 22 October cable: "Sale thirty-three thousand stop Unwise and dangerous now to take dramatic negotiations from Reynolds stop He is shrewd and experienced and is managing them personally and will submit any proposition to you stop Prospects fine" (PUL).

To James Aswell, 21 October 1929

Paris, October 21, 1929

Dear Mr Aswell:—

Your review just came and what ~~the hell~~ can I say—except that if the book made you feel like writing a review like that I'm a lucky bastard to have written the book.[1]

Anyway I never said that to Sisley—nobody ever said any of the things to Sisley that he says they said.[2] I'm awfully glad you said that about the mannered prose.[3] The famous "style" we all vomit to hear about is nothing but the defects caused by the difficulty of stating what you have to say. It's hard to get it said and if I got it so it made you feel that way I'm awfully lucky.

Thank you very much for sending the review. I cant tell you how fine it made me feel.

Yours very truly
Ernest Hemingway.

This is a lousy letter but by Christ the review made fine reading for me.

NWSU, ALS; postmark: PARIS – 2 / R. DANTON, 22 $\frac{30}{}$ / 21 · X / 1929

1 Aswell's review began, "I have finished 'A Farewell to Arms,' and am still a little breathless, as people often are after a major event in their lives." He called it a "tender, brutal, devastatingly simple love story" and concluded, "If anything better has been produced by a native of the New World I do not know what it is" ("Critic Lavishes Praise on New Hemingway Novel," *Richmond Times-Dispatch* Sunday Supplement, 6 October 1929, 3; reproduced in Trogdon *Reference*, 106–7).
2 In his review Aswell wrote of EH, "Years ago in Paris he told Sisley Huddleston that he wanted to divorce language 'from its superfluities.' No wonder poor, old grandiloquent Sisley didn't like him at all!" James Sisley Huddleston (1883–1952), English writer and journalist, stationed in Paris during WWI, chronicled expatriate life in Paris in the 1920s and remained in France for the rest of his life. In *Paris Salons, Cafés and Studios* (Philadelphia: J. B. Lippincott, 1928), Sisley quoted conversations with expatriates and discussed EH, claiming to have met him "years before," when EH was still a journalist for the *Toronto Star*: "He was seeking a simple realistic style. He wanted to set down life as he saw it" (121–23).
3 Aswell had contested "Harry Hansen's remark that he [EH] writes 'the most mannered prose now being written in English,'" countering that EH "has thrown overboard so much of the affectation of Aldous Huxley's dessicated company that his directness seems to be a trick!" and complimenting EH on his "verbal health."

To Ivan Goll, [c. 21 October 1929]

Cher Monsieur Goll:
    Pouviez vous passer chez moi demain matin avant 10.30? J'ai un depeche de Rowohlt et veuillez bien vous consulter

[Translation of EH's imperfect French follows:]
Dear Mr. Goll:

Could you meet me tomorrow morning before 10:30? I have a telegram from Rowohlt and would like to consult you

JFK, ACD

The date is conjectured relative to the telegram EH received from Rowohlt, his German publisher, postmarked in Paris on 21 October 1929 (JFK). EH drafted this cable to Goll, a translator living in Paris, on the back of an envelope he had received from Scribner's (postmark date illegible). In a letter to Scribner's of 17 October 1929, Rowohlt had reiterated his firm's history of German publication of EH's work and requested two copies of *FTA* as well as EH's address (PUL). On 21 October, Rowohlt cabled both Goll and EH. In the cable to EH, he noted that his 8 October telegram and 11 October letter had gone unanswered, asking EH for a copy of the book and his acknowledgment that "WE OWN BOOKRIGHTES AND SERIAL RIGHTES" (JFK).

To Charles and Lorine Thompson, [c. 22 October 1929]

Dear Charles and Lorine:—

How are you both and what about the hurricane? Did it blow away the Overseas Highway?[1] We will come back just the same but the loss of the highway will make Snipe shooting more difficult. It will be grand to get back. The book [*FTA*] came out the 27th—a letter from Max on Oct 7th received today says it had sold 23,000 up till then and on Oct 8th 24,500— on Oct 12 he wired it had sold 28,000 by the 10th of Oct. [*EH circled insertion:* Have to sell 60,000 to clear off my family debts— Then will get a boat!] So I will soon be making money like Bra ~~Kingfishing~~ when we struck the Kingfi[sh].

Keep an eye out for a boat—one like we went out on belonging to that old man—do you remember—to see the race between the King Conch and The Baker Boy would be fine.[2] Wish I could come down in Nov. to get a boat then go to Piggott and come down after Xmas. Well will see. But will see you this winter unless everything goes blooy. Key West is what we talk about all the time. Couldnt have been more worried when reading about the hurricane danger if we'd owned the other ice plant!

Best to you both— Please write—

Ernest.

Pauline is fine. So are Pat and Bumby.

It's the Best selling book in U.S at last report![3] Whoopee Written and re-written in Key West. Interviewed on the subject of his success
Mr. Hemingway said, "I lay it all to the climate of Key West and the fact that it's the only place in America where you get Tropical Beer!"[4]

Profiles in History catalog, Calabasas, California, 19 December 2013, Lot 91 (illustrated), ALS

The conjectured letter date is based on EH's reference to the sales of *FTA,* its appearance on bestseller lists, and Charles Thompson's response to EH, dated 5 November 1929 (a Tuesday), which begins: "Your letter received Sunday" (JFK). Counting back twelve days (to allow for transatlantic crossing) from the Sunday, 3 November, receipt of the letter in Key West produces the conjectured date of 22 October.

1 The Great Bahamas Hurricane of 1929 hit the Florida Keys on 27–28 September, damaging fishing boats and disrupting communications but causing no casualties. The Overseas Highway, built for automobile travel between Key West and the Florida mainland, was begun in 1923 and had opened to the public in January 1928. In his response dated 5 November, Thompson would report that the hurricane "didn't do us much damage. The road was washed a little in places but it is passable, and the state Road Dept is working to get it back in shape" (JFK).

2 EH refers to the Key West boat race of 4 July 1929 in which Walter Maloney's *Baker Boy* won a first prize, and *King Conch,* owned by Charles's brother Norberg Thompson (1884–1951), was unable to compete because it had caught fire early that morning ("Miami Wins Key West Boat Tests," *Miami Daily News and Metropolis,* 5 July 1929, 9).

3 On 2 October 1929, *FTA* was second on the shortlist of "Brooklyn's Best Sellers" in the *Brooklyn Daily Eagle.* On 5 October, it was number one on the *New York World*'s bestseller list, and on 9 October it rose to first place in the *Eagle. FTA* would remain on the *Eagle*'s shortlist until 18 December. On 13 October, *FTA* headed "The Six Best Sellers" list published by the *New York Herald Tribune,* remaining on that list until 19 January 1930.

4 La Tropical was the most popular brand of the Nueva Fábrica de Hielo (New Ice Factory), a brewery established in Havana in 1888 by the prominent Herrera family, then headed by Julio Blanco Herrera.

To Maxwell Perkins, 25 October [1929]

Oct 25

Dear Max:—

Your letter of Oct 14 with the 2nd check for $3000.$\underline{^{00}}$ came today. Am enclosing a copy of a letter I just wrote here in the bank to Pollinger of

Curtis Brown in answer to letters and cables received transmitting an offer from Coward-McCann of $25,000 advance etc. for next book.[1]

I hope you have my letter telling you how I was starting to hear these reports that I was dis-satisfied and telling you they were all lies.[2] This letter of mine to Pollinger I put in to re-assure you if you are hearing them again.[3]

If all this stuff makes you sore it does me too.

I suppose Coward etc are justified in making offers if they hear the reports— But who starts the reports?

The man from Harpers told me it was Bromfield but I thought perhaps that was just an alibi for himself.

Anyway although you dont need it let me tell you again that you have, as always—my full confidence—that I am negotiating with nobody and rely on you absolutely—

I wired yesterday to please accept Modern Library offer and sent the check to Hadley—[4]

Will send this off now—

Yours always
Ernest.

Will you keep the Pollinger copy fo[r] me?

PUL, ALS

1 Laurence Pollinger (1898–1976), literary agent with Curtis Brown Ltd., which represented EH in Great Britain. Coward-McCann, New York publishing house founded in 1928 by Thomas Ridgway Coward (1896–1957) and James A. McCann (1882–1952). Perkins would respond in a letter dated 12 November: "The probability is that these publishers simply want to get you, and they open up by saying they have heard you are dissatisfied. But the offers they make do, of course, put us under obligation . . . We are not in a position to ask you to refuse offers without being willing to equal them ourselves" (PUL).
2 EH refers to his letter to Perkins of 5 October 1929.
3 EH enclosed a copy of his letter to Pollinger, also dated 25 October 1929, which follows in the volume.
4 The Modern Library, established in 1917 by Boni & Liveright, published inexpensive reprints of works by European and American modernist writers. In 1925 the imprint was acquired by Bennett Cerf (1898–1971) and Donald S. Klopfer (1902–1986); two years later they founded Random House, which became the publisher of the Modern Library editions. On 22 October 1929 Perkins cabled, "Modern Library will publish edition of fifty thousand Sun Also in March paying royalty three thousand to author now stop Strongly advise acceptance" (PUL). EH had granted Hadley all the royalties from *SAR*.

To Laurence Pollinger, 25 October 1929

Paris

October 25—1929

Dear Mr. Pollinger:—

Thank you very much for your letters and cables.[1]

I am afraid you have been put to much useless bother, however, as I have never had the slightest intention of leaving Scribners.

About the British situation; I have no intention of changing publishers for the moment. You asked me to disregard your letter in that connection if this was true and so I did.

I'm awfully sorry you have been bothered about the American thing and I would be interested to know how such an unfounded report was started.

Thanking you again for your letters—

Yours very truly—

Ernest Hemingway.

PUL, ALS

EH enclosed this copy of his letter to Pollinger in the preceding letter to Perkins of the same date.

1 Pollinger's 1929 letters to EH remain unlocated.

To Ernst Rowohlt, [25 October 1929]

Rowohlt Verlag

Berlin

Have been sick and waiting for books from scribners to send you stop why should you own first serial rights stop am glad have you publish book and have informed agent negociating serial rights he is not empowered negociate book rights and I will sign nothing prejudicial to you stop however farewell is best selling book in America since published september 27th and cannot regard offer 500 marks advance as serious stop sending book today[1]

Rowohlt Verlag

Berlin

Have been ill and waiting for books and reviews from Scribners to send you stop do not understand why you should consider own first serial rights stop have given Ivan goll fifteen day option negotiate serial rights stating I would sign nothing prejudicial to you stop serial rights certainly my property stop have not empowered goll negotiate book rights stop am glad have you publish book however farewell is long novel best selling book in America since published september 27th and cannot regard offer 500 marks advance as proportional stop am sending book and reviews received today best regards Hemingway

JFK, TCD with typewritten signature

The conjectured date of these two cable drafts, written on the same sheet of paper, is based on EH's receipt "today" of the check and reviews sent by Perkins on 14 October 1929 and received by EH on 25 October (as EH noted in his 25 October letter to Perkins). EH is apparently responding to Rowohlt's 21 October cable, in which Rowohlt, noting that EH had not answered his 8 October telegram or 11 October letter, asked EH to send him a copy of *FTA* and to acknowledge that "WE OWN BOOKRIGHTES AND SERIAL RIGHTES" (JFK).

1 In October 1929, 500 marks were worth about $119. EH had received $16,000 for the serialization of *FTA* in *Scribner's Magazine*.

To R. P. Blackmur, 28 October 1929

Dear Mr. Blackmur:—

If you dont mind waiting until I have one I would be very glad to send you a short story for the Hound and Horn. The trouble is that I write very few of them and have disposed of those I did last summer. But if you dont mind waiting I know I will have one for you sooner or later—[1]

Yours always
Ernest Hemingway
Paris Oct. 28 / 1929
4 Place de la Concorde

PUL, ALS; postmark: PARIS 110 / R. DE RENNES, 2[8] / OCT / 17^{H}30; postmark on verso: BOSTON, MASS R / NOV 9 / 5^{30}PM / 1929

1 Blackmur was the first managing editor for the literary quarterly *Hound & Horn* (1927–1934), founded by Harvard undergraduates Lincoln Kirstein and Varian Fry and officially affiliated with the university until 1929, when it dropped the subtitle "A Harvard Miscellany." The magazine published works by contemporary writers including T. S. Eliot, Gertrude Stein, and Ezra Pound, and took its title from Pound's poem "The White Stag" (1909). In response to its publication of negative reviews of EH's "Hills Like White Elephants" and MacLeish's *The Hamlet of A. MacLeish*, EH referred to the magazine as "The Bitch and Bugle" in a 1929 letter to MacLeish (*Letters* vol. 3, 485–86). No evidence has been found to indicate EH ever submitted a story to the magazine.

To Anton Gud, 28 October 1929

Dear Mr. Gud:

Thank you for your letter. I have no plans for writing any differently—except always to try and write better.

As for immortality, thats something we have to die to find out about. But Joyce for Dubliners and the end of Ulysses is the surest bet for it of anyone now living.[1]

I'm awfully glad if you liked the book and thanks again for writing me.

It's hard enough for me to write at all without having to think about "changing style"— ~~Le style c'est l'homme~~—[2] People writing as well as they can dont change their way of writing any easier than they change their skins.

Yours always

Ernest Hemingway.

Paris Oct28/1929

phPUL, ALS; postmark: PARIS 110 / R. DE RENNES, 29 / OCT / 17^{H}30

1 *Dubliners*, James Joyce's 1914 collection of short stories. Molly Bloom's erotic stream-of-consciousness soliloquy closes the eighteenth and final episode of Joyce's 1922 novel *Ulysses*.
2 The style is the man (French), a variant of *Le style est l'homme même*, employed by Georges-Louis Leclerc, Comte de Buffon (1707–1788), in "Discours sur le Style," his 1753 lecture to the Académie Française: "Writing well consists of thinking, feeling and expressing well, of clarity of mind, soul and taste . . . The style is the man himself."

To Jeanette Mills Littell, 28 October 1929

Dear Miss Littell:—

It would be fine if you could save people's or characters lives with a few words—and maybe sometimes you can—but it never worked that way for me. As for the pictures always laughing that struck me as funny too.[1]

But anyway thank you very much for writing and I'm glad you liked them.

Yours very truly,

Ernest Hemingway.

Paris October 28

1929

Smith, ALS; postmark: PARIS 110 / R. DE RENNES, 2[8] / OCT / 17ᴴ30

1 Littell's letter to EH has not been located. EH's reference to "laughing" pictures is uncertain, but a Helen Breaker portrait of a smiling EH was widely used in Scribner's advertising of *FTA*. The photo accompanying the concluding segment of the novel in the October 1929 *Scribner's Magazine* shows EH on skis, smiling broadly.

To George Frederick Wilson, 28 October 1929

Dear Mr. Wilson:

I cant tell you how happy it made me that you should like the Farewell To Arms so much. I hope very much that you will like the other books too. You were very good to write— I appreciate it greatly.

Yours always—

Ernest Hemingway.

Paris October 28 1929

Knox, ALS; postmark: PARIS / R. DE RENNES, 28 / OCT / 17ᴴ30

To Robert Bridges, 31 October 1929

Dear Mr. Bridges:—

Mr. Victor LLona a South American who has translated Scott Fitzgerald and Willa Cather into French and is a well known man of letters in France has just called and asked me about sending a story (in English) to America. I asked him to send it to you before he sent it anywhere else and told him I would write to you to be on the lookout for it. I haven't read the story and do not vouch for it in any way but know that by sending it to you he will get a prompt and sympathetic reading of it.[1]

With all best wishes.

Yours very truly—

Ernest Hemingway.

Paris October 31, 1929

PUL, ALS

1 Llona had translated Fitzgerald's *The Great Gatsby* (*Gatsby le Magnifique*, 1926) as well as Cather's 1918 novel *My Ántonia* (*Mon Antonia*, 1924) and her 1920 short story "Coming, Aphrodite" ("Prochainement Aphrodite," 1925). His own novels included the *Les Pirates du Whisky* (1925) and *La Croix de Feu* (1928). No story by Llona appeared in *Scribner's Magazine*.

To Maxwell Perkins, 31 October 1929

Oct 31

Dear Max—

I hope to Christ you werent caught in the market. They're liquidating now so Hoover can have brought us out of this slump by 1932.[1] I've been in bed for the last few days. Grippe. Then my kidneys dont work awfully well and I tore a muscle badly in my groin in Spain this summer and had my trousers full of guts like a picador horse. But that is all healed now altho still bandaged— But cant drink anything without my fingers swelling. Need to get down to Key West If I'm to protect your investment. Been too sick to write for a month and worrying about the book—whether it would keep on so could handle things etc. We want to get away by the 1st of Dec. maybe but know nothing about this apt yet and have 3000 bucks tied up in improvements, plumbing, heating, fixtures etc.

I saw in the world that some citizen was <u>lecturing</u> on Farewell to Arms. God it would be ~~beautiful~~ fine to walk in and ask a few questions and then say "Shit Sir I do believe you are mistaken!"[2]

After I got hurt this summer we stayed 3 days in the hottest room you ever saw 115 in the shade—was on the hot side of the house and no shade—only a small single bed for two and I couldnt move— Hotel full for the bull fights in Palencia. Really hot— Pauline was wonderful—.

This letter isnt about anything— Sick of reading and can't think enough to write anything except this tripe to you— What about Waldo? How does he look without the beard? It's a loss to the world.

Hope you're all fine and everyone well.

Best luck always—

Ernest

Oct 31 Paris 1929

I got the two checks for 3000 for Oct 7–14—

One thing you never told me about was whether it would be possible to get the original proofs so I could have one copy without the blanks—

When you get this letter will you wire me what the sale is up to the end of whatever week has been completed?[3]

Will you send one of the presentation copies to—

Owen Wister Esq.

Long House

Bryn Mawr

Penn.

With my compliments!

and one to

Mr. And Mrs. Charles Thompson

c/o Key West Hardware Co.

opposite Thompson Fish Co.

Key West

Florida

with my compliments![4]

Thanks ever so much.

That uses up the 4 copies— I want to buy 3 more— Will you have them hold them for me? I'll send a check or they can deduct them.

PUL, ALS

1 The American stock market crash of 29 October 1929 ("Black Tuesday") marked the worst of several waves of panic selling as stock prices plummeted. As Democrats blamed Republican President Herbert Hoover and Treasury Secretary Andrew Mellon for the financial collapse, the Paris *Tribune* of 31 October 1931 carried a front-page article headlined "Hoover, Mellon Make No Reply; Predict Improvement will Soon Follow Slump."
2 A notice in the 19 October 1929 *New York World* announced: "Tomorrow at 3.30 P. M. Dr. J. G. Carter Troop will lecture on *A Farewell to Arms* by Ernest Hemingway at the Pythian Temple / 70th Street, East of Broadway" (14). Canadian-born Jared Grassie Carter Troop (1869–1930) had taught at the University of Chicago and at Trinity College, Toronto, before becoming a public lecturer for the New York City Board of Education in 1920 and serving six terms as president of the New York Public Lecture Association. Troop's popular weekly lecture series, "The Book of the Hour" (1920–1930), addressed contemporary fiction and nonfiction. Troop espoused the belief that literature should be "spiritually uplifting" ("Literary Morale on the Decline," *Brooklyn Daily Eagle*, [27 January 1929], 80).
3 In his letter of 12 November 1929, Perkins would respond that "the sale to date is just 45,000." Scribner's had printed 70,000 copies and had enough paper ready for an additional 20,000 (PUL).
4 Perkins sent books to Wister and to Charles Thompson on 8 November, accompanying each with a personal letter (PUL).

To Owen Wister, 31 October [1929]

October 31

Dear O.W.—

Did you ever get The Torrents? I wired them from Santiago to send it to you care of Morgans. It's not worth acknowleging but you might laugh at it a couple of times and if you didnt get it I'll cable Scribners to send you one. They said at Miss Beach's that it had been sent but she was away so I couldnt be sure.[1]

Right after that I hurt myself and then got sick and have been more or less so ever since. That's why I haven't written. Fingers swell if I take even red wine and water. When red wine and water—half and half—(l'eau rougi)—have been your best friend and severest critic for years it is not good to stop them—

How are you? Fine I hope. I'll lay you 2/1 (in anything you like) you survive me. (Starters dead from un-natural causes to forfeit their entrys). And in that event the fine set of books to be for my son Bumby—

J.H.N. Hemingway

98 B^{D.} Auguste Blanqui

Paris XIII

This is not a final nor a preliminary testament— It seems to have become very funereal— It's not really— But have wanted to write you for a long time and feel too punk to copy it all over— If you are sick at all in the Autumn— The season its-self makes it seem much more significant than it ever amounts to—

JFK, AL

This letter, which survives among EH's papers at JFK, is apparently unfinished and unsent.

1 In a letter of 14 October 1929, Wister, who did not have EH's address, asked Perkins to write to EH "and thank him for an early book which I found waiting for me at Morgans in Paris," referring to Morgan, Harjes & Cie., the American bank located at 14, Place Vendôme (PUL).

To Isabelle Simmons Godolphin, [c. 31 October 1929]

Dearest Izz—

It was certainly a damned shame not to have seen you last summer. I wired all over hell as you must have heard if you saw Hadley but the sad part was not to see you— And to miss Frisco too.[1] How are you? I hope to god fine. We'll see you in the winter maybe—In December— Where are you going to be?

I want to send you a book but dont know where— Am in bed with the Grippe and if this letter doesnt make good sense lay it to a nose full of scalding snot—

Did you like the book? I hope to god so. I wanted so awfully badly to see you.— It would have been swell if you could have come to Valencia. Pauline sends her love.

Everybody is in swell shape but me and I'm on the bum physically and need to get back to Key West— Got Hurt down in Spain and laid up— Havent had any exercise since and feel lousy— Please write me—love you very dearly—and I am a louse about not writing. Last Spring Pauline was in bed 8 weeks. That's why I wired you instead of writing. Was trying to write and couldnt go in the head at all and carried your letter around to answer meaning to every day took it with me on a trip to try and work and couldnt and never did answer— But I'm damned sorry and you are a fine girl and if you ever get off of me it will make me feel worse than I've ever felt yet— So dont—

Best to Frisco—was it hot in Greece? We hit 120° in shade twice—

Good luck—Really swell luck to you—

Best love—

Ernie

c/o

Guaranty Trust Co. of N.Y.

4 Place de la Concorde

Paris

phPUL, ALS

1 In a letter from Oak Park postmarked 27 June 1929, Isabelle had written that she would sail for France on 10 July and hoped to see EH in Paris before traveling to Rome (JFK). In a letter postmarked 30 August, she wrote, "Terribly disappointed to have missed you" (JFK). Francis R. B. "Frisco" Godolphin (1903–1974), her husband, was a classics professor at Princeton.

To H. Lawrence Lack, Jr., [c. late October 1929]

Dear Mr. Lack:—

After reading your letter I would be shirking my duty if I did not do whatever is possible to discourage you from as you put it "eventually entering the field of authorship." You write abominably; ~~but this may~~ that might be changed, but what is worse—you show a muddled and addled ~~pated~~ mind that, no matter how well you wrote, would deprive what you should write of any real value.[1]

Do you know what "the past few decades" means? Few means more than two. The least it can mean in the way you use it is three. It probably means three or four. A decade is ten years. If, in your orgies of reading, you have found nothing written in the last thirty or forty years which was not

obviously and without anyone having to tell you of permanent value
I should say you should be spanked. ~~for writing to people and taking up their time with foolish questions.~~

In the last thirty years, ie. few decades, you will find books written by Thomas Hardy, Thomas Mann, W. B. Yeats, Knute Hamsun, George Moore, to mention a few writers. All of these except Hardy are still alive.[2]

JFK, AL

This letter, which survives among EH's papers at JFK, is unsigned and probably unsent.

1 EH quotes directly from Lack's letter of 30 September 1929, in which Lack wrote, "One hears on various sides, coming particularly from members of the older generation, the statement that all modern literary work is not worthy of the name, that no true worth has been displayed in literature within recent years, that present-day novels are so much trash and that nothing has been produced in the past few decades which will prove of permanent value." Lack wrote that he had "emboldened" himself "to address a number of present-day writers whose works I have particularly admired and enjoyed" to ask them about the state of modern literature. Lack identified himself as "one of the younger—'and wilder'—set" who harbored "some ambition to further my education by worthwhile reading and study, hoping eventually to enter the field of authorship myself" (JFK).
2 Thomas Hardy (1840–1928), English poet and novelist; Paul Thomas Mann (1875–1955), German novelist and essayist who was awarded the Nobel Prize in Literature in 1929; William Butler Yeats (1865–1939), Irish poet and playwright; Knut Hamsun, Norwegian-born American novelist (né Knut Pederson, 1859–1952) who was awarded the 1920 Nobel Prize in Literature; George Moore (1852–1933), Irish novelist and short-story writer.

To Gustavus A. Pfeiffer, [c. late October 1929]

~~QUICKPILL~~

~~NEWYORK~~

~~GAP AFRAID SHOULD NOT GO RUSSIA THIS YEAR WILL GO BERLIN SEE YOU OFF~~

GAP THANKS LETTERS AFRAID SHOULDNT GO RUSSIA NOW WILL GO BERLIN SEE YOU OFF
    ERNEST
GAP THANKS LETTERS BELIEVE SHOULDNT GO RUSSIA NOW

JFK, ACDS; letterhead: WESTERN UNION CABLEGRAM / SIÈGE SOCIAL EN FRANCE: 2, RUE DES ITALIENS, PARIS

EH apparently intended this cable to reach Uncle Gus in New York before Gus sailed for France on 2 November aboard the *Leviathan*. Gus would visit EH and Pauline in Paris on 8–9 November before he and EH travelled together to Berlin on 10 November. EH returned to Paris on 15 November, and Gus would travel on to Russia (Gus Pfeiffer to Louise Pfeiffer, 21 December 1929, HPMEC).

To Bernard C. Schoenfeld, 5 November 1929

Dear Mr. Schoenfeld:

Thank you very much for writing.[1] The trouble about the Sun is that I had and still have an idea of trying to make a play out of it myself— There's a lot of stuff I cut out of the book that might help in a play and I thought I should try, maybe to make a play of it some lean year.

You were awfully good to suggest doing it and I appreciate it very much— After I've made a mess of it I'll [*EH cancellation, then marked "Stet"*: kick myself for having trying something I know nothing about] be sorry not to have accepted your offer— But I'm afraid I cant accept it now. Although I do appreciate it very much and thank you again for having made it. Please give my best regards to Aiken.[2]

With all best wishes,

Yours always

Ernest Hemingway.

4 Place de la Concorde

Paris

November 5, 1929

Knox, ALS; postmark: PARIS-25 / RUE DANTON, 7 $\frac{30}{}$ / 6 · XI / 1929

1 A 1928 Harvard graduate, Schoenfeld was then studying at the Yale School of Drama. His letter to EH remains unlocated.
2 Conrad Potter Aiken (1889–1973), American poet, fiction writer, and critic, had been Schoenfeld's tutor and friend at Harvard. In his review of *SAR*, Aiken pronounced EH "in many respects the most exciting of contemporary American writers of fiction" and declared, "the dialogue is brilliant." EH had "the dramatist's gift," Aiken wrote, and he asked, "Will Mr. Hemingway try his hand at a play?" (*New York Herald Tribune Books*, 31 October 1926, 4).

To Maxwell Perkins, 8 November 1929

DR MN1 FP693 PARIS 14/13
LCD MAXWELL PERKINS
SCRIBNERS NEWYORK
ADDRESS HADLEY GUARANTY TEUST PARIS WHATS SALE
ERNEST

PUL, Cable; Commercial Cables destination receipt stamp: NOV 8 7 55 PM 29

The cable bears the notation in an unknown hand: "3000+ last report on Sun Also."

To Maxwell Perkins, 10 November [1929]

enroute Berlin
Sunday Nov 10

Dear Max:—

Thanks for the cable about the sale answering the wire I sent giving Hadley's address.[1] She will be over here all winter and her permanent address in care The Guaranty Trust Co. of N.Y, 4 Place de la Concorde, Paris— Am going up to Berlin to see various citizens and German publishers—to arrange about serialization—[2] The German publisher wants to take 37% of what that brings on acct of furnishing the translator (First they wanted 50%) but I am being hard boiled abt it as I have too damn many dependents to split too much with people after the thing is once written and finished— The translator wd have to translate the book in any event for book publication and if it is serialized first 15% on the serialization or 20%—is plenty— Sunny—(my useless sister you met at Key West) now has developed stomach ulcers— (Broke her engagement first— I thot I had her married off)[3] Hope she gets well— I may have to shoot them all to hold down the overhead.

Have been writing well on a story last 3 days so dont give a damn about anything— Saw Scott last week—looking very well and healthy—

If you were me—and Christ knows I need money—not money advanced or loaned but money earned—would you sell the book to movies for cash now or gamble on a play— Reynolds is getting

Laurence Stallings— Scott tells me Stallings no good— Maxwell
Andersen is the goods he says—[4] Play may flop—then movie only bring
20,000 and have to split 3 ways—minus commission to Reynolds and all
his friends— Now I can sell for 10 grand— 1 to Reynolds makes 9 for
me— I <u>would</u> sell for 17 grand— That would net me 15,000. I think that
wd. be better maybe— Then write a play myself sometime. To hell with
plays with other people— May be best tho—

But I think I could write a good play myself sometime— What do you
think about the play or movie business?

Anyway there isnt any news good or bad— Except the 42,000 cockeyed
copies— Once its past 60—it will be fine— If it can come again after
Christmas it will be grand— The Sun did— You all must be sick of it—
If you are I dont blame you— I think we should sell an awful lot of this
though because the whole fiction racket is going to go to hell may be in
a couple of years—

Owen Wister sent me a fine autographed set of his Complete works—
Damned sweet of him to do.— He wrote some fine—very fine—stories—[5]

It's dark outside and train rocking—hot stuffy—wish you were here and
we'd go up to the diner and drink— Must be nearly to Belgian frontier—
Hope the market didnt hit you—

Best to you always—

Ernest

Remember O.W. et al wanting me to tone down or cut out some of the
last chapter? That's why they're reading the damned book. [*EH drew an
arrow pointing to "last chapter" in the preceding sentence*]

It's no fun for me on acct. of the blanks— Now I can never say shit in
a book— Precedent— When you make your own precedent once you make
the wrong precedent you're just as badly stuck by it—

It takes away the interest in writing fiction.

JFK, ALS

This letter and addressed envelope (marked "Personal") survive among EH's papers at JFK,
but the envelope bears no postage or postmark, and a response from Perkins has not been
located. EH may not have sent the letter.

1 In response to EH's 8 November cable, Perkins had wired back that same day: "Sale now forty two thousand" (PUL).

2 EH was traveling with Gus Pfeiffer, who was looking after European operations of the family's business. Before leaving Berlin on 15 November, EH would visit his German publisher, Rowohlt Verlag. *FTA*, translated by Annemarie Horschitz, would be serialized as *Schluss Damit. Adieu Krieg!* in the *Frankfurter Zeitung* from 8 May to 16 July 1930.

3 In letters of 25 and 27 October, Grace Hemingway reported that Sunny was suffering from peptic ulcers and receiving treatment at home (JFK). In an earlier letter Grace expressed regret that Sunny had broken off her engagement to her Oak Park beau Duke T. Hill, Jr. (11 August 1929, JFK).

4 Laurence Tucker Stallings, Jr. (1894–1968), American playwright, screenwriter, editor, and novelist, would write the stage version of *FTA*, which would open on Broadway on 22 September 1930 but run for just three weeks. Maxwell Anderson (1888–1959), American journalist, teacher, and playwright, would be awarded a Pulitzer Prize for Drama in 1933. Stallings and Anderson had collaborated on the successful antiwar play *What Price Glory* (1924), based on Stallings's experiences in WWI, in which he suffered injuries that led to amputation of his right leg and was awarded France's Croix de Guerre. The motion picture version was released by Fox in 1926. In a letter to EH [c. July 1928], Fitzgerald had disapproved of Stallings for "slowly taking to himself the communal exploits of the 5th + 6th Marines" (Bruccoli *Fitz–Hem*, 97–98).

5 The eleven-volume collection *The Writings of Owen Wister* (New York: Macmillan, 1928) included Wister's celebrated western novel *The Virginian* (1902) and many short stories originally published in such magazines as *Harper's Monthly*, *Saturday Evening Post*, and *Cosmopolitan*. The collection formed a part of EH's library (Brasch and Sigman, item 7221).

To Maxwell Perkins, 16 November 1929

NA72 8/7 CABLE (FOLLOWING IS DUPLICATE OF CABLE PHONED TO YOUR OFFICE)
PARIS NOV 16 1929 450P
PU PERKINS
SCRIBNERS NY (PERKINS CHAS SCRIBNERS SONS 5 AVE & 48 ST)
HOWS SALE ERNEST.
    1244P
    1244P.

PUL, Cable.

The telegram bears the handwritten notation: "46000 on Friday."

To F. Scott Fitzgerald, [c. 16 November 1929]

Dear Scott—

Sorry to miss you a[nd] not to have been home when you came around.

When's the best time to get hold of you and have you a telephone?—

Have various things to ask you about but want to see you anyway—

To hell with business. Hope everything is going well—

Yrs always—

Ernest—

PUL, ALS

The conjectured letter date is based on EH's comment in his letter to Perkins of 15 December [1929] that when he returned home from Berlin (arriving in Paris on 16 November), he "found Scott had been here with some alarm."

To Waldo Peirce, [c. 17 November 1929]

Dear Waldo:—

Of all the kike tricks! I'll get the 20 bucks and as much more as I can from them for you or bloody well know why. Why shouldnt they pay something for a ~~drawing~~ painting they used as advertizing in their window— Loan hell. Why should you loan and them not come through! They pay you or I'll pay you and leave them flat. I'll write Max—[1]

Thanks like hell for keeping after Uncle Gus's fish— Got the bill today on return from Berlin— Fred Parke calls it a permit—you a Pompano— Burge a sunfish—Bra an African Pompano —[2]

I'll be damned glad to see you— We're broke too— I am fixing a trust fund to handle my family and have to sell 60,000 before I get any cash for our use.[3] We'll all get together in Key West and at least get actual results from jack spent.

Have seen Ivy a couple of times but she thinks I'm on the Machiavelli side because I claimed to know nothing about you divorcing when we came back from U.S. But hell I didnt know.

Pat and Whitney gone to North Africa. Maude gone around the world.[4]

Went to Berlin to do some business. Had hell of a good time.

Those damn Scribners—

See Charley Sweeney pretty often— He came to Bike races Sundays until found races fixed. Everything's fixed but I dont give a damn as long as I constaté[5] it myself and dont lose any money betting. Charley's a damned good guy though—

We shove for US. first part of Dec. if can get away. If miss you here we'll meet in Key West—

It's Sunday morning and got to go to church—Dimanch C'est l'Eglise et le Vel D'Hiv— Thank God not forced to choose between them— They are wise not to compete— Imagine the priests derriere grosse motos at St. Sulpice—[6]

Thanks for the picture. Give Reneé my love but tell her I'm in the opposite camp— Prefer you with the beard— But then our relations and view point are different.[7] You've got a wonderful target in that chin though— Feel the same temptation to let a right hand go that the sight of Cameron Rodgers always brings.[8]

I hope you find the old 3% Camera. But am cheered by how the luger turned up. God that was a swell pistol to shoot[.][9] I would like to have one when the revolution comes to pick off bycicle Cops with.

So long Chico and hope we see you soon—and anyway we'll all get together in Key West— Write me— Get worried when dont hear from you— I wrote down in Spain and after got back— Must have written one you didnt get. Paulline send[s] her love

Best always— Ernesto

Bumby sends regards too—

I asked him who was the finest man in the world hoping to hear Papa"

But he said, "I think it's Waldo"

Colby, ALS; postmark: PARIS-25 / RUE DANTON, 11 [30] / 19 · XI / 1929

EH wrote "Answered Nov 18" on the envelope of Peirce's letter of 2 November 1929. In 1929, 18 November fell on a Monday. The conjectured letter date is based on EH's remark that it is Sunday and he has to go to church.

1 Peirce had mailed to Scribner's at his own expense a portrait of EH to use for advertising. In a letter of 2 November, Peirce told EH that he had hoped "to collect about $20 for loan of Kid Balzac" but when he asked Perkins "for a piece of coin," it was not forthcoming (JFK).

2 As both Peirce and Parke, the taxidermist, lived in Bangor, Maine, EH had asked Peirce to check up on the fish and ensure its delivery to Gus (see EH to Peirce, [23] June [1929] and 29 August [1929]).

3 The trust fund would be established with the first $20,000 of EH's royalties for *FTA* and $30,000 from Uncle Gus. In a letter to EH of 21 November 1929, Perkins wrote "sale has passed 50,000" (PUL; *TOTTC*, 129). Sales would reach 60,000 by the end of the month.

4 Patrick Morgan and Whitney Cromwell (1904–1930), son of New York Stock Exchange president Seymour Cromwell, had been fellow students and friends at Harvard and at the École des Beaux-Arts; in Paris, they shared a flat. Maud Cabot (1903–1999), member of an aristocratic New York family and herself an abstract expressionist painter living in Paris. The two men had dropped out of the École des Beaux-Arts and gone to Tunis to paint and write. Cabot and Cromwell planned to marry when he returned from Tunis and she from her seven-month trip around the world (Cabot, 80–81, 91). Cromwell would die in Tunis, and Cabot would marry Morgan in 1931.

5 *J'ai constaté*: I have noticed (French).

6 *Dimanche C'est l'Église et le Vel D'Hiv*: Sunday it's church and the Vélodrome d'Hiver (French). Église Saint-Sulpice, the second-largest church in Paris, located a block from EH and Pauline's residence at 6, rue Férou. The Vélodrome d'Hiver, an indoor bicycle racing track near the Eiffel Tower: in *MF*, EH would recall " the smoky light of the afternoon and the high-banked wooden track and the whirring sound the tires made on the wood as the riders passed" ("The End of an Avocation"). *Derrière grosses motos*: behind big motorcycles (French).

7 With his 2 November letter Peirce enclosed a photo of himself, clean shaven, with his arm around a young woman, standing in a garden of gladioli or sword lilies. His handwritten caption reads, "They Soil not neither do they Sin,"a reference to Luke 12:27: "Consider the lilies, how they grow: they toil not, neither do they spin; yet I say unto you, Even Solomon in all his glory was not arrayed like one of these." Peirce wrote: "This photo of me and Renee— Vile libel— She doesn't speak to me—has a regular fellar etc— This is mere photogenic complacency—specially posed for housekeeper." In her postscript to Peirce's 12 August letter to EH, Renee had written that with "his whiskers all shaved off" Waldo "certainly is a regular looking fellow" (JFK).

8 Robert Cameron Rogers (1900–1971), 1923 Harvard graduate, poet, and nonfiction writer whose books included *The Magnificent Idler: The Story of Walt Whitman* (1926), *Gallant Ladies* (1928), and *The Legend of Calvin Coolidge* (1928).

9 In his 2 November letter, Peirce lamented having lost his movie camera, an expensive gift from his father, while attending the August wedding of Kate Smith and John Dos Passos: "Old man's 3%—eclipsed by loss of principle—," he wrote. Peirce had mentioned the camera in three letters to EH sent between 2 February and 15 February 1929, in which he also mentioned his father's Luger and made plans to bring the gun to Key West for shooting practice with EH during his March 1929 visit (JFK). Designed by Austrian Georg Luger (1849–1923), the Luger pistol P08 was used by German and other European military forces during WWI, WWII and later.

To Maxwell Perkins, 17 November [1929]

Sunday November 17—

Dear Max:—

Just back from Berlin arranged for serializing Farewell in Germany— Im enclosing first English review—[1] You can probably use extracts from it—

On arriving here yest. found Pauline worried by news from Scott about the book— Scott seemed very worried. Some contingency which was to prevent a big sale that he had heard from you.

His idea was that if sales started to fall off you should start advertising the book as a love story—which it certainly is as well as a war story— If other war books should start to crowd it— Why not do that?

I have not spoken about advertising and told Scott I would rather not but he said I was a fool not to— So here goes and then I'll drop it— I think the advertizing has been excellent!—

The first ad I would find fault with was the one in the World which started— First choice of Book Buyers in the following cities—[2] You are in competition with people who make such ambiguous statements that any ambiguity is discounted—

I think

The Best Selling Book in —— the names of the cities﹜ is

At The Top of the Best Seller Lists)

at least 10 times as effective as a statement which means that but doesnt say it—

That's all about advertising—

About any reasons that may now keep it from having a big sale—

I know that there were about 3 perfectly valid reasons why I should not have been able to complete it— If I completed it and it ~~recieves~~ gets the reviews it has had and sells as it did for 3 weeks— I'm afraid that no reasons are going to be valid why it should not have a big sale— There are no alibis in a battle— You win it or you lose it in spite of all circumstances that come up— Afterwards it is won or lost. This has reached the battle stage. It is no longer a skirmish, or a preliminary encounter or a trial of strength. It's something to be won or lost. And there are no explanations.

You know I have denied all reports of difficulties, I'm loyal to you in my head and my actions, I've not tried to embarrass you, but I tell you how this book goes is damned serious to me.

About the advertising— I have said nothing— I find it excellent— It is your business—not mine—

If, however, later you would say—"if you had any suggestion to make why did you not make it?" I'll suggest that if the sale does not keep up with what you are doing why not hammer on it as a love story—

These things are from an advertising standpoint—not my opinion or my judgement of the book—

① The action of—	A Farewell to Arms—	①—Takes place in war	Theres more than
② The Background of—		②—Is War—	War in
	But it is The Great Modern Love Story.		A Farewell to Arms.
			It is
			The Great Modern
			Love Story.

What Shit!— It makes me sick to write such stuff and I'm damned if I will— But what sold the Bridge of San Thornton Wilder was ~~the phrase~~ calling it hard, plenty and often— A Metaphysical Novel— Sure and what it was was a well hung together collection of short stories—[3]

You sell the intelligent ones first— Then you have to hammer hammer hammer on some simple thing to sell the rest.

Like this—

There Are Other War Books (or Books of War.)

But

A Farewell to Arms

By

ERNST HEMINGSTEIN

is

A Great MODERN Love STORY.

This (not my opinion or judgement it is only a suggestion for advertizing— You sell the intelligent ones first. Then you have to hammer, hammer,

hammer, on something to sell the rest— I once worked for Richard
H. Loper whose best business was selling whiskey by mail order—
While working under Mr. Loper we did not come in contact with the
intelligent at all.[4]

I only suggest this if you do not continue the sale as you would like with
the present line— I see it's The Sensation of the Season— In the ads— But
there will be other sensations and that is a pretty impermanent
qualification— The thing to do is dub it something The Great or A Great
and then stick to it— Anyone whose opinion matters will have read it long
before— What sold The Bridge of St. Thornton Wilder was (1) It was
a damn good collection of Short Stories (2) They dubbed it A Metaphysical
Novel and stuck to it.

Now a final suggestion from Mr. Richard H. Loper's 2nd in
command:

I would run this entire review in an ad— It has more sales force
(what ~~lovely~~ filthy words) than any damn thing I ever read— In spite
of having written the bloody book and having worked over it so much
that I am completely unable to read it when I read this review
I wanted to go right out and buy one— Dont use the head lines— Just
start the review—

A Farewell to Arms—By Ernest Hemingway—355p. $2.50, Charles
Scribner's Sons—N.Y.

By James Aswell

Then the review.[5] Then at the bottom—In the Richmond-Times
Dispatch. Put any comment you want across the Top and The Bottom—
But I swear that review in its entirety would make a swell ad. You could slug
at the bottom names and comments of various more prominent citizens
who agree with Mr. Aswell—

I'm not trying to interfere— These are two suggestions—

When you get through with the Aswell review will you please send
it back. It's the only one I'm keeping. ~~It makes you see it's written by~~

~~someone who hasn't been worn out and stale by reviewing books~~
~~and has none of the slime of the professional reviewer. He got the~~
~~kick out~~

JFK, AL

Its presence among EH's papers at JFK suggests that this is an abandoned draft of EH's letter to Perkins dated 19 November, which follows in this volume.

1 In the 14 November 1929 *Evening Standard* (London), Arnold Bennett called *FTA* "a superb performance." The English edition had been released on 11 November 1929.

2 The Scribner's advertisement in the 29 October 1929 *New York World* proclaimed *FTA* "The First Choice of Book-buyers" in New York, Chicago, Philadelphia, Pittsburgh, Cleveland, Baltimore, Cincinnati, Milwaukee, and "points west and south" (15).

3 Thornton Wilder's *The Bridge of San Luis Rey* (New York: Albert & Charles Boni, 1927), the bestselling novel of 1928, was awarded that year's Pulitzer Prize for Fiction. The book had been described as a "metaphysical study of love" in the *New York Times Book Review* (27 November 1927, BR7), a phrase repeated in subsequent reviews, advertisements, and announcements. In five chapters, the novel tells the stories of five unrelated people who die in the collapse of an Incan rope bridge in eighteenth-century Peru.

4 Richard Harding Loper (1875–1945) was the publisher of the *Co-operative Commonwealth: The Weekly Magazine of Mutual Help*, a publication of the Chicago-based Co-operative Society of America. EH worked as a writer and editor from December 1920 to October 1921, when the magazine folded and the society went bankrupt amid accusations of fraud.

5 In his review, Aswell called *FTA* a "tender, brutal, devastatingly simple love story" and praised its "emotional tenseness" and "boiling interior life" ("Critic Lavishes Praise on New Hemingway Novel," *Richmond Times-Dispatch* Sunday supplement, 6 October 1929; in Trogdon *Reference*, 106).

To Maxwell Perkins, 19 November [1929]

November 19.

Dear Max:—

Came back from Berlin and found Scott worried about my book—I believe and hope quite needlessly. Something he had heard from you about some contingency that might prevent it having a really big sale.[1]

Scott's idea was that if the sale should start to fall off—other books with war in them coming out—you should start hammering it as a love story—i.e. Farewell To Arms— A Gt. Modern Love Story. (sic) It most certainly is a love story and most of the reviews called it so. This seems a good idea altho I am not mixing in your handling of it—

What ads I have seen have seemed excellent—only two things I would suggest— Many publishers advertisements are so ambiguous that it would always seem better to avoid ambiguity by an exact statement if that is possible—[2]

| The First Choice of Book Buyers |
| in such and such cities |

seems not nearly as effective as

The Best Selling Book or AT The Head of Best Selling Lists— To me, at least, it avoids stating something which another publisher—if he avoided stating it would only be avoiding because it was not true.

That is an awkward enough sentence but I think you see what I mean. The other was—The Sensation of The Season— That makes it old stuff in a month when there is a new sensation. But that is not worth mentioning as I know that was just to be used for a short time— But it's best to dub a thing something and then stick to it—

About any reasons that may keep it from having a big sale—

There were about 3 perfectly valid reasons why I should not have been able to complete the book. If it was completed, gets the reviews it has had, and goes as it did for three weeks I am afraid that no reasons are going to be valid why it should not have a very big sale. There are no alibis in a battle— You win it or you lose it in spite of all circumstances that come up— Then afterwards it is won or lost. That is all that counts. This has reached the battle stage. It is no longer a skirmish, or a prliminary encounter or a trial of strength. It is something to be won or lost And there are no good explanations.

The last letter I've had from you was October 15— The last cable was Nov. 9 giving the sale as 42,000— I wired Saturday, after I'd seen Scott, asking about the sale. Today is Tuesday—may hear this afternoon— [*EH insertion*: P.S. Wire has just come giving 46,000 sale last Friday— So it wd. seem to be going steadily.] One reason I want to keep track is to know how to regard the theatrical and moving picture negotiations. I would rather be writing than doing any of this— But what happens is that I get in the middle of a story and something comes up.

Found a letter from Waldo yesterday who felt pretty badly at not getting 20 dollars for the use of the picture in the window which he framed and shipped at his expense— I will send him $30—[*EH insertion*: if Scribner's doesnt.] but it might be more fitting as I'd asked for the picture not to be used and it was Scribners that used it [*EH insertion*: once it is used I dont care] that Waldo be paid by them rather than me even if a channel has to be opened. Waldo is so damned generous about giving pictures away that he ought to be protected rather than used— He wrote that either the picture was some use or no use— All he wanted was 20 dollars to go to the Harvard Club and spend on liquor and feel he had earned. (He has little enough of that, and it is one of the best of feelings. It's a hell of a life to be taking money from yr. father all the time) I'm willing to pay the money to you to pay to Waldo rather than have any bad feeling— But I do think the money should go to Waldo from Scribners—altho I would rather pay it than make an issue of it.[3]

This seems to be all.

About the sale— I think it is pretty much a matter of objective— At the time of Caporetto the Austrian objective was The Tagliamento. If it had been Milan they would have reached there. Foch said their objective should have been Lyons. As it was they tried for the Tagliamento and reached the Piave and lost the war there.[4]

Yours always—

Ernest

Enclose a bill that I dont know about and review by Arnold Bennett that you might be able to use.[5]

Have a letter from Charles [Thompson] that only a part of the Highway washed away[.] Being repaired now—great flights of snipe and doves— some tarpon still being caught.

PUL, ALS

1 In a letter to Fitzgerald of 30 October 1929, Perkins suggested that "the only obstacle to a really big sale [*of* FTA] is that which may come from the collapse of the market,—what effect that will have nobody can tell" (Kuehl and Bryer, 157).

2 Scribner's publicized *FTA* aggressively, running various ads in every weekly *New York Times Book Review*, among other venues, for months following its publication, praising it as a "novel of love in war" and calling its dialogue "masterly in reproductive realism."

3 In his 30 November response Perkins wrote that he had sent a check for $25 to Peirce and apologized for the misunderstanding (PUL). As a private organization, the Harvard Club, founded in 1865 and located on West 44th Street in New York City, was not subject to the 1919 Volstead Act, which prohibited the sale of alcohol in the United States. Peirce had graduated from Harvard in 1909.

4 At the Battle of Caporetto (24 October 1917–c. 12 November 1917) Austro-Hungarian and German forces quickly advanced from the Tagliamento River in eastern Italy as far west as the Piave River, inflicting heavy losses. French general Ferdinand Foch engineered the defensive strategy that stopped the Italian retreat and kept Italy from defeat. Foch was subsequently appointed Supreme Commander of the Allied forces from 14 April 1918 until the end of the war. In *FTA*, Frederic Henry, suspected of deserting the Italian army during the retreat, escapes summary execution by jumping into the Tagliamento. On 8 July 1918, EH had been wounded at Fossalta, on the Piave.

5 Arnold Bennett (1867–1931), English critic and novelist, praised *FTA* in his review in the 14 November 1929 *Evening Standard*: "The book is hard, almost metallic, glittering, blinding by the reflections of its bright surface, utterly free of any sentimentality. But imbued through and through with genuine sentiment" (quoted in Jeffrey Meyers, *Hemingway: The Critical Heritage* [London, Boston: Routledge & Kegan Paul, 1982], 130–31).

To Grace Hall Hemingway, 19 November [1929]

Nov. 19

Dear Mother:—

I'm so sorry to hear Sunny is ill— Hope she is better now and getting all right. Give her our best and tell her we hope she is on the way to being fine.

Am engaged in trying to fix up a trust fund of some sort so that you will receive a regular amt. each month no matter what may happen to me. This will probably not start working until April. So in the meantime if I seem to be tight it is because I am saving all money toward that purpose— I let you know now so you will not worry— You have no cause to worry from now on— So dont do any—

Thanks for the clippings and news about the book— Glad it is going— Have been to Berlin on business and just got back— All well here but will be glad to get to Key West— Thank you for the invitation but we wont be able to be at Oak Park for Xmas.[1]

Might possibly get to Piggott or Key West late in Dec. but cant make plans until we know about leaving here.

Enclose check for Dec. Wd send more but am putting every cent I have in this trust fund[.] So make out the best you can knowing everything will be set in a few months—

Best to all—

Ernie

Glad to have such good news of Les—[2]

IndU, ALS; postmark: PARIS 110 / R. DE RENNES, [*illegible*]

1   With her letter of 25 October 1929, Grace enclosed a positive review of *FTA* clipped from the Chicago theater magazine *The Playgoer*. She wrote, "By now you must be thrilled with the news of the big splash your book has made. It's headed the best sellers every week since its publication—and the critics are vieing with each other to do you the greatest honors . . . I hope you received the other press notices I sent you" (JFK). In a note on the clipping, Grace had offered "my big room" to EH, Pauline, and Patrick, promising to make them "quite comfortable" if they would come for Christmas.
2   Grace had written that Leicester was playing violin in his high school orchestra, practicing target shooting, and learning to ride a surfboard in Hawaii.

To Madelaine Hemingway, 19 November [1929]

Nov. 19

Dear Sun:

We're all awfully sorry to hear you're sick but hope by now you are much better. Hope the milk diet etc will fix you up. Everyone here sends you their sympathy—[1]

No news— Patrick talks a little now— Everyone well. I try to write but am interrupted all the time by business. Some talk of making A Farewell T.A into both play and movie— Both Brady and Al Woods want to stage it— Richard Barthelmess would like to be the noble hero. All talk and no cash so far. Its going well they say.[2] Thanks for the dope on O.P. and Chicago selling.[3]

Was up in Berlin last week on a business trip— We'll be glad to get to Key West and settle down to work and out door life. Got hurt this summer in Spain and havent been able to take any exercise but am about Jake now.[4]

Book out in England with big reviews.[5] Hope it goes— They're going to serialize it in Germany—

I sound like a real Hemingway reeling off all this accomplishment data[.] But only write it for lack of legitimate news—

Only been to the races once this fall—Longchamp. Wasnt so hot— Give my love to Beef— If they make a movie of the book you must attend it and give me your expert opinion—

I suppose they will have the girl Catherine give birth to the American flag at the end— And change the title to

Star Spangle Whoopie.

Well they say we live through it all— No one seems to know why—

Hope you're much better— It's awfully hard luck to be laid up like that. Hope you're getting O.K.

Your Bro.

Steen

PSU, ALS

1 In her 30 October 1929 letter to EH and Pauline, Sunny wrote that she was being "absolutely faithful to the diet" and getting better (JFK). Grace reported in her 25 October letter (JFK) that Sunny's peptic ulcer was being treated by the "Sippy diet," developed by the American physician Bertram Welton Sippy (1866–1924) and first published in the *Journal of the American Medical Association* in 1915. The antacid diet consisted of milk and cream ingested hourly and powders taken every half hour.
2 William A. Brady had produced the Broadway run of *The Great Gatsby* in 1926. Albert Herman "Al" Woods (1870–1951), Hungarian American producer and theater owner, produced several major stage plays through the 1920s and 1930s. Richard Barthelmess (1895–1963), American stage and film actor who won an Academy Award in 1928. Woods would produce the 1930 stage production of *FTA* without Barthelmess.
3 Sunny had written that *FTA* "heads the best sellers everytime so far in the Trib," and that a saleswoman in the newly opened Oak Park branch of the Chicago-based Marshall Field and Company department store had told her it was outselling all other novels.
4 "Jake," slang for "fine" or "O.K."

5 *FTA* was described in the London newspapers as "glittering" (*Evening Standard*, 14 November 1929, 5); as written by a "very powerful talent" (*Times*, 15 November 1929, 20); and as a "very great" book (*Spectator*, 16 November 1929, 727). Gerald Gould wrote, "I have read few books more terrible; but the beauty survives" (*Observer*, 17 November 1929, 8).

To Charles Thompson, [19 November 1929]

[*Excerpt as published in Christie's catalog:*]

" . . . No news yet about when we leave [to return to America]. Trying to get this apt. [his second wife Pauline's place on the rue Férou] settled up. Have to do that and know where we stand before we can leave . . . Wire from Max [Perkins] says that the book has sold 46,000 copies up to last Friday, the 15th— When it gets past 50,000 copies I'll start to make money. Im going to put $20,000 in a trust fund and Uncle Gus [Pfeiffer, *Pauline's uncle*] is going to put $30,000 to make a trust fund for my mother. Then won't have to worry about that. But it starts us off poor again— Still it is damned good to have it settled . . . Haven't done any shooting—or hardly any exercise all fall—got hurt in the gut down in Spain and have been waiting for it to heal thoroly [*sic*] so will be able to pull properly on tarpon. But have a good alibi now for not lifting any turtles . . ." [*Hemingway spends the next two pages primarily discussing fishing gear he wishes to give Uncle Gus as a Christmas present.*] ". . . When I'll feel good is when we're out in the boat with a lot of those stuffed eggs— Thanks so much for looking after the Xmas business . . . "

Christie's catalog, New York, 9 June 1999, Lot 114, ALS

According to the Christie's catalog description, EH wrote this four-page letter "in brown ink on tan paper creased from folding, two small holes with loss of a few letters." Written in Paris and dated 19 November, the letter is signed "Ernest."

To Maxwell Perkins, 20 November [1929]

November 20

Dear Max:—

Two letters from you Nov. 12–14 this morning. The Bremen is what brings us in closest touch— A hell of a fine fast boat—[1] I'm glad to know Bridges is going—unless it means the Poor house or some hard luck—[2]

Altho I have to thank his complete ignorance of this world for the publication of A Farewell in the Magazine You— were worried about it— But Bridges—being as dumb in one direction as he was in the other about 50 Grand—put it in— So the dumb have their uses. Not that it wasnt publishable— But it took a courage to do it that he replaced with ignorance— Still that's the most prevalent form of courage at that.[3]

About the translations— Thanks for keeping me informed— Give me the information on their propositions as they send them in—or ask them to write me care of The Guaranty—here— That's best. Translation has been signed for Germany and Sweden.[4]

Thank you for sending the checks to Hadley—[5]

About the royalty— You know I am not trying to Shylock—[6] But the contract was the same as for The Sun— There was no provision made for a big sale— I did not even sign it until after I had the proofs— Then only so there would be something of record to protect you in case anything happened to me—

The Sun was a first novel with a First printing of, I believe, 5,000—

In spite of the book club competition etc. This book had the publicity of The Sun, Men Without etc to help it and the first printing was 30,000 instead of 5,000—

I knew that our basis being what it is—one of mutual trust—you would do whatever is usual and just when this came up— (if we would have discussed this contract a provision would have been put in for sales above certain figures)

I've not quoted or tried to bother you with Royalty% offers from other publishers— Have no intention of trying to bid up— It was only when Scott asked me what my arrangements were for a big sale that I mentioned it to you—not quoting an outside elevated percentage but one I knew to be in existance. In the ordinary course I would have waited for you to mention it—

(This paper is too small to write on— They are doing some fumigating to the house and am turned out)[7]

Your suggestion that we wait and talk it over after the 6 mos. is excellent except for one thing— If Scribner's decide now that after certain figures the royalty advances in proportion then we both feel we are making a certain amount— While if we wait 6 months the royalty always being considered 15% then Scribner's when another arrangement is made feel they are giveing up a certain sum they would otherwise have had— I'd rather feel we were both earning it as we went along.[8]

You know we have no fights about money. The only fundamental disagreement was about the words— I <u>knew</u> certain ones could be published because I saw them in proof and they were all right— They shocked no one— I <u>had</u> to have them— It meant everything to the integrity of the book.

I was prepared with the book written and published intact as I wrote it to accept no advance— I didnt ask for one. Everyone to whom I had obligations could take their chances along with me— If the book was suppressed I knew the suppression would not last and that it would be as well and better for all concerned in the end. I wrote about how I felt and how serious the matter was to me— That is our business, yours and mine, and I have talked to no one outside about it. But when I was over-ruled and knew that it was finally a commercial proposition (as of course it is and rightly so to you because you have the responsibility of Scribner's interests) and it was cut so it would be able to sell— I've had no interest in it as a <u>book</u> since. It's something to sell— Some man in town and Country has written that I am the one who made Joyce's integrity saleable and palatable—[9] All right—with the words in they would see whether I was writing to sell or not— But now that I've lost my integrity on it let it sell By God and fix up my mother and the rest of them.

About the book of stories— You must have told me about it and I not paid any attention— I let O'Brien have The Undefeated because of an obligation I had to him— (He dedicated the book to me and broke his rules to publish a story that had never been published in a magazine. or rather <u>did</u> we let him have it? As I recall we refused to let him have it because it was too much a part of the book and made him take The Killers instead— But I may be wrong— He may have published it the year before and wanted Fifty Grand— Anyway we turned him down on something that year and made him take the Killers—[10]

Anyhow the obligation is gone because I read he has a book in which I confide to him on a lonely mt. top that I was a pure young man until the machines in the war turned me against everything etc. Mike Strater and I once spent an evening with him in a monastery above Rapallo—[11] I remember that Mike and I both drank several pitchers of wine— Am capable when tight of telling him I was a pure young girl of course and used to write under the name of Precious Bane[12] but I dont think he shd put such assertions in a serious book— I hope I was a pure young boy once—even if my mother swears I never was—but dont see what that proves—

I'm sorry the book of Stories was published because I dont think I'd have given consent if I'd known—as that story is a big part of Men Without—and at 2 ¢—if it sells only 2,000 copies—it will do at least $40^{00} harm.

Anyway I was damned glad to hear from you— I get so many cables about and hear so many reports of trouble between us that I think sometimes there must be something to it and that you must be sore at me about something. The most purely inventive gossips I know are Bromfield and McAlmon— with both of them in N.Y. any story may start. Never worry about anything you dont hear from me—I'll try to worry you enough personally.

Hope everything goes well with you ~~personally~~ and your family— I'll make some hell of a fuss about something once we're in America so you will <u>have</u> to come to Key West and then once you are there we will never mention any of all this damned business.

Yours always

Ernest

I am fixing up a trust fund for my mother— It's not a problem. Have 30,000 promised from an outside source (<u>This confidential</u>) [*EH insertion*: It's <u>not</u> a publisher.] Will need to call on you for 20,000 against royalties due put in that <u>at that time</u> when the trust is made sometime after the first of the year— (If I get cash from movies in meantime of course will not call on you.) Then the trust will start paying off in April and I will have that off my hands. I wish there was someway I didnt have to pay income tax on that 20,000—there is no money in having to borrow money to pay income tax on money you never see! If you think of any way let me know.
P.S.

On income tax I only get credit for 2 dependents because that is all I have under the one roof— In reality I have 9 dependents! So if you know or hear of any way I can make or receive such a payment and not be liable for tax it will be good— Perhaps it could be sent direct to lawyer making trust and I would simply not declare it and if queried explain it— In the meantime want to take no more money this year if possible as it is all gone—(paid out) and I'll have to borrow to pay tax as it is!

Once this is fixed up am all set though—

PUL, ALS; letterhead: Writing Room / Guaranty Trust Company of New York / 4 Place de la Concorde / Paris

1   The German-built *Bremen* (1929–1941) had become the fastest transatlantic passenger liner at her maiden crossing that summer, breaking the British *Mauretania*'s twenty-year record. Sailing from Cherbourg to New York on 12 July, the *Bremen* made the journey in 4 days, 17 hours and 42 minutes.

2   Robert Bridges would officially resign his editorship of *Scribner's Magazine* in 1930 and become a literary advisor for the firm.

3   In 1926 Bridges had judged "An Alpine Idyll" as "too terrible" for publication in *Scribner's Magazine* and "Fifty Grand" as too long unless it were cut by 1,500 words, which EH was unwilling to do.

4   In his 14 November letter, Perkins enclosed a "Memorandum concerning translations" of *FTA* into German, Spanish, Swedish, and Italian (PUL). *FTA* would be translated into German by Annemarie Horschitz (*In einem andern Land*; Berlin: Rowohlt, 1930) and into Swedish by Louis Renner (*Farväl till Vapnen*; Stockholm: Bonnier, 1932).

5   In his 12 November letter, Perkins said he had sent the checks the day before (PUL).

6   Shylock, the Jewish usurer in Shakespeare's *The Merchant of Venice*.

7   The letter is written on ten sheets of tan $5^1/_2 \times 8\ ^1/_4$-inch letterhead stationery from the Writing Room of EH's bank.

8   In his 12 November letter, Perkins advised EH to accept the contract offering royalties of 15%, noting that Scribner's would generate a financial report six months after publication to evaluate the book's success, and "if you thought we ought, we could then revise the terms of the contract retroactively."

9   Reviewing *FTA* in the 1 November 1929 *Town & Country*, William Curtis wrote: "There is the difference between the work of Mr. Joyce and the work of Mr. Hemingway that there is between pure and applied science. Mr. Joyce is the professor in his laboratory, dealing with abstract principles, concerned only with his thesis . . . Mr. Hemingway is a salesman— manufacturing for the market" (86).

10 The Scribner's anthology *Present-Day American Stories* (1929) included EH's "The Undefeated." The story had appeared in the 1926 volume of *The Best Short Stories* series, edited by Edward J. O'Brien (1890–1941). O'Brien had included EH's previously unpublished "My Old Man" in the *Best Short Stories of 1923* (Boston: Small, Maynard, 1924) and dedicated that volume to EH, misspelling his name as "Hemenway." "The Killers" appeared in *Best Short Stories of 1927* (New York: Dodd, Mead, 1927). O'Brien had requested "Fifty Grand" for the 1927 volume but EH and Perkins had refused,

explaining that the story made up a significant portion of *MWW* (published October 1927) and should appear for the first time there.

11 In *The Dance of the Machines: The American Short Story and the Industrial Age* (New York: Macaulay, 1929), O'Brien discussed the "sense of loss" experienced by writers immersed in twentieth-century "American machine civilization" (236), recalling that "Some years ago on top of an Italian mountain [EH] told me some of his war experiences. He went into the war a pious boy. Then he witnessed the spiritual destructiveness of machinery" (240–41). The meeting would have occurred in February or early March 1923, when EH and Hadley were in Rapallo at the same time as Strater and O'Brien, who was staying at Montallegro, above Rapallo. In a letter of 2 May [1924], EH reminded O'Brien of their meeting "one night at the pub up on Montallegro" (*Letters* vol. 2, 117).

12 *Precious Bane* (London: Cape, 1924), bestselling novel by English author Mary Webb (1881–1927), is retrospectively narrated by Prudence Sarn, whose bane, a "harelip," keeps vanity and ambition at bay so that she develops into a modest and generous character. Her virtue is rewarded with marriage to the man she loves.

To Lawrence Drake, 21 November [1929]

Nov. 21

c/o

Guaranty Trust Co of NY.

4 Place de la Concorde

Paris—

Dear Mr. Drake:

Thanks ever so much for your letter and for the book— I havent read it yet—have been away in Berlin—but look <u>forward</u> to it very much. We were only in N.Y. a few days—when there stay at Brevoort—[1]

I hope the hell the book is as good as you say—if it is we ought to have a big time and celebrate—[2] But the only trouble is you have to die and rot to find out and the worms have a hell of a time to tell you—

Anyway I hope we meet again soon—[3] If you come back here you can always get hold of me through the Guaranty— Thanks again for the book and every sort of luck with it

Yrs always

Ernest Hemingway.

Stanford, ALS

1 Drake had written to EH in care of Scribner's in October 1929, saying he had asked his publishers to send EH a copy of his first novel, *Don't Call Me Clever* (New York: Simon &

Schuster, 1929) (JFK). The Brevoort Hotel, built in 1845 on Fifth Avenue between East 8th and 9th Streets in Greenwich Village, catered to an international clientele. Its café was frequented by artists, actors, and such literary figures as Mark Twain, Edna St. Vincent Millay, and Eugene O'Neill.

2 Drake wrote that in *FTA*, EH had "laid the foundation of an historically as well as psychologically sound conception of modernism—for the first time, I would say, in any literature."

3 Drake reminded EH that they had met "now and then on the terrace of the Dome, in Titus's book shop, and here and there about Paris."

To F. Scott Fitzgerald, [c. 24 November 1929]

Dear Scott:—

Saw Gertrude Stein the other evening and she asked about you. She claims you are the one of all us guys with the most talent etc. and wants to see you again. Anyway she has written me a note asking me to ask you or youse if you would come around Wed. Eve. to her place—after 8.30 or so I fancy—Tate or Tates too—a merchant named Bernard Fay or Bernard Fairy to be there too.[1]

Am going—Tate too—would you or youse like to call by here before 8.30 or then—if not Gertrude's address is

27 rue du Fleurus— But if you came we might go together—

By the way

Gallipoli Memories by Compton Mackenzie (yr. old school fellow) is damned good and the most amusing war book I've read since Repington— wouldnt wonder if it wd go down with G. Moore's Hails and Farewells—[2]

I'll be glad to buy it for you— There are to be 4 more volumnes which is best news I've had in a long time—[3]

Yrs always affect—

Ernest.

[On verso in a different color ink:]

No new news from Max— What about yr. suit against McCalls?[4]

PUL, ALS

Although Baker dates this letter [c. 22 or 29 October 1929] (*SL*, 308), contextual evidence suggests it was written later. This letter postdates Fitzgerald's receipt of the news that *McCall's* had rejected his article "Girls Believe in Girls" (conveyed in a 12 November 1929 letter from his agent, Harold Ober) and Fitzgerald's instructions to Ober to bring suit against the magazine if necessary (in Fitzgerald's 20 November cable and 23 November letter to Ober). As EH was aware of Fitzgerald's threatened suit at the time he was conveying Stein's invitation for "Wed. Eve.," the most likely date for the forthcoming meeting at Stein's is Wednesday, 27 November, as Mellow argues (*Invented Lives*, 351, 534), and not the earlier dates of [c. 22 or 29 October 1929] conjectured by Baker or "October," suggested by Bruccoli (*Fitz–Hem*, 139).

1 EH had seen little of his early mentor Gertrude Stein (1874–1946) since their friendship cooled in the fall of 1925 after she declined to review *IOT*. Allen Tate and his wife, Caroline Gordon, were then living in Paris. Bernard Faÿ (1893–1978), French historian, translator, and a close friend of Stein's, was openly gay.

2 *Gallipoli Memories* (London: Cassell, 1929), by Edward Montague Compton Mackenzie (1883–1972), Scottish writer and political activist who had served in the Royal Marines and the British Secret Intelligence Service (1915–1917). Fitzgerald acknowledged that his own first novel, *This Side of Paradise* (1920), was influenced by Mackenzie's *Sinister Street* (1913–14), though "much more in intention than in literal fact" (26 February 1921, in Andrew Turnbull, ed., *The Letters of F. Scott Fitzgerald* [New York: Scribner's, 1963], 468). Fitzgerald's protagonist, Amory Blaine, has read *Sinister Street*, and Fitzgerald's setting, Princeton University, recalls McKenzie's Oxford. Charles à Court Repington (1858–1925), British career military officer and writer, author of the two-volume work *The First World War 1914–1918: Personal Experiences* (Boston: Houghton Mifflin, 1920). George Moore's trilogy *Hail and Farewell!* (*Ave*, 1911; *Salve*, 1912; and *Vale*, 1914) was published in a two-volume edition in the United States in 1925 (New York: Appleton-Century-Crofts). EH would later name *Hail and Farewell!* among the books necessary for a writer to have read ("Monologue to the Maestro: A High Seas Letter," *Esquire*, October 1935; *BL*, 218).

3 Mackenzie's second volume, *First Athenian Memories*, would be published in 1931. The third volume, *Greek Memories* (1932), would be banned and Mackenzie charged with breaching the Official Secrets Act; a sanitized version would be published in 1938. *Aegean Memories*, the final volume of his WWI memoirs, would be published in 1940.

4 After commissioning Fitzgerald to write a story about "the present day status of the flapper," Otis L. Wiese, editor of *McCall's* magazine, rejected his submission, "Girls Believe in Girls." On 20 November 1929 Fitzgerald wired his agent, Harold Ober, "MCCALLS CONDUCT PREPOSTEROUS BRING SUIT IF NECESSARY," writing him a follow-up letter dated 23 November and cabling again on 24 November. Ober advised against such a suit, however, and the article was sold to *Liberty Magazine* for $1,500, appearing in the 8 February 1930 issue (Bruccoli *As Ever*, 140, 153–63).

To George Slocombe, 26 November [1929]

Nov. 26

Dear George:—

It would be impertinent of me to think that anything I might write would be of any use to your book. I've seen a full page review of it in the Times and know it is well away—as it deserves to be. It is past the point where anything

I might write about it would affect it one way or another. You know I'm no critic anyway and what I might write would not mean a damned thing to anyone—[1]

So I'm returning your ~~courtesy~~ Compliment by sending a copy of my last one— I'll trade you even—book for book—anytime we write them and be sure I'm getting the best of it.

Yours always—

Ernest—

Mine has no illustrations so to even up I'll send you my next one too to catch up.

(Was in Berlin or would have answered sooner.)

PUL, ALS

1 British journalist Slocombe, whom EH had met in 1922 while both men were working as foreign correspondents, had just published *Paris in Profile* (Boston: Houghton Mifflin, 1929), an illustrated guidebook that had been praised in the *New York Times Book Review* of 27 October 1929. In a letter of 29 November [1929], Slocombe would respond, "You are much too modest about yourself as a critic. Possibly you are right. But it's your <u>name</u> my publishers want to put at the end of a laudatory line or two in their Christmas advertising . . . Do it if you can!" (JFK).

To F. Scott Fitzgerald, [c. 28 November 1929]

Friday Morning

Dear Scott

Your note just came and am utilizing a good hangover to answer it.

I was not annoyed at anything you said (you surely know by now, I've written it often enough, how much I admire your work.) I was only annoyed at your refusal to accept the sincere compliment G. Stein was making to you and instead try and twist it into a slighting remark. She was praising her head off about you to me when you came up[.] She started to repeat it and then at the end of the praise to spare you blushes and not be rude to me she said that our flames (sic) were maybe <u>not</u> the same— Then you brood on that—

It is O.K. to not accept the compliments if you dont wish (most compliments are horseshit) but there is no need for me to have to re-iterate that they were compliments not slights. I cross myself and swear to God that Gertrude Stein has <u>never</u> last night or any other time said anything to me about you but the highest praise. That is absolutely true. The fact that you do not value or accept it does not make it any less sincere

As for comparison of our writings she was doing nothing of the kind— only saying that you had a hell of a roaring furnace of talent and I had a small one—implying I had to work a damn sight harder for results obtained— Then to avoid praising you to your face and pooping on me she said she wasnt saying the flame was of the same quality. If you would have pressed her she would have told you to a direct question that she believes yours a better quality than mine.

Naturally I do not agree with that—any more than you would— Any comparison of such a non existant thing as hypothetical "flames" being pure horseshit—and any comparison between you and me being tripe too— We started along entirely separate lines—would never have met except by accident and as writers have nothing in common except the desire to write well— So why make comparisons and talk about superiority— If you have to have feelings of superiority [*EH insertion*: to me] well and good as long as I do not have to have feelings of either superiority or inferiority— [*EH insertion*: to you.] There can be no such thing between serious writers— They are all in the same boat— Competition within that boat—which is headed toward death—is as silly as deck sports are— The only competition is the original one of making the boat and that all takes place inside yourself— You're on the boat but you're getting touchy because you havent finished your novel—that's all— I understand it and you could be a hell of a lot more touchy and I wouldn't mind.

This is all bloody rot to write in bed with a bad stomach and if you succeed in finding any slurs slights depreciations or insults in it the morning has been wasted (It's wasted anyway) Gertrude wanted to organize a hare and tortoise race and picked me to tortoise and you to hare and naturally, like a modest man and a classicist, you wanted to be the tortoise— All right Tortoise all you want— It's all tripe anyway—

I like to have Gertrude bawl me out because it keeps one opinion of oneself down—way down— She liked the book very much, she said— But what I wanted to hear about was what she didnt like and why— She thinks the parts that fail are where I remember visually rather than make up— That was nothing very new— I expected to hear it was all tripe— Would prefer to hear that because it is such a swell spur to work.

Anyway here is page 4—will enclose Max's letter—

I'm damn sorry Bromfield started that rumor but it cant hurt Scribners when I nail it by staying with them—[1] I'd be glad to write him a letter he could publish if he wanted—

Look what tripe everything is— In plain Talk I learned to write from you— In Town and Country from Joyce—in Chic Trib from Gertrude—[2] not yet reported the authorities on Dos Passos, Pound, Homer, McAlmon, Aldous Huxley and E.E. Cummings—

Then you think I shouldnt worry when some one says I've no vitality— I dont worry— Who has vitality in Paris?— People dont write with vitality—they write with their heads— When I'm in perfect shape dont feel like writing—feel too good! G.S. never went with us to Schruns or Key West or Wyoming or any place where you get in shape— If she's never seen me in shape why worry? When they bawl you out ride with the punches—

Anyway will write no more of this—

I'm sorry you worried—you weren't unpleasant—

Yours always affectionately

Ernest

PUL, ALS

Although Baker dates this letter [c. 24 or 31 October 1929] (*SL*, 309–11), the conjectured date of [28 November 1929] is based on the most likely date for the visit to Gertrude Stein being Wednesday, 27 November. EH's reference to a conversation with Stein "last night" suggests that he may be writing on Thursday, 28 November, rather than "Friday," as he dates the letter.

1 EH likely enclosed Perkins's letter of 15 October 1929, a carbon copy of which survives in the Scribner's Archive at PUL. Perkins had thanked EH for denying the rumor that EH might leave his publisher (which Perkins called "the Bromfield matter") and said that although Scribner's would try to match other offers for his next book, EH was free to accept any offer he liked. Perkins wrote, "I told Scott the same thing once and refused to tie him up with options on his 'next ten books.'"

2 *Plain Talk* (1927–1938), a monthly magazine founded by American journalist and critic G. D. (Godfrey Dell) Eaton (1894–1930). In the 1 December 1929 issue, the magazine's

associate editor, Burton Rascoe (1892–1957), who as a regular columnist for the *New York Herald Tribune* had reviewed EH's first two books in 1924, drew parallels between *The Great Gatsby* and *SAR*. He asserted, "It was F. Scott Fitzgerald, I think, who made Hemingway an artistic and commercial success, merely by example." Rascoe speculated that after reading *The Great Gatsby*, EH "sat down to write a lyrical novel himself, celebrating a not quite realizable love in an atmosphere of lust and dissipation" ("The Court of Books," 782). William Curtis, reviewing *FTA* in the 1 November 1929 *Town & Country*, wrote that EH "has adroitly transmuted the technique of James Joyce to the tempo of the American general reader" and that without *Ulysses*, *FTA* "would not have been" (quoted in Stephens, 90–91). In the *Chicago Daily Tribune*, Fanny Butcher called EH the "direct blossoming of Gertrude Stein" ("Here Is Genius, Critic Declares of Hemingway," 28 September 1929, 11).

To Maxwell Perkins, 30 November [1929]

Nov ~~29~~ 30
Saturday anyway—

Dear Max:—

It is two weeks since I wrote you about the ads and all I can say is I am damned ashamed of myself— Will you apologize to Meyer for me even having made any such damn fool suggestions about the First Choice of Book borrower's— You do the advertising splendidly and even if you didnt it's none of my business.[1]

Thought I might hear from you in the mail that came on Leviathan but didn't[2] Scott had a letter. He said the reports of my being dis satisfied hurt Scribner's— But I dont know what I can do to nail them except deny them to everyone who has mentioned them to me and to stay with you. After all that is the most lasting proof. Rumors are very short { lived / lifed but me staying on Scribner's list as long as you stay in the Company should be of some effect.

But would it do any good for me to write you a denial of all these canards that you could use in the publicity notes you send out? I think it might have enough news value due to the other stuff so they would print it—

The book is starting to go in England— Long reviews in the Times, New Statesman, Observer, all the dailies— Cape sent them to me— If you want them I'll send them over—[3]

I might try and write something now for you to use possibly—will try on another sheet— (Have written the letter and enclose it) You may publish it in its entirety— If what I say about Scribners doesnt suit will make it stronger or weaker as you like

Best to you always

Ernest

It may be better to say nothing about The Bookman— It's all over now— let me know what you think before releasing that—BookMan stuff— . In fact—dont use it—[4]

PUL, ALS

1 See EH to Perkins, 19 November [1929].
2 Originally a German steamer named the *Vaterland*, the ship was launched in 1914, captured by American forces in 1917, used as a U.S. Navy transport during the war, and converted for passenger service for the United States Lines in 1923.
3 Reviews of *FTA* had appeared in close succession in the London papers: *Evening Standard* (14 November 1929); *The Times* (15 November 1929); *Spectator* (16 November 1929); *Observer* (17 November 1929); *Times Literary Supplement* (28 November 1929); and *New Statesman* (30 November 1929).
4 EH's postscript, added in black ink to this penciled letter, refers to the following letter to Perkins, also dated 30 November and enclosed with this one. In it EH attacked Robert Herrick's negative review of *FTA* ("What is Dirt?," *Bookman*, November 1929, 258–62).

To Maxwell Perkins, 30 November [1929]

Paris

November 30

Dear Max—

Have read, heard and received cables about a report that I was going to leave Scribners. You offered to publish what I was writing before any one else did. It was only by luck that I was ~~out of the country~~ in Austria and so did not get your letter which was waiting in Paris and accepted the cabled offer of another ~~publisher~~ firm to publish my first book. You published ~~The Torrents of Spring~~ a book which was refused by this first publisher. You published The Sun Also intact with the exception of one word which you have now published in this last book.[1] You have been constantly loyal and you have been wholly admirable. If we have fought over you cutting words out of this last book you at least left blanks wherever you cut and it has been our own

172

fight ~~(it hasn't been a fight anyway but only a~~ and no outsider is going to profit by it. I have absolutely no intention of leaving Scribners and I hope to live long enough so you may publish my collected works if my kidneys hold out and I have luck enough to write any works worth collecting.

Have read an article in the Bookman by a citizen who calls me a swine and one thing and another, to which opinion he is of course perfectly entitled, but what I look forward to is spanking in the physical sense, the editor of the Bookman, who is young enough to know better, for publishing a review of a book written by a reviewer who is also a fellow novelist and who admits having read only a third of the way through the book he is reviewing and then advocates its suppression.[2] Reviewers on a monthly at least should be paid for reading the whole book or not at all. However we must not ask for too much and I will certainly not spank the editor of The Bookman unless he seems in physical condition to support it. In any event the projected spanking is promised entirely in the nature of a moral correction and the physical side will be minimized as much as possible.[3]

Speaking of this book, ~~which I am sorry to do again,~~ will you repeat again that it is fiction, that I lay no claim even to have been in Italy, that I would never attempt to judge or picture Italy or Italians as such, but that I have only taken advantage of the tradition by which writers from the earliest times have laid the scenes of their books in that country.

Yours always
Ernest Hemingway.

PUL, ALS

EH enclosed this letter in the preceding letter to Perkins of the same date.

1 On 25 February 1925, EH received cables from Donald Ogden Stewart and Harold Loeb reporting that *In Our Time* (1925) had been accepted by New York publishers Boni & Liveright. EH had already signed a contract giving them an option on his second book when a letter from Perkins expressing interest in his work reached him in Austria during a ski vacation. When Boni & Liveright rejected EH's novel *TOS*, a parody of *Dark Laughter* (1926) by Sherwood Anderson, one of the firm's bestselling authors, EH was free to move to Scribner's, which published *TOS* in May 1926 and *SAR* in October 1926. Unwilling to print the word "balls," Scribner's edited Mike Campbell's statement to Pedro Romero to read, "Tell him that bulls have no horns" (Chapter 16), prompting EH to remark as he returned the proofs, "The bulls now without appendages" (*Letters* vol. 3, 107). In Chapter 21 of *FTA* the British major says of the war, "It was all balls."

2 The author of "What is Dirt?," which appeared in the November 1929 issue of *Bookman*, was Robert Herrick (1863–1938), American novelist and former University of Chicago professor of English and rhetoric. Although Herrick admitted he did not "stay with the story past the Milan episodes," he nonetheless determined that "no great loss to anybody would result if *A Farewell to Arms* had been suppressed" (261–62). Seward Collins (1899–1952), co-owner of the *Bookman*, was its editor from 1928 to 1933.

3 The literary monthly the *Bookman* (published 1895–1933) provided a forum for the New Humanists, "a group of conservative critics calling for a return to moral values and for decorum in literature" (John Raeburn, *Fame Became of Him: Hemingway as Public Writer* [Bloomington: Indiana University Press, 1984], 34). EH's animosity toward the New Humanism would surface in *DIA* (Chapter 12) and in "A Natural History of the Dead" (*WTN*).

To Louise Lafitte, 30 November [1929]

Nov. 30

Dear Miss Lafitte:—

We are leaving for Cuba in a couple of weeks and I am afraid—as we will be travelling—that it would be too hard to reach me surely with a letter—let alone a Mss.[1] Not having seen the Mss. I cannot advise you where to send it but Scribner's—5th Ave and 48th—Boni and Liveright—whose address you will have to look up and Coward—McCann are all publishers who will give it a reading.

If you do not personally want to change anything in your novel stick with it— Money can only be made writing with the greatest luck— For my book to sell is as though I had won a grand prize in a lottery— But good writing will always be published eventually—and we all have to have some other job to live on in the meantime—

If you want to make a living writing I would say it was easier to make it any other way. If you want to write the only thing is to write and no one can help you—

JFK, AL

This letter, which survives among EH's papers at JFK, is unsigned and probably unsent.

1 In a letter of 7 October 1929, Lafitte asked if EH would consider reading and criticizing her "first, original novel," titled "LEAH." "I personally would not have a syllable changed in it," she wrote, but it had been repeatedly rejected by publishers, and she lamented that her "career and life-work are in ashes" (JFK). Lafitte is not known to have published a novel.

To Struthers Burt, 30 November [1929]

Dear Burt—

Thank you ever so much for writing. I cannot tell you how pleased I am that you liked the book— Nor how I envy you being out in Jackson Hole now—[1] We head for Havana and the Florida Keys in a month and I hope to be out in Wyo. this summer— You probably had the same drought in Italy we had in Spain— Even Galicia dried up—and the streams along with it— Never worked so hard for so few trout— Wyoming will seem pretty wonderful again— Its a damned wonderful place anyway—

Please give our best greetings to Mrs. Burt and thank you again for writing.[2]

Yours always

Ernest Hemingway.

4 Place de la Concorde

November 30 Paris

Penn, ALS

1 Burt, a fellow Scribner's author, had received an advance copy of *FTA* (which he mis-identified as "Call To Arms") from Perkins, and wrote EH from the BAR B C Ranch, which he owned and operated near Jackson Hole, Wyoming, to praise it. The novel's "background was especially poignant" for him since he had spent the summer at Bellagio in northern Italy (10 October 1929, JFK).
2 American writer Katharine Newlin Burt (1882–1977), married to Struthers Burt since 1912, had published nine books of fiction to date, occasionally using the pen name Rebecca Scarlett.

To Archibald MacLeish, 1 December 1929

4 Place de la Concorde

Paris

Dec 1 1929

Dear Archie:

When I got your letter I started right in to work on the thing— Planned to wire you when I was ½ through— However, all the stuff by the citizen you sent was wrong and so I decided maybe they wouldnt want the piece after all—

Who it is that makes the money is the bull fighters— In only ½ doz places in Spain do the promoters make money— So there is no sense me trying to make a great romance of commerce story— It's much nearer a racket— But I have sent to Spain for the figures I didnt have— Govt taxes etc and if they want I can do a hell of a good article on bull fighting as an $\left\{\begin{array}{l}\text{industry}\\\text{business}\end{array}\right\}$, all the aspects you named and the inside stuff all along the line with incidents, statistics, wages, prices of everything etc.[1]

But I warn you that who makes the money is the matadors and of those only the first 6 or 8—as it is in boxing. Rickard never made much compared to Tunney and Dempsey in boxing.[2] But the bull story is very interesting and millions of dollars change hands. However the bull fighters are organized so they make it. They earn it too.

If the article was over 5,000—between there and 6—I would ask $2,500.$\underline{^{00}}$ That is the price I get for a story of that length and I'll have to work just as hard and longer. You know I cant pad nor fake and anything longer than that would be a regular book for me.

If they dont want it it's all right—

Yours always—

Pappy

[*On new page, numbered 3*:]

Dear Archy:

Private letter to you. You know how I hate to pull money terms etc. with you but that is honest to Christ what Colliers offer me for stories that length—$2500—or $750 for 1000 to 1200 words— Its sounds crazy but it's true—[3] Hearst's offer $2000 a story for all stories over 2500 words— I have to keep the price up because thats how they judge you— Although I never give them any stories— I would write the article for $2000.$\underline{^{00}}$ I dont know how much they have to pay and with market slumped and all that may seem ridiculous— I would write it for you for nothing. When you get this wire me what they will pay.

The bad aspect is I pee away stuff I've always collected for my book—[4] I cant write anything twice— The good is that I wont write shit in any event and what you have written is written and what you save for future you die before you write.

Wire me what they will pay—cash—5000 to 6000 words—

The book has to pass 60,000 before I get any—have it mortgaged [bets? into ?] for my family up to that. Hope it goes 64 or so so we can get a boat. I can damn well use this article money if we come to terms. But dont need it. It may sell way to hell up if we can keep Don off of it! Did he write the thing in life? It was awfully funny but why didnt he go on and kid where the girl died? If he starts after me he shouldnt yellow out.[5]

Tell him I thought a writer wasnt to be judged by how much he was like God but by how much he was like the Whitneys. I'm so damned glad you like it—but I have to not ever think about it because it's just so many dead on the battlefield now— Battle's all over. Have to write another book— Good God how do people write? Tell Don I dont know and it's nothing to be jealous about—

Anyway let me know about the article— I can always make up the time it would have saved for me to cable but didnt want you to think I was trying to snot you on the price—or give impression of one kind of article and send another—

Best love to you, to Ada and to my Mimi and to Kenny and Peter—

How are you, really?

Please write again and to hell with business

Pappy.

LOC, ALS; postmark: PARIS – 2 / R. DANTON, 18 [30] / 3 · XII / 1929

1 In October 1929 MacLeish joined the staff of *Fortune*, a magazine focused on business and the economy that had been launched in September by Henry Luce (1898–1967), owner of *Time*. The letter from MacLeish to which EH is responding has not been located. EH's article "Bullfighting, Sport and Industry" would appear in the March 1930 issue of *Fortune*.

2 George Lewis "Tex" Rickard (1870–1929), American promoter credited with making boxing into a million-dollar sport and turning New York's Madison Square Garden into a top venue. He promoted bouts featuring such luminaries as Jack Dempsey (1895–1983; world heavyweight champion, 1919–1926) and Gene Tunney (1898–1978; world heavyweight champion, 1926–1928).

3 In a letter to Perkins of 12 August 1929, EH's agent Paul Reynolds relayed an offer from *Collier's Weekly* of $750 for "short short stories" from 1,000 to 1,200 words and "a good price" for stories of around 5,000 words. In a letter dated 30 August 1929, Reynolds relayed *Collier's* offer directly to EH: "They will pay you twenty-five hundred dollars ($2500) for any short stories of yours that they buy" (JFK).

4 EH had been planning a book-length project on bullfighting since at least 1925, when he first wrote about it to Perkins (*Letters* vol. 2, 318). After years of research, he would begin writing *DIA* in February 1930.

5 The 22 November 1929 issue of *Life* magazine included a madcap parody of *FTA* titled "A Farewell to Charms" by "Very Ernest Dietrick" (11 ff). In the parody, after Catherine tells the narrator he is about to become a father, they bid one another "pip-pip" as he returns to the front. When he later dives into a river to escape being shot, two frightened young alligators cling to him, mistaking him for their mother. Taking leave of the alligators, the narrator remarks, "It was like saying goodbye to a couple of statues," echoing the ending of the novel. EH suspected Donald Ogden Stewart of being the author.

To Jewell Stevens, 1 December 1929

Dear Mr. Stevens:

Thank you very much for the letter. I'm signing the bookplate as we are going to sail for Cuba in a few weeks and sending the book might be awkward.

You seem to have the right view on the Farewell aspect. I'm awfully glad you liked the book and I wish I could sign it for you—[1]

> With best wishes
> Very truly yours
> Ernest Hemingway.
> 4 Place de la Concorde
> Paris
> Dec 1–1929

[*Enclosure: Stevens's bookplate with EH inscription:*]

To Jewel F. Stevens

with all best wishes

Ernest Hemingway

Paris

1929

SIU, ALS with enclosed inscription

1 Stevens had written to EH congratulating him on his "very remarkable book" and wondering if the farewell was "to the arms of Italy, Catherine or the arms of all women" (5 November 1929, SIU). Stevens enclosed a personalized art deco bookplate and asked if he might send his copy of the novel for EH to inscribe.

To Mrs. Wolfenstein, [1 December 1929]

Dear Mrs. Wolfenstein,

Thank you very much for your letter. You were very good to write me about the book and the people in it and I cannot tell you how much I appreciate[1] it.

Yours very truly,

Ernest Hemingway.

University Archives online catalog, Westport, Connecticut, Stock Number 12551–001, ALS

This transcription derives from the University Archives catalog description, which provides the letter date and quotes the text in full. The letter was earlier sold at auction at Christie's, New York, 9 June 1992 (Sale 7498, Lot 89); the Christie's catalog notes that the letter is addressed to "Dear Mrs. Wolfenstein" and gives the letter's return address as 4 Place de la Concorde, Paris.

1 In the Christie's catalog listing, this word is "appreciated."

To Irma Sompayrac Willard, 1 December 1929

c/ Garanty Trust Co of NY.

4 Place de la Concorde

Paris

Dec 1——1929

Dear Mrs. Willard;

You were very good to write me about the book. I cannot tell you how much I appreciate it. The reviewers write the reviews in a hurry for a living and if they get anything wrong it is excusable (if they get something right it's the same!)—but a letter such as yours is about the greatest pleasure a writer gets—

If you ever want to make any sketches and I'm anywhere around it would be a great pleasure— I never knew I read the killers out loud but if I did I must have been drunk so apologise for that and my consequently not remembering you—[1]

Thanks again for writing— I dont know when we'll ever be in N.Y. Going to Cuba in about a month— If you want to make a sketch from a snapshot I'll send one if I can get one—

> With very best wishes
> Yours very truly—
> Ernest Hemingway

NWSU, ALS; postmark: PARIS-[6] / R. DE VAUGIRARD, 15 * / 3–12 / 29

EH addressed the envelope to "Mrs. D. Milne Willard Jr. / 36 Hartley Avenue / Mount Vernon / New York / Etats Unis." At the top of the page is the recipient's handwritten notation: "When I wrote to Ernest Hemingway, I did not tell him I was Irma Sompayrac. I was included in an invitation to Mr. & Mrs. Hemingway's apartment on Rue Notre Dame des Champs, Paris in 1924 while yet 'Miss Sompayrac' Did not sign that name. Wrote Mr. Hemingway (when N.Y. Times review of 'A Farewell to Arms' appeared)—in indignation & refutation of a sentence therein. I. S. W." She apparently refers to Percy Hutchinson, "Love and War in the Pages of Mr. Hemingway," *New York Times Book Review*, 29 September 1929, 5.

1 The recipient added the notation: "(I purposely did not sign Sompayrac)."

To Barklie McKee Henry, 2 December [1929]

Dec. 2

Dear Buz:

It was damned good to hear from you— When we were in N.Y about a month earlier than this time last year I tried hard to get hold of you— The Guaranty Trust claimed not to know you—you werent in the phone book and I'd lost the L.I. address you'd given me— We were only in town about 5 days— Where I was dumb was trying to get you through Guaranty Trust rather than Guaranty Co.— But if you went broke in the market none of this means anything to you anyway—[1]

Usually I get started on a letter and then some completely senseless sentence like the last one writes its-self and I stop, tear up the letter and never get started again— But am going to write you now if none of it makes any sense at all—

I cant tell you how glad I was you liked the book— You know how it is— I worked over and over it myself until finally it didnt make sense to me— Read it for the first time the other day— It's damned fine the way it seems to be going— Started now in England—

Hope after get various things paid off will get a boat out of it— Do youse ever come to Florida? We live at Key West— Did anyway for 9 mos. last year and will this year again—

By god I did name all the characters after you didnt I. McKee was the only one left out— I'll get that in next time—[2]

You've probably made a wise play about the Guaranty— Certainly everything about writing—i.e. publishing, reviewing etc are all bad and pull away from the main thing. But if you want to keep on writing Buz do just that— Keep on writing. You wont be able to stop at 40 and start it again—[3] Shut yourself up and try and do some on Sundays or nights when you cant sleep or anytime— Writing to try and write—not to publish— That's just a by product— It will be hard as hell to do— But you can do it all right— Only the impossible is ever worth doing at all— My god this sounds like the sort of tripe you've undoubtedly fed the troops— But it's damned true— There's no reason you should write or that anybody should— But if you want to— Do it— Any performance is fun— But it is a hell of a lot of fun—

Making a living by it is almost completely improbable if you write honestly unless you are shot in the ass with luck— I was with the Sun—it might just as well have flopped— But before I had any luck with that I had never made 200 bucks in a year in U.S. writing—

Well this is a punk letter. I hope we'll see you Buzz— My very best to Barbara—[4]

Yours always—
Ernie Hemingway.

PUL, ALS

1 In a 13 October 1929 letter to EH, Henry wrote that he was working for "the Guaranty Co. which is the investment end of the Guaranty Trust." He provided his return address as "Westbury, N.Y." (a community on Long Island), asking EH to "note above address, and above telephone numbers" (JFK).

2 Henry wrote, "I note you call your heroine Barkley + your man Henry. Probably a casual quirk of memory, but I hope it meant you were thinking of me at some remote date."

3 Henry had published a successful novel, *Deceit* (1924), and worked for the *Boston American, Youth's Companion*, and *Atlantic Monthly* in various capacities. In his letter he wrote that the Guaranty Trust job enabled him to "make more money, which I need, and read what I like," adding, "I know I will be able to write better at forty than I can write now. I know I can never count on my writing to support myself."

4 Barbara Whitney (1903–1982), an heiress of the Vanderbilt, Whitney, and Payne families, had married Henry in 1924. In 1931 Henry would quit the Guaranty Company to manage the family fortune.

To George Yohalem, 2 December [1929]

Dear Mr. Yohalem:—

Three Stories and Ten Poems—Contact Editions—Paris— In Our Time— Three Mountains Press Paris (19 rue D'Antin) That's all so far but if my kidneys hold up I hope there will be some more—

Yours very truly—

Ernest Hemingway.

4 Place de la Concorde

Paris

Dec 2—

Mills, ALS; postmark: PARIS-[6] / R. DE VAUGIRARD, 16* / 2 – 12 / 29

EH addressed the envelope to Yohalem in care of the Famous Players Lasky Studio, 5451 Marathon Street, Hollywood, California. The incoming letter from Yohalem to which EH is responding remains unlocated. In his reply of 28 February [1930], Yohalem would thank EH for the information, report that both books EH mentioned were "extremely scarce," and express hope that "the kidneys hold out" so that EH could continue writing (JFK).

To Christian Gauss, [3 December 1929]

Dear Dean Gauss—

Thank you ever so much for writing about the book— I cant tell you how glad I am that you liked it—[1]

It was a fine lunch we had that day and a wonderful taxi meter afterwards—
Scott is here now—working hard and looking very well— Thank God you
never wrote your projected conversation between two characters to be called
Scott and Ernest because its bad to quote a man who's been drinking at lunch
even though the names were so carefully disguised as [*EH drew arrows to the
words "Scott" and "Ernest" earlier in the sentence*]—[2]

We'll look forward to seeing you at Princeton if it's ever possible. I was
there for the Princeton Yale game last year and wanted to see you but
couldnt get Scott, whose guests we were, under weigh— Finally saw no
one—[3]

We go to Cuba and Key West in about a month to stay for quite a long
time and we must see you— We'll be North sooner or later—

You were awfully good to write about the book— Ends of books are
always bad if the book is any good so I take it as a compliment if you didn't
like the way it ended— We'll talk it over some time.[4]

In the meantime all good luck to you, and thanks again for writing.

Yours always—
Ernest Hemingway.

PUL, ALS; letterhead: Writing Room / Guaranty Trust Company of New York / 4
Place de la Concorde / Paris

The conjectured letter date is based on EH's notation "Dec 3" on the verso of Gauss's letter to
him of 14 November 1929 (JFK).

1 In his letter, Gauss called *FTA* "a bigger and better piece of work" than *SAR*, which he had
  also admired. He added, "You are really outrunning all of your contemporaries."
2 Gauss reminisced about a lunch in Paris on [9 June 1925] with Fitzgerald and EH, during
  which they discussed "the woes of the world and the sins of the young." Gauss recalled, "as we
  drove home in the old horse taxi, we noticed that the taximeter registered three miles to every
  one we negotiated and we had a little altercation with the old French cabman." In a letter of
  27 July [1925], EH had granted Gauss permission to write about their lunch with Fitzgerald
  (*Letters* vol. 2, 367), probably for Gauss's *Life in College* (Scribner's, 1930), portions of which
  appeared in the late 1920s in *Scribner's Magazine* and the *Saturday Evening Post*.
3 On 17 November 1928, EH, Pauline, Scott and Zelda Fitzgerald, and Henry Strater attended
  the annual Princeton–Yale football game at Princeton. Afterwards the Hemingways stayed
  overnight at Ellerslie Mansion, the Fitzgeralds' rented home near Wilmington, Delaware.
4 Gauss reported discussing *FTA* with Perkins, who "offered some objections to your conclusion." Gauss added, "I had some too but they were entirely different from his so I am
  inclined to think that perhaps we are both wrong and you may be right. I wish I could talk it
  over with you sometime."

To Maxwell Perkins, [8–10 December 1929]

[*Fragment one; beginning on unnumbered partial sheet of paper, the top portion cut away, and continuing on two full sheets bearing EH's circled page numbers 3 and 4:*]

What about this Morley business? Am I supposed to swallow all that? Refering to Isabel P's column of Nov 24— <u>Casts from a Book Worm</u> (It's the only thing people ever send me!)[1] = I havent been at the Dome[2] for 3 years— have never disparaged Morley's knowlege of boxing, boxed with him 5 different times last spring, ordinarily all rounds ended when Morley was winded, the one other time, after the big lunch, I wrote you about at the time—[3] If he could hit he should have killed me—as it was out of about 35 rounds boxed altogether he won one and he gave me a bad beating in one— but then was too light a hitter to put me on the floor or knock me out—

So now I read that I insulted him, he challenged me and knocked me cold! ~~All I can say is that~~ If Morley had anything to do with starting the story— (It may be just malicious gossip by Pierre Loving[4] or some other like rat who lies to appear in the know) I would like to know about it so I'll know what steps to take. After boxing with him five times, stopping everytime he was winded, stopping and apologizing every time I'd happen to hit him with a right hand, always shooting them high up at his head so as <u>not</u> to get his jaw and having him once when I was tight and could hardly see punch me around for 2½ extra minutes (given by Scott) hitting me wherever he wanted whenever he wanted and not be able to do any real damage— (He had about 20 free shots at my jaw and should have killed me) I know what he is worth as a boxer. He is an excellent <u>boxer</u>, but fat and short winded, a very light hitter and easily hurt, ~~and if I find he had anything to do with this story~~. If he has told you any knocking cold story please tell him for me to use a little more imagination in his stories and a little less in his interviews (that should do as an insult) but if he wants it a little stronger tell him I consider his ~~famous~~ novel one of the worst cheap fakes I ever tried to read, that his fight story is another fake, that there is more to knowing the psychology of professional fighters than being a good amateur boxer yourself, that the reason I wrote about the war was to get somewhere he hadn't been and where it was too late for him to go so he couldnt imitate it and that I am always at his disposal for him to knock me cold at any time he wishes. Also please add that if he should knock me cold (providing for every emergency) or if he should knock my young son Bumby cold that I doubt very much if it would make him a writer.

I haven't been worth a damn as a boxer since about 1924–5— But still hope to God I know enough to beat that fat one. I hadnt had gloves on in two years when I boxed Morley—his wife told me he had been boxing 3 or 4 times a week [*EH insertion*: with the Intercollegiate light heavyweight Champion] ~~for~~ all through the winter Evidently preparing his big coup. It was Morley suggested boxing. So now having been unable to do what he wanted to do he <u>claims</u> to have done it instead.

I write this to you instead of to him so that it may be public— as in the story he says I insulted him publicly—all right I'll insult him [once] more— I hope when I see him to ~~knock him~~ beat him up so badly that you'll have to get another Fake Hemingway to fill in on the ~~time~~ seasons when I dont write books—

Please send him this letter. That is the part referring to him—

Yours always—

Ernest

[*Fragment two; on one page bearing circled number 5:*]
harm through malice. One would seem to be Isabel Patterson whom I've never even seen and the other is a Russian jew with a name like Lipipsy who calls himself Pierre Loving. He imitated me, then hated me, have never spoken a dozen words to him but he is almost as great a starter of malicious lies as McAlmon.

Yes there is one more. Some of the damndest stories of all come from a woman named Kay Boyle that I have never even <u>seen</u> in my life. She is also a writer.[5]

Have ~~lived~~ always stayed away from N.Y in order not to make enemies there so that my work might be judged without personality coming in—but when I have this book out 4 of the 5 known enemies I have are concentrated there. And the system those people lie on is that if they tell something monstrous enough there will always be some people who will say "Well where is smoke there is fire!"

McAlmons first theory about me being a homosexual was that I had a "suppressed desire" for him, McAlmon! He finally decided, though, and told freely that I was ~~buggering~~, who do you think? Waldo! I take the word out on acct. of this going through the mail.[6]

[*Fragment three; on both sides of one sheet, bearing the circled numbers 5 and 6:*]

harm through malice. One in a very minor way would seem to be Isabel Patterson whom I've never even seen and the other is a Russian Jew with a name like Lipschitsky who calls himself Pierre Loving and hates and lies about everybody. He is a disappointed writer.

This is not the sort of thing that I care to write about in letters but since you wrote to Scott I ~~feel~~ I ~~should~~ have no great choice. Scott is the soul of honor when sober and completely irresponsible when drunk and as he is sooner or later always drunk—anything you write him is liable to become a public issue. If it's all the same I would rather you wrote me when you hear stories about me—not Scott. Please do not write Scott reproaching him for a breach of confidence as he is not to blame. He is absolutely the soul of honor when sober and when drunk is no more responsible than an insane man. And he is drunk on 4 glasses of wine. He did not say you had written him any definite stories—but told me stories he had heard from Callaghan as the type of thing McAlmon had probably told you.

When McAlmon told one of these stories in the presense of Evan Shipman— Evan called him a liar and fought him. When McAlmon told me Scott was a homosexual—(it is one of his manias)— I told him he was a liar and a damned fool. It was not till after he had left for N.Y. that I heard the story he was telling about Pauline. Frankly I think he is crazy. Callaghan has no such excuse. He is a cheap, small town gossip anxious to retail any filth, no matter how improbable.

[*On verso:*]

This seems to be the end of the letter—

But if you hear any particularly filthy stories about me and have to mention them to anyone please let it be to me— There's nothing you can tell me direct that bothers me in the least—but it is hearing things through other people

Yours always

Ernest.

Your wires about the sale being 57000 and 69,000 came yesterday and today. Thanks ever so much for sending them. I am glad it is going so well[7]

[Fragment four; on one page bearing the circled number 6:]

Now I have no persecution mania—but this is all getting a little too strong. What the hell are they jealous of? I dont want the publicity, I dont get the money—all I want is to work and be left alone and by God you should have a right to be.

Wire yesterday that the sale was 57,000 plus— Thank you for sending it. Dont make up that English press ad until you get the British clippings— I sent them off to Berlin—but they should be back in a day or two and will send them on. But maybe you have them.

Anyway best to you always— I must apologize for having introduced McAlmon to you. Expect I'll live to hear more foul things about myself but doubt if many more foul from anyone that have written a letter of introduction for and was trying to get before a publisher.

Yours always—
Ernest.

JFK, ALDS Frags

The date range of these fragments is conjectured based on the fuller, more polished version that EH sent to Perkins, which follows in this volume.

1 In her weekly column for *New York Herald Tribune Books*, Isabel Paterson had described "a singular encounter between Ernest Hemingway and Morley Callaghan," quoting Caroline Bancroft in the *Denver Post* (ellipses are Paterson's): "One night at the Dome Callaghan's name was mentioned and Hemingway said: 'Oh, you can easily see he hasn't any practical background for his fight stories—shouldn't think he knew anything about boxing.' ... Callaghan, hearing of it, challenged Hemingway ... After arranging for rounds and a considerable audience they entered the arena. Not many seconds afterward Callaghan knocked Hemingway out cold. The amateur timekeeper was so excited he forgot to count and the deflated critic had to stagger up and finish the round" ("Turns with a Bookworm," 24 November 1929, 27). In her column two weeks later, Paterson quoted Callaghan's correction: "Hemingway never sat at the 'Dome' last summer. Certainly he never sat there panning my fight stories." Callaghan maintained he never challenged Hemingway nor knocked him out, adding that he wished Paterson would correct the story "or I'll never be able to go to New York again, for fear of getting knocked out myself" (*New York Herald Tribune Books*, 8 December 1929, 23).

2 The Café du Dôme, on the Boulevard Montparnasse, attracted American expatriates and tourists; it figures by name in *SAR*.

3 See EH to Perkins, 28 August [1929].

4 Pierre Loving (1893–1950), American journalist, translator, editor and writer, joined the
staff of the Paris edition of the *New York Herald* in 1925. Caroline Bancroft (1900–1985),
literary editor for the *Denver Post*, would later tell Callaghan that her source was American
novelist Virginia Davis Hersch (1896–1978), who lived in Paris with her husband, artist Lee
Hersch (Matthew J. Bruccoli, *Some Sort of Epic Grandeur: The Life of F. Scott
Fitzgerald*, second revised edition [Columbia: University of South Carolina Press, 2002],
283).

5 Boyle was a friend of Robert McAlmon, and her sister, Joan Boyle (1900–2004), had worked
with Pauline Pfeiffer at Paris *Vogue*. Kay Boyle and EH never met.

6 McAlmon's remarks about EH were made to Perkins in New York City during a dinner
meeting on 8 October 1929. In a 30 October letter to Fitzgerald, Perkins mentioned but did
not specify the "mean things" McAlmon had said about EH "both as a man and as a writer."
Fitzgerald replied to Perkins that "McAlmon is a bitter rat" who had "assured Ernest that
I was a fairy . . . Next he told Callaghan that Ernest was a fairy" ([c. 15 November 1929]).
(This exchange appears in Kuehl and Bryer, 157–61.) Evidently Fitzgerald elaborated on
these and other rumors at a dinner at the Hemingways' apartment on 9 December 1929.

7 Perkins's cable of 7 December 1929 read, "Sale fifty-seven thousand plus," and his cable of
9 December reported, "Sale today fifty-nine" (PUL).

To Maxwell Perkins, [8]–10 December [1929]

Sunday Dec 7[1]

Dear Max:—

Thanks very much for your letters of Nov 21 and 25th—and the proof
of ad in NY Times which is very handsome—the ad— Glad everything is
going well.[2]

Had a letter from A. Knopf asking to see me so went in order to tell him and
his wife there was absolutely no truth in report I was leaving you—nor was
I dis satisfied—in any way. He is returning to N.Y in a week and I asked him to
deny the report wherever he heard it—which they both promised to do.[3]

Thanks for writing about the salary business— I appreciate it but would
only think of it as a last resort— You know the difficulty I have of working
under contract—

About In Our Time— I wish you would get it from Liveright— There is
no reason why they should hang onto the one book— Remind them that
they promised me absolutely that they would sell the book to you if you
wanted it— I remember wanting to get it settled at the time— The bringing
out of the original Three Mts Press edition again sounds like a good idea—
We can discuss it— I think it should, if issued, have Mike Strater's portrait

189

reproduced as frontispiece— Not the punk woodcut made from it—but a good reproduction—reproduce the original cover also maybe— [*EH circled insertion*: The original edition was only 150][4]

The idea of the English opinion ad sounds fine— Have you all the English clippings? There was a ~~very~~ good one in New Statesman of Nov. 30—and Times Book Supplement of Nov. 27—[5] Glad to have that ad for Mr. R. Herrick to read—just for fun.

Dec 10

Started to write you Sunday—now it's Tuesday— Scott came to dinner last night and while drunk told me he had heard from you that McAlmon had told you various stories about me. He also told me a particularly filthy story Morley Callaghan had told him about me. Morley had gotten it from McAlmon.

So I write to ask if McAlmon has any new stories— His stories that I am familiar with are (1) That Pauline is a lesbian (2) that I am a homosexual (3) that I used to beat Hadley and as a result of one of these beatings Bumby was born prematurely.

Did he tell you these or did he have new ones? I'd appreciate not a general but a particular answer.[6]

Morley, it seems, asked Scott on meeting ~~me~~ him if he knew it were true that I was a homo-sexual. He had just gotten the news from McAlmon! He may therefore be counted on to have spread it fairly thoroughly. He seems also to be having a great deal of success with a story about how I sneered at his boxing ability, he challenged me and knocked me cold.

I sent McAlmon with a letter to you because I have tried to help materially everyone I know who is writing whether a friend or an enemy. Have tried especially to help people I did not like since my judgement might be warped in favor of my friends and hate to see people bitter about never having had a chance even though I may feel sure personally there is good and abundant cause for their failure. I do not try to get them published [*EH marginal insertion*: That's ~~none of my~~ your business not mine.] but to obtain them an extra-fair presentation to the publisher.

But this has gone a little too far. There should be a limit ~~applied~~ to what lies people are allowed to tell under jealousies.

I did not know until last night that Callaghan was definitely in that class. It is all pretty disgusting. Pauline says it is my own fault for having had anything to do with such swine. She is right enough. There will be a certain satisfaction in beating up ~~McAlmon~~ Callaghan because of his boasting and because he is a good enough boxer. There is none in beating up McAlmon— I would have done it years ago if he wasnt so pitiful. But I will go through with it as I should have long ago because the only thing such people fear is physical correction— They have no moral ~~sense~~ feelings to hurt.

I have, as far as I know, only one other—perhaps two other "enemies", that is people willfuly seeking to do you harm through malice. One in a very minor way would seem to be Isabel Patterson whom I've never even seen and the other is a Russian Jew with a name like Lipschitzky who calls himself Pierre Loving and lies about everyone. He is a disappointed writer.

Scott is the soul of honor when sober and completely irresponsible when drunk. If it's all the same I would rather you wrote me when you hear stories about me—not Scott. Please do not reproach Scott with a breach of confidence as he is absolutely incapable of such a thing sober and drunk he is no more responsible than an insane man. He did not say you had written him any definite stories—but told me stories he had heard from Callaghan as a type of thing McAlmon had probably told you.

~~However~~ I had to sit, drinking Vichy, cold sober, and listen to an hour or more of that sort of thing last night. When McAlmon told one of those stories in the presense of Evan Shipman—Evan called him a liar and hit him. When McAlmon called Scott a homosexual to me (It is one of his manias) I told him he was a liar and a damned fool. It was not until after he had left for N.Y. that I heard the story he was telling about Pauline. Frankly I think he is crazy. Callaghan has no such excuse. He is a cheap, small town gossip anxious to believe and retail any filth no matter how improbable.

This seems to be the end of the letter— Your wires about the sale being 57,000 and 59,000 came yesterday and today. Thanks ever so much for sending them. I am glad it is going so well.

Yours always—
Ernest Hemingway.

This is nothing [*EH drew an arrow pointing to two lines above, which he heavily blotted out in black ink*]— I was starting to make a reflexion about people waiting 6 mo. to tell you when drunk some filthy story about you which they ~~should either~~ apparently never challenged physically or in any way but realized that since last night I have reflected entirely too damned much— But Ill be damned glad to be in Key West and see people like Charles [Thompson], Mike Strater and yourself and have no filth and jealousy. What the hell are they jealous of? I dont want the publicity and I dont get the money. All I want is to work and be let alone and I damned well will be.

PUL, ALS

1 EH apparently misdated the letter. 7 December 1929 was a Saturday. The conjectured date range is based on EH's reference to cables from Perkins dated 7 and 9 December, and on EH's comment midway through the letter that he began writing it on Sunday and was continuing it on Tuesday, 10 December.
2 In his letter of 21 November 1929, Perkins reported continued strong sales of *FTA* and proposed "some sort of an arrangement to pay you a minimum sum each year" (PUL). In his 25 November letter, Perkins requested EH's approval for the Scribner's proposal to acquire the publishing rights to *IOT* from Horace Liveright (PUL). Perkins also included an advertisement featuring a photograph of EH skiing, scheduled to run "next Sunday in the Times." It appeared in the 1 December 1929 *New York Times Book Review* (27).
3 Alfred A. Knopf (1892–1984) and Blanche Wolf (1894–1966) established the publishing house Alfred A. Knopf, Inc. in 1915; they married in 1916. Their distinguished literary list included European as well as American authors. Knopf's letter to EH remains unlocated.
4 Initially rejecting Scribner's proposal, Liveright would finally assent, in the hope of keeping his failing firm afloat. On 19 June 1930 he sold the plates, bound stock, and reprints rights to Scribner's (Hanneman A3B, 10).
5 In his 25 November letter, Perkins described plans for another larger advertisement that would "have some such headline as 'English opinion on an American book.'" This ad, headed "Who Reads an American Book?," would feature eight laudatory quotations from English sources (*New York Times Book Review*, 19 January 1930, 18). In his *New Statesman* review, Edward Richard Buxton Shanks (1892–1953), British poet, journalist, and critic, called the novel "a convincing and moving tale" through which "Mr. Hemingway communicates his experience whole and unimpaired" (30 November 1929, 267). The unsigned review in the London *Times Literary Supplement* had praised *FTA* as "a novel of great power ... unlike any other" whose author is "an extremely talented and original artist" (28 November 1929, 998).
6 In a 26 December letter, Perkins would deny that McAlmon had told him any such stories, and say that he himself "would somehow have shut off that line of talk" if McAlmon had even attempted to besmirch anyone. He described McAlmon as "terribly stubborn and he has this idea of his importance as a writer" that leads him to belittle other writers (PUL).

To Hugh Walpole, 10 December [1929]

6 rue Férou
Paris VI
December 10

Dear Walpole:

In case you are in America in February we'll be in Key West from the end of January on. It would be grand to see you there. A wire to me at Key West Florida is enough. Dont know what the address will be until we get a place.

It was a shame you couldnt get over. I'm awfully pleased at the way things have gone for the book in England. This book has been my first experience with getting letters from people who have read it in America. What are you supposed to do? I've answered them all—and have done nothing else. It's a bloody business—takes 20 minutes or ½ an hour to thank them for writing and F.1.50 on the letter. What are you really supposed to do? Do they become angry if you dont answer and go around raking up your past life and getting you indicted? or do they get sullen and never buy another? Do <u>you</u> answer them?

I get none of the moneys my books make but I do have to buy the stamps and between writing the letters and buying the stamps am going to be broke and never have any more time to write. The only way seems to be to go on trips, write like hell, then come back and find more letters. When The Sun Also Rises came out there were only letters from a few old ladies who wanted to make a home for me and said my disability would be no drawback and drunks who claimed we had met places.

Men without Women brought no letters at all. What are you supposed to do when you really start to get letters?

It gets dark in the middle of the afternoon now and has been raining and storming like hell. In the old days I'd sit tight in the house and drink and read my illustrious predecessors—but one day this summer got to the bank of the River Tambre at 7 a.m. and found I had my wife's waders instead of mine—so waded all day without them, it rained like hell and I kept in the stream to keep warm and drank whiskey—[1] So now it seems I have a congested kidney or something as a souvenir and whiskey makes my fingers swell at the tips like little balloons— But it seems too that in a hot climate your pores replace your kidneys— So by the time you get to Key West it will be fine. The problem now is to find something to replace the pores when they go. Am thinking of having an operation performed and a couple of good new box model gas masks, with tubes, inserted in the small of the back.

I remember in the old days how the whores would sleep with the citizens for nothing if they could only show them impressive enough wounds and I imagine, even in times of Peace, a man with a couple of inserted gas masks could practically go around the world on them.

You dont know how fine it is to write a letter in which you thank no one for having been so kind as to write you about your book. I try always to write to them in the style of the late John Greenleaf Whittier.[2]

Look, please come to Key West. There's not a damned thing to do but fish and swim and drink— The Population has dropped to 7,500 from 35,000—[3] You could give a lecture there except they'd probably think you were an impostor— Everywhere I went in America they thought I was an impostor— I gave a woman in a bookstore in the RR. station in St. Louis my card and asked her where was an Italian restaurant with wine. She treated me as an impostor. It seems America is full of impostors.[4] Some say Hoover is an impostor. The real Hoover died in Belgium and was one of the angels of Mons.[5]

This ought to be enough length to a letter— Length without content. Do write if you ever feel like it. It would be fine to hear from you.

Best to you always—
Ernest Hemingway.

NYPL–Berg, ALS

1 The Tambre River in northwestern Spain flows through Santiago de Compostela, where EH and Pauline spent most of August 1929.
2 John Greenleaf Whittier (1807–1892), American poet and antislavery reformer, one of the "Fireside Poets" or "Schoolroom Poets" who advocated American national and moral virtues in rhythmic verse.
3 While EH's statistics have not been precisely corroborated, he correctly observed a decline in the local population. The 1910 U.S. Census for Key West recorded 19,945 inhabitants, making it then the second largest city in Florida. Changes in industrial practices, most notably affecting pineapple canning, cigar making, and sponge fishing, along with the decline of U.S. naval operations on the island and the October 1929 financial crash, reduced the island's population to 12,831 in 1930.

4 In an interview published in the *Kansas City Star* (21 October 1931), EH said he was looking for the man who had been impersonating him for the past year, citing instances in New York City, Paris, and St. Louis. The impostor had autographed books, made and broken appointments with a certain Mr. Lewin (who consequently "gave me hell"), and had even given "a long interview" detailing EH's literary opinions ("The Ghost of a Writer / Ernest Hemingway Seeks his 'Double' in Several Places"; reproduced in Trogdon *Reference*, 118–20).

5 According to a widespread legend, while retreating from heavy German fire during the Battle of Mons (23–24 August 1914), many soldiers saw phantom cavalry, sometimes identified as contemporary English soldiers and sometimes as mounted English bowmen from the 1415 Battle of Agincourt.

To David Garnett, 10 December [1929]

December 10—
6 Rue Férou
Paris.

Dear Mr. Garnett:—

I cant tell you how much it meant to get your letter— I hope to god what you say about the book will be true—though how we are to know whether they last I dont know— But anyway you were fine to say it would.

After I read The Sailor's Return all I did was to go around wishing to god I could have written it. It is still the only book I would like to have written of all the books since our father's and mother's times. As you see I cant write a letter, the tendency as in conversation is always, for me, to replace or indicate emotion with profanity—but you are the only writer of our generation whose writing means a damned thing to me. After I read The Sailor's Return I would not go back to read the Lady Into Fox and Man In the Zoo because if there was any key about how it was done (the writing) I didnt want it. I only wanted the book.[1]

You have meant very much to me, as a writer and now that you have written me that letter I should feel very fine— But instead all that happens is that I dont believe it—dont believe I have the letter, dont believe it when I read it—dont believe a damn thing.

Too many things like that have happened to me in dreams, not about writing, I've never dreamed about writing, and when I woke up they were always gone, and they were as circumstantial as your letter.

I wrote the damned book over so many times to try to get it right that finally it didnt make sense to me when I read it.

If I started to write this letter over it would never be sent to you—

I am so happy you liked the book— You have my very great admiration. Am no good at saying that—but it is Gods truth.

I thank you again for writing and I hope everything goes well with you and that it always will— If you ever decide the book—A Farewell T.A. is no good and want to take back what you said please do it—it will be all right with me— But you were awfully damned nice to write it now.

Yours always
Ernest Hemingway.

UT, ALS

1 Garnett's novels of this period combine social, psychological, and fantastic elements. *The Sailor's Return* (London: Chatto & Windus, 1925; New York: Knopf, 1925) explores racial prejudice as a white sailor attempts to settle in a Dorset village with his black wife, an African princess disguised as a boy. In *Lady into Fox* (London: Chatto & Windus, 1922; New York: Knopf, 1923), a woman and her husband attempt to maintain their relationship unchanged despite her metamorphosis into a fox. *A Man in the Zoo* (London: Chatto & Windus, 1924; New York: Knopf, 1924) follows a man whose prudish beloved calls him an animal because he wants to live with her, whereupon he arranges to be exhibited in a zoo.

To Grace Hall Hemingway, 10 December [1929]

December 10

Dear Mother:—

Enclosed please find 7 checks for Xmas— Will you please mail off at once for me the checks to Leicester, Ura, Uncle and Marce—keep the others for Carol and Sunny until Xmas—use yours whenever you wish.

Please Tell Marce the check is for her 2 children—[1] Merry Xmas to them— And Merry Christmas to you all—

Ernie

Thank you very much for mailing the checks for me!

Hope Sunny is better—

PSU, ALS; postmark: [PARIS 110] / R. DE RENNES, [*illegible*]

1 Carol Hemingway Sanford (1924–2013) and James Sterling Sanford (b. 1929).

To Edward Verrall Lucas, 10 December 1929

6 rue Férou

Paris

December 10—1929

Dear Mr. Lucas,

You were very good to write me about the book. I cannot tell you how much I appreciate it— And I understand and value the very great compliment you paid.

Thank you again for your note— I value it very highly.

Yours very truly,

Ernest Hemingway.

UT, ALS

To Maxwell Perkins, 11 December 1929

FCH 572 LA

PARIS 22

LCD MAXWELL PERKINS SCRIBNERS MAXWELL PERKINS %

CHARLES SCRIBNERS SONS.

FIFTH AVE AT 48TH ST.

NYK

WHATS LETTER ABOUT HOPE NO TROUBLE STOP[1] DONT USE

LETTER ABOUT BOOKMAN[2] MAY SAIL JANUARY NINTH

ERNEST

PUL, Cable; Western Union destination receipt stamp: 1929 DEC 11 PM 6 15

1 Perkins drafted his answer at the bottom of this cable: "All is well (stop) Letter revises contract (stop) Sale <u>62000</u> Wrote Bookman myself / Max." In his 10 December 1929 letter to EH, Perkins revised the terms offered in the first contract for *FTA* (a flat 15% royalties on all copies sold) to royalties of 20% of the list price ($2.00) on all sales in excess of 25,000 copies (PUL).

2 See EH's two letters to Perkins of 30 November [1929] regarding his displeasure with the *Bookman*, which published Robert Herrick's review of *FTA*, "What Is Dirt?" (November 1929).

To F. Scott Fitzgerald, [12 December 1929]

Thursday—

Dear Scott— Your letter didnt come until last night— They'd held it at the bank.

I know you are the soul of honor. I mean that. If you remember I made no cracks about your time keeping until after you had told me over my objections for about the fourth time that you were going to deliberately quarrel with me. The first time I thought I had convinced you. You came back to it and I, and Pauline, thought we had convinced you again. On the 4th time after I had also heard how McAlmon, whom I'd given a letter of introduction to Perkins had lied about me, how Callaghan whom I'd always tried to aid had come to you with preposterous stories I was getting sore.

You'll remember though that I did not, sore as I was about everything in general, accuse you of any such time juggling, I only asked you if you had let the round go on to see what would happen.[1] I was so appalled at the idea of you saying that you were going to deliberately quarrel with me that I didnt know (just having heard this vile stuff from McA and C. which I thought I should have heard a long time sooner, if I was to hear it, and it was to go so long unresented) where the hell I stood on anything.

Besides <u>if you had let the round go on deliberately</u>—which I <u>know</u> you did not—I would not have been sore. I knew when it had gone by the time agreed. It is something that is done <u>habitually</u> at amateur bouts. Often When two boys are really socking each other around the time keeper gives them an extra ten, fifteen or thirty seconds—sometimes even a minute to see how things come out. You seemed so upset that I thought you had done this and regretted it— But the minute you said you had not I believed you implicitly.

You as I say are a man of the greatest honor. I am not, in boxing at least. When I boxed Jean Prevost here in Paris I proposed Bill Smith as time keeper.[2] I was in bad shape and told Bill to call time (we were supposed to box 2 minute rounds) any time he saw me in trouble. One of the rounds was barely 40 seconds long! Prevost just thought the time went awfully quickly. When I had him going Bill let the rounds go 2 minutes and over.

Having done such things myself you cannot expect me to control my reflexes about what is happening to me. But you can believe me when I say that I at once threw out any such idea and coming home told Pauline you had been interested and forgotten all about time.

You may remember too that I put no importance on the incident afterwards and was more pleased than anything. I remember telling it with pleasure at the Deux Magot,[3] praising Morley and giving him all credit for knocking me around. I thought, then, he was a friend of mine. It was only when I read his lying boast that I became angry. Then, being sore, I was sore at your carelessness which had given him the opportunity to make such a boast.

I would never have asked you such a thing if you hadnt gotten me nearly cuckoo with this talk about deliberately quarreling with me.

Let me repeat again— I have not the slightest suspicion of you having been disingenuous— I believe you implicitly and did at the time.

I know how valuable your sense of honor is to you, as it is to any man, and I would not wound you in it for anything in the world. So please believe me.

As an attenuating circumstance though, please look at the different way we each look at Sport— You look on it as a gentleman and that is the way it should be. But look how it has been with me—

One of the first times I ever boxed—A fellow named Morty Hellnick— after the bell for the end of the round I dropped my hands. The minute I dropped my hands he hit me with a right swing full to the pit of the stomach. After the fight I was sick for nearly a week. The 2nd time I boxed him I was winning easily—he had lost the fight anyway— So he fouled me— deliberately—have never had such pain in my life—one ball swelled up nearly as big as a fist— That is the way boxing is- —[4] Look—in so called Friendly bouts—you are never trying to knock them out— Yet you never know but that they will try to knock you out— You get the complete habit of suspicion— Boxing in the gym with a fellow he let his thumb stick out beyond his gloves in the infighting—the thumb caught me in the left eye and I was blinded by it— He blinded, in his life, at least 4 other men. Never intentionally—just the by-product of a dirty trick— I mention this only to excuse my reflex of suspicion which I never carried over for a minute.

It was only when you were telling me, against all my arguments and telling you how fond I am of you, that you were going to break etc and that you had a need to smash me as a man, etc that I relapsed into the damn old animal suspicion—

But I apologize to you again, I believe you implicitly and I have always, and I only wish to God you didnt feel so bum when you drink. I know it's no damn fun but I know too everything will be fine when your book is done.

Callaghan and McAlmon are a couple of shits and as Pauline says our mistake was in having anything to do with such people.

Anyway every kind of luck to you— Did you know Harry Crosby who shot himself yest? He told me about this girl before he went to N.Y. McLeishes introduced her to him. He was a hell of a good boy and I feel awfully bad today about him.[5] One of my best friends died two weeks ago and I'll be damned if I'm going to lose you as a friend through some bloody squabble.[6]

> Best to you always—
> Yr. affectionate friend
> Ernest.

PUL, ALS

1 The letter from Fitzgerald that EH mentions here remains unlocated. EH refers to his infamous Paris boxing bout with Callaghan, when Fitzgerald had neglected to keep track of the time, prolonging the bout to EH's disadvantage.
2 Jean Prévost (1901–1944), French poet, translator, and friend of Adrienne Monnier and Sylvia Beach, who introduced him to EH. Prévost started his literary career as a sports writer and served as literary editor for Monnier's *Le Navire d'Argent*. He published *Plaisirs des Sports: Essais Sur le Corps Humain* (1925) and would write the preface to Maurice-Edgar Coindreau's French translation of *SAR* (Paris: Gallimard, 1933), in which he recalled boxing

with EH (see *Letters* vol. 2, 343). Bill Smith was visiting Paris in the spring and summer of 1925.

3 Café les Deux Magots, at 6, Place Saint-Germain des Prés. Opened in 1885 and named for two Chinese porcelain figures of wise men (*magots*) that decorate the interior, the café attracted journalists, artists, and intellectuals.

4 In his posthumously published African memoir *Under Kilimanjaro*, EH recalls that while still living at home in Oak Park, he had suffered a broken right hand, an injured scrotum, a concussion, and "immense pain" from a boxing match (Chapter 32).

5 Harry Crosby and his lover Josephine Rotch Bigelow (c. 1907–1929), the "Mad Queen" in his love poetry, died in a murder/suicide pact in New York City on the evening of 10 December 1929. Their deaths were widely reported on Wednesday, 11 December.

6 EH's deceased friend remains unidentified.

To Maxwell Perkins, 15 December [1929]

—December 15—

Dear Max:—

Your letter of Dec 3 came yesterday and 2 others written Nov. 30 and Dec 4 came today— Also day before yesterday the wire about letter coming revising contract and the sale. The sale is certainly damned fine. There was no hurry about any revision and no need to do it if it did not seem the thing to you.[1]

I must certainly apologize—I think I have already—for having written that time after Scott got me alarmed about the sale stopping. But came home from Berlin feeling fine and found Scott had been here with some alarm. I went over to see him and he showed me something you had written about the book going well and the only thing to watch was the market slump— I thought there was nothing alarming in what you had written but he knows so much more about the financial side of writing than I do that I imagined, he did not show me the whole letter, but only the part referring to the book that there was some contingencies I did not know about. Also he seemed so alarmed ~~for me~~. Am damned fond of Scott and would do anything for him but he's been a little trying lately. He came over the other day, a little tight, and said "People ought to let you alone. They ought to let you work and not worry you." And then proceeded to tell me the Goddamndest stories about myself that I've ever heard. He has my interests at heart and wants only to help me but really I have been out in the world making a living for a long time ~~and~~ ordinarily get on with people have been ~~used to~~ familiar with slander, jealousy etc. although do not believe it exists as much as people make out and would prefer to ignore things—if they're not true they always die out. But when things are brought to your attention they make you sore as hell. Scott is working hard and well and I know he will be fine when he finally gets his book done.

I wish you would debit my royalty account with the 25$^{\underline{00}}$ to Waldo— Please do—without saying anything to Waldo.[2]

If you are to worry about how you will go down in literary history I will have to write you a series of letters telling you what I really think of you— Am no good at that but will do it to remove any such idea from your head—

But the Xian Science business <u>was</u> something to worry over I can see— Though I dont think <u>they</u> will make any trouble for A Farewell— They arent so smart— They are simply wonderfully organized— If they were more intelligent they wouldnt be Xstian Scientists maybe. Anyway I hope you have luck with the book— The next 2 times that you would in your plans devote a large space to A Farewell please use ½ the space and the other ½ for the Eddy Book—[3] I would be damned pleased if you would—

When I wrote you, angry, about McAlmon and Callaghan it was only personal anger. I can and will handle my personal business with them (only hope I wont have to do any time in jail for making it thorough) but I do not want you to think I am against them as writers— I want them to succeed and would do nothing to hurt them as writers—altho it is dangerous when you have an enemy to do anything but kill him—and that's too expensive a luxury—

Wister is damned nice but all wrong enough— Still there is this great thing about him—he does, personally, seem to belong to the same generation as we do—I mean you, me, Mike Strater, Waldo—for instance— all people of quite different ages— He has written about 3 or 4 damned fine stories—A Gift Horse—Pilgrim on the Gila part of The Honorable The Strawberries— How writing those he could write such a thing as Philosophy Four I dont know— Have just read that for the first time and feel ashamed even to read it—[4] We all write shit but something should prevent you from publishing it or at least re-publishing it— But I am very fond of him— If he wants to think of me as a "projection" there's no harm in it so long as he doesnt try to influence— He could have been a very great writer and the combination of circumstances that prevent that are always tragic—

It's 20 minutes to twelve now—Sunday noon—have to shave and get to mass—

Later—got shaved and to mass and lunch with Pauline Allen Tate and a couple of citizens— Tate is damned intelligent and a very good fellow— Dos Passos and his wife are due tomorrow—

My throat is bad and full of pus and I cant think or write very well— I hope I havent worried or bothered you with letters— I only write when Scott gets me stirred up— I know he does it only because that is his idea of the sort of thing that is exciting to a writer— But it's not exciting—only annoying and when you come to Key West I promise to talk no business at all— The idea that a writer can write a book then become a business man, then a writer again is all —— as we say. It's hard enough to write—and writing prose is a full time job and all the best of it is done in your subconscious and when that is full of business, reviews, opinions etc you dont get a damned thing—

Speaking of all such worries the only fear I've ever had about the book was some Italian action to stop it— That may be cuckoo— But how would it be to run in the front matter that statement I wrote that was published in the magazine when the first number of A Farewell appeared? That seems to cover all aspects— The only thing I dont like is that people might think I was trying to compare myself with Shakespeare by making the crack about the Two Gentlemen of Verona—[5] This only to run if you think so—

Must stop— Am trying to write an article on bull fighting as an industry for "Fortune" Archy MacLeish asked me for it—written in journalese full of statistics— It's a romance of business magazine— There's no romance in the article— They probably wont take it— Am keeping it as dull as possible— Every aspect I touch on if I could go on and write about would make a long chapter in a book— They wanted something between 5,000 and 20,000 words and I told them it would cost $2500— So they want something over 2500 words for $1000^{00} instead— Their magazine came out just at the time of the Crash which was hard luck— But if ever a magazine sounded like useless balls this one does— Am doing it for Archy—how he got mixed up with them God knows—[6]

Well if there's anything unanswered in this letter it's only carelessness— Thanks for your fine letters—and Merry Christmas to you and your family— Best to you always—

Ernest

Please debit me with the Waldo business—otherwise I'll have to send a check to you— The debiting is an easy channel! I <u>really</u> want to pay it— But for Waldo not to know.

The book has stirred up a hell of a business in England— V. Sackville West Broadcasted about it from the official British Broadcasting and the head of the B.B.C. raised hell and she, Walpole etc replied—[7] It's had much better reviews in England than U.S. Damned funny— I want to get to Key West and away from it all— Have never been as damn sick of anything as mention of this book— People write swell letters about it and I am so sick of it that a fine letter only makes you embarrassed and uneasy and vaguely sick.

PUL, ALS

1 In letters to EH of 30 November and 3 December 1929, Perkins discussed advertising, printing, sales of *FTA*, tax matters, and EH's interest in revising his contract with Scribner's (PUL). EH refers to Perkins's cable of 11 December 1929 reporting the sale of 62,000 copies of *FTA* (PUL). Perkins's letter of 4 December 1929 remains unlocated.

2 In his 30 November letter, Perkins reported sending $25 to Peirce, assuming fault for the dispute over payment for Scribner's use of Peirce's portrait of EH.

3 In August 1929 Scribner's had published *Mrs. Eddy: The Biography of a Virginal Mind* by Edwin Franden Dakin (1898–1976), about Mary Baker Eddy (1821–1910), the founder of Christian Science. Church officials and congregants protested its publication, boycotted bookstores, and demanded its withdrawal, prompting Perkins to comment that the firm was "having quite a hot time with the Christian Scientists on account of the book" (Perkins to Owen Wister, 17 October 1929, PUL).

4 EH refers to Wister's stories "The Gift Horse" (1908), "A Pilgrim on the Gila" (1895), "The Right Honorable the Strawberries" (1926), and "Philosophy 4: A Story of Harvard University" (1901), about Harvard sophomores and their tutor.

5 Along with the first serial installment of *FTA*, the May 1929 issue of *Scribner's Magazine* ran EH's disclaimer saying that the novel was "no more intended as a picture or criticism of Italy or Italians than was 'Two Gentlemen of Verona.'"

6 EH's article "Bullfighting, Sport and Industry" would appear in the second issue of *Fortune* magazine (March 1930).

7 Vita Sackville-West (1892–1962), English poet and novelist. Her positive review of *FTA* was part of her "New Novels" program on BBC radio for 28 November 1929. When the review was published in *The Listener*, Sackville-West noted that although she normally refrained from recommending any book that might cause her audience distress, she felt compelled to review *FTA*, calling it "a most beautiful, moving, and human book" even though "the language is rough in parts" and the lovers "have omitted to get married" (4 December 1929, 761).

To Maxwell Perkins, 19 December 1929

M 95 YN
PARIS 19
NLT MAXWELL MAXWELL PERKINS C/O CHARLES SCHRIBER'S
SONS,
5TH AVENUE & 48TH ST..
PERKINS SCRIBNERS NYK
PLEASE DEPOSIT ONETHOUSAND DOLLARS MY ACCOUNT
FARMERS LOAN AND TRUST 22 WILLIAMSST THANKS
  ERNEST
MM18

PUL, Cable; Western Union destination receipt stamp: 1929 DEC 19 AM 4 05

To Gilbert Seldes, 30 December [1929]

December 30.—

Dear Gilbert:—

What would you want from me more convincing than your published denials, Gilbert? What's it all about? You send me the denial but not the accusations.[1] I've never made any. I read D Parker's piece in N Yorker and saw no reference or cracks at you.[2] I don't carry the piece with me ~~unfortunately~~ but believe it mentioned the editor of some now defunct magazine of culture. Why should that be you? Aren't all the magazines of culture now defunct? It all sounds like ball room bananas to me

205

Best to you always
Ernest.

phPUL, ALS; letterhead: PALACE HOTEL SANATORIUM / MONTANA
s. SIERRE

1 The incoming letter from Seldes has not been located, and his "published denial" remains unidentified.
2 Dorothy Parker's *New Yorker* profile of EH, "The Artist's Reward," mentions a "young gentleman who once occupied the editorial chair of a now defunct magazine of culture" who had turned down EH's work (30 November 1929, 30). EH blamed Seldes for the 1922 rejection of his early poems, but Seldes, who had served as managing editor of the *Dial* (1921–1922), later told Carlos Baker that the rejection, if made, must have been by Scofield Thayer (1890–1982) (*SL*, 111 n. 5). EH himself had told Sherwood Anderson in a letter of 9 March [1922] that Pound had sent some of EH's poems to Thayer (*Letters* vol. 1, 331–32). The *Dial* ceased publication in 1929.

To Alan Devoe, 30 December 1929

Dear Mr. Devoe:
   Thank you very much for sending me The Naturalist's Christmas. You were very good to send it to me and I enjoyed it very much[1]

With all best wishes
Yours very truly,
Ernest Hemingway.
December 30, 1929

PSU, ALS; letterhead: Palace-Hôtel / Montana-Vermala (Suisse)

Between 20 and 30 December, EH and Pauline were among the friends who gathered in Montana-Vermala, Switzerland, to spend Christmas with Sara and Gerald Murphy, whose younger son, Patrick, diagnosed with tuberculosis, was a patient in a sanatorium there. The group included Jinny Pfeiffer, the Fitzgeralds, John and Kate Dos Passos, Donald Ogden and Beatrice Stewart, and Dorothy Parker.

1 Devoe had sent EH a copy of his first publication, *The Naturalist's Christmas*, a 24-page monograph privately printed in New York in 1925, inscribing it "To Ernest Hemingway— in admiration, Alan Devoe. 7 December 1929." The volume survives at JFK. An advertisement for the booklet ("Suitable to be read at the Xmas Season"), being sold by the author for fifty cents (or $1.00 for an autographed copy), appeared in the *Brooklyn Daily Eagle* on 18 December 1929 (24).

To Archibald MacLeish, 31 December [1929]

December 31—

Dear Archy:—

Got back from Suisse today and found yours of Dec 18 with bull material—[1]

However had this article finished first— There are 21 typewritten pages and 10 pages in pencil of footnotes—

The foot notes are numbered to go at the foot of pages corresponding with the numbers (1) (2) etc. in the typewritten text.[2]

Look, if this isnt what you want and you want some more color—I've never seen the magazine and that it was facts they wanted—why not run your color description in your piece starting with your page 6— Continuing through page 9—ending where I've marked in pencil— You could run that in a box separate from my fact article or with the box set in it— Marking it—(your color description)—By A. MacLeish or any whatever name you use on the magazine.

Am scribbling this in a hell of a hurry— Have worked like a bastard on facts and figures in the article.

Think the foot notes are a good idea as they give juice to supplement the fact—

Hope the hell you like it— It aint literature— Just article—

Your piece page 6 through page 9 damn good— (The other part of it I more or less cover) Why not use it—6 to 9—as well as mine— Me on the business— You on the picture presented— Damn proud to be associated with you— Like this

Hope to see you in N.Y around Jan 22 or 23— Dont tell <u>anybody</u> at <u>all</u>—
our boat will touch NY two days enroute Havana— Sail Jan 9 on La
Bourdonnais from Bordeaux—[3] Am not even telling Scribners— Want to see
you and Ada and a couple of fights maybe and not be a writer in N.Y— It sure
will be swell to see you— Please don't tell <u>anybody</u> that we're coming— Then
we can do what we want and deny having ever been in N.Y. —

I'll take this now to Bank to mail. We got your swell Xmas wire. Wired
you but to 8 Henderson Place by mistake hope you got it— Up in train all
night—pooped as hell—also hungry—

So long old Archie— Hold the check for me— I'll get it from you in N.Y.—
Will be broke in N.Y and figure on it— Have put all dough from Farewell
direct into Trust fund for my mother and family.

Komroff terrible— I know him but not a friend—[4]

Best love to all———

Pappy——

Hope this piece will be all right for you—

[*On verso in lower left quadrant of the folded letter:*]

Am returning all your Morgue stuff to office

My permanent address care <u>Scribner's NY</u>

LOC, ALS

1 MacLeish's letter and "bull material" remain unlocated. MacLeish's first piece for *Fortune*
magazine appeared in the same March 1930 issue as EH's "Bullfighting, Sport and Industry"
but was completely unrelated; it was titled " . . . and Apple Pie."

2 The 21-page typescript, titled "Bullfighting Business," and the 10-page pencil manuscript of
footnotes survive at JFK (items 296, 297). The letter, handwritten in black ink to this point,
continues in pencil.

3 The French Line's *La Bourdonnais*, originally a German steamer received by the French
government after WWI, served the Bordeaux–New York line from 1923 to 1931.
The Hemingways would sail aboard the ship from Bordeaux on 10 January 1930, reaching
New York City on 25 January.

4 Manuel Komroff (1890–1974), American writer, editor, and translator, had been Boni &
Liveright's production manager and editor of the Modern Library series before moving to
Paris in 1926. EH had admired Komroff's edition of *The Travels of Marco Polo* (1926) and
praised his short stories to *Scribner's Magazine* editor Robert Bridges (*Letters* vol. 3, 122,
126). Komroff admired EH's "Fifty Grand" and offered to shorten it after the story had been
repeatedly rejected by magazines as too long. EH allowed him to do so, but restored the
deletions before submitting it to the *Atlantic Monthly*, which published it uncut (July 1927).
Why EH here deems Komroff "terrible" is unclear.

To F. Scott Fitzgerald, [c. 3 January 1930]

Friday

Dear Scott:

Your note just came. It's tough luck but there are <u>no</u> bullfights in Spain after end of November.[1]

Climate in San Sebastian now on cloudy damp and drisly. Town deserted. Best medium luxe hotel damned good

Hotel Biarritz—

ARANA— More moderate.

Pamplona, now cold, may be raining [*EH insertion*: rain]—comes from the sea—or melting snow— <u>Nothing</u> to do—

Hotels (1) Grand Deluxe deserted

(2) Quintana (The Montoya of Sun Also pretty simple for your tastes, perhaps.)

(3) La Perla—½ way between the two.[2]

In winter Madrid is clear and cold—cold as hell—Hotel Savoy.

Where people go in Spain in winter for good climate—is Tarragona— South on the Coast from Barcelona—Hotel de Paris—Lovely old Town on a hill above sea—

Malaga—further south—Good climate—Hotel Regina—and Ronda— beautiful situation up on the RR from Gibraltar— Lovely place—nothing much to do but beautiful and romantic—where I would go for a honeymoon for instance if had lots of money— Hotel Maria Christina (may be called Regina Christina) It's neither its Reina Victoria![3] and also Hotel Royal.

If I can give you any dope let me know— But San Sebastian and Pamplona would be a hell of a disappointment to you in winter![4]

Ernest

P.S. I forgot to tell you to charge the wire to my account.

Please forgive me. Glad you liked the books. Hope it (Graves) makes you glad

P.S.

—continued from page 3[5]

—You missed the war!

It gives me a hell of a respect for poor Seigfried Sassoon— too![6]

Have read Lady Chatt— It didnt hold me—[7]

PUL, ALS

Although Baker dates this letter c. 5 January 1930 (*SL*, 319–20), that date fell on a Sunday; EH dates this letter "Friday," probably 3 January 1930.

1 The Spanish bullfighting season traditionally ran from March through October, after which many Spanish bullfighters performed in Mexico and elsewhere in Latin America. Fitzgerald's note remains unlocated.

2 During the 1924 Fiesta of San Fermín, EH and Hadley stayed at Hotel La Perla, established in 1881 and located on the northeast corner of Plaza del Castillo. In 1925 they chose Hotel Quintana, on the southeast corner of the plaza, and EH returned to stay at the Quintana during the next four *sanfermines* he attended—in 1926, 1927, 1929, and 1931.

3 On his first visit to Ronda in 1923, EH stayed at the Hotel Reina Victoria (Queen Victoria), opened in 1906 and named after Victoria Eugenia (1887–1969), who that year had married Spanish King Alfonso XIII (1886–1941) and would reign with him until 1931. The Reina Cristina in Algeciras was named for the preceding Spanish queen, María Cristina (1858–1929).

4 In February 1930, seeking a warmer climate for Zelda, who was ill, distressed, and approaching a nervous breakdown, the Fitzgeralds would travel to Algeria rather than to Spain.

5 EH wrote the first portion of this postscript at the bottom of page 3 of this four-page letter and continued it on the last page beneath his signature.

6 Robert Graves (1895–1985), English poet, novelist, and memoirist whose writings include the bestselling WWI memoir *Goodbye to All That* (1929), which was among EH's books in his library at Finca Vigía (Brasch and Sigman, item 2700). Graves had served in the Royal Welsh Fusiliers with Siegfried Sassoon (1886–1967), whose poetry graphically depicted the brutality and senselessness of the war. Sassoon ignited controversy in 1917 with his open letter of protest charging that the war was being deliberately prolonged. Graves persuaded the authorities that his friend was suffering from shellshock, and rather than being court-martialed, Sassoon was hospitalized for treatment before returning to the front.

7 Unable to find a publisher for his sexually explicit novel, D. H. Lawrence (1885–1930) arranged to have *Lady Chatterley's Lover* privately printed in Florence in June 1928. To counter widespread piracy, Lawrence asked Sylvia Beach to publish a Paris edition. She declined but recommended Edward Titus, founder of At the Sign of the Black Manikin Press. Titus produced an edition in 1929 that quickly became a bestseller at Shakespeare and Company. Beach's records show that EH borrowed *Lady Chatterley's Lover* on 19 September 1929 and returned it on 27 September (PUL).

To Morley Callaghan, 4 January [1930]

January 4 1929[1]

Dear Morley—

I traced the story and found that Pierre Loving was responsible for putting it out both in Paris and N.Y.—found out where he lived and sent him this wire to his address, Waverley Place N.Y.C.— "Understand you saw

Morley Callaghan knock me cold answer Guaranty Trust Paris—"

I received no answer.

Scott wired you that he was waiting anxiously to read your corrections of the story (telling you where the story appeared) <u>at my request and against his own good judgement</u>.[2] I did not know whether you had ever seen the story and since over 3 weeks had elapsed since it was first published in NY Post it was up to him to correct it as a witness if you had not seen it and already done so. He, Scott, assured me you would have seen it and did not want to send the wire, (which contained his insinuations against you). Since I had not seen the story in 3 weeks I had no way of being sure you had seen it.

It is, however, <u>entirely my fault</u> that the wire calling your attention to the story was sent; and since some pretty tough words have been passed around apropos of who sent the wire I want you to know that it was in no way an idea of Scotts. It was <u>entirely</u> my fault.

If you wish to transfer to me the epithets you applied to Scott I will be in the States in a few weeks and am at your disposal any place where there is no publicity attached[3]

Yours always—

Ernest Hemingway

PUL, ALScc

In a 10 January letter to Maxwell Perkins, EH would write that Fitzgerald had persuaded him not to send this letter, but Pauline mailed it by mistake.

1 EH misdated the year.
2 EH's handwriting is ambiguous: Baker transcribes the word as "amicably" (*SL*, 318), Bruccoli as "amiably" (*Fitz–Hem*, 152). Callaghan later recounted this episode in his memoirs, paraphrasing this 4 January letter from EH and quoting the cable he received from Fitzgerald just before Callaghan's letter of correction was published in the *Herald Tribune* on 8 December 1929: "HAVE SEEN STORY IN HERALD TRIBUNE. ERNEST AND I AWAIT YOUR CORRECTION. SCOTT FITZGERALD" (Callaghan, 243).
3 In his memoirs, Callaghan confessed to feeling ashamed "to this day" of the outraged letter he wrote to Fitzgerald in reply, charging that "For him to hurry out and send that cable to me collect without waiting to see what I would do was the act of a son of a bitch and I could only assume he was drunk as usual when he sent it" (Callaghan, 241–43).

To Maxwell Perkins, 4 January [1930]

Jan 4.

Dear Max—

Have been pretty sick or would have answered your letters sooner—
The last one I received was the one about revisions of contract— You and
Mr. Scribner are both damned fine about it—

Since you are willing to make it 25% after 25,000 I say make it 25% after
30,000—[1]

I will be in N.Y around between 23–25th of this mo. for 2 days— But for
Christ's Sweet Sake do not tell <u>anyone</u> as I have many things to do and do
not want to be made a dog and pony show—

Enclosed are some British Clippings Cape sent me—I think by quotation
you could get quite a good ad out of them—and scare a few Herricks—[2]
No one in England when they had a war thought the book was written by
a damned amateur who knew nothing about war— However we must all eat
a ton of shit in this life and no one must decline their seat at the table—

While we're in N.Y. we can re-draw the contract putting in the name of
the Trust Co. to whom the first $20,000 is to be paid.

Thank you very much for the review by Thos. Wolfe and the letter
containing it.[3]

Being sick my correspondence has gone to hell but I will see you soon—

Think you can get something pretty good maybe out of these English
reviews— Will you save them please for me? I enclose also a German review
of Men Without Women—[4] Have a lot more (Hot) from other papers sent by
friends etc if you're interested—you might be interested to read this one—

Anyway goodbye and good luck—

Reynolds balled up play and film negociations completely—I kept
insisting I wanted and preferred <u>cash</u> from movies— He stalled until
offers were withdrawn— Get <u>Stallings</u> to do play— I havent seen
a nickel from it yet— Maybe I can collect the advance in N.Y. He
had an offer of $10,000 for movies and let it slide— I'll be lucky to
get $750 now minus his 10%—

He speaks of the book as though he morally disapproved of it—

↑ This <u>entirely</u> confidential— It's not a considered statement— He doubtless has his side to it— But I dont think he's the one to do business for me— No one can sell anything that he does not believe in

Good luck to you— Happy New Year to you and all your family—

Yours always

Ernest

PUL, ALS

1 EH misstates or misremembers the figures Perkins mentioned in his 10 December 1929 letter. Perkins wrote that he and Charles Scribner had discussed revising the terms of EH's contract for *FTA* (which provided 15% royalties on all copies sold), and they were now prepared to offer a 20% royalty after the sale of 25,000 copies. If these new terms did not seem satisfactory, EH had only to tell Perkins what the terms would be (PUL).

2 Scribner's advertisements quoting British praise for *FTA* would appear in the *New York Times Book Review* during January and February 1930, including a half-page ad on 19 January headlined "Who Reads an American Book?" and featuring excerpts from eight British reviews. In a 19 December 1929 letter, Perkins had congratulated EH on his decision not to respond to Robert Herrick's negative review of *FTA* in the November 1929 *Bookman*, saying an author should treat such reviews "with the silent contempt they deserve." Perkins said he suggested to editor Seward Collins that the magazine print a letter Scribner's had received from a reader countering Herrick's piece (PUL). After the *Bookman* refused, Scribner's itself would publish the letter (by M. K. Hare of Tryon, North Carolina) in the magazine's advertising section ("Is It Dirt or Is It Art?," *Bookman Advertiser*, March 1930, xiv–xv).

3 In his 19 December letter, Perkins said he was enclosing a review by Thomas Wolfe "written for some Chicago newspaper which wanted reviews by authors of other authors' books." The piece by Thomas Wolfe (1900–1938), another of Perkins's authors, remains unlocated. Wolfe's first novel, *Look Homeward, Angel*, had been published by Scribner's on 18 October 1929.

4 While the German review is not filed with this letter in the Scribner's Archive at PUL, EH may have sent Perkins a copy of one of the reviews of *MWW* that survive in the Newspaper Clippings file among EH's papers at JFK: B. E. Werner, "Männer unter sich," *Deutsche Allgemeine Zeitung*, 12 November 1929; and Wilhelm Spener, "Ein Dichter, der sein Metier beherrscht" ("A Poet Who Has Mastered His Craft"), *Das Unterhaltungsblatt*, 18 December 1929.

To Bennett Cerf, 4 January 1930

Dear Mr. Cerf:—

Thank you very much for your letter. I am glad you are doing the book but I am sorry I cannot write a foreword for it— I couldnt write a foreword for anything least of all a book I wrote myself— I'm awfully sorry if this puts you to any inconvenience but I feel to write it would be taking $200 out of some critic's pocket—but beside that I swear to God I couldnt write it if I tried.

Best luck to you with the book— I urged Perkins very strongly to let you have it after we met that time in N.Y. and am glad they finally saw their way clear to—[1]

Yours always

Ernest Hemingway.

c/o Guaranty Trust Co of N.Y.

4 Place de la Concorde

Paris

Jan 4—1930

Columbia, ALS; postmark: PARIS – 25 / R. DANTON, 22 [30] / 5 ° I / 1930

The envelope bears EH's notation: "Via Paquebot / 'Ile de France' / partant Havre 8 Janvier."

1 Cerf's efforts to include EH's work in the Modern Library of the World's Best Books would result in the publication of *SAR* on 25 February 1930 as No. 170 of the series. The volume carried an introduction, dated January 1930, by American critic and editor Henry Seidel Canby (1878–1961). While the letter to which EH is responding here remains unlocated, Cerf had first approached EH about adding a book of his to the Modern Library in a letter dated 29 October 1928 (JFK), which EH apparently discussed with Perkins when they met in New York City in mid-November 1928.

To Edward Titus, 4 January [1930]

Jan 4.

Dear Titus:—

Here is the corrected proof. The —Star on last page marks

a footnote—[1] Dont forget the copyright. It is most important[2]

Good luck—

Ernest Hemingway.

UT, ALS

1 This letter accompanied the corrected proofs of EH's introduction to Samuel Putnam's translation of the autobiography of Alice Ernestine Prin (1901–1953), the French model and habitué of Left Bank cafés known as Kiki of Montparnasse. Titus would publish the translation, together with EH's introduction, in June 1930 as *Kiki's Memoirs* (Paris: At the Sign of the Black Manikin Press; Hanneman B7). Prin's memoirs were originally published as *Les Souvenirs de Kiki* (Paris: H. Broca, 1929). On the third and last page of the proofs of his introduction, EH wrote "Foot Note" and drew a five-pointed star in the left margin next to a sentence advising his readers to learn French in order to read Kiki's book, "not Julian Green's nor Jean Cocteau's, nor whoever should be at that time great French writers for Americans." At the bottom of the page, he drew another star next to this handwritten footnote: "I have never read Mr. Green so this reference is probably very unjust. They tell me he is very good. So let me withdraw the advice, or rather change it to urge you, after having learned French, to read both Kiki and Mr Green." The footnote would appear in print as EH specified, marked by an asterisk in parentheses.

2 In order to secure U.S. copyrights to the introduction, Titus would publish it separately in a pamphlet edition of twenty-five copies. EH's *Introduction to Kiki of Montparnasse* (New York: Edward W. Titus, 1930) was copyrighted in Titus's name on 22 January 1930 (Hanneman A9, 31; Grissom, 147–50).

To Grace Hall Hemingway, [6 January 1930]

Dear Mother:———

Enclosed checks for Jan. and Feb— Am sorry not to have sent checks before— But have been sick; worried by leaving, packing and many things— Am arranging trust fund to start in April— Hope to get fixed up by warm climate of Key West, exercise, etc. Havent been able to write since Nov.

Hope you are all fine and Sunny on the mend again— Write me care Chas. Scribner's Sons—5th Ave at 48th Street—N.Y.C. Wish you could sell the house— George R. Hemingway should be forced to take it—[1]

Best Happy New Year to you all— We sail by various ports Jan. 10th for Key West—

Love to all the family—

Ernie

DPL, ALS; postmark: PARIS-25 / RUE DANTON, 13 $\frac{30}{}$ / 6 · I / 1930

The envelope, addressed to Grace Hall Hemingway at the family home in Oak Park, bears this notation in EH's hand: "via Pacquebot / 'Isle de France' / partant 8 Janvier / de Havre."

The envelope also bears Grace's handwritten notation: "Received Jan 18. '30 / Ans same day / c/o care 'Scribners' New York City."

1 Although Grace's response of 18 January remains unlocated, she would resist this advice, claiming in a letter of 2 February 1930 that the Oak Park house served as security for Sunny: "If we sell out here, there would be nothing for her, in Florida jobs are almost impossible to get, and we should live in such small quarters—and have no social standing—she would hate it. Perhaps that's why the Lord isn't letting us sell, because He knows she must be started off in life" (JFK).

To Maxwell Perkins, 8 January 1930

D 16 KC

PARIS 19

NLT MAXWELL PERKINS SCRIBNERS MAXWELL PERKINS, C/O CHARLES SCRIBNERS SONS,

NYK 5TH AVENUE & 48TH ST.

PLEASE HOLD ALL MAIL SAILING FRIDAY WRITING SENDING BRITISH CLIPPINGS IE CUTTINGS TODAY

ERNEST

PUL, Cable; Western Union destination receipt stamp: 1930 JAN 8 AM 3 27

On Friday, 10 January 1930, EH and Pauline would sail for the United States from Bordeaux on *La Bourdonnais*.

To Guy Hickok, [c. 8 January 1930]

Wednesday noon

Dear Guy:—

When we left each other on Saturday I hoped to get out to your place on Sunday—[1] Told you on the phone what happened then— We had 2 francs when Bill Bird[2] came in on Sunday night. Sweeney had said he was coming around and we waited for him but he never showed up— Monday everything went haywired and Tuesday was worse— I tried to get everything done to come in this morning and thought we would have time to go out and feel like hell that it got buggered up so—

In my book trunk were two Mss. that had to be copied corrected and delivered to the shits I'd sold them to—to get money to finance Fangel, Franklyn and our own crossing—[3] They were due Sunday— didnt get here until yesterday morning— Paulines been in bed— It's been pretty bloody—

I appreciate youre going to Berlin with me like hell and I wanted awfully to get out to your place— I know it looks as though I haunted your office when I wanted something done and then never came around but that isn't the way I wanted to do— Havent been able to do a damn thing I wanted truly—

Well So Long Gros— I cant thank Mary enough for all she did for us— I had two books out for you— But Pauline packed them both— Will send them—

But anyway here's your pencil!

Was at Lipps[4] but upstairs—

Good luck Kid—
Ernest

phPUL, ALS

The conjectured letter date is based on EH's reference to preparations for their imminent departure from Paris to sail from Bordeaux on Friday, 10 January.

1 In two letters to EH of 1928, Hickok referred to his new house in the Point du Jour quarter located in Boulogne-Billancourt, on the western outskirts of Paris (PUL and JFK).
2 William Augustus (Bill) Bird (1889–1963), American journalist and founder of the Three Mountains Press (1922–1928), which published EH's *iot* (1924). From 1920 until 1933, Bird served as Paris correspondent and European manager of the Consolidated Press Association, a news syndicate he had co-founded in 1919 with his childhood friend, journalist and news entrepreneur David Lawrence (1888–1973). Bird and EH had met in 1922 while both were covering the Genoa Economic Conference.
3 One may have been the manuscript of EH's article "Bullfighting, Sport and Industry" (published in *Fortune* magazine, March 1930). EH often helped friends in financial difficulties, among them American painter, photographer, and writer Henry Guy Fangel (1875–1943) and bullfighter Sidney Franklin, known for his profligate lifestyle and inordinately high fees that priced him out of many bullrings, resulting in only fourteen engagements in 1929.
4 Brasserie Lipp, at 151, Boulevard St. Germain, established in 1880 by Léonard Lipp, a native of Alsace. EH recalls a meal there in the "Hunger Was Good Discipline" Chapter of *MF.*

To Maxwell Perkins, 10 January [1930]

Jan 10

Dear Max—

Just a note to tell you got your cable and your letter of Dec 27 about Callaghan etc.—[1] Pauline mailed by mistake a letter I'd written Callaghan and then, on Scott's more or less insistance decided better not to send—

It was sent Care Scribners—in my handwriting in a brown envelope[.] Will you hold it for me— I've just cabled you to this effect[2]

In haste

Thanks

Ernest

Thanks for Fine Wire

PUL, ALS; letterhead: COMPAGNIE GÉNÉRALE / TRANSATLANTIQUE / FRENCH LINE

1 On 8 January, Perkins had cabled EH: "Good luck Sale over seventy thousand Signs for future good Max" (PUL). In his letter of 27 December 1929, Perkins recounted his recent lunch meeting with Morley Callaghan, who described the "notorious boxing bout" with EH in "an altogether decent way" (PUL).
2 EH refers to his letter to Callaghan of 4 January 1929, which Callaghan did receive, describing it in detail in his memoirs (Callaghan, 244–47). Callaghan also described EH's letter to him of 21 February 1930, in which EH explained that Pauline had seen the earlier letter on his desk and posted it after EH had left Paris to deliver their car to Bordeaux to be put aboard the ship (249). EH's cable to Perkins remains unlocated.

To Grace Hall Hemingway, 27 January [1930]

N.Y. Jan 27

Dear Mother:—

Our boat has stopped here for 2 days enroute to Havana— Have just gotten your two letters of Jan. 18 and Dec 29— You mention another one about taxes sent in duplicate to K.W. and Paris but have not rec'd it yet so cannot answer it— Hope the taxes are going to be less than last year—

I am terribly sorry you've been ill with sinus trouble and hope it is better now— It must be frightfully painful! You do not mention Sunny or the others so hope they are all well—[1]

Note what you write about sending children to college and that <u>Justice</u> demands they be given same chances we older ones had— Better not, perhaps, to put it on the basis of what <u>Justice demands</u>[.][2] Because you may recall my own experience which was to leave home after a high school education—make my own living and never have received any money or aid ever since—"rather see me dead and in my grave than writing as I am"—"great shame and disgrace" etc.

However I have never been one for strict application of Justice preferring to leave that to those who know more about it than I do—

I've every hope and intention that Carol go to college and have as fine a life as she is capable of making for herself— Not much notice seems to be given to the Trust fund I wrote you we were founding— It goes into operation in April— In it we are putting <u>more</u> money than my book has made <u>entirely</u> and <u>completely</u> in <u>every way</u>— The trust fund totals some $50,000—of the income from it $600 a year will be paid to Carol during your lifetime—(in quarterly installments) The <u>balance</u> i.e. the remainder of the income will be paid to you in the same way— I am relying on you to look after Leicester.

On your death Carol will receive (approximately) $10,000—Leicester $10,000—Sunny and Ura $5,000 each. The balance of the trust fund will go to Pauline— In this way you are assured, no matter what happens to me, of an income of $175 a month for life in addition to the 125 or so you now have from Dads insurance and estate— Carol will have $50 a month— This can accumulate (starting April 1) until she is ready to go to college and will give her 250 or so ahead to start with— This money is <u>entirely her own</u>—but it does not, in my intention, release you from the obligation to provide for Carol as long as she is under age—

Sunny is old enough to earn her own living and even contribute something to family support— Leicester I trust you to look after—

Pauline and I are making this trust fund with money of her own and the money I have gotten from Scribners—

I now have 2 books the profits of which I have given away—The Sun Also Rises and A Farewell to Arms—

So much for what "Justice demands"—

If my book has been sold to the movies I have not been let in on the secret— I have heard <u>nothing</u> of it and received no money for it—

It is to be made into a play by Laurence Stallings for which I will receive an advance of $750.$^{\underline{00}}$ less 10% agents commission—and if the play flops that is all I will get—

We own no home, no property, nothing, and I have 2 children of my own to educate provide for and bring up— ~~So do not have the idea that~~ We have been working on this trust fund since last November when it became sure the book would make a certain amount of money.

If "Justice" demands that anything further be done at the moment to insure Carol all the advantages she and you all should have I think Marcelline, who received these educational advantages and was always a great friend and confidant in the days when I was receiving letters telling me what a disgrace I was and how it would be better for me to be dead etc. than writing as I was; I think Marcelline can help out the cause of Justice.

Anyway now you know what is in the trust fund and what you can count on and I hope you will be able to sell the house and fix things up as well as possible— I'm terribly sorry you've been sick and I hope you are over it now and that Sunny is well too—

Please see that the car is covered by <u>complete liability</u> insurance for <u>all drivers</u> in a <u>good</u> insurance co. or the next thing is liable to be a repetition of the Leicester business which you were lucky to get out of as cheaply as you did—

I am enclosing check for 100^{\underline{00}}$ to use for your immediate needs—

Love to all—
Ernest.

I hope in Key West to get in shape and have some tranquillity to write— What we will live on next year and two years from now I must make now— I've spoken about this trust fund not to complain or belly ache but because people have a way of imagining that if you give them 10^{\underline{00}}$ you must have a million— It is incomprehensible that you would give them 10^{\underline{00}}$ if you only owned $13.$^{\underline{00}}$ And from the way all our relatives, except Aunt Grace, (who I heard damned so much last time I was home.) have acted I see why it is incomprehensible![3]

Your pictures are being sent to the Spring Salon— The big one— And I hope they will be exhibited— Best luck to you—

E.H.

[*On verso in lower right quadrant of the folded letter:*]

Think Marce should give Carol $25 a month at least— Besides other aid to family— What I give is out of my Principle Capital not just superfluous income—and she complains about being delayed in building a new house— My God—

AT ILLINOIS ARTISTS' EXHIBIT

Grace Hall Heminigway of Oak Park, Edward J. Timmons of Chicago and Mrs. Sydney Holmes Langford of Joliet.

PSU, ALS

1 In her letter of 29 December 1929, Grace mentioned suffering from a sinus infection (JFK). Her 18 January letter remains unlocated. EH had not yet received her letters of 9 January, sent in duplicate to Paris and Key West, in which she reported that taxes were due on the Florida investments, provided updates on each of EH's siblings, commented on the state of her sinus infection, and thanked EH for a Christmas check of $100 (JFK). With the copy sent to Key West, she enclosed an undated newspaper clipping headed "At Illinois Artists' Exhibit" featuring a photograph of herself.

2 EH is apparently responding to the unlocated letter. In her reply dated 6 February 1930, Grace would address EH's comments on the phrase "justice demands": "I seem always to be saying the wrong thing or some word or sentence that is capable of a wrong construction. That expression (in all justice) which I meant only to apply to myself and my need to struggle for Carol's educational advantages, has appeared to you to be a demand from me for you to do justice to Carol. All I can say is, that I am most unfortunate in expressing myself—will you try to remember that I never did, and never could have meant that" (JFK).

3 In her 6 February letter, Grace would write that EH resembled her father, "the only man I ever knew who, (as you put it)—was capable of giving 10 when all he had was 13."

To Maxwell Perkins, [c. 28 January 1930]

Dear Max:—

We got off all right— It was fine to see you again and we'll have a fine time when the tarpon start running.

Look— Would you get that $500 courtesy payment from Fox for me at once if possible? If they dont pay it right away they never will— You have my authority to sign whatever release is required—

I think you can bluff them on the matter of there being damages to me— There certainly is——

In N.Y. I heard from several people that my book Men Without Women was being filmed— It's not the same as The Wild Party—which was never published openly— Anyway so long as we're bitched would like the $500.[001]

Will you let me know about this?—

Quiet today—only ten people on the whole boat— Warm outside—5 blackbirds flying along beside the ship—

I'm awfully sorry about Liveright refusing to give up the book— Will figure some way to get it away—[2]

Have been writing Reynolds all morning—

Then want <u>no more negoceation</u> but to get to work again— I've written
Mr. G. A. Pfeiffer that you are sending him the check made out to the City
Bank Farmers Trust—[3]

See you in a month or so—

Yours always

Ernest

Also could Scribners send a check for me to The Author's League—
I dont know how much $30—I think— I've been elected a long time ago but
never joined but now Im in with R. upstairs I better join for protection.[4]

Thanks ever so much for doing all these things— I wanted to buy a lot of
books but never got time— Something awfully funny happened at the boat
that I'll tell you about when you come down— Mike [Strater] bought a gaff
you could land the Bremen with— The little outboard sea skiff we got will
be grand I think for Marquesas and tarpon— I got a ~~scalding snot~~ (no that's
not a pretty figure) cold in the head and think less clearly every minute—

Please excuse

PUL, ALS; letterhead: COMPAGNIE GÉNÉRALE / TRANSATLANTIQUE /
FRENCH LINE

The conjectured letter date is based on EH's travel itinerary. After a two-day stopover in
New York, where EH met with Perkins and MacLeish, the Hemingways continued on to
Havana aboard *La Bourdonnais*, leaving New York City at 4:10 p.m. on 27 January 1930
(according to the passenger manifest) and landing in Havana on 1 February. They would
arrive in Key West on 2 February.

1 A motion picture by the Fox Film Corporation titled *Men Without Women* but unrelated to
   the contents of EH's 1927 short-story collection was about to be released. In a letter to
   Perkins dated 27 January 1930, Fox legal counsel Edwin P. Kilroe enclosed copies of an
   agreement that would grant the studio permission for use of the title in return for a $500
   payment (PUL). *The Wild Party*, a 1929 Paramount film directed by Dorothy Arzner
   (1897–1979), starred Clara Bow (1905–1965) in her first talking picture. A Jazz Age verse
   narrative of the same title by American poet Joseph Moncure March (1899–1977) was
   written in 1926 but remained unpublished for two years because of its portrayal of sex,
   alcohol, and violence. In 1928 it was published in Chicago by Pascal Covici in a limited
   edition of 750 copies and promptly pirated.

2 *IOT*, published in 1925 by Boni & Liveright, would be republished by Scribner's on
   24 October 1930.

3 On EH's instructions, Perkins sent Gus Pfeiffer a $20,000 check for the trust fund on
   29 January (PUL). Pfeiffer would acknowledge receipt in a letter to Perkins of 30 January
   (PUL).

4 The Authors' League of America was founded in New York City in 1912 by Arthur Cheney Train (1875–1945) to represent the interests of writers, advocating copyright protection, fair contracts, and free expression. After receiving notice in late January 1929 that he had been elected to the Literary Council of the organization, EH had consulted fellow member Owen Wister as to whether they ought to resign from "this very silly seeming committee of something or other." Wister advised, "Give the Authors' League Committee the benefit of the doubt. I think those things are always silly" (*Letters* vol. 3, 517, 532–33, 538).

To Mildred D. Giraud, 30 January 1930

To Mildred D. Giraud

—souvenir of 21 days on La Bourdonnais—this book (purchased by herself)—with the best wishes of the author

Ernest Hemingway.

Jan 30 1930

Bookbid Rare Books online listing, Beverly Hills, California, Inscription

EH inscribed a copy of *SAR* (ninth printing, November 1929).

To Robert de Saint Jean, [4 February 1930]

P.O Box 396

Key West

Florida

Dear Monsieur de Saint Jean:—

We left Paris January 10th and I have just gotten your note of the 13th.

It is such a long way from here to the Deux Magots that I am afraid we cannot meet very soon unless you should be coming to America— We will be back in Paris in about a year—

About the article— I am sure writing about the books [*Marginal note in an unknown hand*: *A Farewell to Arms (1929)] you will make no bêtises— and as the life of a writer is usually nothing but bêtises it is better not to mention it![1]

But I am very sorry to miss seeing you again and I hope we will meet in Paris some time not too far away—

Yours very truly

Ernest Hemingway.

RR Auction online catalog, Boston, 14 March 2012, Lot 608 (illustrated), ALS; postmark: [4 February 1930]

The letter bears notations at the top of the page in an unidentified hand: "important / HEMINGWAY / 4.2.1930."

1 *Bêtises*: foolishness, blunders (French). The catalog description translates this as "silly mistakes."

To Waldo Peirce, 7 February [1930]

Box 396

Key West Fla.

Feb 7

Muy Valdo Mío—

We got in N.Y. for 2 day stay on boat same day you checked out of Brevoort— Heard from Max—called up Brevoort— You just gone— Damned tough luck— Sun and Mon—Jan 26-27—

Boat came on down to Havana— Finally arrived here—[*EH insertion*: 6 days after left N.Y.] fine house out near the Casino (swimming place)[1] Working hard— Charles [Thompson] and I caught 3 tarpon first night we went out—

It will be damned fine to see you— That was hell about Whitney— First I knew about it was your letter— We were on water 21 days— Went Bordeaux—Vigo—Halifax—NY—Havana—wired Pat last night to Harvard Club to tell him to come down—[2] This just a note to you— Your girl looks damned nice in the pictures—[3] Saw Max, Mike [Strater], Archie MacLeish in N.Y.— Mikes coming down in March—

Write me the dope— Pauline sends best love—

Ernest

Pauline says how's to send down that picture of me—[4] We've got big house— no pictures— She says if she doesnt get it you'll give it some other woman.

When will you be down?

Colby, ALS

1 After arriving in Key West on 2 February, EH and Pauline moved into a rented house belonging to Charles and Francis Curry at 1301 Whitehead Street. The Coral Isle Casino was located a few blocks to the east and south, on the southern shore of the island. (Although published sources place them at this address in 1931 and in a rented house at 1425 Pearl Street in 1930, EH letters new to print in this volume establish their dates of residency in each house.)
2 Whitney Cromwell had died of pneumonia in Tunis, North Africa, in early January 1930. In a letter to EH of 27 January 1930, Peirce reported that he had met Pat Morgan at Whitney's funeral in New York and invited him to Bangor "for complete change" (JFK).
3 American painter Alzira Handforth Boehm (1908–2010). Peirce wrote, "I'm living in open shame with a sweet young consort of 21 who paints all the time." Alzira appears in four of the five photographs Peirce enclosed with his 27 January letter. She and Peirce would marry on 16 December 1930.
4 EH refers to Peirce's oil portrait of him signed "for Ernest (Alias Kid Balzac), Key West, first April '29, WP." Peirce had loaned the portrait to Perkins, who placed it in Scribner's front window to promote *FTA*. In his 27 January letter, Peirce wrote EH, "I've got your mug back here anytime you want it." The portrait, now part of the Ernest Hemingway Collection at JFK, is reproduced in the plate section of this volume.

To Maxwell Perkins, [7] February [1930]

P.O. Box 396

Key West

Friday Feb ?

Dear Max:—

Have been going well since here— Went out fishing 2 nights ago with Charles [Thompson] and we caught 3 tarpon in the Key West Harbor channels—near where you caught yours— Lost 4 others that threw the hooks when they jumped.

Am mailing the Fox releases— We should get the $500 now it's a fait accompli (misspelled) ~~but~~ evidently nothing else to do— But it is a hell of a bad precedent— What's to prevent them on this precedent naming a picture A Farewell To Arms—or The Sun Also Rises? Those three titles Men Without Women included—are as much my property as the books (no other books were called that)— I should think an injunction could stop their use—[1]

Anyway I'm writing well and that's what matters—[2] Have rented a boat we can live on and fish from for all of March and have Burge hired to run it[.] So will be all set for you— When do you figure on coming?—

I havent received the new contract nor the Spanish offer—[3] No hurry about the Contract but want to communicate with the Spanish citizen as have 2 other Span. offers and must close with one of them by wire— If that man in Baltimore will translate it <u>himself</u> as he did Dos—will take that one— otherwise the Edetorial Espana—[4]

No tourists in Havana—times harder than ever— You'll be able to get a room much cheaper at the Casa Marina I think.[5] Bootleggers in such competition that here absinthe selling only 6$\underline{^{00}}$ a bottle—Best Scotch 4.$\underline{^{00}}$ Red table wine 15$\underline{^{00}}$ the 5 gallons. Whiskey cheaper than in Paris—

Best to you always—

Ernest Hemingway.

That release doesnt give them the right to use any of the stories in Men Without Women does it?

Could the bookstore send me

The Letters of Frances Newman (Liveright)

Escape—by Francesco Nitti (Putnam I think)[6]

PUL, ALS

EH dated this letter simply "Friday Feb ?" The conjectured date is based on the fact that EH is responding to aletter from Perkins dated 3February1930 (a Monday) and that Perkins's reply to this letter is dated 14February (a Friday) (PUL). Tofurther complicate the matter, Perkins's 3February letter bears EH's handwritten notation "Answd Feb8" (a Saturday). EH may have misdated either the letter or the notation, or he may have written the letter on Friday, 7February, and mailed it the nextday.

1 In his 3February1930 letter, Perkins had enclosed four copies of the release granting Fox Film Corporation permission to use the title *Men Without Women*, advising EH to sign them "even though they must have taken the title on purpose, because you will thereby get five hundred dollars, and it is very doubtful if anything at all could be got in any other way." The movie ("a story about men in asubmarine") made no reference to EH's stories, and Perkins felt it would be "very hard" to prove damages in alawsuit. Directed by John Ford (1895–1973), the Fox production had already premiered in NewYork City on 31January and would be released nationwide on 9 February.

2 EH was finishing "Wine of Wyoming" and may have already started *DIA* (1932).

3 Perkins would bring the revised *FTA* contract to Key West in March 1930, where it would be signed by EH and witnessed by Henry Strater, but backdated to 25 September 1929, to precede the 27 September publication date of the novel. The Madrid firm Editorial España had doubled its original offer for the rights to the translation of *FTA*. In a letter dated

30 December 1929, Cape informed EH of this improved offer (£20 and royalty of 10%) and recommended he accept it (URead).

4 No wire has been located, and none of these translations seems to have materialized. *FTA* would not be translated into Spanish until 1940, in Argentina, and would not be published in Spain until 1955 (Hanneman, 199–200). Spanish academic José Robles Pazos (1897–1937), a professor of Spanish literature at Johns Hopkins University in Baltimore, had translated Dos Passos's 1925 novel *Manhattan Transfer* into Spanish, retaining its original English title (Madrid: Cénit, 1929).

5 The luxurious beachfront Casa Marina Resort at 1500 Reynolds Street in Key West, conceived as a destination resort by railroad magnate Henry Flagler, had opened in 1920.

6 Frances Percy Newman (1883–1928) American librarian and short-story writer whose two novels, *The Hard-Boiled Virgin* (1926) and *Dead Lovers Are Faithful Lovers* (1928), both published by Boni & Liveright, were banned in Boston because of their sexual content. The posthumously published *Frances Newman's Letters* (New York: Liveright, 1929), edited by Hansell Baugh and with a preface by James Branch Cabell, was among the books in EH's personal library (Brasch and Sigman, item 4844). Francesco Fausto Nitti (1899–1974), Italian journalist, antifascist political prisoner, and author of the autobiographical narrative *Escape* (New York: G. P. Putnam's Sons, 1930).

To Jonathan Cape, 8 February 1930

Feb 8 1930

P.O. Box 396

Key West—Florida—

Dear Cape:—

Sorry to have missed you in Paris—was on the water enroute here. I'll write in a few days about the Spanish offer— Have had several—a couple of other good ones—will wire you within 10 days whether to accept or not so as not to lose time—

What is the sale of A Farewell to date? It's still keeping up very well in U.S.[1] Best regards to Wren Howard.

Yours always

Ernest Hemingway.

above address will reach me until June— But Guaranty Trust Co. of Paris will <u>always</u> forward mail.

URead, ALS

1 In his 24 February 1930 reply, Cape would report that sales were over 10,000 copies, which "is very good for England" (URead). According to Perkins's letter of 14 February 1930, American sales were 79,251 (PUL).

1. Patrick, Ernest, and Pauline aboard the *Yorck*, returning to France after a year in the United States, April 1929.

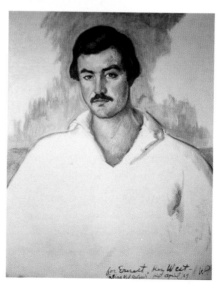

2. Waldo Peirce signed this oil portrait "For Ernest (alias Kid Balzac), Key West—first April '29. W. P."

3. Morley Callaghan in *Scribner's Magazine* (January 1929). His first novel, *Strange Fugitive*, was published by Scribner's in 1928.

His first novel listed among outstanding works of the year— Morley Callaghan.

4. F. Scott and Zelda Fitzgerald with their daughter, Scottie, in Cannes, summer 1929.

5. Hemingway and American bullfighter Sidney Franklin near Madrid, c. September 1929.

6. Virginia Pfeiffer, Guy Hickok, Pauline, and Ernest at a bullfight, 1929.

7. Harry and Caresse Crosby, founders of Black Sun Press, with their whippet, Clytoris, Le Bourget, France, 1929.

8. EH's longtime friend Kate Smith and John Dos Passos, who met in Key West in 1928 and married on 19 August 1929.

Just Published

© *Helen Breaker, Paris*

Ernest Hemingway's
New Novel

A Farewell to Arms

A novel of love in war; of the bitter fighting in the frontier mountains of Italy in 1917; a profoundly moving romance of a young American officer serving in the Italian army and an English nurse, written with a power and brilliance that surpasses even "The Sun Also Rises." $2.50

10. The unretouched portrait by Helen Breaker (Paris, 1928) used in Scribner's publicity. Hemingway had been injured when a broken skylight fell on his head.

9. Advertisement for *A Farewell to Arms* in the *New York Times Book Review* (29 September 1929). First serialized in *Scribner's Magazine* (May–November 1929), the novel was published as a book on 27 September and quickly became a bestseller.

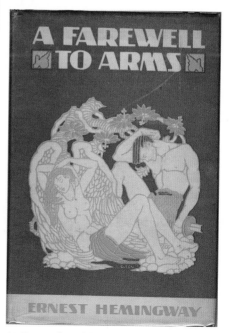

11. Dust jacket of *A Farewell to Arms* (New York: Scribner's, 1929), with cover art by Cleon.

12. Ernest and Honoria Murphy,
Montana-Vermala, Switzerland.
The Hemingways spent Christmas
1929 with Gerald and Sara
Murphy, who were visited by
many friends at the sanatorium
where their son Patrick was being
treated for tuberculosis.
*Photo © Estate of Honoria
Murphy Donnelly/Licensed by
VAGA, New York, NY.*

13. Hemingway wrote an
introduction to the translated
memoirs of Left Bank denizen
Alice Prin (known as "Kiki of
Montparnasse"), published in
Paris by Edward Titus (1930).

14. Hemingway, Berge Saunders, Henry (Mike) Strater, and Maxwell Perkins at Fort Jefferson in the Dry Tortugas, March 1930.

15. Archibald MacLeish on a visit to Key West in the spring of 1930.

16. A reunion of the Pfeiffers—Paul, Mary, Pauline, Karl, and Jinny—at the family home in Piggott, Arkansas, summer 1930.

17. Patrick with his French nanny, Henriette Lechner, Piggott, Arkansas, June 1930.

18. Pauline wearing waders on a fishing trip near the L-Bar-T Ranch, Wyoming, where she, Ernest, and Bumby vacationed in July–September 1930.

19. Posing with the head of a mountain ram, Wyoming, September 1930.

20. Bumby posing in front of the skin of one of two bears Ernest killed while hunting in Wyoming, August–September 1930.

Nordquist Ranch,
Near Yellowstone Park Country,
Cody, Wyoming.

21. Hemingway and his family first vacationed at the L-Bar-T Ranch, owned by Lawrence and Olive Nordquist, in the summer of 1930.

22. *A Farewell to Arms*, adapted for the stage by Laurence Stallings, starred Elissa Landi as Catherine Barkley. The play ran on Broadway from 22 September through 11 October 1930.

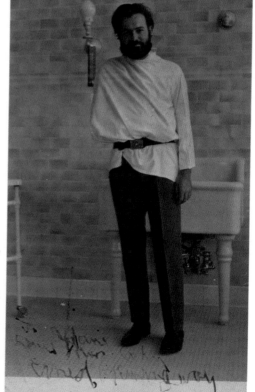

23. On 1 November 1930, Hemingway suffered a badly broken arm in a car accident near Billings, Montana. He was a patient at St. Vincent's Hospital until 21 December 1930, undergoing several surgeries. This photo bears his left-handed inscription to bibliographer Louis Henry Cohn.

24. Ernest and Gus Pfeiffer on the dock at Fort Jefferson during a fishing trip to the Dry Tortugas, February–March 1931. Gus enclosed this photo in a letter to his sister with this description: "Ernest and me ridiculing the sign 'Forbidden.' I suppose because there was no one there to enforce the 'forbids.' Ernest is holding his broken arm, which at that time was paining him almost constantly" (HPMEC).

25. Hemingway with a shark, probably the one caught by Uncle Gus, on the trip to the Dry Tortugas, February–March 1931. Hemingway's right arm is still not fully healed after the November car accident.

26. Charles Thompson in front of Fort Jefferson, constructed in the mid-nineteenth century on Garden Key in the Dry Tortugas but never finished.

27. Waldo Pierce with his wife, Alzira Boehm, and their twin sons, summer 1931. Peirce's caption reads "Crossing los altos Pireneos" ("Crossing the high Pyrenees").

28. Ernest and Bumby at the bullring in Pamplona, July 1931.

29. Hemingway with Sidney Franklin (on his left) and Franklin's *mozo* Luis Crovetto (on his right) among other bullfighters and friends, picnicking by the Manzanares River near Madrid, July 1931.

Don Ernesto, el de los Toros   Luis Quintanilla

30. Portrait by Luis Quintanilla, painted from memory in the mid-1950s and titled *Don Ernesto, el de los Toros*. Quintanilla added the caption below, "Ernest Hemingway in Madrid in 1931—We called him Don Ernesto of the bulls." In 1931 Quintanilla had done a portrait of Hemingway in Madrid. It hung above the bed in Hemingway's Key West home for years but was lost in the fire that destroyed Patrick Hemingway's house in California in 1967. Courtesy of Paul Quintanilla.

31. Ernest, Bumby, and Patrick
with attorney Maurice Speiser,
Hendaye, France, August 1931.

32. The Hemingway home at 907 Whitehead Street, Key West, photographed from
the lighthouse across the street. The family moved in on 19 December 1931.
Hemingway's writing room was on the second floor of the carriage house, visible behind
the main house.

To Milford Baker, [10 February 1930]

Box 396
Key West—Fla

Dear Bake:—

I'd be only too glad to sign the books— We've just gotten here from France and if you send them to me c/o P.O. Box 396— Key West Fla I'll sign them and return them promptly— I'd love to have any Italian pictures— Either of Sect 4 or the Piave—You'd be very good to send them—[1] By the way I will be shooting in ~~Nyasaland~~ Tanganyika next year and would appreciate any advice you can give me on rifles— What should I pay for a good rifle to shoot the 30–06 Springfield Cartridge—[2] What is most dependable action?— Where best to buy— Can you recommend any hunting Scope for hard usage? Have you had any experience with double Express rifles?[3] What do they cost?

If these questions are too much bother dont answer— Bake—

Send the books— And best to you always—

Yours always
Hemmie

PUL, ALS; postmark: KEY WEST / FLA., FEB 12 / 1 PM / 1930

The conjectured letter date is based on EH's notation "answered Feb 10" on the back of Baker's letter to him of 13 January 1930 (JFK).

1 In his letter, Baker reminded EH that when they ran into each other in New York the previous spring, Baker told him that he had begun collecting first editions of EH's work, and EH "kindly offered to put an inscription in any of the books I would send to you." In return, Baker offered to send pictures of scenes on the Piave River, where both had served in Italy during WWI in the American Red Cross Ambulance Service, EH in Section 4 and Baker in Section 5.
2 The Springfield rifle and its cartridge were developed and initially produced in 1903 at the government armory in Springfield, Massachusetts, as the primary infantry weapon of the U.S. Army. The ammunition, officially designated as "Cartridge, Ball, Caliber.30, Model of 1906," was known as the .30–06 and became a popular hunting cartridge.
3 EH refers to a double-barreled rifle that uses "the unique Nitro Express cartridges developed in Britain around 1900, which generate massive shock and—with the right bullets— penetrate the thickest skin, muscle, and bone" (Calabi "Safari," 107).

To Archibald MacLeish, [12 February 1930]

Dear Archie:—

My god kid you didnt put me off Don or say anything against him. I've always known and heard what you thought of his literary judgement and "serious thinking". Good God he's frightful when he "<u>thinks</u>"—and he's damned callous about <u>other peoples</u> troubles or feelings anytime. We had a swell visit in N.Y. and would have been completely happy if we hadnt been worried about Ada.[1] Dont worry about Don— You didnt say one damn thing to put me off him and Dont get any idea you did— The shit I referred to writing Dotty had <u>nothing</u> to do with that— I thought you were God damned <u>wonderful</u> in N.Y. So did Pauline.[2]

About here— Swell weather now and mosquitoes practically gone—at Casa Marina where Ada'd stay I'm sure there'd be no mosquitos anyway— But about you— You are always swell while things are happening but they take hell out of you afterwards and I wish you'd come down here now or next week if only for a week— It's not a question of Jack— I'll stake you the jack— My God didnt you feed and clothe me for years?— Didnt you keep me and Jinny at the Alpina? Didnt you buy me R.R. tickets and Pullmen? Youre damn right you did.[3] Now we're potentially <u>rich</u>. Your prologue is damn good and a week out in the old gulf and shooting with the sun and swimming would put you in shape—really[4]—on the train it's nothing to get here[.] Train leaves 5.30 or something like that—Havana Special—the Mallory boat takes longer—[5] But is cheap— I'd advise the train—you could make entire trip all expenses on train and here for 200^{\underline{00}}$ Probably less— Probably a lot less.

Come on— Dont be a bastard—

Glad you liked Dotty— Who she likes best of all is Benchley and in all the time I've known her have never known her to pan Benchley— She's no great double crosser— Her hard luck is she always falls in love with shits— That can make about as much hard luck as anything except of course raising Turkeys—[6]

Come on down and send or bring Ada. But you come too damn you— Come right away. Old Doctor Pappy's orders.

All our love to Ada—tell her she certainly looked beautiful that day in the hospital— Hope she's fine—

Yours always

Pappy

You dont need any clothes or outfit— We have everything— [*EH insertion*: Bring] Just a pair of old trousers and sweater [*EH circled insertion*: dont really need] and sneakers— We've got plenty of sweaters, 9 shotguns— 12 rods 9 reels etc.

If you dont come I'll <u>never</u> come to Conway nor go any place with you— You must come— Do I have to write Ada to make you?

Our best to Adele if you see her.[7]

LOC, ALS

The conjectured letter date is based on EH's notation "Answered Feb 12" written in the margin of MacLeish's letter to him postmarked 10 February 1930 (JFK).

1 EH had visited Ada MacLeish in the hospital, where she was recovering from a hysterectomy.
2 In his 10 February letter, MacLeish wrote that he feared EH's New York visit had been "a good deal of a flop" and expressed worry that EH might think MacLeish had meddled in EH's relations with Donald Ogden Stewart and Dorothy Parker. Stewart's comments on *FTA* "made me sore because I thought it was bunk and I told him so," MacLeish said, but "I am sorry as hell if I seemed to you be making a situation" by having told EH what Stewart said. Regarding Parker, MacLeish added, "Dotty says everything you heard in New York was shit and I guess I told you most of it. Try to forget about it and forgive me."
3 In 1926 the MacLeishes had invited EH and Jinny Pfeiffer to join them at the Grand Hotel Alpina in Gstaad, Switzerland, for a Christmas ski holiday while EH awaited Pauline's return from the United States after their three-month separation, which Hadley had stipulated as a condition for granting him a divorce.
4 MacLeish had begun work as early as June 1927 on what would become his epic poem *Conquistador*. In his letter of 10 February, he wrote that he "hadn't been able to work at my poem since I finished the prologue."
5 The Havana Special train of the Atlantic Coast Line offered deluxe accommodations and daily service, in February 1930 departing from Pennsylvania Station in New York City at 6:50 p.m. and arriving in Key West almost thirty-seven hours later at 7:40 a.m. (*The Official Guide of the Railways and Steam Navigation Lines of the United States Porto Rico Canada Mexico and Cuba*, National Railway Publication Company, February 1930, 586). Mallory Line steamships traveled between New York City and several cities in the American South, including a weekly route to Galveston that in February 1930 left New York on Wednesday and made a stop in Key West on Saturday.
6 In his 10 February letter, MacLeish wrote, "met Dotty Parker Saturday night and think she's swell." Parker and Robert Benchley met when both worked at *Vanity Fair*, she as drama critic (1917–1920) and he as managing editor (1919–1920). The two were among the founding members of the Algonquin Round Table (1919–1929) and joined the

New Yorker when it was established in 1925. Dorothy had left her husband, Edwin Pond Parker II, in 1919 (divorcing him in 1928), and she had been romantically involved with *Bookman* editor Seward Collins, among others. Her poems about her unsuccessful love affairs, depression, and abortion appeared in magazines of the period. EH refers to the turkeys the MacLeishes were raising at their farm.

7 Adele Quartley Brown (1899–1986), daughter of New York investment banker James Brown, married Robert Abercrombie Lovett (1895–1986), son of the chairman of the Union Pacific Railroad, in April 1919. Lovett and Archibald MacLeish's younger brother, Kenneth (1894–1918), had been classmates at Yale and served together in the U.S. Naval Air Force in WWI. The Lovetts began a close friendship with Archibald and Ada MacLeish in 1919 when both men were attending Harvard Law School.

To Milton Leidner, [12 February 1930]

Box 396
Key West
Florida

Dear Mr. Leidner:—

Thank you very much for your letter.

My first book was Three Stories and Ten Poems published in Paris in, I believe, 1922—by Contact Editions—19 rue D'Antin Paris—the 1st In Our Time was published by Three Mountains Press—Quai D'Anjou—Paris— Their address is 19 rue D'Antin— I believe now too—[1] These have both been out of print for some years— The other books are the Liveright In Our Time— Torrents of Spring— The Sun Also Rises— Men Without Women— and A Farewell T.A— These with the pamphlet you speak of—(which by the way has a funny history)— They wrote me and asked me for a story and I sent it telling them it was the only Mss. I had and would they please return it to me—[2] They only paid me $10^{00} for the story on a tale they were doing it as a non-profit venture etc. And last year in Chicago—in the Walden Bookshop—I found the Mss. of the story with my letter asking them to please send it back as it was the only one I had—Which they had sold!— Both Mss. and letter.[3]

I'm afraid it was a racket after all—

Anyway good luck to you and if you get all the first editions you'll have more than I have!

Yours very truly,
Ernest Hemingway

Karpeles, ALS; postmark: [12 February 1930]

1 Robert McAlmon's Contact Publishing Company and Bill Bird's Three Mountains Press, both established in 1922, had shared quarters at 29, Quai d'Anjou on the Île Saint-Louis. McAlmon published EH's first book, *TSTP*, in 1923. Bird sold his press in 1928 to Nancy Cunard, and in 1929 McAlmon closed Contact Editions and moved to North America. As European director of the Consolidated Press Association, Bird had an office at 19, rue d'Antin, which had served as a mailing address for both presses.
2 The pamphlet "Today Is Friday" was published on 10 November 1926 by the As Stable Publications of Englewood, New Jersey, in a limited edition of 300 numbered copies. The story, which takes the form of a one-act play, was included in *MWW* (October 1927). EH received a "small honorarium and several copies of the pamphlet in lieu of the manuscript Hemingway had requested to be returned" (Smith, 155).
3 Walden Books, Chicago bookstore where writer and editor Georgia Lingafelt (1898–1957) worked in the late 1920s. In a letter of 3 October 1927, EH had asked Lingafelt to inform him whenever rare editions of his early work became available. The typewritten envelope, addressed to Lingafelt at "The Walden Book Shop / 311 Plymouth Court / CHICAGO / ILLINOIS / ETATS UNIS," bears EH's handwritten notation "not for sale" (*Letters* vol. 3, 302–3).

To Ernst Rowohlt, 18 February 1930

P.O. Box 396
Key West
Florida.
February 18, 1930

My Dear Herr Rowohlt,

Thank you for your letter of January 16 enclosing the contract.

I am sorry that I cannot sign the contract yet as I have no dictionary and so cannot be sure I read it all correctly.[1] There is no one on this island that knows German any better than I do. I have taken your letters to an old man who gives lessons (out of a book) in German, French and Spanish and he says that is not the kind of German he knows! So please send me the English translation too.

Things to remember in the contract too are— That you were only to get 35% of the amount received for serialization if the amount paid to me was at least 5000 marks. In case I received less than 5000 marks net your percentage was only to be 25% I believe. Herr Mowrer will remember this.

You may have forgotten it when drawing up the contract. Speak to Herr Mowrer about it if you do not remember it.[2]

I think too the royalty per-centages are too low. If that is what I accepted for the Fiesta, Männer, In Our Time, and Torrents of Spring then I suppose they must hold good for those books. But in no country, even France and Spain, do I have a lower royalty per-centage than 10% and I do not think I should accept a lower royalty% than that on A Farewell To Arms. Especially as I have taken only a small advance.

As yet I have received <u>no</u> copies of Men Without Women!

Will you send me too, please, an accounting of the sales of Fiesta up to January 1 and a check for the royalty due me and also an accounting of the sums received for stories from Men Without Women and In Our Time which have been published in newspapers and magazines and a check for the amount due me.

About the title in German for A Farewell to Arms. <u>Krieg und Liebe</u> I do <u>not</u> like. <u>Vorbei mit Krieg und Liebe</u> I do <u>not</u> like either. It is too long and tells too much. <u>Krieg und Liebe</u> is not a good title for that book. If I wrote a book called Krieg und Liebe I would have much fighting in it and also much fornication. Fahrwohl Krieg und Liebe I do <u>not</u> like either. It tells too much and does not give the spirit of the book.

I like better <u>Liebe im Krieg</u> if you must have that sort of title. <u>In Another Country</u> would have been a good title as it translates well into German In ein andere Lande (I probably spell it wrong)[3]

In principle I believe a title should always be a poem in its-self. In Our Time, Men Without Women, The Sun Also Rises, A Farewell To Arms—those all make poems in themselves in English. The title is as important as the book.

<u>In Another Country</u> is good because it comes from The Jew of Malta by Marlowe— The quotation is "I have committed fornication, but that was in another country, and besides, the wench is dead."

If you called it In Another Country you could print the quotation from The Jew of Malta, by Marlowe, in one of the front pages as the quotation from Ecclesiastes was printed in The Sun Also Rises.

If you think it would cause confusion because one of the stories in Men Without Women had that title do not use it.[4] But I think it is a <u>beautiful</u> title and one that would be very good for the book. Liebe im Krieg may be all right. It is certainly better than the others.

I will hope to hear from you soon about the contract and the serialization. The book still sells very well and is being translated into Spanish, Swedish, Norwegian, Polish, Hungarian, etc. I will not let the Nouvelle Revue Francaise publish it in French until they pay me the money they owe me. I have many French and Italian offers.[5]

Please excuse this letter being so full of business. We are settled here until June, am working very hard and having fine fishing. Mrs. Hemingway joins me in sending you our best regards and good wishes in every thing. I look forward very much to seeing you again.

With all best wishes,

Yours always,

Ernest Hemingway.

I am glad the Männer was so well received.

phDLA, TLS

1 The contract for the German publication of *FTA*, translated by Annemarie Horschitz and published as *In Einem Andern Land* (Berlin: Ernst Rowohlt, 1930).

2 American journalist Edgar Ansel Mowrer (1892–1977), with the Berlin office of the *Chicago Daily News*, had acted as EH's German agent since July 1926. He was the brother of Paul Scott Mowrer (1887–1971), the journalist and poet with whom Hadley was romantically involved and whom she would marry in 1933.

3 *Krieg und Liebe*: War and Love; *Vorbei mit Krieg und Liebe*: Finished with War and Love; *Fahr wohl Krieg und Liebe*: Farewell, War and Love; *Liebe im Krieg*: Love in War; *In einem andern Land*: In Another Country.

4 *The Jew of Malta* (c. 1590), play by English poet and playwright Christopher Marlowe (1564–1593). The title for the German edition of *FTA* is taken from the epigraph quoted on p. [6]: "*Bernardine*: Thou hast committed– / *Barabas*: Fornication: but that was / in another country; and besides / the wench is dead" (Hanneman D89, 182–83). EH's short story "In Another Country," first published in the April 1927 issue of *Scribner's Magazine*, was collected in *MWW*. EH took one of the epigraphs for *SAR* from Ecclesiastes (1:2, 4–7 in the first American edition; the second verse was omitted in the third printing and all later issues [Hanneman A6, 14]).

5 *FTA* eventually would be published in translation in each of the languages EH mentions, appearing in Norwegian in 1930, Polish in 1931, Swedish in 1932, Spanish in 1940, Italian in 1945, and Hungarian in 1958. The French translation would be published in November 1931 under the Nouvelle Revue Française (NRF) imprint as part of the Du Monde Entier series in a limited edition of 1,180 numbered copies, and in 1932 by Gallimard. In 1928 Les Éditions de la Nouvelle Revue Française had published *Cinquante Mille Dollars (Fifty Grand)*, a collection of six of EH's stories, in a limited edition of 110 numbered copies. For bibliographic details of these and other translations, see Hanneman, 175–205 and Grissom, 687–733.

To Henry Strater, 18 February [1930]

Feb 18th

Dear Mike:—

The harpoon gun and sht gun shells came along last week and Charles [Thompson] just called up to say your motor was down at the store— Thanks ever so much for sending them—

The 2nd night we were here Charles and I went out with Bra [Saunders] and caught 3 tarpon—around 25 lbs apiece in the channel between the Marie and the old iron Barque[1]—had 5 other strikes or fish on— Since havent fished much— The little boat is a K.O. for fishing— But the 4 horse motor isnt powerful enough to really drive her altho it is swell for trolling— The 12 would have been better— But it starts as simply as a bicycle and runs swell— Will drive her about 7 knots with 2 people— The guns are swell— I got first 5 shots at snipe straight—a couple of them hard ones—with the little 16—

Look Mike— When are you coming down? Any time we would be damned glad to see you— Theres nobody here and everythings cheap— Good Cuban table wine 15\frac{00}{}$ the 5 gal jug. Absinthe 6$\frac{00}{}$ a bottle— Bourbon 4\frac{00}{}$ Scotch 4$\frac{00}{}$— Have only been drinking wine <u>But</u> my gut is <u>fine</u> now.

Have arranged to get Luther's[2] boat—32 ft. (same length as Bras) With a cabin that will sleep 4 and a good low stern for fishing for $125 a month— Will hire Burge to run and look after her for $125 a mo. That makes $250 a mo— So we'll have a boat can live on on trips— Cruising all day she only uses $3.75 worth of gas and oil—and is comfortable to sleep on at Marquesas—up the Coast etc. I thought I'd better arrange to have one so we'd always have one and could take harpooning and bottom fishing trips and all kinds of monkey business without a $30 a day angle and maybe having to use Mimi—

When Uncle Gus is down and we take trips to Marquesas can get Bra too. and use ours to live on. Last year we hired Happys[3] to live on <u>alone</u> (fishing from Bra) and it was $15 a day. I tried to get Bra by month— He said he'd carry us cheap but naturally he'd be a fool to tie up by month if there are going to be lots of parties and he can work by the day. But if there arent parties will try and get him some work anyway.

We went out in the Gulf stream Sunday and caught bonitas and mackerel— Charles lost a big King— Then I hooked into something—fought it 45 minutes without it showing and the hook straightened— Had just started trolling again— Hooked into something again—took all my line 300 yds—(3 times) after an hour 10 minutes he showed—a damn mackerel shark— I fought him one hr. more (by clock) and we landed him— Didnt have your gaff and he broke the harpoon line, I'd get him up to boat— they'd strike him and out he'd go again— I was pooped— Finally gaffed him and I shot him a magazinefull of 22 hollow points—weighed only 205 lbs. but was 8 ft. long and slim and a hell of a fighter—on 6 oz. sailfish tip—15 thread line—2 hrs. 10 minutes. About 40 times he did that circling under the boat— There were 4 others followed him most of the time— We certainly wished to hell we'd carried your Gaff—

Write when you're going to come— What about Max? When is he coming? Waldo has to go to Paris first—[4] Henriette is cooking <u>wonderfully</u>—
Love to Maggie— Pauline is still raving about Young Mike—[5]
Bra sends his best to you and to Miss <u>Maggie</u>—

Dont know any other news especially— I had a hell of a grippe caught it leaving N.Y when first got down—that's why didnt write— Finally went to bed with it for 4–5 days and now am all over it and feel swell—

There were a lot of mosquitoes when we came down but they're about gone now—

The Johnson 4 runs and starts beautifully but wish we'd gotten the 12— Boat is steady as a rock to fish from and more room than Charles—

Everybody sends you their best—594 turtle Came in Sat—Hope we see you soon—

Yours always
Hem.
Box 396 Key West—

We got a swell house right near swimming beach and Athletic club—[6]

PUL, ALS

1 Presumably sunken vessels that served as markers in the waters off Key West.
2 Captain Thomas Luther Pinder (1884–1961), coast guard pilot and Key West fishing entrepreneur.

3 Appleton "Happy" John Saunders (c. 1880–1948), Key West fisherman and brother of Bra and Berge Saunders.

4 Waldo Peirce's estranged wife, Ivy Troutman, was living in Paris, where their divorce would become final in October 1930.

5 Mike and Maggie's son Michael Henry Strater, then about nine weeks old.

6 The Key West Athletic Club, on the waterfront at the southern end of Duval Street, played host to frequent amateur and professional boxing bouts, as well as tennis matches, basketball games, dances, concerts, picnics, and other community gatherings. It would be demolished in 1935 by the Federal Emergency Relief Administration to provide more beach space.

To William D. and Frances Horne, 18 February 1930

Box 396
Key West
Florida
February 18 1930

Dear Horney and Dearest Bunny:—

We certainly would love to see you men down here—why not? You ought to come down— There is no use you men working yourselves to the bone in the filthy book and Store rackets—

Old Bunny! Come on down— There's nobody here in town now—only Pauline, Pat Henriette [Lechner] and me— Henriette is cooking wonderfully— The good red wine is only $15.$^{\underline{00}}$ a five gal demi-john— Swimming is swell— Pauline is in grand shape— I'm in swell shape again— We'd have a swell time and it certainly would be fine to see you all—

Caught 2 tarpon the other night— Gulf full of sail fish—

We feel terribly about how we were all sick and in bad shape when Bunny was in Paris—but if you men come down here now we'll show you the gay free high life of the Carribbean—

We're going to Wyoming this summer— What about you guys?

Why dont you leave for Key West on receipt of this? We're here until June— Western Union address just Key West— Why dont you come now before a lot of merchants get here—[1]

Love from Pauline
and Ernie

Newberry, ALS; postmark: KEY WEST / FLA, FEB18 / 1 PM / 1930

1 In their reply of 2 March 1930, the Hornes lamented that they had missed EH and Pauline's letter by a few hours and had gone on a skiing vacation instead, but Bill responded enthusiastically to the mention of Wyoming: "Sure we are going with you, if that's jake with you—gosh!" He recommended a ranch just east of Yellowstone and about 8 miles south of the Montana border, "where they say the fishing is simply godwonderful" (JFK).

To Grace Hall Hemingway, 19 February 1930

February 19—1930

My Dear Mother:—

I have received your extraordinary letter in answer to my letter in which I sought to advise you about your financial affairs which had become complicated through (1) The purchase of a motor car for a sum equal to nearly half of your assured yearly income at the time of purchase (2) The necessity to pay a sum over a fourth of your assured yearly income as of next April for taxes on boom-bought Florida property of no fixed value and from which you derive <u>no income.</u>[1]

My efforts have been to get your financial affairs on a sound basis and to provide an income on which you can live comfortably. If this is to be achieved certain fundamental things must be agreed to— I outlined some of these in my letter. One is that you must not sell or borrow money on securities you hold to pay taxes on property of doubtful value from which you receive no income. To do this is economic suicide. Another is that you must not use more than a certain percentage of your income to pay taxes on this property. I went into this in detail in my last letter and what I said in that letter still holds good.

It is beside the point to bring into this effort to give you economic stability any discussion of our Lord or our Heavenly Father. I am glad you are on such excellent terms with Him. It is one of the important things of life and I congratulate you. However that is not what we are going into at present.

You tell me not to threaten you. [*EH insertion*: appropos of my making certain stipulations for the safe-guarding of your capital for your own

safety.] We have not had many financial dealings until this past year so
I understand that your saying that comes from unfamiliarity with dealing
with me and I overlook it. You will find in your dealings with me that I do
not threaten.

You say you are a free soul and will not be owned by [*EH insertion*: any
man] neither husband nor son.

To provide an income for a person from whom you ask <u>nothing</u> in return
except that they shall not imperil the adequacy of this income ~~except~~ by
spending or mortgaging the capital from which it is derived is not trying to
<u>own</u> them.

I would not have mentioned this contingency in my letter except that
I know you to have sold securities in the past and also to have mortgaged
your home to buy land in the Florida Boom. I am not reproaching you for
these things in any way. It is only to guard against such contingencies that
I made the statement I did and to which I strictly adhere.

The other parts of my letter were practical advice to you about how to live
on a quarterly income which I am providing. They are not attempts to
"own" you.

I am sending you 150.$\underline{^{00}}$ on the first of March and stand ready as I wrote
you—To finance your trip to St. Petersburg to try to sell your lots— [*EH
insertion*: I regard this as necessary and a good investment on my part.]
If you cannot sell these lots do not be discouraged as you will have plenty to
live on if you get nothing from them—provided you do not [*EH insertion*:
continue to] pay for them several times over in taxes. What is happening in
Florida on that boom land is that most people are not paying any taxes at
all— The people who do pay taxes are assessed for those who do not— Here
in Key West the tax assessor gets $7500 a year—which is paid him out of the
first $<u>7500</u> of taxes collected— It is nothing more nor less than a racket.
If you held the land 10 years—if the taxes were not raised—you would pay
out over $8,000.$\underline{^{00}}$ plus the interest on your money. It is a rat hole to avoid
and I have made it possible for you to avoid it— If you cannot sell the land
for what the taxes ~~will be~~ are for 3 or 4 years no one will buy it when it is
offered at the end of that time for tax sale. I would be happy to see you get
$5,000 for the whole business. Whatever you get is a profit.[2]

Do not feel backward about asking me for the expense money to make a trip to St. Petersburg to see what your property there will bring. I have no worries of any sort and do not waste any time feeling sorry for me. The only reason I mentioned my financial status—which is no ones business—is because I could tell from your two or three previous letters and clippings enclosed that you were under the impression I was making large sums from movies etc. Fox stole the title Men Without Women, then made me a "courtesy payment" of $500 and then announced in the papers they had bought the title from me for $5000.

Lay it to my eccentricity or anything you like but when I write a business letter would rather you would try and answer with a business letter. And please do not write anything silly about threats. I never threaten. If I say I'll do a thing that is what I'll do and certainly so in financial matters. Giving is a matter of the heart but after giving administration and keeping capital intact is a matter of the head and I have a hard head about this and mean exactly what I say. I don't want to "own" you and I appreciate your being a "free soul" but putting in some $50,000 to get you on your feet so you can be a "free soul" am entitled to give advice and to make stipulations to insure the capital you have is kept intact. Praying for advice and guidance is an excellent thing but advice an[d] guidance even though unprayed for when accompanied by cash can be an excellent thing too.

Glad you are all well. Tell Sunny we didn't get the Piggott present as Pauline's family had gone to Arizona but thank her very much for it and will appreciate it when we get it. My throat is O.K. Keep sensible, don't get tragic and don't write me silly things.

Best to you always,
Ernest

I will send you $150 March 1st in any case.
Please keep my letters so you can refer to them.

PSU, AL/TLS with autograph postscript; postmark: KEY WEST / FLA, FEB 19 / 4³⁰PM / 19[30]

1 The letter from Grace to which EH is responding remains unlocated, as does EH's letter to her that had provoked her "extraordinary" response. In a letter to EH of 20 December 1929, Grace announced that she had traded in her old Ford and paid an additional $725 for

a second-hand Pontiac, adding, "We hope you will not think us extravagant, or misusing what you so generously give us" (JFK). In her letter of 9 January 1930, Grace had written that "It will take $816.73 for this years taxes; they keep creeping up a little every year, but this amount will answer if you can get it to me, by latter part of February" (JFK). According to the terms of the trust fund, Grace would be assured of an annual income of $2,340 and a supplement of $600 per year for Carol starting April 1930, when the trust fund would go into effect (see EH to Grace Hall Hemingway, 10 March [1930]).

2 The remainder of the letter is typewritten, with autograph postscripts.

To Morley Callaghan, 21 February [1930]

Feb 21

Dear Morley:

The letter you received was written when I was still sore (and if you put yourself in my place, throwing out all question of resposibility for the story; I know you were not responsible and your disavowal was prompt, courteous and friendly; you can see how I was sore and plenty sore at the story its-self and anxious to fight) and there was no intention of mailing it. The facts in the letter were quite correct but, as you point out, there was no point in me offering to try to beat you up for having written a very courteous and correct disavowal of a piece of malicious author baiting put out by a third party. Put that down to Berserker-ism.

I wrote the letter, decided not to send it for obvious reasons and put it away in the drawer of my desk. I left in the car for Bordeaux to deliver the Ford to the boat and Pauline stayed in Paris superintending moving our things out of the apt. Cleaning out the desk she found the letter, thought it was something I had forgotten to send and stamped it and mailed it.

Once you had the letter there was nothing for me to do. You can't write a citizen, intentionally or not, suggesting you have a good brawl and then send him a wire asking him to disregard your letter.

I know of course you are not afraid of me and I don't blame you a bit for being sore if you got that cable from Scott collect. I'm sure it wasn't sent collect from Paris but if it was sent through N.Y. they may have forwarded it collect.

There is no use denying I was plenty sore about the story. How do you think it feels to read and have people send you from all over the country a syndicated story in which you sneer at some one, poop on their stuff, then get called by them and knocked cold. Especially when it is someone whose stuff you have praised and tried to get published[1] and whose boxing you have enjoyed and admired.

So I was good and sore. In all friendliness and with no idea of anyone being afraid of anyone else I honestly believe that with small gloves I could knock you out inside of about five two minute rounds although I'm sure you would pop me plenty. [*EH insertion:* I say this not being sore and ~~I'm sure~~ not in an unfriendly way.] But unless you hold a contrary belief I don't want to have to try to stay in shape the rest of my life on a chance of our running into each other. So if you want us to disarm let me know. In the meantime best luck with your book and my regards to Lorretta

Yours always,
Ernest Hemingway.
P.O Box 396
Key West
Florida.

phMason, TLS

This letter was among those concerning the infamous Paris boxing bout that were exchanged among Callaghan, EH, and Fitzgerald and that were stolen from the safe of Toronto bookseller David Mason in 1993. The originals remain unlocated. For Mason's vivid account of the theft, see "The Hemingway Heist" in *The Pope's Bookbinder: A Memoir* (Windsor, Ontario: Biblioasis, 2013), 371–402.

1 EH had encouraged Callaghan's early efforts to write fiction. In 1926 EH had sent the manuscript of Callaghan's first novel to Robert McAlmon, recommending Callaghan as "a kid that is worth doing something about" and offering to go "50–50" with McAlmon on the cost of publishing it. Callaghan was able instead to place his book with Scribner's, which published it as *Strange Fugitive* in 1928 (*Letters* vol. 3, 73–74).

To Maxwell Perkins, 28 February [1930]

P.O Box 396
Key West
Fla.
Feb 28

Dear Max:—

The weather and fishing are excellent and we look forward to you coming—

Thanks ever so much for the books you sent—

Could you let me know by return mail how much money I received from Scribners in 1929—(for my income tax)

The $5,000 advance on the serial was received in 1928—Do you remember if I put that in my 1928 tax return? I hope so—

Otherwise—as I remember—there was $11,000 for the serial—

$6,000 advance on Farewell in 2 checks of 3000 Sometime in Oct or Nov.

$1,000 advance on Farewell that you deposited in my City Bank Farmers Trust account.

And whatever royalty I received from Men Without Women, the use of stories etc. during 1929— Will you let me know how much that was?[1]

> Hope to see you soon.
>
> Best to you always—
>
> Ernest

PUL, ALS

1 Perkins's response, dated 4 March 1930, would confirm EH's reckoning: Scribner's paid EH $18,416.94 in 1929, this amount including the sums EH mentions, which total $18,000, plus two smaller sums labeled "Feb 1 report" and "Aug 1 report." Perkins also confirmed that the first payment for the serial rights for *FTA* had been $5,000, paid with a check issued on 2 October 1928. As for EH's question about tax payment on the 1928 advance for *FTA*, Perkins wrote, "I should think you must have done it. You have always gone on the plan of paying a tax on the amounts you received during the year, and I think that is much the safest way to do" (JFK).

To Ezra Pound, 28 February [1930]

> P.O. Box 396
> Key West
> Florida
> Feb 28—

Dear Ezra:—

Damned glad to hear from and of you. I'll get a photo of the Shark and remains and send it—for Van H. Plate is sold but I can get one O.K. Also any other good ones I can get. What language is he going to Translate into?[1]

What do you want to use of mine? You're welcome to anything that isnt disposed of. Have sold all german rights on stuff up till now. Only things unavailable in French are what was in that book 50,000 Dollars—(What a shitty title—but I suppose they figured French would pay 12 francs for $50,000—) I have a contract with N.R.F. but am not going to give them any more books until they pay me the 2,000 francs they owe me as un-received advance on publication of $50,000—[2]

So if Van H. is in French take anything you damn please. If he wants a Chapter from Farewell etc anything he pays is all right with me that's all right with you.

If he's Norswegian or Swenish I have sold A Farewell to Arrums and The Sun Alsos to them countries already but everything else free.[3]

Have sold Spanish, Polish and Hunkgarian rights on Farewell.

I am damn glad you liked it— what you write about the S. Story conv. and the novel is damn true— I will try to get it better—think I <u>have</u> made a difference but maybe not—

[*EH insertion*: re Gert. <u>Stein</u>]

Neither do I believe in her— She was a smart woman and, <u>if she had worked</u>, [*EH insertion*: i.e. accepted the old disciplinary establishment of prose.] could have written damned good stuff but instead she got a way by which she could write <u>every day</u>, without corrections, and by writing make herself feel swell— (Instead of like us poor bastards (I speak for myself) who can usually not write at all, fail all the time, feel like hell, work like bastards— She found this way whereby she could turn it out every day and feel fine— Then, though, to keep on feeling good—she had to get it approved and accepted and accoladed etc. Otherwise she would start to feel punk writing it. So for some years now she has been organized in an effort to get it approved, accepted etc. and it has all more or less left what realm of belles (sic) lettres and become a racket.

I think at the start she had something and was writing good stuff— i.e. Melanctha, the First part of Making of Americans, but it was simply panned and so she got bitter and thought all right if the reader is so damn dumb to hell with the reader and wrote for herself— Then because she did not have to make it give a kick to the one who reads as well as the one who writes she could do it right off like automatic writing— However some of the short pieces in Geography and plays and some others are damn good legitimate stuff— (To me)[4]

This opinion (all of above) not for publication or quoting—if it was I'd have to go into it and organize it— I think she had a good period at the start— then another period where she took it all lightly and it pleased her— Now this period of trying to get into the Academy is pretty awful—

I'll read H.J. [Henry James] ~~again.~~ As you know I've read damned little of him. Have had hard luck and hit the wrong ones. I know you wrote an outline to him but I havent it here.[5] What ones do you say I ought to read?

Certainly the interior monologue is shit— It always takes place in the mind of the <u>yauthor</u>—not the citizen he is writing about. I think it is legitimate for the Irish because their minds go that way— But I know <u>personally</u> I have never had one going on in my mind in my life. As you say a dream is different— The dopy state of more or less complete exhaustion also different— I know the interior monologue is a trick because it is the easiest damn thing to write— I have cut out thousands of them out of Mss. <u>All shit</u>. You write that stuff when you wont bite on the old nail—

Anyway I am damned happy you liked the bloody book— It is damned hard to write a novel (—trying never to fake—) just physically— I would have been glad to pay my esteemed father a good sum or give him a share in the profits to postpone shooting himself until the book was completed— Such things have a tendency to distract a man— However les voyages forme la jeunesse—(doubtless misspelled)[6]

D'America is in throes of Humanism— I have been read out of the practice of letters by them as immoral— Also it seems I was once a reporter—and it has been proved, by the editor of The Bookman, that I only went to High School and so am uneducated and illiterate (He went to Princeton)[7]

A Humanist was once a man who knew his Latin and his Greek— It does a man no harm to know French, Wop, German and Spanish too— If youve read Eng. D'American, Wop, Spanish, French literature in the original, can understand the languages referred to and overhear conversations in the

countries involved why the hell are you uneducated— However since
D'American literature consists of yr. friend H. J. and part of one book by
Mark Twain (Melville is shit but isnt it better to read him and find that out
than be told what a great writer he is in College? What the hell is education?
If you ever mention book make me out an educated feller— There's
a Campaign going on now that I cant either read nor write and dictate these
books to a trained stenographer. Any patent medicine, patent religion or
new system of Ethics always sure to go big in D'America.

Also any system whereby the non-writers can try and put the boots to the
writers and discuss writing about writing rather than writing is always popular.

Give my love to Dorothy—

The Key West address is good until June— Then we move North through
Fla, Louisiana, Miss. Tenn to ARKansas— Then to Wyoming— Liquor
(whiskey) cheaper and better here than Paris— Good Spanish red wine—
(what they make the St. Estephes and St. Emilions out of by adding water at
Bordeaux) $13.50 the 5 gallon demi john— Pinch bottle Haig $4.00 a qt.
Gilbey's gin—3.^{00} champagne less expensive than Montmartre but ~~cheaper~~
dearer than at Depot Nicolas—[8]

The Hon. Cape is a business man— That's why he didn't publish
Torrents— Also no reason now— The citizens it killed off havent risen from
the sepulcher.

Am sending shark—

Best always—

Hem

Yale, ALS

1 Paul-Gustave Van Hecke (1887–1967), Belgian journalist, art dealer, and art critic who promoted Dadaism and surrealism and edited the short-lived illustrated monthly *Variétés: Revue mensuelle illustrée de l'esprit contemporain*, published in Brussels from May 1928 to April 1930. Van Hecke had asked Pound to help him make up an American number, and Pound was soliciting material, including "really funny photos. representing the habits of the american peepul" (Pound to E. E. Cummings, 17 February 1930, in Barry Ahearn, ed., *Pound/Cummings: The Correspondence of Ezra Pound and E. E. Cummings* [Ann Arbor: University of Michigan Press, 1996], 17). *Variétés* ceased publication before Van Hecke could publish the projected issue of American works in French translation. Pound's letter to EH remains unlocated, but EH responded by sending Pound the jawbone of a shark he had caught in February.

2 Translations of EH's "Fifty Grand" and five other stories were collected in *Cinquante Mille Dollars*, published in Paris in 1928 by Les Éditions de la Nouvelle Revue Française in a limited edition of 110 copies (Hanneman D69).

3 Both novels appeared in Norwegian and Swedish translations. In Oslo, Gyldenal published *SAR* in 1929 and *FTA* in 1930 (Hanneman D232 and D233). In Stockholm, Holger Schildt published *SAR* in 1929 and Bonnier would publish *FTA* in 1932 (Hanneman D329 and D330).

4 "Melanctha," one of the three stories in Stein's *Three Lives* (New York: Grafton, 1909); *Geography and Plays*, a collection of poems, stories, and plays (Boston: Four Seas Company, 1922); and *The Making of Americans*, a novel (Paris: Contact Editions, 1925). EH's laudatory review of *Geography and Plays* had appeared in the 5 March 1923 Paris *Tribune*.

5 The "outline" is likely Pound's essay on Henry James, originally published in the *Little Review* (August 1918) and collected in *Instigations of Ezra Pound* (New York: Boni & Liveright, 1920). The essay is a reader's guide to James, "a Baedecker to a continent," in which Pound recommends particular works in answer to the imagined query, "Where the deuce shall I begin?"

6 *Les voyages forment la jeunesse*: Travel broadens the mind (literally, "travel shapes the young"); proverb attributed to French philosopher Michel de Montaigne (1533–1592).

7 Seward Collins, editor of the *Bookman*, was a 1921 graduate of Princeton. EH had complained about Robert Herrick's negative review of *FTA* in the November 1929 *Bookman* in two letters to Maxwell Perkins, both dated 30 November [1929].

8 St. Estèphe and St. Emilion, full-bodied red Bordeaux wines. Haig & Haig Scotch Whisky, sold in a distinctive dimpled three-sided "pinch" bottle. Gilbey's, a dry London gin. Dépôt Nicolas, wine shop established in 1822 and located at 64, rue Saint-Louis en l'Île in Paris since 1921.

To Grace Hall Hemingway, 10 March [1930]

March 10.

Dear Mother:

Enclosed please find two copies of Trust Agreement; one for you and one for Carol. Attached is also a statement of the securities in the trust, the amounts of income and dates on which income is payable. The income will, however, be paid to you quarterly by the Trust Co.[1]

You will see from the trust agreement that Carol is to receive 600 dollars a year and you are to receive the balance less 2% the fee charged by the trust company. The trust yields $3,000.00 a year minus carol's $600 and the $60 which represents the 2% taken by the Trust Co. This leaves you $2340.00 a year which makes your quarterly income $585 which corresponds to a monthly income of $195.00.

I would suggest that you have the City Bank Farmer's Trust Company remit the proceeds each quarter as soon as received to your bank with the request that your bank credit the amount to your account. I would suggest also that Carol open an account and folow the same procedure. You will declare the sums you receive in your income tax return for next year but I do not believe the W.R. Warner Stock or the Electric Bond and Share Stock are taxable. They must be declared however. Whoever assists you in making out your income tax return can tell you where they should be listed.

Since Carol's income is only $600 a year she will not be required to file a return. Please file this deed of trust in your safe deposit box. You have no disposal of the securities in this trust fund but you are to have the income, as stated, as long as you live.

Am enclosing check for 150 dollars I promised for march. Hope you are all well and that everything is fine. Best regards to Carol, Les, and Sunny—

Yours always—

Ernest

It is understood that the money paid you from this trust fund is to be used with the income you derive from the securities purchsed from Dad's estate for your support and the support and education of the unmarried children.

Payments will commence from the trust fund in April and quarterly thereafter.

PSU, TLS; postmark: KEY WEST, FLA. / REGISTERED, MAR / 11 / 1930

1 EH sent this letter and the enclosed trust agreement by registered mail to his mother at 600 North Kenilworth Avenue in Oak Park, Illinois. Drawn up by the law firm Baldwin, Hutchins & Todd in New York City, the document identifies EH and Pauline as the "Donors" and the City Bank Farmers Trust Company as the "Trustee." Signed by EH and Pauline on 18 February 1930, and by a trust officer of the City Bank Farmers Trust Company on 4 March 1930, the trust agreement is archived in the Special Collections Library at PSU.

To Carol Hemingway, [10 March 1930]

[*Excerpt as published in Herman Darvick Autograph Auctions catalog:*]
Enclosed please find copy of Trust agreement whereby you will receive $600 a year during Mother's lifetime. . . . I would try to let these payments accumulate until you are ready to go to college so you will have that much

money ahead. Pauline and I want this money to help you to go to college. It is not intended for your support in the home as a sufficient sum is being paid monthly to Mother for her to support herself, you and Leicester. We want you to have this fixed sum though so that when you are through college you can save it when you are earning money and use it for travel or what-ever will be of most help to you in your writing or whatever you decide to do. Good luck to you.

Yours always

Ernie

Herman Darvick Autograph Auctions catalog, New York, 4 October 1990, Sale 23, Lot 236, TLS; postmark: [Key West, Florida, 10 March 1930]

According to the catalog description, this letter was accompanied by the original envelope sent by registered mail, addressed by EH in ink to "Miss Carol Hemingway / 600 N. Kenilworth Avenue / Oak Park / Illinois," with the return address "E. Hemingway / Box 396 / Key West / Florida." The lot also included a copy of the Trust Agreement between "Ernest Hemingway and Pauline Pfeiffer Hemingway with City Bank Farmers Trust Company," signed by both EH and Pauline.

To Henry Luce, 10 March 1930

Box 396

Key West, Florida.

March 10. 1930

Dear Mr. Luce,

Thanks for writing me but there was really no necessity. I have been an editor in a minor way and understand the exigencies of make-up. However, if there had been time, I would have been glad to cut the article for you myself. I wrote it because Archie asked me to and I know he felt more or less responsible for it and of course I would have been glad to cut it for you and to correct any typographical errors in Spanish etc. but the demands of daily, weekly or monthly journalism have nothing in common with pure literature (where we have these fights about mis-placed and omitted words) and certainly this article had nothing to do with it either. The illustrations were fine, especially the Goya in colors.

With best wishes,

Yours very truly,

Ernest Hemingway.

Weinberg, TLS

Although the incoming letter from *Fortune* editor Henry Luce has not been located, EH's reply suggests that Luce had addressed the editing and layout of EH's article "Bullfighting, Sport and Industry" as it appeared in the magazine's March 1930 issue. A passage concerning the injuries inflicted on horses and bulls (about 1,200 words), included in the typescript EH would later send to John Herrmann with his letter of [13 June 1930], was omitted from the published version. The magazine inserted section headings, provided estimated dollar values for EH's pricing in pesetas, and added several sentences that do not appear in EH's typescript (PUL). The magazine also transformed EH's footnotes (mentioned in his letter to Archibald MacLeish of 31 December [1929]) into a separate Appendix. A 21-page typescript of the article and a ten-page manuscript of the footnotes also survive at JFK (items 296 and 297). The first of the article's three full-color illustrations, *Bullfight*, as well as its ten black-and-white etchings, are by Spanish painter Francisco José de Goya y Lucientes (1746–1828).

To Maxwell Perkins, 10 March [1930]

March 10

Dear Max:

We'll be damned glad to see you. Mike is staying over and we will take a trip either to the Cape of Florida, tarpon fishing along near the everglades or to Marquesas and Tortugas. Have a boat, equipment etc. prepared and Burge to run the boat and guide us.

So we will never mention it while you are down here I think it is too early to abandon the book and lay off advertising, most of the sale of the Sun etc. was after the first of the year and as you will see by the enclosed they are still keeping after it in England.

Wire or write me when you are leaving. We'll be at the train.[1] Have a fine tub of a boat that sleeps 4 in great comfort. Fine shooting and wild stuff along the Cape and Burge says wonderful tarpon.

Pauline and I each caught Tarpon two nights ago.

Best to you always—

Ernest

PUL, TLS

1 In a cable draft dated 14 March, Perkins responded that he would arrive in Key West on Monday [17 March] and would not need to be met at the train (PUL).

To Milford Baker, 14 March 1930

March 14, 1930

Dear Bake;

I certainly appreciated your letter and would have answered sooner, but have been trying to combine working with fishing. This means getting out on the water as soon as I'm through with the actual writing and coming back too pooped to write a line. But have been thinking about the rifle question and here goes.

First; if you send me the books any time I'll autograph them to anyextent and fire them back. Or if you want to wait until I'm in N.Y. in May or so you could bring them into town and I'd sign them at lunch.[1]

I'll put myself in your hands on the Springfield. As to measurements, I'm six feet tall, weight 190 pounds, have small hands for my size (have smashed them boxing many times on that account) but I suppose they have a standard measurement for 6 ft and 190 lbs. I would like to get a good job on the Springfield and, if you suggest, a Griffin and Howe mount on the scope.[2] I wish I could try a few scopes and see what went best with my eyes. I shoot without glasses, right eye is good, left eye only 2/20 vision.

However I don't care about the job being too ultra, would prefer fit and sturdiness and absolute dependability of action to finish. I-ve been shooting shotguns since ten years old and have about a dozen and have finely gotten to the ultra point on them on 25inch bbl.light Purdeys and they keep me broke.[3] Would like to start in Rifles in a modest way, especially since I'll shoot it an awful lot to get ready for the trip and may have shot the rifling out pretty well before we start. The way it looks now we will start a year from this May and I'd like to get the rifle as soon as possible so I can shoot it enough so that I will have some sort of confidence before we start.

How many rounds can I figure on firing from the gun you outlined my getting before it will affect the rifling?

If it will not bother it to shoot it plenty before-hand may I send you a check for the original Springfield cost and will you order it for me and have either Griffin and Howe or Owen get started on it?[4] How long after you order it will it be before I can have the rifle?

Thanks for the dope on double guns. If I can get so I shoot the Springfield well enough I will not worry about one but it may be a good thing to have anyway. Doubtless. Perhaps we can get them 2nd hand at Mombassa or Nairobi and save both the duties. ~~If it is a question of a knock down life saver~~[5]

I would be damned pleased with anything you send me as information

What about this Springfield that Sedgeley are getting out?[6] Have you seen or shot one? Would it be a good idea for me to get one of those now and start shooting it to get used to it? I find I can shoot pretty well with any shot gun if it isn't too heavy. I make a practice of shooting all my damned guns as much as possible. You do not get as good results but it makes you feel more like a shot and less like a specialist. If you can really play billiards you should be able to put up some sort of a game with almost any cue. However, as you see, I don't know a damned thing about rifle shooting and am glad to be given the Decalogue.[7]

Let me hear from you, Bake. I would welcome the chance to meet Captain Curtis; he being one of my favourite authors.[8]

Yours always,
Hemmy.

PUL, TLS; postmark: KEY WEST / FLA., MAR 15 / 1 PM / 1930

1 In a letter of 17 February 1930, Baker wrote that he planned to send copies of *MWW* and *FTA* (and possibly *SAR*) for EH to sign, and he invited EH to join him for lunch at the Harvard Club on his next visit to New York City (PUL).
2 In a letter of 17 February 1930, Baker had recommended that EH have "a sporting Springfield rebuilt to your measurements and specifications," saying that, if equipped with a telescope, it was "the finest sporting rifle in the world," suitable for most African game (PUL). This weapon, the standard U.S. Army rifle since 1903, was made available for civilian use in 1905 and was introduced in game hunting by Theodore Roosevelt during his 1909–1910 African safari. Responding to Roosevelt's praise and criticism of the Springfield in *African Game Trails* (1910), New York cabinetmaker Seymour Griffin (1885–1966) and

metalworker James V. Howe (1889–1969) formed Griffin & Howe, which specialized in converting the military weapon into a hunting rifle. In 1927, the company patented a popular scope side mount that allowed quick removal and reattachment of a scope without the need to readjust the sights.

3 EH refers to top-quality lightweight guns with 25-inch barrels (as opposed to the heavier, conventional 30-inch models) manufactured by the London firm of James Purdey & Sons. Established in 1814 by James Purdey (1828–1909), the firm "occupies the same exalted position in gunmaking as Rolls-Royce does in automobiles" (Calabi "Safari," 117).

4 In his 17 February letter, Baker had recommended either Griffin & Howe or Robert Owen (1884–1959) of Sauquoit, New York ("unquestionably the finest rifle builder in this country today") to customize the Springfield for EH.

5 Regarding EH's question in his previous letter (10 February), Baker responded that he had no personal experience with double rifles but advised that "the heavy double express rifle is essentially an English product" and ought to be purchased in England from the makers—both because "they are very tricky guns" and to avoid 50% import duties. He wrote that EH would probably not need the double express "except for close shots at dangerous game or to stop the charge of a wounded lion, elephant, or buffalo."

6 The R. F. Sedgley Company of Philadelphia, which manufactured firearms accessories, also customized Springfield rifles, launching the Sedgley Springfield Sporter in the mid-1920s.

7 The Ten Commandments, a reference to Baker's detailed letter of advice, which ran to five single-spaced typewritten pages.

8 Paul Allan Curtis, Jr. (1889–1943), American writer, gun authority, and WWI veteran. From 1919 to 1934 he worked at *Field and Stream* magazine as an associate editor and held additional positions as both Gun Editor and Arms and Ammunition Editor. EH owned two books by Curtis: *Sporting Firearms of Today in Use* (New York: Dutton, 1922) and *American Game Shooting* (New York: Dutton, 1927) (Brasch and Sigman, items 1603 and 1604). Baker mentioned in his 17 February letter that he had talked with Curtis, a close friend, who confirmed Baker's judgment "with regard to the proper battery for African shooting."

To Otto Barnett, 16 March [1930]

March 16
P.O. Box 396
Street address—
Corner of Whitehead and
United Streets.

Dear Mr. Barnett:—

It will certainly be very nice to see you again and to see Laury and his wife.[1] We are off for a cruise around Cape Sable etc. but expect to be back by March 24—[2] I've spoken to Capt. Bra about his boat for you— He expects to be back from Tortugas March 25— If anything should happen to him there is always Burge who sends you his best regards.

Pauline will be at the house and will be very glad to see you and give you information in case we are not returned— With best regards to Laury and his wife and to yourself— Looking forward to seeing you—(you must get a B i g Tarpon this time!

Yours always

Ernest

Thank you very much for the invitation to Dinner. If it's at all possible we'll be there!

JFK, ALS; postmark: KEY WEST / FLA., MAR 18 / [*illegible*] PM / 1930

1 EH addressed the envelope to "Messers OTTO or Lawrence Barnett / Hotel Bristol / Havana / Cuba." Lawrence Barnett, who had served with EH in the ARC Ambulance Service during WWI, married Elizabeth Groves (1901–1972) in 1923. He worked with his father, Otto, as a patent lawyer in the Chicago firm of Barnett & Truman.
2 Cape Sable, the southernmost point of mainland Florida and of the continental United States, is a peninsula about 64 miles northeast of Key West across Florida Bay.

To Gustavus A. Pfeiffer, 17 March [1930]

March 17—

Dear Uncle Gus— Thank you very much for sending the Trust agreements and enclosures—and for your good letter from Washington—[1]

I have been working—and fishing—very hard and so havent written— Max Perkins of Scribners has arrived and am taking him on a cruise early tomorrow morning— When we come back I'll write— My work has been going the best it has gone for over a year— Am well into it and going very well.[2] You must realize how much I appreciate and how very very deeply I thank you for all you did for the Trust fund for my mother and children. But please let me pay the amount over par you paid for the securities purchased with the 20,000. I would appreciate it if you would let me know how much it was.

Please excuse this hurried badly written letter. I appreciate what you wrote about me keeping the Mss. but I would rather give it to you. I know you'll always let me see it anytime I need to but would like to be able to give you something in a gesture, anyway, of return for all the things you have done for us. It is no more than a gesture for nothing we could ever give would equal your generosity. So please consider the Mss. yours. I will be so pleased if you will accept it.[3]

Two people have written me who are publishing bibliographies of my extant works—[4] Max Perkins tells me the last sale of a 1st (Paris) edition of In Our Time—was for $160.$\underline{^{00}}$ which is quite an advance over $3.$\underline{^{00}}$ in less than seven years. It may be only a bull market but I'll try to write nothing that will lower the value of yours Mss. and first editions. If I have good luck I hope to write a hell of a lot better than I have.

Anyway will answer your letters in detail when we come back from this trip— We are counting absolutely, as Pauline told you, on making a cruise together sometime before the middle of June—

Yours always—

Ernest

I was very sorry to hear about Uncle Jake. It was fine that you all had the reunion when you did.[5]

Am becoming a book-learned authority on African rifles and equipment. I wrote Fortune to send you a copy.[6]

JFK, ALS

1 EH is responding to Gus's letter of 8 March 1930, sent from Washington, D.C. (JFK).

2 EH had begun writing *DIA* in February.

3 EH had offered Pfeiffer the manuscript of *FTA*. After demurring, Pfeiffer would accept the offer in a letter to EH of 24 March 1930, "with the understanding that it is yours for the asking" (JFK). Pfeiffer would keep the manuscript all his life (Hawkins, 261, 275–76).

4 In a letter to EH dated 14 February 1930, Georgia Lingafelt enclosed a copy of the bibliographic listing she had prepared based on their previous correspondence and asked him to provide details about *FTA* (JFK). When Perkins arrived in Key West on 17 March, he delivered a letter to EH from American bookseller Louis Henry Cohn (1889–1953), who requested EH's cooperation in the preparation of "a definitive bibliography of your work" (UDel).

5 Gus's older brother, Harvey Jacob (Jake) Pfeiffer (1864–1930), owner of the Pfeiffer drugstore and one-time mayor of Cedar Falls, Iowa, died on 27 February 1930. In early October 1929, Paul and Mary Pfeiffer had "hosted the first family reunion since 1906 in Piggott," where "the seven living Pfeiffer brothers and one living sister gathered with their spouses" (Hawkins, 117). Gus's letter of 8 March indicates that he, Pauline's parents, and her brother, Karl, attended the funeral.

6 EH's letter to *Fortune* remains unlocated. In his 8 March letter Gus wrote, "I bought a March Issue of 'Fortune' yesterday haven't read Ernest's Contribution ["Bullfighting, Sport and Industry"] yet but will."

To Grace Hall Hemingway, 17 March [1930]

March 17

Dear Mother:—

Thanks for your good letter.[1] Hope by now you've received my letter enclosing Trust agreement. Have been very busy. Please thank Sun and Carol for Splendid barometer just arrived.

Always

Ernie

PSU, ALS; postmark: KEY WEST / FLA., MAR 18 / 5³⁰ PM / 1930

1 Grace reported in a letter of 9 March 1930 that all was well with Leicester, Marcelline, Sunny, and the weather. Regarding the trust fund, she wrote, "It seems <u>too</u> wonderful to think you are doing all this for us; I'm simply overwhelmed. And dear Pauline—it is noble of her to be a party to it." She signed herself, "Lovingly and gratefully, Your Mother" (JFK).

To Pauline Pfeiffer Hemingway, 30 March 1930

9WS 0Q RADIO
YACHT CAROLINE WS KEYWEST FLO 12 535P MAR 30 1930
MRS ERNEST HEMINGWAY
WHITEHEAD AND UNITED STS KEYWESTFLO
STILL STORMBOUND LOVE
 ERNEST
 547P

JFK, Cable

The cruise that began on 18 March ran into a storm off the Dry Tortugas, leaving EH, Max Perkins, Mike Strater, Archibald MacLeish, American writer John Herrmann (1900–1959), and Berge Saunders stranded. They were rescued on 30 March by the *Caroline*, a yacht owned by American businessman Eldridge Reeves Johnson (1867–1945), and would return to Key West c. 5 April.

To Milford Baker, 5 April 1930

April 5

1930

Box 396

Key West

Fla

Dear Bake;

Thanks ever so much for your two letters and what you have done about the Springfield. We were on a three weeks fishing cruise, held a week longer than we expected at Dry Tortugas by a bad blow and I am writing now as soon as returned. The books haven't come yet but will sign them as soon as they do and return to you.[1]

About the rifle. I enclose check for 100 dollars to you for the initial expense and for a deposit with G. and H. if that is necessary.

Get the rifle as you specify in your letter of March 28— also the sole leather case and case for scope. Also I'll need a good cleaning outfit, rod, brush, and flannel patches and would like to get a can of Fiendoil if you can recommend it. Ordered one from VLand A. my chicago dealers but they didn't have one.[2]

Am enclosing snap shot and measuremeant from ear to collar bone—base of ear to top of collar bone. This measurement is 14 centimeters— From the hollow of my arm to the end of my trigger finger is 74 centimeters—that is length of right arm. Would give this in inches but have only a metric tape measure. Can't measure best guns as they are in Arkansas.

Look, Bake. One of the two fellows who is to shoot with me in Africa is Henry H. Strater. He has been down here fishing and has just returned to N.Y. I told him how you were helping me out and he asked me if you would mind if he asked you out to lunch some day and you could give him some dope. His address is 115 East 86th street and he would like to order a G.and H. job too and perhaps order one at the same time for Charles Thompson who will be the third member of out party. He wouldn't bother you or bore you but I know would appreciate meeting you if it wouldn't annoy you to talk with someone who is as much of a neophyte about rifles as I am myself.

If you would be willing to have lunch with him I'll write him your address and he could make an appointment.

It will be grand to get the rifle and start learning to shoot it. Thanks ever so much for offering to loan me your Marlin 22 with scope but I couldn't think of it as the sea air is so damned hard on a gun here that I wouldn't have a gun in the house that I didn't own and could consequently accept the damage to finish etc. on.

We have had wonderful fishing lately and back from this cruise I am trying hard to work. Excuse the filthy bad typing of this and believe how much I appreciate your damned generous help on this rifle business.

The chances are that I won't be in N.Y. until middle of June so better figure on shipping the rifle as soon as ready.

Box 396 is a correct address until June. Piggott Arkansas will always reach me as will the Guaranty Trust Co. of N.Y. 4 place de la Concorde, Paris. But any of those will forward so the box 396 is as good as any.

You are certainly being damned good to me on the gun question. I know if you meet Mike Strater you will like him. He is a good painter and an old friend of mine from Paris.

Best to you always,
Ernest Hemingway

If it's better to have the balance on the rifle paid in advance please let me know. or G. and H. can send me bill here—

PUL, TLS; postmark: KEY WEST / FLA., [*illegible*]

1 In a letter of 28 March 1930, Baker summarized his recent conversation with Seymour Griffin (of Griffin & Howe) about the ordering and converting of the Springfield rifle, outlining alternatives, making recommendations, and itemizing estimated costs (total about $235, which includes "a gold disc set in the bottom of the stock on which your initials will be engraved"). He relayed Griffin's request for a photograph of EH, to establish the distance between EH's ear and shoulder, and reported his progress with EH's application for membership to the National Rifle Association, without which he could not acquire the military surplus rifle (PUL). In a letter dated 1 April 1930, Baker wrote that he had sent three books for EH to autograph, specifically requesting that EH write something in Baker's copy of *FTA* "which will associate our days on the Piave in 1918 with the inscription" (PUL). Baker also wrote that Griffin was awaiting EH's approval for crafting the gun.
2 Fiendoil, brand name for an oil-based rust preventive lubricant. Von Lengerke and Antoine, a prominent Chicago sporting goods firm established by Oswald von Lengerke (1860–1932) and Charles Antoine (1859–1939) in 1891.

To Georgia Lingafelt, 6 April 1930

Dear Miss Lingafelt:

I hope I havent held you up on the bibliographical thing—we were on a 10 day cruise and got caught in a storm at Dry Tortugas—another 10 days wonderful fishing— But when I got back my correspondance was hopeless— I have paid the bills, now, and yours is the 1st letter. Use the note, of course— Hope I can see you in Chicago this fall— I'm awfully glad you liked the book— Am trying to write another one maybe you will like it —

Yours always

Ernest Hemingway.

Box 396

Key West

April 6 1930

[*On envelope verso:*]

Somebody told me they paid $160 for a Paris In Our Time— What do you sell it for? Maybe I better buy one before it's too late—[1]

Private Collection, ALS; envelope at UDel; postmark: KEY WEST / FLA., APR 7 / 1 PM / 1930

1 In a letter to EH of 4 May 1930, Louis Henry Cohn would enclose "an extract from an auction catalog which might interest you," adding that he had bought the book for $160 (UDel). The listing for the "Mint Copy" of *iot* in the catalog for the 10 March 1930 auction at the Ritter-Hopson Galleries in Newark, New Jersey, is reproduced in facsimile in Bruccoli and Clark's *Hemingway at Auction* (1), bearing the marginal notation "160.— / H of Bks." The sale receipt, dated 3/10/30 and made out to "Miss Arnold," survives in the Louis Henry and Marguerite Cohn Hemingway Collection at UDel. Cohn and Marguerite Arnold (1887–1984) would marry in September 1930 and together establish the House of Books in New York City.

To Laurence Stallings, 6 April 1930

Box 396

Key West

Florida

April 6 1930

Dear Mr. Stallings:—

We were out on a cruise in 28 ft. tub and ran into a blow that held us 10 days overdue at Dry Tortugas— So I've just gotten your letter. I'm awfully sorry to have been delayed answering it—

About the play— The best way is to act as though I'm dead— You're making the play and you have the responsibility— I cant give permission to anything except to you to make the play— God be wit you—[1]

You see I dont know a damned thing about the theater— So you take the book as though it were by some citizen that is dead all ready and let all your responsability be to the book—

I would like to go in with you and help on it and learn something about the theatre— But I'm trying to write another book— So it's your show—

Do you know anything about that Metro-Goldwyn business that went on for a while? Mr. Reynolds and I both speak the English language to a certain extent but I do not always understand what he says. All I know so far is that I've received $750 less 10%—less attorneys fees—less cables—less telegrams—while my creditors, families and miscellaneous responsabilities write me feeling that I have held out on them on the moneys I have received from all the things they have read I have sold to the pictures.[2]

My father, who was a marvelous shot at grouse, ducks, quail and clay birds, shot himself with equal success last year and ever since I have been broke as hell— I have been slipping the family what money I have made— But since they had no cause to trust me in the past they do not believe me when I deny having made the vast sums from the films— Have had Scribners turn over all money so far from the book to them— I thought maybe it would be all right for me to write and ask you, confidentially, what the picture possibilities are—

If this is one of those things that gents can only inform each other about through their agents—all right— But anything you can tell me confidentially I will keep that way.

Anyway I wish you all luck with the play—

Yours always—
Ernest Hemingway.

Wake Forest, ALS; postmark: KEY WEST / FLA., APR 7 / 1 PM / 1930

1 Stallings was writing the stage version of *FTA*, which would open on Broadway on 22 September 1930. The letter from Stallings to which EH is responding remains unlocated.
2 Producer Al Woods paid $1,500 for the dramatic rights to *FTA*, which EH and Stallings split evenly minus a 10% commission to EH's literary agent Paul R. Reynolds, Jr. (Reynolds to Stallings, 8 March 1930, Wake Forest). Metro-Goldwyn-Mayer had offered $10,000 for the film rights to *FTA* in late 1929, but Reynolds thought the offer too low and held out for more money, which upset EH. However, Reynolds proved right, as in September 1930 Paramount would buy the film rights to *FTA* for $80,000.

To Waldo Peirce, 6 April [1930]

Box 396—Key West
April 6

Dear old Waldo:—

I'm a bastard not to have gotten a letter to you— Didnt know your boat went so soon— Planned to wire— Mike and Archie came down— We went on a cruise for 10 days— Got in a storm at Tortugas and 10 days over due from there— So far I've got 8 tarpon— Pauline 5— Biggest 120 lbs. Maxie (Dead Pan) Perkins caught a Kingfish that weighed 58 lbs. Tarpon are coming in thick as hell now— Mike, Max, Burge and I had best damned Cruise we've ever had.

Alzira is here and seems a damned fine girl—we tried to look after her feed her a few times etc. She seems in good morale. Suppose you have her news from her.[1]

Maxie (Dead Pan) Perkins stayed 3 weeks— All of which we were on a Cruise— Went to Cape Sable— But Mosquitos ran us out— Went to Marquesas and Tortugas- Now reduced by guest losage and breakage to 1 rod and 1 (damaged) reel— Have another rod—

Pat Morgan here— Damned glad to see him— Why I dont write letters is I have only about 18 minutes a day between arrival of early morning trains—seeing off merchants—unhooking fish—putting on baits—taxing in car—ordering tackle—getting mullets etc Cleaning guns— And have been using those 18 minutes to write on new book—

A lot of merchants we never did more than nod to in cafés have turned up in the role of old friends and taken houses—our next move will be to west coast of Mexico— Plan to spend all time possible at Tortugas—

My simple little idea of coming to Key West to write See no one and fish <u>when through writing</u> appeals to no one—

Dos and Nuestra Katy[2] arrive Friday—wire from them from Santiago— We'll all go to Tortugas if weather is good— Pat ought to be able to water color well there— Sure as hell will be glad to see Passos and Kate— It isnt seeing your friends like you, Archie Pat, Mike, Passos—Katy that destroys work. Nor Max either because he's damned good— But everybody I've ever met or had any business, commerical or literary dealings with thinks it's damned good idea to drop in and have us show them a little tarpon fishing—

Figure on drowning somebody next time out and that may cast a pall over the business— After all we picked Key West as a quiet place to live and work— I have to work or tousands starve— We'll have to move that's all—

Hope everything goes well with you in Paris and you get everything all O.K. Best to Ivy— Tell Charley [Sweeny] ~~why I havent written~~— I'm writing him— Come on Kid— The tarpon are so thick you can walk across the jack channel on their backs—

Excuse this lousy letter— If tried to write decent letter would never get it off—

> See you soon—
> Best luck to you—
> Ernest.

Everythings swell— I'm only crabbing at not working.

Thanks for letting us take the pictures.

Colby, ALS

1 In a letter of 21 February 1930, Peirce wrote from Bangor, Maine, that he would be leaving for Paris in a few days and Alzira Boehm would go to Key West "to paint, establish a little gay home in Key West etc." (JFK). Peirce was waiting for his divorce from Ivy Troutman to become final, and Alzira was pregnant with the twins who would be born in October.
2 Our Katy (Spanish).

To Cyril Clemens, 6 April 1930

Box 396
Key West
Florida
April 6, 1930

Dear Mr. Clemens:

I am greatly honored by your offer of an Honorary Vice-Presidency in the Mark Twain Society and accept with great pleasure.

With all best wishes,

Yours very truly
Ernest Hemingway.

MHM, ALS

Cyril Clemens, a distant cousin of Mark Twain (né Samuel Langhorne Clemens, 1835–1910), founded the International Mark Twain Society and later the *Mark Twain Journal*, which he edited from 1936 to 1982. This letter was reproduced on the front cover of the journal's Ernest Hemingway Memorial Number (Summer 1962), featuring tributes to EH, who had died the previous summer.

To Milford Baker, 8 April 1930

Dear Bake:—

Enclosed is my N.RA membership card that has just come.[1] Got in last night from the tarpon after the post office was closed but found a notice of an insured package in the box. It is probably your books and I will sign them and ship them right out.

So far have taken 8 tarpon—largest 120 lb. 6 ft 2″— Biggest ones not in yet. All on 6 oz tip—15 thread line— Mrs. H. has taken 5—we go to Tortugas next week again so if you dont hear from me dont lay it to lack of interest in getting the rifle out.

Yours always—
Hemmie
Key West
Box 396
April 8 1930

[*On envelope verso:*]

Please deduct what I owe you from the check.

PUL, ALS; postmark: KEY WEST / FLA., APR 8 / 1230PM / 1930

1 Public Law 149 (1905) permitted members of accredited civilian shooting clubs, such as the National Rifle Association (established 1871), to acquire surplus military rifles, ammunition, and equipment at cost. Baker used EH's membership card "to order, from the office of the Director of Civilian Marksmanship, a new, unfinished and un-stocked National Match-quality Springfield barreled action" (Calabi, Helsley, and Sanger, 125–27).

To Maxwell Perkins, [c. 11 April 1930]

Dear Max:—

Thanks for your two letters and the royalty statement— Havent received the present but if in your magnificent statement it's in view of bathing beauties, lions and buffaloes it sounds like an indispensability. I feel like before Christmas when ~~I was a~~ we were kids. We had a wonderful trip didn't we?[1]

The In Our Time was advertized on the 3 Stories and 10 Pms. because it was announced to appear in 1923 but didn't get out until 1924— It was the last of a series of 6 books—the 3 Mts published— It was an old handpress and they were always months late—[2]

Ernest Walsh was a citizen who had tuberculosis and a very varied career— Edited with Ethel <u>Moorehead</u> This Quarter and died a couple of years ago—

I would like very much to have the letters— Will you please send them to me? I got out the 1st number of his magazine for him when he got hemmorages and had to leave Paris— Did him many favors—was bitched by him in true Irish fashion— He wrote the attack on The Torrents—in the New Masses—The Cheapest book I Ever Read—after I'd told him I couldnt let him serialize it in This Quarter— Anyway I would like to have the letters— If you cannot sell the 3 Stories and 10 Poems for £35 I will pay you the difference between what you paid and what you sell— I do not believe the letters are shameful but they are probably libelous[.] Send them to me without reading them and if I read them think they wd amuse you will send them to you—[3]

Walsh got up a prize The This Quarter Award of $^\$$2000.$^{\underline{00}}$ to be given to the Contributor who printed the best stuff in his mag. He promised the award to Joyce, to Pound and to me I found later— He got swell things from all of us on strength of this promise! I have his letter promising it to me—[4]

I'd like to keep my letters to him— But there must be more than 6—damn it—and will publish them and his sometime when we're all broke—[5]

Thanks ever so much for getting them for me— Always write me about anything like that— There are some I've written to girls I will be prepared to pay a good price for if you ever hear of them coming into the market—

Yours always

Ernest—

Ask them to buy any other letters from me to Walsh that come up for sale— I'll trade you something else for them or write you some letters—

Have caught 3 tarpon since you left— Now another North Easter blowing like the devil— Have been working hard—

PUL, ALS

1 In one of two letters dated 8 April 1930, Perkins wrote he had sent EH a gift "in memory of one of the happiest episodes of my life," the fishing cruise. He said the gift would enable EH to "get the first possible glimpse" of some future rescue yacht "and the lions and buffaloes of 1931," a reference to the African safari EH was planning (JFK).

2 In his second letter of 8 April, Perkins reported that he had received a copy of *TSTP* and a half-dozen letters written by EH to American poet and editor Ernest Walsh (1895–1926) that had been sold in London for £30. Charles Kingsley, Scribner's London manager from 1919 to 1940, had acquired the lot from the buyer and sent the materials to be sold in the rare book department of Scribner's New York store. Perkins asked EH if he could explain why an advertisement for *iot*, published in 1924, appeared on the back of *TSTP*, which was published in 1923 (PUL).

3 Together with Scottish painter and suffragist Ethel Moorhead (1869–1955), Walsh co-founded and co-edited the little magazine *This Quarter*. EH had served as their on-site liaison in Paris, overseeing the production of the first number, published in May 1925. Shortly after Walsh died of tuberculosis on 16 October 1926, his negative review of EH's *TOS*, titled "The Cheapest Book I Ever Read," appeared in *New Masses* (October 1926). Perkins said he did not know who Walsh was and had not read the letters, but Kingsley had described them as being "of a more or less intimate character" (Kingsley to Perkins, 19 March 1930, PUL). Perkins told EH, "we thought you might well not wish to have them sold, and if so we shall gladly destroy them, or send them to you, or whatever you say."

4 In the first number of *This Quarter*, Walsh had announced that $2,000 would be awarded to the contributor of the best work in the first four numbers. He died after publication of the second number, and the award never materialized. Walsh and his empty promise were

the subject of EH's unflattering sketch "The Man Who Was Marked for Death" (*MF*). The letter EH mentions receiving from Walsh remains unlocated.
5 Between 7 January [1925] and 7 April 1926, EH had addressed six located letters jointly to Walsh and Moorhead, and twenty-eight more to Walsh alone (see *Letters* vol. 2 and vol. 3).

To Milford Baker, 15 April [1930]

April 15—

Dear Bake:—

The books are all written in and ready to send back— I'm trying to get you a Sun Also Rises to go with them—

Yrs always—
Hemmy—

If you dont hear from me it is because we leave today for Tortugas again, Mike Strater ran into Capt. Paul Curtis at the Players— So that will save you the bother.[1]

PUL, ALS; postmark: KEY WEST / FLA., APR 15 / 1 PM / 1930

1 In a letter of [11] April 1930, Strater told EH that he had run into Paul Curtis at the Players Club in New York City just as Strater was completing paperwork proposing EH as a member (JFK). Founded in 1888 by actor Edwin Booth (1833–1893; brother of John Wilkes Booth) and located at 16 Gramercy Park South, the private social club restricted membership to men associated with the dramatic or other creative arts. EH would be admitted into the Players Club in 1930 and remain on the rolls until 1951, when Charles Scribner informed the club that EH wished to resign. EH would mention his membership in "The Sights of Whitehead Street: A Key West Letter" (*Esquire*, April 1935, 23).

To Henry Strater, 15 April [1930]

April 15

Dear Mike:—

It's a bloody shame about the films but what the hell we took none that I cant remember better in the head. I remember the tarpon and I dont give a damn about proving it.[1]

We are going to Tortugas again today—Dos, Pat [Morgan] Pauline and Co.

Caught 5 tarpon since you left but only 3 days of fishing—all the rest a bloody norther—

I've been working or I'd have written—

Thank Maggie for the two swell clippings!

Tell the committee I'm a kike—[2] Family changed from Hemingstein when they got off the Mayflower— My mothers family were Hall and Hancock's—another kike name— Originally Hamcockskinoff— He changed his name on becoming Gov. of Massachusetts— The Halls were the Rabinowitchs.

My paternal grandmother was an Edmonds—(Edsmutz)

maternal grandmother Caroline Hanckock—

maternal Grandfather Ernest Miller Hall (of the Hall room boys)[3]

Tell the committee I'm a Kike and I can prove it—

If they have to see me to know if I'm a jew or not it aint worth while— Wd rather go aboard yachts—

We had a swell trip didnt we— By God yes—

We'll have a damned good one in Africa too— I wish we could take Dead Pan Maxie [Perkins]—might be possible— Would set a precedent on relations between authors and publishers! Miss you very much—wish the hell you were going now.

> So long Kid—
> yrs in Kosher
> Hem—
> Love to Maggie

PUL, ALS

Typewritten upside down at the bottom of the second page: "Now is the time for all g / men to co,"

1 In his letter of [11] April 1930, Strater explained that his camera had malfunctioned, ruining the pictures taken on their recent fishing cruise. He especially lamented losing photos of EH's tarpon catch (JFK).

2 Referring to EH's prospective membership in the Players Club, Strater had written, "When you are in town you will have to come down here & meet the committee. They don't trust anyone on the kike proposition nowadays." Exclusion of Jews was common among private clubs.

3 EH's maternal grandparents were Caroline Hancock (1843–1895) and Ernest Miller Hall (1840–1905); his paternal grandparents were Adelaide Edmonds (1841–1923) and

Anson Tyler Hemingway (1844–1926). John Hancock (1737–1793), president of the Second Continental Congress (1775–1777), the first signer of the Declaration of Independence (1776), and the first governor of Massachusetts (1780–1785). According to Grace Hall Hemingway, her mother was descended from the same Hancock line in England as the American patriot (Sanford, 113). The popular comic strip "The Hall Room Boys" by Harold Arthur McGill (1876–1952) appeared in national newspapers from 1906 to 1921.

To Louis Henry Cohn, 23 April [1930]

Box 396
Key West
Fla.
April 23

Dear Mr. Cohn:

Thank you very much for your letters. I am sorry not to have written before but did not know what to answer— About the bibliography— If you would send it to me— a carbon of it— I'd know whether I could sign and what there would be that I could write as a foreword or epilogue—(the latter might be better)[1] Too I could and would be glad to correct anything or give you any information about published things that I know about— Have you any record of the so called obscene poems published in English in Germany?[2] Flechtheim wanted to collect them and bring them out with drawings by Pascin— But I didnt know whether it was completely advisable—[3]

About the Up in Michigan— It might be better for it to be reprinted in any re-issue they should ever make of the complete In Our Time—in which it was originally included—and in which the text of the Mr. and Mrs. Elliot should be published as it was originally in the Little Review—[4]

If you send me the text of the bibliography I'll tell you if I can sign it and if there's any thing I can write— If I do the $350 will be all right as long as I get it in cash and whenever I want it.

With all best wishes
Yours always—
Ernest Hemingway

UDel, ALS; postmark: KEY WEST / FLA., APR24 / 1 PM / 1930

1 In an undated letter to EH that Max Perkins delivered on his March visit to Key West, Cohn wrote that Random House had asked him to do a definitive bibliography of EH's work, to be published in a limited edition of 350 copies. Random House would "pay liberally" if EH would be willing to write a foreword to the book and sign the copies (n.d. [March 1930], UDel). Although EH refers to Cohn's "letters," no other letter from Cohn has been located that pre-dates EH's 23 April response.

2 EH refers to his poems published in the November 1924 and February 1925 issues of the literary magazine *Der Querschnitt*, founded in Berlin in 1920 by publisher and art gallery owner Alfred Flechtheim (1878–1937). The poems included "The Soul of Spain with McAlmon and Bird the Publishers," "The Earnest Liberal's Lament," "The Lady Poets with Foot Notes," and "The Age Demanded."

3 In a 22 April 1925 letter to Dos Passos, EH reported, "The 'Schnitt also publishing a book of my dirty poems to be illustrated by Pascin" (*Letters* vol. 2, 323). Jules Pascin (né Julius Mordecai Pincas, 1885–1930), Bulgarian-born French painter, had contributed two illustrations for EH's "Stierkampf" (translation of "The Undefeated"), published in *Der Querschnitt* in the Summer [June] 1925 and July 1925 issues. The plan to publish a volume of EH's poems illustrated by Pascin never materialized. EH would later recall the painter in a chapter of his Paris memoirs (*MF*, "With Pascin at the Dome").

4 Cohn had written that Random House was interested in bringing out a limited edition of EH's story "Up in Michigan," which appeared in *TSTP* (Paris: Contact Editions, 1923) but had never been published in the United States. "Mr. and Mrs. Elliott," first published in the *Little Review* (Autumn–Winter 1924–1925), was altered for inclusion in the 1925 Boni & Liveright edition of *IOT* at the insistence of Liveright, who feared censorship. The story would appear in its original form in the 1930 Scribner's edition of *IOT*. "Up in Michigan" would not be reprinted until 1938, in *The Fifth Column and the First Forty-nine Stories*.

To Paul and Mary Pfeiffer, 23 April [1930]

April 23

Dear Mother and father Pfeiffer:—

This is the great pen and if I'd had anything worthy of being written by it this letter would not have been so long delayed.[1]

We are all well— Pat has commenced to talk fluently in French and can also say "I dont know" and "Hobo" in English. Pauline is fine and very strong and healthy. We have a fine time fishing together. She has caught 5 tarpon— She looks the best I have ever seen her.

Waldo is still in Paris. Bumby is fine and will come with Jinny when she comes in June or July.

Key West is increasingly unprosperous altho the sponging industry is reviving. I dont know whether this means more people are taking up bathing or whether sponges are now being used to manufacture home brew—

The Literary Digest poll is very instructive—as is the advice by the noted (Paid) Dry leader to all good drys to "vote as many times as they can obtain ballots) A reaction against Prohibition seems to have set in over the country. I hope to live to see it replaced by Temperance.[2]

Dos Passos and his wife arrived about ten days ago from Spain. They were in Madrid the day Sidney Frankin the American bull fighter was gored but it rained so they did not go to the fight. I saw a lot of him last summer. He was a very nice fellow and I feel terribly badly that he should have something so bad (the horn wound almost destroyed the sphincter muscle) for his first wound as it is liable to take away his Courage and make him useless.[3]

We were at Tortugas so were not counted in the census so they will have to add 3 to the official figures.[4] Have been very busy working on my book, looking after business and income tax matters with a few too many visitors staying a little too long. Do you want any books? We could make up a box now to send to Piggott—or bring a trunk load when we come.

You will like Henriette I think. Speaking no English she stayed with Patrick while we were both gone for 8 days to Dry Tortugas—and enjoyed herself.

She can do more things with less bother than anyone I've ever seen— She is a splendid cook.

This is a dull letter. But we are like happy countries with no history—

Did you see that a Farewell to Arms was in the books selected for the White House Library? If we could have gotten Al in they would not have had to worry about a White house library—[5]

The pen writes much better than I do as you can see—

But we will be seeing you now in six weeks or so— Patrick can say Grandmother and Grandfather in French—and he'll learn all the English you will teach him—

With best love from us all—

Ernest—

Thank you ever so much for forwarding my mail and papers—

PUL, ALS; postmark: KEY WEST / FLA., APR24 / 1 PM / 1930

1 Paul Pfeiffer had ordered a premium Sheaffer writing pen and desk set as a 1929 Christmas gift for EH. Founded by Iowa businessman Walter A. Sheaffer in 1912, the company produced superior fountain pens whose gold nibs were insured for the lifetime of the owner.

2 In February 1930 the *Literary Digest* (1890–1938) began polling 20 million voters on their views of Prohibition (the Eighteenth Amendment) and the Volstead Act (Amendment enforcement). Clarence True Wilson (1872–1939), general secretary of the Methodist Board of Temperance, Prohibition, and Public Morals, declared the poll "outrageous, for it is conducted by wet propagandists" and advised dry voters to submit more than one ballot (*Chicago Tribune*, 1 April 1930). On 24 May 1930 the *Digest* would present the results of roughly 4.8 million responses: 30.46% supported Prohibition, 29.11% supported modification of the Amendment to allow beer and wine, and 40.43% supported its repeal.

3 Severely injured on Sunday, 16 March 1930, Franklin was not fully healed when he next performed, on 4 May, at a minor bullring. Complications from the wound would effectively end his career.

4 The 1930 U.S. Federal Census, conducted every ten years.

5 U.S. President Calvin Coolidge (1872–1933) had housed his personal book collection in the White House Library, taking it with him at the end of his administration (1923–1929). When it became public that there was no home library at the White House, the American Booksellers Association selected and donated 500 books. The list of titles, published in the *New York Times* (10 April 1930, 26), included *FTA*. Alfred Emanuel "Al" Smith (1873–1944), four-time governor of New York (1923–1928) and an anti-Prohibitionist, had been the Democratic Party's 1928 presidential candidate. The first Roman Catholic to run for the office, Smith lost to Herbert Hoover.

To Laurence Stallings, 23 April [1930]

April 23

Dear Mr. Stallings:—

Thanks very much for your letter. Was out at Tortugas again so just got it today.

About the M.G.M. business— It would be fine to be out with you and the Great MacArthur but I've got to keep going on this book I'm writing—not write anything else until it's finishes—and It will take me through next fall anyway.[1]

About their terms— I wouldnt go in on any proposition whereby you get the alleged real money if you make good— I would never go into it at all except if I were going to do it as well as I could— Anybody takes a chance if they hire you— But they dont get anymore speed out of a race horse, however punk, by promising him a big meal or holding a lump of sugar out in front of him.— If you do the work they've got the stuff whether they accept it officially or not— I might be lousy or I might be good— But that's their risk— They'd make plenty of money if I was good that I wouldnt cut in on.

It's very long odds against ever going out there— Although I know I would have a fine time if you and Charley were there— But if I ever went it would have to be on a straight weekly contract basis for 10 weeks with money that sounded like money and no splits with any agents. Would not work to make money for any agent on acct. of a letter being forwarded through him.

One reason I asked about the money picture chances was that when I was broke last fall I wired Reynolds to sell the novel outright and named a certain sum which made it, then, a bargain at that price. I needed that amt of money. He, on his own authority, not mine, (I named a sum at which I wanted it sold) prefferred to gamble on it as a play. You say they offered $15,000. 15 G. at that moment were worth 30 now and 50 in the future. So I was sore at instructions not being followed. But I hope you get a swell play and have luck with it.

You were damned nice about not wanting to split the advance— But the ½ of advance is yours and there's no way I'd take it.

What I hated was to see 15 G in cash become 675 and a stack of chips.—[2] It's been a long time since 675 one way or another could complicate or solve my major economic problems. And the only way I like to really gamble is to go with a little money into a crap game where there's a <u>lot</u> of money.

But anyway good luck to you and God Bless MacArthur. Tell him there is a fine opening for a young man here in the commercial fishing and drinking business. We were making good money around 250 seeds a day when we hit the kingfish until we got in a hell of a storm, couldnt run our fish, and the ice all melted and had to throw the bloody fish all overboard. Fishing is like farming. You could make money except for the number of acts of God.

Tell him there are a couple of other good businesses here he would like. Have a fine pugilist here named Willie Jackson who, like Tantalus, is strengthened every time he hits the canvas. But am afraid it cant last. He is getting to walk a little funny already.[3]

With best regards,
Ernest Hemingway.

Wake Forest, ALS; postmark: KEY WEST / FLA, APR24 / 2 PM / 1930

1 Although his incoming letter remains unlocated, Stallings presumably had proposed that EH join him and Charles Gordon MacArthur (1895–1956), American journalist, playwright, and screenwriter, in Hollywood to write for the Metro-Goldwyn-Mayer Studios. After working as a reporter for the *Chicago Herald-Examiner*, in 1924 MacArthur moved to New York City, where he joined the Algonquin Round Table and married actress Helen Hayes (1900–1993) in 1928. MacArthur collaborated with Ben Hecht to write the hit Broadway play *The Front Page* (1928) and in 1930 began writing Hollywood screenplays for M.G.M. Hayes would star in the 1932 film production of *FTA*.
2 EH and Stallings each received $675 as their share of the $1,500 advance royalty payment for dramatic rights to *FTA* (minus the 10% commission for agent Paul R. Reynolds).
3 Key West boxer Willie Jackson, Irish-American welterweight known as the "Fighting Fool." Jackson would knock out Tampa welterweight Kid Camero in a bout at the Key West Athletic Club on 28 April 1930. Several months later the *Key West Citizen* would report, "Jackson has a wonderful record, he has engaged in 18 or 20 scraps and has dropped only three decisions" (13 September 1930, 3). Tantalus, Greek god punished with eternal thirst and hunger and tormented by the sight of water and fruit that appear within reach but continually recede just beyond his grasp.

To Maxwell Perkins, [c. 24 April 1930]

Dear Max:—

Thanks ever so much for the books and the glasses. Dos has been reading the Trotsky ever since it came. He says it is damned good. The others are good too— The Dinali is the kind of book I like very much.

The glasses are damned fine—[1]

We found the Kings all gone at Tortugas— Not a one <u>anywhere</u>— Birds hadnt started to lay yet— But hundreds of man of war hawks gathered waiting for them—

Am trying to work— So wont write much— Will send you the Ernest Walsh letters that you sent me for you to read if you like— Am glad to have them out of circulation since they curse out too many merchants—
It certainly is a crappy business to find your own personal letters up for sale— am going to quit writing letters—

Is a Farewell still selling? I hope they will try to get it to the 100 tousand mark that Mr. Scribner spoke of—

I wrote Cohn to send me the Bibliography and I'd know then if I could sign it—

Have you tried to get the I.OT. from Liveright again?— It sh'd be brought out, when it is in new edition, with the <u>Up In Michigan</u> story and <u>The Mr. and Mrs. Elliott</u> as it appeared in original in the Little Review—

Best to you always—

Ernest

It was a shame there were no pictures out of all those Mike took—

I had a nice note from Morley C.

Hope his book goes well.[2]

John left a week ago for Pennsylvania.[3] Have heard nothing from Scott— Waldo writes of him from Paris—

The boat broke her pump just as we got opposite Marquesas coming home from Tortugas night before last— Anchored there about 4 miles off Marquesas all night and I brought Pauline and Dos up to Key West in the outboard in the morning—24 miles— It was good and rough until we got to Boca Grande—

PUL, ALS

The conjectured letter date is based on EH's 23 April return to Key West after an eight-day fishing trip, having spent the previous night (22 April) at anchor in the damaged boat. That night, EH tells Perkins, was "night before last."

1 Scribner's published both *My Life: An Attempt at an Autobiography* (1930), by exiled Russian revolutionary Leon Trotsky (1879–1940), and *The Wilderness of Denali: Explorations of a Hunter-Naturalist in Northern Alaska* (1930), by American conservationist Charles Sheldon (1867–1928). Edited by C. Hart Merriam and Edward Nelson and published posthumously by the author's widow, Louisa Gulliver Sheldon, Sheldon's memoir was among the books in EH's personal library (Brasch and Sigma, item 6015). Perkins had sent EH a pair of binoculars as a thank-you gift after the fishing trip to the Dry Tortugas.
2 Callaghan's novel *It's Never Over* was published by Scribner's in February 1930.
3 John Herrmann and his wife, American writer and journalist Josephine Herbst (1892–1969), had married in 1926 and since 1928 had lived in Erwinna, Pennsylvania.

To Guy Hickok, [c. 25 April 1930]

Dear Guy:

We're so damned sorry to hear about your mother. She was very lovely and so sweet and good. I hope she did not have too much pain from the foot before she died.[1] Anything I try to write sounds no good but I know how much you loved her and how bad it must have been and Pauline and I both send you our love and sympathy—to you and Mary both. She was so good and sweet and so very pretty— I always felt she was so fine I was too lousy a guy to ever be around where she was.

Everything has been o.k. here. Got the trust fund fixed up for my ~~mother~~ family etc. Paid U.S. income tax on all moneys recd. Have been working pretty steady but fishing even steadier. Caught 8 tarpon so far Pauline 5. She is in the best shape she has ever been. Strong and brown and swell and a grand companion.

Henriette has worked out better than ever expected. Does al work formerly done by two jigs and my dumb sister Sunny and has lots of time besides. She stayed alone with Pat for 8 days while Pauline and I were at Tortugas. Jinny is bringing Bumby over in June. Pat Morgan is here now. Also Dos and his wife. Pat is going to Paris pretty soon. He'd go to Pamplona with you I think.[2] [*EH autograph insertion*: Whitney Cromwell— the boy who was such a great friend of his—died in Tunis— Pat had to take care of him—bring back body etc.]

Yeah books nor nothing don't sell. My gut is in excellent shape though and I can and do drink anything and no bad effects. Have never been in better shape.

Waldo was to come here many different dates but have about given him up. So I don't beat my wife don't I? And what else don't I do? My God all those lousy literary libellings seem remote when you are going out in the old boat to Tortugas— We were on one cruise 3 weeks. 10 days stormbound at Tortugas. It's the best place I've been any time anywhere. I'll tell you about it. Flowers, tamarind trees, guava trees, cocnut palms with cocnuts till your urines clear as gin. maybe it was gin. we drank enough gin. [*EH autograph insertion*: No mosquitoes, nor flies.] got tight last night on absinthe and did knife tricks. Great success shooting the knife underhand into the piano. The woodworms are so bad and eat hell out of all furniture that you can always claim the woodworms did it. Have to stop and try to write.

The reason I haven't written letters is that I get no time to work on acct. visitors and these cruises. Took paper and envelopes to write you from Tortugas but it was trying to write from Pamplona with Kingfish instead of bulls.

Love to Mary and take care of yourself and please write.

Ernest

Ruano Lopez is a good friend of mine— I would have given a lot to have had a chance to buy some of those pictures—[3]

> Box 396
>
> Key West until middle June—
>
> then Piggott

phPUL, TLS with autograph postscript

The conjectured date is based on EH's 23 April 1930 return to Key West from the cruise to the Dry Tortugas, and his reference to doing knife tricks involving a piano "last night."

1 Clara E. Hickok (née Falkner, 1868–1930) died suddenly on 2 April. "She fell in the garden and broke the bones of her right foot; and while a surgeon was setting them an embolism killed her," Hickok wrote in a letter to EH of 9 April 1930 (JFK). She had lived with Guy and his wife, Mary, in Paris.

2 In his 9 April letter, Hickok wrote that he wanted to go to Pamplona in July "but guess that without proper guidance I'd better not."

3 Spanish painter Carlos Ruano Llopis (1878–1950), who had formally trained as a draughtsman in Valencia, worked at the Ortega Lithographic Workshop painting large oil canvases that were used to illustrate bullfight posters. Although EH did not acquire an original painting, a large poster titled "Toros en San Sebastián" by C. Ruano Llopis, announcing bullfights on 4 and 11 September, hangs in his library at Finca Vigía in Cuba.

To the editor of the *New York World*, [c. 25 April 1930]

To The Literary Editor of the World

Sir:

In the New York World of Easter Sunday under the heading of A Sometimes Absent Author Mr. Harry Saltpecker writes that no one in New York knows precisely where Mr. John Dos Passos is.[1] Mr. Saltpenis goes on to state that Dos Passos is "of slight build, inclined to stoop a little, thin haired where he is not bald, inclined to a student-like pallor and timidity. He has a smallish face, expressive eyes etc. To look at and to listen to him is to realize how much more daring he is in print etc."

Mr. Saltpeter goes on to state how Mr. Dos Passos has two unfinished projects—a novel and a play. He described these projects so they sounded pretty terrible.

All right. No one in N.Y. may know precisely where Mr. Dos Passos is but his publishers and his agents, there are at least two of them since they have a double barrelled name and they take ten percent of all his royalties, address him care of General Delivery, Key West, Florida. ~~On the easter Sunday in question he was at the Dry Tortugas. As I write this he is in the Overseas (Half seas over) Hotel, Key West, Florida.~~[2]

Hoping to enlighten Mr. Saltpeter I asked Mr. Dos Passos why he travelled. He answered ~~Cryptically s~~, always the man of mystery, "Why does a chicken cross the road?"[3] As far as I know he travels for pleasure. He gets more pleasure out of it than anyone I know and he travels more. He can speak English, French, Spanish, German, Italian, Russian, and Arabic and he has been to most of the places the other boys have only read about. This makes them very critical of his observations. ~~since what he writes has seen may not agree with what they have read.~~

I started to write this ~~bloody~~ letter on account of Mr. Saltpeter's description of Dos Passos's physical appearance about which there cannot be much question. Anything else may be a matter of opinion but I have observed Mr. Dos Passos's appearance. Since I have known him ~~and~~, I first saw him in 1918 or 1917, he has been of solid build, weighing between 170 and 185 pounds, with a wide, rather round face. I have read ~~the same libel in other places~~ too that he is pale, academic and a user of words in his books that would never think to use himself. ~~As a matter~~ Really his face is dark, he is not academic but educated, a rare thing, and he has a full Elizabethan vocabulary. He uses all the four letter words properly and correctly.

He is a humanist in the old sense that he knows his latin and his greek, that he is travelled, that he speaks the languages of the countries where has travelled and has read ~~their classics and~~ as well as latin and greek a good part of French, Spanish, German and Italian literature in the original. He can also hold his liquor which is a form of decorum.

On the other hand Mr. Seward Collins who is a spokesmen for the Humanists who part their hair with a capital H ~~and speak no foreign languages~~ is not so good with Latin nor with Greek, nor with the foreign languages I have heard him attempt and I have seen him vomit while drinking socially which is surely not a part of the decorum Professor Babbitt wishes us to acquire. He happens however to own the first literary review ever purchased with United Cigar Store Coupons ~~which~~ (this is fantasy; it wasn't the coupons it was the profits from the Cigar Store business) and ownership of a review almost inevitably results in the owner becoming an editor, and, with luck, a Spokesman.[4] Death or the private sanitarium for nervous diseases usually rids us of most of these editors if we are only patient. Mr. Collins claims to be tubercular, at least he offers this alibi to those lady friends of mine that he has ineffectually bedded with, and so, men, we can but hope for the best.[5]

In the meantime there remains Mr. Dos Passos ~~known as John (Mutton Fish) Passos who travells widely and writes well~~ who has lived ~~very~~ much in many places ~~and~~, writes very well ~~and knows a few things to write about~~, who owns no magazines and belongs to no parties, who does not project one novel but ~~two more~~ three of which the 42nd Parrallel is the first volumne, who was nearly as blind as James Joyce but whose eyesight gets better every year amd who writes better every year, who is a good friend, a good cook, a good traveller, a fair fisherman, a hell of a good climber and one of the best eaters and drinkers of all times and, again, a damned good writer and, personally, gentlemen I would rather have my money on Mr. Dos Passos. ~~than~~
I remember in school they had what were called Older Boys Conferences which were sort of moral and ethical prayer meetings and I often wondered what had become of all the boys who went to these Conferences and now I find that they are all Humanists. There were many boys like that in school but there was nobody in school like Mr. Dos Passos and afterwards in life there was nobody like Mr. Dos Passos either except him himself while the critics are very hard to tell apart and are even confused by themselves sometimes it seems and even get into the wrong beds with each others wives ~~I don't know which the story~~ or their own wives I don't know which, the story came in a very garbled form, but anyway, gentlemen, maybe it isn't bad for a country to have a few artists and writers as well as critics. The idea is very unfashionable now and I apologise for offering it but it may have some value and if you want a writer and an artist and no critic, his criticism is lousy, gentlemen, I give you Mr. Dos Passos. He travells gentlemen, we must apologize for that, but he travells in a damned good direction

Yours etc.
Ernest Hemingway.

JFK, TLS

No evidence has been found that this letter was ever published in the *New York World*. The heavily revised typewritten letter, located among EH's papers at JFK, may have been unsent.

1 EH refers to an article by Harry Salpeter (1895–1967), American writer, art critic, and gallery owner, that was published in the Sunday book section of the *New York World* on 20 April 1930. Salpeter had interviewed Dos Passos, whom he described as "the most elusive and the most unpredictable living American author," who "has been everywhere and he is still restlessly searching" ("A Sometimes Absent Author / All Parallels the Province of Dos Passos, / A Wanderer in Forms of Self-Expression," 10 M). EH quotes accurately from the two-column article.
2 The Over Sea Hotel at 917 Fleming Street in Key West.
3 Salpeter reported that when he had asked, "Why do you travel so much?" Dos Passos replied, "Either to leave the place in which I am, or to go elsewhere."
4 The 20 April 1930 *New York World* also featured an acerbic article by Burton Rascoe titled "The New Humanists / First Aid to Table-Talkers Relates the History of Tempest Brewed by T. S. Eliot, St. Louis Poet Turned Briton" (1 M, 6 M). Rascoe quoted Irving Babbitt (1865–1933), Harvard professor of French literature and one of the founders of New Humanism, as having declared, "Decorum is supreme for the humanist even as humility takes precedence over all other virtues in the eyes of the Christian" (6 M). Seward Collins, owner and editor of the *Bookman*, a mouthpiece for New Humanism, was heir to the United Cigar Stores fortune; the national chain had been founded by his father. Collins and Rascoe had purchased the *Bookman* in 1927, but Collins assumed full ownership and editorship in 1928.
5 Probably a reference to Dorothy Parker, with whom Collins was romantically involved in the mid-1920s.

To Jefferson B. Browne, April 1930

To Judge Jefferson B. Browne
remembering a very pleasant evening
Ernest Hemingway.
Key West
April 1930

PBA Galleries catalog, San Francisco, 17 November 2002, Lot 132 (illustrated), Inscription

EH inscribed a first-edition copy of *Men without Women* (1927).

To Milford Baker, 5 May [1930]

May 5

Dear Bake:

Glad to hear the gun is coming along and will get it so soon. You certainly have been swell about it. I will take good care of it and keep it in good shape down here.

Would have written before but had an accident and cut the right (trigger and writing finger) of my right hand— Six stitches, still in a splint)[1]

The Sun Also I am trying to get but hasnt come yet. The other books are all signed ready to send.

If you will tell me how much I owe you on balance of gun, case, cleaning outfit, N.R.A. etc. will send check immediately— Look at same time could you send me 100 each of the two weight bullets you recommend?—[2] I may shoot a few Cranes—illegal but splendid long shots—maybe better have a couple of cans of Fiendoil—also bullets better be hard point so if I should break law there wd be something left of Crane. Did you ever eat them? They are as good and better than Turkey— It is a great native dish along the keys—

I cant wait to see the gun— They take stitches out of my finger tomorrow— Will start supple-ing it up as soon as possible— I've never shot anything except a 22 cal. Marlin—and a 30–30 Winchester hunting— Must learn this game properly— There is a 100 and 200 yd. range down here at the old fort— we can start it there—

A N.E. wind has blown for 3 weeks and ruined tarpon until last 2 nights— My wife caught one 74 lbs. Dos Passos caught one around 50 lbs last night— The Giant Kings were all gone at Tortugas when we got there— But a swell trip— Fishing around the reef with fly rod— Snapper—mutton fish— yellow tail— Tortugas is a great place—

Best to you always—

Let me know for what to write the check—

Yours always

Hemmy.

Am counting the days till the gun comes.

PUL, ALS; postmark: KEY WEST / FLA., MAY 5 / 1230PM / 1930

1 In a letter to EH of 30 April 1930, Baker wrote that he expected the gun to be ready to ship within a week, adding, "I will go ahead and get it, giving Griffin my check for the b[a]lance which will be about $150 and you can settle with me." Baker's only reservation was that the salt air could ruin the gun unless EH worked on it every day (PUL). EH had split the knuckle of his forefinger on a chain attached to a punching bag.
2 In his 16 April 1930 letter, Baker told EH he would sight the gun for him using 180-grain and 220-grain Western bullets (PUL).

To Maurice-Edgar Coindreau, 7 May [1930]

May 7
Box 396
Key West

Dear Mr. Coindreau—
I have just sent this wire to Gallimard—[1]

Gaston Gallimard
5 rue Sebastien Bottin
Paris
Accepterai Maurice Coindreau comme traducteur lui ecrire 413 1903 Hall, Princeton N.J. stop regrette impossible accepter LLona[2] Ernest Hemingway.

Dos tells me you are disgusted with the N.R.F. and the way they act about paying.[3] I thought this would be a good way for you to get paid in any event. You do not have to accept Gallimard's conditions but in any event do not accept them unless they first send you a check for royalties due.

Because they want to publish a Farewell they have sent me the money due me and if I insist on you as translator they must pay you too before you will translate. Doubtless the demenagement[4] of the bureau will be a good excuse why you haven't been paid.

I enclose a letter from Gallimard which is self explanatory. The M. LLona referred to is a translator who also sometimes acts as an agent. I do not care for his translations. Would you send me back this letter?

Thank you very much for writing and please excuse brevity and lack of protocol (misspelled) in this letter. Have six stitches in right forefinger making the pen impossible and the machine difficult. Dos left here for Mexico day before yesterday.

yours very truly
Ernest Hemingway

PUL, Typewritten transcription of EH letter

This transcription of EH's letter, preserved in the Carlos Baker Collection at PUL, bears the notation "Typed letter on ⅔ sheet of typewriter paper."

1 In 1911, French publisher Gaston Gallimard (1881–1975), together with the editors of the literary review *La Nouvelle Revue Française*, co-founded the publishing house Les Éditions de la Nouvelle Revue Française, which was renamed Librairie Gallimard in 1919. Coindreau's translation of *FTA* would be published as *L'Adieu aux Armes* in 1931 under the NRF imprint as part of the Du Monde Entier series of translations and in 1932 by Gallimard, which would also publish Coindreau's translation of *SAR* as *Le Soleil se Lève Aussi* (1933).
2 "I will accept Maurice Coindreau as translator. Write him at 413 1903 Hall, Princeton N.J. I regret that it is impossible to accept Llona" (French).
3 N. R. F., La Nouvelle Revue Française-Librairie Gallimard, publishers of Coindreau's 1928 translation of Dos Passos's *Manhattan Transfer*. The translation, Coindreau's first for Gallimard, had not sold as well as expected.
4 *Déménagement*: move, relocation (French).

To Waldo Peirce, 9 May [1930]

May 9
Dear Waldo—

Have been going to write every damned day but what with so many merchants here—two trips to Tortugas—then cut my right forefinger and had six stitches and couldn't pound the machine nor grip the pen.

We had two swell trips to Tortugas. Maxie (deadpan) Perkins broke the worlds record for Kingfish on rod and line with a 59 pounder. He lost at least 6 bigger ones as did Mike 4. I got one tarpon on way down at Marquesas. Weighed 120. Have caught only 8 tarpon altogether Pauline 7[.] Her biggest 74 lbs.

Dos and Kate were here Dos about a month Kate a couple of weeks. She went to visit relatiffs while we were at Totugas[.] Dos, Pauline, Pat [Morgan], Burge and I went to Tortugas but the giant Kings were all gone. Since then they've gone to Mex. Pat to France presumably he left for N.Y. to sail last Sat and aint heard from him since. He got in good shape down here physically and in the head. Was in pretty bad shape all around when came down. He's a damned good kid and it was swell having him here.

Alzira and her two sisters have been here a long time.[1] They live economically but with r.r. fare etc. for three of them and living expenses A ran out of Jack about two weeks or so ago and we loaned her 260 seeds. Loaned 100 again today. She wanted money to buy a ford they have been renting as three of them can go North or two anyway in it for damned near what the r.r. fare is and still have the Ford. Seems a sound move but as I have less'n 800 seeds in bank and no more Jack until August I told her to write you about it and you would send money direct or through me or cable me if you approved. I am glad to loan any dough I have to you or yours on your sayso. But can only afford to loan up to a certain amount unless know when it is coming back due to being close to bed rock due to having staked family to Trust Fund etc. Also spent 1200 in one month on taxes and entertainment—hired this boat for season thinking lots of merchants would be down, men of wealth etc. and we would split on it as formerly but aside from Mike all visiting firemales have been lads in the last stage of financial depression and couldn't think of asking them to split nor wouldn't have accepted it from them. So what with the boat at 125 a mo. Burge at 130 a mo. two or three hundred gallons of gas and an comparative amt. of wines likkers and key west smokers etc. it all runs into money especially when it blows a couple of weeks at a time and you drink instead of fish with no reduction of overhead. Must rectify figures— Last month was 1200 what with boats trips and tackle. Month before was when had to pay income tax on all dough I gave away and never even handled- that Mo. was 2300. Today is May ninth and check book only shows expenditure of 509 seeds so far with tackle bill and boat rent yet to come so are being economical.

Pat left in swell shape. We were damned glad to have him here. Archie MacLeish was down too. He is a hell of a good guy too. Dos and Kate were in fine form and pulled out Monday morning. I couldn't fish Sat or Sunday nights on acct finger—but there was a good tide and swell breeze for tarpon. Dos lost one gigantic one—was biggest I've seen in two years. He caught one and Pauline caught one. Between three of them had 11 strikes. Haven't taken Alzira tarpon fighing nor to Tortugas because it has been steadily rough and I thought if you were playing for offspring no reason to echouee (you spell it) on acct. of Noman's land. That is no trip to help provide heirs.[2] We were storm bound once there for damn near two weeks—ran out of everything but got supplies when a yacht belonging to the bird who bought the Mssof Alice in Wonderland came in.[3] He had never heard of us and we looked bad but when Max asked about the market they knew we must be gents. A true gent is one who knows about the market. Hope A. wasn't disappointed about me writing to you about how much jack to loan. I told her I din't want to write about it nor to have anything to do or say with your money affairs and could loan her 100 seeds any time and as often as she wanted it but for any bigger sums will have to borrow from Maxey myself and so you might just as well dig up the dough to start with.

Alzira ran the movies beautifully and they sure were fine.[4] Don't think I think she's been financially unsound, not at all. They-ve done no buying nor blowing but with R.R. expense about 100 seeds a head N.Y. Key West and a long stay 700 seeds gives out. She's had and has a hell of a difficult show what with having to go to the Dr. who is also director of the bank in as small a town as this and the sisters being here have been a help to her. If you think you could come here where your as widely known as say the Eiffel tower and live with her alone with her looking about 16 and things the way they are without getting into a jam or anyhow getting Charles and Lorine into one you're crazy. In Bangor youhave droits de Seigneur (misspelled) but they don't run below the Macy Dixie line. A big town's the place for that or somewhere you haven't got friends that live on permanently. Paris or N.Y. or Madrid, no not Madrid. Havana say or Mexico City or Paris. What's simple as hell in Paris is complicated as same in U.S.A. or K.K.K.[5]

Hope the hell haven't offended you by saying this. Know you've been having plenty of troubles and we've been trying to keep everything going o.k. Everything has gone swell. But I tell you if you-re planning to stay somehwre and have a baby K.W. is too small a place now that you know or anyway are known by so many local merchants. Nothings my damned business but there's a certain responsibility to Charles and Lorine as with Chrles position it doesn't take much scandal to give his relatives excuse to hold him down even further Guys like you and me that live and have lived around and don't give a damn what people say about anything so long as the law aint invoked are one thing and merchants that have to live on in a town and have people say to them "so your swell friends just turned out to be a bunch of scandalous bastards" are another. Needless to say I thought this up out of my own head and din't get it from Charles or Lorine who are good loyal friends to you and to me and to us all.

Key West as a place to work is pretty well a thing of the past for me. Having your good friends that you want to see is one thing but in addition there has been a couple of domeites around, two or three merchants I've always detested, and a bird who got in a jam and turned up and had to be shipped out of town as well as Provincetown drunks etc. The hot weather is driving them out—they haven't noticed it is 90 and over in N.Y. too and am getting some work done now. Anyway forgive this lousy letter. Wish the hell could see you. Glad to do any damned thing can do for you and all luck in Paris. Give my best to Charley [Sweeny]. Aint going to Spike Hunts ranch nor any damn place where I know a living soul.[6] I got to work or tousands won't eat.

They are ruining this place just like they did Pamplona. Got my gut and physique in swell shape though. Tortugas is damned wonderful. Can drink fine again. The Lipp stationery was swell to see.

Best to Pat if you see him and any other of the old time merchants. The Deux Magots must be a good cafe if 100,000 lesbians can't be wrong. The D.M. doesn't say anything to me but Lipp's beer does. God if you could have a barrell of that on the boat.

So long Chico and if I've spoke out of my turn it's easy to tell me to shut up.

Best always to you

Tu amigo

Ernesto

Colby, TLS

1 Alzira's younger sisters, Rebecca Boehm (1910–1969) and Rachael Handforth Boehm (1912–2003).

2 *Échouer*: to run aground (French). EH had previously written to Peirce about fishing in "No man's land," which he describes as a "2hrs/ and 45 minutes run beyond Marquesas" (*Letters* vol. 3, 506–7). Alzira was pregnant.

3 Eldridge R. Johnson, owner of the yacht *Caroline*, which had rescued EH and his fishing companions when they were stranded in the Dry Tortugas. In 1928 Johnson had acquired

the original manuscript of *Alice's Adventures Under Ground*, the earlier title for *Alice's Adventures in Wonderland* (1865), by Lewis Carroll (né Charles Lutwidge Dodgson, 1832–1898), along with two first-edition copies of the book, for just under $150,000.

4 In his 17 April 1930 letter, Peirce had written EH that Alzira was taking a projector and "all the movies with you in em—& damn good too" to Key West (JFK).

5 *Droit du seigneur*: the right or custom of a feudal lord to have sexual relations with a vassal's bride on her wedding night (French). K.K.K., Ku Klux Klan, a white supremacy group that arose in the aftermath of the American Civil War.

6 Frazier ("Spike") Hunt (1885-1967), American journalist and associate editor of *Cosmopolitan* magazine, owned Eden Valley Ranch in Alberta, Canada. In 1929 Hunt rejected EH's "Fifty Grand" as unsuitable for *Cosmopolitan* (PUL).

To Maxwell Perkins, [c. 10 May 1930]

Dear Max:—

I wonder if you could have the book store send me these books (and a bottle of spirits)

Assorted Articles —	D.H. Lawrence —Knopf —	2.50[1]
The Open Door —	Mary Roberts Rinehart — Farrar and Rinehart	$2.$\underline{^{00}}$[2]
Rogue Herries —	Mr. Walpole — Doubleday Doran	2.50[3]
The Bridge —	Hart Crane — Liveright	2.50[4]
The Gentleman in the Parlor —	Somersault Maugham — Doubleday etc.	3.$\underline{^{00}}$ [5]
Byron —	By Andre Maurous (<u>In French</u>—)	(They must have this in french dept)[6]
Long Hunt —	By James Boyd	(Hope I get this free) you must have plenty on hand)[7]
Gloustermen—	J. B Connolly	(Maybe I can get this free but will pay for it if he's hard up.)[8]
The Fools' Parade	JW Vandercook — Harpers	2.$\underline{^{50}}$[9]
To the Best of My Memory	—A. P. Terhune Harper	4$\underline{^{00}}$ (My God)[10]
Confessional —	Frank Harris Panurge Press—	5.$\underline{^{00}}$[11]
Blue Rum —	E. Souza J. Cape H. Smith	2.$\underline{^{50}}$
Vile Bodies	Evelyn Waugh J Cape H. Smith	2.50
Bystander—	Maximus Gorkibus J. Cape H Smith	3.$\underline{^{00}}$[12]

Wister on Roosevelt (?) (?)[13]

A book by some merchant on Africa — (A Dr. in Miami —) who shows up Trader Horn etc.[14]

The Catholic Church and Current Literature — MacMillan   1.$\underline{^{00}}$

George N. Shuster[15]

A Book published by <u>Liveright</u> of war stories by odly enough a <u>German</u> (who could have give them that idea)[16]

Anyway send me these with Bill and all those we cant read will present to Key West Library—

Nearly cut my right finger off—suggested to Dr it wd be easier to take it off than take month to heal it but probably will heal O.K.

We're in the S.H. now ⟨drawing⟩ as far as right forefingers are concerned—for a while.

Hope youre fine— Burge— Charles— Pauline send their best

Yrs always

Ernest

Am writing well

PUL, ALS

The conjectured letter date is based on EH's mention of his cut finger, which he first noted in his 5 May [1930] letter to Milford Baker, and on Perkins's response of 17 May, saying, "You will have heard from the bookstore about the books you wanted. Most of them went on to you and should have arrived some time ago" (PUL).

1 *Assorted Articles*, a collection of essays and newspaper articles by D. H. Lawrence, was published posthumously in 1930 by Martin Secker in London and Knopf in New York. Unless otherwise noted, EH accurately identifies the publisher of each book listed in this letter.

2 Mary Roberts Rinehart (1876–1958), popular American author of murder mysteries, including *The Door* (1930).

3 Hugh Walpole's novel *Rogue Herries* (1930) is the first book in his series *The Herries Chronicle*, set in England's Lake District, where he resided.

4 Hart Crane (1899–1932), American poet whose modernist masterpiece, *The Bridge: A Poem* (1930), takes the Brooklyn Bridge in New York City as its central setting and metaphor.

5 William Somerset Maugham (1874–1965), English novelist and short-story writer who achieved fame with *Of Human Bondage* (1915). His travel memoir *The Gentleman in the Parlour: A Record of a Journey from Rangoon to Haiphong* and his novel *Cakes and Ale* were both released in 1930.

6 Maurois's biography *Don Juan ou la Vie de Byron* (Paris: Grasset, 1930) was published in English translation as *Byron* the same year (London: Cape; New York: Appleton). The English edition was among the books in EH's library at Finca Vigía (Brasch and Sigman, item 4421).

7 American writer James Boyd (1888–1944), author of five novels, all published by Scribner's. *Long Hunt* (1930) was his third.

8 James Brendan Connolly (1868–1957), Irish American Olympic athlete, prolific maritime story writer, and author of *Gloucestermen: Stories of the Fishing Fleet* (New York: Scribner's, 1930).

9 *The Fool's Parade* (1930), a collection of short stories set in the tropics by American author and journalist John Womack Vandercook (1902–1963).

10 *To the Best of My Memory* (1930), an autobiography by Albert Payson Terhune (1872–1942), American novelist and short-story writer who bred and wrote about collies.

11 Frank Harris (1855–1931), Irish-born novelist and editor with an international reputation and a problematic relationship with the law because of his erotic publications including the four-volume autobiography *My Life and Loves* (1922–27). His *Confessional* and *Pantopia* (a novel) were both published in New York in 1930 by the privately owned Panurge Press, which produced lavish limited editions.

12 In 1929 English publisher Jonathan Cape and American editor Harrison Smith (1888–1971) formed the short-lived New York publishing concern Cape & Smith (1929–1931). Among the company's publications in 1930 were *Blue Rum*, an adventure story set in Portugal written by Evelyn Scott (née Elsie Dunn, 1893–1963) under the pseudonym Ernest Souza; *Vile Bodies*, a humorous romantic satire by English novelist Evelyn Waugh (1903–1966); and *Bystander* by Russian political activist, journalist, playwright and short-story author Maxim Gorky (né Aleksey Maksimovich Peshkov, 1868–1936), a long novel about pre-Revolutionary Russian society.

13 Owen Wister's bestselling novel *The Virginian* (1902) was dedicated to his friend and Harvard classmate Theodore Roosevelt, also the subject of Wister's *Roosevelt: The Story of a Friendship: 1880–1919* (New York: Macmillan, 1930). "N.Y.P" is written in pencil in another hand next to this title, likely meaning "not yet published."

14 *African Drums* (New York: Farrar & Rinehart, 1930), a memoir by Fred Puleston (c. 1860–1940), an Englishman who spent fourteen years (1882–1896) as a merchant in equatorial Africa before taking a medical degree at Iowa State University in 1901 and settling in Florida in 1916. A review in the *New York Times* on 6 April 1930 compared *African Drums* to *Trader Horn* (New York: Simon & Schuster, 1927) by Alfred Aloysius Horn (1861–1931), English merchant, itinerant peddler, hunter, gold prospector, and ivory trader, whose book Puleston said inspired his own.

15 George Nauman Shuster (1894–1977), American Roman Catholic author, educator, and editor; his 1930 book *The Catholic Church and Current Literature* was part of the Calvert Series, whose general editor, Hilaire Belloc (1870–1953), provided a preface for the volume.

16 Probably *Loretto, Sketches of a German War Volunteer* (New York: Liveright, 1930) by Max Heinz (b. 1891), translated by Charles Ashleigh (1888–1974); originally published as *Loretto. Aufzeichnungen eines Kriegsfreiwilligen* (Berlin: Rembrandt-Verlag, 1929).

To Maurice-Edgar Coindreau, 12 May 1930

Key West

May 12 1930

Dear Mr. Coindreau:—

Thank you very much for your letter. If you prefer to deal with me about the payment for the translation rather than Gallimard what would be your idea of a fair ~~split~~? recompense.

In Germany, Norway, Sweden, on my other books I have never had anything to do with this— I get a royalty of 10%—increasing after a certain number of copies—an advance—and the publisher pays the translator a flat sum for making the translation.

What did you do about Manhattan Transfer?

If I have nothing to do about arranging for the translation the lowest royalty I can receive is 7%— If I pay the translator I receive 10% and 12%—

I should think if you wanted to work on a percentage basis your share would be the difference between 7% and 10% and between, say 8% and 12%

In other words 3% on those copies for which 10% royalty are paid and 4% for those on which 12% are paid.

Does this seem equitable to you? I would be glad to divide the cash advance of 3500 francs when it is made 2000 to me—1500 to you and only apply the percentages above to moneys received <u>after the cash advance</u>.

Let me know if this seems all right to you— If you prefer a fixed sum you can doubtless arrange with Gallimard. However the book might sell very well and in that case a percentage of the royalties would be good to have.[1]

Yours very truly

Ernest Hemingway

PUL, Typewritten transcription of EH letter

This transcription of EH's letter, with the notation "Handwritten letter," is preserved in the Carlos Baker Collection at PUL.

1 In a letter of 23 May 1930, Coindreau would respond that he intended to accept Gallimard's "quite fair" offer of 3% on the first 10,000 copies of his translation of *FTA*, 5% on succeeding copies and a cash sum of $2,000 upon receipt of the manuscript, which Coindreau expected to submit in September. He thanked EH for "your generous offer which I was ready to accept in case Gallimard would have refused to treat directly with you" (JFK).

To John Herrmann, [c. 12–17 May 1930]

Dear John:

The suit is fine and fits perfectly except for length of trousers that tailor can fix in an hour. It is a damned handsome suit. Look, I have the Mss of that bull fight piece in Fortune for you—if you want it—[1] Want to copy off some of the notes they didnt use—

I am your man for any suits— Yr old man is an Ace in the clothes racket— That's as fine a suit as I ever saw—[2]

Every damn king was gone from Tortugas—we had a good trip though— Broke down coming home off [*EH insertion*: Mooney Harbor at] Marquesas and I brot Dos and Pauline home in the outboard— Did you know Eldridge Johnson the Big Yacht and Victrola King gives $12,500 twice a year to the association against Prohibition Amendment.[3] A bottle of Spirits indeed.

Cut hell out of my right forefinger—6 ~~stichhes~~ stitches— That's why didnt write until now— Still not so good— Dos and Kate left for Mexico last week—

Best to Joe—

Love to you both from Pauline—

Good luck kid and thanks ever so much for the suit—

Yrs always—

Hem

UT, ALS

The conjectured letter date is based on EH's comment that John and Kate Dos Passos had left Key West "last week"; the couple had departed on Monday, 5 May 1930.

1 The manuscript of EH's "Bullfighting, Sport and Industry" (*Fortune*, March 1930).
2 Herrmann's grandfather Johann Theodor Herrmann (1837–1898) founded the John T. Herrmann Merchant Tailor Shop, established in 1878 in Lansing, Michigan, and renamed John Herrmann's Sons after his death. Herrmann's father, Heinrich (Henry) Herrmann (1865–1943), worked as a designer and cutter in the firm, which counted Michigan's politicians and business elite among its customers.
3 Johnson's yacht, the *Caroline*, had rescued EH's fishing party in the Dry Tortugas in March. A machinist from New Jersey, Johnson designed a motor for the gramophone in the late 1890s and in 1901 co-founded the Victor Talking Machine Company, which quickly became the leading manufacturer of record players and records. Johnson was a generous contributor to and director of the Association Against the Prohibition Amendment (established 1918).

To Waldo Peirce, 16 May [1930]

May 16

Muy Waldo Mio:—

Have just received check for 500 from you to me delivered by Alzira and given her check for 500 in exchange— Damned sorry if we arent going to see you. But it's hot now anyway— Still we'll stay till middle of June unless it gets too damned hot—

Charles [Thompson] caught one that weighed 100 lbs night before last— Lorine caught 1 60 lbs last night— Have seen 15 tarpon lost and 4 landed since I've hooked a good one— So dont try and cut yr. right forefinger off if you are in tarpon country—

Hope all going well with you— Give our best to Pat [Morgan]— He's a damned fine boy— Imagine youve seen him by now— Salute Sweeny— I wd give a lot for a hogshead of Lipp's beer— Tropical too damned strong—also it's 20 francs a bottle— I'd give 25 francs a distingué for Lipps though—[1]

Good luck to you—

Excuse punk letter— Finger hurts on typer and pen—

Ernesto

Colby, ALS

1 In his Paris memoirs EH would recall the beer at Brasserie Lipp, where he ordered "a distingué, the big glass mug that held a liter" ("Hunger Was Good Discipline," *MF*).

To Milford Baker, 17 May [1930]

May 17

Dear Bake;

Your two letters of May 14 and 15 just came. Am enclosing check for $184.10.

Thanks ever so much for getting me the Crossman book. By all means get the other books and send them. I have The Hunting and Spoor of Central African Game by Denis Lyell but nothing else would be liable to duplicate.[1]

Am very anxious to see the gun. The 375 Magnum sounds like an excellent buy if it fits. Being made specially it might not, I suppose, but I would like to try it and would appreciate it ifthey could put it aside. Perhaps you could let me know how the measurements are compared to mine. If it fits I imagine I ought to get it.[2]

You have certainly been damned fine about getting the Springfield and outfit and I appreciate it. Have an order in for A Sun Also first but so far one has not turned up. Perhaps I had better send on the others that are signed and not wait for it. When we get to Paris I believe I can get you an original edition of Three Stories and Ten Poems. It is pretty bloody rare. If you don't want it you could always sell it and buy a gun with the proceeds.

My finger hasn't done so well. The cut healed all right and stitches out with no infection but being over the joint it cracks open, that part across knuckle, whenever I use it or if I close my fist unconsciously in the night. Will have to put it back in a splint for a while. Have been shooting with the second finger all right for shotgun but pretty useless with the pistol. Have always felt I should learn to shoot a pistol properly with left hand but never done so. Only way to shoot oneproperly, I don't mean for target so much as much as snap shooting and general monkey business, is shooting thousands and thousands of rounds. I've never had patience to shoot with left hand. The Colt Woodsman model 22lr. is the most accurate for that I've ever known. Out west we shoot Prairie dogs usingthe hollow point long rifles. That is the best pistol sport I know. They talk about the Colt 45, 38 on 45 frame etc. being such swell guns and I have seen fine shooting done with them but the only pistols I can be _sure_ of hitting like a rifle with are the Luger.30 and the 22 Colt Automatic and they don't weigh so bloody much. I-ve shot partridges, ducks, prairie dogs, woodchucks, squirrels, rabbits, porkies, moccasins, bull frogs, crows, plenty of them, and God's own quantity of sharks with the 22 Colt.[3]

Must stop this and get to work. Will appreciate the cartridges and anything else you send along. Anything I owe you let me know.

Look could you send in Charles P. Thompson, care Thompson Fish Company, Key West, Florida for membership in the N.R.A. [National Rifle Association] They can send him the paper etc. at that address. I not you haven't my N.R.A. membership down. Am adding 6.00 to the check to cover my membership and Charles T.s.

Best luck to you always and thanks enormously for all of your trouble,

Yours always,

Hemmy.

PUL, TLS; postmark: KEY WEST / FLA., MAY [17] / 5 [PM] / 1930

1 In his letter to EH of 14 May 1930, Baker itemized the cost of the Springfield rifle ($175) and miscellaneous accessories as totaling $284.10, of which $100 had been paid on account; Baker had paid Griffin the balance. Among the items Baker purchased for EH was *Small-Bore Rifle Shooting* (Marshallton, Delaware: Small Arms Technical Publishing, 1927) by American sportsman Edward Cathcart Crossman (1881–1939). Baker offered to buy additional books he thought EH should have (PUL). EH mentions *The Hunting and Spoor of Central African Game* (London: Seely, Service, 1929) by Scottish big-game hunter and author Denis Lyell (1871–1946).
2 In his 15 May 1930 letter, Baker reported meeting a sportsman who had gone broke in the stock market crash and wanted to sell his custom-made weapons, among them a .375 Magnum that Baker thought might interest EH (PUL).
3 EH had owned a Colt Woodsman pistol, model 22LR (chambered for firing the .22-long rifle cartridge), since at least 1920. Colt .45: a handgun made by Colt that fires a .45-caliber round .38 on 45 frame: a pistol or revolver of sufficient size and sturdiness to fire a .45-caliber round but chambered instead for the smaller, less powerful, and easier to shoot .38-caliber cartridge. Luger .30: a German pistol whose 7.65 mm bore barrel diameter converts almost exactly to 0.30 inches, hence .30 caliber.

To Guy Hickok, [c. mid-May 1930]

Dear Gros:

Thanks for Player Support. Yes I heard about the picture. They stole the title and gave me $500 as a courtesy payment—then announced they'd bought it for $5000.^{00}

Who should I start a trust fund with the 500 for?

Best to you always—
Ernest

phPUL, ALS

To Henry Strater, 20 May [1930]

May 20

Dear Mike—

You write a fine letter kid.[1] I havwn't answered on acct. being pooped always after working and then cut my bloody forefinger—punching Charle's bag. It suspended by chain and fastened with bolt and nut. 6 stitches to close it and just across knuckle. A bludy nuisance.

Thanks for the caps, and for sending the clay. It was for Alzira. Let me know how much it was and I'll add it to my ledger acct. with Waldo. Considerable acct.

Charles is excited as the devil about the trip next fall. I might very well be able to go but won't know until then. I think Charles will go if you bring pressure on him. I'll probably be coming to N.Y. about then with Bumby. But may hunt in Wyo first so long as out there and just come to N.Y. to work. Going to write a play.[2] Don't tell anybody or my creditors will want the dough from it before it's written.

Been working pretty well lately. Excuse orthographic faults in this. Hot as hell now. Imagine Pat told you about Tortugas. Every damned King gone but a fine trip. I bought a 12 orse johnston. We broke down off Souwest Key coming home and I brought the Merchants to K.W. in the Outboard. The 12 orse is very good for fast going and trolling both.[3]

My gun hasn't come yet but is due any minute. We are both anxious as hell to see and try it.

Baker wrote he had lunch with you. He was never what you would call an intimate of mine but has worked hard on this gun racket. Think he knows something about guns altho much of it he may have read in same sporting journals you and me read. The proof of how much he knows will be how my gun turns out. He wanted you to see it before shipping it.[4]

Hickock writes the Players have written him about me. He says he gave them a filthy report. Hope I can get in that Cloob.[5] Am having nose straightened.

Looks now as though wouldn't go to N.Y. until fall. Bumby arrives the 24th. I have to drive the damned car to Piggott so gues Jinny will bring him direct to Piggott. Have financed Bra on trip to Bahamas to replace my invitation to him to go to N.Y. Will do that another time. He claims he would rather go to Bahammies anyway.

Lots of tarpon lately. Pauline has caught 10 now. Biggest 74 lbs. Charles largest 100 lbs. Lorine 60 lbs.

Dos lost one that looked like 200. It jumped 7 times. Ran out every bit of line 4 times and we had to chase it. Just at dusk. It was biggest I have ever seen jump. Finally threw it. Kate lost some big ones too. I couldn't fish on acct. of my finger. Dos finally caught one that weighed 54.

Did you see DeadPan [Perkins] again before leaving?

Somebody poisoned Jack Cowles's dog.[6] Rotten hard luck. Everybody is gone even the little Alziras.[7] We would go too but am waiting for Uncle Gus.

I have 74 pages done on the book am working on but it gets so damned hot hell to work. Would shove if wasn't waiting for Uncle Gus. His arrival delayed by purchase of 4million dollar business. I tell him all right to do anything with his cash except spend African Money. He is damned nice. You'd like him. He won't come before 7th of June or so now.[8] Happy brought up 3000 eggs from Tortugas. They are leaving for the Bahams. Braward can't sleep nights thinking of the report that they pay a dollar apiece bounty on wild hogs killed.[9] I am loaning them a shotgun to use on the great Saunders Pidgen and Wild Og Scientific Expedition.

Isn't there some way we can make our African trip a Scientific One. We could measure the amount of urine secreted by members of the party when 1 drinking tea 2 drinking schlitz in brown bottles to avoid that skunk taste. 3 when drinking elephant milk. We could measure the amounts by the men being required to urinate their names on the sand. That ought to make it a scientific expedition and then if anyof the men are mauled by hippopotamus they will be martyrs to Science.

Write me Kid. Best love to Maggie and all your outfit from us all.

Hem

Box 396—Key West—Florida

PUL, TLS

1 EH is responding to Strater's eight-page letter of 4 May 1930 (JFK).
2 An unclear reference. In a letter to Bernard C. Schoenfeld of 5 November 1929, EH noted that he had thought of trying to make a play of *SAR* "some lean year."
3 EH refers to a 12-horsepower Johnson outboard motor.
4 In a letter of 14 May 1930, Baker reported meeting Strater for the first time, liking him, and discussing guns with him (PUL).
5 While this letter from Hickok remains unlocated, in a 26 May 1930 letter to EH, Hickok would write, "It was very difficult to reccomend you for the Players, considering that I had nothing but recommendations to get myself in, thanks to F. E. Mason, I felt like a ferronier reccomending a grand seigneur" (JFK). In a letter to Perkins of 24 May 1930, Strater would write, "Geoffrey Parsons seconded Hem for the Players. There are a lot of men there who like Hem's work, but very few who know him; and so I appreciate your assistance" (PUL).
6 Presumably John (Jack) Cheney Cowles (1894–1972). A grandson of *Chicago Tribune* co-owner Alfred Cowles, he had worked for the Paris edition of the *Chicago Tribune* newspaper in the early 1920s and probably met EH through Donald Ogden Stewart, a former Yale

classmate of Cowles. While visiting New York City in February 1926, EH had socialized
with Cowles and inscribed a copy of *IOT* for him (*Letters* vol. 3, 28–29).
7 Alzira's younger sisters, Rebecca and Rachael Boehm, who had come to Key West with her
in late February.
8 In a letter of 8 March 1930, Gus thanked EH for his invitation to come to Key West but was
unable to make firm plans, saying, "Last week we bought a business in Des Moines + now we
are negotiating to buy a New York business. That means staying at the helm or near it" (JFK).
9 Happy Saunders, his wife Nettie (1883–1938), and their son Broward (1911–1953) would
travel to the Bahamas aboard the cabin cruiser *Pureta*.

To Maxwell Perkins, 22 May [1930]

May 22

Dear Max:—

Thanks for having the books sent. They all arrived O.K.

Im awfully sorry to hear Scott has had trouble again. Hope things are all
right now.[1]

Pauline is typing a story out and I'll send it as soon as it's done. I think
you'll like it.[2] Would have sent it before but my finger has made writing
hard— Had 6 stitches and the joint is still stiff—

Have been working hard but it is getting too damned hot—

May come to N.Y in June—Maybe not— Waldo isn't coming here—all
the jeunes filles have left—[3]

Tarpon have been biting like Sharks— We have 400 some odd lbs. in the
ice box now— Burge busy butchering all morning— I write mornings fish
them in the evening— Everybody in fine shape but its getting damned hot—

Sorry the book racket is on the bum— If you want to get out we could get
a boat and go fishing and turtle-ing— Get John and Burge—we could live at
Tortugas and only leave when the Coast Guard would run us out—[4]
The smacks could bring us liquor and we'd go into Key West every couple of
months for grub and to get the Wister articles— We could get a smack and
live aboard her for damned near nothing— Think about that before you
take any definite steps like joining the Marines—

Yours always

Ernest

PUL, ALS

1 In a letter to EH of 17 May 1930, Perkins reported that he had a letter from Fitzgerald "which implied that the novel would not be ready to be published until next year, but I think he knows what he is about now, and he is right in not hurrying it through just to get it published." Perkins added, "He said Zelda had had a nervous breakdown on account of overwork. That knocked him out for two or three weeks, and then some friends turned up which meant a series of parties, I judge. All this sounds bad, but the tone of the letter really was good" (PUL). Zelda, who had been writing short stories and taking ballet lessons, had suffered a breakdown and was admitted to the Malmaison Hospital in Paris on 23 April 1930.
2 "Wine of Wyoming."
3 *Jeunes filles*: girls (French). In his letter, Perkins had said that he felt Waldo Peirce should be in Key West "to chaperone the three school girls," referring to Alzira Boehm and her sisters.
4 Perkins reported seeing John Herrmann, who was concerned about not getting a job with the Macaulay publishing company in New York City because "business is so bad." Macaulay, which published eighteen books in 1929, would publish fourteen in 1930 and only nine in 1931.

To Maxwell Perkins, 27 May [1930]

May 27

Dear Max:—

Will you have $500.$\underline{^{00}}$ deposited in my account—City Bank Farmers Branch

43 Exchange Place

N.Y.C.

It has gotten very low—(The account)

I understand from reports that the book business is practically a thing of the past—

Am I to understand that we are all in the ——— house now?

Pauline has the story nearly copied—

Best to you always—

Ernest

PUL, ALS

To Maxwell Perkins, 31 May [1930]

May 31

Dear Max:

Enclosed is the story. I think you'll like it. It is nearly 6,000 words long.

Dont let anyone tell you it's not a good story or has too much French in it.

Everybody that reads Scribners knows some French—or knows somebody that knows some French. The French is necessary in this—[1] I've never given you anything that wasnt good have I? This is a <u>1st flight</u> story. I promise you.

I should have fed all those Doubledays poisonous gum drops the day they came up to the place.[2] After June 7th will you please hold all my mail?

You hold the Worlds' Record for Kingfish all right but by God you should have broken it so far that it would stand for 50 years— It was 58 lbs— Yours and Mike's that 1st day would have weighed 80-100—[3] Next year we'll spend all of March there—

Yours always
Ernest

I may go on a trip to the Bahamas —— running with Bra.

PUL, ALS

1 The Fontan family in "Wine of Wyoming" speak French to each other and to the narrator.
2 In a letter to EH of 28 May 1930, Perkins wrote, "Your friend Nelson Doubleday, with his dollar book announcement, has smashed about all that was left of the market" (JFK). Nelson Doubleday (1889-1949) played a leading role in a move by four major U.S. publishers (Doubleday, Doran, & Co.; Simon & Schuster; Farrar & Rinehart; Coward-McCann), announced on 22 May, to cut book prices by 50% and issue novels for $1.00, aiming to increase sales. Despite their claim that the price reductions would not affect the quality of the books nor authors' royalties, the plan was strongly opposed by another group of publishers led by Alfred Knopf, who called it "short-sighted, unwise and likely . . . to have a very disturbing effect indeed on the industry as a whole" (*New York Times*, 23 May 1930, 21).
3 In a letter of 24 May 1930, Strater had written to Perkins, "You now hold the world's record for kingfish. The old world's record was 58 pounds" (PUL). In his 28 May letter to EH, Perkins had quoted Strater's comment.

To John Herrmann, [c. late May–early June 1930]

Dear John:

Sorry to hear you are undergoing an occupation by The Canadian Northwest mounted. But it is all for literature. You really ought to board him though because then he wd get swell food at 3 seeds and also an opportunity to write one of those stories about your and Joes droll efforts to be happy.[1] Is he writing ~~Harry Trotter In the Alps~~ about Paris? ~~Harry Trotter on the Bank of the Seine?~~

The tarpon have been biting 2 nights almost the way the King's did—
weve caught 4 just under of just over 100 lbs this week— Lots of medium
and small ones—

After an actual 3 mo. visit to Paris he ought to be able to turn out some
pretty hot old world Stuff—[2]

The Canadian Proust

A la recerche du Harry Trotter—

A L'ombre de Harry Trotter en Fleur—

La Coté du Chez Trotter—

Trotter Disparu

The Trotters in Sodom and Gomorrah

Madame Trotter Prisonniere[3]

Will send the Mss when get the bloody notes copied—

Its getting too hot to work— My lousy finger still stiff—

Best to Joe and to you from us merchants—

Write me if the Pride of the Frozen North is writing Old World Stuff—
I need something to look forward to now that Flaubert and Proust are gone—

It is damned fine to know your father and brothers will clothe us all from
now on.[4] I wont need another one now until Fall— Break in something
natty in a dark blue for October wear—

Best to you always

Hem.

UT, ALS

1 EH refers to Canadian writer Morley Callaghan, who visited Herrmann and Josephine Herbst
at their home in Erwinna, Pennsylvania, several times while seeking a house to rent in that area.
2 This sentence and the following list of titles are written at the bottom of the page,
perpendicular to the rest of the text.
3 Harry Trotter, a lumberman and bootlegger in Toronto, is the main character of Callaghan's
Strange Fugitive (New York: Scribner's, 1928). EH plays on the volume titles of *À la Recherche
du Temps Perdu* (*Remembrance of Things Past*) by Marcel Proust (1871–1922). The volumes
were published in Paris between 1913 and 1927, the first by Grasset and the others by
Gallimard. By 1930 all but the last were available in English: *Du Côté de Chez Swann* (1913),
A L'ombre des Jeunes Filles en Fleurs (1919), *Le Côté de Guermantes I* (1920), *Le Côté de
Guermantes II: Sodome et Gomorrhe I* (1921), *Sodome et Gomorrhe II* (1922), *Sodome et
Gomorrhe III: La Prisonnière* (1923), *Albertine Disparue* (1925), and *Le Temps Retrouvé* (1927).
4 John Herrmann's father, Henry, and paternal uncle Christian (1868–1949) carried on the
family's tailoring business after their father died in 1898. John's brother Richard
(1904–1979) joined the firm of John Herrmann's Sons in 1928.

To William D. Horne, Jr., 1 June [1930]

June 1—

Dear 'Orny:—

It's filthy to wait a month before answering your swell letter but—how's this for an alibi—I smashed and cut index finger of right hand so that 6 stitches were needed and writing bloody near impossible— You may not believe it Article[1] but have scar to prove it— Was so lousy difficult to write that only wrote what I had to on book— Always gyp you first Article because you never hold anything against me—

By God it will be fine to see you merchants— Pauline goes to Piggott next Friday with Henriette and Pat— I go to N.Y to get Bumby—he's arriving on the 23rd of June— Probably go straight from N.Y to Piggott— to K.C. to Wyo. So chances are we wont see you and Bunny till out at the ranch—

Look— Since seeing all these pictures in the paper— Is it really Rudy Vallee or is it Pardee?[2]

About the tackle— I'd already ordered from Hardys—[3] Dont buy any leaders— I've got plenty— If you want to get a fly reel for you or for Bunny the one I've checked on the torn out page is O.K. Either of the 2 rods I've checked should be O.K.[4] All depends on if you want to spend the jack— But you merchants dont fish enough to spend too much on tackle— If you buy a rod buy one for Bunny only— I've got a damned good rod or couple of D.G. rods you can always use— Fitted with everything—

I think you should get a <u>dealers discount</u> on the Catologue prices— I'll have plenty of junk—

Excuse this punk letter— I should be working— But will send this off—

Best to you old Article— Love to Bunny from us both—

What about whiskey? Are you going to bring some—or buy it out there?

Wont it be swell to be at the ranch drinking a good old Scotch and soda before supper after a fine day in the woods and on the stream?— Yeah Citizens—

Best love to youse

Steen

If I come through or near Chicago will descend on you—

[*EH insertion in left margin*: Thanks ever so much for sending the catalog—
and for all your trouble taking about the reservations—]

[*EH insertion in right margin*: Best to the <u>Carper</u>. Was he the unidentified
guest when they shot Georgy Druggan?][5]

[*Enclosure*:]

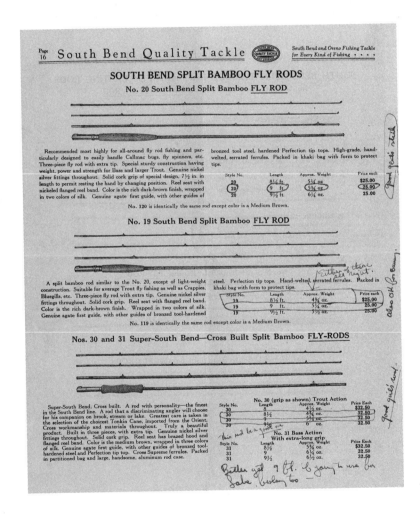

PUL, ALS; postmark: KEY [WE]ST / FLA., JUN [illegible] / 1 PM / 1930

1 Among EH's nicknames for Horne were "Horny Bill" (hence "Dear 'Orny"), and "Horned Article." The letter to which EH is responding has not been located.

2 Rudy Vallee (né Hubert Prior Vallée, 1901–1986), American crooner, bandleader, and host from 1929 to 1936 of the weekly radio variety program *The Fleischmann's Yeast Hour*. EH's reference to Pardee is uncertain.

3 Hardy Brothers, English manufacturer of premium-quality fishing tackle, was founded in the 1870s by brothers William Hardy (1853–1917) and John James Hardy (1854–1932).

4 EH enclosed five double-sided pages torn from a catalog of the South Bend Bait Company of South Bend, Indiana. In black ink he circled, checked, or commented on listings for an Oreno Fly Rod Reel, three Split Bamboo Fly Rods, a Cross Doublebuilt Dry Fly Rod, a Double Tapered Enameled Line, and Fuzz-Oreno single spinner flies.

5 Just before 2 a.m. on 1 June 1930, three gangsters were killed in a machine-gun attack at Manning's Hotel in Fox Lake, Illinois, a summer resort 50 miles north of Chicago. A fourthman, George Druggan (1901–1945), brother of wealthy Prohibition bootlegger Terrance (Terry) Druggan (1903–1954), was seriously wounded. Howell G. Jenkins (1894–1971), nicknamed Carper, a friend of EH's and Horne's who served with them in the Red Cross Ambulance Service in Italy, was from Evanston, a northern suburb of Chicago.

To Waldo Peirce, [2] June 1930

June 1st 1930[1]

Box 396

Key West

Florida—

Dear Old Shyte:—

Hadnt written on acct. of thinking you might be shoving off— I'll send this to Alzira— She ought to know where ~~the~~ you are— Got 3 damned fine letters from you—[2] I felt like a sonof after I wrote thinking you might think I was bellows acheing or trying to tell you what you should or shouldnt do. Hope you didnt think it because all dough I have on hand or able to borrow is yrs. always or anytime and anything you do anywhere is right with me.

Got the check. Sent balance to Alzira. Hope everything's fine with her. The weather went haywired here a week ago— It's rained 5.9 inches in 3 days now— Damned storm—bastardized us out of this good tide for tarpon—

Pauline leaves Friday for Piggott— This is a Monday— I'll shove off after in a few days— If can get somebody to drive car up I'll maybe go to N.Y and meet Bumby— He gets in on the Lafayette on June 23 or thereabouts—[3]

Town carried away with new hatched frogs with the rain—

Book Racket is just about belly up— Publishers cant move the volumes even at 1$\underline{00}$ prices— Hang onto your dough— Dont give it all to the Harry Daughertys—[4] This was evidently the last year in the book racket— What we've got now is called Hoover Prosperity—
If youre in Paris give our love to Pat [Morgan]— He was damned good down here—

Is Tanya the Tanya I used to know—out of Joe Bennett? and who?[5]

Best to Sweeney [Charles Sweeny]. He's a damned good Bird— Even if he's only done ⅛ things he's supposed to have done he's a hell of a citizen— I'm damned fond of him—

Have been drinking too since the damned heat came— Had to drink on acct. the heat— Then when the rain set in found damned good excuse drink on acct of the rain—

Couldnt write with any comfort with my bloody index finger— Cut from the root over the joint— [*EH insertion*: 6 stitches] look in and see the bone white and clean as when I was boy by God— Still stiff and cant make a fist of it yet—Painful— But will make a fist of it the first time have to sock any merchants—

We had one cockeyed wonderful cruise to Tortugas— Maxie (Dead Pan) Perkins lost at least 6 <u>Giant</u> Kingfish that would knock the worlds records higher than a kike— Landed one <u>medium sized</u> one that was still 1 lb. over World's Record— Now held by our Maxie— We had a fine damned time— out nearly 3 weeks—out of everything— Never ate nor drank better in my life—

All wives worried sick except Pauline— She never has worried yet— Damned good trait in a woman— Love you and not worry about you— We sure eat damned well— Get jug wine— Gilbey's Gin down to $\$$30 a case now all the merchants gone—

Happy Saunders went on a cruise to Bahamas—caught in Saturdays storm— Lost his boat— Escaped with nothing but their lives (The Paper States)[6] Loss will include one 62$\underline{50}$ Shotgun I loaned to the H. Saunders Wild Hog shooting and Scientific Exposition— Bra and I were going to join them— Burge has been damned fine— When I found he was drinking up all his wages got him to drink with me— Thus participated in his profits— If he's going to drink and throw it all away let him do it with his Employer—Old Hem—

So long Chico— Hope I see you soon— May be in New York— I know you've had a hell of a time— I've felt like hell about it— You've written swell letters and I havent written a damned thing—

Su Amigo

Ernesto

Pauline sends her love.

Thought Maybe Send this to Harvard Club— Just as quick— Save A. the trouble— That's what a cloob is for—

Write to Piggott.

Arkansas—

Colby, ALS; postmark: KEY WEST / FLA, JUN [*illegible*] / 1 PM / 1930

1 EH apparently misdated the letter, in which he writes "this is a Monday" and refers to a newspaper article dated Monday, 2 June 1930.

2 EH is responding to Peirce's letter of 22 May 1930 (saying he had cabled $500 to EH), a letter of 23 May 1930 (noting he had sent additional funds to Alzira), and an undated one in which Peirce responded to EH's letter of 9 May [1930], again mentioning a mailed check and cabled funds (JFK).

3 The *Lafayette*, on which Bumby and Jinny Pfeiffer sailed from Le Havre to New York City, would arrive on 21 June, two days ahead of schedule.

4 In his 22 May letter, Peirce mentioned that after cashing in Liberty bonds worth $25,000 to invest in two companies that he later heard were worthless, he rushed to the bank and "was assured the Bonds were allright—Dohercy or Doherty & Co are behind them—Warren Gamaliel's friends—crooks mebbe—but I don't give a damn . . . as long as they pay." Harry Daugherty (1860-1941), a lawyer and political manager for U.S. president Warren Gamaliel Harding (1865-1923), had been tried on charges of graft, fraud, and conspiracy to sell illegal liquor permits and pardons. Although Daugherty was not convicted, Harding's successor, Calvin Coolidge, forced him to resign.

5 In his 23 May letter, Peirce reported attending a boxing match with "Pat [Morgan] & Tanya Bennett." EH likely refers to Frances Woodruff Bennett (1905-1990), nicknamed Tanya. She was a daughter of American activist Josephine (Jo) Beach Day Bennett (1880-1961), a Paris friend of EH and Hadley, and Connecticut attorney Martin Toscan Bennett (1874-1940), who were divorced in 1926. Peirce had also mentioned "Tanya" in two other recent leters to EH, noting Charles Sweeny's infatuation with her ([May 1930] and 15 May [1930], JFK).

6 In a 2 June 1930 article headlined "'Happy' Saunders, Wife, and Son Are All But Drowned," the *Key West Citizen* reported that Happy's cabin cruiser, *Pureta*, ran aground in a storm on Saturday, 31 May, and the family escaped to Grand Bahama in a dinghy.

To Maxwell Perkins, 2 June [1930]

June 2

Dear Max:—

What would you do about this if you were me?

Please keep it confidential.

Yours always
Ernest

I must answer right away I imagine. I trust Cape as much on a sale as on a royalty report and believe he makes this offer to help me— But is there any way I would be protected in case of him being out or dead? or is there a form by which I could offer to sell him an edition of a certain number of copies? or best to leave it all alone. The loss by tax is certainly enormous. We are most certainly broke.

PUL, ALS

In a letter to EH of 7 May 1930, Jonathan Cape offered to purchase the rights to *FTA* for a lump sum of £850 instead of paying EH royalties on every copy sold, as these royalties were subject to English income tax, which reduced them considerably. Cape added that if the book continued to sell, he would make further payment to EH in a year, "and if and when we decide to do the book in a cheaper edition I will make you then a payment for the right to do such cheap edition." Cape noted, "It will mean of course that you are trusting me completely because you are selling the rights to me instead of giving me a licence, and so you must decide for yourself whether you will face the deduction or whether you are content to take a chance on my doing the right and fair thing by you" (URead). In his response to EH of 5 June 1930, Perkins would advise against accepting Cape's proposition because "an author ought to have control over his books" and because, even if EH had the most complete confidence in Cape, difficulties could arise if Cape were to die or sell out—or if EH later wished to change publishers (PUL) .

To Giles P. Greene, 2 June 1930

Key West
Florida
June 2 1930

Dear Mr. Greene

We are leaving here in a few days so it wouldnt be practical to send the book here— But if you will send it to Scribners in my name—marking it—

To Be Autographed—Please Hold— I'll be in New York fairly soon and would be delighted to write in it for you—

With all best wishes
Yours always—
Ernest Hemingway.

USCar, ALS

In a letter dated 21 May 1930, Greene expressed his admiration for *FTA* and asked if he might send EH a copy to be autographed (JFK).

To Evan Shipman, [3 June 1930]

Dear Evan:—

You are just in a dumps about writing I think— Everybody gets it— Maybe now it's over—[1]

I tried to write you a couple of times but you know what a lousy correspondent I am— Then smashed and cut index finger of right hand—6 stitches—still stiff—buggered up writing completely—

Did you ever get La France Chevaline? I sent it to Keswick— It was subscribed to only through June— Dont mention if you got it only if you didnt so I can bawl out Brentanos[2] Have had a fine winter— Never been in better shape except this finger—

How's Paris?— Wish you'd eat a Cervelas, a pomme a l'huile and Drink some beer for me at Lipps—[3] Thats what I miss most— Love to André [Masson]— Give my best to Harold [Stearns]— Please write me about everything and how you come out with the horses— Forgive me not writing—

Pauline sends her love— I meet Bumby in N.Y June 23— Wyoming this summer— Be in N.Y in Fall— When will I see you?

I wish to hell you'd finish your novel— Nobody can write—

I've been working hard some of the time— Been too hot lately—

Best luck to you always—

I wanted to write you but was working all the time or else on a cruise—mea culpa mea maxima culpa—

So long Kid and good luck—None of us can write—but if anybody can you can— I'll bet I've felt worse about it than you have 1 million times—

Probably I havent but every body thinks they feel worse than the others—
It's only those bastards who cant write that think they can—

Hem

Channick, ALS; postmark: JACK & KEY WEST R.P.O. / S.D., TR76 / JUN / 3 / 1930

1 EH is responding to a letter of 5 May [1930], in which Shipman reported that he he had been
unable to write; he worried that he had lost his enthusiasm or "may be just impotent" (JFK).
2 EH had promised to send Shipman a subscription to *La France Chevaline* (see EH to
Shipman, 24 August [1929]). Shipman had been residing with his sister and brother-in-law
at their Marletotz Farm in Keswick, Virginia, where she bred and trained horses (Sean
O'Rourke, *Grace Under Pressure: The Life of Evan Shipman* [Santa Monica, California:
Harvardwood Publishing; Nashville, Indiana: Unlimited Publishing, 2010], 67, 69).
Brentano's, an independent bookstore founded in New York City in 1853 by Austrian
immigrant August Brentano (1829–1886), had a Paris branch at 37, avenue de l'Opéra.
3 In his letter, Shipman wrote that he was about to sail for France. Shipman had been invited
by Jim Hamilton, a trainer he met at Keswick, to accompany him to Paris to scout for horses
to race in America, the trip funded by Pittsburgh department store magnate Edgar Jonas
Kaufmann (O'Rourke, *Grace Under Pressure*, 69). EH would recall such a meal at Brasserie
Lipp in the "Hunger Was Good Discipline" chapter of *MF*, describing cervelas as "a sausage
like a heavy, wide frankfurter split in two and covered with a special mustard sauce" and
pommes à l'huile as "potato salad."

To Archibald MacLeish, 8 June [1930]

June 8

Dear Otchy:—

They kept your fine letter in the General Delivery from May 28
until June 7—or we'd have gotten together in N.Y.[1] Pauline left last night for
what Pat calls Baggott— He calls Chasser les lions— Tater les Bions—
Cocteau could found something on that—[2] I go to N.Y. sometime before
Bumby arrives on the Lafayette on the 23rd.

When do you come to town again?— We pull out a day or so after Bum
arrives— Jinny is bringing him— A merchant has driven my car (Ford) to
Cincinnatti— will pick it up there and drive to Baggott and get Pauline; then
on to Wyoming—

Send me the New Found Land for Christ's Sake—[3]

The book racket has gone belly-up— Maybe now if it is demonstrated that nobody can make money honestly from the practice of letters (except like hitting the Xmas lottery) it will limit the number of practicioners—

It was wonderful how the dollar book announcement killed Humanism— As when war was declared in 1914 and Vorticism fell—[4] Writers all such shits that anything like the $1^{\underline{00}}$ book racket would end all political, religious, sexual, military, millinery, ethical, technical etc. discussions— Maybe the writers will all become Xistian Science healers, Chiropractors or Gurdieff[5] massagers now that the bottom has fallen from Pooblishing—

It isnt that we arent meant to drink— It's that to drink we need exercise— Drinking in cities is bad— Drinking skiing—drinking out in the boat are fine— But guys like you and me that used to take exercise then we stop and half our elimination stops—

What the hell is this? Chiropracty?

When will you be in NY till—when will you be back?

We sent Mimi a sea garden— Love to her, to Kenny and to Ada— I dont know Peter yet— Love to him too—

Hope we'll see you— Maybe I could come to Conway for a couple of days—

Have a lion, Tiger and Elephant rifle with telescope sight— Have you any woodchucks Mister?

Yrs

Pappy—

LOC, ALS

1 EH may be responding to MacLeish's undated letter [c. May 1930], thanking him and Pauline for their hospitality in Key West: "I got more out of those days on the water and my clumsy efforts at trolling than I've gotten out of anything in years" (JFK).

2 EH is apparently repeating Patrick's baby talk for *chasser les lions*: to hunt the lions (French). EH seems to enjoy the surreal image of groping them (*tater*), which would have appealed to Jean Cocteau (1889–1963), French avant-garde artist, filmmaker, and author.

3 MacLeish's *New Found Land: Fourteen Poems* was published by Houghton Mifflin on 4 June 1930.

4 Vorticism, the short-lived but influential avant-garde movement (c. 1912–1915) led by Wyndham Lewis (1882–1957) and named by Ezra Pound. The group members established a magazine, *Blast*, which published only two issues (1914 and 1915) and presented one exhibition (in London in 1915).

5 George Ivanovich Gurdjieff (c. 1872–1949), Armenian spiritualist who founded the Institute for the Harmonious Development of Man (established in 1922 in Fontainebleau, France) to teach certain movements, postures, and dance forms that would enable his followers to realize their inner potential.

To Allen Tate, [c. 8 June 1930]

Dear Dr.

We are bitched on coming to Clarksville this Spring.

Pauline has written the details to Caroline.[1] It is a damned shame but we will see you in the Fall and shoot quail together.

I'll do everything I can for K.A. Porter. I will have to see a copy of the Horny Hound to know what I'm talking about and will then see or wire Harcourt about Katherine Ann Porter— Swear to God if I can do any good can do more good if I know her stuff—[2] The book racket is on the bum they tell me and the publishers are all in the S—t house now— I will do what I can in N.Y. Can do more by word of mouth than writing—

On Death (anticipated) of Collins, More, Babbitt—[3]

Then worms shall try their ill preserved dignity

and their quaint pamphlets gone to bust

and into footnotes all their lust.[4]

No need to worry about those merchants— It's all over— The dollar book killed off Humanism like when they declared war in 1914 and Vorticism fell—

All writers all such s—ts that when a financial issue was raised all creative, philosophic, ethical, religious, military and sexual issues disappeared permanently—

More and Babbitt will have to go into another racket now—

Just when they get it started 25¢ books will come along and put it on the bum—

What do you say Doctor?

I have felt the writing racket stinks for a long time and am going into wholesal and retail fish business where you know it stinks and can throw the fish overboard—

Am teaching Patrick to Say "Pas des livres!" Have offered Maxie (Dead pan) Perkins a job sweeping out the fort at Tortugas—[5]

I feel like hell not to see you now but we'll get together before (chez toi) and during (chez Pauline) the Quail Season—

Best to Caroline—

Ernest

Patrick calls Chasser le lion— Tater le bion— Cocteau could found a whole religion on that.

PUL, ALS

1 In letters dated 16 April and 17 May 1930, Tate invited EH, Pauline, Patrick, and Henriette to visit him and his wife, Caroline Gordon, in Clarksville, Tennessee (JFK). Writing separately on "16 May or something," Gordon repeated the invitation, extending it to Jinny and Bumby as well (JFK).

2 Katherine Anne Porter (née Callie Russell Porter, 1890–1980), American journalist, essayist, and fiction writer, whose short story "Flowering Judas" had appeared in the April 1930 issue of *Hound & Horn*. Tate, Gordon, and eminent American critic Edmund Wilson (1895–1972) were among those who recommended Porter to Harcourt, Brace & Company, which would publish *Flowering Judas and Other Stories* in September 1930 in a limited edition of 600 copies. Tate's letter requesting EH's support for Porter remains unlocated, as does any letter EH may have written to Harcourt, Brace on Porter's behalf.

3 Journalist, critic, and essayist Paul Elmer More (1864–1937), along with Seward Collins and Irving Babbitt, was associated with the New Humanism.

4 EH would echo this satiric critique of the Humanists in *DIA*, claiming he hoped "to see the finish of a few, and speculate how worms will try that long preserved sterility; with their quaint pamphlets gone to bust and into foot-notes all their lust" (Chapter 12). EH alludes to the poem "To His Coy Mistress" by Andrew Marvell (1621–1678): "then worms shall try / That long preserved virginity, / And your quaint honour turn to dust, / And into ashes all my lust."

5 *Pas de livres!*: No more books! (French). EH refers to Fort Jefferson, constructed between 1846 and 1875 to protect the harbor at Dry Tortugas and never finished.

To Guy Hickok, [8 June 1930]

Dear Gros:—

What you trying to do Kid— Drive <u>down</u> my prices?

A merchant paid 160 for a copy of I.O.T. the 3 and 10 has now brought 150— (Wish I had some—you'll be rich if you didn't give yours away.)

The merchant offered me 500 for the S.A.R. mss. not 150— Old Hickock trying to smash prices—[1] Merchant offered 500 for the Killers Mss. I've never sold one.

I give them all [*EH insertion*: the mss.] to Uncle Gus or the Poor—[2] He's done more for ~~me~~ us than all the bloody merchants in the world— He's damned fine—

How was the Somme? Wish we were Going to Pamplona—[3]

Pauline, Pat, Henriette left for what Pat calls Baggott— last night— I go to N.Y. to meet Bumby— He comes in the 23rd of June ~~on Lafayette~~— It's been regular hurricane weather here last 2 weeks— Damn we had some swell trips though—

Book racket on the bum— Wish I had a few copies of my 1st edition so would always know I could eat for a couple of weeks—

Write to Piggott— Arkansas— They'll forward to Wyoming— Best to Mary—

Drink me a beer (Distingué) at Lipps— That's what I miss—

So long Gros—

Wish you were here to drive with me the car— (Goiman influence) to Arkansas— F.T.A. being serialized in Frankfurter Zeitung—

Best to Ezra—

Hope you're fine—

Ernest

Uncle Gus sent me the Clipping about prices—

You better write another saying theyve gone up— (Dont quote me)

You can sell on the rise!

phPUL, ALS

1 In a newspaper article datelined "Paris, May 16," Hickok had reported that a copy of EH's *TSTP* "with a couple of Hemingway's letters included, sold recently for $150" and that EH had been offered $150 for the manuscript of *SAR* by a London dealer ("Hemingway's Books Take on Classic Halo," *Brooklyn Daily Eagle*, 24 May 1930, 4). EH refers to higher prices paid by Marguerite Arnold for *iot, TSTP*, and *SAR*.

2 In 1928 EH had received an offer of $500 from collector Burton Emmett (1871–1935) for the manuscript of "The Killers" and other short stories, but EH returned Emmett's check, explaining that he preferred to give manuscripts to his Uncle G. A. Pfeiffer and to friends (*Letters* vol. 3, 353, 371). On 16 March 1928 EH had sent the manuscript of "The Killers," the first typescript of "The Undefeated," and an unpublished section of

"Fifty Grand" to Uncle Gus as gifts (*Letters* vol. 2, 370), and in March 1930, he gave Gus the manuscript of *FTA*. The "Poor" may refer to John Herrmann, to whom EH would send the corrected typescript of "Bullfighting, Sport and Industry" (EH to Herrmann, [13 June 1930]).

3 In his 26 May 1930 letter, Hickok wrote he was going to the Somme with a group of "gold star mamas," mothers of American soldiers who had died in the war. He also mentioned running into Jinny Pfeiffer, who had been with EH and Hickok in Pamplona the previous summer (JFK).

To Henry Strater, [c. 12 June 1930]

Dear Mike:—

The Springfield finally came and you ought to see it kid—[1] Comes up as naturally as pointing your finger—hit about a 6 inch piece of paper 3 times at 100 yds first time tried it— Most beautifully made and finished and simple, practical, gun I've ever seen—

But Dr. the telescope sight is the works!— [*EH insertion*: Charles said, "Write Mike right away about the telescope."] Easier to put on than to shove in a shell—nothing complicated—and is the damndest, simple, classy, easy to shoot with thing I've ever seen— No kick to gun—not as much as a 16 ga—one shot with the 220 grain bullet that went through about a foot and ½ thick palm tree tore out a place the size of your head and shoulders—hell—my head and your shoulders—

Nothing but rain and hurricane weather here for 3 weeks— havent wet a line in 2 weeks— Before that we were butchering them every night— Charles caught on 3 nights (1) 92— 1 (99) (1) 102 lbs— Pauline caught 12 on season—only lost 3—

I am going to meet Bumby in N.Y. he comes in on Lafayette—June 23 (expected) (Dont tell anybody I'm going to N.Y) Any chance you being there then? May be there a few days before (2 days after he arrives for sure)

Dont make trip specially— I can see the Club Kings in the fall— Dont feel any obligation or any such tripe to come down— I only mentioned I'd be there because you said you might be coming and didnt want to miss you— I'll stay at Brevoort or Uncle Gus's—

Bra not coming— I gave him the dough instead—he didnt make much jack this year and wanted to go sponging and diving for liquor dumped by chased speed boats near Miami— Seems they've located 100,000 cases—

Happy [Saunders] lost his boat in storm at Bahammys— Later reports he's recovered her though sunk— I had a shotgun aboard (20 ga)— Sad end of Saunders Scientific wild hog and pigeon shooting Expedition—

Write me to Chas. Scribners Sons—Fifth Avenue at 48th— I wrote Maxie (Dead-Pan) and asked him if it was true that the publishers were all in the S——T house now— He said in answer that they were in the Place I mentioned. I guess Publishing is a thing of the past. I am offering Maxie a job at sweeping out the fort at Tortugas if he can learn to keep things neat.

Archie said the portrait you did of me was swell he said—[2] I tell you I never saw a classier gun in my life than the Griffin and Howe Springfield— I'll bring it to N.Y in case you sh'd ~~want to see it~~ be there— Charles and I are going out to shoot it now—

Love to Maggie— So long— What's the sporting news?

Best always

Hem.

For Christ Sake Dont come to N.Y unless you have to for some reason—

PUL, ALS

The conjectured letter date, which differs from Carlos Baker's date of c. 20 June 1930 (*SL*, 324), is based on Milford Baker's letter of 4 June 1930 telling EH that the Springfield rifle had been shipped to Key West and he ought to have it by that time (PUL), and the fact that EH was still in Key West. He would leave Key West for New York City on 14 June.

1 In his 4 June letter, Baker explained the delay in the gun's arrival: Griffin & Howe had mislabeled the package and the gun had to be reshipped to EH in Key West.
2 Strater's third portrait of EH shows a "clean-cut three-quarter-face bust in a blue shirt" (Baker *Life*, 208). In a 4 May 1930 letter to EH, Strater wrote, "The portrait of you didn't look so good later, so I spent four or five days on it, and now it is right" (JFK). On 24 May, Strater wrote to Perkins from Ogunquit, Maine, that it was finished and framed (PUL).

To John Herrmann, [13 June 1930]

Dear John:

Enclosed is an even more original original Mss of the article the merchant offered to buy the supposed original— This is the genuine guaranteed original just found by the Mahatma on looking through the Sacred unanswered letter trunk.[1]

It is hot here brother— Pauline left a week ago tomorrow— I shove off tomorrow—

Best to you and Jo—

Yours always—

Hem—

What about the Menace from the Open Spaces?[2]

Write care Scribners'—

I wrote Maxie I understand the publishers were in the S—T House now—

This piece was published in Fortune—Very unique— It has that Jenesayqua[3] you used to put in the beans.

[*EH notation on the last page of the enclosed typescript:*]

(The bum guy got gored in the anus (ass) tore sphincter muscle etc etc.) Is at it again now.[4] This article maybe not much good John but maybe you can turn a not too honest penny by selling this Mss.

PUL, ALS

1 EH enclosed a twenty-page hand-corrected typescript of the article published as "Bullfighting, Sport and Industry" in *Fortune* magazine (March 1930).

2 Reference to Morley Callaghan.

3 *Je ne sais quoi*: a certain something (French).

4 The typescript of the article concludes with a description of Sidney Franklin, who "has never been gored or badly wounded" and who had told EH that "it is not the bull who gores the man but the man who gores himself on the bull by some mistake in technique." Franklin was gored in Madrid on 16 March 1930 when he made precisely such a mistake, turning his back on a dying bull that lifted its head and gored him. Franklin returned to bullfighting on 4 May, only partially healed of the wound that would bedevil him for years.

To Charles Thompson, [14 June 1930]

[Excerpt as provided in Christie's catalog:]
"Don't forget your measurements! Enclosed is the 35 seeds [dollars?]—
Thanks ever so much— We had a good time all right— I feel like a shyte
saddling you with those things to carry and ship— There was a drawing of
Waldo's [Waldo Frank[1]] too–you can keep it or put it in the Photobook—
Been raining all the time—no mosquitoes but carried away with frogs
shrilling— Drink up all the wine . . . get plenty of exercise and keep in good
shape for Africa [their planned African safari, which was postponed until
1933] . . . Remember to talk French to the mutt. Appreciate like hell all your
kindness . . ."

Christie's catalog, New York, 17 May 1989, Lot 74, ALS; postmark: [New York, New
York / 15 June, 1930]

The catalog description of the letter reads: "Autograph letter signed ('Ernest') to
Charles Thompson ('Dear Dr.') in Key West, 'Enroute / Harvard Special / (nearing
Savannah),' [June 1930]. It is accompanied by an envelope addressed by Hemingway
postmarked "New York, June 15, 1930" and giving the return address as Scribner's in
New York. EH was traveling to New York City aboard the Havana Special train. In
June 1930 the Havana Special left Key West at 5:30 p.m., arrived in Savannah,
Georgia, the next morning at 10:57, and arrived at New York's Pennsylvania Station at
6:55 a.m. the following day (*The Official Guide of the Railways and Steam Navigation
Lines of the United States, Porto Rico Canada Mexico and Cuba*, National Railway
Publication Company, June 1930, 597). The conjectured letter date is based on the
train schedule and the letter's postmark: presumably EH wrote the letter on the
morning of 14 June and mailed it after arriving in New York the next day.

1 EH almost certainly refers to Waldo Peirce.

To Milford Baker, 20 June 1930

23P TL 26
NNW NEWYORK NY 254 P JUNE 20 1930
MILFORD BAKER
ATLANTIC BLDG

RIFLE ABSOLUTELY SPLENDID COULD YOU LUNCH WITH ME SATURDAY OR MONDAY ANYWHERE YOU SAY ANSWER CARE PFEIFFER 277 PARK AVENUE NEWYORK HOPE YOU CAN

HEMINGWAY

323P

PUL, Cable

To Louis Henry Cohn, 24 June [1930]

June 24

Dear Captain Cohn:—

I have had the questions answered for quite a long time but didnt send them because I could not make up my mind about the introduction and signing—[1] Rather my mind was always made up and I have tried, without success, to convince myself that it was of no importance and that I might do as you wished.

The reason I cannot is this:— I believe formally that a writer of my age should not have anything to do with limited editions of his writings, bibliographies of his writings or, in fact, anything but his writings themselves— I signed the Scribner edition of A.F.T.A. under protest but— All right to do once but A hell of a bad policy to follow

I might elaborate on this but I believe you see what I mean.

I appreciate your interest very truly and accept it as a compliment—but a compliment, like all compliments to a proffessional in any line of work, that may be accepted, truly appreciated— But not pondered over—

You are damned good to be doing what you are doing— I tell you that I appreciate it very much— But for my self respect I can take no cognizance of it or it loses what significance it has— I've tried, always, to keep my self separate from my work so that, ~~as much as possible,~~ I could get the only truly valid evaluation (very bad phrase, by God) ~~possible~~—an impersonal one— I've not let Max give out any personal publicity, I've tried not to meet critics— You know yourself how something you write makes you feel but you cannot tell if you are conveying it completely to another person if that person knows you, likes or dislikes you, or has any personal prejudice, explanation, like or antipathy.

317

For instance:— Most people who have met Gertrude Stein are so impressed with her, her intelligence, good sense etc. that they accept more or less completely her writing— Altho. before, much of it may have meant nothing to them— Well Miss Stein may not always be here to, in person, convince people of the value of all of her writing—

The other way it works is that several people having met me have been convinced by the experience that my writing must be, shall we say, shit—

The point is that I want to keep outside of it in every way— To be judged without personal prejudice or appeal—judged as though I you were dead— or knew no one—

You compete only with dead men— And you cannot tell how you are going if you are being judged by friends—or enemies—or acquaintances—

My only pride is of a certain artistic and financial integrity—in all other ways in life I have made an ass of myself— To keep this self respect— which is of great importance—since without some self respect it is not worth (to me) continuing to exist I can neither sign nor write introductions to, nor take any cognizance of bibliographies nor iconographies, of my work

But I appreciate very much the interest that you take and would be glad as a return of the compliment to give you a page of unpublished Mss. which you can have, reproduce or do any bloody thing you want with—

I hope my answers to the questions were not too curt— I did not mean them at any time to be offensive to you personally—

> Yours always
> Ernest Hemingway—

About critics— The two I know of complete integrity are Edmund Wilsen and Allen Tate— That does not mean they are infallible—

The personal element in criticizm is—

Mr. Lohrke, with whose opinions you disagreed is a friend of my former wife—

Mr. Collins a friend of Miss Parker—[2]

[Enclosed are thirteen half-sheets bearing Cohn's typewritten questions (here italicized) and EH's responses—typewritten on the eight numbered sheets and handwritten in pencil on the five unnumbered sheets:]

1.

Did the publication of "in our time" actually precede that of THREE STORIES &
TEN POEMS? The latter volume has a printer's note that it was printed at Dijon
in 1923 and has a mention of IN OUR TIME (Three Mountains Press) on the
rear wrapper. Why, then, was "in our time" dated 1924?
[EH:]

   3 stories and 10 poems was published in summer of 23. In Our Time was
announced before that and expected to be published but being hand printed
at Bill Bird's press and he having plenty of other things to do it was delayed
until 1924. Was also delayed a couple of months in bindery.

2.

THREE STORIES & TEN POEMS carries a note on the page opposite the
title-page: Copyright 1923, by the author. I can find no record of the copyright
in Washington except for the January issue of POETRY; A Magazine of Verse,
which contained six of the poems. Did you ever personally copyright the book
in Washington? Why does the note on the contents page state that five of these
poems appeared in POETRY, when actually six appeared?
[EH:]

   Copyright etc attended to by Contact Publishing Co. You will find in
addition to the Poetry copyright My Old Man copyrighted in Best Short
Stories, of 1924 I believe, by Edward J. O'Brien Vol dedicated to me and
named spelled Hemenway.[3]

   answering 2nd question, I haven't the least idea.

3.

Did you edit more than one number of THE TRANSATLANTIC REVIEW?
From the text of the editorial comment, I figured that you had edited only the
number for September 1924. Am I right?
[EH:]

   Have no files of T.R. here so cannot answer. I edited 2 I believe. I think
Aug. and Sept. Anyway the numbersthat ran Paul Valery on Leonardo, The
Baroness Elsa Von Freytag Loringhoven and a story by Dos Passos called

July. Also Ring Lardner's I Gasparri. If those are spread over two numbers I edited them both. If all in one I only had one. Think I had one complete, another all ready to print before leaving for somewhere and Ford added editorial comment on his return from U.S.[4]

4.

In THE EXILE, No. I, Spring 1927 on page 1, I find the heading
NOTHOEMIST. In every copy I have seen there has been a pencil marking
indicating a transposition to NEOTHOMIST. Can you throw any light on
this for me? What did you intend it to read and what does the title mean?
[EH:]

Neo-Thomist is correct. Nothomist is a printers error and was corrected in pencil by Pound. The title means Neo-Thomist. Poem Refers to temporary embracing of church by literary gents.[5]

5.

My records show that you wrote an article "THE REAL SPANIARD" for No. 8
of the BOULEVARDIER. The month is given as October but no year is given. I
believe it is 1927. Am I correct? Did anything else of yours appear in the
BOULEVARDIER?
[EH:]

The article was written partly by me, mostly by my wife and re-written by a citizen named Arthur Moss who put in all the funny cracks. Anyone familiar with the worksof Moss can pick out his funny cracks. He was editing the Boulvardier and his policy was to improve the work of contributors by inserting funny bits of his own.[6]

6.

In the October 1924 number of THE TRANSATLANTIC REVIEW there
appears PAMPLONA LETTER by you and also an appreciation of Joseph
Conrad. There also appears a letter from the U.S. presumably by Krebs
Friend. Does such a person exist? I have always had a queer feeling that it was
a pseudonym of yours.
[EH:]

The Pamplona letter is foolish and the appreciation of Conrad was written by request while Mr. Ford Madox Ford who had requested it and would not take no for an answer, I knew I could not write an appreciation, waited in the next room. It did Mr. Conrad no good and gratuitously insulted Mr. T. S. Eliot.[7]

Krebs Friend is a man of that name. He assisted Ford for a while with the T.R. in the fall of 1924.[8] Am not greatly honored that you should have felt it was a pseudonym.

7.

Were your articles in the K.C. Star about conditions in the City Hospital there signed? Did they appear in early 1917?
[EH:]

Nothing signed in K.C. Star.[9]

Were your articles in Montreal Daily Star signed? What year?
[EH:]

Nothing signed in Montreal Star.[10]

When you were writing for Universal Service from Geneva in 1923, were all your articles signed JOHN HADLEY or were there any others under other names?
[EH:]

When working for Hearst wrote no articles. All cabled dispatches.[11]

It is the height of silliness to go into newspaper stuff I have written which has nothing to do with the other writing which is entirely apart and starts with the first In Our Time. Have written thousands of columns in newspapers. Also sent much in condensed cable-ese to be re-written in U.S. and Canada. This has nothing to do with signed and published writing in books or magazines and it is a hell of a trick on a man to try and dig it up and confuse the matter of judging the work he has published. If anyone wants to do that after a man is dead he can't defend himself but while he is alive he can at least take no part in it and oppose it as far as possible. The first right that a man writing has is the choice of what he will publish. Everybody writes shit and plenty of it but the place for it is the waste basket. If you have made your living as a newspaperman learning your trade, writing against deadlines writing to make stuff timely rather than permanent no one has any right to dig this stuff up and use it against the stuff you have written to write the best you can.

The way I would oppose it would be to have nothing to do with it, if anyone still insisted on using or listing newspaper stuff of any kind would then put in someone else's hands enough information that the first one could not obtain as to render the first book incomplete and valueless.

[*EH autograph insertion:*]

Don't mean this in any way as a threat—rather a statement of policy—

8.

In the bibliographical note in TRANSATLANTIC STORIES, there is the statement that some of your work has been translated into Russian. I have no record of that at all. Can you give me any data on what, when and where?

[*EH:*]

Dos Passos knows what the books are. So does Robert Woolf I don't. But they sent word through them that I could have the royalties if I came to Moscow.[12]

[*The following five unnumbered sheets bear EH's pencilled responses:*]

My records on Der Querschnitt show the following:

> *iv Jahrgang Heft 4 Autumn 1924*
>   *The Soul of Spain with McAlmon & Bird.*✓
>   *The Earnest Liberal's Lament.*✓
> *iv Jahrgang Heft 5 November 1924*
>   *The Lady Poets with Foot Notes.*✓
> *V Jahrgang Heft 6 Summer 1925*
>   *Stierkampf Part 1 (The Undefeated)*✓ *Translated by B. Bessmertny.*
> *V Jahrgang Heft 7 July 1925*
>   *Stierkampf Part 2 (The Undefeated)*✓
> *V Jahrgang Heft 2 February 1925*
>   *The Age Demanded.*[13]✓

Is this everything that appeared in this publication?

[*EH:*]

Am not sure. Other things paid for but possibly not published.

The appearances here are the actual first of "The Undefeated", are they not?

[*EH:*]

Believe so.

Have any of the other items above mentioned ever been reprinted with the possible exception of the Flechtheim book which I doubt ever appeared? I wrote Flechtheim but have not yet had a reply.[14]

[*EH:*]

Most stories in IO.T.—Men Without Women—appeared in various German periodicals and newspapers especially Frankfurter Zeitung— If you write to Edgar A. Mowrer—Chicago Daily News Bureau Berlin [*EH insertion*: He is an excellent fellow and a good friend of mine.] he can tell you a great many of them— Farewell To Arms now being published in Frankfurter Zeitung— Can get Information from Ernst Rowohlt— Ernst Rowohlt Verlag—Berlin[.] Rowohlt is my German Publisher.

I have written to Adrienne Monnier as you suggested to me but in the meantime I located some files of the "Navire D'Argent" here in the Public Library. I found only one contribution by you "L'Invincible" in the number for March 1926 in a translation by Georges Duplaix. There were only 12 numbers all told in the library and if my dope is correct, I believe that is all that were ever published. There are no files of "Commerce" in the library, so I will have to wait until I hear from Mlle. Monnier on that.

Do you recall if this is all that appeared in the "Navire"?

[*EH:*]

Believe so.

Did Ott de Weymer *use this translation of "L'invincible" in his book or did he translate it in his own [b]ook again?*

[*EH:*]

Used this with a few corrections by me— [*EH underlined "Ott de Weymer" in Cohn's query and ran a pencil line from the name to the bottom of the page, where he wrote:* is Georges Duplaix.[15]]

I expect to run down to Washington to the Library of Congress to look at that book. Is there anything I can look up or do for you down there? About copyright or otherwise?

[*No response by EH*]

On the verso of the title-page of "Men Without Women" among the copyright acknowledgments there is one to Doubleday, Page & Co. Miss Comstock who looks after the copyrights of that firm tells me that the only thing that she can find a copyright on is "The Killers" which they used in the O. Henry Prize Stories of 1927 and in Mirrilies' Significant Contemporary Stories. Both of those books, however appeared after "Men Without Women".

Do you recall anything other than this which might have been copyright by Doubleday?

[EH:]

<u>No</u>[16]

My records on La Nouvelle Revue Francaise show the following:

Cinquante Mille Dollars appeared August 1, 1927 in a translation by Ott de Weymer

[EH:]

=Georges Duplaix— Belive Ott de Weymer is his mother's name—

Le Village Indien appeared June 1, 1928 in a translation by Ott de Weymer.

A review of the book "Cinquante Mille Dollars" by Victor Llona appeared January 1, 1929.

As far as you can recall, is this all that appeared in this publication?

[EH:]

As far as I know—

The Killers appeared in La Nouvelle Litteraire

Hills like White Elephants in Bifur

Now I Lay Me in, I believe, La Revue Europeene—

The Battler in ?

Several others in various places—[17]

I can find no record of the following stories having appeared previous to their appearance in "Men Without Women". Was this their first publication?

A SIMPLE ENQUIRY.

TEN INDIANS.

A PURSUIT RACE.

NOW I LAY ME.

[*EH:*]

<u>Yes</u> [*with a pencil mark encompassing all four of the listed titles*]

UDel, ALS with AN and TN questionnaire responses; letterhead: HOTEL BREVOORT / Fifth Avenue / At Eighth Street / New York; postmarks: NEW YORK, N.Y. / STA.D, JUN 24 / 1030AM / 1930; [*on envelope verso:*] NEW YORK, N.Y. REC'D: / [GRAND]CENT.STA, JUN24 / 1130AM / 1930

EH sent this letter by Special Delivery mail.

1 In a letter dated 4 May 1930, Cohn thanked EH for offering to correct his bibliographical notes and said he was sending some questions on "separate slips" (UDel). Cohn had enclosed thirteen half-sheets with typewritten questions and space for EH's answers, which EH returned with this letter.

2 EH seems to be responding to Cohn's remark, "it amuses me to see the Farewell treated by some of the critics as a war book," when Cohn viewed the war as "only a shadowy background" to the love story. American novelist and critic Eugene William Lohrke (1897–1953) included Chapter 30 of *FTA* (under the title "The Retreat from the Isonzo") in his collection *Armageddon: The World War in Literature* (New York: Jonathan Cape and Harrison Smith, 1930). The February 1930 issue of *Bookman*, edited by Seward Collins, featured an unsigned critical article titled "Inflammatory Topics" speaking of the unfairness of Robert Herrick's negative review of *FTA* in the November 1929 issue.

3 EH's "My Old Man" was first published in *TSTP* (Paris: Contact Editions, 1923) and reprinted in O'Brien's *The Best Short Stories of 1923* (Boston: Small, Maynard, 1924), that volume dedicated to "Ernest Hemenway."

4 Ford Madox Ford (né Ford Hermann Hueffer, 1873–1939) founded the literary magazine *Transatlantic Review*, the first issue of which appeared in Europe in December 1923 and in the United States in January 1924. EH served as the magazine's subeditor beginning in February 1924 and oversaw preparation of the July and August issues while Ford was traveling abroad. The July issue included "Three Poems" by Elsa von Freytag-Loringhoven (1874–1927) and the mock-play "I Gaspari" by Ring Lardner (1885–1933), in addition to "Variations sur une 'Pensée'" by French poet and essayist Paul Valéry (1871–1945). The August issue included the short story "July" by Dos Passos. As guest editor of the August issue, EH excluded Ford's own work, which was being serialized in the magazine, and offered what Ford would term in his editorial commentary an "unusually large sample of the work of that Young America whose claims we have so insistently—but not with such efficiency—forced upon our readers." Ford promised that the next issue would "re-assume its international aspect" ("Chroniques," *Transatlantic Review*, August 1924, 213).

5 EH's "Neo-Thomist Poem" (misspelled "Nothoemist") appeared in the first issue of Pound's magazine the *Exile*, published in four issues in 1927 and 1928. In the bibliography, Cohn would quote EH's explanation here verbatim (89).

6 EH's article "The Real Spaniard" appeared in *Boulevardier* 1, no. 8 (October 1927) with unauthorized revisions made by editor Arthur Moss (1899–1969).

7 In the September 1924 *Transatlantic Review*, EH famously declared that if he could resurrect the recently deceased Conrad (1857–1924) "by grinding Mr. Eliot into a fine dry powder and sprinkling that powder over Mr. Conrad's grave," he "would leave for

London early tomorrow with a sausage grinder" ("Conrad, Optimist and Moralist," 341–42). In "Pamplona Letter," which appeared in the same issue, EH commented on his editorial policy while editing the magazine (300–2).

8 Harold Krebs Friend (1896–1967), a WWI veteran and EH's colleague at the *Co-Operative Commonwealth* in Chicago, 1920–1921. In August 1924 Friend became the chief financial backer of the *Transatlantic Review*.

9 EH's writing for the *Kansas City Star* primarily consisted of short news stories generated by routine assignments, and he was not credited in the bylines. EH began work at the *Star* in October 1917; the first article attributed to him is dated 16 December 1917 (Matthew J. Bruccoli, ed., *Ernest Hemingway, Cub Reporter: Kansas City Star Stories* [Pittsburgh: University of Pittsburgh Press, 1970], xii, 15–19).

10 EH contributed more than 170 articles to the *Toronto Star* between 1920 and 1924, the majority of them signed "Ernest M. Hemingway" (*DLT*, xxix).

11 In violation of his exclusive contract with the *Toronto Star*, EH cabled spot news stories to Frank Mason (1893–1979), manager of the Paris office of the International News Service (INS), which was part of the Hearst publishing empire. The news stories appeared in several Hearst newspapers under the byline "John Hadley, International News Service Staff Correspondent." EH also filed one item under the byline Peter Jackson (Hanneman, 141).

12 Cohn refers to *Transatlantic Stories: Selected from the "Transatlantic Review,"* with an introduction by Ford Madox Ford (London: Duckworth, 1926; New York: Dial Press, 1926); the collection includes "A Story" by EH, first published as "The Doctor and the Doctor's Wife" in the December 1924 *Transatlantic Review* (Hanneman E4, 209). The biographical note for EH in the volume's appendix states that "his work has been translated into German and Russian" (257). Both Dos Passos and American poet and novelist Robert Wolf (1895–1970) were regular contributors to the leftist journal *New Masses* (1926–1948), which followed cultural events in Russia. Joseph Freeman (1897–1965), a founding editor of the magazine, recalled that on his 1926 trip to Moscow he gave a copy of *IOT* to Ivan Kashkin (1899–1963), a professor of American literature at the University of Moscow, who translated one of EH's sketches for *Nasha Put* (*Our Way*), a bilingual educational publication Kashkin edited (Freeman, "A Year of Grace," *New Politics*, 1965: 110–11). In a letter to EH of 26 August 1930, Cohn would mention that Russian publication, adding that he had told Perkins about continuing Russian interest in EH and that Perkins was going to send over a copy of *FTA* "with a request to know what other work of yours they want" (UDel). Hanneman and Grissom date EH's first translation into Russian to 1934 (Hanneman D287; Grissom I772).

13 *Jahrgang* indicates the year or volume number and *Heft* the issue number (German), hence the first entry is volume 4, issue 4. EH placed a check mark beside each item Cohn listed.

14 In his 23 April 1930 letter to Cohn, EH had mentioned Flechtheim's plan to publish a volume of EH's "obscene" poetry to be illustrated by Pascin.

15 "The Undefeated" had been translated by Georges Duplaix (1895–1985) and published as "L'Invincible" in the March 1926 issue of the magazine *Navire d'Argent* (*Silver Ship*), edited by Adrienne Monnier. Duplaix included this translation in the 1928 collection *Cinquante Mille Dollars* (*Fifty Grand*) under the pseudonym Ott de Weymer.

16 New York publishing house Doubleday, Doran & Company (formerly Doubleday, Page & Company, 1900–1927) included "The Killers" in two anthologies: *O. Henry Memorial Award Prize Stories of 1927* (1928) and *Significant Contemporary Stories* (1929), edited by Edith Ronald Mirrielees (1878–1962), a professor of English at Stanford University. Lillian Adele Comstock (1878–1962), longtime secretary to company founder Frank Nelson Doubleday (1862–1934).

17 No record has been located for the appearance of "The Killers" in *La Nouvelle Littéraire*; in the published *Bibliography*, Cohn would list the French translation of this story as "previously unpublished" prior to its appearance in 1928 as "Les Tueurs" in *Cinquante Mille Dollars*. EH correctly recalls that Alice Turpin's translation "Les Collines Sont Comme des Elephants Blancs" ("Hills Like White Elephants") appeared in the third issue of *Bifur* (30 September 1929), and that Llona's translation of "Now I Lay Me" ("Je Vous Salue Marie") appeared in the first issue of *Revue Européenne* (January 1930), as had "Le Batailleur," Jean Georges Auriol's translation of "The Battler."

To Milford Baker, [30 June 1930]

PAUL M. PFEIFFER, Pres.   G. A. PFEIFFER, Vice-Pres.   MARY A. PFEIFFER, Sec.-Treas.

These lands grow fine Clover, Corn, Cotton, Wheat, and Truck Crops. Minimum insect damage, mild winters, and fine pastures make this an ideal Hog, Cotton and Poultry Section. Served by both the Cotton Belt and Frisco Railroads.

Piggott Land Co., Inc.

Owners of over fifty thousand acres highly improved and cut over lands in rich St. Francis, Cache and Black River valleys. Well drained. Located in Clay County, Northeast Corner of Arkansas, two hundred miles due south of St. Louis, Missouri.

Near to good roads, schools, and markets. State highways adjacent and through these lands, built and maintained by State of Arkansas through gas and auto tax, free of any cost or direct tax on lands.

Piggott, Ark., ———————————— 19 ——

Dear Bake:—

Take the above letter head with a grain of Salt Except for the extent of the land which is really something over 70,000 acres and the finest quail shooting in America.

Am laid up with summer grippe— Dosed up with quinine—[1] But what I wanted to write you about is what a great pleasure it was to see you again— You have been so extra damned fine about helping me on this gun matter and I cant tell you how happy it made me to see you again face to face.[2] You've been so damned patient and intelligent in your letters and I cant tell you how much I appreciate it.

It was very interesting at Griffin and Howe's— I acted less receptive, perhaps, than necessary because I know he must sell and make so many guns for very wealthy men etc who need to be sold etc. on the other hand I believe a.416 Magnum Mauser to really fit would be a damned good buy and most useful— I hope, eventually with your aid and advice to own a <u>light</u> 7. MM on Springfield action with same Scope as my Springfield—to use wherever I must climb—i.e. Wyoming, B.Columbia, Hymalayas, etc. and

327

for a deer rifle, coyotes etc. The Springfield for <u>everything but Elephant in Africa</u>. The.416, if we decide that is best, for Elephant and emergencies—

But I will be damned if I would want to carry it for Buffalo or lion or any other junk— And from all I hear no Rhino should get you sober—as long as you can side step or climb thorn trees—

Have killed bulls with a sword and if I can learn to shoot the Springfield would feel pretty ashamed to go beyond it for anything it will kill if moderately well placed—

> I.O.U.
> one copy original edition
> 3 Stories and 10 poems—
>
> Ernest Hemingway
> To Milford Baker—   June 29—1930

This [*EH insertion with arrow pointing to boxed text above*: legal document!] to help me to think may be able to try to make some return for your great patience, trouble taking— I have two of them in the vault of Guaranty Trust in Paris— Have never seen a 1st Edition that could compare with a good rifle or a good shotgun but as I said if values dont drop you can always exchange the one for the other.

It was grand to see you again Bake—

Best to you always—
Hemmy—

We shove in 2 days to L.T. Ranch
Painter Wyo[3]
But wont be there for a couple of weeks as plan to stop in K.C.—Sheridan etc—at LT from July 17 on—

If I send you a check will you buy me those glasses we saw at G and H?

PUL, ALS; letterhead: Piggott Land Co., Inc. / Piggott, Ark.; postmark: SAINT LOUIS, MO. 5, JUN 30 / 8[30]AM / 1930

1 Quinine, the standard treatment for malaria, which manifests flu-like symptoms of fever, headache, and weakness. Arkansas consistently reported the most malaria-related deaths of any state throughout the 1920s and 1930s.

2 In a cable dated 20 June 1930, Baker had set their meeting for lunch at the Harvard Club in New York City for Monday, 23 June 1930 (PUL).

3 The L-Bar-T Ranch, owned by Lawrence (1886–1963) and Olive (1902–1932) Nordquist, located just inside the Wyoming border, about 16 miles from Cooke City, Montana, and 19 miles by trail from Painter, Wyoming (EH to Baker, [21 July 1930]). The name of the ranch derived from the first and last letters of Lawrence Norquist's name (Baker *Life*, 212). EH and Pauline would return to the L-Bar-T in 1931, 1932, 1936, and 1939.

To Archibald MacLeish, 30 June [1930]

June 30

Dear Archie:—

I wanted like hell to come to Conway but Jinny and Bumby got in a day and ½ earlier than expected and so it was off until next fall— In N.Y. I started to clip notices of the book but there were so many and as good as reviews can be [*EH insertion*: So I figure H. Mifflin would send them—][1] (which is a long way from anything good— My Christ but—reviewers are a shitty folk and Pappa hopes they will all choke) But they were about the best reviews I ever read of a book— I.E. they could tell it was a fine book

That's the way it is Kid— When you are disgusted with them and expect nothing will happen they make much noise— When you have something you know is the absolute works they never mention it except to, perhaps, point out how you derive from Maurice Dekobra[2]

You are the best living writing poet— There are a couple of other good poets but not writing or writing tripe and you are living and writing too—

It has been very dry here—bad for crops but wonderful for quail— Have spotted any quantity of coveys and we'll shoot them in Dec. Season opens Dec. 1— Am shoring up local wines, moonshine etc. You'll come and we'll have great shooting—

We leave in 2 days for Wyoming— Bumby Paulinoes and me— Stop at K.C. at my cousins a couple of days—[3]

I am going to read the book in Wyoming—

Saw Galantiere, Author of Brushwood Boy at The Front—Wanted him to check some french (spelling) in a story I have in August Scribners— He did as much with aid of a dictionary— Maybe you'll like the story—[4] He is a little fellow I trust as long as I'm in the room with him but while he has doublecrossed me in mean and petty ways 3 times now I still like him—when I'm with him—

You Mac—I feel the same way about when with and away from—
We'll shoot a lot of quail too— Ducks auch—[5]
I hope Ada's fine—
Pauline sends her love—

I've had some 40 consecutive hot nights and havent slept for a long time— It will be fine in the mountains—need like hell to work too—

Good luck to you Andy Marvell—remember when you die it will be a unique experience for the worms to try a good half back, classy diver, lawyer and great poet combined—[6] Become a quail shot this fall Mac and give the worms an extra treat—

Pappy—

LOC, ALS

1 The glowing reviews of MacLeish's *New Found Land* in the *New York Evening Post* and the *New York Times* (21 and 22 June 1930 respectively) would be followed by similarly extravagant praise in the *Nation* and the *New York Herald Tribune Books* (2 and 6 July 1930 respectively) (Donaldson *MacLeish*, 555).
2 Maurice Dekobra (né Ernest Maurice Tessier, 1885–1973), popular French journalist and novelist.
3 EH refers to Ruth White Lowry (1884–1974) and William Malcolm Lowry (1884–1953), who lived at 6435 Indian Lane, Kansas City. Ruth was the younger half-sister of Fanny Arabell White Hemingway (1876–1963), widow of EH's paternal uncle Alfred Tyler Hemingway (1877–1922).
4 Lewis Galantière (1895–1977), American-born French translator, journalist, playwright, and one of EH's first expatriate friends in Paris, published a positive review of *FTA* titled "The Brushwood Boy at the Front" in *Hound & Horn* (January–March 1930). EH had asked Galantière to check for French idiomatic usage and accent marks in the galleys of "Wine of Wyoming," which would appear in the August 1930 *Scribner's Magazine* (Baker *Life*, 210–11).
5 *Auch*: also (German).
6 EH refers to MacLeish's poem "You, Andrew Marvell," included in *New Found Land*, and alludes to Marvell's "To His Coy Mistress": "then worms shall try / That long preserved virginity." MacLeish had played football at his prep school, Hotchkiss, and as an undergraduate at Yale. He had graduated from Harvard Law School in 1919 and worked as a trial lawyer with the Boston firm of Choate, Hall, and Stewart before abandoning law for poetry in 1923.

To Jonathan Cape, 1 July 1930

Piggott
Arkansas
July 1 1930

Dear Cape:—

I appreciate very much your efforts to help me hold down on income tax but I'm afraid I cannot make the arrangement you suggest.[1]

The difficulty is that I would have no protection in case anything happened to you— Nor would my heirs— As long as you were alive I know things would be all right but so many of my friends have died lately that I must take that possibility as well as that of any mergers, amalgamations etc into account. I hope you'll live long though and prosper unmergered and unamalgamated.

A few years ago many writers here thought they had found ways of holding down the bloody tax but it cost most of them more in the end. The hell of it is that under any system by which I would be protected in case of anything happening to you—such as sale of a definite number of copies outright or other plan— Sooner or later the Gov't might step in— Bugger the Govt I say—but stay inside the law—impossible to do here of course where we're law ridden past all decency— Here you must break them for your own self respect—

It is altogether wrong to consider what a writer makes from a book as income anyway— It is Capital and when it is spent is capital gone any way you may look at it—

Thanks very much for the trouble you took though— The thing is that the income from my books is the only estate I'll leave and I must leave it in as good order as I can— You must sell enough of them to satisfy the bloody tax and me both—

With best wishes
Yours always
Ernest Hemingway—

URead, ALS

1 In his 2 June letter to Perkins, EH had asked his advice about Cape's offer to purchase the copyrights to *FTA* instead of paying taxable royalties on each copy sold (Cape to EH, 7 May 1930, URead). In his 5 June reply, Perkins had advised EH to retain copyright (PUL), for the reasons EH notes here.

To Maxwell Perkins, 10 July 1930

VA5 16 NM=SHERIDAN WYO 10
MAXWELL E PERKINS=
CHARLES SCRIBNERS SONS 5 AVE AT 48 ST NEWYORK NY=
FORWARD ALL MAIL L BAR T RANCH PAINTER WYOMING WAS
108 SHADE CROSSING NEBRASKA=
ERNEST.

PUL, Cable; Western Union destination receipt stamp: 1930 JUL 10 PM 10 01

To Maxwell Perkins, 14 July 1930

VB648 11 NM=CODY WYO 14
MAXWELL E PERKINS=CHARLES SCRIBNERS SONS
597 FIFTH AVENUE NEWYORK NY=
PLEASE FORWARD ALL MAIL CARE LAWRENCE NORDQUIST
COOKE MONTANA WORKING WELL=
ERNEST HEMINGWAY.

PUL, Cable: Western Union destination receipt stamp: 1930 JUL 14 PM 11 58

To Milford Baker, [21 July 1930]

L-T Ranch
Cooke City
Montana

Dear Bake:

You may have written and I not rec'd it on acct been enroute for 10 days or so and find only one mail a week into Cooke City and no mail out of Painter— Wyo—which was address they gave me— Ranch 16 miles from Cook City— Must go 19 miles trail to get mail at Painter[.] Cooke City Mont.—care of Lawrence Nordquist is best address—

I send the measurements for the Springfield for Charles Thompson— Plaque to be initialled C.T. Gun same as mine, same case, same scope and mount—Scope case—

Weight 190

Height 6ft. 1 inch

Lobe of ear to shoulder 4 ½ inches.

Shoulder to end of trigger finger 29 ½ inches.

he has good sized hands—bigger than mine but not gigantic— If you drop a note to Strater—Henry H.—Ogunquit Me. he will send the deposit etc. His town address 115 East 86th Street N.Y.C.

Gun to be sent to Charles Thompson care Thompson Fish Co. Key West Florida—

Look Bake I'm going to hunt sheep here Sept. 15— There are a couple of fine bunches on two Mts near here— Pilot and Index—?[1] Am afraid the 9 lb. Springfield wd be too heavy to lug up mtsides— Know damned well it will be! What do you advise? one of the 6.5 mm Manlichers? Could G. and H. [Griffin & Howe] put on a Scope and sight it in for 200 yds? Could you pick out a good 6.5 for me at Abercrombies? Would it be accurate? Will it take a G.H. mount and 2 ½ scope such as I have on Springfield? If get it will want one of those sole leather cases as on my Springfield—

I'm afraid to order a 7 M.M. on Springfield action from G.H for fear he wouldnt have it done in time— Would love to have a good short light one but seems like a lot of money if the Mannlicher is O.K. What would G. and H. charge? I want it for a saddle gun and to carry climbing way up— This is grand sheep country—many big rams—

Lots of woodchucks eating clover and oats to practice on— Stream still muddy from heavy cloudbursts— Caught 10 yesterday but had to use a spinner on the fly— All cut throats—

Would you ask A and F. [Abercrombie & Fitch] if and when you are in to send me a Tackle and Gun and Ammunition catalogue— I may stay out through Oct. Saw a good big moose—nice head still in velvet— Elk still high up— Lots of bear— You can see sheep with glasses from the ranch— Ranch at 6800 feet—

What about those glasses? Do you want me to send a check— Have had no mail since July 2nd at Piggott—

Hope everything is fine with you—

Best to you always—

Hemmy.

Nordquist tells me most sheep shot at between 50 and 200 yds— Says you can get very close sometimes—

PUL, ALS; postmark: COOKE / MONT., JUL / 21 / PM. / 1930

1 Located in Park County, Wyoming, just to the east of Yellowstone National Park, Pilot Peak (elevation 11,708 feet) and Index Peak (11,699 feet) form part of the Absaroka Range.

To Maxwell Perkins, 24 July [1930]

c/o Lawrence Nordquist

Cooke City

Montana

July 24

Dear Max:—

Mail only once a week here— If you want to wire send it c/o Lawrence Nordquist—Painter—Wyo— There is a ranger phone in that direction—

The I.O.T. came just now from Piggott— I am going too well on my new book [*DIA*] now to stop and flay dead horses— Have done 700 to 1200 words a day every day since I got here—July 14—except one—

But if you will send me a copy of 3 stories and 10 poems and the number of the Little Review that Mr. and Mrs. Elliott appeared in I will copy them out, correct and mark the book as soon as I am stalled on the present book or have a rainy day— But do not want to interrupt this one to go back—

I do not think much of putting in another piece beside the original matter— The Up in Michigan was originally included [*EH insertion*: So it should be in]—will look at the other piece when it comes through— But doubt if will include it— Maybe it is all right but cant tell without trying it and if it does not make the book better will certainly not include it.

About grouping the Chapters together = Max <u>please believe me</u> that those chapters are where they belong— They make a complete unit by themselves—sure—but in The In Our Time as issued by Liveright they <u>belong where they are as they are</u>— Later on some time we can make the In Our Time as issued in Paris—[1]

You can borrow the 3 and 10 from Capt. Cohn— As well as The Little Review— They can be sent carefully packed registered to the Cooke City address if anyone is worried about them and I will take good care of them and send them back— I think Capt. C. will be willing to loan them for this—

In August, I believe, when the A.F.T.A. royalties are due will you please have the check split up as follows— If is not too much trouble—

First deduct what I owe the retail dept:

according to their bill it is $543.97—

$243.^{97} of this is books I have bought

$300 is billed as letters from me to Walsh purchased by them and delivered to you—

By the way since I am billed for this will you please return me the letter I wrote to you as a first payment in kind on these letters— Ill pay the cash and cancel the obligation—

2nd will you please send a check for $921^{00} to G.A. Pfeiffer 113 West 18th Street mentioning that it is sent at my request.

3rd will you split the balance due me into 2 checks—(1) for $7,000^{00} and the other for the balance?

I plan to stay here until I get the book finished— Will pass up N.Y. for this fall— Am spending too much money and interrupting my work travelling—

Oh yes—one thing more— Mr. Whitney Darrow told me the retail dept had 2 copies of the limited edition of Farewell to A's they were holding at $20— He said he thought they would sell them to me somewhat cheaper— perhaps, if on no other basis, on that of my being a good customer.[2] I'd appreciate it if you would have these books bought for me and sent to Piggott marked—To Be Held—<u>Not To Be Forwarded to Montana</u>—

Hope your hay fever is not too bad and that you have a good vacation— I hope everything is fine with you and that your family is all well— This is a good place and not getting mail is a hell of a fine thing and very good for working— Havent seen a paper since July 10—am in best shape, physically etc in years— Hope to get book all finished except appendices which I can work on anywhere—

About the In Our Time— I want it to be the book as I wrote it and as it was intended to be published— That is its only value— I will not doctor it up for any other purpose—

Yours always—

Ernest—

When you write Scott give him my love—

Tell him I'd write him but am working and cant write anything else—

Tell him we're all fine—

Havent heard from Waldo— Sorry to hear he's broke— Wish to hell we were all broke the same way— Somebody ought to kick his ass about money and models—[3]

PUL, ALS

1 In a letter of 1 July 1930, Perkins wrote that he had sent a copy of *IOT* to Piggott so EH could revise it and suggested that in the Scribner's reissue "it might be wise to rearrange the book so that all the original 'In Our Time' [*iot*] pieces, with the new one, came together under a half title, perhaps at the beginning of the book" (PUL).

2 Whitney Darrow (1881–1970), a Princeton graduate who had joined the sales staff at Charles Scribner's Sons in 1917 and became its sales manager by 1924.

3 In a letter to EH from Paris of 15 May, Peirce had written that his divorce from Ivy would be costly. He also mentioned Chantal, Alzira, and his new "goil friend" Gilberte, a model for French painter André Derain who also had posed for Pat Morgan (JFK).

To Louis Henry Cohn, 29 July [1930]

July 29

Dear Capt. Cohn:

Thanks for the letter [*EH insertion*: came today] and wire for my birthday. Damned nice of you to wire— Mail only comes here once a week—wires the same—unless wires sent via Cody when they are telephoned in to Ranger Station—[1]

Am going very well in my book—

Wrote several days ago about a matter to Max that he will probably speak to you abt—The loan of the text of Up in Mich and original Elliott— I would take good care and return them if you were willing—

Titus said nothing to me about pamphlets— I will write Titus for 2 and give you one— I wrote the introduction to please Kiki—look at a couple of the photographs of her in old days and youll see why— But would not have written it if it was not, in parts, [*EH insertion*: the early childhood and [first] Quarter] a damned fine extraordinary book— Read it in French—[2]

Max didnt get IOT. from Liv. [Liveright] He had tried to for a couple of years— Dont let him think he did J'ai fait ca[3]

I am staying here until finish my book— Maybe Nov.

My book trunk hasnt come yet and the Mss. is in it— Will send it when it comes—[4]

Please Keep the Russian address for me—[5] Thank you so much for the offer of the Galsworthys Conrad but it is doubtless too valuable for you to give— I'll take the Scotch or Rye and let the first editions go—nor heed the rumble of the distant drum—[6]

Did you know Kiki— Did you ever see her bare? Did you once see Shelley plain and did he stop and speak to you? I'd rather have seen Kiki than Shelley—[7]

Best to you always—
Ernest Hemingway.

[*On verso, Cohn's typewritten questions (here italicized) and EH's handwritten responses:*]

Vaguely I recall that you were one of the signers of a letter protesting against the piracy of Joyce's "Ulysses" by that lousy crook Roth. Do you remember where that letter of protest was first published?
[*EH:*]

No.[8]

By the way, I heard that Roth is doing time in Atlanta and will be collared on another charge when he gets out.[9] When I spoke to you about copyrighting the poems from Der Querschnitt if possible, I had birds like that in mind. There is one operating now up in St. Paul under the name of the Casanova

Book Shop. He just got out a pirated thing of Siegfried Sassoon's—the
suppressed letter poem in Robert Graves' "Good-bye to all that."[10]
[*EH:*]

Probably we should copyright them. But in edition of not over 10 copies.

If you have any scheme for copyrighting the Querschnitt poems let me
know—

[*EH underlined Cohn's words* "By the way, I heard that Roth is doing time in
Atlanta" *and commented as follows:*]

If am glad to hear anybody in jail it would be Roth—will tell you an
interesting yarn about him sometime. Might as well write it. It's not very
interesting without the dressing. When I was in N.Y in winter of 192(?) to
arrange for S. Also publication. He offered me $250 to reprint Up In
Michigan in his 2 Worlds Mo. I refused. He then said he would print it
anyway getting it photostated from Pub Library (I dont know which one).
I said OK. but I would promise him entirely extra legally to beat the shit out
of him and would make a trip to N.Y to do So. He never printed it altho
he announced several times—once in an ad in The Nation—stuff To come
by me.[11]

UDel, ALS and TN questionnaire responses; postmark: COOKE. / MONT., JUL / 30
/ P M. / 1930

EH's letter is written on the verso of the typewritten questionnaire Cohn had enclosed in his
letter to EH of 21 July 1930 (UDel).

1 EH's thirty-first birthday was 21 July 1930. In his letter of that date, Cohn said he had tried
to wire greetings to EH's Cooke, Montana, address, but Western Union claimed to know
of no such town in Montana.
2 Cohn wrote that Bennett Cerf had just returned from Paris with an eight-page "copyright
pamphlet" containing EH's introduction to *Kiki's Memoirs*, given to him by Edward Titus.
After Titus refused to sell another pamphlet to Cerf, saying only twenty copies had been
printed, Cohn sought EH's help in persuading Titus to sell him a copy for his collection.
Alice Prin's memoir was originally published in French as *Les Souvenirs de Kiki* (1929),
with photographs by Man Ray (né Emmanuel Radnitsky, 1890–1976).
3 *J'ai fait ça*: I did that (French).
4 Cohn had asked if EH would send him the page of unpublished manuscript EH had
offered in his previous letter (24 June), as Cohn was "having all the cuts made very
shortly."
5 Cohn reported that Dos Passos had sent him the name and address of a man in Russia
whom EH could consult about Russian royalties.

6 Cohn, who collected first editions of the works of English novelist and playwright John Galsworthy (1867–1933), had offered EH "a copy of that limited edition of Galsworthy's TWO ESSAYS ON CONRAD." Cohn also wrote that he had a birthday gift for EH but could not send it "because it might leak, or break, and Uncle Sam would pinch me if he caught me sending it." EH alludes to *The Rubaiyat of Omar Khayyam*, translated by Edward FitzGerald (1809–1883) and published in English in 1859: "Some for the Glories of This World; and some / Sigh for the Prophet's Paradise to come; / Ah, take the Cash, and let the Promise go, / Nor heed the rumble of the distant Drum!"

7 EH alludes to the poem "Memorabilia" (1855) by Robert Browning (1812–1889), which refers to Percy Bysshe Shelley (1792–1822) in the opening lines: "Ah, did you once see Shelley plain, / And did he stop and speak to you? / And did you speak to him again? / How strange it seems, and new!"

8 Samuel Roth (1893–1974), publisher of the American literary magazines *Two Worlds* (1925–1926) and *Two Worlds Monthly* (1926–1927) and notorious literary pirate. Without permission, Roth reprinted portions of James Joyce's "Work in Progress" (later *Finnegans Wake* [1939]) in *Two Worlds* (September 1925–September 1926) and published a bowdlerized serialization of Joyce's *Ulysses* in *Two Worlds Monthly* (July 1926–October 1927). EH was among 167 artists and writers who signed "An International Letter of Protest" against the piracy of *Ulysses*. First printed in Paris by Sylvia Beach as a broadside dated 2 February 1927 and circulated to press agencies, the letter was reprinted in *The Humanist* and *transition* as well as in the *New York Herald Tribune Books* (6 March 1927, 21; facsimile reproduced in Bruccoli and Baughman *Mechanism*, 9–10). Undeterred, Roth published the complete *Ulysses* in 1929, introducing corruptions into the text.

9 Roth was convicted on state and federal obscenity charges and sentenced to several months' imprisonment in 1928 and in 1930; he later served two longer terms (1936–1939 and 1956–1961), spending a total of nine years in jails in New York and Pennsylvania.

10 Graves had included Siegfried Sassoon's "letter poem" ("Dear Roberto") in his autobiographical *Goodbye to All That* (London: Jonathan Cape, 1929), but when Sassoon objected, Cape excised the poem from late copies of the book's first printing. Shortly thereafter, an unauthorized edition of "A Suppressed Poem" was published in London as a four-page leaflet in fifty numbered copies by "The Unknown Press" and dated on the cover "A 1919 D." The Casanova Booksellers in Milwaukee, Wisconsin, founded in 1927 by Harry W. Schwartz (c. 1903–1984) and Paul Romaine (1906–1986), also brought out an unauthorized printing of "A Suppressed Poem."

11 In 1926 Roth had advertised that EH's work would appear in *Two Worlds Monthly*, but nothing by EH ever appeared in the magazine.

To Waldo Peirce, [c. late July 1930]

Care Lawrence Nordquist

L-T ranch

Cooke City

Montana

Muy Waldo Mío:—

Pauline says <u>not</u> Dr. Bove under any circumstances. The class of the maternity line medics is a Dr. Saint Something or other— You will recognize it instantly— A very high flown name— We've tried to recall it all day ever since your letter came— But it it starts with Saint— Archie could tell you— Anybody can tell you—

Think you are probably playing it right— Damned good luck go with you and all our best to A. Good hunting to you—[1]

I'd hoped you'd be able to come out here and spend the fall with me— Plenty of elk, Deer, Mt. Sheep— Best trout fishing in the world— No kidding— Am going to stay until book is done or dung—

Good luck kid I hope this gets to you in time—only one mail a week here— Thats what delayed your letter—

Pauline sends all her best to you and to A.

tu amigo

Ernesto

Colby, ALS

1 Peirce had left for Paris in late February, and Alzira probably joined him there when she left Key West in late May; their twin sons would be born in France in October. EH refers to the eminent French obstetrician Gabriel Bouffe de Saint-Blaise (b. 1862), who in the 1920s was head of obstetries at the Hôpital Saint Antoine, Paris, and whose publications were widely quoted in international medical literature. Ada MacLeish may have seen an obstetrician in Paris while pregnant with Peter, who was born shortly after the MacLeish family returned to the United States from France in 1928.

To Maxwell Perkins, 31 July 1930

July 31—1930

Dear Max:—

Have just rec'd a copy of The Sun Also in Grossett and Dunlop edition very kindly sent me by Mr Whitney Darrow. The book is gotten up very handsomely and at a dollar ought to effectively put the original edition out of business.[1]

Would you be so good as to ask Mr. Darrow or someone having influence with G. and D. to ask them to at once remove that biographical <u>crap</u> i.e.

SHIT about me on the back wrapper explaining to G. and D. what my position is about personal publicity and telling them for me that unless that material comes off all the wrappers immediately and any reference to war service or my private life such as marriage etc removed I will never publish another book with G. and D. So HeLp Me GoD. I do not blame G. and D. for putting it on— If it was served out to them— But what I want is for them to take it off—

It is no good my trying to keep my private life out of things and avoid bullshit publicity if it is then to be spread in mass production.

Yours Always

Ernest.

None of that was ever put out by me at any time— If you remember your original biographical material was gotten out of Scott [Fitzgerald] and was as accurate as most things gotten from Scott when tight—and because publishers get that lousy sort of crap from their authors everyone thinks I gave it to you— I tell you [*EH insertion*: (this sort of thing)] it takes any possible pleasure out of writing—

PUL, ALS

1 New York publisher Grosset & Dunlap published *SAR*, priced at $1.00, as part of the Grosset & Dunlap Novels of Distinction series in September 1930 (Hanneman A6C).

To Frieda Inescort Redman, 31 July [1930]

July 31

c/o Lawrence Nordquist

Cooke City

Montana

Dear Mrs. Redman:

I'm sorry not to have gotten your letter sooner—but it was forwarded several times and there is only one mail a week up here.

A man named Stalling, Lawrence Stallings—has made the play and Al Woods is the producer. I haven't a thing to say about it or to do with it and have heard nothing about it except that Stallings has the script done (I haven't read it) and Woods is rumored to be enthusiastic about it. They would be the ones to see if you still want to play the Catherine.[1] A word from me would do you no good and might do harm as I think they know I haven't been to the theatre twice in ten years. This an apology, not a boast!

I'm awfully glad that you and your husband liked the book. I wish we had been at Pamplona with you. It's the first one I've missed in 9 years—this letter is getting ~~damned~~ very statistical. I hope it was good and that you had a fine time. Tocon should have been good if nothing else was—[2] Felix Rodriguez, the kid who was so good last year, has been pretty bad with the ~~Scribner for syphyllis~~ and they write me he has gone off very badly—[3]

I wish you best luck with Woods and Stallings— Will try to get this off in the morning mail and hope you get it in Paris—though it's of no use— I wish I could do something—but it's better to say I can't than pretend I can—

Please remember me to Mr. Redman.[4]

Yours very truly

(signed) Ernest Hemingway

PUL, Typewritten transcription of EH letter

This transcription of EH's letter, preserved in the Carlos Baker Collection at PUL, bears the notation in Baker's hand "Received from Mrs. Ben Ray Redman, 8640 Lookout Mt., Los Angeles 46, California."

1 In a letter of 1 July 1930, actress Frieda Inescort Redman had written to Laurence Stallings from Paris, saying she had heard he was adapting *FTA* for the stage and asking, "Can you by any happy chance see me as Catherine?" (Wake Forest). On 20 July 1930 the *New York Times* reported that "a leading woman for Mr. Stallings's dramatization of 'A Farewell to Arms' continues to be one of the chief concerns of the Woods office" ("Gossip of the Rialto," X1). Austrian-born Elissa Landi (1904–1948) would ultimately play Catherine Barkley in Stallings's adaptation, opening on Broadway on 22 September 1930.
2 Saturio Torón (1898–1937) was promoted to the rank of matador in Pamplona on 8 July 1930. Injured by his second bull of that afternoon, he had to cancel two additional corridas scheduled in Pamplona. Frequently gored, he would renounce the rank of matador in 1933.
3 During the 1929 season, Félix Rodríguez Ruiz performed in sixty-five bullfights, but in 1930, weakened by syphilis, he managed only twenty-six performances. Rodríguez would be gored in 1931 and retire the following year.
4 Ben Ray Redman (1896–1961), American writer, editor, and literary critic. He and Frieda met in New York City while she was working as an assistant at the Putnam Publishing Company, where he was assistant editor, and they married in 1926. The couple moved to Hollywood when he took a job as a writer and literary advisor at Universal Studios.

To Maxwell Perkins, 6 August 1930

NA182 8=CODY WYO 6 1120A

MAXWELL E PERKINS, CHARLES SCRIBNER SONS=

597 FIFTH AVE=

=THANKS VERY MUCH HATED AWFULLY TO BOTHER YOU=

    ERNEST.

PUL, Cable; Western Union destination receipt stamp: 1930 AUG 6 PM 1 41

Upon receiving EH's letter of 31 July complaining about the "biographical crap" on the jacket of *SAR*, Perkins had written to F. L. Reed of Grosset & Dunlap concerning the "enraged letter" he had from EH requesting that "if there is anything reassuring I can tell him from you, please for Heaven's sake let me know" (PUL). Reed responded on 6 August that the firm would "immediately reprint new jackets for this title and destroy those that have already been printed" (PUL). Perkins cabled EH that same day: "No Suns have been or will be sold with jacket as it is stop All destroyed" (PUL).

To Hemingway Family, [early to mid-August 1930]

c/o Lawrence Nordquist

Cooke City—Montana

Dear Family:—

Glad to hear you are all well and everything O.K. Have been working very hard and consequently not writing letters. Carol's present is still enroute. Hasnt come yet. We'll have to get her something else— Tell her to expect it for some time but it will come finally.

Thanks for the birthday wishes and invitation to Windemere—[1] Wish we could come but it is impossible—

Bumby, Pauline and I are here until Sept. 15 anyway— I may stay until my work is finished—am sick of moving around—

Rc'd picture of Carol taken in K.C. but Couldnt like it even with much effort— Tell her I like a girl or woman to be good looking as well as intelligent— She is both and no sense to sacrifice the first to make the 2nd more obvious.

Hope you all have a fine summer—

Excuse brevity of letter and lack of general correspondence but when working cant write letters— Had to write so many this winter that ruined my work— Am sticking to work for a while—

We are all in best of health etc.

Yours always
Ernie

PSU, ALS

1 EH's sister Carol's birthday was 19 July, EH's was 21 July, and Pauline's was 22 July. The letter to which EH is responding has not been located.

To Maxwell Perkins, 12 August [1930]

August 12—

Dear Max:—

Have gone over the I.O.T. also the Up In Michigan. I've rewritten it to try and keep it from being libelous but to do so takes all its character away. It clearly refers to two people in a given town, both of them still alive, still living there and easily identified— If I take the town away it loses veracity—[1] But I can leave out enough of the first part to eliminate libel. However I know you will not publish it with the last part entire and if any of that is cut out there is no story.

I do not feel much like getting into a libel action or being suppressed now for the skin of a dead horse. The Farewell was worth making a fight on and I was willing to make it and take whatever came but this is an old story, one of the first I ever wrote, and I've published it once as I wrote it and do not feel like stirring up trouble with it now when I'm working.

What I would suggest is that you get Edmund Wilson, if he is willing, to write an introduction to the In Our Time. He is, of all critics or people, the one who has understood best what I am working at and I know an introduction by him would be of much value to the book as you are getting it out now. As I understand it you are getting it out somewhat as a new book i.e. you want new material from me and it is not fair to do this without explanation since it is not new but my first and earliest book. I'll be damned

344

if I will write a preface but Wilson, if he would, could write what it would need as an introduction. If he wouldnt care to it would be better to have none— Allen Tate might write one— He is a good critic but Wilson knows my stuff very well and writes so damned well and it would be a shame not to have him do it if he were willing.[2]

Please let me know what you think of this—

I know I am not going in for putting out books because there should be something from me on the Scribners list— The Our Time is, I really believe, a hell of a good book [*EH insertion*: The stories, when I read them now, are as good as ever.] and worth anyones two dollars but I am not going to jazz it up with any things of another period and try to make it sell as a new book— If you could publish the Up In Michigan without any trouble O.K. But show it to anyone and ask them. I'd like to have it published so people could see Morley's source book[3] but its not worth getting into trouble over when I am still able to write and am writing— What it needs [*EH insertion*: The In Our Time] is a good introduction— What you are doing is making it really available for the first time to the people who have read the other books— I am too busy, too disinterested, too proud or too stupid or whatever you want to call it to write one for it. If you can get Wilson to it would be excellent— He is a damned fine critic of prose and he writes well— I believe that is the way it should be published—my 1st book, now made generally available with an introduction by Wilson.

Anyway I will return the book to you with a few corrections, the original Mr. and Mrs. Elliott, and with or without a couple of short pieces of the same period depending on how these seem in the book between now and then—not later than the 1st week in September.

However we had better figure out a formula to put in the front about no living persons which will absolutely prevent libel as there are three people who might, if they were in desperate enough straits and the book sufficiently prominent try a libel action.[4] The reason most of the book seems so true is because most of it is true and I had no skill then, nor have much now, at changing names and circumstances. Regret this very much.

Am going well on the new book [*DIA*]— Have something over 40,000 words done— Have worked well 6 days of every week since got here— Have 6 more cases of beer good for 6 more chapters— If I put in an expense account on this bull fight book it would be something for the accounting Dept to study.

The checks came and your letter with them— Thanks ever so much—also for the telegram about G. and D. jacket— I hated like hell to bother you about that— You have enough to worry about without Grossett and Dunlop— I'm so sorry to hear bad news of Scott— Please let me know what you hear and let me know <u>anything</u> you think of that I can do— I'd go over if you think it would do any good—[5]

Best to you always— Please if I speak rudely in letters never take it personally— I'm working damned hard and a letter about some bloody problem or other is only a damned interruption and curse. Dont let me get on your nerves— We'll have a good time in March at Tortugas!

Yours always

Ernest

PUL, ALS

1 In one of the surviving typescripts of "Up in Michigan" at JFK, several characters share the exact names of people EH had known in Horton Bay, including the blacksmith Jim Dilworth, Liz Buell (the maiden name of Jim Dilworth's wife, Elizabeth), and A. J. Stroud (Item 800). On another typescript (headed with the address 74 Cardinal Lemoine, EH and Hadley's first residence in Paris, 1922-1923), EH has crossed out some characters' last names, changing "Jim Dilworth" to "Jim Gilmore" and "Liz Buell" to "Liz Coates," the names that appear in *TSTP* (JFK, Item 799). Paul Smith identifies a third typescript (Item 798) as EH's summer 1930 attempt to revise and expurgate the narrative to make it suitable for the Scribner's 1930 reissue of *IOT* [3–4]). EH's markings in a copy of *TSTP* (1923), now in the Cohn Collection at the University of Delaware, further evidence his attempts at revision for republication as he changed "Jim Gilmore" to "Jim Dutton," "Liz Coates" to "Mary Coates," and deleted or emended some sexually explicit references (*TOTTC*, 145). "Up in Michigan" would not appear in the 1930 Scribner's edition of *IOT*. It was finally republished in *FC* (1938) in a form nearly identical to that in which it had originally appeared in print in 1923.
2 The 1930 Scribner's edition of *IOT*, released on 24 October, would include an introduction by Edmund Wilson. Wilson had favorably reviewed EH's first two books, *TSTP* and *iot*, in the October 1924 *Dial*.
3 EH had been irritated by critical comparisons of his work and Callaghan's, such as R. P. Blackmur's declaration that Callaghan's first novel, *Strange Fugitive*, was "very much in the Chicago-Paris-Hemingway measure of hardboiled realism" (*Hound & Horn*, July-September 1929, 439).

4 The 1930 Scribner's *IOT* included the disclaimer that "there are no real people in this volume: both the characters and their names are fictitious. If the name of any living person has been used, the use was purely accidental" (Hanneman, 9).

5 In his 1 August letter, Perkins wrote that he was "dividing up the royalty as you directed" and enclosed two checks. Perkins confided his worry about Fitzgerald, quoting a letter from Scott saying that "Zelda is still sick as Hell" and Scott himself felt "somewhat harrassed and anxious about life." Perkins wrote to EH, "I sometimes even think of going over there,—but I never could do anything with him anyhow,—and anyhow, what's to be done?" (PUL).

To Milford Baker, 12 August [1930]

August 12

Dear Bake:—

Thanks for your three excellent letters.[1] Have been working like a horse and also waiting for your final verdict on the Sheep gun to write—

Of course I'd like to shoot them with my Springfield but it is damned hard climbing and I'm afraid I'd get too pooped with the big gun— So I'd better get the Mannlicher—6.5— If you think that a better bet than the 7. mm.

I tried one in Abercrombie Fitch and the stock seemed a good deal too short— Wouldnt That bring the scope too near my eye? Anyway I'll get it and Pauline can always use it when we shoot big game together— So will you get me the 6.5—with sling strap—scope—case—scope case?

Would it be possible for you to sight in the scope for me for 200 yards? I'm afraid I'd never get it right. I suppose it would vary some between you and me but I could find how much it shot off and allow or if it was too much try to correct it— When you buy the gun—or ship it rather—could you have them pack in a cleaning rod and 300 rounds soft nosed cartridges?

Express address is c/o Lawrence Nordquist

Gardiner—Montana.

Would you get me the 8x glasses too? If they want to send the glasses right away I'll be glad to have them— The Cooke City address is OK. for parcel post—

I enclose check for $220.$\underline{^{00}}$ Let me know if that doesnt cover it—

You would like this country I believe— If you should decide you would want to come and hunt let me know and I'll make all arrangements— You

347

know how glad I'd be to see you— The sheep hunting might entail too much climbing— But Elk—deer—bear—dont need that—

Cloudbursts have put the river on the bum for a week— I'm working hard on my book—

My God you are a damned fine woodchuck shot—

Best to you always and thanks eternally for the constant trouble you take—

Hemmy—

PUL, ALS; postmark: [COOKE] / MONT., AUG / 15 / 10AM / 1930

1 Baker's letters of 14 July, 29 July, and 6 August offered advice, information, and prices for firearms and accessories of interest to EH (PUL).

To Archibald MacLeish, [c. early to mid-August 1930]

c/o Lawrence Nordquist
Cooke City
Montana.

Dear Archie:—

How would you like to go to Africa to hunt and see the country? We'll kill all the dangerous ones and have a fine time— See the jigs, the country all the birds and beasts You and me and Mike and Charles— Leave next May—the end of it—or 1st of June— Be in Africa 3 months— Uncle Gus is financing it and it's all settled and It's just you, and the two other merchants and old Pappy— You wont have to spend a sou after we leave N.Y. This is a formal invitation, all expenses paid N.Y to N.Y.[1]

I know no reason why you cant you bastard. It will be swell for work and we ought to see the world before we die. Us 4 can have a good time on the boat and the whole time— What do you say kid. It's all settled

You can save yr. income or let Ada spend it while yr. gone— It is really a way to save money because you will be withdrawn from circulation for 5 mos. or so— Mike and Charles can go—yr the last man tapped for Bones— Buffalo bones— Lion bones—[2]

We'll go and purify ourselves with a little danger then and not shoot the lions until we can smell their breath—if they ve been drinking we'll spare them—

If you want to go why the hell dont you come out here in Sept? I'm staying through on into Oct. Not coming east at all till my book is finished— There is the best trout fishing in the world— I caught 6 successive doubles and then a triple— Big fish in wonderful fast water— Smash your tackle— Can see Mt. Sheep from the ranch— Deer tracks all along the river— Hunting season opens Sept 15th— Many elk— We saw a bear on the road yesterday coming home from fishing— Come on out and you can get in good practice with a rifle— We'll go after Mt. Sheep Sept 15th—

It's the loveliest country you've ever seen— An open valley with Mts like around Pamplona— I've never worked better— Work <u>swell</u> everyday— We could drive home by Piggott— I'll loan you the dough—to come— You come on the train to Gardiner—Mont. Pauline and Bumby leave Sept. 15th— She is going to take Henriette and Bumby to N.Y. If you came out for Sept. you could work a.ms. and we could fish p.ms. until 15th— Then can hunt—

I'll be all alone—ranch will be deserted—

Anyway you are going to go to Africa— All you have to furnish is a Springfield rifle— I have a guy will get it made and fitted when you give me yr. measurements— We'll pick up big 2nd guns out there— Ada wont have to worry—we can hunt together and you will undoubtedly get to be a classy shot but anyway I am a trick shot (modest old Hem) and will shoot her initials in the charging brutes— What we want is to see the country— Maybe Uncle Gus isnt a swell fellow to do this—

We'll all have a swell time knowing it isnt a part of life wasted and if you get low about working I will bust a rifle over yr. head— If you never wrote another thing your God damned <u>name would live forever</u> with at least 3 of the poems in the book. Ill take no more complaints from you you bum[.] Youre in the big time now and you have to accept the same lot as the late Shakespeare, Mr. Marvell, and the rest of us boys—i.e. death, and you have to accept it because youre going to get it but we'll go to Africa in the meantime

Pappy—

Since I've accepted it I'm swell— They cant scare you in the night and if your father's ghost comes fuck yr. fathers ghost— Well put a sword through him and see what hes made of—[3]

Pauline wrote a long letter to you and to Ada about your book— But tore it up because it is so fine that anything you say turns out shit—

LOC, ALS

1 EH, Pauline, and Charles Thompson would arrive in Mombasa on 8 December 1933 to begin the much delayed safari. MacLeish and Strater would not join EH in Africa.
2 Skull and Bones, a prestigious secret society restricted to seniors at Yale University, established in 1832. In its annual Tap Day ritual, the society selects fifteen undergraduates for membership. Particular honor is reserved for "the last man tapped," who in May 1914 had been MacLeish.
3 The prologue to MacLeish's 1928 poem *The Hamlet of A. MacLeish* begins, "No man living but has seen the king his father's ghost." In the last section the following line is twice repeated: "It is time we should accept."

To Henry Strater, [25 August 1930]

Swell you hooked one Kid— It was a grand letter— Why cant you and Charles come here to hunt? Season opens Sept 16— I saw 12 Mt Sheep— Many big rams here— Elk and deer guaranteed— Bear too— Jai tué un ours avant hier qui a mangé douze vache! 2 coups de fusil[1]—offhand 105 yards— Deadern hell— Youse guys would have wonderful hunting here in fall— Nobody else will be hunting—

Best Sheep hunting in States—

Stream in wonderful shape for trout Full of rainbows and cutthroat Bite like grunts!

Love to Maggie—
Hem.

If you come Ill stay through October— Guarantee Shots at Sheep—elk— deer—bear— Guarantee swell trout fishing—

PUL, A Postcard S; verso: photograph of stream, meadow, and trees; postmark: COOKE / ADDRESS / MONT., AUG / 25 / 19[30]

1 I killed a bear day before yesterday that ate 12 cows! 2 gun shots (French).

To John Herrmann, [c. 31 August 1930]

Care Lawrence Nordquist
Cooke City
Montana

Dear John:—

Which book is it kid? You write the blurb for the book and send it to me and I'll try and improve on it. I'll write something about you in general too. Is it the one about the Salesman?[1]

Damn glad Maxie Dead Pan took the story—[2] He hasnt written me in a month— Maybe I insulted him or something— Hope not—

Am on page 170 of my book— Never been in better shape—never gone better— Going to stay here thru October— Went on a bear hunt and horse got crazy and bolted through timber— Had my gun in scabbard on saddle and was afraid to let him go for fear he'd smash it[.] So stayed on too long and got my pan all cut to hell—

Scar like this—stitches just out— Morley [Callaghan]

will probably claim he gave it to me— Killed 2 damn big old boar bear— Killed one with one shot—other 2—at 85 and 100 yds. They had eaten over 20 head of stock in last 2 mos. Stockmen claimed they killed them but that probably horshit— Stock could die of poison and then bears eat them— But anyway we ate the bears— When it gets cold I'll ship you a quarter of elk. I'll sign it in the rectum and you can sell it as an original Hemingstein—

We're terribly sorry Jo [Herbst] has been sick— Give her our best love and I hope to hell she is much better—

Will sign the Mss anywhere it means the most dough—

Give me the dope on the book—

Yours always—
Hem.

UT, ALS

1 Dos Passos had been trying to help Herrmann find a publisher for his second novel (with the working title *Woman of Promise*) and had written to EH the previous summer to say he might be asking EH to write "a note to some damn publisher or another about it" (1 July 1929, JFK). Herrmann's letter to EH requesting a blurb remains unlocated. EH would send a blurb to Herrmann in his letter of 28 September [1930]. EH's endorsement would be quoted in advertisements for Herrmann's novel, published as *Summer Is Ended* (New York: Covici, Friede, 1932). Herrmann's third and last novel would be *The Salesman* (New York: Simon & Schuster, 1939).
2 Herrmann's story "The Man Who Had Two Stars" had been accepted by *Scribner's Magazine* (Herrmann to Perkins, 21 August 1930, PUL) and would be published in the August 1931 issue.

To Archibald MacLeish, [c. 31 August 1930]

Dear Archie:—

It's grand you'll go kid and we will have a fine trip—

I wish the hell you could come out here— The East aint for me this fall— I'm on page 170—and I'm fighting it out in this terrain— Have to get this book done and as long as I'm going good in this latitude and longitude it would be bad to shift—

It would be grand to be at Conway and bang around and go to the games— But must stick here thru Oct—then Piggott until after Christmas— We are not too rich just now but that isnt why I cant come— It's just that I cant shift again until I get the book done— Out here mail only once a week—no papers—no news and I have the damned book in my head so that cant even write a letter— But we will have a swell time in Africa and take Charles to Lipps on the way and drink Xeres Seco[1] at the Deux Magots and see the pictures and one thing and another—

I've never been so damned healthy— Ranch lost 20 head of stock killed, or anyway eaten by bear last mo. I went hunting and shot 2 big old males just after Sunset—a week apart— Damned exciting to see them come out of the woods to feed on the carcass— Killed the first one with two shots at 85 yds— So dark could hardly see the sights— The other at 100 yds with one shot— My horse bolted through the timber on the first hunt—was afraid to let him go for fear of busting or losing my gun which was in Scabbard and so stayed on too long— Got all cut up pretty badly—legs—arms—and one like this from my mouth down onto chin— Gives the mouth

an expression, permanent, as though it were saying "Ta hell you say."

Took stitches out a couple of days ago— It was the hell of a bloody nuisance—werry bloody— Funny to be scarred all over and never a mark on the pan and then be cut up by Fairies and Horses—[2]

No dont write Uncle Gus yet— Later on will be fine— I told him I was asking you— You can write him later on— I'll tell you when if you want— He is ~~about~~ the most generous and understanding citizen I know—

I wish the hell you could come out here— I'd love to come to Conway but cant now— Maybe we can come in the Spring before we shove for Africa and shoot a few rounds—

My love to Ada and to you all— Pauline takes Bumby to N.Y to put on the boat in Oct. Maybe you'll be there then.

Maybe you'll go to the Farewell play and tell me how it is— Have you heard who is going to play in it?[3] I havent heard anything— Snow on the hills this morning—we were watching a carcass for bear and a big cow elk came right out and up to within 22 yards of where we sat— Bumby whispered to me— "Is it a camel Papa?"

Love to you all—

Pappy.

Would you forward this letter to Charley Curtis— <u>I have lost his address</u>— Read his book on Africa— It is <u>damned good</u>—[4]

LOC, ALS

1 *Xérès sec*: dry sherry (French); *seco*: dry (Spanish).
2 EH's reference to being "cut up by Fairies" is uncertain but may refer obliquely to his infamous June 1929 boxing bout with Morley Callaghan, which left "a big scar on my lower lip," as EH told Perkins two months later (28 August [1929]). EH also bore a prominent facial scar from an earlier incident in Paris: in March 1928 a bathroom skylight fell and gashed his forehead, requiring stitches.
3 Laurence Stallings's stage adaptation of *FTA*, produced by Al Woods and directed by Rouben Mamoulian (1897–1987), would star Glenn Anders (1890–1981) as Frederic Henry and Elissa Landi as Catherine Barkley.

4 Charles Pelham Curtis, Jr. (1891–1959) and his brother Richard Cary Curtis (1894–1951) wrote *Hunting in Africa East and West* (Boston: Houghton-Mifflin, 1925) about their 1923 safari. Both had attended Harvard Law School with MacLeish, Charles graduating in 1917, two years before MacLeish, and Richard in 1921. The three were also colleagues at the Boston law firm of Choate, Hall and Stewart until 1923, when MacLeish left to write poetry and the Curtis brothers left to establish their own firm. EH would praise the Curtis book as "very honest" in Chapter 10 of *GHOA*.

To Maxwell Perkins, 3 September [1930]

Sept 3

Dear Max:—

Your letter of Aug 18th just came last night due to it going to Painter instead of Cooke City— Glad you saw old John [Herrmann]— Pauline is typing now on the Mr and Mrs. Elliott and I'll send the book to you tomorrow if possible— Dont see how I can conscientiously put anything else in—have tried all day yesterday and this morning—will try again <u>this</u> aft—

Later— Have been working all day on it— The Smyrna chapter can go as an Introduction by The Author— To follow Wilson's introduction. It goes pretty well that way. The original Mr. and Mrs Elliot is enclosed— I hope you could get Bunny [Edmund Wilson] to write the introduction—[1]

Now we must get this straight— The book has been out 5 years and I've had no trouble about it but, also, it has had only a limited circulation so anyone tempted to make trouble ~~would~~ might not have seen it nor thought it worthwhile to do so—

It is not worthwhile for me to now run any danger of trouble, censorship or libel— I'd sooner let the book go out of print— Its done its work and when Im dead they can always revive it if they want—or it can come out in my collected woiks—

So if you bring it out now you bring it out at your own risk— If you change the Elliot you change it at your own risk— You had better put a iron clad protective notice in the front that there are no ~~living~~ actual characters and that the names are not those of any living people— You work out the wording and be responsable for it—

I'm on page 174 of this book I'm writing and have had it knocked out of my head for two days working on this In Our Time again and I've no interest in publishing it now, will take no risks and give no guarantees against libels nor slanders. All I'll guaranty is that Mr and Mrs. Elliots name was not Elliot nor anything like it— But half the other characters in the book have their real [*EH insertion*: Christian] names although there are no other last names—or real last names used and I have fixed up the name in A Very Short Story—[2] So you had best be thoroughly covered—

It is all skinning dead horses to me.

You have seen me worried about possibility of libel and slander in past and nothing has ever happened so it may be all nonsense again. But the above is how I feel about it. I'd rather write this book than get out anything— It is you that want to get the book out— Last Spring I came to N.Y to work and not see anyone and instead just ran around doing business with one jew and another— I <u>have</u> to stick at one thing when I'm writing a book and keep that in my head and nothing else and when I get to worrying and thinking and trying to fix up this old book it gets into my subconscious and buggars up everything— The Example of Scott ought to be evidence enough that a man has to stay in a book in his head until its finished— I dont want excuses for not finishing my present book— <u>I want to ~~finish~~ write it.</u>

Anyway am through with it now and I send the book to you with corrections, the Elliott Mss. and an Introduction By The Author to come after Wilsons Introduction but not to be mentioned on jacket nor in advertising but simply to be included in the book. You can advertise it as "new material" if you like. I've other stories but I've tried them—they break up the book, destroy the unity and being of a different period stand out in a way they shouldnt—

Best to you always—

Yours, in haste—

Ernest

The real reason I wanted to get the book from Liverights for you was so you would have it if you ever wanted to bring out my collected works—a certain number of people are bound to buy whatever book I bring out after the sale of A Farewell— If that sale is pee-ed away on this getting out of In

Our Time then the bull fight book will have to start from scratch again—
Young Thornton harmed the sale of his book <u>enormously</u> by getting out
that collection of 1 act masterpieces[.]³ But then neither the book nor the
masterpieces were of much account anyway. Correct me in this if I am
wrong— But I believe <u>any</u> attempt to bring this out as a new book or as
anything new from me in any way will be altogether harmful[.] That's why
the Wilson introduction is necessary—to make it clear this is an old book
and what sort of an old book!— Most people are ~~so dumb~~ dont follow the
production of litrachoor as we do any any new book out is a new book. But
this is really a <u>damned good book</u> and if they dont buy it under false
pretences they'll get their 2 dollars worth— Maybe 2 and a half.

Please dont think I'm getting to be a bloody crab— Its just that I go
bughouse when I'm interrupted.

[EH writes in the top, left, and right margins of first page:]

<u>Later in the evening.</u>

My God Max I seem to write you the lousiest letters— But if I rewrite this
and make it as decent as I wish it would sound it will take all tomorrow and
the last mail for a week goes at breakfast—

Pauline sends her best and says pay no attention to me. I'm all smashed
up from an accident it would take too long to write about— Have 6 inch
gash in my jaw— But never healthier or in better shape in my life— Killed
two big bear— Maybe its fine to get the book out—what the hell do I
know— I just re-read it and its a damned fine book— Especially the
Battler—Cat In The Rain—Out of Season and the first couple of stories—
Those three I couldnt write any better now.

PUL, ALS

The letter was written in at least three stages over a long day, the first two stages written in
black ink and the letter completed "Later in the evening" in pencil in the top and side margins
of the first page.

1 In his 18 August letter, Perkins had told EH that he would ask Edmund Wilson to write an
introduction to *IOT*. Perkins deemed the book "very great as it stands" and said that EH
need not write anything new for the 1930 Scribner's edition, but suggested that EH could
perhaps "put in things that belong, like that additional 'In Our Time' sketch you read me in
Key West" (PUL). The 1930 edition would include EH's sketch titled "Introduction by the

Author" (retitled "On the Quai at Smyrna" in *FC* [1938]) and "Mr. & Mrs. Elliot," restored to the original form in which it appeared in the Autumn–Winter 1924–1925 *Little Review*.

2 In manuscript "Mr. & Mrs. Elliott" was originally titled "Mr. & Mrs. Smith," a jibe at American expatriate poet Chard Powers Smith (1894–1977) (Smith, 75–79). In "A Very Short Story" the character Luz was originally named "Ag," a reference to Agnes von Kurowsky (1892–1984), the Red Cross nurse with whom EH fell in love in 1918 and who jilted him in 1919.

3 Thornton Wilder's 1927 novel *The Bridge of San Luis Rey* was followed by his 1928 collection of sixteen three-minute plays, *The Angel That Troubled the Waters and Other Plays* (New York: Coward-McCann). EH is mistaken that publication of Wilder's plays hurt sales of his novel: *The Bridge of San Luis Rey* topped the *Publishers' Weekly* list of fiction bestsellers for 1928, and Wilder's next novel, *The Woman of Andros*, would be third on the bestsellers list for 1930.

To Louis Henry Cohn, [3] September [1930]

September 4—[1]
Cooke City—Montana—

Dear Captain Cohn:—

First may I congratulate you on your marriage and wish you and Mrs. Cohn all good luck and happiness.

About the other and very minor things you write of—[2]

There exist handwritten Mss. of nearly all my stories and of The Sun Also and A Farewell, so I dont know where this typescript of The Undefeated hailed from unless it was the one sent to Walsh for This Quarter— If you want me to sign it I'd be glad to if that will make it of any value— If the printing and corrections are not in my handwriting I probably didnt make them—it might be a carbon that someone got hold of and is trying to make some money out of. Perhaps I should see it before you buy it—[3] [*EH drew a line to a heavily cancelled marginal insertion that is indecipherable*]

About the Four Poems— First it is not complete— There was a second part to The Soul of Spain etc. published in Der Querschnitt— 2nd— If it cant be copyrighted without incident and without <u>any</u> copies getting out there seems no sense in publishing it no matter how limited— In Der Querschnitt where they are safelly buried no one is liable to dig them up while if printed and not copyrighted anyone can get them out. I do not wish to have any publicity or stink by now getting out poems written years ago and published only in Germany— So perhaps it would be best to let it drop— You have the one galley proof— I rely on you to pull no more unless you want to pull one for me—and if you have one and I one that is sufficient and perhaps two too many— The galley proof should be worth the cost of setting it up— If it makes no difference to you I'd prefer to have the type pi-ed and the poems left in Der Querschnitt where they belong since the only reason, really, for publishing them now was to prevent them being published.[4]

I am writing Titus again.

Wine of Wyoming I wrote a month or so after I finished A Farewell to Arms— Glad you liked it and that Galsworthy liked the book—[5]

Edgar Mowrer may be on his vacation— Rowohlt is a bad letter writer— But you should hear from both of them— I know that nearly all of In Our Time and several of Men Without Women were published in German periodicals because I had checks for them— The translators were principally a man named Hauser— Great friend of Liam O'Flaherty's and a Frau Anna Marie Horschitz— Rowohlt has her address.[6] Carlo Linati who translates Joyce in Italian has translated stories of mine in IL Convegno of Milan and written reviews of my books in Il Corriere de la Sera of Milan—1 Col. and ½ review I remember—[7]

Ezra Pound has had to do with publishing various things of mine— recently he wrote about some Belgian revue[8]—his address is 12 Via Marsala Int 5—Rapallo—Italy— He always answers letters at once altho he may not answer them politely— Cape writes that A Farewell to Arms has been barred from Sale of importation into Australia whatever that means.[9]

My book trunk did come but did not have the Mss in it I wanted or I would have sent it long ago— It was the first page of a story I'll probably never publish—a story of the Greco-Turkish war of 1921–2 called Death of The Standard Oil Man—[10] If it is imperative that you have it to go to the engravers with and not practical to wait until I get back to Piggott the end of Oct or 1st of November I can send something else. The Mss. that turned up in the book trunk are not particularly interesting— Three or four stories I was working on or wanted to work over— I think you would rather have a page of a damned good story than just a page of Mss. Quelconque.[11]

I thought that story was in the book trunk but after it arrived found I'd put it away in the Safe at Piggott with some others to make more room for stuff I was working on— If one page is as good as another for you write me and I'll send one by return mail—

About Mss.— the last I gave away was to John Herrmann of Erwinna— Pa. a writer and very good friend who wants to keep it but who might well have to sell it— His wife has been ill and I'll give him some more when I get some— If you got in touch with him, he might sell it—

I am on page 174 of my book and going well— Have never been in better health nor worked better. was rather badly cut up two weeks ago—horse bolted through the timber when we were hunting bear which had eaten 20 head of stock in last 2 months— Had 6 stitches to close a cut from the corner of my mouth to the base of jaw bone— I shot two big old male bear— Will stay here until November and not come East this fall—

Hope you enjoy the book shop and have good luck with it It should be a lot of fun.

Give my best to Max when you see him— ~~Today~~ Yesterday, [*EH insertion*: Sept 2,] I received his letter mailed August 18— And again my best congratulations and wishes for great happiness for you

Yours Always
Ernest Hemingway.

New punctuation on face

I'd be curious to know what you paid for the books— I got nothing NOTHING for writing either of them— Either 3 and 10 or the first In Our Time

I asked [Ma]x to give you the corrected copy of In Our Time when it comes back from for the printers if it wd be of any interest to you to have.

UDel, ALS; postmark: COOKE / MONT., SEP / 5 / P M. / 1930

1 The dating of the letter is uncertain, as EH later mentions having received a letter from Perkins "Yesterday, Sept 2."

2 In his letter to EH of 26 August 1930, Cohn wrote that he would marry Marguerite Arnold on 18 September and that they planned to open a bookshop called House of Books, Ltd. in New York City. Cohn wrote that he was acquiring Hemingway items "at fancy prices" and that he would give his Hemingway collection to his wife "so that we will never be tempted to sell it even if business is lousy" (UDel).

3 Cohn wrote he was undecided about buying a typescript of "The Undefeated" with handwritten corrections that did not resemble EH's "ordinary handwriting at all."

4 Cohn had enclosed a set of privately produced galley proofs for an edition titled "Four Poems by Ernest Hemingway." Cohn explained that in order to secure copyright, the collection would have to be put on sale, and he had considered printing a run of twelve copies and making a "phony sale" of all of them to EH. However, Cohn had been told it was doubtful the government would grant copyright "because of some of the words used." The galley proof included four of EH's poems published in *Der Querschnitt*: "The Soul of Spain with McAlmon and Bird the Publishers" (Part One) and "The Earnest Liberal's Lament" (autumn 1924); "The Lady Poets with Footnotes" (November 1924); and "The Age Demanded" (February 1925). It was missing Part Two of "The Soul of Spain with McAlmon and Bird the Publishers" (November 1924). The edition was never published; the manuscript and galley proofs survive in the Cohn Collection at the University of Delaware.

5 In his letter Cohn quoted from a letter he had received from John Galsworthy: "I certainly read Ernest Hemingway's 'Farewell to Arms.' I thought the end portion extraordinarily good. He certainly has great talent and possibilities."

6 EH's story "The Undefeated" was published as "Stierkampf" in *Der Querschnitt* (June and July 1925) in a translation by B. Bessmertny. Heinrich Hauser (1901–1955), German journalist, novelist, photographer and translator, translated O'Flaherty's novels. Rowohlt had published Annemarie Horschitz's translations of *SAR* as *Fiesta* (1928), *MWW* as *Männer* (1929), and *FTA* as *In Einem Andern Land* (1930), and would publish her translation of *IOT* as *In Unserer Zeit* in 1932.

7 A translation of EH's "Soldier's Home" ("Il Ritorno del Soldato") by Italian writer, critic and translator Carlo Linati (1878–1949) appeared in the Milan magazine *Il Convegno: Rivista di Letteratura e di Arte* (30 June–30 July 1925). Linati was a regular columnist for the Milan newspaper *Corriere della Sera*, for which he reviewed *IOT* (4 March 1926).

8 In the summer of 1922, Pound invited EH to contribute to the six-book series called "An Inquest into the State of Contemporary English Prose" that he was editing for Bill Bird's Three Mountains Press; EH's contribution was *in our time* (1924). In the absence of Pound's incoming letter, the Belgian review that EH mentions here remains unidentified.

9 In a letter to EH of [18] July 1930, Cape reported, "Australia has judged your book improper and its sale, publication and importation into that county is prohibited" (URead).

10 Manuscript fragments of this unfinished, unpublished story survive at the JFK. Cohn used a facsimile of the holograph manuscript page EH sent to him as the frontispiece of *A Bibliography of the Works of Ernest Hemingway* (New York: Random House for the House of Books, 1931).

11 *Mss. quelconque*: a mediocre or second-rate manuscript (French).

To Henry Strater, [c. 3–4 September 1930]

Dear Mike:—

I wish to hell you and Charles could come out here to hunt— Take RR. to Gardiner Mont. Stage will bring you to Cooke City— I'll meet you there with horses— If you wire you're coming will have everything set and arranged—

So far I've killed two damned big old cattle eating bear— 1 with one shot—at 90 yards—paced—never moved— The other two shots at 85 yards—paced— Got up after 1st one and I nailed him dead with 2nd—through shoulder—

There are lots of grouse, ducks and geese— <u>Nobody else will be hunting here this fall</u>— Hunting in the mts is more damned fun than anything you can imagine— I saw 12 mt Sheep a week ago— I can guaranty you shots at Elk, deer, bear and Bighorn sheep—wonderful rainbow trout fishing— I caught 28 yest aft between 2.30 and 5.30— All big ones—all on fly—

Am going damned well on my book—page 174— I can shoot the Springfield as well as a shotgun nowPauline and Bumby leave the 13th— I stay on through Oct. Hunting season opens Sept 16 but from then on all through Oct is swell— Charles could get train to Kansas City from there to Gardiner— I wish the hell you'd come— I've got all trout tackle— All you need is your rifles, heavy old clothes—bring plenty of 220 Grain Western Ammunition—

This is the most beautiful country you ever saw— Grizzlies are best training for Africa—only dangerous animal in North America— I'll pay whatever difference it would cost you between Canada and here—

Wire me as soon as you get this if you can come— Wire Care Lawrence Nordquist—Painter—Wyo—

Write Care Lawrence Nordquist

    Cooke City—

    Montana

You must have had the top in excitement with the big tuna— Wish the hell I'd been there—

I've asked Archie to go to Africa too to make a fourth—

Why the hell dont you come out here— It is the best hunting this side of the upper Peace river country—

Licence 60 bucks gives you 1 elk, 1 deer, bear, Game birds and trout— Mountain sheep 15 bucks extra licence. You ought to see the West anyway.

Hope I'll hear you're coming—

Best always—

Hem.

Charles can drive back with me in the car as far as Piggott and get train from there— That will save car fare.

PUL, ALS

Although Baker dates this letter c. 10 September 1930, the conjectured date of c. 3–4 September is based on EH's remark in his 3 September letter to Perkins that the weekly mail would be picked up the following morning and that he was on page 174 of *DIA*, a figure he repeats in this letter to Strater. In his 12 September letters to William and Frances Horne and to Jonathan Cape, EH would report being on page 188.

To Milford Baker, 10 September 1930

12P TR 19

CODY WYO 1055A SEPT 10 1930

MILFORD BAKER

609 ATLANTIC BLDG

BAKE HAS GUN BEEN SHIPPED EXPRESS ADDRESS CARE NORDQUIST GARDINER MONTANA STOP TELEGRAMS CODY WYOMING BEST REGARDS AND THANKS

HEMINGWAY

134P

PUL, Cable

In letters of 22 and 28 August 1930, Baker had reported on the progress of his efforts to have a 6.5 Mannlicher rifle customized and shipped to EH by Griffin & Howe (PUL). Baker would respond to EH's query the same day, cabling back: "GUN COMPLETED READY TO SHIP WILL BE TARGETED THURSDAY SHIPPED FRIDAY" [12 September] (PUL).

To Jonathan Cape, 12 September [1930]

c/o Lawrence Nordquist
Cooke, Montana
September 12—

Dear Cape:—

I'd be glad to have the 167 odd pounds paid into my £ account in the Guaranty Trust, Paris any time you wish. Ask them to please keep the sum in £ as I lost quite a bit the last time on it being changed into francs and then back into the dollar.

About the Travellers library—a selection of stories is all right if you have Edward Garnett make the selection— Although I do not believe Men Without Women would do badly in the Travellers library— What advance can you give me on a selection?[1]

Am on page 188 of my new book and going damned well—bagged 2 big bear the past two weeks that had killed some 20 head of stock—am going after mt. sheep for 2 weeks starting tomorrow then back to the book again— Piggott—Arkansas will be a permanent address until after Christmas—

With best wishes for the season,—it seems Christmas weather; snowing hard in the mountains—to you and to Mrs. Cape and, if you see her, to Norah James, and to Mr. Wren Howard—[2]

What advance would you be prepared to make on a good bear hide for the offices?— There is a grizzly here that leaves a 14 inch track that I hope to get before October is out.

Yours always—
Ernest Hemingway.

URead, ALS

1 In a letter to EH dated 7 August 1930, Cape proposed publishing an edition of short stories selected from *IOT* and *MWW* for his firm's reprint series, The Travellers' Library, with a publication date of early 1931, a price of 3s 6d, and royalties of 10%. Among his suggestions for story selector was English novelist, critic, and literary editor Edward William Garnett (1868–1937), Cape's literary advisor from 1922 to 1937, married to Constance Garnett (née Black, 1861–1946), whose translations of Dostoevsky EH admired. In a letter to EH dated 24 September and addressed c/o Scribner's in New York, Cape would suggest instead a plan to reprint *MWW* complete in The Travellers' Library, under identical terms. The edition would be published in May 1931.

2 Olyve Vida Cape (1895–1931) had worked for the firm since its inception and married Cape in 1927; it was a second marriage for both. Norah Cordner James (1896–1979), English novelist and journalist, oversaw Cape's advertising from 1926 to 1929, when her first novel was banned and she resigned to pursue her writing career. Cape's founding partner, George Wren Howard, was in charge of book production.

To Milford Baker, 12 September [1930]

September 12

Dear Bake:—

The glasses, as I wrote you, are splendid. Ideal in fact. Thanks ever so much.

Did I tell you about the 2nd bear?[1] Bears had killed, or at least eaten, 20 head of stock. Whether they kill it I doubt—but one cow was still alive and badly clawed—looked like lion to me— But anyway we hunted bear to pacify stockmen and keep from bringing in a govt. hunter who would kill everything. The first one I got at 85 yards—nearly dark—2 shots—first through ribs knocked him down—he got up and started for timber and I killed him with 2nd shot through the shoulder [*EH insertion*: Killed instantly]—220 grain bullet—2nd bear at 100 yards—1 shot through the neck— [*EH insertion*: all—Killed instantly] bullets went all the way through mushrooming perfectly not going to pieces— Both were old male bears— The 220 grain bullet has a terrific wallop— I don't see how those birds in Am. Rifleman article—could shoot their sheep so many times—[2]

It's a bad break not to get the 6.5 by the 15th as we leave for the sheep country on that date— Still I wouldnt have time to get used to it anyway— If I dont get a big ram will go out again in oct anyway. What are the chances of you coming out? I write this in haste. Excuse me if I've repeated the bear dope— I'll write you all dope when I get back from sheep trip—

Thanks ever so much for the damned bother you've taken— I am Constantly more deeply endebted to you—

Best to you always—
Hemmy

In case any of your friends want the information— Nordquist's terms are $25 a day a head for hunting parties of two or more. He is a really fine hunter—

I could see this on the bear hunting we did— Has guided McGuire of Outdoor life numerous times—[3] Country is full of game—

[*On verso in lower left quadrant of the folded letter:*]

Enclose check for balance—let me know if any more additional expense—

PUL, ALS; letterhead: LAWRENCE W. NORDQUIST / THE L-T RANCH; postmark: COOKE / MONT., SEP / 12 / [P M.] / 1930

1 In his 12 August letter, EH had enclosed a check for Baker to buy the 8x binoculars they had seen at Griffin & Howe, and Baker reported in a 22 August letter that he was sending them that day (PUL). In a letter to EH of 24 September, Baker would write, "I was glad to get your letter of September 12th and delighted to have your account of the bear hunt. There must be a slipup somewhere in our correspondence for in your letter you say that 'the glasses, as I wrote you, are splendid,' but this is the first mention I have received from you of the safe arrival of the glasses" (PUL). Nor had Baker heard about the first bear.

2 An illustrated article by Elmer Keith (1899–1984) titled "The 7-MM. .30–06 and .300 Magnum On Game" in the July 1930 *American Rifleman* reported on a two-month hunting expedition in British Columbia during the fall of 1927. Keith observed that while a 220-grain Western bullet was used to fell a caribou during the hunt, three members of the party pursued large rams using rifles with smaller bullets that required as many as eleven shots to kill them.

3 John A. McGuire (1869–1942), founder and editor in chief of *Outdoor Life* magazine. An avid hunter, McGuire was an outspoken proponent for the conservation of bears and other overhunted animals.

To William D. and Frances Horne, 12 September [1930]

Sept 12

Dear Bunny and Bill:—

You were damned noble about getting the 2 vols. and am enclosing check which probably wont cover cost of same. By God it was grand having you out here and we missed you like hell when you left. The day after you left I went up and shot big old male bear on the bait—and a week later another [*ditto marks:* big old male bear]— The stream cleared up and fishing was splendid— Pauline and Bumby leave tomorrow— Sidley's Monday—[1] I go Saturday to hunt [*EH drew an arrow to words he circled in the letterhead:* "ELK, DEER, BEAR AND MOUNTAIN SHEEP"] with Lawrence— If you will write stating your preference I'll send Bunny a quarter or a haunch of the finest meat available as soon as it gets cold enough to ship— Am on page 188—

I felt cockeyed sick all the time you were here about how the bad weather gypped our fishing— It was a crime— you were both so damned nice about it but I know it was pretty terrible—

Anyway we love you very much and I hope we see you soon— Thanks an unwriteable amount for sending the Gaelic— I'd been out 3 days when I wired! Love to you both— I've never seen people finer married—

Ernie.

Newberry, ALS; letterhead: LAWRENCE W. NORDQUIST / THE L-T RANCH; postmark: COOKE / MON[T.], SEP / 12 / P.M. / 1930

1 Chicago lawyer William Pratt Sidley (1868–1958) and his wife, Elaine Dupee Sidley (1872–1959). EH would write a new will dated 13 September 1930 and witnessed by Elaine Sidley and Lawrence W. Nordquist. The will named William P. Sidley as Pauline's successor if she were unable to act as executrix.

To John Herrmann, 28 September [1930]

Sept 28

Dear John—

Your letter came while I was up in the high mts. for 2 weeks. Shot a hell of a fine Big horn ram—stalked him, crawling on my belly—from noon until 4 pm—way up above the timber line—trying to get within range—wind blowing "between the worlds"—[1] I'd crawl when he'd put his head down to feed— watching them with the glasses— killed him with 1 shot at 350 yards—couldnt get any closer— Swell ram all right— Got a big bull elk too— When and if the weather in general gets colder will try and send some meat—

Well here goes for the endorsement————[2]

[*EH crossed out the following two paragraphs:*]

John Herrmann is a creator and originator who has ~~been~~ remained unpublished while the imitators ~~were~~ have all been

John Herrmann writes a prose that is empty and without charm and as bitterly true as the telephone directory. He writes of ~~an~~ the America that his immediate ancestors have made and it is an America as barren as his way of writing of it. It is the America you now have and that you will live and die in and ~~the Humanists will not~~ no literary religions will be able to abolish it with footnotes.[3] John Herrmann writes of the tragedies of the human heart and of the lack

[*EH bracketed the following paragraph*:]

John Herrmann writes of the tragedy of the human heart as truly as any writer that has ever lived. While his contemporaries have been imitating literature with more or less skill he has been creating it in a prose empty, without charm and as bitterly true as the telephone directory. He writes of the America his immediate ancestors have made, the America that we have now, that he has made his living in as a salesman, not as a writer, a damned good salesman, if that means anything to you, and I congratulate any publisher who has the courage to publish him.

—— | | ——————

Will that be all right kid?

If not let me know— They can take any sentence from it— but would like, also, for them to somewhere give the complete content.

Send this in a hurry—hope it's not too late[.] It's Swell Max took the story— But write the book about the Salesman and dont ever lay down in telling truth on acct. of chance to make money presumably writing— (I'll get you the dough someway if you have to have it) You are one of few honest bastards we have—

What about Key West this winter? By God you'd better come—

We'll be there By January— Hope the above is all right— Let me know if it isnt and I'll try again— I mean every damned word of it and could make it stronger but have no felicity in these matters—

Hem—

(Kick Morley's ass for me.) My very best to <u>Jo</u> [Herbst]

Pauline is gone to N.Y to put Bumby on boat then to Piggott.

UT, ALS; postmarks: COOK[E] / MONT, SEP / 29 / 1930; CHICAGO [ILL], JUN 6 / 6 PM / AIR MAIL / 1931

Postal markings on the envelope indicate that Herrmann did not receive this letter before the following summer. The envelope, addressed to "John Herrmann, Esq. / Erwinna / Pennsylvania," evidently made its way to France, where it was stamped "RETOUR A L'ENVOYEUR" (return to sender), and was finally postmarked on the verso CHICAGO ILL / AIR MAIL, JUN 6 / 6 PM / 1931. In the fall of 1930 Herrmann and Josephine Herbst travelled to Russia to attend the International Congress of Revolutionary Writers. In a letter dated 1 December 1930, Herrmann wrote to Perkins from Munich saying, "We are now on the way back from Russia after a very interesting trip. All the time we have been gone we have received no mail and have no idea what is happening back home. It must take mail a couple of months to get to Russia . . . Now we are going to Paris for a short time and I wonder if you will drop me a line there, c/o American Express Co., 4 Rue Scribe" (PUL).

1 Herrmann's letter to EH remains unlocated. In Rudyard Kipling's poem "Tomlinson" (1891), the refrain "The Wind that blows between the Worlds" is echoed as the eponymous narrator, who has died, is taken by a Spirit to both Heaven and Hell, and is eventually returned to life.
2 *Summer Is Ended* would be accepted by New York publisher Covici, Freide in December 1931 and published in the fall of 1932. Advertisements for the novel would feature EH's endorsement: "John Herrmann writes of the tragedy of the human heart as truly as any writer that ever lived" (*New York Times* [2 October 1932]; *Contact* [October 1932], reprinted in Bruccoli and Baughman *Mechanism*, 20).
3 The material EH deleted here would echo in Chapter 12 of *DIA*: "I want to see the death of any self-called Humanist . . . I hope to see the finish of a few, and speculate how worms will try that long preserved sterility; with their quaint pamphlets gone to bust and into footnotes all their lust."

To Maxwell Perkins, 28 September [1930]

Sunday Sept 28

Dear Max:—

I was up in the high mts from Sept 14 to 28th— So that's why I didnt answer your wire sooner— Anyway the telegraphic address here is Lawrence Nordquist— Cody, Wyo— They phone them from there to the ranger station— Wires to Cooke City come with the weekly mail—

Havent heard how the play is— Maybe it will sell some books anyway—[1]

Am nearly to page 200 in the book— Trailed two grizzlies but didnt get a shot— I killed a Mt. Sheep, fine old big ram at 350 yards—(1 shot) He has a fine head— Got a good bull elk too—

Am enclosing a letter from Ford Madox Ford for you to act upon as you see

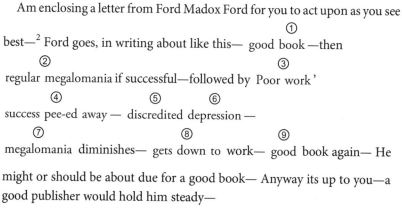

best—[2] Ford goes, in writing about like this— good book —then regular megalomania if successful—followed by Poor work ' success pee-ed away — discredited depression — megalomania diminishes— gets down to work— good book again— He

might or should be about due for a good book— Anyway its up to you—a good publisher would hold him steady—

A man named Trumbull White who was a great friend of my father has a son just out of college (name ~~Owen~~ Kenneth) who is looking for beginning work in Editorial or Magazine job. Do you need any worthy young men to start in at the bottom and work their way to the top? Anyway will you write me. If you want to see such an young man will you let me know and I will write his father who has written me. I will guaranty him to be presentable, literate and willing and Brought up among Books.[3]

Glad you have better news of Scott and that Bunny Wilson will do the Introduction.

What in hell was the objection to calling my piece Introduction by The Author— You can call it Preface if you like but it is not nearly as good—[4]

Write me what the damned play was like would you— I know nothing about it—

What I want to do is get this book finished and get to TORTUGAS— Then Africa— Am getting to be a hell of a rifle shot— Killed with 4 shots 2 bear and 1 mt. sheep— Stalked the old ram from noon until 4pm crawling on my belly trying to get within range—way up above timber line with the wind blowing like a knife— Give me that and they can have the theater and all the by products of the practice of letters—

If you want to hold the book over until 1931 its all right with me— I must have the illustrations for the bull fight book and cant get them without going to Spain and cant go to Spain until Oct 1931[.] So that would bring the book out in 1932—[5] Unless I could go to Spain and get the illustrations en route to Africa— In May or June 1931— Maybe have to do that— The

illustrations—photographs and reproductions are damned important—
Anyway I hope I'll have the 1st draft finished by Christmas— It will be a
damned fine book I hope— Have only laid off it 2 weeks since left Key West
except for that week in N.Y. The country is wonderful out here now—

Best to you always—

Ernest

PUL, ALS

1 Perkins would cable in response on 30 September: "Play not going well stop Though hopes for improvement run likely to be short but movie sale went through" (PUL). The Stallings dramatization of *FTA* had opened on 22 September 1930 and would close after twenty-four performances.
2 In a letter to EH dated 20 September 1930, Ford had written that he was dissatisfied with his publishers and asked EH to recommend him to Scribner's (PUL).
3 Trumbull White (1868–1941), American journalist, foreign correspondent, editor, and founder of *Red Book* and *Adventure* magazines. In 1917 he was the manager of the Chautauqua-style "Summer Assembly" in Bay View, Michigan, where EH had met his sons, Owen Sheppard White (1893–1970) and Kenneth Sheldon White (c. 1905–1973). In his reply to EH of 14 October 1930, Perkins would write, "I canvassed this whole concern to see if there is any possible opening" and offered to give the young man advice, adding, "But this is about the worst time to get a job in publishing that ever was" (PUL).
4 In a letter of 9 September 1930, Perkins had confirmed that Edmund Wilson would write an introduction to *IOT*, and in a letter of 10 September he relayed Fitzgerald's report that Zelda was "almost well." In a cable dated 24 September 1930 Perkins had suggested changing EH's title to "prelude" or "foreword" (PUL).
5 In his 9 September letter, Perkins wrote that publication of *IOT* might have to be postponed until 1931, which "might then conflict with the new book [*DIA*], which would be bad" (PUL). *IOT* would be published by Scribner's on 24 October 1930 and *DIA* on 23 September 1932.

To Maxwell Perkins, 29 September 1930

NA170 57 DL=CODY WYO 29 838A
MAXWELL E PERKINS, CARE CHARLES SCRIBNER SONS=
597 FIFTH AVE=
CALL IT PREFACE IF YOU MUST CHANGE FROM INTRODUCTION
BUT INTRODUCTION FAR PREFERABLE UNLESS OBJECTIONABLE
TO WILSON STOP OK TO BRING OUT IN 1931 IF SUITS YOU BETTER
SINCE IMPROBABLE HAVE BULL FIGHT ILLUSTRATIONS BEFORE
NEXT FALL STOP JUST RECEIVED YOUR INTRODUCTIONS WIRE

HOW IS PLAY GOING TELEGRAPH ADDRESS HERE LAWRENCE
NORDQUIST CODY WYO=
    ERNEST.

PUL, Cable; Western Union destination receipt stamp: 1930 SEP 29 PM 1 07

To John Hemingway, [c. early October 1930]

Happy Birthday to
Bumby from Papa
and Patrick

JFK, ANS

EH wrote this greeting to Bumby, who would celebrate his seventh birthday on 10 October, on the verso of a photograph by American photographer, artist, and historian Elsa Spear Edwards (1896–1992), who worked as a guide for guests at the Spear-O-Wigwam Ranch, located near the Crow Indian Reservation. In September 1928 EH and Pauline stayed at this dude ranch, owned by Elsa's father, Willis Moses Spear (1862–1936), a Wyoming cattleman and a state senator, 1918–1932. The tinted photograph depicts a seated American Indian wearing a feather headdress, fringed jacket, and several necklaces, captioned on the verso: "White Man Runs Him © Elsa Spear Edwards." A penciled note, not in EH's hand, reads: "1^{25} colored / White Man Runs Him— / 76 years old / last of Custers Scouts alive 50 yrs after the Custer battle / June 25, 1926" (JFK).

To Milford Baker, 2 October [1930]

October 2nd

Dear Bake:—

    The Mannlicher came in splendid order and one of the boys from the ranch rode up to camp—2 days ride—with it and my mail. It shoots beautifully both with iron sights and scope and is very handsome too. So far its record is 100% as I have only shot it twice—not game (sic) 1 camp robber high in the top of a spruce—1 Blue jay ditto— Both demolished. The guides call it my bird gun!

It would have been swell for sheep or, indeed any game out here since I belong, as you do, to the school that believes in shooting at some particular spot on the animal and if you hit them there the 6.5 is plenty— But I got my ram the first day— Way up above timber line we located them[.] I saw them first with the little glasses—2 white spots in a pocket below a high wind swept verge— Then 2 more— The white spots their rumps— We stalked from noon until 4 pm—due to lack of cover and the direction of the wind and the way they were feeding couldnt get closer than about 700 yards— So went around the spur of the top of the mt and the big ram of the 4— I'd located him so as to make no mistake in a hurry if I couldnt see the horns well—by the length of his white ball sac—was below us—350 yards— I sat got a good bead and fired— He rolled over and never moved— The others couldnt see where the shot came from and stood perfectly still— <u>Then came over toward the old leader</u>. If he didnt run they didnt see why they should— They stayed there until we we went down within 50 yards of them! I could have shot all 3 easily— We paced it down to him— I taking big ones in a hurry counting leaps and paces made 299— The Guide made it 352— Anyway it was a good full 300—iron sights— Bullet—220 grain—went clean through just under spine back about 2 inches of fore shoulder— Butchered, skinned out the head and started for our horses about 3 miles away—(to come back next day for meat—dropped a couple of shells to keep coyotes away) and damned if one of the rams didnt come up over the side of a precipice to look at us. The ram we killed was very old, 13 years by his horns, 17½ base—36 inch curl— He was so much the boss that the 3 younger rams didnt know what to do when he was gone—

You could have done the stalking O.K. if the ride to the hunting country was not too long 36 miles of up Down up and up—

Shot a bull elk—6 points each horn—at over 500 yards—running across a high hill side— Too far to shoot but we had stalked them all afternoon and the bull kept hidden in timber with 12 cows around— When the wind finally changed and they winded us and broke from the timber on far side and across hill side I emptied magazine— First shot threw up a cloud of dust—over him—2nd cloud this side— 3rd hit him and anchored him— He stood very sick and the cows went on— I missed him <u>twice</u>—shooting too fast— Then squeezed off carefully and broke his fore shoulder and he rolled about 70 yards down the hill side— I filled up the magazine and as he was trying to get up shot and broke his neck—well back.

The 1st bullet was about 5 inches back of foreshoulder and 8 below the spine— Went clean through and was under the skin on the other side, perfectly mushroomed. 2nd broke shoulder into bits took top off lung and was in the other side perfectly mushroomed and well held together— 3rd went clean through neck and into dirt—

220 grain soft point western am.

We tracked 2 grizzlies but didnt get a shot— Country full of elk— Many extraordinay heads— Country very rough and broken up with heavy timber— Elk werent starting to bugle yet[1] and very difficult to still hunt in thick timber—

Saw gray wolf and 2 eagles— Much bear but we only had 2 days of tracking snow—

I believe you could hunt this country well in oct when the elk leave the heavy timber for open grassy mt. meadows— All depends on how much of a nuisance a horse is to you—

Elk take a lot of lead— But of course at 500 yards the 220 gr. would not have the knockdown it would at 100 to 200— I didnt use the scope at all— used glasses constantly—even in timber— They are simply splendid—

The hell of a scope is that in game hunting as I've had it so far you are winded, or have to snap shoot and your own physical condition makes an instrument of too great precision damned difficult to use. The Springfield or Mannlicher are so accurate and easy to shoot that you can hit damned near anything with the iron sights if you can get any shot at all—and until you are shooting you use your glasses all the time so there is no question of needing scope to tell buck from doe, good head from bad etc.

I'm damned glad I have the scopes and will learn to use them— But so far in my damned limited experience— I dont need them on game—

About the set trigger— I like it. I have learned to touch it off and made 7 consecutive bulls on the 100 yd target with it and scope— But I would be afraid of it in promiscuous hunting since I'm a squeezer and when not thinking of gun—but of game am sure I would get in trouble with it sometime—and would <u>never</u> be sure Pauline might not shoot me with it by mistake. So believe I will sacrifice it and have G. and H. put on trigger with same sweet pull my Springfield has—

Now about the play—

I had nothing to do with it—my agent made the arrangement for dramatization and I never even saw the script— I figured it was nothing for me to get mixed up in—am working on another book— Sorry it was bum—and thank you for telling me so frankly— It must be pretty bad—[2]

Do you remember what Griffin said he would build the .416 Mauser Magnum for? I think perhaps I'd better get it—with leaf sights sighted at 50 yards say— Seeing the old elk stand on his feet gave me the idea that you might have to hit a buffalo pretty hard even in the right place— Can the damned .416s (cartridges) be bought in Africa? Will you ask Griffin what he will make it for me for? Dont make a point of it. Only if you are in N.Y and around there.

Do you know if you can buy the western 220 gr. open points out there? In Tanganyika— In Nairobi— I hate to carry shells through Europe.

I wish the hell you could have come out here. Nordquist is a splendid guide and hunter. We will hunt together sometime but I wish it could have been this fall.

Thanks again for all your many great kindnesses—

Hemmy.

Please let me know how ever much more I owe you— The case came and is very good l[oo]king— I'm delighted with the 6.5, scope and all equipment— Hope to blood it with a buck or a coyote before I leave—

PUL, ALS; postmark: COOKE / MO[NT.], OCT / 6 / PM. / 1930

1 Bull elk "bugle" during the fall mating season by emitting a squealing bellow.
2 After seeing the play *FTA*, Baker had written in a letter of 24 September 1930, "Honestly, Hemmie, it is an awful mess and I say this without knowing whet[h]er you had anything to do with the dramatization or not" (PUL).

To Grace Hall Hemingway, 2 October [1930]

Oct 2
L-T Ranch
Cooke City
Montana.

Dear Mother:—

Thank you for your letters, for the fine birthday nuts and candy and for the clippings—[1] Unfortunately the play hasnt done much financially—few of the critics liked Stallings dramatization much— However it might pick up—

Give my best to Sunny and Les—also to Carol when you write— We will be in Key West, I hope, after the 1st of the year and I hope to stop and see Carol enroute—[2] Am working hard on my new book—page 205— Have had a couple of accidents and new scars (my face is cut up) but am in Splendid health— Pauline has gone to N.Y. to put Bumby and Henriette [Lechner] on the boat— Have shot 2 bears—big cattle killing ones—also a mt sheep ram and a bull elk—tell Les—

We are all in good shape—hope you are all well and happy—

Ernest

Please thank Les for the present from Aunt Grace and the fish just arrived today.

E.

Hope you are receiving your income regularly.

PSU, ALS; envelope letterhead: THE L-T RANCH / LAWRENCE W. NORDQUIST PAINTER, WYOMING [*EH cancelled letterhead text and added*: "Cooke—Montana"]; postmark: COOKE. / MONT., OCT / 6 / P M. / 1930

1 The letters from Grace have not been located.
2 EH's sister Carol graduated from Oak Park and River Forest High School in June 1930 and started her studies at Rollins College in Winter Park, Florida, that autumn.

To Maxwell Perkins, 3 October 1930

NA198 94 DL=CODY WYO 3 1002A

MAXWELL E PERKINS, CHARLES SCRIBNER SONS=
597 FIFTH AVE=
ANSWERING YOUR LETTER SEPTEMBER TWENTY SEVENTH
BELIEVE MUST INSIST ON INTRODUCTION BY AUTHOR STOP
WILSON HAS GOOD SENSE IS ARTIST AND WOULD NOT BE
OFFENDED WHERE NO OFFENSE INTENDED OR POSSIBLE STOP
CALLED ANYTHING ELSE IT LOSES ALL FORCE AND
SIGNIFICANCE STOP I WANTED CONTRAST OF TWO
INTRODUCTIONS HAVE NOT READ WILSONS HAVE GREAT
RESPECT FOR HIM SO WHY WOULD I INSULT HIM STOP
CHANGING IT RUINS IT STOP AFTER ALL IN WRITING YOU GET
YOUR EFFECT ONE WORD AT A TIME AND IF SOMEBODY
CHANGES THE WORDS FOR YOU THE EFFECT IS GONE=[1]
ERNEST.

PUL, Cable; Western Union destination receipt stamp: 1930 OCT 3 PM 1 21

1 In a 27 September letter, Perkins had written that since EH's piece "is not in any usual sense an introduction," titling it as such might seem a rebuff of Wilson's "regulation introduction" to *IOT*. Perkins suggested the title "By the Author" (PUL). In the 1930 Scribner's edition the piece would be titled "Introduction by the Author" (Hanneman A3B, 9).

To Archibald MacLeish, 6 October [1930]

October 6

Archie:

I'll send a book from Piggott showing just where to shoot them and why—you cant shoot worse than Charley in the book[1] and you might be a hell of a fine shot— We'll shoot like flies in Key West— You wont get scared [*EH insertion*: Shooting is how you learn to shoot—Hell!] because it isnt alone (I'm always scared alone) and what scared me and you and everybody in the war was the fact that there was no bell at the end of the rounds— You could be scared on a boat with Gerald and Vladimir [*EH insertion*: possibly though I doubt it] but you couldnt be scared on a boat with me and Bra [Saunders]—[2] I dont mean that bragging nor pooping— I just mean that the nervous organization of the merchants around has damn near everything to do with it— Except if you dont like the guys then a man can get scared as his only form of protest against the bastards he's with— We'll have a swell time—you'll be kicking lions in the ass—

Glad the moccassins fitted— We werent trying to shower you— They'd been promised for 2 years—and ordered for one—[3]

From what the boys tell me Stallings didnt make much of a play— Suppose it's quit running by now— I'd hoped to get 500 bucks from it— Wonder if it will have made that— They sold the moving picture rights for fairly good money—

Did you see Pauline— I havent heard from her since she left Piggott ten days ago— The freighter quit and the mail dont come any more—

I shot a Mt. Sheep Ram— Big old one— way to hell above timber line in wonderful country—350 yards—1 shot— Stalked on my belly half the day[.] Bull elk running at 530 yds—too far to shoot—but threw up a dust spot on the hill behind him—then one in front—then hit him— Then when I had him anchored missed him three times! Excitement— Then filled magazine, eliminated excitement, squeezed off on him and down he came— Game hunting sounds like nothing to hear about but by God its the best fun I've ever had— The country is damned wonderful—

Am on page 216—

Write me the news from N.Y.

Love to you and your family—

Pappy

My god youve got a swell place for trophies at the farm—

LOC, ALS

1 In *Hunting in Africa East and West*, MacLeish's friend Charles Curtis reports a number of misses, even titling one chapter "I Miss a Buffalo." EH would praise the book in *GHOA* as "very honest" (Chapter 10).
2 Vladimir Orloff, a longtime employee of the Murphys, was a Russian émigré whom they originally hired in the early 1920s as a studio assistant. Among other household duties, he oversaw their boats. An ardent sailor, he had persuaded Gerald to buy the *Picaflor* in 1925 and had himself designed the *Honoria* in 1927.
3 In a letter of 25 September 1928, Waldo Peirce told EH that he wore "the royal Big Chief Shiting Bull Bison Beaded Buskins with great comfort & delight" (*Letters* vol. 3, 460). EH may have sent similar moccasins to MacLeish.

To Madelaine Hemingway, 6 October [1930]

October 6

Dear Sun:—

Your letter and one from Mother came tonight in the weekly mail. I'm answering yours without any reference to hers!

About the money business— It isnt exactly the same as it is with other girls who are working and paying a certain amount for board and room and toward the family as ours is a rather different fix due to Dads hard luck. You cant fix it completely logically since I paid last year about 88⅔ percent of what I made—

But this is the dope as I see it—chip in the amount that you can <u>without</u> it destroying your sense of making something for yourself and having certain pleasures and the things you need— Put in what, if you were alone, you <u>should</u> save for the always liable rainy day.

I've provided a sum for you in the disposal of the trust fund if Mother should ever die—which I hope she wont ever. No huge sum but more than you'd save in ten or twelve years if you banked every month what you are contributing now— Dont say anything about this and dont not save if you have a chance— you'll need it— But continue to put in the money that you can—toward family support—

I'm no one to tell you how much it should be— If $30 is all you feel you can contribute that is enough— I leave it up to you— But dont put it on a basis of pleasure to give it to Mother— It is on basis of what you can contribute to relieve the situation our parents including poor Dad left us—

The play so far is not much of a financial success— However I should get a good sum for moving picture rights— You will all be surprized to know what I'm going to do with this— invest it for [*EH insertion*: myself and immediate] my own family—ie Bumby, Patrick Pauline etc.

I'm awfully glad you had the Bermuda trip— You wrote a fine letter from there— Good luck to you always—

Ernie

I've just read Mothers letter— She says you are making 150 a month— good work even if it isnt true! 30 out of that doesnt seem so much—but even if it's only 140 perhaps you could raise the ante a little— I leave it up to you—

PSU, ALS; postmark: CODY, WYO., OCT 10 / 7$\underline{^{30}}$AM / 1930

EH addressed the envelope to "Miss M. Hemingway / c/o Dr. A.H. Parmelee / 715 Lake Street / Oak Park / Illinois" and added the notation "Personal." Sunny was then working as a doctor's assistant (M. Miller, 125).

To Grace Hall Hemingway, 6 October [1930]

Oct 6

L-T ranch

Cooke—Montana

Dear Mother:—

Your letter of Sept 30 came today— I'm sorry you and Sunny have been having trouble about what she can contribute to the family— I trust she will do the right thing—

About the mortgage— The house and lot must be worth much more than that or you would never have gotten that sum— on the other hand you've been paying a lot in interest— Who would the $300 commission go to— Uncle George?— I would hate, if I were you, to let the house go for the mortgage when you can perhaps get something [*EH insertion*: substantial] more if you hang on a year— If I were you would have Marce and Co. or Uncle George or whoever has carried you on the interest pull it off for another year even if it is an effort for them—[1]

That is my urgent advice

Mention your noble son Ernie and sacrifices of capital made by same— If you have any idea of selling or letting the property go dont pay any more taxes—

Thanks ever so much for the notices— So far the play has not made money, enormous caste, people prefer book etc.

I will get $^1/_3$—$^1/_3$ to Stallings—$^1/_3$ to producer, of the motion picture rights and intend to invest them for myself and family— Must look out for my own rainy days—

I enclose check for $250.$\underline{^{00}}$ to be used for repairs and your own expenses— Have made check for $300 instead—

My congratulations to Les on his shooting— Best to you and Sunny—

Ernest

Tell Less I shot the 2 bears with

(1)st 2 shots—Foreshoulder and back at 100 yards

2nd 1 shot neck at 100 yards

Mt Sheep—1 shot—back—at 350 yards—

Springfield 30—06—220 grain Western soft point—lubaloy bullet—[2]

Have made check for $300 instead of 250.^{00} Now its up to Marce and Co.

I paid $992^{00} premium that I owed on the bonds in your trust fund in August— The fund was $50,000 but that was the amount over par and covered interest over that sum.

[*On verso:*]

Dont tell anyone you've heard the play hasnt made money as they might want to play Chicago— And it might be a success there if not given a bad name—

[*On envelope flap:*]

900 interest a year is ~~less than~~ 75 a month rent—not bad as rents go.

PSU, ALS; postmark: CODY, WYO., OCT 10 / 7^{30}AM / 1930

1 EH refers to his sister Marcelline and her husband, Sterling Sanford, and to his paternal uncle George R. Hemingway.
2 The announcement that Leicester had recently qualified as Expert Rifleman in the Junior Rifle Corps appeared in the August 1930 issue of *American Rifleman*. Lubaloy bullets, made with a patented copper lubricating alloy, were manufactured by the Illinois-based Western Cartridge Company.

To Matthew Herold, 10 October 1930

L-T ranch

Cooke, Montana

October 10—1930

Dear Mathew:—

Thank you very much for your letter of September 29th with enclosures.

There is no notary public here, it has been raining steadily for two weeks and the road in both directions was impassible yesterday for a wagon and 4 horse team, let alone a motor car. In addition I've been in bed with ulcerated throat. So it looks as though Paramount would have to accept the power of attorney signature which is certainly legal and which they appear to have accepted in the case of Stallings.[1]

I was glad to hear [Paul] Reynolds had paid in the money. Sorry the play did not turn out better. The easiest and simplest way is for Reynolds to send me the box office reports and checks for receipts, when and if any, to my permanent address c/o Charles Scribners Sons, 597 <u>Fifth Avenue, New York</u>. They always have my forwarding address and are in the same building as Reynolds.

$80,000 is a good sum even with 10% off and divided by three. It is interesting to know that is the sum your office got for the Journeys End rights.[2] Please remind them though, when they are making out my bill on this that an offer of 77,500 to net me 23,000 odd with agents commission paid was already made me before you were called in to transmit it to me. That I was prepared to accept this offer and did not seek legal advice or counsel on it. I would have taken 20,000 and last fall I would have taken 15,000. I needed it badly then and coming this year it will take a considerable bit of it to pay the increase it will make on my income tax. There was no reason for Reynolds not communicating it to me direct and, eventually, he would have. You know, of course better than I (I've heard nothing about it) what part you had in having the figure of 77,500 raised to 80,000—

If when the contract was submitted to me there was anything in it that I did not understand or was doubtful on I would certainly have submitted it to you. I probably should have in any case if there had been no one here to advise with. I'm very glad you went over it. But I was furious that something it was the agents business to inform me of, and the expenses of telegrams etc that he should have born for such informing, should have come to me through a third party.

Anyway I appreciate very much what you did and regret you should have been put to the trouble of trying to call long distance and other annoyances.

The way things have gone with the critics there is probably no use discussing the matter of the Sun Also Rises dramatization possibilities that you wrote about previously at present. If you run into Stallings give him my best wishes and tell him I'm sorry we had bad luck with the press on it. I meant to send him a wire when it opened but it wasn't until I came back from hunting that I learned it had already gone on. Perhaps it will run long enough to cover the advance and make us a few thousand apiece. Hope so.

I'll be here until the 28th of the month— If it's imperative that I sign the agreement as well as yourself I can do it on the way out. But I believe the power of attorney is sufficient.

With best wishes

Yours very truly

Ernest Hemingway

OPPL, ALS

1 Herold, Pauline's second cousin, a New York attorney, represented EH in contract negotiations concerning the Stallings stage adaptation of *FTA*. The play would close on Broadway the day after EH wrote this letter.
2 The British–American WWI film *Journey's End*, based on the 1928 stage drama of the same name by English playwright R. C. Sheriff (1896–1975), was released in the United Kingdom and United States in mid-April 1930. The film was directed by James Whale (1889–1957), who had directed both London and Broadway productions of the play in 1929.

To Maurice-Edgar Coindreau, [12 October 1930]

L-T ranch

Cooke, Montana

October 12—1930

Dear Mr. Coindreau—

Answering your questions:—[1]

a — V.E. soldiers were Infantry designated as shock troops which wore those initials (Victor Emmanuel) on their left sleeves—after 1917 these were incorporated into the Arditi—[2]

B — The regiment is, as you suspected—the 69^0 fanteria

C — I'm sorry I don't— 606 six cent six is the ordinary designation I believe—it is arsenical—not mercurial—you might correct that—

D. Shit is the word—

I wish you would send me the book to sign and let me fill in the blanks— I would have done that before as I did for the German and Norwegian translation if I had remembered— I didnt use any dashes—the —— publishers put them in—

Sometimes of course there must be free translation but often, mostly too, I hope you could take it literally especially in paysage, action and I should think much conversation—[3]

~~I know~~ In Russian all translations were spoiled for a long time by being too free—~~a type named~~ a certain Georges Duplaix (Ott De Weymar) ruined stories for me in French by putting in slang words in the main body where I would never use anything but English and never use any slang in conversation even that is not at least 200 years old. What makes writing journalistic, "timely" and quite worthless rather than permanent is the use of quickly outmoded / (page turns here) expressions. If you ever write in the mode you will quickly be old fashioned and as unreadable as a last years Vanity Fair—

I have tried hard never to do that and I am sure that you will not make me—

After all a translation is a translation and gain its merit as such— you do not want to make Bovary an American story nor translate it into American terms—unless you are Mr. Sinclair Lewis—[4] ~~and then~~

I'll write Scribners to send you a Men Without Women— Did you ever read In Our Time? If you would care to have it I will have them send it to you—

Please excuse me writing about translation it's your show—not mine— But I care for French very much, most of my friends are ~~there~~ in France and I have had to face them as a writer in the worst Jack-off London translations that turn my stomach to read—[5] I am counting on you for a sober, true honest ~~translation~~ rehabilitation if possible— It's hell to have someone popularize your work for you when the only merit it has is that you have tried to keep it entirely and absolutely honest and what popular success it has had has been luck.

Farewell to Arms was finished before any war books were published of the lot that started with Sergeant Grisha— It was not written to write a "war book"—the road to fortune— It was being serialized when <u>All Quiet etc.</u> came out—[6]

Well good luck to you— I would like to fill in the blanks and dedicate the
book— Please write me if I may do anything to help—

Yours always—

Ernest Hemingway

PUL, Typewritten transcription of EH letter

This transcription of EH's letter is preserved in the Carlos Baker Collection at PUL and
reproduced here verbatim. At the top of the first page are typewritten notations indicating that
the letter was "handwritten on deckle-edged pinkish-buff stationery" and that the envelope
was addressed to "Maurice E. Coindreau / 413 1903 Hall / Princeton, New Jersey," and
"postmarked Cooke, Montana, October 15, 1930."

1 In a letter to EH dated 4 October 1930, Coindreau wrote that he had finished translating
   FTA "yesterday" but still needed EH's explanations in order to translate four items: (a) the
   phrase "V. E. soldiers" (Chapter 9); (b) the reference to a sexual activity "like the number of
   the first regiment of the Brigata Ancona" (Chapter 10); (c) the drug Salvarsan (Chapter 25);
   and (d) the words replaced by dashes (end of Chapter 27). "I usually knew what you had in
   mind when you used dashes," Coindreau wrote. "There won't be any dash in my translation. Thank God French readers are no prudes" (PUL).
2 Victor Emmanuel III (1869–1947), king of Italy from 1900 to 1946. The Arditi were the elite
   special assault forces of the Italian Army during WWI.
3 Coindreau had written, "A good translation has to be free, I think in order not to sound like
   a translation." *Paysage*: landscape (French).
4 Many critics had drawn parallels between *Madame Bovary*, the 1857 novel by Gustave Flaubert
   (1821–1880), and *Main Street* (1920) by American writer Sinclair Lewis (1885–1951).
5 Some French translations of books by Jack London (1876–1916) distorted the originals by
   rearranging the text, summarizing passages instead of translating them, and omitting or
   adding entire sentences and paragraphs. (Pierre-Pascal Furth, "Traduttore, Traditore,"
   Europe [January–February 1976], 117–33, offers detailed textual analysis.) Notwithstanding
   the quality of the translations, London's work was popular in postwar France.
6 EH finished the first draft of *FTA* in late August 1928. The English translation of Arnold
   Zweig's novel *The Case of Sergeant Grischa* (New York: Viking) was published on 29
   October 1928, and that of Erich Maria Remarque's *All Quiet on the Western Front* in
   March 1929 (London: Putnam) and June 1929 (Boston: Little, Brown). The first serial
   installment of *FTA* appeared in the May 1929 issue of *Scribner's Magazine*.

To Archibald MacLeish, 12 October [1930]

Sunday October 12

Dear Archie:—

Who is the producer?[1] ~~I'm going to write one~~ I have a damned fine one!
Play I mean. Dont you remember the one that turned out to be Hamlet?

About equipment— You ought to have a Springfield 30—06 for everything but the giant stuff— I believe it's worth getting one made to fit you by Griffin and Howe—now G. and Hobbs—202 East 44th Street—[2] Mike [Strater] will be back from hunting in N. Brunswick by now maybe and he could go with you. He is 115 East 86th Street. If you go there they will give you all the dope— I know I can shoot better with mine than any rifle Ive ever handled— Then we can use the same shells[.] The 220 gr. is a wonderful bullet— I think ~~you~~ we can get a .450 double used much cheaper in either ~~Kenya or~~ Nairobi or Arusha wherever we go— I've got one borrowed—may be able to borrow another—and may get Griffin to build me a .416 Magnum on a Mauser action— It has a little more wallop than the .450— Sounds improbable but is true—

I wont know exactly where we go until I hear from Philip Perceval—[3]

If you go to France get your Springfield first— You'll need a pair or two pair of light hunting boots—such as <u>Beans</u> make— Soft leather—<u>not high</u> Crepe soles are OK. I think—[4] You'll need a pair of field Glasses as powerful and small as you can get— If necessary we can get every thing else out there or enroute— I've glasses you can use if you havent a pair— G. and H. have a swell little 8x [*EH insertion*: J. D. Moeller.] hunting glass—for $60 if anybody wants to buy you a present— I've used them all this fall and they are super-good.[5]

Dont let them sell you a telescope on your rifle unless you are feeling plenty rich— You can shoot em as far as you can see 'em with the regular Lyman 48 sight they will put on—[6]

It's a hell of a note if you're not coming to Key West— We'll be there from Jan 1—on— I may have to spend May in Spain to get the illustrations for my book— Am on page 246— Will be done the 1st draft by Xmas— As it looks now we wont leave for Africa [*EH insertion*: ie from Marseilles] before June 1st to 15th subject to obstetrical variations by any members of party— I have to wait until all obstetrical reports are in before signing up with Perceval— Dont you clap up on me either—you've never had it I believe— Dont get it now— This is no time for the clap Mac—

The riviera in winter aint the riviera in Spring, fall and Summer—the only time I was ever there in winter it gave me the horrorrors—[*EH*

insertion: motors nose to ass on all roads and English the same way]
although it might work if you need Europe bad enough— I get damned
homesick for Paris every afternoon at 5 o'clock— But when we were there it
was not as good as you think when you are away. Evan [Shipman] is back
and says it is bad too— But it is the only city in the world to live in and I'd
feel like hell and that a lot of life was gone if I thought I could never live
there again— Ada may need it too

Did you see Pauline? She called you at Henderson Place but drew the
Seldes instead—[7] My God I miss her—Pauline—not the Seldes—and am
God damned lonesome but getting a lot of work done— Hope it wont
be shit—

Give my love to the Murphys— I've written them a couple of times but
never hear— This is the country if they ever want to come west—

Well I'm lonely as hell but sleepy as hell too—

So long keed— I look forward to what you will tell me about the play—
My love to Ada

Pappy

LOC, ALS

1 In the absence of MacLeish's incoming letter, EH's query about "the producer" is uncertain.
   EH makes snide reference to his own play, *FTA*, which had ended its brief run on Broadway
   the night before, on 11 October 1930.
2 After the stock market crash severely depressed custom rifle orders, Seymour Griffin's
   partner sold his shares in the company. In March 1930, American stockbroker Anson
   Wales Hard (1884–1935) and his secretary, Harry Hobbs, acquired those shares, and in
   June the board of directors changed the name of the company to Griffin & Hobbs. On 22
   July Griffin & Hobbs was wholly acquired by Abercrombie & Fitch, which restored the
   prestigious former name, Griffin & Howe, to their subsidiary that October. Very few rifles
   were manufactured under the name Griffin & Hobbs.
3 Renowned professional hunter Philip Hope Percival (1884–1966), an English expatriate in
   East Africa who guided Theodore Roosevelt and his son Kermit (1889–1943) on their 1909–
   1910 safari. After having guided EH and Pauline on their safari, 1933–1934, he would
   become the prototype for Jackson Phillips (Pop) in *GHOA*.
4 The iconic "Bean Boot," or "Maine Hunting Shoe," developed in 1912 by Leon Leonwood
   Bean (1872–1967), combined lightweight leather tops with waterproof rubber soles and
   became the cornerstone product of the mail-order and retail company L.L. Bean of
   Freeport, Maine.
5 German optician Johann Diedrich Möller (1844–1907) established the J. D. Möller Optical
   Works in 1864.

6 The Lyman Gun Sight Company, formed in 1878 by American inventor William Lyman (1821–1891), first issued the popular Model 48 gun sight in 1910. Designed specifically for the Springfield rifle to improve aim and accuracy, it was popular with Griffin & Howe customers.

7 On 13 September Pauline and Bumby went to New York City, where Bumby and Henriette would embark for Europe. Early in 1930, soon after Archie began working for *Fortune*, the MacLeishes moved into a rented house at 10 Henderson Place, New York City, but the noise and expense caused Ada and their children to return to her father's home in Farmington, Connecticut, while Archie moved to different quarters in the city (Donaldson *MacLeish*, 203). The 1931 New York City Directory lists the address of Gilbert and Alice Seldes as 10 Henderson Place.

To Maxwell Perkins, 28 October [1930]

October 28

Dear Max:—

Just got back and have your two letters of the 15th and 14th—

I enclose one from Curtis Brown— You figure out what to do and communicate with Curtis Brown please.[1]

The dope on it from my end is— It was in January not March that I came through N.Y. and told your Foreign rights King (Wm III) that Czech rights were unsold.

On In April, having heard nothing more from you about Czech rights I accepted the Curtis Brown— The end of June when I was in the office you told me Scribners had sold the Czech rights— I said I thought (I cant hold all foreign dealings of $75^{00} a throw in the head permanently) that Curtis Brown had already sold them. You said it couldnt be. If I'd had any sense I'd have remembered. Next I heard was on my royalty statement.

To hell with them both.

Will you arbitrate with Curtis Brown not making me out too much of an irresponsible swindler of the Innocent Czech. I should think the one who made the first offer should get the book and Messers Curtis Brown be roundly reproved for not being in better touch with the situation and knowing it was already sold.

Tell them you didn't inform me because I was working and you did not want to bother me and that was how the mix up happened. I will have to turn back the money to one or the other but will be damned if I'll pay any damages. I can't go into Yugoslavia nor Italy and might as well add Czecho-Slovakia—[2]

(Please return me the 2 memoranda for my files[.]) I wish to Christ I had them. The files. Not the piles.

Enclosed is something demanding immediate attention by your lawyers— Can they (the lawyers) write that such publication is impossible— If it is possible for them (the Medusa Press) to dig up or buy up all the filthy journalism I made a living by and publish it over my refusal the lawyer will have to find grounds for enjoining them.[3] But first a letter from a lawyer, not giving his position but telling them such publication is impossible should scare them or make them think not enough money in it with legal difficulties as an overhead.

Please

What is B. Wilson planning to say that he thinks I wont like? He ~~ought to~~ must realize that having read his criticism I ask that he write an introduction to this book, I put myself completely in his hands and trusting he will confine himself to this book that there must be a certain amount a noblesse oblige on his part not to try and ruin me—[4]

Oh well to hell with all that— I'm in this racket to write new and better ones rather than try to preserve the old ones—although that is how they make their reputations. But I will kill Mr. Melrich V. Rosenberg rather than let him dig up all my old journalism— So if they want to keep me out of jail and pen in hand (which they probably, like lawyers, dont give a damn about) let them do their duty—

Have hunted 8 days in the high mts.—ridden 40 miles today— Am on page 280 on my book [*DIA*]—nearly through— 2 more chapters and the 4 appendice to do at Piggot—

Dos [Passos] is out here— We leave for Piggott via Billings—Sheridan K.C. in 3 days

Thanks for your two damned good letters— Alzira (by Waldo) had twin boys[5]—

Will write about the magazine question—

Look—will you please arrange it so I wont get any more money due me until 1931? I wont to be able to pay my income tax as it is and will need the money then to do it—

Glad Scott is better—

Best to you always—

Ernest

What about that $61,000 merchant—[6] How much of that was all our royalties? They aughtnt to be snotty anymore in the acct. dept anyway.

PUL, ALS

1 The letter from Curtis Brown remains unlocated.
2 EH had written critically of Benito Mussolini and his Italian Fascist Party, as early as 1922 ("Fascisti Party Half-Million" and "Italy's Blackshirts" [*Toronto Star*, 24 June 1922; *DLT*, 172–75]). Under Mussolini, both the novel and film versions of *FTA* were banned in Italy, and the novel would not be translated into Italian until 1945. Although some of EH's short stories would be translated into Czech in 1933 and *FWBT* in 1947, *FTA* would not appear in Czech translation until 1958.
3 EH enclosed a letter dated 18 October 1930 from Melrich Vonelm Rosenberg (1904–1937), a publisher's agent in New York and owner of the Medusa Head, a private press. Rosenberg requested permission to reprint sketches and interviews that EH had written for the *Toronto Star* and asked EH to contribute an introduction for the proposed limited reprint edition to be published in 1931. Rosenberg wrote that he had learned about these early EH items from "a man who worked on the Toronto 'STAR'" and EH commented in the margin of his letter, "not Morley I ~~hope~~ feel sure" (PUL). In a letter dated 7 November 1930, Perkins would inform EH that he had consulted a lawyer and written to both Rosenberg and the *Toronto Star* and did not expect any further attempts to publish EH's journalism (PUL).
4 In his 14 October letter, Perkins had written of Wilson, "Bunny is very sensitive, and he had already got a little cold-footed about doing his own introduction [to the 1930 edition of *IOT*] for fear he would say something you would not like–which I told him was bunk—and so I was very sensitive to any conceivable danger. But it is all right and I am sorry I worried you about it" (PUL).
5 Mellen Chamberlain (Bill) Peirce and Michael Peirce were born in Neuilly-sur-Seine, a suburb of Paris, on 3 October 1930. In his 7 November reply Perkins, who had five daughters, would comment, "I am overcome with admiration of Waldo's feat."
6 Possibly a reference to the unlocated memorandum that Perkins had mentioned enclosing in his 15 October letter, commenting, "don't let it worry you too much. Just tell us what you think is right and we will straighten it out somehow, or tell us you will leave it to us" (PUL).

To Ford Madox Ford, 28 October [1930]

L-T ranch
Cooke, Montana
Oct 28

Dear Ford:—

I wrote to Scribners as soon as your letter came and no doubt you have heard from them.[1]

Dos Passos is out here and we go to Piggott Ark., to rejoin my family, this week— Will you be getting out that far west? I should always love to see you— Have been working well and am in very good health— Wonderful shooting—2 bear, wapiti bull, Mt. Sheep ram other edible beasts.

I hope you get the publishing thing fixed as you want it—

Best to you always—
Ernest Hemingway.

Cornell, ALS

1 In his 28 September letter to Perkins, EH had enclosed Ford's letter requesting that EH recommend him to Scribner's. In his 14 October reply to EH, Perkins wrote that although he liked Ford and his novels about the war, he feared that such an established older writer would expect a big advance. "The great interest in publishing," Perkins wrote, "is to take on an author at the start, or reasonably near it, and then to publish not this book or that, but the whole author" (PUL).

To Caresse Crosby, 28 October [1930]

permanent address
Piggott
Arkansas
Cooke, Montana
Oct 28th

Dear Caresse:—

I never got the other letter but I would be very happy to have you do the story and will send one when I get one that seems the right thing.

I hope everything goes well with your press and with you—

Yours always

Ernest Hemingway.

SIU, ALS

In letters of 17 February and 15 August 1930, Crosby had asked to publish one of EH's stories. The first letter was addressed to EH in care of Archibald MacLeish at 10 Henderson Place, New York City (SIU). In the second letter she wrote that she was "anxious to know if you are going to let me do a story of yours as you once told Harry and me you would." On that letter, EH noted "Answered Oct 28th" (JFK). Crosby would reply on 15 November 1931, "I am perfectly delighted that you are going to send the Black Sun Press a Hemingway to publish" (SIU).

To Samuel Putnam, [c. 28 October 1930]

c/o L. Nordquist

Cooke—Montana

Piggott

Arkansas.

↑

(permanent address)

Dear Putnam:—

Today I had a request from Guggenheim Foundation for a statement or report or some such thing on your candidacy for a Gu—heim Fellowship— your having given me as a reference—[1]

I wrote them as follows—

I believe Mr. Putnam would do very valuable and sound work and that the Guggenheim Foundation would be very proud of having aided him—

Ernest Hemingway—

Since I hadnt seen you for a long time and didnt know what you were up to thought that brevity would be the best— If you would like me to write them at greater length please let me know and I'll be glad to but hope the above will

Give my best to Titus will you please? And ask him to send me a copy of the Kiki and of the pamphlet he reprinted my introduction in—[2] I've never seen either. Would you mind doing that? I want them to complete my complete Woiks—

Tell him I'm on page 280 of a new book and was never in better shape— Kidneys A-1— Have shot couple very good bear, Mt. Sheep ram, elk etc. Damned fine country here—

He can send me the books to Piggott—Ark. I've never gotten any This Quarters since I left.[3] Hell this letter seems mostly to Titus— But my best to you always—

Ernest Hemingway—

Hope to God you get the Fellowship!—

PUL, ALS

1 In a letter dated 26 September 1930, Henry Allen Moe (1894–1975), secretary of the John Simon Guggenheim Memorial Foundation, asked EH to provide "a full and frank statement of your opinion of the applicant's abilities" (Guggenheim). Samuel Putnam would not be granted a Guggenheim Fellowship until 1949.
2 EH refers to *Kiki's Memoirs*, published in Paris by Edward Titus in June 1930 with an introduction by EH; and to the separate pamphlet publication of EH's *Introduction to Kiki of Montparnasse*, which Titus had printed in New York in January 1930 to establish copyright.
3 Titus had taken over the little magazine *This Quarter* in early 1929 and published fourteen issues between the July–August–September 1929 number and the last in December 1932. Putnam had served as associate editor for the January–February–March and the April–May–June 1930 issues until he and Titus quarreled (Karen Lane Rood, ed., *Dictionary of Literary Biography*, vol. 4, *American Writers in Paris, 1920–1939* [Detroit: Gale, 1980], 390) .

To Dorothy Connable, 28 October [1930]

L-T ranch

Cooke, Montana

Oct 28—

But permanent address is

Piggott—Arkansas

Dear Dorothy:—

Worse luck we wont be in N.Y. this fall—[1] Pauline took young Bumby there from here and put him on the boat for Paris but I've stayed out here working (and hunting) [*EH insertion*: 2 Bear, Bighorn Ram, Bull elk and other edible beasts.] and go from here to Piggott until Christmas— Then to Key West—until April—

Why dont you come to Key West? It has a fine hotel (Casa Marina) and nothing to do but <u>play tennis</u>, swim, fish and talk— We'd love to see you— I would have given very much to have seen you in Paris— Do come to Key West, Dorothy— I think you'd like it[.] We'll be there from January on— Will you be in New York in the Spring?

Will you give my love to your mother when you write her and remember me to your father and Ralph?[2] It was fine to hear from you.

Yours always

Ernest Hemingway.

phPUL, ALS

1 In a letter of 16 October 1930, Dorothy had invited EH to visit her in New York, where she would be all fall. Her letter bears EH's handwritten notation "answered Oct. 28" (JFK).
2 Dorothy's parents, Harriet Gridley Connable (b. c. 1870–1945) and Ralph Connable (1865–1939), financier and head of the Canadian branch of F. W. Woolworth. After meeting Harriet Connable in December 1919, EH worked in the family's Toronto home as a live-in companion to their son, Ralph, Jr. (1900–1957), in early 1920.

To Ray Long, 29 October 1930

Cooke, Montana.

October 29, 1930

permanent address

Piggott—

Arkansas

Dear Ray:—

I found your wire when I got back from a hunting trip and it made me feel like hell that you didnt have the stories.

What happened was this— When I got through re-writing the Farewell To Arms book, fighting about the proofs etc went to Spain to work on some stories. Went trout fishing one day and found I'd brought Pauline's waders instead of mine and so waded the stream all day without waders in a cold rain. Caught cold in the kidneys, got congestion of same and damn near passed out. Couldn't drink, write nor anything. If I'd take a drink my fingers would swell up like balloons.

When I was convalescing wrote three stories but you wouldnt want them. I'd be afraid to even send them through the mail let alone ask you to publish them.

Then we went to Key West and I got in fine shape again, kidneys better than ever, and felt I'd been losing time and plunged in on this long bull fight book I've been working and getting dope on for years. Now have worked steadily at it, except for two hunting trips, ever since February and am nearly finished.

You must think me a lousy bum on the stories and I dont blame you a bit but you know I've tried never to publish or try to sell any that weren't as damned good as I could do them. The only thing I've published since the book was the one story in Scribners which was so full of French that it was altogether unsuited for general publication ["The Wine of Wyoming"].

The three I have now you'd have to get out a special asbestos edition to print—[1]

I have some damned fine stories to write and might have done better to write them but the bull fight book was the hardest thing I had to handle and when I had laid off and gotten in bad shape I thought I ought to bite into that to get going again. Now am in better shape than I've ever been in every way. Sooner or later I'll have some swell stories for you. But if you want to curse me out in the meantime you certainly have a right to. You have the best writer of short stories in the racket anyway in Somerset Maugham.[2] By the time he starts to slip on you I'll just be getting in my prime. So you're not losing anything and think of the money you save!

Anyway I hope everything goes finely with you and I wish you'd give my very best regards to Mrs. Long—[3]

Yours always

Ernest Hemingway.

SIU, ALS

1 Probably "The Sea Change," "A Natural History of the Dead," and "After the Storm." After rejecting Long's generous offer for the serialization rights to *FTA*, EH had offered to "write some good stories and send them" to Long (EH to William Lengel, 24 June [1929]).
2 Between 1923 and 1929, Somerset Maugham published twenty-nine short stories in *Cosmopolitan*, of which Long was editor.
3 Lucy Virginia Bovie (1898–1942) and Ray Long were married in 1922.

To Maxwell Perkins, 3 November 1930

VA187 20 NM=BILLINGS MONT 2
MAXWELL PERKINS, CARE SCRIBMERS=
597 FIFTH AVE NEWYORK NY=
PLEASE FORWARD ALL MAIL FOR TEN DAYS SAINTVINCENTS
HOSPITAL BILLINGS MONTANA GETTING ALONG ALL RIGHT
MAY BE HERE THREE WEEKS=[1]
  ERNEST.

PUL, Cable; Western Union destination receipt stamp: 1930 NOV 3 AM 1 48

1 On the evening of 1 November 1930 while driving on a gravel road west of Billings, Montana, EH overturned his Ford, suffering an oblique spiral fracture above the elbow of his right arm. EH had been traveling with John Dos Passos, who was uninjured, and Floyd Allington (1904–1967), a cowboy from Red Lodge, Montana, whose shoulder was dislocated in the accident. EH reported that he was blinded by the headlights of an oncoming car and swerved to the right, landing in a ditch. Pauline traveled from Piggott to join him at St. Vincent's Hospital in Billings, arriving on 4 November. On 6 November Dr. Louis William Allard (1887–1971) would operate on EH's arm, ordering that EH remain immobilized for several weeks to allow proper healing.

To Maxwell Perkins, 14 November 1930

NAE138 28=BILLINGS MONT 14 1014A
MAXWELL PERKINS, CARE CHAS SCRIBNER SONS=
597 FIFTH AVE=
THANKS WIRE PLEASE SEND NEW IN OUR TIME TORRENTS
ARTHUR TRAIN TUT BOOK[1] AND LIAM OFLAHERTYS TWO
YEARS[2] TWO MEN WITHOUT TWO FAREWELLS AND LIST NEW
FRENCH BOOK=
    ERNEST HEMINGWAY.

PUL, Cable; Western Union destination receipt stamp: 1930 NOV 14 PM 12 44

1 *The Adventures of Ephraim Tutt* (New York: Scribner's, 1930), a collection of short stories
  by Arthur Train (1875–1945), American lawyer, criminologist, bestselling fiction writer,
  and creator of the lawyer-detective character Ephraim Tutt.
2 *Two Years* (New York: Harcourt, 1930), autobiography by Irish writer Liam O'Flaherty.

To Henry Strater, [c. mid-November 1930]

Dear Mike,

The day I left the ranch for here came a letter from the Players with a bill
for forty-some dollars. It had been sent to Paris and forwarded to the ranch
and the day it got to me the time was up for paying the dues. I've sent for
a check book but it hasn't come and if you would pay this bill at the Players
and explain why it's late, I'll send you a check to cover it if you will tell me
how much you paid.

Pauline is writing this on a new three-dollars-a-month noiseless,[1] and the
doctor says we'll have to stay here a month. Don't let anybody ever mix you
up in this broken bone racket because it hurts like hell all the time. On the
other hand, letters from friends are gratefully received. Answering yours of
Oct. 25th, I8 m sorry they didn't have Charles' gun sighted properly, but don't
judge the gun by how it shoots when it wasn't sighted. A good gun can be
sighted t[o] shoot perfectly, so bludy well that it surprises you, but you can
never tell how a punk gun will shoot. If you like open sights, leaf sights, get

them and stick to them. Open sights are capable of greater accuracy, but a man shoots best with whatever he practices with and uses. It's like hours in the air, or number of tarpon caught, or anything like that. Confidence at close range only comes with lots of shooting. They look so big and so easy close that you simply don't draw a bead, that's all. You go back to shotgun shooting and shoot the whole gun at them. Any time you draw a bead with a properly sighted rifle and squeeze off—not jerk off—you ought to hit at close range.

Be darn careful— I'm dictating this letter, and that's what may make it sound dictatorial—about getting a light gun to shoot heavy loads. I think it's bloody nonesense to have the Springfield weigh under nine pounds. You simply make a gun which you cannot stand to shoot. Everybody out here in the WEST HAS TRIED IT [*Pauline writes in margin*: unconscious Emphasis] at some time or other, getting light 9pt. 5mm Mannlichers, light seven and a half pound Springfields, and so forth, and they've all had to throw them away or give them away, because they gun punishes you so that you cannot squeeze. You jerk and pull off in spite of yourself. Remember, we're not going to be doing New Brunswick deer hunting. The ideal rifle for you and Charles to have had for quick running shots—it shoots just like a shotgun—is the old 30–30 Winchester. Or, if you have to take long range shots and want a light gun, the 6pt. 5mm. Manlicher. It has no kick, I shot the heads off numerous grouse with it and didn't miss any. And it has 160 gr. bullet that is plenty powerful enough to kill moose. The trouble is, they make them with a set trigger and this is fine for target shooting, but a deadly handicap to carry hunting.

This is a swell shooting gun tho. [Milford] Baker got one for me to use sheep hunting but it came two weeks late and I'd already shot the ram with the Springfield. I was glad I had the Springfield, because the set trigger might have bitched me.

Your 404 should be a good calibre, but don't get it so light that you can't shoot it, and don't let them kid you with a lot of ballistics. Shoot a gun of the same cartridge and the same weight gun and see how you stand up under it— not just once but several times.

I shot both 180 and 220 gr. bullets all summer and the difference of a couple of inches isn't worth worrying about. The 220 from the elk I saved and can show to you. It seems like a swell cartridge. Everybody out here was strong for it. The hollow point 180's go all to pieces and ruin the meat. I have enevr shot 405 Winchester. You say it was good enough for Roosevelt, and the old 44 sharps was good enough for Buffalo Bill.[2] If they've stopped using them in Africa, where a lot fo guys hunt for meat, as well as moving pictures, there must be some reason for it. I imagine it is the box magazine. All the guys who hunt out here claim they are bad. Anyway, if you want to get one, I hear they give them away free in Nairobi to anyone who will buy a box of shells. White didn't use the 405. He developed the 406 [*Pauline circled "406" and drew a line to the marginal notation*: 30–06] as a sporting rifle.[3] A lever action shoots fast but can't handle the heavy loads safely, and I honestly believe that you'll get to think of rifle shooting as a one-shot-does-it business than fullilade. You'll probably shoot too fast, that is faster than you'll aim properly. no matter what action you have.

A big bull jumped at a hundred and fifty yards and ran straight toward me through the timber, coming into the clear at about seventy, and giving time for a shot absolutely certain with a Springfield, but I had the little Manlicher and the minute I concentrated on the game, could only go by reflex, so acted exactly as though it were the Springfield, sqeezed off without setting the trigger, nothing happened, except I lost the shot. I agree with you absolutely that the gunsought to be the same action or else be thoroughly familiar with both. When you see the game you so concentrate on the shot that everything else is out of your mind and any small similarites or differences in action will only gum things up. Hope you can get some kind of brace for your knee to hold it so that won't be a problem.

I saw Santa fight in Paris the night Stribling fought Carnera and he was lousy—too thin for his height clubbed with his arms, and seemed slow in reflexes[4] He fought in Paris several times and was a flop. Dos Passos and Vasco de Goma are the only good Portugese.[5] I can't write very well, and dictate lousy and would like to write Charles some reassuring gun dope on the 30–06, which shot really swell for me all summer, so maybe you'll send him this. Tell him I can sight his telescope for him when I get down there Once it's sighted in, it shoots really swell.

Well, so long kid. I hope to God this arm won't put us off a year, but if it does, we'll be better at hitting the beasts, anyway. In the meantime, I'd shipped two thousand shells to Piggot for the opening of quail and duck shooting—best quail year they've ever had—first time I'd had a chance to shoot the full season. Oh hell. Best love to Maggie, you and your family. It's getting to be quite a family.

[*Handwritten by Pauline*:]
    Ernest dictated, but not read nor signed
    E.H./P.H

PUL, TL [dictated] with ANS from Pauline

1 The Connecticut-based Noiseless Typewriter Company began manufacturing its first commercially successful model in 1917, based on a patent granted in 1916 to American inventor and manufacturer Wellington Parker Kidder (1853–1924), whose design involved the type bars making a gentle "thrust action" that produced less noise and a lighter mark. Both Remington (which acquired the Noiseless Typewriter Company in 1924) and Underwood (under contract with Remington) were producing noiseless models by 1929.

2 William Frederick "Buffalo Bill" Cody (1846–1917), famed American frontiersman, scout, and entertainer. In 1883 he launched Buffalo Bill's Wild West Show, which toured the United States and Europe from 1883 to 1916.

3 EH used 180- and 220-grain bullets in his recently acquired Springfield .30–06 rifle, which he would bring on both his 1933–1934 and 1953–1954 safaris. Theodore Roosevelt used a customized Springfield .30–06 during his 1909–1910 safari as well as a Winchester Model 1895 rifle, chambered for the Winchester .405 cartridge; Roosevelt described using both guns in *African Game Trails* (1910). A friend of Roosevelt's, American novelist and travel writer Stewart Edward White (1873–1946), brought a .30–06 on his 1911 safari, and he described the gun as "remarkable" for its accuracy and "killing power" in his book *The Land of Footprints* (Garden City, New York: Doubleday, Page, 1912), 410.

4 Portuguese heavyweight boxer José Santa (1902–1968) beat French heavyweight Robert Villard on 7 December 1929 at the Vélodrome d'Hiver in Paris, the same day the American boxer Young Stribling beat Italian heavyweight Primo Carnera (1906–1967) in the same arena. At 6 foot 9 inches tall and weighing around 260 pounds, Santa went on to win a number of fights in Germany and in East Coast U.S. cities in 1930.

5 John Dos Passos was one quarter Portuguese, his paternal grandfather, Manoel Dos Passos (1812–1882), having immigrated to the United States from Madeira. Vasco da Gama (1469–1524), legendary Portuguese explorer who discovered the sea route from Europe to India in the 1490s. A three-part series titled "Equipment for African Hunting" appeared in *American Rifleman* (September 1929, November 1929, and January 1930) under the byline "Count V. da Gama." Photographs of the author with his bounty bear such captions as "Buffalo shot by Vasco da Gama in the Great Forest" (November 1929, 14).

To Maxwell Perkins, 17 November [1930]

Nov. 17

Dear Max,

Thanks ever so much for the books. I enjoyed them all very much except the John Riddle, which I couldn't read but which I hope for your sake somebody can.[1] My arm seems to be coming along all right. They set it a couple of times at the start, but it wouldn't hold, so finally the doctor operated, notched the bone, and tied them together with kangaroo tendons. Three days afterwards they took an x-ray and it was holding well. The break is about three inches above the elbow and the ends of the bone churned up the flesh a good deal.

How it happened was we were driving along the road just after sundown, coming into Billings and a number of cars were coming from the oposite direction. One car pulled out of line to pass. I had to pull over and there wasn't enough road. The road was flat gravel, ungraded, without room for three cars to pass, and a deep ditch on the side. The car turned over.— Dos [Passos] was sitting beside me, but was not hurt. The car only had the doors sprung and scratches from the rocks. Dos went out and drove it in a few days later. He stayed here with me until after the operation and until Pauline came out.

Why don't you have Scribner's insure me against accident and disease? I believe there would be big money in it. It might pay better than publishing my books. Since I have been under contract to you, I have had anthrax, cut my right eyeball, conjestion of the kidney, cut index finger, forehead gashed, cheek torn open, branch ran through leg, and now this arm. However, on the other hand, during this whole period I have never been constipated.

A Mr. Snook, who seems to be a great buddy of Will James and Whitney Darrow, is here in town, and has come up to see me several times, making himself very pleasant and bringing papers and other things.[2] A Mr. Raymond, who sells parts west of here for your limited edition and first edition racket, also come in and was damn nice.[3] He brought a fine pint of whiskey, two highly readable detective stories, and if my recommendation of him can ever advance him in your esteem, I would like to advance him a long way.

It is fine to have Pauline here, but outside of that life is pretty dull (and I have never seen any one behave so beautifully.—P.H.). I was in such swell shape and on page 285 of the book and confident of finishing it before Christmas, that it is lousy to have my one writing tool, my right arm, busted in the way that it is. However, don't let any of the boys suggest that you sell me down the river because if it turns out that I couldn't write with my right hand, will learn to write with the left, or with my big toe, and still outwrite anyone to whom the news that I was laid up was good news. But as you see from this letter, I can't relie on dictating, but that's all I can do now, as I am still in bed in the same position that they put me in two weeks ago, and cannot move from side to side. There is some numbness which may come from a pinched nerve, but that will either clear up, or can be relieved by a small operation.

Don't let Reynolds tell you that I got two and a half times what the book would have brought for movies alone last fall a year ago. Fifteen thousand was offered, which he turned down, and that, last year, would have done me some good while this year the twenty-four added to all I must pay income on, but haven't received, will make an income tax that wil be something formidable. $80,000 was paid for the picture rights, which was negociated by Stallings, Woods, and their attornies, but Reynolds, by his own accounting received $8,000, that is a third as much as I got for writing the book or Stallings for making the play, or Woods for producing it. He manoeuvered it with the movie angle always in mind, so that he got the maximum possible commission, and I got a flop on Broadway that didn't ever cover the advance.

If all goes well, we'll get away from here some time in December, early December. I'll write you about the In Our Time after I've read Wilson's introduction. Have you read Cakes and Ale by Somerset Maugham?[4] I thought it was damn good. Have you any news from Waldo? I've heard nothing since the twins. Take care of yourself and we'll all go to Tortugas in March. I may get Chubb Weaver who's been cooking for us here in the mountains, to drive the car down to Key West and cook there on the trip.[5]

Yours always,
Ernest

PUL, TL with typewritten signature [dictated]

1 On 3 November 1930 Perkins had cabled: "Terribly sorry for accident Hope I may hear more Sending some books" (PUL). These included *The John Riddell Murder Case* (New York: Scribner's, 1930), written by humorist Corey Ford (1902–1969) under the pseudonym John Riddell.

2 Earl E. Snook (1883–1951), owner of an art supplies business in Billings, Montana, was a friend and patron of Will James (William Roderick James, né Joseph Ernest Nephtali Dufault, 1892–1942), Canadian-born cowboy, artist, and Scribner's author who portrayed ranch life in art and fiction. EH would autograph at least six books for Snook, whose estate included inscribed copies of *IOT, TOS, SAR, FTA* (2 copies), and *FWBT*. When the books were appraised for auction at Sotheby's in 2001, specialists at first doubted the authenticity of certain inscriptions before realizing that EH had written them with his left hand (*Billings Gazette*, 14 December 2001).

3 Cranston D. Raymond (1896–1991), a Seattle-based salesman for Scribner's.

4 Maugham's *roman-à-clef Cakes and Ale; or, The Skeleton in the Cupboard* (New York: Doubleday, Doran & Co., 1930) recognizably parodied Hugh Walpole, Thomas Hardy, and Maugham himself.

5 Leland Stanford "Chub" Weaver (1899–1974), a ranch hand, hunting guide, and cook whom EH met and befriended at the Nordquist L-Bar-T Ranch. In Chapter 30 of *FWBT*, Robert Jordan recalls riding with "Chub" in the high country, above Red Lodge, Montana; alone with Chub, Jordan rids himself of the gun his father used to kill himself by dropping it into a lake.

To Maxwell Perkins, 20 November 1930

NBN297 50 DL=BILLING MONT 20 1126A

MAXWELL PERKINS CHARLES SCRIBNERS SONS=

59 FIFTH AVE=

=MAX PLEASE SEND DAILY MIRROR AND EVENING SUN FOR TWO WEEKS ALSO THE REAL WARS BY CAPTAIN LIDDLEHART OMNIBUS OF CRIME BY AGATHA CHRISTY[1] CATALOGS FRENCH BOOK SHOP 556 MADISON AND OVERSEAS PUBLICATION 118 F SIXTH AVENUE XRAY SHOWS ARM HOLDING FINE THANKS EVER SO MUCH=

ERNEST.

PUL, Cable; Western Union destination receipt stamp: 1930 NOV 20 PM 3 38

1 Perkins would cable in response the same day, "Am sending books and newspapers" (PUL). The Hearst-owned New York *Daily Mirror* (1924–1957) featured the popular and widely syndicated gossip column by Walter Winchell (1897–1972) beginning in June 1929; a representative of the newspaper would reply to Scribner's on 21 November 1930 confirming EH's subscription through 4 December 1930 (PUL). The Baltimore *Evening Sun* (1910–1995) was closely associated with journalist, editor, literary critic, and social commentator H. L. Mencken (1880–1956).

The Real War: 1914–1918 (Boston: Little, Brown, 1930) by English military historian Basil Liddell Hart (1895–1970). *The Omnibus of Crime* (New York: Payson and Clarke, 1929), edited by detective novelist Dorothy Leigh Sayers (1893–1957); the volume contains no work by the English mystery writer Agatha Christie (neé Agatha Mary Clarissa Miller, 1890–1976).

To Archibald MacLeish, [22 November 1930]

Dear Archie,

It certainly was fine to hear from you, kid, and if this is the worst letter you ever got, it's because Mussolini is the dictator, not old Pappy. But if you want to do a good deed in this Nobel Prize World,[1] sit right down and write me again, because nothing happens here except the mail comes, and today it stopped coming.

The arm is coming on fine, but I haven't changed my psotion for three weeks tomorrow, except to have them set it three times and operate on it once, which took two hours and was very satisfactory, the doctor notching the bone, boring a hole through one side and then tying it together with kangaroo tendons—which ought to help me to land awfully hard on the jaw of Morley Callaghan some day.

It is awfully fine to have you write me what a fine writer I am, and even if it's horseshit it is the stuff to feed the troops when their writing arms are busted. Certainly I can't write anything now, nor for some time, to make you out a liar. There is some kind of numbness that will either clear up or can be relieved by another operation, but in a couple of months I'll know how she's turned out, and whether we shoot 'em in Africa this summer or next summer. I hate like hell to hold up your plans for the summer, but we'll do something anyway.

Don't let Mike [Strater] tell you anything about guns. Every thing he has written me about guns is utter nonsense. As a matter of fact, don't let anybody tell you anything about guns except old Pappy. I will not get onto guns because Pauline is taking this dictation and when I get on guns she gets off me. In other words, you can see I'm getting to be an authority on guns. When I get started on guns we run out of paper, and the little woman's fingers wear out. I wrote Mike a long letter on guns which you might ask him to let you read, if he did not destroy it. I dictated it with the tag end of five days of morphine in me and a pleasant delusion that I had a numer of right arms, like the Goddess Siva or whatever the goddesses name is, you may know the goddess, Mac, but I know the principles therein expressed were sound.[2] You see, the thing is that the English have a certain way about guns, and they high tone us always so that the majority of big game hunters get buffaloed by them. Any gun that you're used to, and throws a good heavy bulletthat won't go to pieces, ought to be all right. Pauline says she sees we're on guns. But the principle is that foot ball players aren't made by fancy pants, nor baseball players by eight dollar catcher mits, and shots are made by shooting; but a Springfield made to fit you, and heavy enough so it doesn't kick is sure a lovely gun. I got so I thought so I got I couldn't miss with mine because they always fell when I squeezed the trigger, and then when I saw a big bull elk at sixty yards it was so easy I just shot it at himlike a shotgun. But that isn't what you do in rifle shooting, Mac. There's only one bullet, and it goes wherever you point the gun, and if you point it in the right place, that's the only one you need. Enough about guns.

There is a raddio here, and any time day or night I can get Rudy Valee, the somethingless crooner—remember I'm dictating—singing in a thin voice about that Big Blue TEAM.[3] He is the favorite thing they have on the raddio out here, except a phonograph record which is played a good deal by the local broadcasting company and which they call Largo. It's by Handel, I believe.[4]

There is a Russian across the hall who was shot through the thigh at the same time that a Mexican across the hall was shot through the stomach. The Russian groaned a good deal at first but is now very quiet. The Mexican, on the other hand, has three tubes in him, and drains a good quality of high-grade pus. Two Mexicans came into visit him today—one of whom was a lousy crook if I ever saw one, and they also visited me.[5] I gave them a drink of Scotch for a bottle, three drinks from which had nearly killed me two nights ago, and then two drinks of rye, which isn't bad, poisonous, that is, but is pretty lousy and green; and they have promised to come and visit me tomorrow, bringing the finest beer in the city—if they recover from the Scotch, that is.

How is your wife Ada and all your children. Bumbi got back to France safely and Patrick says his father doesn't love him because he never comes to see him. They get these French ideas quick.

This is the Will James country out here. Anybody who comes into see you, outside these two Mexicans, who talked about howmany tubes there were in the radio, talks to you about Will James. They feel what you must talk to one writer about is another writer. I have met Will James, one time in Scribners', and he is a sort of dog-eared moth-eaten, shifty-eyed, fake imitation of old C. W. Rossell, who was a real cowboy artist.[6] However, desiring not to speak ill of a local boy, I talk about Will James for hours, but am about through doing it. The next time anybody comes in I'm going to claim to be Will James myself, and present them with an autographed copy of Smoky, that classic for boys.[7] How are

you yourself, Mac? Of course Ezra is an ass, but he has written damned lovely poetry. I don't think he intended any cracks at me because he wrote me how much he thought of my last book and even mentioned it in the same breath as the only other authors he's ever read. He just makes a bloody fool of himself 99 times out of 100, when he writes anything but poetry, and 40 times out of 100 when he writes poetry but the good stuff sentence by sentence certainly deserves a hell of a lot more Nobel prizes than Dr. Lewis. That was a hell of a blow to me because I'd always thought of the Nobel prize as something that you got when your beard was long and white and you needed to put your grandchildren through Devil's Island.[8] But now I know that there's nothing that you get except maybe they operate on you for gallstomes, and that the only difference between the Nobel Prize and all the other prizes, is that it's just more money. So maybe we won't get any prizes, Mac, except the grave. And hope they won't give us that until we're so old we can't wipe our own bowels—or even each other[']s bowels—in case they've segregated all writers by then.

I've finally solved the mystery of why there were fifteen curtain calls the night Farewell to Arms opened, and yet it only ran three weeks. They must have all been by people who wanted to sleep with either Mr. Anders or Miss Landi,[9]

I'll send thes to Conway, although you wrote from Farmington, because I don't know the Farmington address.[10] My love to Ada, Mimi and yourself

Pappy

LOC, TL with typewritten signature [dictated]; postmark: BILLINGS / MONT., NOV 22 / 12[30] PM / 1930

1 Sinclair Lewis received the 1930 Nobel Prize in Literature, becoming the first American to win the award. The news was reported on 5 November in European papers and on 6 November in the *New York Times* and other American papers.

2 The Hindu god Siva or Shiva is often depicted with multiple arms, as is the Hindu goddess Kali, an incarnation of the wife of Shiva.

3 Singer Rudy Vallee, Yale class of 1927, performed with the Yale Collegians, led the Yale Band, and became known as the "First Crooner" and "Dean of the Crooners." He hosted the popular weekly radio show *The Fleischmann's Yeast Hour* (1929–1936). In September 1930 he and his band, the Connecticut Yankees, recorded a Yale fight song, "Goodnight Poor Harvard," which included the lyrics "When the big blue team gets after you / Harvard, goodnight!"

4 The opening aria "Ombra mai fù" from the opera *Serse* (*Xerxes*, 1738) by German composer George Frideric Handel (1685–1759) is commonly known as Handel's *Largo*.

5 Rudy Vallee, the Mexican, and the Russian would appear in EH's story "The Gambler, The Nun, and the Radio" (*WTN*, 1933).

6 Charles Marion Russell (1864–1926), painter, writer, and sculptor who portrayed the activities of cowboys and Native Americans in western landscapes.

7 *Smoky, the Cowhorse* (New York: Scribner's, 1926), written and illustrated by James, won the 1927 Newbery Medal for children's literature.

8 Part of a prison complex off the coast of French Guyana, where political prisoners and violent criminals were incarcerated during the French Revolution and until the early 1950s. Its most famous inmate was Alfred Dreyfus (1859–1935), the Jewish French army captain wrongly convicted of treason in 1894 and sent to Devil's Island in April 1895.

9 Glenn Anders and Elissa Landi had starred in the stage production of *FTA*.

10 The envelope was addressed to "Mr. Archibald MacLeish / Cricket Hill Farm / Conway / Massachusetts" and forwarded to "Farmington / Ct.", with a forwarding postmark from Conway of 26 November 1930.

To Grace Hall Hemingway, [22 November 1930]

Dear Mother,

Thank you for your letter of November 6 which was forwarded to me here.[1] I'm glad to see that bad news does not travel as fast as supposed good news, for it was in all the papers on November 2 that I had my right arm broken and was in the hospital in Billings where I still am and will be for some time, yet you did not hear about it for nearly a week while I received great congratulations on the success of the play which closed after three weeks and in fact first heard of this so-called success from you.[2] So far I've heard nothing from any other member of the family about this arm racket, but have received wires and heard from all my friends. The arm that was broken was my right. The bone was broken completely off between elbow and shoulder. It would not hold when set several times, and was finally operated on and the bone fastened together. It is now holding well, and we should be able to leave here in a couple of weeks. I will not, however, be able to write with it for some time.

So Marce is having another child[.][3] I hope it will be a great comfort to her and will support her and Sterling in their old age. Glad to hear news of Sonny, Carol and Leicester, and that they're all doing so well. If Ursula is still with you, please give her my best love. I would have written her before but was working so hard on my book trying to get it done before Christmas that all my intentions in correspondance went wrong. I'd planned to drive through Winter Park en route to Key West to see Carol but will not be able to drive now so will have to make other plans. We will not be at Key West until after the first of the year. I hope Carol will be able to spend part of one of her vacations with us. If the Christmas holidays are impractical perhaps she could come during Spring vacation.

Hope you are all well, and that everything is going well with you and that you will be able to sell the house for a good figure. I did not understand the financial transaction involved in renewing the morgage, nor why Uncle George [Hemingway], through the bank, should be getting commission on it and you putting up the securities and will be glad to have you explain this to me some time in detail when I'm feeling better. I hate to see the insurance principal being decreased in any way.

Do not write me off the books as being of no further use on account of this arm business, as I am quite capable of learning to write with my left hand if need be, although I doubt if there will be any need for this.

Best to you always

Yours, Ernest

PSU, TL with typewritten signature [dictated]; postmark: BILLINGS / MONT., NOV 22 / 12³⁰ PM / 1930

1 Grace's letter has not been located.
2 EH's accident was reported in the Helena (Montana) *Independent* on 1 November and in the *Billings Gazette* and the *New York Times* on 2 November. A short paragraph about the accident appeared in the 12 December 1930 Oak Park and River Forest newspaper *Oak Leaves*.
3 John Edmonds Sanford (1930–2016), born on 27 December in Detroit.

To William D. Horne, Jr., 23 November [1930]

Dear Horny,

Both your letters were fine, kid, and there wasn't any need for a second one to apologize for the first, although I was damn glad to get it.[1] You were right in surmizing that it was my hoisting arm, shooting arm, writing arm, and so forth. They couldn't get the bones to hold together when they set it, and the doctor operated, notched the bone, bored a hole in it, and tied them together with kangaroo tendon. Not it's two weeks since the operation, and the x-ray shows the bone is holding fine, and we shall probably be able to pull out of here in two weeks more, but we will have to go to Piggott direct, and I am afraid Chicago is off. It would have been swell to see you men, and also to drink a little good liquor. Some pretty horrible stuff has been produced here in the name of Scotch and Rye, that's never been any nearer Scotland than the fusel oiler's barrel.

Any time you do decide to lay off, or you and Bunny [Frances Horne] to take a long vacation in the winter, Key West would be swell. You could live for as little as you want, and we'd have a fine time.

Don't worry about the Carper's [Howell Jenkins's] political affiliations. Remember, he voted for Hoover, too, and brought us all this prosperity, and he is as incapable of voting for a Democrat as—but I can't find a comparison. But he ought to vote for wet. J. Ham. is a swell fellow anyway. There's a fine lot of wet sentiment in the country now, but what I'm afraid of is that it will reach it's peak and subside and nothing will have been done.[2] Certainly Hoover'll never do anything.

Pauline got a fine letter from Bunny and has been on the point of writing her ever since, but I keep her going down town and trying to buy papers and one thing and another, and have about worn the girl out. (Ed. note: Not at all) This is a lousy letter, Horny, but I wanted to answer yours and tell you how much I appreciated it, and let you know everything is fine. As you see, I have not been able to learn to write by dictating, and will take up writing with my big toe before I take up dictating permanently.

So long, kid. Give my love to the mis-voting Carper and Bunny. Thank Mr. Wilcoxen for his kind message.[3]

Yours always,
Steen
Nov. 23

phPUL, TL with typewritten signature [dictated]

The letter is typewritten on an "X-Ray Department" form. In the space for "Interne Attending" is typed "Pauline P. Hemingway."

1 These letters from Horne to EH remain unlocated.
2 James Hamilton Lewis (1863–1939), Democratic U.S. senator from Illinois, 1913–1919 and 1931–1939. Lewis campaigned as a "wet" (anti-Prohibition) candidate and won in the elections held on 4 November 1930.
3 Fred S. Wilcoxen, Jr. (1899–1934), nicknamed "The Blight" when he and EH were high school classmates, lived in Oak Park and worked as an advertising copy man. His father, Fred Sr. (1866–1948), was a salesman for railway supplies, specializing in brass.

To Maxwell Perkins, 23 November 1930

VB167 43 NL=BILLINGS MONT 23
MAXWELL E PERKINS=
CARE CHARLES SCRIBNER SONS 597 5 AVE NEWYORK NY=
BOOKS WIRED FOR NOVEMBER FOURTEENTH NEVER ARRIVED
WERE THEY SENT HERE STOP MAIL DEPT STILL SOMETIMES
SENDS MY MAIL TO PARIS HAVE NEVER YET SEEN WILSONS
INTRODUCTION ANY SPECIAL REASON FOR KEEPING THIS FROM
ME[1] GOING BUGHOUSE OUT HERE WITH NOTHING TO
READ=
    ERNEST.

PUL, Cable; Western Union destination receipt stamp: 1930 NOV 24 AM 1 15

1 Perkins would cable back the same day: "Sent books October seventeenth and others twenty-first Four Our Time sent Cooke City before accident one Billings seventeenth Introduction quite all right stop Mailing proof special" (PUL).

To Henry Strater, [c. 23 November 1930]

Dear Mike,

It sure was swell to get your letters, and if you send me that Players' bill you'll get a check by return mail. This is still being typed by the little woman, and I haven't changed my position in bed come three weeks yesterday, except for settings, operation and so forth. But listed, doctor, do you think there is any connection between the fact that Yale hasn't won a game in three years and Rudy Valle singing over the radio WHEN THAT BIG BLUE TEAM GOES SOMETHING SOMETHING SOMETHING HARVARD GOOD*NIGHT! You might take this up with Archie.

Pauline says there is to be nothing about guns in this letter so we won't say anything about guns. It is the subject she cares least about typing about.

I hope the snuff racket is holding up well.[1] I have noted a number of snuff users, and congratulated them all on their habit. As a matter of fact, I purchased four cans of snuff in Cooke City for a fellow called Rudy—not Rudy Vallee—and thought as I did so that this would probably help send your offspring to schools for exceptional children. I have thought deeply about taking up snuff, myself, and if the racket is falling off any let me know and I will take it up now, because God knows there's nothing else to do here, and if you were ever depriving of your writing tools when on page 285 and ready to finish up before Christmas, with 2,000 shells waiting at Piggott, and more quail than has ever been, you know what I mean. But I may have taken up snuff without knowing it, because the last bottle of Scotch we had was flavored by something that tasted very like your product. I hope you understand, Mr. Strater, that I can't write you as dirty a letter as I feel like because I am dictatint through my wife. That may be why Mr. Hoover is unable to express himself on any topic, because he has to speak through so many push buttons.[2] Not that my wife is any push button, I hasten to add.

If you see Maxie Deadpan [Perkins], would you tell him I wired for some books on the 14th of Nov. and on the 23rd of Nov., there was no sign of them. His office has a way of sending everything to any former address that you once had, and as all I do every day is wait fro thise books to show up, I'm thinking of leaving Scribner's if I can find any publishers that will send your mail to where you are and not charge you two hundred pounds apiece for libelous letters you once wrote to Ernest Walsh which they dig up at auctions. Also this bloody new edition of In Out Time has been out a month and I've never been sent a copy—only word from Max that Wilson didn't want to publish the introduction because he'd said things about me that I wouldn't like. So tell Max I'm upset about this whole racket if you run into him.

I've got a couple of stories for the magazine to publish just as they are, and if they won't, why to hell with them. This must all be verey interesting to you, but it is only old Hem bellyaching around because he has to stay in bed. And this bloody arm hurting like hell today. But what bloody use are publishers that can't deliver books you order and won't send you your own books when they come out.

Well, in a couple of weeks we ought to be able to shove off from here. Then in another month or so I'll know what kind of arm I've got, and we'll know whether we shoot 'em in 1931 Or 32. I8 m keeping a lot of dope for you from the Fishing Gazette on the tuna fishing off Scarborough[3] This is the first year they ever fished for them there with rod and reel, and in the summer they come at thick as grunts. One fellow using Hardy rod and reel caught three, the largest 700 and some pounds. It seems that they bite like tarpon, and the whole secret is getting on the grounds before darlingt. If you fish for them in daylight, you run a chance of hooking one occasionally, just as you do tarpon, but before it's light, they'll bite a bait on a hook every time. I'll bet that's been the main trouble with tuna fishing all along. One fellow hooked 12 one morning before daylight. Another fellow who was doing dayling fishing only hooked three the entire season. It's just a question of getting up a couple of hours earlier. I'll bet you could get them off Agunquit before it was light and they'd bite like tarpon on an ebb tide with the flats coming out of water. Fishing for them in the daytime, is like trying to catch those tarpon up in Jewfish that are rolling around after they've seen you.

That Scouting on Two Continents was a fine book. I bought one for Dos, and one for Ivan Wallace, a fellow up here.[4]

So long, Mike. Best love and luck to Maggie.

Yours,

Hem.

P.S. I've got a 14 ft. Salmon rod coming from Hardy's to sue for tarpon.

PUL, TL with typewritten signature [dictated]; letterhead: St. Vincent's Hospital /
CONDUCTED BY THE SISTERS OF CHARITY / Billings, Montana

The conjectured letter date is based on EH's reference to his 23 November wire to Perkins and
his complaint that he had still not received a copy of the Scribner's edition of *IOT* (published
on 24 October), which "has been out a month."

1 In 1891 Strater's father, Charles Godfrey Strater (1856–1937), along with Charles's brothers, William Edward Strater (1866–1908) and Henry Strater (1852–1912), founded the
  Strater Brothers Tobacco Company in Louisville, Kentucky, manufacturing chewing and
  smoking tobacco products. In May 1912, as sole remaining owner, Charles sold the business
  for roughly $500,000 to the Burley Tobacco Company, retaining a viable business entity as
  a corporate branch called Strater Brothers.
2 While Herbert Hoover was widely regarded to be a poor communicator, his wife, Lou
  Henry Hoover (1874–1944), was an experienced public speaker and made a number of
  regular nationwide radio broadcasts. To improve her speaking voice she practiced with
  a recording system she had installed in the White House.
3 Scarborough, a town in northeastern England, became known as a prime location for tuna
  fishing after a 560-pound *Thunnus Thynnus* ("Tunny") was caught 50 miles off its North
  Sea coast in August 1930 by a man using a rod. *The Fishing Gazette: Devoted to angling,
  river, lake and sea fishing, and fish-culture*, a popular London-based weekly (1877–1962).
4 *Scouting on Two Continents* (Garden City, New York: Doubleday Page, 1926), memoir by
  Frederick Russell Burnham (1861–1947), American hunter, tracker, mining engineer, gold
  prospector, and archeologist who hunted and explored California and parts of the south-
  western United States and Mexico. From 1893 to 1904 Burnham lived in South Africa,
  where he led mining and exploring expeditions and worked as a scout during the Second
  Boer War. Canadian-born Lawrence Ivan Wallace (1901–1976) worked as a hunting guide
  for the Nordquists at the L-Bar-T Ranch.

To Waldo Peirce, [c. 27 November 1930]

Billings—

Dear old Waldo,

I wired you when I got the letter about the twins, but maybe you never got
it. Now Max says you're in Bangor.[1] Pauline and I are out here in a fine
hospital, curtesy of a gravel road about 22 miles outside of Billings. Dos
[Passos] was in the car with me, but you know that the Portuguese are never
injured except in one way. So Passos escaped unscathed. I am now the
victim of all the latest inventions in science but we may be out of here inside
of two weeks, but meantime write to the address on this letter.

When are you going to come to Key West this winter? Remember that the
bearing and up bringing of twins is not a fulltime job for a man and we

missed you last winter very much. Pauline came out here from Piggott and she is writing this letter. There is no news outside of the fracture racket, but write and tell us how you are and how Alzira is and how the twins are.

From here we go to Piggott and then to Key West the first of year. So long kid

Su amigo

Ernestito, con el brazuero roto[2]

[*Handwritten by Pauline:*]

N.B. Ernest is very nonchalant about this arm affair, but he's been having a rotten time, with lots of pain and it's three weeks today since the operation and he hasn't even been able to change his position.

Love to Alzira. Would like to express my admiration and amazement of her to her personally. Will you give me her address when you write

Ernest

Pauline

Colby, TL with typewritten signature [dictated] with ANS from Pauline

The conjectured date is based on Pauline's comment that "it's three weeks today" since EH underwent surgery (on 6 November).

1 In his 21 November letter to EH, Perkins reported that "a Bangor girl who happened to turn up here" told him that Waldo was in Bangor with his infant twin sons, and the whole town was "considerably scandalized" because he and their mother were not married (PUL). In a letter of 2 December, Perkins would correct himself, saying he had learned Waldo was still in Paris (PUL).

2 EH uses the diminative form of his Spanish name, Ernesto. *Con el brazuelo roto*: with the broken upper foreleg (Spanish); EH refers to his arm injury in taurine terminology.

To Ernst Rowohlt, 30 November 1930

St. Vincent's Hospital

Billings, Montana,

Nov. 30, 1930

Dear Herr Rowohlt,

Any time you want to write or wire me you can reach me at Piggott Arkansas. I have been here in hospital for a month with my right arm broken clean off below the shoulder, so I have not answered your cables or letters.

About the play, it was dramatized by a man named Laurence Stallings and produced by A. H. Woods. You would have to write A. H. Woods in New York for permission to produce it in Berlin. Someone can tell you his address. I have not got it.

Until I broke my arm, I had shot a big horn mountain sheep ram, two bears, and a bull elk, and written 285 pages on my new book. Dos Passos was with me when the accident happened, but he was not hurt.

Will you send me money and the revised contract to Piggott, Arkansas, where we do hope to go in two weeks. Will you please send me press reviews of Farewell to Arms and some copies of Manner [a]nd In einem andern Land. I have never yet received even one copy of Manner.[1] If you do not treat me better about books and make me more money I will have to get another publisher, some big Jewish one. I was surprised you got so little money from the serialization of In einem andern Land.[2] I could have gotten five thousand marks myself.

I hope you are very well and happy and that everything goes finely with you. Business cannot be as bad in Germany as it is in America. Soon we will have another war and everyone will be happy and prosperous. I wish you could have been with us in the mountains. Give my best regards to Herr Meyer[3] and Mme. Horschitz—such a beautiful name for a translater.

Please send me the clippings, the books, a contract that I can sign, and a lot of money if you have it. I am happy for you that Sinclair Lewis got the Nobel Prize.[4]

Please write me at Piggott at once. My arm has been very bad. They have had to operate on it and I can do no work and feel angry all the time.

Mrs. Hemingway joins me in sending best regards. She says you are her favorite publisher, but they you never make us any money. See what you can do about this. Everyone tells me the Germans are a very ingenius people. You should be ingenius enough to make us a little money. If I write such fine books, why don't you try to sell a few.

My very best to you always,
Ernest Hemingway
Per P.H.

phDLA, TLS [dictated]

1 *Männer* (Berlin: Rowohlt, 1929), the German edition of *MWW*, translated by Annemarie Horschitz.
2 *FTA*, translated by Annemarie Horschitz, was serialized in the *Frankfurter Zeitung* from 8 May to 16 July 1930 under the title *Schluss Damit. Adieu Krieg!*
3 Paul Mayer (1889–1970) was an editor for Rowohlt Verlag from 1919 to 1939.
4 Rowohlt had published German translations of Lewis's *Elmer Gantry* (1927) and *Dodsworth* (1929), published as *Sam Dodsworth, Roman* (1930), translated by Franz Fein. Lewis was the first Rowohlt author to have been awarded the Nobel Prize in Literature.

To Maxwell Perkins, 1 December 1930

Dec. 1—

Dear Max

The enclosed introduction you can show to Wilson if you want, at the same time letting him see this letter. I have only the one complaint—that he should have said "we cease to believe in them as real people" because I believe that is exceeding his authority, since it is not an editorial we.[1] He has a perfect right to say whatever he wants, and you know that I did not ask to see what he wrote, or have anything to do with it. There has never been a word written in criticism or explanation of Miss Gertrude Stein's, or Mr. James Joyce's work which was not a reflection or a derivation of something explained by Miss Stein or Mr. Joyce to some critic in conversation. All interpretations of what they have done, explanations and glorifications, have originated with the writers themselves. This does not detract from the value of their work per se, but it is something which would make the practice of letters unbearable to me. I do not explain because of some noble virtue in myself nor cultivate the friendship of critics, but only because to do so would make writing not worth doing and altogether disgusting. Writing is made to be read; the writer should keep out of it. If he explains some thing into it which is not there, it will only lose in the end. Shaw is an example of the explaining mountebank who will be ridiculous within his own lifetime.[2]

I hope you will tell Wilson that he is the only critic for whose writing I have any respect, but that I believe he is sometimes as wrong as when he claimed that Pound derived from Eliot, and when he speaks seriously of Dorothy Parker, who is also a friend of mine, and of Edna Millay as poets.[3] If he were always right he would have been snatched to heaven in a chariot of fire long ago, but in the meantime reading him whenever I have the oportunity he seems nearly always right— If I disagree with him about the "romantic" ending of "A Farewell to Arms" it does not mean that I think him an ass, but that possibly I've seen more people die than he has and that we differ in our attitude toward the pleasures of sexual intercourse.[4]

Something—this for your own information—has been wrong with the main nerve in my arm and I have been having hell with it for four weeks. The only thing that I've discovered about pain—the subject Wilson says I'm so interested in—is that I cannot stand it as I could in my twenties. I was all right for three weeks and then it got to me. I dont know whether this discovery is worth the field work I've put into it. I would like to ask one favor though of Scribner's and that is if I should ever be bumped off in any of these various affairs, that you would not as a good business venture have either Morley Callaghan or W. R. Burnett[5] write my biography. This last is a joke. In case I do not make any jokes clear, lay it to the fact of an unfamiliarity with dictation.

I am not in the least angry at Wilson who has a right to put in anything he wants, but it gives me a pain to think of the wires I had to send because you feared I might hurt Wilson's feelings by calling my introduction an introduction, and the fact that you thought I would feel fine to have some one in my own book make me out a faking romanticist. Well, this seems to be all.

Yours always,

Ernest

Per P.H.

P.S. You know that the only reason I asked for an introduction was not for any self glorification, but simply that it might be more clear to people buying the book that this was a re-issue of an old book and not a new book. I told you why I wanted an introduction at the time, and I hope you explained this to Wilson.

E.

Dear Max—

This is the voice as well as the pen of Pauline. Ernest is really in pretty bad shape, after pain all the time for a month, and not sleeping nights. He's had nothing to do but think, always lying in the same position, and he's pretty nervous and depressed from the pain and worry. The numbness in the elbow and the paralysis in the wrist still persist, but the doctor expects this to be cleared up when the splint is taken off and the position of the arm changed. Today Ernest sat up for the first time, and tommorrow he will get up again, and we may leave a week from today, the 8$\underline{th}$, but of course we may not, too. Thank you for sending all the books and papers. They have been a great help. Poor Ernest, its very sad to see him lying here so long. I wish you'd write him when you can. The mail's about the only thing that breaks the monotony

PUL, ALS [dictated] with AN from Pauline

This five-page dictated letter was handwritten by Pauline on the verso of "X-Ray Department" forms.

1 In his introduction to the 1930 Scribner's edition of *IOT*, Edmund Wilson wrote that the story of Frederic Henry and Catherine Barkley "lacks the conflict of impulses which makes the real drama in Hemingway, and when they emerge from the stream of action, when they escape together after the Caporetto retreat, we cease to believe in them as human personalities" (xii).

2 George Bernard Shaw (1856–1950), Irish dramatist and critic, who received the 1925 Nobel Prize in Literature.

3 In his review of T. S. Eliot's *The Waste Land* (New York: Boni & Liveright, 1922), Wilson had described Pound as Eliot's "imitator" ("The Poetry of Drouth," *Dial*, December 1922, 616). Earlier he pronounced that Pound "copies" Eliot, adding "the comparison goes all against Pound" ("Mr. Pound's Patchwork," *New Republic*, April 1922, 232). American poet Edna St. Vincent Millay (1892–1950) had a brief but intense romantic relationship with Wilson in 1920 that cooled after his failed marriage proposal; he later called Millay "one of the only poets writing in English in our time who have attained to anything like the stature of great literary figures in an age in which prose has dominated" (*The Shores of Light: A Literary Chronicle of the Twenties and Thirties* [New York: Vintage Books, 1952], 751–52).

4 In his introduction to *IOT* Wilson termed the ending of "A Very Short Story" "perhaps more convincing than the rather romanticized idyll" of *FTA* (ix).

5 W. R. (William Riley) Burnett (1899–1982), American novelist and screenwriter whose tough-talking male protagonists specialized in violent activities. Burnett achieved popularity with *Little Caesar* (1929), which featured a vicious mob boss; *Iron Man* (1930), about a prize-fighter; and *Saint Johnson* (1930), about frontiersman and gambler Wyatt Earp.

To Henry Strater, [c. 2 December 1930]

Dear Mike,

Enclosed is the check for the Players [Club]. Thanks ever so much for paying it. They sent me a receipted bill.

It looks as though it would have to be 1932, kid. I'll know by the time I get to Key West definitely, but the doctors are talking six months now before the nerve may come back. If it shouldn't come back, it can be relieved by an operation. It may come a lot quicker, of course, but there is still complete paralysis of the wrist and she hasn't stopped hurting like one of those hells that Ezra writes about, but has never been in, since the first of November.[1] What happened technically was that when the ends of the bone were broken off and the arm bent back on itself, the nerve was stretched so that it put it on the bum. Today they fooled with the fleuroscope and took the splint off to look at it and found the bone is coming finely, straight and starting to be solid, but the incision between biceps and triceps was something over nine inches. Oh hell, I'm sick of talking, thinking, writing, or dictating about, but a damn sight more sick of having it.

I hate like the devil to make Pauline pound this typewriter, and I wonder if you'd send this letter to Charles to give him the army dope. I had a swell letter from Braw [Bra Saunders], who said he must have got hold of some bad liquor because he had fallen outside the door, but thank God he had not broken his arm. He advised us all to be careful as men are dying this year who have never died before.

Well general, there's not much news from here. I hope you saw Mclarnin and Petrolle. I would have given my last hundred bucks to have seen that fight.[2]

We may leave here in a week now for Piggott and go to Key West the first of the year. Hope you and Archie can get some shooting. If he wants double guns let him get them. I don't care what the men shoot as long as they learn to shoot them. I don't think it makes a hell of a lot of difference what you shoot as long as it isn't some freak gun made too light, so that it punishes you so that you can't hold on. We will provide jigs to carry the heavier guns.

I sure appreciate you writing such swell and such long letters because the mail is the only excitement. Do you notice where Hoover is going in for child welfare now and filling the White House with the patter of little feet.[3]

They will doubtless runn him as a great humanitarian—above mere business problems. I see where his organs are begining to refer to the unemployed as the idle. Well, your old friend Hem is among the unemployed, or the idle and everybody in the hospital tells me I should just accept this as a good long vacation.

I figure Maxie [Perkins] has double-crossed me pretty badly, but that may just be my diseased condition of mind.

Love to Maggie and best to yourself from Pauline and me. I can't tell you how terribly lousy I feel to have delayed the trip. If dope didn't constipate you I would most certainly become a dope head. I only had five days of it when they got scared that I liked it too much, but it certainly was wonderful, not as an active pleasure but as a means of passing out. What gets you bughouse is to lie awake all night with nothing to think about but how old Max, who you'd trust as far as you would Charles [Thompson], had double-crossed you. All this is probably a form of bed sores. So long, Mike. Remember me to all the unemployed club mates. I am thinking of taking an hour over the radio at Billings here as the Strater Snuff hour with the Strater Snuff Revellers. This is a great field for snuff as I believe I told you before.[4]

Hem

[Handwritten by Pauline:]
Dear Mike,

You'll never know how much Ernest has enjoyed your letters. He's been having a very bad time. I think he really suffers now more than he did at first, as he's been in bed so long and had so much pain that it's worn him down. He got up this morning and walked a little, and the doctor still seems to think we can leave Monday, but I dont know. I dont think he should try to travel while he still has so much pain. The doctor is going to change the splint and that may ease the arm. The doctor and the nurse seem to take the pain as a matter of course—"fracture case always has lots of pain; fracture case doesn't sleep nights—but Ernest and I dont, and we are sick of it.

To this gloomy postscript I add my love to Maggie and you.

Pauline

PUL, TL with typewritten signature [dictated] with ANS from Pauline

This was typewritten by Pauline on the verso of "X-Ray Department" forms. Although Carlos Baker dates this letter to c. 15 December 1930 (*SL*, 335–36), EH's and Pauline's remarks about the condition of his arm, about EH's being able to get up and walk "a little," and about their expected departure for Piggott in a week (i.e., 8 December) make the conjectured date of [c. 2 December 1930] more likely. Similar remarks appear in the preceding and following letters in this volume.

1 Pound's "Hell Cantos" (XIV–XVI) were collected in *A Draft of XVI. Cantos* (Paris: Three Mountains Press, 1925). Strater had illustrated the volume.
2 Irish-born welterweight James "Baby Face" McLarnin (1907–2004) and lightweight William Michael Petrolle (1905–1983), nicknamed "the Fargo Express." On 21 November 1930 in New York City, McLarnin went ten rounds against Petrolle, who was trying to make a comeback after having retired. Although McLarnin was heavily favored, Petrolle won by unanimous decision.
3 Herbert Hoover convened his second White House Conference on Child Health and Protection on 19–22 November 1930. That same month his three young grandchildren— Margaret, known as Peggy Ann (1926–2011); Herbert III, nicknamed Peter (1927–2010); and Joan (1930–2002)—moved into the White House while their father, Herbert Hoover, Jr. (1903–1969), recovered from tuberculosis in Asheville, North Carolina. The children would live with their grandparents through the following May.
4 The Revellers, a quintet of four male crooners and a pianist, performed on such sponsored commercial radio programs as *The Palmolive Orchestra Hour* (1927–1931). EH makes joking reference to the Strater family tobacco business.

To Archibald MacLeish, [c. 4 December 1930]

Dear Ochie,

This will certify that the bearer is an intimate friend of the writer and competent to speak on his religious, sexual and economic deficiencies, and that the writer is of sound mind, and possessing of all the intellect

he has

ever possesed

when writing

this, so help

him God.

(Signed)

ERNEST HEMINGWAY,bart.

Well, Mac, you've saddled a great responsibility on my slightly bedsored shoulders in refusing Antibes for the winter, but I like that place very much and went there once in the winter and started vomiting

just the other side of Cannes and was still retching violently when we
reached Bordighera. The lines

> of motors were as tightly
> packed as Fifth Avenue.
> You couldn't have thrown
> a stone in any direction
> without knocking out a
> round half dozen of vac-
> uum cooled teeth from
> the faces of the most ho
> rrible bloodies I have
> ever seen, all en route
> to Monte for a go at the
> tables. All of it
> looked no more like the
> fine Riviera we used to
> lie on the beach and
> drink Cinzano on than
>> the old Cafe du
>> Dome which

was always deserted and where you went with somebody to play billiards
looks like the ediface with a thousand never deserted tables which is now at
the corner of Montparnasse and Raspail.

If I have led you astray in this, you can cut off my right arm and will be
very pleased to have you do so anyway, because it looks as though it had
definitely delayed our African trip until 1932. The doct-

> ors are talking six months
> now before the nerve comes
> back, and having studied
> the dung of the grey-brea-
> sted hyena you know we
> must have the nerve back
> before we start shooting
> them down like the dogs

they are. If you aren't going to what I have learned to refer to as the Philip Barry country[1] when whill we see you in Key West? We go there the first of January. Ze fish are zere now. (I got to talk that was from hearing Rudy Vallee imitate Maurice Chavelier on the radio last night. It was a good deal like hearing La Gish imitate La Parker.[2] I have got a fourteen foot salmon rod from Haridy's, with

> four different tips to try on king
>> fish and tarpon.
>> We will
>> go to Tortugas
> and anywhere else. A citizen named

Chub Weaver from Red Lodge in this state, is driving the car down from here to Key West, he being a high-grade cook who also holds an embalmers license but without employment in either of these professions and he will cook on all trips.

> He cooked
>> for us in
>>> the mountains
>>> and was very
>>>> good. Pauline
>>>> does not care
>>>>> for him be-
>>>>>> cause he calls
>>>>>>> her Pauline

but since I addres her at all times as Mrs. Hemingway, Chub may come to call her that too, in which event he could cook in the home as well as for us on trips. I read an introduction written by your old buddy Wilson which seemed to me all an introduction shouldn't be, in that it made the author out a crook, a faker, a romanticist and a lover of grasshoppers. Did you see it on the In Out Time
Scribners has got out.

> It seems that old Hem
>> is not the devout Bud-
>>> dist that we all know

but a pain worshipper.
Well, had Herr Wilson
been here he could have
seen the Master at his
orisons. This bludy
arm started in to hurt
like holy hell on November
first and kept it up
steady for a month.
It would have been
a gala for Wilson
to see the master
study it. As a
matter of fact, my
system was after
the third week to
wait until every
body was out of the room
at night and then cry like D
otty Parker at the mention of an
injustice to some small defenceless
animal. All that I have learned about
pain is that if kept up long e-
nough, it wears you out and I knew this before. It also wears your wife
out, and if you had any children or friends around it would wear them
out too.

By the way,
could you
see Dotty
and ask her
to write to
Piggott. Tell
her I know
that she's

more of a co than a cor respondant, but give her a few details of the state of my arm which the doctor said when he opened it up looked like the part of the meat of an elk that you have to throw away where the bullet smashes the bone, and ask her if she doesn't want to write to me as just a mite of suffering humanity. Or, as she's a great dog lover,[3] tell her old Hem admits to being a son of a bitch. He can prove it at any time by production of his mother.

We go from here to Piggott some time next week. I can't tell you how terribly I feel about putting the trip on the bum. I imagine you have some idea of it, but the doctors say that you can't expect the nerve to be good before six months, and it isn't until then that they know what they will have to do about it in case it shouldn't come out all right. But there's no danger of our missing out on the trip, and I believe general impovrishment will keep the hunters away from the beasts, and a year from this summer we'll be better able to recognize their excrement and shoot them. The beasts not the excrement. If you want to shoot excrements, New York is the place. Although since Stewart refused to shake hands with Griswald it may be that there's pretty good excrement hunting on the continent.

There was a

guy here who says

YOU CAN GET THE BEST

DOUBLE*BARRELED RIFLES IN THE WORLD AT NAIROBI second hand for under two hundred dollars.

So that's where we'll buy our double-barreled rifles. He said you would get guns worth two

thousand dollars for a song. So it might pay to take Mrs. Macleish along. Unfortunately, Mrs.

Hemingway doesn't sing, but we could secrete a small phonograph on her person and between

the two of

these splen-

did women

get enough two thous-

and dollar riffles to
set up as Macleish
and Hobbs, Gunsmiths[4]
and fresh water
pimps.

Well. Mac, I feel I've abused Pauline enough
at pounding this mill, although she has been

trying to amuse herself by typing it very fancy,
and I hope you will show it to Mrs. M. as an

example of what a good wife can do in case you
should ever become an ex-writer like Papa.

Write to Piggott and see if you can get Dotty to
write to Piggott, too. Give my best to Benchley,

and my love to
Mrs. MacLeish and Mimi.

Papy[5] or if you prefer,—
to you Mr. MacLeish
Pappy

Ernest has just seen the way I've typed this and he doesn't seem to like it,
so if you could-can imagine it as just the ordinary typing it would-will make
it a lot easier for me, and I wont do it again

P.

LOC, TL with typewritten signature [dictated] with AN from Pauline; letterhead:
St. Vincent's Hospital / CONDUCTED BY THE SISTERS OF CHARITY / Billings,
Montana

1 Philip Barry (1896–1949), American playwright whose best-known works included *Holiday* (1928) and *The Philadelphia Story* (1939). He and his wife, Ellen Barry (née Semple, 1898–1995), owned the Villa Lorenzo in Cannes, about 8 miles from the Murphys' Villa America in Antibes.
2 Maurice Chevalier (1888–1972), French singer and movie star whose French accent EH imitates. EH presumably refers to Dorothy Parker and Lillian Gish (1893–1993), American actress who starred in silent films including *The Birth of a Nation* (1915), *Way Down East* (1920), and *La Bohème* (1926).

3   A well-known animal lover, Dorothy Parker owned dogs all her life, treating them with affectionate humor in such poems as "To my Dog" (1921), which begins "I often wonder why on earth / You rate yourself so highly; / A shameless parasite, from birth / You've lived the life of Reilly."

4   EH alludes to the gun-manufacturing company Griffin & Hobbs.

5   The remainder of the letter is handwritten by Pauline.

To Guy Hickok, 5 December [1930]

Dear Gros,

Well Gros, it certainly is satisfactory to read of your success at outwitting the French and pitting them the one against the other. I've often thought that if you would have been at 6 rue Férou it would have cost de Juvenal over a million francs to take possession, and it would have ended by his not marrying this widow at all but merely turning the hotel over to Hickok as the easiest way out of the whole ghastly business.[1] The French are always bitched in foreign politics and invariably outwitted by any statesman and you, Gros, have discovered the secret. If you would only operate on a big scale instead of confining yourself to mere domiciliary transactions, you would have been able to drive every Frenchman out of the country by now and we would probably have Ezra Pound back living in Paris. It certainly is a filthy business for them to give the Nobel prize to Mr. Lewis when they could have given it to Ezra or to the author of Ulysses. Or is it that the Nobel prize is supposed to represent the best aspects of Swedish life in America, or anywhere, and that is why the give it to Lewis? Well, I suppose we should be thankful they didn't give it to Dr. Henry van Dyke or William Lyon Phelps, both of whom, I'm sure, felt that they were in line for it.[2] Also, it eliminated the Dreiser menace, although of two bad writers, Dreiser certainly deserves it a hell of lot more than Lewis.[3] It has occurred to me that the only difference between the Nobel prize and all other prizes is simply a matter of quantity of money and since all prizes are lousy, what's the difference except in the extent of the sum. Although last year when they gave it to Thomas Mann, and when they gave it to Yeats, it made me damned happy.[4]

If this typing is usually neat, or if there are any words mis-spelled that you would expect me to know, or if you detect an understanding feminine touch, it is because it is being typed by Pauline. We have been in ST. VINCENT'S HOSPITAL, Billings, Montana for the last five weeks, and hope to leave next week for Piggott. Coming into Billings with Dos en route to Piggott, had a spill brought on by loose gravel and Saturday night drivers and six days later when the doctor operated on my upper arm to fasten the bone together by boring a hole through it and then lashing the end with kangaroo tendon, the inside of the arm looked like the part an elk that you have to throw away as unfit for human consumption when you butcher it out. So now it is all fine except that it is lousy and has hurt like holy hell ever since it happened, but will be all right in six months or else won't be. The bone is knitting very well and they have it straight and any trouble is in the nerves.

We go from here to Piggott and then to Key West the first of the year and will see you in Paris sometime in the spring, the first of May, maybe. I had my book on bull fighting about three-quarters done and we figured on going to Madrid in May and June to get the illustrations, would have had the first draft of the book done by Christmas. Now it will be done pour Paques or le Trinité. (Ernest told me how to spell Paques, because he thought I might put down Paques the composer.[5] You can see he has great confidence in my, augmented by being in bed).

An average of 63 banks a day failed in Arkansas. Things are pretty prosperous here in Billings due to the sugar beet racket. Everyone else in America is unemployed including the writer of this letter. If you want to know what kind of car it is that tipped over—it was the same car we put on the boat at Bordeaux and that we used to drive out from Pamplona in.[6] If you're contemplating going into the theatrical business would advise that I received an advance of 750 dolars on A Farewell To Arms, that Mr. [Paul] Reynolds, who obtained this munificent offer, received seventy-five of that, that the lawyer employed to check up on Mr. Reynolds activities, took 102.50, the dramatist Guild took 18 something and several assessments I have refused to pay, and with the rest we bought our Beverly Hills Mansion. The play, according to the producers, Mr. Reynolds who handled the money, and the lawyer employed to check up on Mr. Reynolds, never made the advance. On the other hand, the movie rights sold for 80,000 dollars, of which Mr. Reynolds, who had no part in the negociations, received 8,000, according to his accounting, the lawyer employed to check up on Mr. Reynolds was content with a modest 200 odd, Mr. Woods, who produced the play just long enough to sell it to the movies, and Mr. Stallings who dramatized it ditto, each received 24,000 and Mr. Hemingway received 24,000 also, which will be good news to all his friends, relatives and dependents, and the Billings Hospital.

In case this letter should not seem sweet in tone, it is because it's being dictated. Pen pencil, or glass in hand I am the sweetest tempered of mortals (Mrs. Hemingway may refuse to type this). But dictating that old Primo de Rivera strain comes up.[7] If you hear any reports that we are backing any Left Bank magazines, will you kindly shoot whoever brings them to you as an objest lesson. We are not backing anything. We are in bed paning in the Far West and finding no gold. Several weeks ago, people stopped writing out here because they were all sure that with a simple little thing like a broken arm, we would have shoved off long ago. Even the Billings Gazette sent a reporter up to find what this fellow Hemingway was still doing in the hospital with nothing more than a fractured arm.[8] The report was at the Billings Gazette that he must have been in frightful shape when he came in, cirrohsis of the liver, probably. Well Gros, knowing your interest in ghastly details, and the pleasure with which you watch a tumor extracted from anyone, whether you know them or not,[9] let me tell you that the humerus was broken clean off so that my arm was bent back on itself so that the knuckles touched the shoulder, that it was put in place by Mr. Hemingstein himself, and held between his knees during a 22 mile drive into Billings. You could see the point of the bone under the skin, but a compound fracture was avoided. It was set three times, and the ends would not hold because the muscle would draw them out of place. The operation took two hours and the incision of nine and one-half inches long, and the kangaroo tendons used came from contented kangaroos. The arm busted is the right one and I believe that we have written you enough and even perhaps a little too much about it. But while the family does not desire wreaths or couronnes, and I would be glad if you would keep my present condition from the Messrs McAlmon, Callaghan, [ect]., any anount of letters that you may send to Piggott Arkansas, in the heart of the ex-banking belt, would be very well received. And as long as Mrs. Hemingway's hands hold out, would have a good chance of being answered.

Best to you, to Mary, and good luck with your family. I have scrutinized a number of sinister looking former hotel keepers, broken by drink and other excesses, and even whispered Hickok into the ears of several in an effort to surprise them into an admission that they were your father, but so far have been able to get no one in this great Western country to admit to it. However, we are pursuing our searches diligently and will send in an expense account the first of the year. What would you like done with your old man if I could locate him?

So Long Gros. Love to you both from Pauline and me.

Ernest

Dec 5th

phPUL, TL with typewritten signature [dictated]; letterhead: St. Vincent's Hospital / CONDUCTED BY THE SISTERS OF CHARITY / Billings, Montana

1 French journalist and statesman Henry de Jouvenel (1876–1935), after whom a short stretch of the rue Férou, from the rue du Canivet to the Place Saint-Sulpice, would be named in 1936. In a letter to EH of 12 August 1930, Hickok had enclosed a clipping and reported "that your old land–lord has gone and got himself marries [sic]. He marries very frequently these days" (PUL). On 4 August 1930, de Jouvenel married his third wife, Germaine Sarah Hément (1882–1964), widow of wealthy industrialist Charles Louis–Dreyfuss, who died in 1929. De Jouvenel was previously married (between 1912 and 1925) to the French writer Colette (née Sidonie–Gabrielle Colette, 1873–1954).

2 On 28 November 1930, speaking at a luncheon in Germantown, Pennsylvania, Henry Jackson van Dyke (1852–1933), American clergyman, professor, poet, and member of the American Academy of Arts and Letters, protested the awarding of the Nobel Prize in Literature to Sinclair Lewis, claiming Lewis painted a mean, negative portrait of America: "It shows the Swedish Academy knows nothing of the English language. They handed Lewis a bouquet, but they gave America a very back-handed compliment" ("Nobel Prize Award to Lewis Is an 'Insult' to America, Says van Dyke, Hitting Scoffers," *New York Times*, 29 November 1930, 1). Lewis responded to van Dyke's criticism, saying, "I am honored no less that American colleagues have attacked my work and I am particularly honored that the attack came from where it did" ("Sinclair Lewis Off, Hits Back at Critic," *New York Times*, 30 November 1930, 5). Admitting that he had hoped for the award, Lewis mentioned other deserving American writers, including EH. In his Nobel Prize Lecture, "The American Fear of Literature," delivered on 12 December 1930, Lewis would describe EH as "a bitter youth, educated by the most intense experience, disciplined by his own high standards, an authentic artist whose home is in the whole of life" (quoted in Horst Frenz, ed., *Nobel Lectures: Literature 1901–1967* [Amsterdam: Elsevier, 1969], 288).

3 Theodore Dreiser (1871–1945), author of *Sister Carrie* (1900) and *An American Tragedy* (1925), had also been nominated for the 1930 Nobel Prize in Literature. He never received it.

4 Thomas Mann was awarded the 1929 Nobel Prize in Literature and William Butler Yeats the 1923 prize.

5 *Pour Pâques or Le Trinité*: by Easter or Trinity Sunday (French). In 1931 Easter would fall on 5 April and Trinity Sunday on 31 May. Désiré Pâque (née Marie Joseph Léon Désiré Pâque, 1867–1939), Belgian pianist, organist, theoretician, and composer of eight symphonies, four masses, an opera, and several other chamber and orchestral pieces.

6 Hickok had driven with EH from Paris to Bordeaux to deliver the Ford Cabriolet to *La Bourdonnais*, which sailed for New York on 10 January 1930 with EH, Pauline, Patrick, and Patrick's nanny aboard. Hickok described the drive in two articles for the *Brooklyn Daily Eagle*, "'Do I Beat My Wife? No,' Says Hemingway" (28 January 1930, 19) and "Bum Hotel's Gaudy Door Fools Tourists" (29 January 1930, 19).

7 General Miguel Primo de Rivera (1870–1930) seized control of the Spanish government in September 1923 and ruled as dictator until January 1930, when the nation's bleak economic situation and the army's dissatisfaction with his management caused him to resign. He went into exile in France, and died in Paris in March 1930.

8 The *Billings Gazette* published an unattributed report of the accident on 2 November 1930 ("Noted Novelist Is Injured in Auto Accident"). Although the newspaper may have sent reporter Franklin Long Gregory (1905–1985) to interview EH (see EH to Perkins, 28 December [1930]), no additional mentions of EH's accident have been located in the *Gazette*.

9 In 1928 EH and Hickok exchanged letters about a medical procedure Hickok witnessed as a news reporter (*Letters* vol. 3, 359–60). Hickok had described the excision of five fibrous tumors from a woman, including one "as big as your two fists," another "about as big as a fist and a half; and three little ones like hen's eggs with lumpy jaw" (2 February 1928, JFK).

To Maxwell Perkins, 8 December 1930

NBN394 22 DL=BILLINGS MONT 8 239P

MAXWELL PERKINS,CARE CHARLES SCRIBNERS SONS=

597 FIFTH AVE=

DEAR MAX IGNORE MY LETTER ABOUT INTRODUCTION[1] SORRY I EVER NOTICED IT THINGS NOT SO GOOD HERE SO PLEASE CONTINUE NEWSPAPER SUBSCRIPTION=

    ERNEST.

PUL, Cable; Western Union destination receipt stamp: 1930 DEC 8 PM 5 01

1 EH refers to his letter to Perkins of 1 December 1930.

To Louis Henry Cohn, 8 December 1930

NBF268 38 DL=BILLINGS MONT 8 243P

CAPTAIN LOUIS HENRY COHN=

52 EAST 56 ST=

YOUR LETTER UNRECEIVED HERE INDEFINITELY BOOKS MOST
WELCOME ADVISE HOLD FIRST EDITIONS AS MAY NOT BE ANY
MORE WILL SEE THAT LITTLE REVIEW AND THREE STONES ARE
RETURNED TO YOU THEY WENT AHEAD WITH MY LUGGAGE
TO PIGGOTT=

    HEMINGWAY..

UDel, Cable: Western Union destination receipt stamp: 1930 DEC 8 PM 5 15

1. Responding to an unlocated wire from Cohn, EH refers to copies of the *Little Review* and *TSTP* that Cohn had loaned to him (see EH to Cohn, [19 December 1930]).

To Maxwell Perkins, 18 December 1930

NBN 168 10=BILLINGS MONT 18 948A
MAXWELL PERKINS=
597 5 AVE=
PLEASE FORWARD MAIL PIGGOTT HOPE ABLE LEAVE SATURDAY
OR SUNDAY=

    ERNEST HEMINGWAY.

PUL, Cable; Western Union destination receipt stamp: 1930 DEC 18 PM 12 17

Perkins would cable back the same day, "Delighted receive telegram suggesting great improvement" (PUL).

To Louis Henry Cohn, [19 December 1930]

Dear Captain Cohn,

Thank you very much for the books which you sent that arrived today. If there are any of them which are first editions or that you value I will be very glad to return them. It was very kindof you to send them.

When your wire came asking if I had received your letter, I did not know what letter was referred to, since the last I had received came via Cooke City

Montana to the ranch and I answered it there. Your copy of Three Stories and Ten Poems and of the Little Review which you had loaned to me, I had sent on to Piggott Ark?, with my books when Dos Passos and I left the ranch by car. They are still there or you would have received them long before this. I made arrangements, however, for them to be sent to you in case I should not have been able to get to Piggott to send them myself.

We plan now to leave for Piggott in time to arrive there for Christmas, and I will have the books registered and sent to you, along with the peice of manuscript if it is not too late for this. You might let me know at Piggott on receipt of this if you still want the page of mss. I hope everything is going well with you and yours and with your shop.

Yours very truly,

UDel, TL [dictated]; letterhead: St. Vincent's Hospital / CONDUCTED BY THE SISTERS OF CHARITY / Billings, Montana; postmark: BILLINGS / MONT., DEC 19 / 3³⁰PM / 1930

To Bennett Cerf, 26 December [1930]

Piggott Arkansas

December 26

Bennett A. Cerf Esq.

20 East 57th Street, New York

Dear Mr. Cerf,

Thank you very much for sending me the Modern Livrary books.[1] They were very fine to have and the proper size for one-handed reading.

Please excuse this dictated and unsigned note and its brevityas I have not yet gotten the arm into use yet. With best regards and many thanks again for the books, yours very truly,

Ernest Hemingway

Columbia, TL with typewritten signature [dictated]; postmark: PIGGOTT / ARK., DEC 27 / 1930 / 6 PM

1 In a letter of 10 December 1930, Cerf had expressed concern over EH's accident and said he was sending "several of our recent Modern Library books in the hope that they may help you to while away a few of the tedious hours" (JFK).

To William D. Horne, Jr., 26 December [1930]

Piggott Arkansas

December 26

Dear Horney,

The only reason you haven't heard from me, article, and why we haven't written you what grand news it is to hear about Bunny and you and the heir[1] is that I was too bloody sick to write and Pauline had a full time job organizing possilbe funeral arrangements, packing, unpacking, writing checks, many checks, Also, article, you advised me not to dictate but that advice though sound, was uneeded because I can't dictate as this letter will easily prove. But you were grand to write such fine letters and to get the old carper [Howell Jenkins] to write and I wonder if you could call him up and tell him how much I appreciated getting his letter but that I was in such lowsy bloody shape that I couldn't write; then when I tried to the nurse had put his letter somewhere and I couldn't get the address.

This is all, kid. Except to wish you all good luck again. We left Billings in time to get here for Christmas eve and when we can travel again will shove off for Key West. So long kid and excuse a lowsy letter,

Heming stein

P. S. This arm is nothing to worry about. Its just turned out to be one of those long things you hold like the stock market.

P.S. I hope you guys had a swell time over the hollow days but make Bunny be careful. You shouldn't ski after seven months, Doctor Hemingstein noted obstetrician signing off,. Ladies and gentlemen of the radio audience you have been listening to Doctor Hemingstein speaking. Thank you, Doctor Hemingstein. Now we will hear again the Lucky Strike Dawnse orchestra.[2]

phPUL, TL with typewritten signature [dictated]

1 One of EH's nicknames for Horne was "Horned Article." The Hornes were anticipating the birth of their first child in January 1931.
2 Sponsored by the cigarette brand Lucky Strike, the *Lucky Strike Dance Orchestra* was launched in September 1928 as a nationwide weekly radio program on thirty-nine stations of the NBC (National Broadcasting Company) network; in September 1930 the program expanded to three weekly broadcasts. It would run until 1934.

To Maxwell Perkins, 28 December [1930]

Piggott, Dec. 28th

Dear Max,

Got here Christmas eve and am still feeling pretty punk, but hope we'll be able to leave for Key West by January third. Thanks ever so much for your letters, wires and the fine books. This is just a note to tell you about Archie Mac Leish, who is leaving Houghton Mifflin of his own accord and who has received offers from Harcourt Brace, Harpers and so forth, but who wants, on my advice, to come to Scribners instead. I think he is w[i]thout any doubt writing the best poetry written in America, and that he has the biggest future. He's working on a long poem called Conquistador, about Cortez in Mexico, which wont be ready for some time, but which you could make arrancements about publishing when it comes out by writing to him to Archibald Mac Leish, care Fortune magazine, New York, and making an appointment for him to see you. You couldn't get a better name, a better writer, or a better guy for your list of what ever I may call them, and his future is ahead of him instead of behind him.[1] He will be as bashful to talk about money as you will be to offer it to him, and will deprecate any monetary arrangement, but for God's sake offer him as much advance as you can afford because it will cheer him up like hell and you will get it back many, many times over in the end, no matter what you give him. Some poetry that he's written all ready will be good a couple hundred years from now as it is.

You know how I usually write to you recommending somebody, if doing it out of "goodness of heart" or friendship. I usually say to be very polite and not hurt the gentelman's feelings and throw him out as pleasantly as possible. This about Archie is something different. He is the best bet you could have as a poet right now if you had your choice of the whole works, and do not let let Edmund Wilson tell you differently. I promise you this before God. He has come on steadily while the others have stood still or gone backwards. It would be a tragedy if he went to any other publisher.

Don't think from this that I'm for God, for Scribner and for Yale,[2] or actuated by patriotic motives, but you yourself have been damn good to me, whether or not your outfit can sell any books, and Archie is the biggest favour I could do you.

This seems to have gotten longer than a note. Did you ever talk to Wilson about the introduction or not. I hope you got my wire in time so that you did not. If I hadn't had a lot of fever and one thing and another I would not have paid any attention except to register it myself for future reference. Oh yes, a fellow named Gregory, a newspaper man in Billings, sent you a novel about which I know nothing.[3] He was a very nice fellow and was damn pleasant to me, and I wish you could give it a good reading and write him a letter about it. I look forwardvery much to seeing you at Key West in March. If Johnathan Cape comes in and asks you anything about my next book, don't tell him anything. Except that you know it was nearly done when I got hurt. It was, too, by God. I'll let you read some of it when you come down to Key West, if you want to, and are a very good boy in the meantime, and don't shoot any birds on Federal Bird Refuges.

When you get this letter, the forwarding department might start forwarding my mail to Key West. Hope we'll be there to receive it. I'm still in bed most of the time, but count on Key West to fix everything up finely.

Best to you always,

Ernest

Dictated—

PUL, TL with typewritten signature [dictated]

1 Disappointed with Houghton Mifflin's advertising for *New Found Land*, MacLeish was receptive to EH's suggestion that he publish *Conquistador* with Scribner's, but when Houghton Mifflin made a favorable bid for it MacLeish accepted. The poem would be published in 1932 and would bring MacLeish the Pulitzer Prize for Poetry in 1933.
2 Yale University's alma mater anthem, "Bright College Years" (lyrics written in 1881 by Yale alumnus Henry S. Durand), ends with the watch-cry "For God, for Country and for Yale!"

3 Franklin Long Gregory worked as a reporter for the *Billings Gazette* from 1929 to 1935; he then accepted an editorial position with the *Philadelphia Record* (1936-1947). His mystery novel, *The Cipher of Death*, would be published by Harper & Brothers in 1934. His second novel, a horror story titled *The White Wolf*, would be published by Random House in 1941. Any correspondence between Perkins and Gregory remains unlocated.

To Archibald MacLeish, 28 December [1930]

Piggott, Dec. 28th

Dear Archie,

Just a note to let you know I've written to Max Perkins telling him you are free, what I think of your stuff, and that it would be tragic for you to go to any other publishing house than Scribner's. All publishing is an unfortunate business, but they are so much the best house that there is no comparison with others. I told him to write you care Fortune.

We got here Christmas eve, had Christmas, and went to bed. Feel punk but think it is weakness and lack of exercise. Maybe it is a good sign. Anyway, hope to be in shape to travel by January third or fourth. When will you be in shape to travel, Doctor. What about your little woman? Will she be in shape to travel? All you little people know the direction to travel, I hope, or must teacher get out that nasty switch again? The direction to travel is south.

I swear to God, Mac, I would like to write to you for an hour, but my own little woman has been doing trained nursing since we left Miss O'Day,[1] and I'll be damned if I have the heart to make her do stenography, too. So this is all of the letter. You know, if you've got any sense, how much it meant to us your coming out there.[2] I'll write soon.

Love from Pauline, Jinny and
Pappy

LOC, TL with typewritten signature [dictated]

1 Harriet Marie O'Day (1890-1976), the nurse assigned to EH at St. Vincent Hospital in Billings, had been a Red Cross nurse during WWI, stationed in France. According to Michael Reynolds, it was she who provided EH with a radio in the hospital (*1930s*, 54).
2 Earlier that month, MacLeish made the long trip from New York to Billings to visit EH while he was convalescing. EH reportedly greeted MacLeish saying, "So! You've come to see me die, have you?" (Donaldson *MacLeish*, 207).

To Donald Ogden Stewart, 28 December [1930]

Piggott, Dec. 28th—

Dear Don,

I couldn't urinate when your wire came, let alone telegraph, and by the time I could do both Christmas was passed and we were ready to start on the new year. We sent you the wire about Merry Christmas and so forth before the one came that you'd sent to Billings. The funny thing was, Kid, that MacLeish didn't read us any poetry. He came out because he happened to call up Pauline on the long distance on the day that the trained nurse was crying in the hall, that the sisters advised Pauline to pray to St Jude, the saint of the impossible, and that your old buddy had just produced a quart of puss that would have made the fortune of a chocolate eclair manufacturer. I imagine Archie, who is a damn good friend of mine, thought he might be some use to Pauline in the disposal of the body. Anyway, his coming out there seemed to me about as white a thing as anybody ever did, and if it seems otherwise to you you might mention it to me when I get this arm fixed up. No offense, Stewart, no offense. Mention it now if you like.

We're going to Key West soon after the first of the year. Address there: Key West. Thanks ever so much for the wire and I hope you and Bee have a grand year.

Ernest

(dictated)

Yale, TL with typewritten signature [dictated]

To Maurice-Edgar Coindreau, 31 December [1930]

Piggot Arkansas
December 31

Dear Monsieur Coindreau,

I have just today seen your letter of October 25th. As you may have heard, Dos Passos and I had a motor accident on November first near Billings Montana which put me in hospital in Billings for two months and will keep me from using my right arm for several months more. Your letter I had picked up with some others at Gardener Montana and put in a pocket of the car intending to read them that night in Billings. After the accident Dos could not find the letter and I had it very much on my mind to write you explaining the circumstances and asking if you would be good enough to write to me again and summarize what was in it. But they were obliged to operate to tie the ends of the humerus together and afterwards with complications fever and one thing and another, my good intentions were lost. Yesterday, when the car arrived here from Sheridan Wyoming where Dos had driven it they told me there was an unopened letter in one of the pockets and it turned out to be yours. I am very sorry that it has been unanswered so long.

First thank you very much for sending the books. I will mark the blanks today and have the books sent off to you to-morrow.[1] The sentence that you ask about has no masturbatory intent. Corks off means simply sleeps in this connection. I will get a picture for you to send to Gallamard (sic) but can not furnish him any biographical material.[2] I write fiction and I find that all publishers want biographical material only so they can use it to make your fiction seem a "document". I do not claim even to have been in the war and it is impossible for me to furnish a military history to a publisher. If he wants to he can say that I served on the Italian front which is true enough and ample but I would prefer no military mention at all. I have forbidden Scribners ever to use any personal publicity because I want the stuff to be judged as fiction without any attempt to tie it up with documentation. They don't need any of that stuff and there is no reason to encourage them in publishing it.

This is just a note to thank you for your letter and explain why you haven't heard from me. My address will be Key West Florida for the next couple of months.

With very best regards, yours always,
Ernest Hemingway

PUL, Typewritten transcription of EH letter

This typewritten transcription, located in the Carlos Baker Collection at PUL, bears the following descriptive note: "Single-spaced / Typed with typed signature (no handwriting) on buff deckle-edged stationery. No envelope."

1 In his letter of 25 October 1930, Coindreau wrote that he was sending a copy of *SAR* for EH to dedicate and one of *FTA* for EH to fill in the blanks and sign. He asked EH for copies of *MWW* and *TOS* (JFK).

2 Coindreau had written, "I found another sentence which I don't quite understand—'I am going to sleep in the major's bed, I am going to sleep where the old man corks off. Is 'cork off' just a slang word for sleep or is it more . . . naughty? I noticed that the sentence has been left out in the Tauchnitz Edition." Coindreau also relayed Gallimard's request for "biographical notes" and a photo of EH.

To Mr. Small, 31 December 1930

> Piggott Arkansas
> December 31, 1930

Dear Mr. Small,

I can not tell you how much your letter meant to me and I feel very badly not to have answered it but I was in the hospital myself for two months with a smashed right arm. The people were real enough. Don't worry about that. I hope you have good luck and get well soon. Thank you again for writing to me.

> Yours always,
> Ernest Hemingway
> Ernest Hemingway
> left hand
> writing![1]

Clean Sweep Auctions online catalog, Port Washington, New York, 2 June 2004, Lot 79 (illustrated), TLS with autograph postscript

1 EH added his penciled signature and postscript to this typewritten letter in a wobbly hand, marking an early attempt by the right-handed author to resume writing after the accident.

To Don Carlos Guffey, [c. late December 1930–January 1931]

To Dr. Don Carlos Guffey with much admiration and grateful remembrance of a Caeserean that was beautifully done and turned out splendidly—[1]
Ernest Hemingway

written with the left hand due to fracture of right humerus, with open reduction, etc. I have the wilder walpole letters[2] for you and will get them to you sooner or later. Havent been in touch with my files for many months! EH.

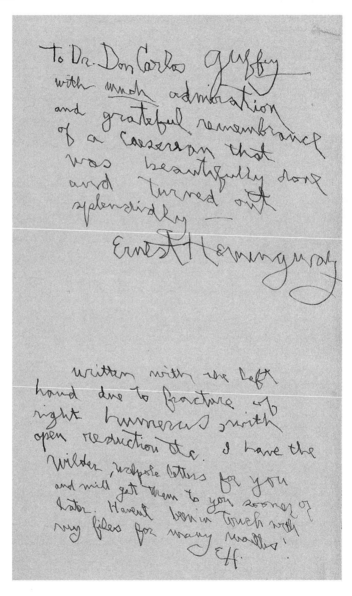

UMKC, Inscription

EH wrote this inscription on one of the front endpapers of presentation copy number 3 of the limited first edition of *FTA* (printed in 510 copies of which 500 were for sale and 10 for presentation). EH's shaky handwriting closely resembles that in other letters from late December 1930 through January 1931.

1 Guffey had delivered Patrick Hemingway by Caesarian section on 28 June 1928 at Research Hospital in Kansas City, Missouri.

2 In a letter to Guffey of 12 April 1931, EH would promise, "in Paris I will get you the letters Wilder—Walpole—from my stored correspondence." Any request by Guffey for these letters remains unlocated, as do any letters from Hugh Walpole to EH. The Hemingway Collection at JFK holds ten incoming letters from Thornton Wilder to EH dated 1926–1929.

To Maurice-Edgar Coindreau, 1 January 1931

[Carlos Baker transcription of EH inscription:]

Inscription in Maurice Coindreau's copy of A Farewell To Arms.

To Maurice Coindreau / with very best wishes, / this sample of left- / handed writing by a righthanded / writer— / Ernest Hemingway / Piggott / Arkansas / Jan 1, 1931.

Note: Hemingway wrote this with his left hand since his right arm was still either in a cast or still unusable following his car accident in November, 1930 near Billings, Montana.

[On separate page:]

On or before Jan. 31, 1931

Hemingway fills in obscenities left blank in Coindreau's copy of FTA, and sends same to Coindreau for his guidance with translation.

page 35 — f--k

page 50 — s--t

page 186 — Rinaldi calls salvarsan a mercurial product. Hemingway has crossed out mercurial and in the upper margin with his left hand has written "an arsenical", as explained in his letter to Coindreau.[1]

page 201 — f---ing

page 204 (twice) s--t

page 205 — s--t

page 209 (four times) f---ing

page 211— s--t (EH missed one on 219 evidently f---ed)

page 221 — f---ing

page 222 — f--k

page 228 — c---s---er

page 238 — same as 228

There are no others in the book. Note that of the sixteen actual obscenities used in the book, 14 are to be found within a single section of less than 40 pp. The reason is clear: this is the section dealing with the common soldiers and the trench-mortar episode and its aftermath—occasions when in their rage and pain these soldiers would use that kind of language. The use of the obscenities here, with only two early uses, helps to create the special atmosphere of evil and suffocation that is intended for this section of the book. The relative clean-ness of language elsewhere contrasts thus the more sharply with this section's language.

PUL, Transcription of EH inscription and typewritten notes

This typewritten transcription and notes concerning EH's inscription and annotations of Coindreau's copy of *FTA* are preserved in the Carlos Baker Collection at PUL and reproduced here verbatim. Replying to EH's 12 October 1930 letter, Coindreau had thanked EH for offering to fill in the blanks and write a dedication in a copy of *FTA* and said he would be sending the book to EH that afternoon ([25 October 1930], JFK).

1 See EH to Coindreau, [12 October 1930].

To Karl Pfeiffer, 1 January [1931]

Piggott Arkansas

January 1

Dear Karl,

That was a lovely sweater you and Mathilde gave me for Christmas and I have wanted to write you every day about it but it is difficult to fit in the time with the stenographer and find the stenographer and having found her keep her in the room but what this is really is a joint letter to the boat from Pauline and me wishing you good luck and a grand time and containing as much practical ~~advice~~ information on the practical side of wine drinking as we can get in when we can get a stenographer to put it down.[1] Speaking of putting it down, the enclosed is to buy some of the recommended vintages and put them down.

Allright, although you probably know a great deal about them and have most of this information already, I'll write this as though you knew wines whiskeys an[d] liquers only by heresay.

You're going on a British boat so the Bordeaux, light red French wines will probably be listed in the wine list as Clarets and the white wines from the Rhine and Moselle will probably be called Hock. The ordinary clarets are St. Estephe, St. Emilion, Pontet-Canet, Margaux, these will do to begin on. They're inexpensive, do not make you bilious and are good to drink at any time of the meal except with oysters and fish. You can drink a full bottle of any of them yourself at any time without having to worry about it going to your head or upsetting your stomach but remember to drink all wines slowly, smell them as you drink them if you want to appreciate the taste. The quality of a Burdeau or Clare[t] is not necessarily determined by its price. A high price usually indicated a higher degree of alcohol in a wine or a rarer vintage, that is an especially good year, or wine made from grapes that grow on a very small area, or restricted area of ground, producing a wine that because of its scarcity and subtlety and bouquet is in great demand by connoseurs. The chances are when you start you cannot tell one claret from another regardless of price but if you commence with St. Emilion, then go to St. Estephe and then to Margot you will find you will be noticing the difference in no time. When you get so that you[r] palate appreciates them, try a bottle of Chateau Margot, which is about as good as you can get but not as good for steady drinking at meals as any of th[e] three lighter wines that I've named above.

Most people when they start drinking wines prefer sweet wines and especially sweet white Bordeaux. This is natural because the education of the palate in any thing always proceeds from sweet to dry. White Bordeaux will probably be called on the British wine list white clarets, and I suggest that you try them in this order: Graves, Barsac, Sauterne, and finally Graves Monopole, which is a dry white Brodeaux. These wines are fine to drink at the start of the meal with oysters, fish and chicken, but when the roast comes on, switch to the red Bordeaux, which you can then drink all the way through. You can't get tight on either of these wines, but don't try to prove me a liar.

You can get tight on Burgundy, and I'd only drink it when you're getting plenty of exercise, because otherwise it can put the liver on the bum and make you billious and ruin your capacity to drink all the other fine things. But when you are getting plenty of exercise, and are in good shape, and want to try some Burgundy, which is the fullest bodied, noblest wine of all, drink either Richbourg, Pommard, Beaune, Hospice de Baune, Volnay, Moulin au Vent. These are wines that are wonderful with game, roast, steaks, or any good red blooded meat. I've named them starting with those that are least heavy, but they are all plenty heavy, but are all noble wines that will never do you wrong until well passed the middle of the second bottle. But while you might be able to drink two bottles yourself of a good red Bordeaux, if you ever drink two bottles of Burgundy yourself, you ought to spend the next day drinking Vichy water.

White Burgandies are very diggerent from red. Where the red are full bodied and have a faint burr, sort of like that you get in good Scotch whiskey, the whites are very dry, cool and with a delightful nutlike taste. They are to be drunk with oysters, all shell fish, fish and fowl. The best of them all is Montrachet; then comes Pouilly, Pouilly Fusee, then Chablis. I would try them in reverse order, saving the finest for the last, because any of them are excellent. You can drink from a bottle to two bottles of any of them, but a bottle is plenty.

That is a quick glance at Clarets and Burgundies. Other French wines which you will want to try, will be Vouvray, a moderately sweet white wine with a very delicate flavour, that is inexpensive but good; Saumur, a drier version of the same thing; Reisling, a dry Alsatian wine in a tall thin necked bottle. Don't drink too much of this last or it will sour your stomach, but a bottle of it is very pleasant. Also, I wouldn't drink any sparkling Burgundies or other bastard combinations in a country where you can get good Champagne. Which brings us to Champagne and where as Ginny and Pauline have to go down stairs to play bridge, we will knock off for the moment. You understand, Karl that this is only a birds eye view and that you'll make all kinds of discoveries for yourself. Also, I'm not including Matilda in the writing of it because you'll know more about what she would like to drink than I possibly could. She may not like to drink wine at all, but usually girls like Graves, Sauternesand Vouvray the first time they try them and none of them are at all heavy and have very little alcohol in them. It isn't nece[s]sarily the amount of alcohol that determines the cheering effect yo[u] will get from a wine, but rather how much the makeup of the wine opens up the pores of your stomach so that what alcohol there is may be absorbed.

Well Karl, with your permission we'll leave Champagne alone for a minute except to say that it is really very good if you have a tendency to sea sickness or if you get low in your mind or when you are traveling on railroad trains or any time you and Mathilde think that the trip maybe wasn't worth while after all and Jinny hasn't written and you wonder how the children are and Orange seems like a pretty good place[2] and tennis a fine game, why then drink a bottle of Champagne between you but be sure it is well iced and no matter what the brand that it is marked on the neck of the bottle BRUT. Champagne is labelled according to its degree of sweetness and its degree of sweetness is determined by the amount of syrup and brandy that's added to it. If you insist on BRUT, pronounced brute, you get the driest that there is, and the driest is the healthiest because its pure wine with nothing added and it won't give you the morning after that sweet Champagne will. The other thing that I've found that goes best with the stomach on ship board is a dry martini or two dry martinis before meals but when you're in Europe its a shame to drink cocktails when you can get so many other things that you can drink before the meal as aperitifs, as they are called, or appetite producers, that do not have any hard liquor in them. We usually drink Cinzano vermouth either with or without seltzer. I know you'd like that. There is another aperitif too to try called Chambery, a French vermouth. These are often served with a dash of fruit syrup, either cassis which is a black raspberry or some other, such as grenadine. If you want a vermouth Chambery with cassis you simply ask for un Chambery cassis and the waiter brings it in a big glass and you add your own water and ice. You will be introduced to plenty of aperitifs yourself but all the vermouth ones are pretty healthy and all the others pretty unhealthy. The unhealthy ones which ruin your palate, your large intestines and everything between are the various false absynthes such as Anis del 'Oso, Pernod and the amer picons. I think you ought to try an Anis del 'Oso once if you want and then let your conscience be your guide but the amer picons are really poisonous. You get just as good a kick from the vermouths which have a healthy wine base and they do you no harm.

Gin is the great hot weather drink. The best is Gilbey's and it is nothing like gin as we know it in America. The English call a Tom Collins a John Collins but they make it very well and I think it would make you a good drink in Egypt. They have never done me any wrong.

It's just occurred to me that if this valuable document should fall into any ones hands it would probably be evidence that I was trying to make a drunkard out of my brother-in-law so remember that I do not advise you to drink any of them at once nor even advise you to drink any of them at all, am merely summarizing my own experience for your doubtful benefit in answer to your request to Billings. The Continental and American idea of drinking are so different that it would take a whole essay to go into them. The continental idea is that something such as vermouth may be taken before you eat, wine or beer drunk with a meal and possible a liquer afterwards with the idea of making you feel better, changing your ideas, stimulating conversation and in general giving you a sense of well being and a pleasant feeling in your head and in your body. There is no moral aspect to drinking at all in this way. It is not regarded as moral not to drink or as immoral to drink. If a person does not drink he does not regard himself morally superior to those who do not but abstains because of a weak stomach or kidneys or liver or because he finds that any form of drinking goes to his head. It is recognized abroad that the drinking of wine and its products are healthy and a source of happiness, while the drinking of spirits is looked down on. This does not hold true in England nor in any British possession where because they have no wine and consequently is very expensive and in no sense a drink of the people they have become great drinkers of spirits and of beers and ales. Personally I find that English beers and ales are much too strong for me to drink. Most of them contain almost as much alcohol as Burgundy and if instead of sipping them as you would a wine you drink them down as you would beer, they will stop your digestion and go to your head. On the other hand the English drink their spirits very well. Their whiskeys are aged long enough so they are not poisonous and they drink them with water and drink them slowly so that in a way they get the same results as in drinking wine although any form of spirit drinking cannot be compared to wine drinking for health or in the effect on your own feelings. Most of the whiskeys that are nationally know[n] brands are very inferior and are made principally for export to our own unfortunate country. No Johnny Walker nor Black and White is fit to drink. Nor is White Horse. Dewars Fold Label is a good whiskey. Doctor Maccullums is a fair whiskey, Vat 69 was alright the last time I tried it. Haig in a pinch bottle is no longer reliable. As a matter of fact, the only scotch whiskey in recent years of any real quality that I have tried has been Dewars Gold Label. The way the distillers do when they bring out a new grade of whiskey is to produce a very fine old well-mellowed and well-blended article. Then when it has received of those people who know whiskey and can make its reputation and has been established in popular favor they put in the same green whiskey, they use in their other brands. Theres nothing new or good about the product except its label. The same holds true with brandy/ Neither Martel nor Hennessey are fit to drink.

I might as well finish up with French wines and ligueurs or this thing will go on forever and you will have no room for it in your trunk. The best Champagnes are Moet and Chandon, Mumms, Roederer, Paul Roger. They are labelled demi-sec which means sweet, and isn't healthy to drink no matter how pleasant it tastes, sec, which is slightly less sweet but which has still been sweetened, Gout Americain, which is dry but usually has had brandy added to it and is a great night club Champagne, and BRUT the kind I tild you about and which is the only one I would counsel you to drink. If they haven't got BRUT in one brand, they will usually have it in another. If you want the taste of a sweet champagne and it is a very good taste, and still want it to be healthy, get Asti Spumonti which isn't a champagne at all but is the natural sweet wine of Asti in Italy, made sparkling. It will cost only about a fifth as much as champagne does[.] You can get the same thing in France also very cheaply under the heading Vins Mousseux in the wine list. These are the natural sweet wines of the Loire bottled sparkling. None of these wines will give you the same effect as Champagne which produces a brisk heady exhileration but they are pleasant to drink after a meal and have a nice taste. The Liqueurs are also easiest divided into dry and sweet. The Dry ones are those that are simply distilled from fruit or grape products and they are, Vieux Marc, which is distilled from the residue after the grapes have been pressed to make Burgundy, Kirsch, which is made from cherries, Calvados, which is applejack, Mirabelle which is made from plums, Quetsch which is also made from plums. These are all the natural alcohols. distilled from fruits, and if they are properly made are the healthiest liqueurs a man can drink. There is only one proper time to drink them and that is with coffee after a meal/ Armagnac is drunk at the same time and is the best and healthiest brandy there is. There are various sweet liqueurs which are well-made and healthy but which usually appeal more to women that to men, such as Cherry brandy, apricot brandy, Benedictine and Cointreau. You ought to try all of those if you don't know them already and I think Mathilde will like them. The best Cherry and Apricot brandy are made either by Rocher or Bols. These are really good and about the only ones that are safe, since many synthetic drinks are made in France. Kirsch and so forth, when it is synthetic, must be labelled Fantasy on the bottle and is to be avoided. The general rule is that those which are cheap are bad. A good bottle of Kirsch costs about 20 or 26 francs.

The wine of Italy that I like best of all is white Capri. They have some fine sweet wines, such as Orvietto, Lacrima Cristi etc. Of the red wines there are no really good ones outside of Chianti, Barbera, Fresa and so forth are poor enough compared with French wines. And Chianti is too strong to drink all the time. They have lots of little known wines which do not travel and are served locally in hotels and pensions, which are excellent and in general in Italy the thing to do is to drink the local wines putting water in it if it is too strong.

The Greek wines are some of them very good and most of them have a faint pine taste of resin which is very pleasant when you know you can get away from it. Remember that you can't drink any wine too slowly. When you pour it out look at it in the glass, for its color, hold the glass in the palm of your hand and revolve it slowly, then smell it for its bouquet, then taste it/ Theyre are as many flavors in a good red wine from Bordeaux or Burgundy as there are variations of color in Nature. Remember too that good red wines have their vlavor ruined if they are drunk cold. They should be drunk the temperature of the room. Being cold will make them bitter. This is true especially of Burgundys. If you order a bottle of Burgundy and it is served cold, ask the wine waiter, called a sommelier in French to take it back and Chambree it or heat it too the temperature of the room.[3] On the other hand most qhite wines are improved by being chillled and all the white burgundy should be drunk very cold except the Montrachet. You will find many Americans probably who will seek to impress everyone with their knowledge of wines by claiming that about half the bottles of wine that are served to them are corked, because there will be a few pieces of cork or the bottoms of the cork will be slightly worn away. This is all nonsence. You don't get one bottle of really corked wine in France out of a thousand. If there are a few specks of cork in your wine take it out with your finger. When you open a bottle of wine yourself and are pouring it for other people, always pour a little in your own glass first so that you will recieve this cork and then serve the other people. If they are boobs, they will think you are being rude in thinking you are serving yourself first but if they know anything they will see that you know how to serve wine.

In Paris if you want good beer go to the Brasserie LIPP on the Boulevard St. Germain across from the cafe des Deux Magot. I'll tell you the simplest way to dine in this and all other places in Paris. When you get to Paris write a note to Guy Fangel, The Guarantee Trust Company of New York, 4 Place de la Concorde, Paris. Just say in the note that you are Virginia and Pauline's brother about who[m] I have written to him. And tell him where your hotel is and that you would be gla[d] to have him come there to dinner.

He is an old friend of ours and he can tell you any places you want to get there, take you to any cafes or restaurants and take you to the races. The only thing is that he is dead broke and so will not be able to entertain you as I know he would like to. But he has lived in Paris twenty years out of

449

his life, knows it thoroughly, and can show you anything in it that we could. He is also a very nice fellow and I know that you would like him. He is a painter and a writer but happens at the moment to be broke and when I say broke I mean broke. That is he probably lives on fifty dollars a month or less. He is not a guide nor sponger nor an object of charity but just a very good fellow with a fine knowledge of Paris who happens to be broke but who if you wanted to ask him to take you to various places explaining that you wanted him to be your guest because I'd told you that I understood that writing and painting business was on the bum just now, could take you to the restaurants, the cafes and the races as I would myself except that I won't be there to be able to pay the bill.

But you could maybe use some of this check to do so. Ask Guy to take you to eat once at Lipps, where they have the good beer, to take you to see Montparnasse a dismal enought ~~sight~~ site, to take you to eat at the Quatre Sergents de la Rochelle on the Place de la Bastille— And when you go there drink the Richebourg—to have a drink at the Deux Magots. A fine place to eat too, especially lunch in the Cafe de la Regence where they have wonderful Hors d'oeuvres.[4] And be sure and go to the races. You won't have seen Paris if you haven't done that and Guy Fangel knows them as well as anyone can.

Well this has gotten to be a very unweildy letter Karl, but we certainly hope you have a grand and wonderful trip and we both want to thank you and Mathilde again for the fine Christmas presents.

We had planned to get this check and letter to you for Christmas but perhaps you can imagine the difficulties that prevented it. I wish we could be in Paris when you are there but I know Guy Fangel can show you the things we would and you will have seen so many ruins and wondersby that time under the auspices of the messieurs Cook[5] that it will be good for you to go out to Auteuil and see the steple chases, even though you miss an afternoon of sight-seeing. That side of life is also a part of our educations. Well good bye and good luck and all our love and best wishes on the trip, to you both.

Yours always,

Ernest

N.B, Have a good time, both of you, and don't worry about the home and thnk yo for all the lovely Christmas presents. And remember the word to use

about food, customs, continions, etc, in another country is DIFFERENT—
not FUNNY!

Love, Pauline.

Stanford, TLcc with typewritten signature [dictated]

This joint letter was dictated by EH and typed by Pauline on the versos of eleven sheets of letterhead stationery imprinted "KARL G. PFEIFFER / Piggott, Arkansas."

1 Pauline's brother Karl Pfeiffer and his wife Matilda were about to sail to Europe for the first time; they would return to the United States in late April.
2 Jinny was staying at Karl and Matilda's home in Orange, New Jersey, to care for their small children: Barbara (1925–1961) and Paul Mark (1928–1962), who had been born with spina bifida. The couple's first child, Margaret (1923–1927), had died of the same condition.
3 *Chambrer*: to bring to room temperature (French).
4 EH recommends two Right Bank establishments: Restaurant des Quatre Sergents de la Rochelle at 3, boulevard Beaumarchais in the Place de la Bastille; and Café de la Régence at 161, rue St.-Honoré.
5 Thomas Cook & Son, the London-based travel agency specializing in group tours.

To Megan Laird, 1 January [1931]

January 1,1930[1]

Dear Miss Laird,

This is being written with the left hand, the right arm being at present and for some months to come, useless, so with your permission I'll let the caps go and you will not mind spelling etc. I'm glad you saw some bullfights and you were damned lucky tonbe able to in November because ordinarily the season is over when you got to Spain but this year Dominguin rented the Plazacto to put on this Domingo Ortega and Carnicerito of Mexico and both kids were very good the first, 2ndand even the 3rd time although after the first time the bulls weren't much.[2] all of which you probably know but which I learned in the hospital in Billings, Montana which is more difficult. Maybe you were there in time too to see Marcial Lalanda. I hope you were.

Naturally I dont give a damn whether you like my books or not but it is very pleasant that you liked the bull fights because all people that like them have that much in common, and it is a great deal. While I have nothing in common with people who like or dislike what I have written except a profound wish that if they dis;ike it they wont feel they have to mention it, because if itwasnt as good as i could make it at the time would not have published it, and that if they like it they will be very brief. But please dont put Cervantes in with the two you mention because his Spain exists as much as it ever did while they never had any Spain at all but only local color writing though some fair enough as la barraca.[3] Anyway if it interests younI have been working on a book on the bullfight for some years but steadily all this year until smashed the arm and was only 2 chapters from the end. I tell you this so if you work very hard and very fast you will probably be able to get a book out on this subject yourself before I get these two chapters done but on the other hand if you wait a few months you will be able to read mine and profit by its mistakes.

This was meant to be a very pleasant letter in answer to your very pleasant letter but evidently have not yet mastered the art of being pleasant with the left hand only. But let me tell you something; when you are writing and trying to do something that has not been done before what people will praise as your style will be only your more visible awkwardnesses caused by the difficulty of what you are trying to do. Ifvyou have no appetite for praisevthose awkwardnesses will gradually disappear as you learn to make it smoother and yet keep what you want. Ifvyou have an appetite for praisevthose unfortunate characteristics will come to seem very fine to you and you will never get rid of them. I dont mean you personally I mean anybody. You sound as though you had a very good head but you know damned well that while you could visit any part of the bull ring with a little backsheesh while it was unoccupied you couldn't study the bull fight from the quarters of the matadors while any matadors were in them. They would be afraid of you if you werent goodclooking and they would especially not want to see you then if you were because they have something else to think about.

Anyway even if I disapprove of your technique it would be very pleasant to meet you and hear about the fights. Mrs. Hemingway znd I will be in Madrid in May and June. My address is always the Guranty Trust, Guaranty rather, 4 place de la Concorde.

Thanks for the letter,
Yours always,
Ernest Hemingway.

Comini, TL with typewritten signature; postmark: PIGGOTT. / ARK., JAN / 3 / 6 PM / 1931

Although stray characters in typewritten letters are not generally reproduced in transcriptions, they are retained in this particular case to illustrate EH's difficulty with one-handed typing. This is his first known attempt to type a letter himself since his car accident.

1 EH misdated the year of the letter.
2 Spanish bullfighter, manager, and impresario Dominguín (né Domingo González Mateos, 1895–1958) presented the previously unremarked *novillero* Domingo Ortega (1908–1988) to important bullrings in September, October, and November 1930, thus sparking the career of one of the century's most important matadors. Mexican Indian *novillero* Carnicerito de México ("Little Butcher of Mexico"; né José González López, 1905–1947) would be promoted to *matador de toros* late in September 1931 (Mandel *HDIA*, 186–89, 320–26).
3 The letter to which EH is responding has not been located. Spanish novelist Miguel de Cervantes Saavedra (1547–1616), author of *Don Quixote de la Mancha* (1605; 1615). *La Barraca: Novela* (Valencia: Prometeo, 1898) by Spanish journalist and bestselling novelist Vicente Blasco Ibáñez (1867–1928) depicted life on a farm on the outskirts of Valencia; the novel was published in English translation as *The Cabin* (New York: Knopf, 1917). EH owned a copy of the 1898 Spanish edition (Brasch and Sigman, item 655).

To Louis Henry Cohn, [2 January 1931]

Dear Captain Cohn;

The reason you have not received this before is that on getting here to Piggott I had to go to bed with fever. My mss. was in two leather trunks in the vault of the bankb along with all business etc. papers. My keys were misplaced or lost and I too sick to hunt for them properly Finally had the lock cut off one of the trunks with a cold chisel, this town has no locksmiths, and am enclosing the page of mss.

Have been picking this out on the typewriter with the levt hand so please pay no attention to spelling and general construction. Please do not take the typewrtten notation on the mss. personally. It was my opinion when youfirst wrote me that you were doing a bibliography, it was my opinion when you asked if I would see you in NY, and it remains my considered opinion today. So I would like it recorded since otherwise I might seem to favour such a compilation. A bibliography may be of interest to you because you love books but I do not love them at all.

We leave here January 5 if I can travel then. It looks as though it would take six months or so to get the arm in proper shape again since the muscle was all cut to pieces and sluoghed off finally as puss and broken down tissue.

The nerve which controlls the wrist is starting to work again. With the nerves functioning it will be a simple matter to get the arm back in shape.

I hope everything is going well with you,

Thank you very much for the wire at Christmas,

Yours always,

Ernest Hemingway.

[*Enclosure: a page of holograph manuscript titled* "Death of the Standard Oil Man" *in EH's shaky left-handed writing and bearing EH's typewritten introductory note:*]

Dear Captain Cohn,

You may have this for your book if you want it but truly, very truly, I think it is all balls to publish bibliographies of living writers. E.H.

UDel, TL with typewritten signature; postmarks: [PIGGO]TT. / ARK., JAN / 2 / [*illegible*] / 1931; [*on verso:*] NEW YORK,N.Y.REC'D / G.P.O., JAN / 3 / 830PM / 1931; NEW YORK,N.Y.REC'D / GRAND CENT.ANNEX, JAN 3 / 930PM / 1931

A facsimile of the enclosed manuscript page with EH's typewritten notation would be published as the fold-out frontispiece in Cohn's *A Bibliography of the Works of Ernest Hemingway* (New York: Random House, 1931). Cohn would quote the second paragraph of EH's letter (minus the opening sentence) in his introduction, dated 3 June 1931. Fragments of the pencil manuscript of EH's unfinished story "Death of the Standard Oil Man" survive at JFK (items 360, 361, 362, 362a). The envelope, addressed in Pauline's hand, bears her notation "Air Mail = Special Delivery."

To Henry Strater, 2 January [1931]

Jan 2

Dear Mike,

Well dr. we got here for xmas and went right back to bed but plan to shove for Key West the 5th if can travel all right. Am pecking this off with the left hand. Capitols are the big difficulty zso may abolush them. you can have david go over and put the caps in. you were damned swell to write so many and such high grade lettwrs. i hope the hell we didnt have you too wprried. .your gun sounds damned good. look, tell maggie that it wasnt the fault ofvthe docs that i was laid up so long but the fault of what happened to the arm. the bones were broken completely off and the angle of the break was so long it was impossible to set them so they would hold it was broken as long and as sharp as the way one of those greenheart 4.00 rods splinters.[1] and you cou[l]dnt make it hold without splicing it. i know because we tried that three times. when you break an ankle, a bone in the forearm or your pelvis the other bones hold it in shape. when you break the humerus or the femur it flops like washing on the;line and every time the sharp ends of the bone move they cut up the meat. My arm was broken so that it was bent back and the back of the hand was underneath my shoulder. When it kept hurting for weeks and began to swell so the dr. thouhgt it might be thekangaroo tendon setting up an irritation but it was only the completely chopped up musclesof biceps andtriceos which had gone rotten, broken down inoto puss and had to sluff offb. which they did. but nobody could tell it was that and not an infection until it happen4d and they could put the ~~blood under a~~ stuff under a microscope. Now the nerve has started to come back that controls the wrist and there is nothing to do but wait ten days untul we know the bone is solid, then start to get movement in the stiff elbow and bring back the muscles with massage, erxercise etc. the nerve was all i was afraid of as it seemed completetly dead but it has started to come back already. but please tell maggie the operation wasnt malpractice but was an absolute nece[s]sity. it was the sort of a smash dr. that in war they would have taken the arm off as sure as hell. u could have put it in a splint or a cast forever and it wouldnt have helped it any. The only thing now is that im weak asvhell from two months on the back in same position but am picking up every day. had three fingers broken which never noticed in general swellingv until they were knit.

well to hell with all this army writing. ~~when are~~ but thought you might want the final, i hope, dope. love to maggie. thanks for the swell xmas book. have wanted that mexican dope for a long time. will get you that new Florida book. when will you be down? its 100 to 1 i&ll be jake to go to tortugas in march. chub weaver who c[o]oked for us hunting all fall has driven the ford down to key west. left here yest and will stand by to cook on trips. that will make things damned good.

write the dope to k.w. yrs. al3ways Hem

PUL, TL with typewritten signature

1 In the early twentieth century, fishing rods were often made of imported greenheart wood, a less expensive material than the more flexible split cane. 4.00 rod: a four-foot rod.

To Archibald MacLeish, 14 January [1931]

January 14

Dear Mac:—

a norther blowing outside and Pauline Chub [Weaver] and Patrick gone to shoot snipe— The silver fish was fine—we have an gigantic old house for $40 a month but 6,000 income tax to pay on money that mostly never saw— well wont have <u>any</u> to pay next year—and anyway am 1 swell Gris ahead![1]

I'd wondered what language Pat would speak—his first rimark was—"Whatchasay Papa?" Hope you're going good.

My arm I guess is coming along—northers have killed the mosquitoes[.] The gulf is full of sailfish and big schools of Kings—

Charles [Thompson] sends you his best— He is grand—

We all send our love and hope we see you soon—

Pappy—

LOC, ALS

1 A reference to EH's purchase of *Le Torero* (*The Bullfighter*, 1913), an oil on canvas by Spanish painter Juan Gris (né José Victoriano Carmelo Carlos González Pérez, 1887–1927). A color lithograph of the painting would appear as the frontispiece to the first edition of *DIA*.

To Maxwell Perkins, 15 January [1931]

Jan 15

Dear Max;

I cannot decide about The Killers business. My inclination is to have nothing to do with it but certainly I wouldnt touch it on the terms outlined in the letter you enclosed. All I ever recd from the Farewell to Arms dramatization was the initial 675 advance. The Am play co. man admits a value of 2500 for the Killers if sold as a story to the movies. All right if I take a 250 advance and a third share on royalties my share of the movie rights would be only a third or a ½ of one third of a three way movie split. You know most of these plays are produced only for the purpose of selling them to the pictures and the Am Play Co. and doubtless the producer knows Farewell To Arms brought 80,000 and netted a profit to Woods, Stallings and the agents although a lousy flop.

My terms if I would decide favourably would be at least 1000 advance to me to protect me in case of a flop for they, if the play flops and I get nothing, still have the lions share in the movie rights of the story. One half the royalty to me. One-third of the picture rights to me. It is not my fault that they need more than one dramatist and there is no reason I should be penalized for that. I might want to make it into a play myself sometime. If the terms were satisfactory and I decided to let them do it they could say based on or suggested by the Killers by Ernest Hemingway but I'm damned if any of it sounds attractive to me. Selling the by products of your writings may be o.k. but I see no reason to sell the Killers for 250 dollars to make a bum play when I could shop around and get up to 5,000 for it from the moom pitchers.[1]

You can show them my letter up to this point.[2] Am typing this with one hand and it goes damned slow about six words to the minute maybw less. The other one I didnt type. It was Jinny; Paulines sister. The Gulf is lousy with Sailfish. Arm is still pretty bad. All I'm trying now is to get it so we can spend March in Tortugas. Will do that all right. Arm still in splint pretty painful

Look Max, will you have them send me a list of moneys paid me, itemized, including money I paid for books, the money that was due in Dec, would have been paid then ordinarily, as well as the 20 G, paid to NCB as trustee and the 900 odd paid G A Pfeiffer. I want to list wvweything for income tax. You might as well send me a check for that qhich was due in Dec. but that you held up when I said didnt want any more money in nineteen thirty. Dont want to have anything they can kick about. Though it is tough not to be able deduct the huge amt have given away, nor any depreciation on this arm nor the 6 months work it will cst me besides the

2500 in cash I've spent on it so far. Can they send me the figures on my complete earnings so I can get this tax business done so we wonyt have to worry about it in March.

Charles and Lorine send you their best, Burge too. Thanks ever so much for your two letters and the Sportsman. A norther uis blowing outside like the one we had at Tortugas.

So sorry Zelda is still ill.

So long max. excuse punk one handed letter.

Ernest

PUL, TL with typewritten signature

1 In a letter of 9 January 1931, Perkins summarized the script of a proposed three-act play titled "Murder" and described its resemblance to EH's story "The Killers." Despite some misgivings Perkins wrote, "Still, there is this possibility of making a great deal of money on these byproducts of your writing" (PUL). Perkins enclosed a letter from playwright agent Leland Hayward (1902–1971) that remains unlocated. Perkins named Erskine (likely Chester Erskine, 1905–1986) as the hopeful producer and speculated that "they would want to say, 'Suggested by Ernest Hemingway's famous story, "The Killers."'" The American Play Company, a theatrical agency formed in 1914 by Elisabeth Marbury (1856–1933) and John Williams Rumsey (1877–1960), represented writers and managed script sales to producers.
2 A typewritten transcription of the first portion of this letter, ending here, survives in the archives of Charles Scribner's Sons at PUL.

To Waldo Peirce, 17 January [1931]

Jan 17

Dear Waldo,

It was a damned shame you had the picture trouble. Mrs. Cromwell always seemed one of those things to me.[1] Couldn't stand her the first time I saw her nor any subsequent times. Hope you had a good trip to the B.P. without too much rain fog brume and pluie.[2] Everybody here misses you and sends you and Alzira their best. They've had a lot of northers that have killed the mosquitoes.

Am typeing this with one hand and it goes damned slowly. By the time you get something to say and have it ½ typed have forgotten the rest of it. By god

I hope you have good luck with the two boys. Write me kid and dont pay any attention to what a bum letter I write because this method is just about as slow as building with blocks. Why dont you get a lawyer of your own instead of using I's lawyer and only go to Hill as a sort of *conseille de famille* intermediary. How in hell is one man to protect two peoples conflicting legal interests? Especialy if he should be a twirp as you describe H?[3]

Pauline wrote Alzira the other day. Look, IJll tell you something you can do for me. See that Guy Fangel doesnJt starve or have to hit the Seine will you? I try to look after him but am not there. He hasn't a sou I know and lives on nothing. Don't ever let him know I told you this. He can do good and intelligent typeing for one thing if you ever need any one to type what you write. Any money you can ever loan him tell me and I will repay you. I have him on my mind and thought if you would keep an eye on him it would relieve Pauline and me both.

There has been a big norther blowing. We have a big old house out near the mullet seller for 45 bucks a month.[4] Arm still pretty bad. Havent done any work since Nov.1 and wont be able to maybe until April. My best to Sweeney. Could you abonne me to L'Auto for 3months   Box 404   Key West   Florida   EU[.] You can do it at Brentanos.[5] Will send you a check. Will save me writing a letter.

Is there anything we can do for you here? Bra send his best.

Siempre tu amigo[6]

Ernesto.

Colby, TL with typewritten signature

1 Most likely a reference to Whitney Cromwell's mother, Agnes Whitney Cromwell (1874–1959), an active suffragist and civic leader who was the first woman to serve on the New Jersey State Board of Education.
2 B. P.: Basses Pyrénées; *brume*: fog; *pluie*: rain (French).
3 Ivy Troutman Peirce's lawyer, Hill, remains unidentified. *Conseil de famille*: family council (French).
4 EH and Pauline had rented a house at 1425 Pearl Street, where Josephine Herbst and John Herrmann lived the previous year. In a letter of [c. 29 March 1930], Herbst wrote to Katherine Anne Porter from that address: "the mullet man is a good neighbor and sells mullets for bait and eats fish three times a day" (UMD). According to Lorine Thompson, the house was later torn down (Baker *Life*, 600).
5 *Abonner*: to subscribe (French). *L'Auto*: French sports magazine founded in 1900 by cyclist and journalist Henri Desgrange (1865–1940). *L'Auto* launched the Tour de France in 1903

to boost its circulation and dominated sports journalism in France until it ceased publication in 1944.

6 Always your friend (Spanish).

To William Lengel, 21 January [1931]

Key West—Florida

January 21

Dear Lengel:—

Thanks for your two letters to Billings and Piggott—was too sick to answer the first one—

This scrawl to let you know we've left Piggott— Sorry I'll not see you my arm still pretty bad— Had to be operated etc.

My best to Ray Long to yourself and to Spike—[1]

Yours always

Ernest Hemingway

SIU, ALS

1 Frazier "Spike" Hunt, literary talent scout for the Hearst magazines and a colleague of Lengel and Long.

To Ezra and Dorothy Pound, 21 January 1931

Jan 21

Dear Ezra:—

I'm a shit not to have written before but I was working like hell— [*EH insertion*: compound fracture of right Index finger last May.] Then out in Montana— Shot 2 bear—bull elk—mt sheep ram— ~~Then~~ a horse went through the timber with me when we were bear hunting and cut my face up pretty bad Then in a car broke my right arm between Elbow and shoulder— Had to ride 25 miles to hospital— Bone cut the muscle all to hell— That was November 1st—arm still in Splints [*EH insertion*: Broke 3 fingers again at same time] They had to open arm up and Splice the bone with Kangaroo tendon— now it is all fine except wrist paralysed— No can write—ni fish— ni shoot[1] Had book nearly done— Well what the hell

460

If there was any justice in Dis world You'd have gotten the Nobel prize. You'll get it yet.[2] I was damned sore.

we are coming over in the Spring—where can we see you? Dont think I can go to Italy under present regime

Write to P.O. Box 404

Key West

Hem.

Dear Dorothy:—

Hope you are fine, ~~Much love Hem~~ would write more but it is as slow as building with blocks Have wanted to write you for a year and now have no good excuse not to.

You were damned good to like the book and I can understand the wench being annoying[.] I tell you though it is god bloody annoying just when you have learned to write a little to bust your writing tools altogether. How are you?

Would like to talk to you sometime before I break my jaw!

Much love

Hem

Yale, ALS; postmark: KEY WEST / FLA., JAN[?]1 / 1PM / 1931

1 *Ni*: nor (Spanish).
2 The Nobel Prize had been awarded to Sinclair Lewis in November 1930. Although nominated eight times between 1955 and 1965, Pound would never receive a Nobel Prize.

To Paul and Mary Pfeiffer, 28 January [1931]

Jan 28

Dear Family;

It is fine to hear that you are having such a good time. The weather, which was cold when we first came, has become ideal and we are all well. Thank you very much for packing the books and toys. Theyvwere packed very professionally and I am very much in your debt for all the trouble you took as well as for the express.

My mother came here for two days.[1] Pauline and she got on splendidly. Henriette is to land in NY February 12.

By now Karl and his wife must be well out on the ocean. He sounded very excited in his letter. Am very sorry to have been as much trouble as he intimates he heard from Virginia I was and solemnly promise never to inflict myself on you as a convalescent again. It was a dirty trick I know to come to someones house when you should have stayed in a hospital and I have nothing but admiration for the way you put up with me and took care of me. I want to tell you again how very sorry I am to have made you so much trouble and to promise that it will not happen again.

Can't promise, of course, not to go in the ditch again but will try to see that the car is one of the kind that kills you when it turns over on you instead of merely making you a nuisance to friends and relatives.

Patrick is very well and very manly and cheerful. He misses you all very much but he has one of his true loves, Monkey, or rather what is left of Monkey, to console him.

When we first came it looked as though Key West after losing the cigar factories, the Naval Base, was to, as a final blow, lose its climate.[2] But the last few days have been unbeatable. My arm as we know might have been worse and is bound to get better, like business, so the less said about its actual condition the better.

Pres. Hoover spent 500,000 of the peoples money to get his Wickersham report and then weazled again. He sees his only salvation in the organized support that elected him before, and may, for all we know, still believe in him. He will run no chance of losing that no matter what his commissions may tell him. They are all backing him since his statement on the W report anyway. He needs that Moral Issue to run on since continued Prosperity by having an ENGINEER in the White House to control the gigantic prosperity machine has gone up the spout. What we actually have is an ambitious, cowardly amateur politician. It doesnt take an engineer to run a political machine.[3] Mark Hanna was no engineer. He was a politician and any man in politics who is not a good politician must take orders ratherc than give them. Of course he is only reaping the whirlwind causedc by the wind that Coolidge sowed. He was supposed to be a silent man but he never lacked words to inflate the marketv.when they asked him for them.[4]

Glad you saw some good fights. Revolution is going on in Cuba with Machado sitting tight on the lid still. Many political exiles here now. When things are better organized politically here we will jail all political refugees as fast as they arrive.[5] All have forgotten that this country was organized by a revolution.

Dont get in with any of those Faro dealers thatvtook 50,000 from the poor U.S. Govt collector of internal revenue for Chicago.[6]

Love from all,

Ernest

Onehand typeing.

Please excuse mistakes.

PUL, TL with typewritten signature

1 The *Key West Citizen* reported on 27 January 1931 that "Mrs. Clarence E. Hemingway, Oak Park, Ill., mother of the well-known author," was registered at the Casa Marina and had "entertained at luncheon Monday" (26 January).
2 The U.S. Naval Air Base in Key West, established in 1823 to combat pirates, was decommissioned at the end of WWI.
3 In 1929 President Herbert Hoover created the National Commission on Law Observance and Enforcement, chaired by George Woodward Wickersham (1858–1936), to examine the federal system of criminal justice. In January 1931 the Wickersham Commission issued twelve reports on Prohibition, some endorsing the Eighteenth Amendment, others criticizing it as unenforceable, and others suggesting a variety of revisions. The $500,000 cost of the inconclusive report was widely publicized and criticized. Hoover, a successful mining engineer who had received a degree in geology from Stanford University in 1895, had his own mining consulting business and had become a millionaire by 1914.
4 Marcus Alonzo Hanna (1837–1904), American businessman, U.S. senator from Ohio (1897–1904), and chair of the Republican National Committee (1896–1904), was known for promoting the candidacy of William McKinley in the 1896 presidential election and as a pivotal figure in the growing alliance between business and politics. President Calvin Coolidge, nicknamed "Silent Cal," was noted for proclaiming "the chief business of the American people is business."
5 Gerardo Machado y Morales (1871–1939), president of Cuba (1924–1933). As Machado's regime became increasingly corrupt, repressive, and dictatorial, hundreds fled Cuba, settling mostly in Miami and New York City. Machado would be forced into exile on 12 August 1933.
6 On 22 January 1931 Myrtle Tanner Blacklidge, collector of internal revenue for Chicago, borrowed $50,000 from Edward R. Litsinger, a member of Chicago's Cook County Board of Tax Review, claiming she needed the cash as guarantee to collect the proceeds of a winning streak in a faro game and promising to share her winnings. Litsinger agreed and sent his nephew, Fred Litsinger, to deliver the cash. After Fred was robbed of the money, Edward accused Blacklidge of complicity in the robbery and participation in a swindle. Although Blacklidge denied the charges, claiming that she had been the victim of card sharps, she resigned her post on 24 January "to Avoid 'Embarrassing' Friends" (*New York Times*, 25 January 1931, 5).

To Owen Wister, 26 December [1930]–[31 January 1931]

Piggott Arkansas
December 26

Dear O. W.,

It was very good of you to write and I was a bum not to answer but I can't dictate and there was no good news and the discussion of casualties always bad business, especially in letters. I enjoyed your letters greatly and it was fine to hear from you.[1]

Keep on giving me good advice; but don't expect me to take it! We have to make our own mistakes but I like advice so long as there is nothing that binds you to take it since while one must make his own mistakes there is no reason to make any one else's and you might tell me several things with which I could neveragree and then one which would be very fine [*EH autograph insertion*: and valuable]. If this has any ring or smell of snootiness please eliminate it as you read because it was not intended but is the result of trying to dictate. The principle technical reason as I see it against a writer trying to dictate anything; is that to write at all you must be alone and, better still, lonely and I can not be alone with anyone in the room with me. Then, having spent your life learning to do something with your ~~write~~ [*EH autograph insertion*: right] hand it would take a good deal of egotism, which is I believe ~~the~~ a predominant characteristic of all writers who dictate, to imagine you could do this task as well with your mouth. What's meant to be read with the eye should be written with the hand and checked by the eye and the ear as it's written. Rhetoric or particularly involved sentences can be easily constructed with the mouth but they do not untangle so wellwith the eye. [*EH autograph insertion*: Or do they?]

"Also there is no particular reason to teach your god-father to suck eggs," [*EH autograph insertion*: you can justly say.]

I will get some sort of an arm out of this buisness and will know what sort by the end of six months. I wanted to write you about the Roosevelt book[2] but I couldn't becasue the way it worked out finally was that [*EH autograph insertion*: it seemed to me,] a man must not write about another man of whom he has been very fond after that man is dead because it can not be done. You may be able to prove to me that it can or has but I do not believe it can any more than a man can write about his wife if she is dead and if he has loved her. A detailed portrait I mean. It is only by staying miles outside that you have any chance to recreate the person. Any how you can't recreatea person, you can only create a character in writing. You can record an actual person's actions and re-create them in a sense, i.e. present them through this recording but it takes great detail.

Why I should write to you like this, God knows, except that I had to clear this up before I could write at all. In French it would be very simple.

We would meet at one of those horrible [*EH autograph insertion*: insincere] meetings of men of letters and I would say "Je n'ose pas vous dire, cher maitre, combien j'etais affecte par vos[3] etc.

My god what tripe this letter is! I send it only that you should know I was thinking of you on Dec. 26!

How are you?

Arm is getting better although musculospiral nerve still paralyzed.

Shot a fine ram, 2 bear[,] a good bull.

You were damned good to write. I was quite sick or I would have answered.

You can see was still running a fever when wrote the other two pages of this.

Best to you always
Ernest Hemingway

what was it about Balaam that Roosevelt made you take out? It was <u>that</u> made me <u>furious</u> against him.[4]

LOC, TL [dictated] / ALS; postmark: KEY WEST / FLA., JAN 31 / 1 PM / 1931

The first portion of this letter was dictated by EH and typed out on 26 December 1930 in Piggott, but the final portion, as well as numerous corrections and additions to the typewritten text, are in EH's still shaky handwriting, as is the hand-addressed envelope.

1 Wister's letters to EH of this period have not been located.
2 Wister's biography of Theodore Roosevelt, *Roosevelt: The Story of a Friendship, 1880–1919*, was published by Macmillan on 10 July 1930.
3 *Je n'ose pas vous dire cher maître, combien j'étais affecté par vos*: I dare not tell you, dear sir, how affected I was by your [...] (French). *Maître*: honorific for a lawyer or professor (French). The remainder of the letter is handwritten.
4 Wister's short story "Balaam and Pedro," first published in the January 1894 issue of *Harper's*, presents a graphic description of how the rancher Balaam gouges out the eye of his horse Pedro. Theodore Roosevelt objected to the details as "sickening" and advised Wister that in republishing it, he should "throw a veil over what Balaam did to Pedro, leave

that to the reader's imagination, and you will greatly strengthen the effect" (*Roosevelt: The Story of a Friendship, 1880–1919*, 34). Echoing the story in his novel *The Virginian* (1902), Wister obscured the nature of Balaam's violence against Pedro.

To Louis Henry Cohn, [31 January 1931]

Box 404
Key West
Florida

Dear Capt Cohn:—

Did you ever get the page of mss and the books I sent fom Piggott? They were sent to 320 East 53rd Street, NYC. I could not find your House of Books address.[1]

With all best wishes
Yours
Ernest Hemingway

UDel, ALS; postmark: KEY WEST / FLA., JAN 31 / 1 PM / 1931

1 EH addressed the envelope of this letter to Cohn's home address. Cohn's bookshop, House of Books, was located at 52 East 56th Street.

To Maxwell Perkins, 5 February [1931]

Box 404
Feb 5

Dear Max;

When will you be down? Fishing is the best it has ever been. The cold weather of Nov. Dec. has held the migratory fish down here and brought down other fish that you hardly ever see here. Big schools of tuna in the gulf, acres big.. Sunday and Monday weather was perfect and we caught nine tuna, any number of bonita and many kings and Pauline caught a sailfish 7 feet 1 inch. Saw five and hooked three. My arm is coming along with massage and heat although it will be 4or 5 months possibly before I can write with it. You can see it when you come. But it will be ok to go to Tortugas March first. Can steer boat alright with other hand.

Mike [Strater] cant come but am counting on you. John [Herrmann] is here already and Paulines Uncle [Gus Pfeiffer] is coming down to leave for Tortugas March 1st. So let me know I can figure on you for that date. A boat has come b[a]ck from Tortugas and reports the giant kings are there already in same place. They smashed away many big ones and fifty pounds was largest they caught so your record is still safe. We must get there while they are still there.

I may hit you for up ton5,000. to pay my income tax some time this month. Please let me me know if this is inconvenient so can make other arrangements in time.

Thanks for the two very fine books.[1]

Ernest

This one hand typing is so damned slow.

PUL, TL with typewritten signature

1 In a letter to EH of 22 January 1931 (PUL), Perkins wrote that he was sending *The Grass Roof* (New York: Scribner's, 1931) by Thomas Wolfe's friend Younghill Kang (1903–1972) and a book "with some good fishing pictures," probably *Atlantic Circle: Around the Ocean with the Winds and Tides* (New York: Scribner's, 1931) by Leonard Outhwaite (1892–1978).

To John Dos Passos, [c. 5 February 1931]

Dos,

Damned glad to hear from you. Gen Smelly Buller may have last word yet. Musso vcant drive all over Italy that fast and not run over dozens of babies—hundreds more likely.[1] I daresay you've run over dozens yourself. I've run over eight ten a day myself when I wasnt ever hitting fifty. Musso hits 150 habituslly. Bet he runs over e four thousabd a year.

Stewart.

He sent the lousiest wire you ever read out to Billings puking on A. MacLeish for having come out there. It couldnt have been sent by a man sober and it wasnt funny enough for a man drunk. All I freplied was that

467

I thought it was damned fine for MacLeish to come out there and for Stewart if he didnt think so to tell me when I had two good hands or now and I would knock the whitney out of him with one hand or something cheery like that.[2] Heard nothing further from Stewart. You cant call that having words with a man or can you. If Stewy is mouthing about that tell him to mouth to me.

From present indications arm will be solid, strong, and crooked. But if elbow breaks down will be no worse than the average case of jamaica ginger poisoning. No I think it will be jake if you know what I mean.[3] Nerve is coming on well.

We went out in the gulf Sunday and monday. Alive with fish. Schools of tuna and bonita acres big. We caught 17 bonita, 9 tuna, as good to eat as shell fish, weigh about 14 lbs, fight like hell, gold coloured, big sicle fins, purple backs,. Pauline and Chub [Weaver] each hooked big sailfish at same time. Chubs broke away jumping and Pauline landed hers. 7 feet one inch. A swell fish. I caught 3 bonita and a big king with one arm. Also shot a snipe and 2 clay pigeons on fly with one handed shot gun shooting. Am going to try to be a 2nd Cendras.[4] Steer the boat; drive car etc, already. Everything but write. So goddamn slow to write. May get a dictaphone. Ever try a dicaphone Pasos?

Well kid I wish the hell you and your goddamn fine wife were coming down here. Let me have all the dope on Mejico.[5]

Best love to Katy and my best to Bill,

HREMINGSTEIN

UVA, TL with typewritten signature

1 In a speech of 19 January 1930, the highly decorated American general Smedley Darlington Butler (1881–1940) referred to Italian dictator Benito Mussolini as a hit-and-run driver. According to an unidentified American who claimed to have accompanied Mussolini on his tour of Italy, "The automobile was driven at a high speed and when it struck a child did not stop, the Premier saying, 'What is one life in the affairs of the state?'" (*New York Times*, 30 January 1931, 1). Mussolini denied both the presence of the American and the accident, the Italian Ambassador to the United States made a formal complaint, and Butler was scheduled for a court-martial by President Hoover. The international scandal would end in mid-February with the cancellation of the trial and a reprimand for Butler, who had consistently refused to retract the accusation. On 19 February Butler would announce his resignation from the U.S. Marine Corps.

2 EH refers to his letter to Donald Ogden Stewart of 28 December 1930.

3 "Jamaica ginger," also known as "Jamaica Gin," "Ginger Jake," or simply "Jake," was a widely available patent medicine containing ginger extract in a solution of 80–90% alcohol, which made it a popular intoxicant during Prohibition. Excessive consumption as well as toxic additives and substitutions intended to lower its price unexpectedly produced an epidemic of "jake paralysis," a severe weakening or partial paralysis of the extremities. EH plays on *jake*, American slang for excellent or fine.

4 Blaise Cendrars (né Frédéric-Louis Sauser, 1887–1961), Swiss-born French poet and novelist who lost his right arm in 1915 while engaged in trench warfare.

5 John and Kate Dos Passos would leave their Cape Cod home in February 1931 for a brief trip to Mexico City.

To Donald Ogden Stewart, [7 February 1931]

> Box 404
> Key West
> Florida

Dear Don,

Naturally [*EH typewritten insertion*: or un-naturally] I never said or wrote anything to Archie about that bloody wire that I went sour about but about a week ago had a letter from him where he said you had told him about it [*EH typewritten insertion*: and that it] was a joke that I didnt take nor get correctly.

That is okeh with me, or perhaps you say oke in the east but when I was in Chi last—but that's another story, Rudyard.

Anyway Stew— If I may call you Stew since I've so often seen you "stewed"—if it was a joke, a schwantz as we call it in Flemish,[1] then I'm a sonofabitch to have gone for wormwood on it and regret mine of recent date.

It rests with you. If you want to be sore no one will be sorer than me if I can succeed in remembering the incident correctly. [*EH typewritten insertion*: which is doubtful] [*EH autograph insertion*: as the memory goes first, followed by blindness, insanity and death.] If you want us not to be sore no one will be less sore than your old pal.

Just a postcard will do. Cross out any phrases that do not apply. You are an ass, signed Stewart.

I am good and sore, signed Stewart.

My ass is sore, signed Stewart

Let's not be sore—signed Hemingway—or anything you say—

You are probably my wealthiest friend Stewart and I canJt afford to lose you. Since I heard how you gave MacLeish a radio receiving set and then to think I have deliberately jeopardized our friendship. Well they say born to hang will never drown. Am picking this out letter at a time on the typer so if it lacks spontaneity and sparkle dont lay it to the languorous southern climate. My gd arm wont be any good for six months the drs. say while it takes only nine months to make a baby or two babies if you have twins. three for triplets. Six for septuagenarians. 87 for marechal Joffre.[2] three weeks for rabbitts and a tiger for old cornell.[3] I have a cake of babbitting metal that I carry in a sock though. Well the whole of life is confusing even to a man like me endowed with poetic vision.

Yours always

Ernest

Yale, TL/ALS; postmark: KEY WEST / FLA., FEB 7 / 5 PM / 1931

1 *Schwantz*: Yiddish slang for penis, particularly a limp one; derived from the German *schwanz*: tail, also slang for penis.
2 Joseph Jacques Césaire Joffre (1852–1931), who had died in Paris on 31 January, was a highly decorated French military officer who had risen to the rank of Commander-in-Chief of the French Army in 1915. Upon his dismissal from that post in 1916, he was given the ceremonial title Marshal of France.
3 The tiger is the mascot of Princeton University, whose school song is "Old Nassau." Cornell University's unofficial mascot is the bear.

To Patrick Morgan and Maud Cabot, [c. 7 February 1931]

NEWS WONDERFUL STOP BEST LOVE TO YOU BOTH STOP PAULINE CAUGHT A SEVEN FOOT SAILFISH STOP ARM BETTER STOP DON'T STAY TOO LONG CHARLESTON STOP YOU AND MAUD CERTAINLY BOTH SPLENDID CHOOSERS—PAULINE ERNEST.

From Maud Cabot, *Maud's Journey: A Life from Art* (Berkeley, California: New Earth Publications, 1995), 95, published transcription of cable

Patrick Morgan and Maud Cabot were married in New York City on 7 February 1931. In her memoirs, Cabot quotes this congratulatory cable from EH and Pauline and recalled that after the wedding she and her husband traveled to Key West to visit the Hemingways, stopping en route in Charleston, South Carolina, to visit the Arthur Whitneys (Cabot, 95).

To Evan Shipman, [9 February 1931]

Box 404,

Key West, Florida

Dear Evan,

I wrote you fromout in Wyoming last Fall when you wrote giving me an address. Sorry you never got it. Amdictating this to Pauline—my armis still on the bum. I saw the poem in Scribners. It is really a splendid poem; one of the best I've ever read.[1] If you come down to Orlando that is not such a hell of a way fromhere. We'll be here until the end of April; then to Paris and Spain for the summer. Don't know whether we'll go through New York or leave from Havana.

Johnny Herman is down here and told me he saw you in New York. I wish I had.

As you see from this letter, I can't dictate, and writing with the left hand is like pulling teeth if you're no dentist. I hope to hell you're well. Keep on working hard.

I don't want to even talk about McAlmon.

Id you've got any other poems you would like me to try to get published tell me, will you, because I would be very proud to have anything to do with getting themprinted. Write me, kid. I must have written you twice that you didn't get.

Who is this Victor Emanuel that is starting Rhyticere in the Grand National. Is he the guy you bought the horse for?[2]

I was on horses all summer, on and off them that is, and find them the same bastardly animals as ever. A horse to really win old Hem's love must pay about 146 francs to ten. That was the noble aspect of our old friend Uncus. When they pay like that I see all their beautiful qualities.[3]

It would be fine if we could see you. The difference bewteen you and a horse is that you don't have to pay anything on ten feancs to hold Pauline's and my affection.

Yours always,

Hem

Channick, TL with typewritten signature [dictated]; postmark: KEY WEST / FLA., FEB 9 / 5 PM / 1931

1 Shipman's "Third Heat, 2:12 Trot," published in the February 1931 issue of *Scribner's Magazine.*
2 Victor Emanuel (1898–1960), New York businessman and owner of a stable of race horses on Long Island that included Rhyticere, the fourth-place winner in the Grand National Steeplechase on 27 March 1931.
3 Uncas, a half-bred gelding foaled in 1920, won the Prix du Président de la République at Auteuil on 4 April 1926 at odds of 45 to 4 (Mandel *HDIA*, 438–39, 560–61). In Chapter 1 of *DIA*, EH would recall the "profound affection" he felt for Uncas "when he won a classic steeplechase race at Auteuil at odds of better than ten to one, carrying my money on him." In a footnote EH adds, "Mr. Shipman having read this informs me that Uncas after having broken down is now used as a hack by Mr. Victor Emanuel."

To Henry Strater, [c. 14 February 1931]

Dear Mike,

You and Denny must have had good fun. Jinny, Paulines sister, had about the same experience. I'd planned to shoot at them in Piggott all the fall and was going to use that light sixteen with the 26inch bbls but arm put that on the bum.

We surely miss you here kid. The gulf has never been better. Big schools of tuna, acres big sometimes. We caught ten one day. largest 15 lbs. All kinds of kings. largest so far 41 lbs. Pauline czught a 7 ft 1 inch, measured, sailfish. Biggest here so far this season. The gulf, due to such a cold Dec. and Jan, is alive with bonita, kings, tuna and many sailfish altho the Casa marina hasnt been catching any. Have been out 4 times and haven't seen a dolphin yet. But day before yesterday saw 12 of the giant mantas and watched two feeding right up a stream one behind the other. Ten fathom bar alive with amberjacks.

Havent seen your Bro[1] yet altho Charles has. He is reported fishing for big kings exclusively with a bonefish reel and 9 thread line. I see that ideology runs in the family.

Would have looked him up but felyt any body using that outfit was probably happy as he was. also at one time arrived to be fished and entertained Lawrence Nordquist who guided us in Wyo, a Mr. Outhwaite, seems a good bird, sent by max, and Pat Morgan and bride.

We plan to go to Tortugas March 1. The big kings are there now. Max, the bum, says he cant come until after a sockholders meeting March tenth.[2] Uncle Gus on the other hand arrives March first. So we will go down in two shifts mainataing a camp there unless run out by the Coastgurad.

Charles is in splendid shape. The trip was wonderful for himalright.

Hope Maggie is fine. Give her our love and wishes for the best of luck.

My arm is getting strong but elbow movement very limited, no good massager here but use what there is and bake it under lamp daily. Have what seems to be a good old neuritis coming on at point of shoulder which gives holybhell. Doubtless all passes art alone endures.[3]

Armhowever gettting strong better every week. Strong grip in hand, once adhesions broken down in elbow etc. will be practically as good as average artficial arm if not better. much better.

You are damned fine to write so damned good letters with nothing from old hem.

You ought to have a hell of a fine show. I wish I could see it.

Best always and love to Maggie. See you in tarpon season.

Hem

My arm will be most certainly jake for Africa next Spring. If it never bent anymore I could shoot with it. Would like, however, if possible to get it so can write with it.

Thanks ever so mch for Mr.Kuniyoshi lovely male cow!⁴

PUL, TL with typewritten signature

1 Strater had two brothers, Charles Helme Strater (1884–1944) and Leonard Godfrey Strater (1892–1952).
2 EH refers to Perkins's letter of 11 February 1931 (PUL).
3 These words derive from "L'Art" ("Tout passe-L'art robuste / Seul a l'éternité") by French writer Pierre Jules Théophile Gautier (1811–1872), from his 1852 poetry collection *Émaux et Camées* (*Enamels and Cameos*).

473

4 Yasuo Kuniyoshi (1889–1953), Japanese American artist born in the Year of the Cow, often incorporated images of cows in his early paintings.

To Evan Shipman, 16 February [1931]

February 16

Dear Evan:—

Splendid to know youre coming down!

We can put you up, or hotel you anyway—

The only thing— I wont be here between March 1–7th—

Come before or after that—or if you come then Pauline will be here and you can come with her to join me at Dry Tortugas after March 7—

Best to you always and luck to Mazeppa—[1]

Yours always

Hem—

It will be grand to see you—

First writing with right hand! Still very difficult—

Channick, ALS; postmark: KEY WEST / FLA., FEB 17 / 4 PM / 1931

1 Shipman worked on his epic autobiographical poem "Mazeppa" for a decade, taking its title from the hero of the 1819 narrative poem of the same name by George Gordon, Lord Byron (1788–1824). Shipman's poem would be published in the annual anthology of poetry, *The New Caravan* (eds. Alfred Kreymbourg, Lewis Mumford, and Paul Rosenfeld [New York: W. W. Norton, 1936], 290–96).

To Edward Titus, [mid- to late February 1931]

Box 404

Key West

Dear Titus:—

Thanks for the pamphlet— I wrote about it to Putnam because I'd no answer to two letters I wrote you—one from Key West asking about the Review and one from Montana—[1]

Hope everything goes well with you— This hand writing is caused by compound fracture my right humerus—Nov 1st with paralysis of musculo spiral nerve etc—arm is getting along now and will be as good as ever— But process has been damned slow—

Am not writing a history of B.F.[2] Is much more complicated—will tell you when I see you—

Will be in Paris in the Spring. Look forward to receiving the Kiki—

Look. Since the pamphlet is by me and the agreement was it was not to be published in U.S. without another arrangement between us—wouldnt it be better if it was copy-righted in my name if it were to remain my property?[3]

You can reach me at the above address for a couple of month's— Have missed seeing your review— Last remember I saw was Spring of 1930—

With best regards always—
Ernest Hemingway.

Karpeles, ALS

1 See EH to Samuel Putnam, c. 28 October, 1930. EH's two letters to Titus have not been located. The "Review" is *This Quarter*, which Titus then owned and edited.
2 Bullfighting. In his letter of 6 February 1931, Titus had had asked, "Are you ever coming back again to Paris? Someone told me that you are now working on a history of bullfighting—is that correct?" (UDel).
3 Putnam's translation of *Kiki's Memoirs* with an introduction by EH was published in Paris by Titus in June 1930. EH's introduction, published separately in pamphlet form in New York in January 1930, had been copyrighted in Titus's name (Hanneman A9, 31). In his 6 February letter, Titus said he had delayed sending a copy of *Kiki's Memoirs* because he had been "waiting for a possible clearing up of the situation resulting from the seizure in New York of an important shipment of Kiki to Random House." He also reported hearing that a pirated edition had appeared in America.

To Maxwell Perkins, 21 February [1931]

NH14 73 NL=KEYWEST FLO FEB 21
MAXWELL E PERKINS=
NEWCANAAN CONN=
GIANT KINGS NOW TORTUGAS WE GOING THERE FEBRUARY
27TH YOU COULD LEAVE NEWYORK TUESDAY ARRIVE KEYWEST
THURSDAY ARRIVE TORTUGAS FRIDAY EVENING BE BACK
IN NEWYORK FOR STOCKHOLDERS MEETING IF YOU HAD

TO STOCKHOLD STOP IF YOU WANT COME AFTER
STOCKHOLDERS WILL TORTUGAS AGAIN THEN STOP NEED 6500
FOR INCOME TAX WIRE ME IF YOU CANNOT DEPOSIT THAT
TO MY ACCOUNT NATIONAL CITY BANK 43 EXCHANGE PLACE
ON MONDAY=

ERNEST.

846A.

PUL, Cable; WESTERN UNION destination receipt stamp: Received at 35 Railroad
Ave., New Canaan, Conn.

To Edgar Stanton, [26 February 1931]

[*Excerpt as published in Schulson Autographs sale listing*:]
"As it stands now some of us go down to Tortugas tomorrow—the 27th . . .
I have to come back for an X-ray and to pay income tax. Tortugas has no
accommodations—you live on the boat or on the dock . . . you could fish a day
or so here and we can go down to Tortugas the 19th or 11th—If that's too long
a trip for Hollie . . . we can go to Marquesas en route for tarpon (Best there is)
Tortugas is 60 some miles— Marquesas about 25 miles from here en route to
Tortugas . . . Anyway we can plan the trip when you get here— Tortugas is for
the big kings— Marquesas is wonderful tarpon fishing—we could spend 2
nights there—then go to Tortugas . . . This arm writes a bum letter— Don't
hire any boat when you get here unless for a day or so fishing . . . I have two
chartered for this trip . . . we can get grub before starting . . . we have never
failed to get tarpon at Marquesas altho [*sic*] I don't guaranty [*sic*]—caught 13
one night—7 another . . . excuse the hurried lousy letter . . ."

Ernest.

David Schulson Autographs online listing, ALS; postmark: [Key West, Florida, 28
February 1931]

According to the catalog description, this letter is signed "Ernest." Edgar Stanton and his wife,
Harriet Campbell Rew Stanton (1875–1983), along with other "prominent society members
from Chicago," were in Florida in February attending the annual George Washington's
birthday charity event in St. Augustine to benefit the local Flagler Hospital ("St. Augustine
Prepares for Annual Ball," *Chicago Daily Tribune*, 22 February 1930, H2).

To Maxwell Perkins, 12 March 1931

MZA1123 54 NL=KEYWEST FLO 12
MAXWELL E PERKINS=
597 FIFTH AVE NEWYORK NY=
BEEN STORM BOUND AGAIN JUST BACK MANY KINGS BUT
BELIEVE BIGGEST NOT YET ARRIVED WE CAUGHT ELEVEN
HUNDRED POUNDS AVERAGE THIRTY POUNDS PLAN LEAVE
STAYING MAY WHY NOT COME TO GO TORTUGAS FIRST APRIL
SEEMS BEST FOR KINGS BUT SPLENDID HAVE YOU NOW OR
ANYTIME TARPONS WILL BITE WITH FIRST WARM WEATHER
COMMENCED TODAY=
    ERNEST.

PUL, Cable; Western Union destination receipt stamp: 1931 Mar 12 PM 11 27

To Archibald MacLeish, 14 March [1931]

March 14

Dear Archie:—

We just got back from Tortugas—13 Days—3 of fine weather the rest blowing a gale— Caught about 60 big Kings—lots of yellowtail, snappers grouper etc. I hooked some Kings and turned them over to others—arm getting fine—writing this with it—all right but still difficult—can use to catch all small fish—

Didnt write you to Montana because I thought you'd be back before it could reach you— Then found your letter from there and feel like hell not to have a letter at Farmington for you when you got there

Look— We have a room for you (quiet) in Charles [Thompson] House— (he insists)—or if you dont want it there at Pat Morgans—house—or in the house where Chub [Weaver] lives— Either Charles or the room where Chub is good bets— Charles Free— $5 a week at Chubs place— Henriette be cooking finely—

Weather turned fine and warm yesterday— When are you coming and for how long? Swell fishing now— Tarpon starting— Lots of fish still in Gulf Stream—

I shot 27 out of 30 clay pigeons thrown hard holding gun with left hand against right shoulder right arm by side—raising gun each time— Also two terns on wing with pistol in left hand. Papa bragging again—

I'd be glad to let Caresse have the Natural History for the 1500— You can read it when you come— I didnt answer because I couldnt write nor go over the story—will write her soon—[1] Your news of Murphs very good—we had fine wire from them yest.[2]

You come down and tell me all about every thing— Pauline sends her best love— I am strong and healthy as a pig— Dans la vie il faut (D'abord) durer—[3] Cant write French— Excuse such a rotten letter— Hand still slower than the eye—

Glad Red Lewis was nice—we'll all be gt. men when we're dead and well travailleyed by the ver (I hope youze knows your Baudelaire) [*EH marginal insertion*: Les morts, le pauvris morts, ont de grandes douleurs][4] I wd like to be gt. writer but same very difficult— Shooting a shotgun with one hand makes you discoloured all over your chest— May never be a gt writer but by Christ I am a hell of a fine shot with shotgun— Shot one handed against Edgar Stanton shooting regular at 20¢ a target and won twice—lost twice— tied once[.] Shot 9×10—9×10—7×10 9×10—8×10—6×10— Shoulder too sore finally— Pappy the bragger—

Love from Pappy.

He's a damned good shot. Edgar Stanton that is.

our address

   Box 404

We leave for Spain in May.

LOC, ALS

1 In January 1931, Crosby had wired EH in Key West, "Archie thinks Black Sun should publish Natural History of Death" and invited EH to name his own terms (SIU).
2 Archibald and Ada MacLeish visited Gerald and Sara Murphy in February 1931 at Montana-Vermala, Switzerland, where their younger son, Patrick, was being treated for tuberculosis.

3 *Dans la vie il faut (D'abord) durer*: In life one must (first of all) last (French).
4 During his recent return voyage to the United States from Europe, MacLeish sailed on the *Europa* with Sinclair Lewis, nicknamed "Red" for his hair color. Lewis reportedly remarked of EH, "I'm afraid he's a great man" (Donaldson *MacLeish*, 209). *Travaillé par des vers*: worked on, or eaten, by worms; *Les morts, le pauvres morts, ont de grandes douleurs*: The dead, the poor dead, suffer great sorrows (French). The line is from "La Servante au Grand Coeur" ("The Servant with a Big Heart") in *Les Fleurs du Mal* (1857) by French symbolist poet Charles Baudelaire (1821–1867). EH owned an 1894 French edition of Baudelaire's book (Brasch and Sigman, item 424).

To Maurice-Edgar Coindreau, 16 March [1931]

Box 404
Key West Fla
March 16 (1931)

(am just back from Tortugas and find your letter)
Dear Mr. Coindreau:—

a few cuts in chap 26 will not bring the book from 667,920 lettres to 400,000 and anyway and in all ways I am unalterably opposed to any cutting of any sort—[1]

If there is to be any cutting of any sort I prefer not to publish—

It is enough to make me try to write a sentence in French a language which I cannot spell nor write correctly—

C'est de la litterature, mon vieux, et ca on ne coupe pas[2]

Only time can prove whether it is or not but that is my standpoint and I cut everything cut-able in Mss. myself and will not destroy its integrality (if there is such a word) to suit M. Gallimards always short sighted and doubtful convenience—if he will not publish it as it is we will get someone else to take the translation,

excuse this very hasty scrawl,
Yours always—
unsigned

Even if it has "de plus grande vente"[3] which he desires to acquire by cutting you know perfectly damned well we would never get the money. What is he supposed to be doing? Publishing a book or enough extracts from that book to make an ideal size vol for manufacture and sale?

PUL, Typewritten transcription of EH letter; postmark: [Key West, Florida, 17 March 1931, 5 pm]

This transcription of EH's letter, reproduced verbatim from the Carlos Baker Collection at PUL, bears the typewritten notations "handwritten letter unsigned on off-white deckle-edged paper" and "Postmarked Key West 5pm March 17, 1931."

1 In a letter to EH of 1 June 1931, Coindreau would report that Gallimard had respected EH's objection and published the complete text of *L'Adieu aux Armes*, saying, "They have not left out a single word" (PUL).
2 *C'est de la littérature, mon vieux, et ça on ne coupe pas*: It is literature, old boy, and it is not to be cut (French).
3 *De plus grandes ventes*: greater sales (French).

To Laurence Stallings, 16 March [1931]

Box 404

Key West—Fla

March 16

Dear Stallings:—

You are a hell of a white man all right and I appreciate very much your wanting somebody else to try to do something with the book— It may be altogether impossible. It was a damned shame that you worked so hard on it and then that we had ~~the double zero turn up for us~~ no luck with it but I'm equally damned glad that we both got some money from the movies and I only wish there was some unendictable way that we could stand Mr. Paul Reynolds et fils, who received ⅓ as much as you for Dramatizing, me for writing and Al Woods for producing,[1] [*EH insertion*: for them doing nothing] up against something where they wouldnt fall too easily and let me plant my good hand on their stern and constipated countenances and you, with the aid of an engenious mechanical device which I would be prepared to contribute, kick them neatly and profoundly under the chin with your better leg in such a manner as to rupture their prominent Adams apples each time they exhibited a tendency to go to the floor on us. If you could promise me your whole hearted support in this we could put on something in the nature of a Paul Revere's Ride which would do much to improve the breed of horses patoots.[2]

I believe my operatives could for a nominal expenditure put through a bill in Arkansas making mayhem only a misdemeanour in which case we could put the Reynolds Boys on the dotted line in The Crown Jewel state perhaps for the benefit of some local hunger fund.

If any of these projects appeal to you let me know and I will commence production on the Adams apple rupture-or.

Anyway I am, in the meantime, your grateful ex-dramatee and present well wisher

Ernest Hemingway.

Wake Forest, ALS; postmark: KEY WEST / FLA., MAR 17 / 5 PM / 1931

EH addressed the envelope to Stallings c/o Howard E. Reinheimer, 11 East 44th Street, New York City, and marked it "Personal / Please Forward."

1 In late September 1930, shortly after Stallings's play opened on Broadway, Paramount purchased the film rights to *FTA* for $80,000. The amount was split equally among EH, Stallings, and Al Woods. *Et fils*: and son or sons (French), a reference to the agency Paul R. Reynolds and Son.

2 EH's literary agent, Paul Revere Reynolds, Jr., was a descendant of American patriot Paul Revere (1735–1818), who rode on horseback from Boston to Lexington on the night of 18 April 1775 to warn the American militia that the British were coming.

To Edward Titus, [20 March 1931]

[Excerpt as published in Christie's catalog:]

"perhaps the reason that a letter from me might miscarry is that my were sent out in the pockets or rolled slickers of people leaving the ranch for Red Lodge, Montana, Cooke City, Montana, and Cody, Wyoming and that all other mail was sent to a cabin at Painter, Wyo. Where it was all left in an open box to be picked up once a week and taken 63 miles to Cody." Then, turning to Titus's recently published *Kiki's Memoirs*, to which he had contributed an introduction, he writes: "I'm sorry you lost money on your Kiki (thanks very much for sending me the copy),[1] and for all the reviews which I look forward to reading) We've all lost money in 1929–30—and may lose more in 31—But hang onto a pamphlet or two and you'll get some of it back. My arm is coming along well and I'll be hard at work in another two weeks."

Christie's catalog, New York, 14 June 2006, Lot 296, ALS

According to the catalog description, this letter is signed "Ernest Hemingway."

1 *Kiki's Memoirs* (Paris: At the Sign of the Black Manikin Press, 1930), containing EH's introduction (Hanneman B7).

To Archibald MacLeish, [c. 25 March 1931]

Dear Archie:—

I cant write a letter because we are going to Tortugas tomorrow— Max has come to do that (I wanted him to come 1st of March or late in April but he's come now) and I am Commander Birding around getting chow and everything else ready and am sick pooped of seeing merchants of all sorts.[1] I wish to hell you were going kid— I counted like hell on seeing you— Have never been tired of seeing you Mac but I certainly as hell get tired of all these other bastards— except Charles— Evan Shipman was here and he is no strain either— Uncle Gus was damned fine too— He's no strain either— But there have been 100s of others that are[.] I get tired of ~~anybody~~ people that acts like a child[*EH insertion:* ren] no matter how old they are and there have been thousands of those here it seems like— ~~They~~ have damned near driven old Hem bughouse—all fine people but Christ how sick I am of people[.] Suppose it was best to have gone and cheered up the Murphs but that doesnt make your friends miss you any less —we have been <u>swamped</u> with every kind of goddam people— ~~Cant offer~~ we are broke or I'd have wired you dough and made you come— But its been bad weather all winter for fishing— Never more than 2 good days together—

I paid $6661.<u>84</u> income tax mostly on dough never even saw— That's why we're broke—

Well wont need to pay any next year!

Arm is steadily better but cant yet write unconsciously of the movement enough to make a decent letter—

I wish to Christ you were going on this trip— When we come back I start work again on the book— If you cant do it now we'll go to Tortugas absolutely next year— Anyhow were going to go to Africa— Maybe we can hunt together in the fall— It depends on how soon and how well I get going on the book— Uncle Gus may buy us that house here—[2]

About Caresse Crosby—if you havent done anything I'll write you when I get back—[3] My head is so damned muddled with Checklists— Forgive a lousy letter— Love to Ada— Love to you from us both— I wouldnt send such a lousy letter as this except that I'll be gone 2 weeks maybe and otherwise you wont hear from me at all— Can you work all right?— If you cant to hell with every thing and well get you down here— I hope to Christ I'll be able to write when I start—

Pappy—

LOC, ALS

1 Commander Richard E. Byrd (1888–1957), American polar explorer whose first Antarctic expedition (1928–1930) had included forty-two men, eighty-four sled dogs, two ships and three airplanes. EH's recent cruise to the Tortugas had included about a dozen people, or "merchants."
2 In late April 1931 Gus Pfeiffer would help EH and Pauline finance the purchase of the house at 907 Whitehead Street that Lorine Thompson had shown Pauline the previous year.
3 See EH to MacLeish, 14 March [1931].

To William D. Horne, Jr., [26] March [1931]

March 25 (?)

Dear Horney—

We got back from Tortugas finally and foun[d] your 2 fine letters— [*EH insertion*: were west bound again] but as the 2nd seemed to cancel the need for taking action on the 1st and as I went bughouse on the income tax—was late for it—about then—havent answered— I am a skunk, a maxima culpa skunk— But you relieved my mind so swell I havent worried and so havent written—

We have been <u>swamped</u> with merchants and I have not had one minute— Max arrived and wanted to go to Tortugas and am leaving again today—

I'll write and do whatever you say when get back— Should be in 10 days—

It is now 6 a.m of the morning we are to leave at 8 and must get 8 cubes of ice and the dinghys aboard— Forgive me not writing article— My best and our best love to Bunny and your daughter—[1]

If there is any new dope—or when you get the original letters you want me to sign shoot me a line and I'll do as you say— will write you fully when we get back— (It will be about Easter)

Best love—

Steen

[*On verso:*]

The Nordquists,

The Stantons

The Doles

The Buffingtons

The Sidleys—including Mrs. S. nearly drowning)[2]

Evan Shipman

Max Perkins

have been here—

All <u>damned</u> nice

PUL, ALS; postmark: KEY WEST / FLA, MAR 26 / 1230PM / 1931

1 EH is addressing Horne by an abbreviated form of the nickname "Horned Article." The Hornes' first child, Louise, was born on 20 January 1931.
2 The Stantons, Doles, Buffingtons, and Sidleys may have been among the "large party of well-to-do Chicago businessmen" that the *Key West Citizen* noted would be visiting the city in March (19 March 1931, 2). Andrew R. Dole (1857–1940), founder and president of the Dole Valve Company in Chicago and chairman of the Hooker Glass and Paint Manufacturing, and his wife, Mary Durand Hooker Dole (1875–1968), lived in Oak Park and were active in civic affairs. E. J. (Eugene Jackson) Buffington (1863–1937) and his wife, Drucilla Nichols Moore Buffington (1866–1931), lived in Evanston, Illinois. He had become president of Illinois Steel in 1899 and was a director of the U.S. Steel Company, as well as a trustee of the Chicago YMCA and the Chicago Community Trust. A front-page article in the *Key West Citizen* reported that Pauline Hemingway and "a Mr. Shipman, visitor to the city" had rescued Mrs. Sidley from drowning ("Visitor Nearly Drowned in the City Park Pool," 19 March 1931, 1).

To Laurence Stallings, 10 April [1931]

Box 406

Key West

Florida

April 10

Dear Laurence,

It's pretty bad they get to writing anonymous letters accusing a man of plagiarism isn't it? Or isn't it. Listen Doctor the mistake you made was in kidding a jewish reviewer and poet. Isidor. No higher minded purer devotee of art exists than Isidor, truly, but this is the way those gents work. In the Sun Also I had a jew who was not like Our Lord, completely that is, so Schneider Broke with Me.[1] It takes a jew to break with you in capital letters and anyway Isidor who had been an unsought buddy of mine—broke with me so completely that he would never read another line I pooblished. This, however, did not impede him from writing a long attack on me and my work and the poor bloody bastards that imitate its more glareing faults for the Nation last Spring. Josephine Herbst wrote to good old Isidor and said what about Men without Vimmen and and Absheit to Arms which didn't have all the same defects that showed when old Hem was first warming up before he started working the corners and Isidor answered (,I swear this to God), that he had read nothing I had written since the Sun Also Rises! Yet that did not keep him from a long analytical explanation of why I wouldn't do written most solemnly for the Nation.[2]

Listen, maybe you are listening, well pull up your goddamned chair then— MacLeishes publishers wrote me sending proofs of the poem and asked me to say something about the poem which I thought was as I said or wrote as they published in Jacket although not as good as New Found Land which has poems as fine as any of any time[.] But literature if any is written. I wrote MacLeish and said it was bad for one friend to write about another—bad for the friend he writes about if his stuff is good since a friend is cramped in talking about his friends stuff—also people would say log rolling etc. and every little constipated or dioehreic (mis-spelled) enemy I had would be transferred to him and that his poem was too damned good to need anything said on the jacket anyway. But as you know you have to be careful not to let a guy think you won't back him in public because you do not believe in him or won't take chances. So I said to myself to hell with all that and wrote what I thought about it advising them to read Newfound Land as well. Did you ever read that? God it is fine poetry— Great bloody poetry.

Well that wasn't worth pulling your chair much closer for. but read this Newfound Land and you'll be damned happy you went to bat for him. Why don't you put something in your column about them even writing anonymous letters—[3] Goddamn them all to hell. The bastard is the most honest, ethical, incabable of taking an advantage let alone cheating guy I have ever known. I remember when he first read the Bernal stuff and he was goofy with it.[4] He writes a swell poem and then those little literary worms all in their same bottle without dirt;[5] hungering for a system, a church, anything to direct them—with no knowlege or feelings of their own, natural older boys conference, ymca workers—all try to knife him even with anonymous letters.

I never read the Spanish book but would be glad to and report accurately on same in interest of science. They've written plenty and badly about the Cid and the Conquistadores—naturally—but I dont know this book—[6]

If hadn't been plenty cockeyed would not have sent the Faulkner wire. He had a piece in the bookman that made him sound like a damned good skate.[7] He's lousy with talent; but a streak of phony that you can push a pencil into if it really exists you can drive a horse and carriage through in two years. To me it seems as though he had this streak but there must be plenty of kids who must have known Jack Sharkey when he was a yellow little bastard as a kid who could not lick him now and plenty of get over streaks, as you must know, having been around. We all write too bad to start with and too lousy plenty long after to poop on any body in the same racket and I wish him plenty of luck.

I wish we could drive by your place[.] Afraid it won't be possible. Going out north west from here. But the next time you come to Miami Beach come down here instead. If we ever go northeat I'll come. Thanks very much for asking us.

The bull book isn't until fall. Cutting crap out of the proofs now. According to Dos a writer should judge the excellence of a book for himself by the quality of the stuff he is able to remove without losing anything.

I'll send MacLeish the letter and yours with it if you dont mind.

Yours always—

Ernest

Wake Forest, TL/ALS

1 Isidor Schneider (1896–1977), American poet, translator, critic, and editor, had served as publicity director for Boni & Liveright in the 1920s. Although Schneider had expressed to EH his dislike of *SAR*, saying he could not care about any of the people in the book except the bullfighter ([November 1926], JFK; quoted in *Letters* vol. 3, 191), the two continued a cordial correspondence into April 1927.

2 In the 18 February 1931 *Nation*, Schneider decried "the Hemingway school of writing" with its "overemphasis on simplicity," specifically mentioning Herbst as a writer who, in her commitment to the simple, has "not realized to the full her narrative powers" ("The Fetish of Simplicity," 184–86). Herbst responded to Schneider's critique in "Counterblast" (*Nation*, 11 March 1931: 275–76).

3 Stallings was a book reviewer for the *New York Sun*. He would favorably review MacLeish's *Conquistador* in his "The Book of the Day" column for 7 April 1932, at the same time dismissing Isidor Schneider's negative review of the poem in the previous Sunday's *New York Herald Tribune Books* (3 April 1932).

4 In summer 1927, MacLeish discovered the writings of Bernal Díaz del Castillo (1492–1584), Spanish writer and soldier whose *The True History of the Conquest of New Spain* (1632; translated in 1908 by A. P. Maudslay) became the principal source for *Conquistador*. In early 1929 MacLeish had invited EH to accompany him to Mexico "to get a little dope in them parts on the conquistadors" and in a letter of 11 March 1929 MacLeish described to EH his month-long sojourn in Mexico (R. H. Winnick, ed., *Letters of Archibald MacLeish: 1907–1982* [Boston: Houghton Mifflin, 1983], 201 n. 3, 223, 225–26).

5 In Chapter 1 of *GHOA*, EH would declare, "Writers should work alone. They should see each other only after their work is done, and not too often then. Otherwise they become like writers in New York. All angleworms in a bottle, trying to derive knowledge and nourishment from their own contact and from the bottle."

6 In the unlocated letter to which EH is responding, Stallings presumably named a Spanish book that MacLeish had been anonymously accused of plagiarizing.

7 William Faulkner (1897–1962), whose novel *Sanctuary* had been published on 9 February 1931. EH's wire remains unlocated. EH likely refers to Alan Reynolds Thompson's effusive review of *Sanctuary* in the April 1931 *Bookman*; none of Faulkner's own work had appeared in the magazine.

To Evan Shipman, 11 April [1931]

Box 404

April 11

Back from Tortugas yest. Gone 16 days.

Dear Evan:—

Got your letter last night—

Listen:—

That extract is <u>not</u> lousy— It is <u>god damned good</u>. For Christ sake finish the novel or at least do not lose or destroy it— I dont want you to interrupt your long poem but please please (and that is not a word I am in the habit of doubling with that way) finish it, the novel, afterwards.[1]

You must remember that in prose there is a time when it <u>always</u> seems like shit—but that stuff of yours isnt and I <u>know</u>

It was great having you here— We are both damned fond of you—

Chub leaves tomorrow—with Wobert—a good bird allright[2]

This is only a note—

Best from Pauline, Business Monkey[3] and me

Hem—

Channick, ALS; postmark: [*illegible*] R.P.O. / S. D., APR / 12 / 1931

On the envelope flap EH wrote, "Send anything to me to send to Max."

1 Shipman's novel about horse racing, *Free for All*, would be published by Scribner's in 1935; his epic poem, "Mazeppa," would appear in the annual poetry anthology *The New Caravan* in 1936.
2 In a letter dated 31 July 1931, Gus Pfeiffer would write to his sister, Emma Pfeiffer Merner (1860–1945), detailing his fishing trip with EH in the Dry Tortugas. He enclosed several photos, including one with "a little dog" named "'Worbert,' Patrick's name for 'Robert.' He was mascot on our trip and enjoyed it" (HMPEC).
3 Likely a playful inversion of "monkey business" used as a nickname for Patrick, whose attachment to a toy or stuffed animal named "Monkey" EH had noted in his 28 January [1931] letter to the Pfeiffers.

To F. Scott Fitzgerald, 12 April 1931

April 12—1931

Box 404

Key West—Fla.

Dear Scott:—

We're both terribly sorry that Zelda had such a rotten time and I would have written long ago. I hope to God she's getting along well now and that you are too. I know you had hell. You have our deepest sympathy—[1]

Outside of the arm have been having a damned fine time and was going well on book until accident on Nov 1— Didnt write a line after that until this week— Feel in damned good shape now to go well—nerve in arm has regenerated and paralysis all finished—

We come abroad in May— I'll be working all summer in Spain finishing book and will look forward like hell to seeing you— If youre still in Switzerland will come down there to see you in the fall— We might take one of those topless motor trips— I havent kept up with Arland or any other of the boys and you could give me cultured synopsise of what the lads have been doing.[2] My operatives in N.Y report you have become a grave, courageous and serious citizen— This all sounds like horseshit to me and have cut my operatives wage scale accordingly— Give my best to John Bishop when you see him or write him— I would write him but can only write about 400 or so words still before arm poops out and am putting those 400 or so into reducing our national debt to Max— Will write him anyway—arm is getting well fast—

Have you become a Communist like Bunny Wilson?[3] In 1919–20–21 when we were all paid up Communists Bunny and all those guys thot it was all tripe—as indeed it proved to be—but suppose everybody has to go through some political or religious faith sooner or later— Personally would rather go through things sooner and get your disillusions behind you instead of ahead of you—

Ah Fitz but we are profound chaps—we word lads—

Enclose latest passport picture showing new alterations in pan caused by last summers defective horsemanship—[4]

Best always to Zelda—tell her not to feel any worse than she can feel about dancing— She started it too late anyway—[5] You start it at 6 as in bull fighting—to get well up in it— She wouldnt have wanted to start late and be the Sydney Franklin of the Ballet would she?— You know us word merchants—Fitz— Always ready to give comforting advice to others while pewking with the other hand about our own troubles—

By Christ my only trouble now is to have pen and ink (pencil O.K.) and paper and 3 mos. clear to write in— But imagine troubles will be furnished—

So long Scott and our best love to you both—

Ernest—(The man who discovered Curro Carillo)[6]

How does your Ex-Marine write?[7]

I'm sorry you had a trip to U.S. on such sad business— Hope to read your acct. of it between board covers—rather than in Post— Remember us writers have only one father and one mother to die [*EH heavily inked out one and a half lines*]— But dont poop away such fine material—[8]

[*Enclosure:*]

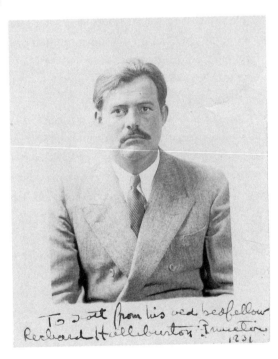

490

PUL, ALS

1 After suffering a nervous breakdown, Zelda was hospitalized at French and Swiss clinics from April 1930 to September 1931. Scott's father, Edward Fitzgerald (1853–1931), had died in Washington, DC, on 26 January 1931; Fitzgerald returned alone to the United States for the funeral.

2 In his Paris memoirs EH would describe the trip he and Fitzgerald made to Lyon in 1925 to retrieve the Fitzgeralds' Renault. The car's top had been removed at Zelda's insistence, and while driving it back to Paris the men were repeatedly caught in the rain. Fitzgerald had passed the time by giving EH plot summaries of the books of Michael Arlen (1895–1956) (*MF*, "Scott Fitzgerald"). Arlen was best known for his novel *The Green Hat* (1924), to which *SAR* had been compared by some critics.

3 Edmund Wilson had recently criticized American capitalism as a dead end and called for "some new manifesto and some new bill of rights" to replace the American Declaration of Independence and the Constitution ("An Appeal to Progressives," *New Republic*, [14 January 1931], 238).

4 EH inscribed the enclosed photo "To Scott from his old bedfellow Richard Halliburton. Princeton 1931." Adventurer and travel writer Richard Halliburton (1900–1939), Princeton class of 1921, was author of the bestselling *The Royal Road to Romance* (1925), *The Glorious Adventure* (1927), and *New Worlds to Conquer* (1929).

5 Zelda, who had taken dance lessons as a child, decided in 1927 to become a professional dancer. She practiced incessantly and studied under Russian prima ballerina Lubov Egorova (1880–1972) in Paris in 1928 and 1929. Asked to assess Zelda's dancing, Egorova wrote to Scott that Zelda could become a very good dancer but had started too late to become a first-rate one (Matthew J. Bruccoli, ed., *F. Scott Fitzgerald: A Life in Letters* [New York: Scribner's, 1994], 185–87).

6 Possibly a reference to little-known Spanish matador Francisco (Curro) Carrillo Ordóñez (b. 1868).

7 In a letter to Perkins dated 21 January 1930, Fitzgerald wrote that he would send him "some memoirs by an ex-marine, doorman at my bank here. They might have some documentary value as true stories of the Nicaraguan expedition" (Kuehl and Bryer, 163). The U.S. military intervened in Nicaragua from 1912 to 1933.

8 Edward Fitzgerald's death would surface in *Tender Is the Night* (1934) when Dick Diver returns to the United States for his father's funeral.

To Don Carlos Guffey, 12 April 1931

Box 404
Key West—Fla
April 12—1931

Dear Dr. Guffey;

I would have answered your letter long ago but this week, only, I have started to write again with this arm. Have not written a thing since November 1—

The musculospiral nerve has regenerated finally and can work the wrist but it still is on the awkward side to use— So this will be only a short note to let you know we are going abroad for me to finish this book, and that in Paris I will get you the letters Wilder-Walpole—from my stored correspondence[1]

Also I would like very much to give you a copy of <u>Three Stories and Ten Poems</u> which is one of the books you mentioned in your letter as hard to get I believe— I own one and would prefer for you to have it since I am not a Collector and you are—

Anyway this letter is an I.0.U. for one copy of the above book—and you will have it before we return to U.S. next fall— I'm sorry not to have a 1st of the In Our Time but believe the 3 and 10 is the harder to get of the two— certainly it is the first I ever published— If there's any delay in sending it will be because I go first to Spain to work in Madrid through June, July-August and it will probably be Sept before I will get to Paris, get my stuff out of the trunk and send you the book—

Am enclosing card from Dos Passos—

I hope everything is well with you and your family—

With best wishes always from Mrs. Hemingway and myself—
Yours always
Ernest Hemingway.

phJFK, ALS; postmark: KEY WEST / FLA., APR 14 / 5 PM / 1931

1 Guffey's request for these letters remains unlocated, as do Hugh Walpole's letters to EH. Thornton Wilder's letters to EH are located in the Hemingway Collection at JFK.

To Maxwell Perkins, 12 April [1931]

BERLIN.
or here—
April 12—

Dear Max:—

Havent heard from you but hope you are all right. We were there 16 days— Day after you left the worst gale of all winter came—after it was over John and Burge left on a Thursday for ice, coffee and supplies—[*EH insertion*: to be back next day—] they broke down—mechanically as well as morally and physically— And were gone 5 days— We sent Pat and Maude [Morgan] back on a boat that came in and tried to catch snappers to cover overhead. I caught 47–42–50 on three nights— Burge and John [Herrmann] had bad weather and turned up on a Tuesday night—

It was grand having you down and I hope you had a good time—44 lbs. was largest King— $5\frac{1}{4}$ largest yellowtail— My English rod was broken by some son of a bitch day before we left and gears on reel stripped— I thought for a time of shooting Pat on general economic principles when grub ran low but decided to spare him as a product of your Alma Mater—[1]

Look—I have been consious stricken about talking business to you when we were both drunk and please understand that nothing you promised me holds. I have never believed in the "lunch" method of doing business and you have my greatest respect and admiration as one of the best guys on Earth and I feel a shit for having mentioned business and wouldnt have if the time hadnt suddenly got so short—

Carol had no trouble at college—[2]

I have started to work again and hope to outwrite all these bastards— outwriting living merchants too damned easy—prefer to compete with, and be beaten by, the dead— Faulkner <u>damned good</u> when good but often unnecessary—only true competition is against time—[3]

Anyway will the Retail Department send me—for reading on boat— which we take May 1–4 or 15—

Men and Memories— By Sir or Lord Wm Rothenstein—[4]

Whistler— By James Laver — (not by Anders Zorn or Pennell or any others of Mr. Royal Bengal Cortizoz's buddies)[5]

This Our Exile — By D. Burnham (You might give me this if feeling generous) I will promise to present it to Public Library.[6]

Autobiography of Lincoln Steffens— ~~By~~ Harcourt Brace— (Will present this too no matter who pays for it)[7]

Poems of Gerald Manley Hopkins (Oxford) $3^{\underline{008}}$

Your new Baedeker for Spain—[9]

So Your Going To Spain by Clara McLaughlin (Pour rire)[10]

Papa never despises information from no matter whom she be the source—

Wrote 4 pages today, applied for passport, fixed door of car, wrote for steamship information, paid off Burge, (a godsend to the rum ~~kings~~ dispensers) inspected Bras boats bottom—(a plank dropped out coming home) and so to write you and to bed—

So long, Max, it was fine to have you down and I wish we'd had better fishing for you—

Yours always

Ernest

PUL, ALS; letterhead: Conrad Uhl's / Hotel Bristol / Berlin W.8 / Unter den Linden 5 u. 6

1 Perkins graduated from Harvard in 1907 and Morgan in 1926.

2 EH's sister Carol, a student at Rollins College, had returned late from the trip to the Dry Tortugas (see EH to Perkins, 1 August [1931]).

3 EH owned copies of Faulkner's novels *Soldiers' Pay* (1926), *As I Lay Dying* (1930), and the recently published *Sanctuary* (1931) (Brasch and Sigman, items 2104, 2114, and 2115).

4 *Men and Memories: Recollections of William Rothenstein, 1872–1900* (New York: Coward-McCann, 1931), the first of three volumes of memoirs by Sir William Rothenstein (1872–1945), English painter, writer, and educator who was knighted in January 1931.

5 James Laver (1899–1975), English critic and art historian, author of *Whistler* (New York: Cosmopolitan Book, 1930), a study of American artist James Abbott McNeill Whistler (1834–1903). Anders Zorn, Swedish painter and etcher (1860–1920) whose works were then being featured in New York shows along with etchings by Whistler. American writer Elizabeth Robins Pennell (1855–1936), author of *Whistler the Friend* (Philadelphia: Lippincott, 1930). Royal Cortissoz (1869–1948), art critic for the *New York Herald Tribune* from 1891 until his death, had written the introduction to Edward G. Kennedy's *The Etched Work of Whistler* (1910) and remained an advocate for Whistler's work.

6 *This Our Exile* (New York: Scribner's, 1931), autobiographical novel by American author David Burnham (1907–1956).

7 *The Autobiography of Lincoln Steffens* (New York: Harcourt, Brace, 1931) by American journalist Lincoln Steffens (1866–1936), whom EH had met in 1922 while working as a journalist at the Genoa Economic Conference.

8 *Poems of Gerard Manley Hopkins* (London: Oxford University Press, 1930) by English poet Gerard Manley Hopkins (1844–1889), edited by Robert Bridges.

9 EH's reference to "Your new Baedeker for Spain" is uncertain. Many of the guidebooks for travelers published by the Leipzig firm of Karl Baedeker were issued simultaneously in New York by Scribner's, which published nine Baedeker guides between 1929 and 1931, but none on Spain. EH owned Baedeker's *Spain and Portugal: Handbook for Travellers* (1913), the most recent English-language edition at the time of this letter (Brasch and Sigman, item 302). In its May 1931 issue *Scribner's Magazine* launched "The Books of the Month," a listing of books by various publishers that could be ordered through the magazine; in addition to *The Autobiography of Lincoln Steffens*, that listing included *Highway into Spain* (New York: Alfred H. King, 1931), a travel narrative by Australian geologist Marcel Aurousseau (1891–1983).

10 *So You're Going to Spain! And If I Were Going with You These Are the Things I'd Invite You to Do* (Boston: Houghton Mifflin, 1931) by American author and radio broadcaster Clara Elizabeth Laughlin (1873–1941). The book was in EH's library at Finca Vigía (Brasch and Sigman, item 3742). *Pour rire*: for a laugh (French).

To Archibald MacLeish, 19 April [1931]

Sunday morning
April 19

Dear Archy:—

Youve not been officious but goddamned fine and looking out for the troops.

You see I started to work the day we got back from Tortugas—we went for 10 and stayed for 16— For 5 had to give up a couple of the citizens as drowned [*EH insertion*: (They'd left on a Thursday to bring back needed Supplies on a Friday and never showed up until following Tuesday night!)] and found it surprizingly easy to do they both being drunks[.] But they were not drowned—only pursued by the hard luck that interferes with drunks performance—[1]

Then anyway we came back in 60 miles of open sea in 30 ft boat in hell of a storm and the bottom opened up— But not until we were almost to K.W. So my own luck has started to run good again—

Listen Keed— We missed you like hell— I had counted on you altogether and cursed be Der Schweitz that kept you from the Dry Tortuges[.][2] But anyway I started to work and have been working like a bastard— Did some more on that Natural History ["A Natural History of the Dead"] then went on with book [*DIA*]—

We sail probably on Mexique May 15 for Spain—me going direct to Madrid Pauline, Pat and Henriette continuing on to Havre to go down to Hendaye and install H and P. there where Bumby can come for Summer and we come up to see them etc. I have a June, July, Aug and Sept. of work to do in Spain—

Probably cant get back to hunt at L-T in Sept. but wish the hell you could for the sake of how fine it is as well as the experience— They are going to build a road into that country from Red Lodge and this fall and next fall will be the end of the hunting—we'll be in Africa next fall and I wish you could hunt there this— The fishing in the Clarks Fork is perfect from Sept 1 on—[3] Hunting season opens Sept 15— I believe Charles or Mike would go with you— It is the L-T ranch— Cooke City Montana— Laurence Nordquist Prop.

I wd rather fish and hunt there next fall than anything in the world and might be able to— But cannot plan on anything except finishing this book and dont want any fixed dates ahead—

About the King—it was his own bloody fault—[4]

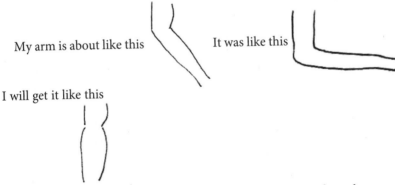

My arm is about like this   It was like this

I will get it like this

before I am through— It is getting strong and the nerve is altogether regenerated— It still hurts somewhat at nights—otherwise I am in <u>swell</u>

shape[.] Have lost the overweight I put on from no exercise and am swimming an hour a day and working fine—

Paulinoes is grand—

All the merchants gone or going— Jinny is coming down the last of the month to stay until we go— I wish to God we could see you before we go— Why dont you come down and catch some tarpons?

My best love to Ada—

Thank you very much for the Caresse business— I need the money and will be bloody glad to have it—would have accepted by cable but couldnt sell what was still working on—nor accept something on acct. and then be unable to agree to the conditions— For instance for my own self respect dont believe will ever sign anymore limited copies—all that stinks so and money is only money—[5] ~~Money is a shotgun~~ If they would offer you a double Express rifle or a boat or a suit of clothes at O'Rossen[6] you'd bastardize yourself easily— But I've never been able to take a check seriously—a check is no temptation— But will be broke when hit Europe and will take what cash can get—

So long old Archie— I just let Max see a little to cheer him up on acct he having put money in it—had been treating him rough— Think may be he is sore at me—he never wrote whether hed had a good time or not— ~~Maybe that was the easiest way to~~ well when you can write the rest doesnt matter— When you cant too many things get important—

yrs always

Pappy

LOC, ALS

1 EH refers to John Herrmann and Berge Saunders, whose supply run from Key West to the Dry Tortugas was delayed by bad weather and engine trouble.
2 *Der Schweiz*: the Swiss (German); alternatively, EH may mean *Die Schweiz*: Switzerland. On 5 February 1931 Ada and Archibald MacLeish sailed for Europe, where they visited the Murphys in Switzerland. They landed back in New York City on 4 March 1931 aboard the *Europa*. EH set out for the Dry Tortugas on 26 March.
3 Intended to provide access between Red Lodge, Montana, and the northeast entrance of Yellowstone National Park, near Cooke City, Montana, the Beartooth Highway would officially open on 14 June 1936. The 68-mile portion of U.S. Highway 212 crosses the Beartooth Pass at an elevation of 10,947 feet and passes through northwest Wyoming. A long fast-flowing trout stream with its headwaters near Cooke City, Montana, Clarks Fork is

a tributary of the Yellowstone River named for William Clark of the Lewis and Clark expedition (1804–1806), which explored newly acquired U.S. territory west of the Mississippi River.

4 In mid-1931 it was rumored that Swedish industrialist and stock swindler Ivar Kreuger (1880–1932), owner of the world's largest match company, was facing financial difficulties. Upon the collapse of his multifaceted empire early in 1932, Kreuger would commit suicide in March 1932. MacLeish's three-part series, "The Swedish Match King," would appear in *Fortune*, May-July 1933.

5 EH may refer to a note MacLeish had written to him on the verso of a 3 April 1931 telegram MacLeish had received from Caresse Crosby concerning her wish to publish a work by EH. Crosby's cable reads: "ONE THOUSAND DOLARS IMMEDIATELY BUT MUST KNOW CONDITIONS DO I HAVE EXCLUSIVE RIGHTS OR DOES HE LIMIT EDITION MUST HAVE SIGNED COPIES ALSO MANUSCRIPT IF ANY THESE THINGS MAKE DIFFERENCE IN PRICE PLEASE CABLE HIS IDEAS COLLECT." In his note, MacLeish wrote that he had wired Crosby back to say that $1,500 would be the minimum, and he asked EH to let him know if he could do anything else (Stanford).

6 O'Rossen, a haute couture shop at 12, Place Vendôme, Paris, established by Louis O'Rossen and specializing in men's and women's tailored suits.

To Don Carlos Guffey, 27 April [1931]

April 27—
Box 404
Key West
Florida

Dear Dr. Guffey:—

I'm afraid there isnt time to send the books for autographing because I am leaving day after tomorrow for Havana to get a boat direct for Spain— I didn't know exactly when I was going—expected to sail May 15th and was going to wire you to send the books as soon as I was sure— But have a chance to get this Dutch boat and must get to Spain as soon as possible—[1]

However we will <u>surely</u> be in Kansas City in November— Mrs. Hemingway will probably be writing you soon to give you aditional assurance that we will be and to ask your advice— And I will autograph the books then—[2]

In case anything should happen to me—in the bull ring or any other dumb way—I have told Pauline where to find the copy of the 3 Stories and 10 poems and that it is to go to you— Do not expect any disasters nor have any premonitions but have had so many accidents lately that should take that step to protect your interests. If anything <u>should</u> ever happen to me write to Pauline and remind her— Tell her I told you to!

About Mss. I either lost them or gave them away as I went along— Have always been completely opposed to selling them since to the person writing them himself they are only so much scrap paper once the work is accomplished— And for him to think of them as anything else would be damned bad for future work— But since people began buying them up have given some to friends who were writers and broke telling them to sell them if they wanted and keep whatever they would bring— I will go through my stuff in Paris and see if I can find anything you would like—

But don't worry— I'm not through writing by a damned sight, barring acts of God, and will have some Mss. of stories as soon as I get going again that I will be very happy to give to you—

Am somewhat worried about Pauline making the trip to Europe and return— Would prefer for her not to; except that she wants to very much and feels sure it will not be hard on her. She does not expect to be confined until early November and plans to return to U.S. in August—has many things she needs to do in Paris—and is going direct via New York to Paris— [*EH insertion*: (all our things are there—] to join me in Madrid where I go direct from here as soon as possible to finish this bullfight book— She will probably come back to U.S. before I do unless I can get the book done— Mention this not to talk shop but so you will be au courant[.] Pauline doesn't plan to sail until May 20th from N.Y— Leaving here about May 16—

The Kiki book is a lousy—a <u>terrible</u> translation— The original was really very good— I will get a copy of the original French edition in Paris and translate a couple of chapters for you while we are in Kansas City— You can paste in the translation and that should make a good item for your collection and will justify <u>or fail to justify</u> my opinion of the translateability of the book[.] The Translation as it is ~~filthily~~ misses every quality the original had— Well enough of this— Goodbye—and I hope you have a splendid summer— yours always

Ernest Hemingway.

Think of that damned In our Time selling for $200.$^{\underline{00}}$ I got <u>not one cent</u> for its publication— Bill Bird printed it for the pleasure of printing on a hand press [*EH insertion*: He sold the press to Nancy Cunard finally] and while all the copies sold out at once what they brought went to pay for the cost of printing the other books he made that didnt sell.[3]

I only got $200 from Liveright for the original In Our Time as published in U.S—with all the stories. Could not sell a single one of the stories in it to magazines—[4]

It is a strange business

phJFK, ALS; postmark: KEY WEST / FLA., APR 30 / 4 PM / 1931

1 The *Volendam* of the Holland-America Line would sail from Havana on 4 May 1931, with stops in Vigo and La Coruña.
2 Dr. Guffey would deliver EH and Pauline's second son, Gregory Hancock Hemingway, in Kansas City on November 12.
3 Bird's inventory shows that only 170 perfect copies of EH's *iot* (1924) survived the printing and binding process, of which thirty were supplied to Shakespeare and Company. Sylvia Beach's records indicate that only twenty-five copies of *iot* had been sold by the end of 1925, and that Bird's bestselling book that year was his own *A Practical Guide to French Wines* (Hugh Ford, *Published in Paris: American and British Writers, Printers, and Publishers in Paris, 1920–1939* [New York: Macmillan, 1975], 105, 114–15).
4 EH had received an advance of $200 from Boni & Liveright, whose publication of *IOT* (1925) carried an acknowledgment to the editors of the *Little Review*, the *Transatlantic Review*, and *This Quarter* for "permission to reprint some of the stories in this volume" (Hanneman A3A).

To Maxwell Perkins, 27 April [1931]

Monday April 27—

Dear Max:—

Thanks ever so much for sending the Shotgun book and Trout stream book and the ones I asked about.[1] Am trying to help business in the retail Dept but greatly appreciate the gifts.

I am sailing from Havana on Monday on the "Volendam" for Coruña—

—leaving here Saturday May 2— Must get to Spain as soon as possible and get this book completed— Pauline will go direct to France to get Henriette and Patrick settled and join me in Madrid— About the revolution there— So far it is in its honeymoon period. It may get rough as you say but the only thing I would ~~have to~~ fear in that case is the possibility of loss of my Mss. so am having it copied as it is to have a carbon somewhere safe.[2]

About business

The February royalty report shows 2192$\frac{59}{}$ due me (I don't know exactly when) and me owing you $6500 which I borrowed as an advance on this next book— If you are willing to let that stand as advance on the book— (It does not seem exhorbitant to me but that is a matter for you to decide) If it does please say so and I'll borrow from the bank and pay it back to you. Will you please deposit $1,000.$\frac{00}{}$ of the Royalty due in my account City Bank Farmers Branch, 43 Exchange Place, N.Y.C. on receipt of this and I will only call on you for the balance when and as I need it.

About the Cerf and Grosset business—[3]

Since the putting of a book in these reprints amounts, as much as I can gather from looking at the royalty figures, to saying good bye to all further income from its sale for an outright cash payment, at least for some time, [*EH insertion*: (possibly, since there is no check up on their honesty, forever,) I know nothing about that— They may be honest—] I do not want to do this unless the payment is considerable. Nor can I afford to.

5000 G and D [Grossett and Dunlap] must be sold to bring in the same royalty as 1000 regular copies— Maybe 10,000— (Later—it amounts to about 7,500)

The Cerf business does not wipe out the ordinary sale as completely as the G and D. does— Because it is a different format for one thing— Also I like the Modern Library and do not give a damn about G and D. Some are novels of distinction and some merely stink— In the whole lot there are only 6 truly 1st rate ones—

In any event if the regular sale of the book is to be wiped out after such a short time I do not think it should be done without having <u>both</u> Cerf and G and D. take editions. Of course G. and. D. have the favor of the business end since if the publishers make a concession to them on one book G and D. will reciprocate on another book. While Cerf takes only good books [*EH insertion*: (or what are supposed to be) Some of them aren't.] so is not in a position to be of as much use. For myself I dont want to have it go to G and D. without assurance that Cerf will also take an edition. Dont you think this is correct? G. and D. want it because it is going to be in the Moom pictures—

If they want it let them pay for it—[*EH insertion*: of course they are taking a good big edition as it is]

Write this so you will know my standpoint as I might be on the water or difficult to come at by letter when you were deciding this.

Also I'll find and sign the In Our Time Contract and send it to you—

Can't think of any more business—

[*Bottom quarter of page 2, which was torn off, was reattached by an archivist*]

When I was first in this racket, and steadily until it has been proved to me that it is not that way, I thought that if I could write good books which were true and would last they would all sell a certain amount each year say $363 apiece on an average and when I had 7 of them written say and was 50 with my life work done and inside them they would, if they had turned out to be good and had lasted, bring me in, say 2541\frac{00}{}$ a year which with what I had been able to save during any times they had made money would be fine But instead you find, or rather I've found so far, that a book of stories is sold out piecemeal for the original $40 it brings from the anthology and the 40¢ a year thereafter until it has lost its cohesion and its capital is all disbursed.

That a novel exists only for a few months and that what you get from it is entirely dependant on how violently it is pushed during those months and principally how long the push is kept up. And the chances are that when you are fifty if you should have written 7 good books your income from them will probably be about $300 a year—if that—and that if you do not save the chunks of capital that come into your hands—they will be giving benefits for you— It may be that the economic salvation of the aged writer is the collected works racket about which I know nothing yet— Anyway I'm not worrying— But you see why I want the best terms possible in the disposal of my capital to Messers Grossett and Cerf— Because I am not in the writing business with one to sell each year— I am not crabbing about the above— I have made more money already than a writer deserves to make— or than is good for him— But have been protected from that by not getting most of it—

As for the Communism that everybody is so spooked about— What the hell? If we are <u>all</u> broke it is all right— If we dont like it we can get out of the country— If we hate it enough we can fight it and die— But I'll tell you something; we wont have it. We are the most cowardly people in the world. Let business be a little bad and <u>everyone</u> is spooked about Communism. Personally I dont like it as a regime to live under. But if you dont like it you can get out— The trouble in the world is overpopulation—plagues and wars will handle that— If you have studied the history of Communism you will note that no country has ever had a Commune without first being defeated in a war— You need that to break down "Sales resistance"— We will have no Communistic govt. here until after a military defeat— Such a defeat would be the greatest thing that could ever happen to us—

But at the Dry Tortugas Max you gave me such confidence in the inherent military genius of America that I feel we need never fear this defeat— So you neednt think about the fate of five daughters under Communism—[4] First we must have the war, then the defeat— You can argue that a sufficient economic defeat might do instead— You would have a point— But I dont think it would be enough—

Now about the Story for August—

I would have sent you one before but have not published anything for sometime and it is best not to publish anything after a long absence.

[*Bottom half of page torn off and missing*]

[*On verso of torn page:*]

This is some valueless pooping on financial aspects of the literary life and some sage observations on Communism which I tore out to go on with the letter when your Grosset and Dunlop letter came and then thought you might be amused by—

[*EH starts a new page, which he numbers 3, circling the number*]

Have just received yours of April 25—[5]

Note that 75,000 of Grossett and Dunlop will bring in to me the same as about 9000 sale of the regular edition—

I would not expect Cerf to match their offer of number of copies guaranteed— But believe would be much better off if they each took 50,000— Cerf to publish <u>without</u> an introduction— [*EH insertion:* To hell with introductions. Though I read Bunnys over and it was fair enough.][6] or get Cerf to take 25,000 later if that is the best they will do— I dont think the number means much except as size of advance— Why cant they publish simultaneously?

Well I will do what you say to do— But have put down my viewpoint to guide you—or anyway to acquaint you with it—

About the story for August—

The only two stories I have that are in shape to publish without re-writing (which would hold up work on my book on which I am going well)— are [*EH circled insertion*: There is a lot of going over on the Standard Oil Man one—]

A Natural History of the Dead—

[*Rest of page torn off*]

[*EH begins a new page, which he numbers 4, circling the number*]

You read this one upstairs and you know whether the magazine will publish it or not— Black Sun Press in Paris have offered $1500 for it but I dont want to sign any limited editions— That is a lousy racket— will probably save it for in the B.F. book anyway.[7]

A Sea Change—

This is a damned good story—would be better in a book though— However since I promised one you can have it— But publishing it is against my judgement—[8]

I could try to write one in Madrid— [*EH insertion*: or on the boat]—once wrote 3 there in 2 days [*EH insertion*: in Madrid] including The Killers, Today is Friday and I forget the other—[9] Started a hell of a good one here and stopped it because I thought it was a ~~hell of a~~ mistake to write anything but on this book until it is finished— How late could you have one and still publish it in August? Whats the matter with [*hole torn in center of page; text missing*] Callaghan and the rest of your jackals? Cant they crack a few old bones up for the August number? Or get Mr. Thomas Wolfe to kill for you. He's no jackal. [*illegible cancellation*] He really kills by himself. I'll bet he'll write swell books for you.[10]

Anytime I don't write a book for over a year you get a Faux-Hemingway complete with mis-spelled words, ~~bad~~ mustache, inability to punctuate, naive rythms and all the visible faults of the original. [*EH insertion*: carefully photo-stated.] The only trouble with them is that they're lousy. You ought to have more confidence in me, Max, and spend that money some other way.

Am not pooping on Caldwell— Just read him. He seems very honest. Glad you're publishing him.[11]

Just received Special Delivery package of Two Novels of Distinction

[*lower edge of page torn off and missing*]

[*Upper edge of EH's numbered page 5 torn off and missing*]

My god Max I must knock off from writing this slop to you and get to bed—

But look— What about Capt. Cohn? I suspect the worst there— What is the Cap cooking up? He hasnt replied to me at all— When he wanted something he replied by return airmail Special Delivery envelopes enclosed. So I think he's selling us short somewhere— I have gotten a pamphlet Titus printed for him but damned if I'll send it unless he writes me—

My address will be care of

The Guaranty Trust Co of N.Y.

4 Place de la Concorde

Paris—France—

The only part of this letter you have to answer or read even is that about the reprint business—and give me a late report on Cap. Cohn—

Best luck to you—

Ernest—

John [Herrmann] didnt get drunk on the trip— It was Burge— John was OK.[12]

Max if I ever sound rude in a letter please forgive it. I am naturally a rude bastard and the only way know not to be is always to be formally polite. You stopped me doing that when you asked me to un-mister you.[13] So please remember that when I am loud mouthed, bitter, rude, son of a bitching and mistrustful I am really very reasonable and have great confidence and absolute trust in you.

The thing is I get so damned tired of being careful in letters— Christ, here I am starting to loud mouth again— But—anyway goodbye and good luck—

Ernest

PUL, ALS

This nine-page letter is in fragments, with portions of some pages torn away and missing.

1 Recent Scribner's publications included *The Modern Shotgun*, vol. 1: *The Gun* by Gerald Burrard (1888–1965) and *Better Trout Streams: Their Maintenance, with Special Reference to Trout Habits and Food Supply* by Edward Ringwood Hewitt (1866–1957).

2 In a letter of 23 April 1931, Perkins had asked about "the revolution there which might become Communist and get really rough" (PUL). In Madrid's 12 April municipal elections the monarchist candidates suffered an overwhelming defeat, resulting in the self-exile of King Alfonso XIII (1886–1941), who had reigned since 1902, and the proclamation of the Second Spanish Republic headed by Niceto Alcalá Zamora (1877–1949), who would serve as its prime minister and then president until 1936. The *New York Times* had recently reported post-election violence ("Civil Guards Kill Two / Demonstrators Shot in Madrid and Seville — Many Others Hurt in Revelry," 14 April 1931, 1). The Republican coalition included socialist, anarchist, and communist elements.

3 In his letter, Perkins wrote that Cerf (co-owner of the Modern Library) and Grosset & Dunlap (publisher of inexpensive reprints) had offered $50,000 and $53,000, respectively, for the rights to a reprint edition of 75,000 copies of *FTA*; Perkins was waiting for Cerf's counteroffer.

4 Perkins and his wife, Louise Saunders Perkins (1887–1965) had five daughters: Bertha (1911–2005), Elizabeth (1914–1974), Louise, known as Peggy (1915–2013), Jane (1918–1979), and Nancy (1925–1984).

5 In a letter of 25 April 1931, Perkins enclosed a memorandum from Whitney Darrow detailing the Grosset & Dunlap offer and reporting that Cerf would not be able to match it but might be interested in publishing an edition six months later (PUL).

6 Reference to Edmund Wilson's introduction to *In Our Time* (Scribner's, 1930).

7 "A Natural History of the Dead" would appear in Chapter 12 of *DIA* and would be included, with revisions, in *WTN*.

8 "The Sea Change" would first appear in the December 1931 issue of *This Quarter* and would be included in *WTN*.

9 EH's log of his May 1926 Madrid sojourn indicates that he wrote "The Killers," "Today Is Friday," and "Ten Indians" on May 20 and 21; manuscript evidence indicates that only "Today Is Friday" was written entirely on those two days (Smith, 154).

10 Both Callaghan and Wolfe had published and would publish in *Scribner's Magazine*, although neither published a story in the magazine in 1931. EH's prophecy would be realized with Scribner's publication of Wolfe's bestselling *Of Time and the River* (1935).

11 Perkins had sent EH a copy of *American Earth* (Scribner's, 1931), a collection of short stories by Southern writer Erskine Caldwell (1903–1987). Scribner's would publish Caldwell's novel *Tobacco Road* in 1932.

12 The remainder of the letter, primarily written in ink, is written in pencil.

13 In a letter of 15 January 1929, Perkins had written to EH, "For Gods Sake un-Mister me anyhow" (JFK).

To Waldo and Alzira Peirce, 30 April 1931

MZB284 45 NL = KEYWEST FLO 30

MR AND MRS WALDO PIERCE=

ARRIVING SS DEGRASSE MAY 2 NEWYORK NY=[1]
WELCOME HOME SAILING VOLENDAM FROM HAVANA MAY 4
ITS A TOUGH BREAK TO MISS YOU LIKE THIS WE WILL SURELY
GET TOGETHER NEXT WINTER BRO [Bra Saunders] CHARLES
[Thompson] AND ALL SEND THEIR BEST ADDRESS GUARANTY
TRUST PARIS THANKS EVER SO MUCH FOR LOOKING AFTER GUY
[Fangel] BEST LOVE=
ERNEST PAULINE.

Colby, Cable; Western Union destination receipt stamp: 1931 APR 30 PM 5 33

1 The *DeGrasse* departed from Le Havre, France, on 24 April and docked in New York City
on 2 May 1931 with Waldo, Alzira, and their twin sons, Mellen and Michael Peirce, aboard.

To Maxwell Perkins, [1 May 1931]

Friday—packing to leave Sat. morning—No Sunday boat to Havana.
Dear Max:—

Thanks for the wire and I just rec'd your letter about the Cerf business—
go ahead and close with them both if you think its best—glad if we must
have one that we are to have both—[1]

About the enclosed— I do not want to hurt Mr. Griffith's feelings but
am altogether opposed to a <u>condensation</u> having condensed it all I could
myself— Who in hell will read a condensation? Why a condensation?[2]

I wish to god I might get a swell story for you on the boat or in Madrid—
am getting to be as bad a promiser as President Harding since I've promised
<u>both</u> Ray Long (long ago) and the Magazine—[3] The result is that to keep an
honorable citizen and not break my promises I write no stories at all!—

Good luck, Max, the wind is blowing hard and I'd rather go in Bra's boat
than that rolling bitch of a Gov. Cobb—[4]

Did you know that Bra's bottom did open up, his boats bottom, one
whole plank—the day we came home— Didn't open until we were almostat
the dock— [*EH insertion*: Would have] Also I caught 5 tarpon one night out

of 5 strikes and 2 the next out of 2 strikes—4 of them good big ones—
72 lbs—64 lbs largest— So my luck must be in again—

Have had 3 typists working steady along getting a rough copy of my
original Mss of this book—one carbon to be left in U.S. Have original in my
book trunk and a copy in my other trunk so that we will not have to worry
about losing it if the revolution gets good. Thus Max do I protect your $6500
because if I lost the only Mss. I wouldnt be able to do a bloody thing but write
it off the books—can never remember anything when once written—

Have to pack now— So long and good luck again— My best to John
[Herrmann] when you see him— I was unjustly hard on him about Burge's
breakdown—

Yours always—
Ernest

Could you send me to Madrid when I get an address there—marking
them books only—

The Glass Key— Dashiel Hammnet—Knopf—

Green Hell—By some Irishman—(about Jungles)

The book of Mandariagas that you published?—[5]

If I got this book all done by Sept or Oct or Nov. when would you
publish? Spring is bad isnt it? That's what I always heard— But we wont
worry about anything but getting it done yet—

PUL, ALS

1 In his letter of 29 April 1931, Perkins reported Bennett Cerf's new proposal for a Modern
   Library edition of 15,000 to 20,000 copies of *FTA*, explaining that it would not interfere with
   a Grosset & Dunlap edition of 75,000, as the two publishers targeted different audiences.
   Perkins provided the proposed royalty details, saying, "I think this makes the whole
   proposition a very good one indeed" (PUL). In a 1 May 1931 cable, Perkins wrote,
   "Think we should accept both Grosset and Cerf" (PUL).
2 EH enclosed a letter of 28 April 1931 from editor William Griffith (1876–1936) requesting
   permission to include a 4,000–5,000-word condensed edition of *SAR* in a forthcoming
   volume of *Author's Digest*. Perkins would relay EH's refusal in a letter to Griffith dated 5
   May 1931 (PUL).
3 Harding, earlier accused of being "long on promises and short on performance" (*New York
   Times*, 22 September 1921, 1), had promised the position of Chief Justice of the Supreme
   Court to both former president William Howard Taft (1857–1930) and to English-born
   jurist George Sutherland (1862–1942). Harding appointed Taft, but a subsequent resignation from the Supreme Court enabled him to nominate Sutherland as Associate Justice in
   1922.

4 EH and Pauline had first arrived in Florida on 4 April 1928 aboard the *Governor Cobb*, which then served the Key West–Havana route. The 290-foot, four-deck, turbine-propelled passenger steamship was built in Eastport, Maine, in 1906, and named after William T. Cobb (1857–1937), governor of Maine from 1905 to 1909.
5 *The Glass Key* (New York: Knopf, 1931) by Dashiell Hammett (1894–1961). *Green Hell: Adventures in the Mysterious Jungles of Eastern Bolivia* (New York: Century, 1931) by English author Julian Duguid (1902–1987). In 1930, Scribner's published *Spain*, an historical overview by Spanish writer and historian Salvador de Madariaga y Rojo (1886–1978). EH owned the 1931 English edition published by Ernest Benn (Brasch and Sigman, item 4149).

To Henry Strater, [c. 1 May 1931]

Dear Mike:—

I'm a tripe not to have written. Was damned pleased Uncle Gus bought the portrait.[1] Once my arm got so it could write was so bloody swamped by mail that I owed that I didnt write you because didnt think you'd read me out of the party if I delayed answering—

I guess Uncle Gus told you about the 1st Tortugas and Max probably the 2nd—

We hooked 3 that jumped in the air at once—2 lines and the teaser—all over 30 lbs— They are not hard to hook in the air— Have found a system— Will explain better than on paper— Largest King was 44 lbs— My arm is OK now except will not straighten completely— That will come all right— Shot 24 × 25 at 200 yards standing on Marines' rifle range—23 × 25 [*Ditto marks*: at 200 yards standing] rapid fire—with the Springfield—

I think I'll get a double 2nd hand Express out in Africa—for heavy gun— Cant think about that until get this damned book finished— Is at its worst now and must now perform miracle of taking lousy muddle of 1st draft and make it into a good book—will need a miracle— Go to Madrid direct sailing May 4 from Havana by way of Coruña—going to stay in Spain until I have the bastard whipped— Pauline is going to Paris first—then settle Pat and Henriette and Bumby at Hendaye— Then join me at Madrid—

Admiral I am very pleased that you have a fine child and a swell show[2] and are still a fine unspoiled Southern Gentleman of the old School and for Christ sake forgive me either not writing or writing such a foul scrawl as this because until I get this book done I am unfit for human consumption—

But will get it done and we will have a swell trip to the land of the Jigs—

Listen why dont you hunt out with Lawrence Nordquist this fall—L-T ranch—Cooke City—Mont— The best trout fishing in the world is there between Sep 1–15th and hunting season opens 15th— He is a swell hunter and if there are two of you will take you for $25 a head a day all found—you can get a bull elk and a ram and a buck— Elk hunting in the mts is damned exciting— No pushover— Damned swell exciting hunting— If I can get finished and get back I will certainly go out because they are building a road in over the mts and when that is completed (in 2 years) the hunting will be gone— There are some wonderful big moose heads too— I saw one alive that would go 60 inches— Had no moose license— It's the finest mt. country Ive ever seen—

Well so long Mike old kid—

I appreciate the gun present offer very much and will take it out in a 2nd hand 465 or something like that in Africa if that's all right—[3]

My best love to Maggie—

Write to Guaranty Trust Co. Paris— they will forward to Madrid when I get an address there—[*EH insertion*: Will be plenty lonely and damned glad of a line until Pauline gets there] Am all balled up packing etc.

Please forgive me not writing— Have been working like hell until arm would poop each day— Arm will be OK. for everything except possibly boxing—Pro Football and human fly work—

Yours always

Hem—

Thanks for the grand reproductions— You are going <u>damned</u> <u>well</u>. But you know that—

PUL, ALS

1 Strater's third portrait of EH, begun in Key West and finished in New York City in April 1930, portrays EH in three-quarter view, sporting a moustache and wearing a loose-fitting blue shirt. In a 30 April 1931 letter to EH, Strater wrote that Gus Pfeiffer had praised the portrait (JFK), and Gus himself would later tell EH that Strater "has expressed your spirit and to me thats the important thing in a picture" (16 July 1931, JFK). The location of the painting is unknown, but the image, dated and signed, is reproduced in black and white in *Works of Sixty Years by Henry Strater / American Artist—born 1896 / Rocks, Nudes & Flowers* (Ogunquit, Maine, 1979) and in Colette Hemingway, *in his time: Ernest*

Hemingway's Collection of Paintings and the Artists He Knew (Naples, Florida: Kilimanjaro Books, 2009), 29.

2 Henry and Maggie's fourth child, Nicholas Appleby Strater, was born on 16 March 1931. An exhibit of Strater's paintings was held 16–28 March 1931 in New York City at the Montross Gallery. An American artists' show held there in May also included several of Strater's works.

3 In a letter of 4 May 1930, Strater asked EH to let him have the pleasure of buying him a gun for their planned safari as a birthday gift (JFK). A .465 is a caliber of Nitro Express cartridge for use in a high-powered rifle. EH would rent a .470 Nitro Express double-barreled rifle for his first safari (Calabi "Safari," 107–10).

To George Albee, 1 May [1931]

Box 404

Key West—Florida—

May 1—

Dear Albee:—

I was damned sorry to have missed you then in Paris and I'm a son of abitch not to have written you long ago— But am going to now in the boat—that am taking Monday to Spain— The reason I didnt write was that I was working and then got in a jam and was laid up 5 months—arm paralyzed etc. Am in good shape now. Please forgive me for never answering your letter— I'll read the story, send it back and write you from the boat—[1] Best luck to you always—

Yours

Ernest Hemingway—

I wish you had looked me up in Paris— They will forward mail from the above address or from the Guaranty Trust, Paris— Have no Spanish address yet—writing is a tough thing without trying to make a living from it— To write honestly and live by it needs gamblers luck for a long time—

UCalB, ALS

1 In his reply to EH of 6 May 1931, Albee would identify the story he sent as "Initiation," writing, "Why I picked 'Initiation' God only knows, unless because there was enough of yourself in it so that I thought you might like it" (JFK).

To Ezra and Dorothy Pound, 4 May 1931

This historic photo of our president for your files.[1]

Hem

Yale, A Postcard S; verso: photograph of U.S. Navy ship TEXAS, captioned "Llegada de Mr. Coodlige a la Habana" and "Mr. Coodlige arrived at Havana Jan 15/1928.";
postmark: HABANA, CUBA, MAY 4 / 10-AM / 1931

EH addressed the postcard: "Signo / Ezra Pound / Via Marsala 12 / Int 5 / Rappalo / Italia." Coolidge's name is misspelled in the postcard caption.

1 Calvin Coolidge visited Cuba on 15–17 January 1928 to address the Sixth International Conference of American States. His trip marked the first visit to Cuba by a sitting U.S. president.

To Waldo Peirce, 4 May [1931]

[S.S.] Volendam

May 4—

Dear Old Waldo:—

Thanks ever so much for the cable Chico—wish the hell you were on this thing and we were going to Spain together—

It looks like a dull voyage—all sacerdotes[1] so far— Hope you and A. are swell and the twins—

We have bought that old house with the iron rails and balconies opposite the lighthouse in K.W.[2] Alzira will know the one I mean.

I'll write you from Madrid— Guaranty Trust Paris will forward mail— I've been lousy about writing but it was my damned finn— Has only been out of paralysis class for 3 weeks—

Absolutely O.K. now—

Best always

Tu amigo

Ernesto

Colby, ALS; letterhead: HOLLAND-AMERICA LINE / ROTTERDAM.

1 *Sacerdotes*: priests (Spanish).
2 On 29 April 1931 EH and Pauline purchased the house at 907 Whitehead Street in Key West for $8,000, the funding supplied by Uncle Gus. Built in 1851 by shipping magnate and salvage wrecker Asa Forsyth Tift (1812–1889), the Spanish colonial-style house had wrought-iron railings surrounding the second-floor balcony, a large lawn, several fireplaces, and a carriage house.

To Charles Thompson, 4 May 1931

[*S.S.*] Volendam
May 4, 1931

Dear Dr.:—

Muggy day to leave here— Few tourists in Havana— But very quiet Boat packed—returning Spaniards— Thanks ever so much for looking after the guns and rods—

Left Key West at 196—201 yesterday—205 today—at that rate will hit 300 by June 11th—

If you drank beer, Dr. you'd weigh a ton—

Pauline just told me over the phone that Jinny was coming tomorrow—

Maybe she could go shooting with you to Cottrells (Scottrells) Key[1] and tarponing a couple of times— I'd appreciate it like hell if she could— She can shoot my 16 ga— Browning—

Tell Sully[2] his friends on the boat entertained me very royally—

So long Dr. I'll write you later— Looks like a blow coming— Had a wire from Waldo from N.Y. My very best to Lorine— I certainly appreciated her big help in getting us off—

Best to you always—
Ernest—

Take care of yourself.
Best to Bra—

Yoken, ALS; letterhead: HOLLAND-AMERICA LINE / ROTTERDAM.

1 EH refers to Cottrell Key, the northernmost of the uninhabited islets comprising the Mule Keys, 9 miles west of Key West.
2 James Bernard (J. B.) Sullivan (1886–1965), a Brooklyn native who had been a construction worker on the Flagler railroad connecting the Florida Keys and owned a machine shop in

Key West, the East Coast Electric Welding Company. EH would dedicate *GHOA* to "Sully," Charles Thompson, and Philip Percival, the professional hunter who served as guide for EH's 1933–1934 African safari.

To Frank McCoy, 4 May 1931

[*S.S.*] Volendam
May 4 1931
Major General Frank R. McCoy
Fort McPherson
Ga—

Dear General McCoy:—

You were very good to write about the fishing when it was so very poor— But I hope sometime you will come to Tortugas when we are there and the weather is good so that we can have some real fishing together.

I enjoyed greatly meeting you. Please remember me to Lt. Biddle.[1]

Yours very truly—
Ernest Hemingway.

LOC, ALS; letterhead: HOLLAND-AMERICA LINE / ROTTERDAM.

1 Major General Frank R. McCoy visited Key West on 2–8 March 1931 to inspect Fort Taylor. He was accompanied by his aide, Lieutenant William S. Biddle (1900–1981). The *Key West Citizen* quoted McCoy as saying that he regarded fishing in Key West and the Dry Tortugas as the "finest in the world" ("Key West to Have Troops Each Season," *Key West Citizen*, 7 March 1931, 1).

To Thornton Wilder, 6 May [1931]

[*S.S.*] Volendam
May 6—

Dear Thornton:—

What the devil has become of you? For two months in the hospital (Nov. Dec.) I read nothing but assaults on you and defences of you,[1] My Christ Dr. but you have impassioned admirerors, assaulters and defenders—, and listened to the radio. I've spoken for you in conversation a couple of thousand times and wd defend you in print if your goddamned writings needed any defence. But you write pretty well, Dr. Pretty well.

But what the hell has become of you personally?

The last I heard you were going to Berlin and you said, sadly, that my present, then, attitude toward God did not sound like a true religious viewpoint.— (I probably misquote)[2]

But since then if you, too, are Curious will say that had a couple of bad months with a stopped Kidney, got perfectly well, had 3, fair months of work, then 3 damned fine ones—hunted a month in the high mts.—then broke my upper right arm and all but lost it. Was paralyzed in it 5 months. Got all all right and am working again—or rather interrupting it for a week or 10 or 11 days to go to Madrid on this bloody boat—to go on working there—

Am writing a damned sight better than before and know a couple of things more—hope so anyway—

What the hell are you doing?

Listen, while I give you that most precious to give and shit to receive—

Dont try to write exclusively great ones—write them good, as good as you can, and then if they should ever turn out to be great they'll be great— But if you start out to write masterpieces you will get so constipated that even Nujol wont save them or get the golden eggs out—[3] While if you just keep ahead opening oysters if your on the proper beds may find almost anything.

If this is of no use throw it out—

Dos and I were writing a play when broke my arm— It may have been a sign from the maker—

Why dont you write me care of

Guaranty Trust—4 Place de la Concorde—Paris—

They will forward it to Spain— Will you be in Europe or where? Why dont you come to K. West some winter?

Good luck to you—

Ernest

Yale, ALS; letterhead: HOLLAND-AMERICA LINE / ROTTERDAM; postmark: PLYMOUTH DEVON, MAY 18 / 4 – PM / 1931

EH addressed the envelope to "Thornton Wilder Esq. / c/o Albert and Charles Boni, Publishers / New York City / Estados Unidos," with the notation "Please Forward." The letter was forwarded to 50 Deepwood Drive, Hamden, Connecticut, with a forwarding postmark from New York City of 22 May 1931.

1 In 1930 left-wing critic Michael Gold (né Itzok Isaac Granich, 1893–1967), editor in chief of the *New Masses* (1928–1939), denounced Wilder as elitist, escapist, and reactionary, referring to Wilder's accumulated work as "an historic junkshop" ("Wilder: Prophet of the Genteel Christ," *New Republic*, 22 October 1930, 266). The article provoked significant controversy about the social and political role of writers. Edmund Wilson, associate editor of the *New Republic*, took an active role in the debate, which included significant reader involvement. For Wilson's detailed critical analysis of the controversy begun by Gold's attack on Wilder, see "The Literary Class War: I," *New Republic*, 4 May 1932 (319–23).
2 The letter EH refers to remains unlocated.
3 Nujol was an orally administered mineral oil advertised as a remedy for constipation.

To George Albee, 7 May 1931

[S.S.] Volendam
May 7, 1931

Dear Mr. Albee:—

This is to answer yours of Dec 7th enclosing the story—

It seems like a good story to me— But the hell of it is that it doesnt come off someway— Certainly disease is a legitimate subject and a first dose of clap an excellent one— But did he kill himself— You made him do so and plenty of people have done so—but still it doesnt seem to come off— Did that particular kid kill himself? That's the problem—[1]

I'll tell you what I'd do— I'd put it away and forget about it— If you can write that well you can and will write a damned sight better—

You see in all writing when you first start to do it you, writing, get a terrific kick and the reader instead of getting that only feels that you, the writer have it— As you go on you learn to give it all to the reader— There is no short cut to learning how to do this. You only can learn to do it by keeping at the damned thing— All of a sudden you have it—

I'm trying to think what it is that makes the story weak and this is it I guess— The kid sounds as though he had caught the disease without having intercourse— You never believe in the intercourse— In the disease, yes. After intercourse a man's, or a boys, head clears and is cold— If he thought the girl had given him gonorrhea he would be not only frightened but angry—

Am saying this arbitrarily— Maybe not with your kid— But believe the trouble is you dont make the intercourse come true—

Since that is probably the hardest thing to do in all writing why the hell should you be discouraged—

Keep on writing— You will write damned good stuff— But I cant take that story and go to bat for it because it isnt right yet— But it's better to write a new one than re-write an old one—

If this advice is punk—remember you asked for it—

Best luck to you—
Ernest Hemingway.

UCalB, ALS; letterhead: HOLLAND-AMERICA LINE / ROTTERDAM.

1 "Initiation" would appear in the March 1932 issue of *Story*, a literary journal founded in 1931 by Martha Foley and Whit Burnett. In the published version, the protagonist is a seventeen-year old college student in love with a woman he calls his "little silver goddess." When he is diagnosed with a sexually transmitted disease, the protagonist commits suicide by jumping out of the window.

To Guy Hickok, 7 May [1931]

[*S.S.*] Volendam—
May 7

Dear Gros:—

Well Mr. Hickock—here is a rare thing—a leter from your old Pal asking no favours, not exposing you to expenditure, and returning the photo of yr. old man— I need no photo to identify him now— I suppose pretty soon you will be so fond of your old man we wont even be able to Kid about him. But listen—speaking of rubber checks—if you are so you could use some cash I can let you have it up to whatever you say. You would seem a better placement D'Argent[1] as far as chance goes to get it back than any U.S. banks the way things look. I cannot tell you what a privelige it would be to loan dough to some guy you could figure on getting it back from—

Also Listen Gros— When my kidney was haywired had to give up drinking for about 6 weeks but now can drink and have drunk for ever since a year ago last February— I may have made a certain amt. of dough which has all been give away, loaned or spent but I am a son of a bitch if I have become respectable and no later than last winter was forced to sleep all night on the front porch—not being a good size for Pauline to carry up stairs—and on going to church the next morning was surprized to be treated [. . .]

[*Catalog description: "The relating of a drunken stumble into a holy water fount and Spanish villagers spying the '3/4 empty' bottle in the front seat of his convertible provides further evidence"*]

The reason I didn't write you about the book is because it is hard enough to write it without writing about it. But listen if you will come down to Madrid you can read it typed in Mss as far as it is to date[2] besides which we could see who can drink and who not and see the bull fights—

[. . .] We bought a damned fine home in K. W. [. . .]

[*Regarding his book in progress:*] Worked steady on it from last Feb— went well all summer—worked until I broke my wing— [. . .]

I'll wire Guaranty, Paris, who [are] holding my mail, my address as soon as have one—

Will wire you too—but you'll get the wire before you get this letter—

Henriette has been wonderful—you were swell to look after her— I couldnt write then because my arm was still paralysed— Have only been able to write since 3 weeks—

Can nearly straighten arm now—
Was like (1) Now most of
the time like (2) but
can straighten to (3)
with massage—

It will be absolutely all right if keep after it. Anyway can shoot, fish and write with it now—but cant sock anybody— [. . .]

This is written 3 days out from Havana— 7 more to Vigo—will mail it there— You'll get it in a week maybe—

I'd planned to come to Paris first— Then realized when got to Madrid at once would miss all the bull fight season (May and June)— Then this boat came along and took it in a hurry—

We'd just bought the house and Pauline wanted to do some looking after it and then miss this 16 day to France route— It is a hell of a fine old house

Like this

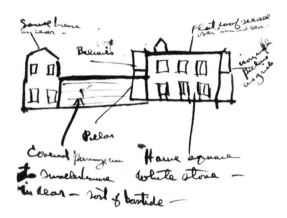

[*EH's labels with arrows pointing to various parts of his drawing*: Small house in rear— / Balconies / Flat roof see all over town and sea— / ironwork pillars and grills / Covered passageway to smaller house in rear—sort of bastide— / Pillars / House square white stone—][3]

Well so long again Kid and again Love to Mary—

Yours always

Ernest

I hope see you pretty soon— If you cant come now you could come later in the summer maybe—

Sotheby's catalog, New York, 11 June 2013, Lot 192; Kotte Autographs online catalog, Rosshaupten, Germany (partially illustrated), ALS; letterhead: HOLLAND-AMERICA LINE / ROTTERDAM.

This transcription derives from the catalog descriptions and partial illustrations of the nine-page letter. Bracketed ellipses indicate unavailable portions of the text.

1 *Placement d'argent*: investment (French).
2 The 280 pages of *DIA* that EH had finished before breaking his arm (see EH to Perkins, 28 October [1930]) had been typed in Key West.
3 In a letter of 1 June [1931], Hickok wrote that when Pauline visited him in Paris, "I showed her your drawings of your Key West estate. She said that though she always thought you were a great pen and ink artist that didn't look like the house. You had omitted it seems the iron gallery and a number of other things that make it nice" (JFK). *Bastide*: small country house (French).

To Cranston D. Raymond, 8 May [1931]

[S.S.] Volendam
May 8—1930

Dear Mr. Raymond:—

I got your letter too late to wire you to send the books on. But if you dont mind waiting I'll be glad to sign them when we get back in the fall— I'll get Dos to sign the two for you too— His address is 571 Commercial Street— Provincetown, Mass. He's not back from Mexico yet but I'll write him and tell him you're writing him— He should be back in a couple of weeks—

You were damned good to me in Billings and I'll never forget it. We were there two months—arm got pretty bad and was more or less paralyzed up until about a month ago— Think it will be as good as ever now—

This is one of those bum overfed underbrained letters you write on boats but I want you to know how very very much I appreciated your kindness and how much I look forward to seeing you again sometime.

With best regards to you and to Mrs Raymond (and thanks for your Christmas card!)

Yours always
Ernest Hemingway.

[*Enclosure: picture postcard of S.S. Volendam. EH wrote on verso*: "Postcard for the Kids"]

HOLLAND-AMERICA LINE.   ROTTERDAM-NEW YORK } DIRECT
                         ROTTERDAM-HALIFAX (CANADA) } SERVICE

T.S.S. **VOLENDAM.** 15430 Tons Register – 25620 Tons Displacement.

Stanford, ALS; letterhead: HOLLAND-AMERICA LINE / ROTTERDAM.

To Mary Pfeiffer, 13 May 1931

[*S.S.*] Volendam
May 13—1931

Dear Mother Pfeiffer:—

We've been on this boat 9 days now and tomorrow Night are due at Vigo. The boat has been very steady and dull—like voyaging on Queen Wilhelmina's ample bosom.[1] For three days there has been fighting and riot in Madrid according to the wireless. The Revolution has passed out of its honeymoon stage and may be entering on a period of terror. This occurrs in all successful revolutions and if they really want to do away with the King they may burn the Royal palaces, kill or exile the aristocracy and seize their lands. Burning churches is silly and criminal.[2] Still by two days after tomorrow if the trains still run will be in Madrid.

If they stop the bullfights can write about the Revolution. Will not shut up the sausage mill as long as there is meat of any kind available.

Am glad not to have anything to worry about—had my Mss. copied and one carbon in U.S. for this emergency and Pauline will be safe in France and will go to her rather than have her come down if things are bad enough. Believe, though, that they will be pretty well quieted down after this first exuberance for a while. None of the real problems have yet come up. Burning a few churches is hardly a settlement of the religious problem in what has been a 92% Catholic country.

This is only a note to thank you for your letter and tell you both how much I hope for a good weather summer at Piggott; one that will make up for the drought.

Jinny will give you all the family news from us since I left. Let her get out one of the guns and execute the woodpecker if he is too much of a nuisance. I'll write from Madrid and give you any news there is.

The 3rd class passengers, inspired by the church burning news, sent a revolutionary Committee to demand no more rice and that potato omelets be served every day. This was granted after much argument. and over 15,000 gestures.

There are 7 Spanish priests on board, expelled from Mexico, and they are pretty gloomy about the Spanish news. But believe they feel nearer Rome here than they were in Mexico.

Am leaving the boat in Vigo rather than Coruña to get to Madrid a day earlier. Should arrive there May 16—

Best love to you all—

Ernest—

Pauline and Patrick were Splendid when I left Key West— Hope to see them in 3 weeks now.

Please thank Pauline's Father for me for sending the boots and breeches. I owe him a letter and will write when I have news. I sent the book to the W R. Warner man in Mex. City.[3]

PUL, ALS; letterhead: HOLLAND-AMERICA LINE / ROTTERDAM.; postmark: PLYMOUTH DEVON, MAY 18 / 4 – PM / 1931

1 EH was aboard a Dutch passenger liner. The Dutch queen Wilhelmina Helena Pauline Maria of Orange-Nassau (1880–1962) reigned from 1890 to 1948.

2 On 10 May, when monarchists attempted to reclaim power and Republicans rioted in opposition, violence erupted in the streets of Madrid ("Madrid Swept by Riots," *Chicago Daily Tribune*, 11 May 1931, 1). The violence spread quickly and included attacks against the Catholic Church, which was traditionally allied with the deposed monarchy and the army. On 12 May 1931 the *New York Times* reported "Riots in 7 Spanish Cities; Churches Looted, Burned; Martial Law is Declared / Nuns Beaten in Madrid / Headquarters of Jesuits Raided – Attacks Spread to Provinces / Provincial Troops Called" (1).

3 William R. Warner & Company, a pharmaceutical firm, was acquired by Gus and Henry Pfeiffer in 1908. The Pfeiffers retained the Warner name as they acquired other companies and established branch offices in other countries, including Mexico.

To Waldo Peirce, 14 May [1931]

[*S.S.*] Volendam—

May 14

Dear Waldo:—

Thanks ever so [m]uch for the wire to the boat. Hope you find everything fine at Bangor. It was a damned shame not to see each other in Paris or N.Y. When I heard you were leaving Paris decided go straight to Spain. Get off at Vigo tomorrow and hope can get train straight to Madrid. Want to get there before they set up the guillotine in the Plaza Mayor—

I'll write you the dope. Write me care of the Guaranty Trust—Paris— They will forward as soon as have a Spanish address—

Best to Alzira and to you Chico—

Ernest

Colby, ALS; letterhead: HOLLAND-AMERICA LINE / ROTTERDAM.

To Pauline Pfeiffer Hemingway, [c. 18 May 1931]

Mrs Ernest Hemingway

Hotel Brevoort

NewYork

LCD wonderful Bargains here now working well You can shop mornings we both afternoons see you Hendaye Seven letters Citibank Paris Dearest Love Ernest

JFK, ACDS

The conjectured date is based on the facts that Pauline had left Key West for New York City on 16 May with Patrick and Henriette, and that they sailed for France on 20 May. EH had arrived in Madrid on 16 May, and probably cabled this for it to reach Pauline while she was in New York. EH wrote this cable draft on the verso of a letter he received from Merle Armitage (1893–1975), manager of the Los Angeles Grand Opera Association, dated 18 February 1931 and requesting that EH sign his copy of *FTA*. The verso also bears EH's notation "Answd / May 14." EH's letter to Armitage remains unlocated.

To Maxwell Perkins, 15 June 1931

BN1/15 C MADRID 15 / 9AM
MAXWELL PERKINS SCRIBNERS 597 FIFTH AVENUE NYK.
GOING FINE PLEASE DEPOSIT 500 DOLLARS MY ACCOUNT
CITYBANK FARMERS BRANCH 22 WILLIAM STREET ERNEST.

PUL, Cable; Western Union destination receipt stamp: 1931 JUN 15 AM 5 03

The cable bears Perkins's handwritten notation: "Okay / Max."

To Ezra Pound, 16 June [1931]

June 16

Dear Ezra:—

It was a damned shame I didnt know you were in Paris or would have gone up there— The card you wrote the Guaranty sent to U.S. and back— Got it here at same time as a letter from Hickock saying you'd just left—[1]

Would come to bathe but there are better men than me in jail in your country already— Why couldnt we meet somewhere this fall and take a walk somewhere? I'll meet you at any border— Walking, however, best from North border— Things are pretty good here now— Still revolutionary honeymoon stage— All brothers— 5 bullfights this week and free outdoor performances of La Vida es Sueno and so forth in ex-royal palace patio every night with fireworks to fiesta the republic—[2] As one of old original republicans am well received— Goddam it we would have had the republic long ago if you hadnt persuaded me they would stop the bulls— all the ex newspaper men and bum writers are now ministers— If you were a Spaniard you could be president easily— The great qualification to hold office is to have been in jail— Have you ever been in jail? If so send details and I can easily arrange your naturalization and appointment—

I am holding out for the Court of St. James myself— Perez de Ayala wont last long there—[3]

They are putting the boots to Cristo Rey and civil war— Don Jaime (formerly Don Carlos) is promising to come over the Pyrenees with the Sword in one hand the Cross in the other and the Sacred Heart of Jesus on his chest—[4] 23,000 people cheered this announcement on Sunday in Pamplona—[5] a Carmelite nun destroyed with kicks a local lad who viva-ed the Soviet Republic and a prelate shot down a citizen from the top of an autobus for insults to religion— Things are warming up in Navarre.

In Madrid everything is very quiet—overwhelming Republican sentiment—

In Andalucia will be big blowup if the Cortes does not distribute land to peasants—[6] It will distribute though and then peasants will be broke on their own hook probably in no time as in Arkansas—

Whats the news in Litrachur?

Do you still have anything to say in the available languages or have you been forced to invent new ones? (This is a swing at our illustrious contemporary—[7] I know you have several things to say still) Understand there is a great movement on foot or on hands and feet in America for you to again become fashionable as Great American Poet— This denying and affirming the worth of gents goes in Cycles—

By paying nothing and being polite to no-one a gent will be great and lousy 1/2 doz times in his life and cycle continue after his death indefinitely— By paying heavily and being polite to all who matter citizen stays great as hell during his life to at once become and stay lousy from death straight on— ie Amy — Galsworthy etc etc etc.[8]

Well Dr. what about our old fellow Ape with God Wyndham Lewis— Is he trying to pick a winner with Hitler? The world and the German being as it is he may well have a winner— But somebody should tell Wyndham it is no good writing about a guy <u>before</u> he gets into power—[9] That never pays— That only gets you barred from the country later for knowing too much— Havent read the book— The chances are he doesnt know too much—

What about Major Eliot? Has the Major found comfort in Angleworm Catholicism, George and Mary Royalism and J. B. Priestly J. C. Squire Classicism? Are his supplys of early sermonaters holding out? At the hour when the thought of approaching sexual intercourse warms the evening after the 2nd bottle I picture the Major taking down his copy of Launcelot Andrewes—[10] For me the Major is a skillful poet, damned skillful, and a yellow bastard—

     A poop on the Major—

   With his quaint pamphlets gone to bust

   and into footnotes all his lust—

Originally written for the humanists—capital H—but the Major is an naturalized Humanist—[11]

Have been reading the late James, (Henry Jr.) You are right [*EH insertion*: very very right] about the late James although at the very end his sphincter muscle was lax, most lax—that is if the premise be accepted that we all write shit—

Anyway I feel like hell not to have seen you—

McAlmon is Dreiser without the industry or experience—

I tried like hell to get him published in N.Y. [*EH insertion*: Wrote numerous letters, appealed, etc.] but He would get tight at lunch with the publishers and tell them what a shit I was, interesting them at first, but finally boring them— For a couple of the things he said am justified in beating shit out of him now that have only one good arm—

Well So long—Senator— You might write to Hotel Biarritz—Calle Victoria 2—Madrid—

Love to Dorothy—

Hem—

Yale, ALS

1 In a letter of 19 May [1931] from Paris, Hickok wrote, "Old Ezra was sitting there when your wire came in and he took your address off it," adding that Pound was returning to

Rapallo on Thursday (21 May) (JFK). Both EH' wire (mentioned by Hickok) and Pound's card to EH remain unlocated.

2 In spite of earlier violent clashes, the Madrid newspaper *ABC* of 18 June 1931 would devote an entire page to describing the crowded cafés, streets full of strolling citizenry, and general holiday feel in Madrid. Bullfights were held on 14, 16, 17, 22, and 23 June, and *La Vida Es Sueño* (*Life Is a Dream*) by Spanish playwright Pedro Calderón de la Barca (1600–1681) was presented on 13 June at the open-air Plaza de la Armería, beside the south facade of the Royal Palace.

3 Ramón Pérez de Ayala, Spanish novelist, poet, and critic (1881–1962) nominated for the Nobel Prize in Literature (1931, 1934, and 1947), served as the Spanish Republic's Ambassador to the United Kingdom from 1931 to 1936, when the Spanish Civil War broke out.

4 "*¡Viva Cristo Rey!*" (Long Live Christ the King!) was the rallying cry for pro-Church, anti-secular uprisings such as Spain's three Carlist Wars (1833–1840, 1847–1849, 1872–1876). Don Jaime (Jaime de Borbón y Borbón-Parma, 1870–1931) was a descendant of Don Carlos (Carlos María Isidro de Borbón, 1788–1866). Carlos had been the presumptive heir to the throne of his older brother, Spain's Ferdinand VII (1784–1833; reigned 1808, 1814–1833). When Ferdinand's daughter, Isabella (1830–1904), was born and designated his heir (reigning as Isabella II, 1833–1868), Carlos claimed that under Salic Law, which recognizes only male succession, he was the rightful or legitimist heir to the Spanish throne. The Carlist uprisings were unsuccessful, but in 1931, as the establishment of the Republic caused the reigning King Alfonso XIII to retreat into exile, the Carlists re-emerged, with the support of their traditional ally, the Catholic Church, to claim the Spanish throne for Don Jaime, then living in France. The Sacred Heart of Jesus: distinguishing insignia of the *requetés* (Carlist militiamen), who were particularly strong in the conservative northeastern provinces, including the Basque provinces and Navarre.

5 The Catholic newspaper *El Siglo Futuro* reported attendance of 28,000 at the Carlist rally in the Pamplona bullring held on Sunday, 14 June 1931. A crowd of Republicans gathered outside the bullring shouting slogans and threatening violence, which was largely controlled by the police ("Al grandioso mitin de afirmación católica asistieron 28,000 personas," 15 June 1931, 1).

6 An important platform of the Second Republic (1931–1939) was agrarian reform, a particularly touchy subject in the southern province of Andalusia where estates were large and the peasantry particularly poor. Spain's national legislative assembly, the Cortes, passed confusing and contradictory agrarian reform laws on 29 April, 19 May, 11 July, and 6 August 1931.

7 Probably a jibe at James Joyce.

8 American poet Amy Lowell (1874–1925). Pound was instrumental in establishing the Imagist movement in 1912. After he turned his attention to Vorticism, Lowell became the chief proponent of Imagism, which Pound then dismissed as "Amygisme." Lowell was awarded a posthumous Pulitzer Prize in 1925. John Galsworthy was nominated for the Nobel Prize five times (in 1919, 1920, 1921, 1922, and 1931) before receiving it in 1932.

9 *The Apes of God* (London: Arthur, 1930), a novel by Wyndham Lewis satirizing the contemporary literary and social scene, particularly the Bloomsbury Group. In his next book, *Hitler* (London: Chatto & Windus, 1931), Lewis praised Adolf Hitler as a "man of peace." At the time, Adolph Hitler (1889–1945) and his National Socialist German Workers' (Nazi) Party were gaining power in Germany; in 1933 Hitler would be appointed Chancellor by President Paul von Hindenberg (1847–1934) and would establish himself as absolute dictator of the Third Reich in 1934. Lewis would later recant his support for Hitler in *The Hitler Cult* (1939).

10 T. S. Eliot allied himself with Anglo-Catholicism (the branch of the Anglican Church that favors the Roman Catholic tradition over the Protestant); with the British monarchs King George V (1865–1936) and Queen Mary (1867–1953) who reigned from 1910 to 1936; and

with J. C. (John Collings) Squire (1882–1958), British journalist, author, and editor (1919–1934) of the influential monthly *London Mercury*. Launcelot Andrewes (1556–1626), scholar who while dean of Westminster Abbey oversaw the translation of the King James Bible.

11 EH would echo this parody of Andrew Marvell's poem "To His Coy Mistress" in Chapter 12 of *DIA* as part of his attack on the Humanists. Proponents of the conservative literary movement rejected the contemporary focus on realism and argued that literature should reflect morality and decorum.

To Guy Hickok, [17] June [1931]

June 16[1]

Dear Gros:—

It was a damned shame to miss in Paris[2] But I had a berth on the train and another to take Pauline to Madrid. But look— If you come down here you wont be spending much money with the peseta a 10 to $— Prices are down—

We pay 15 pesetas apiece for full pension and room here at Hotel Biarritz—Calle Victoria, 2—

Are going to Sierra de Gredos—3 hrs in car from here—on Tuesday 22nd for 3 or 4 days— Then will be at Hendaye July 5—to go to Pamplona on 6th— Pauline is staying at Hendaye— I'm taking Bumby to Pamplona—

If you want to study the revolution from Pamplona it is not such a bad bet—

Don Jaime is preparing a new Carlist war with Pamplona as base— 23,000 people in the ring there Sunday at Jaimist rally — Viva Cristo Rey— etc. Read a message from Don Jaime in which he promised to cross the Pyrenees with sword in one hand, cross in other and sacred heart of Jesus on his chest— He and the ex Bishop (Expelled) of Victoria (Mateo Mugica) crossed the border a few days ago for him to take the oath on famous and sacred tree of Guernica as King of Navarre and defender of the religion—[3]

Both now back in Bayonne— But things are getting hot in Navarre— When the Cortes votes separation of Church and state if hell should be popping in Andalucia over the land settlement they might shoot the works—

That was the history of the first Republic—[4]

Madrid very quiet (and noisy) and overwhelmingly Republican— I believe the trouble in the south will be settled by the distribution of land to peasants— But this Navarre thing is new— The above Navarre dope is not exaggerated but as straight as could be got from source. If you decided to come to Pamplona we could go up together— or may see you here for election's—[5] Write to Hotel Biarritz

Calle Victoria, 2

Excuse this letter— Am trying to work—

Best always—

Ernest

Felix badly gored yesterday—through and through right thigh—

See a lot of Sidney Franklin here—

phPUL, ALS

1 EH's reference to the goring of Félix Rodríguez "yesterday" establishes the date of this letter as [17] June [1931]. The matador was gored by his second bull on 16 June 1931 in Madrid.
2 In his letter of 19 May [1931], Hickok wrote, "That you should leave Paris at 8:40; and that I should arrive in Paris at 9, is one of those things that happens only in the wood-pulps" (JFK).
3 The Pamplona meeting was headed by José Selva Mergelina (1884–1932), the political secretary and representative of the Carlist claimant of the throne, Don Jaime, who remained in Paris. Mateo Múgica Urrestarazu (1870–1968), Spanish cleric and monarchist, appointed Bishop of Pamplona in 1924 and of Vitoria in 1928, had been expelled from Spain on 17 May on suspicion of organizing a counterrevolutionary movement. A newspaper report with the byline Madrid, June 13, reported an intense search for the bishop, suspected of having returned recently "to attend a mass meeting at Pampeluna to-day, at which the Catholic Party's election campaign will be initiated" (*North-China Herald and Supreme Court & Consular Gazette* (1870–1941) [Shanghai], 16 June 1931, 383). The sacred tree of Guernica (*Gernikako Arbola* in Basque): an iconic oak tree associated with the swearing in of Basque officials as they commit to uphold the Basque *fueros*, or the traditional freedoms.
4 The First Spanish Republic (11 February 1873–29 December 1874) was so torn by these issues that it had five presidents in its twenty-three months of existence.
5 Elections for representatives to the Constituent Cortes would be held on 28 June 1931.

To John Dos Passos, 26 June [1931]

June 26—

Calle Victoria, 2

Madrid.

Dos:—

Things are pretty well steamed up with the elections day after tomorrow— over 900 candidates but less than 100 of the right—23 different parties— Republican landslide in various colors Red White and Black Republicans—[1]

The govt has rightly stopped work on the Coruna-Orense R.R. (Motor trucks and buses are killing R.R.S) and in consequence the Gallegos are proclaiming the Social Republic of Galicia (until work begins on RR. again) and are General Striking on election day and refraining from voting—

Andalucia is coming to boil but will not probably boil over until after Cortes in order to see what land partition will amount to— The workers comitees have gotten all harvesting machinery banned—

(You see it isnt much like Russia)

Navarra has gone for el Cristo Rey in the biggest possible way—and it is no uncommon thing for a prelate to shoot down a good republican from the top of an autobus or for a Carmelite to destroy with kicks an agitator—

23,000 Navarros in Pamplona bull ring 2 weeks ago enthusiastic for Don Jaime who has promised to cross the Pireneos with the sword in one hand, the Cross in the other and the Sacred Heart of Jesus on his chest—

He came into Spain incog and swore an oath as King of Navarre and defender of faith on Sacred tree of Don Carlos etc. Is now in Bayonne—all that is being directed from Bayonne—

Catalonia is waiting to do business—

Madrid loves the Republic—which, as soon as any one takes power— Lerroux etc. they shift from left to right faster even than in France—[2]

The King is permanently out—[3]

Ramon Franco etc. are well bughouse and are being read out of the party— Their great ambition is to really bring off an air revolution (Cuatros Ventos-ism) against Anybody in power.[4]

Sunday may prove me all wrong on all of this— Am sending big collected bunch of papers for backhouse reading— Have been saving ones with dope— La Libertad is now Le Temps[5]—consequently all my buddies are prosperous—

Have been working like hell until it got too hot 42°–46° in Shade— Been following politics Closely— Seen a few funny things—

Most bull displays lousy— Present republic all for bulls but ganaderos[6] have just about ruined the bloody bulls—

How the hell are you? We could have a fine time here now— Communists have no money at all—or could make a pretty good show—

Except for Andalucia—which had an Arkansas crop season last year—very damned few out of work— Chances for Marxian revolution nil— May yet have a terror though—

If worst comes to worst history of 1st Republic will repeat—

Pauline and Pat and Bumby all fine— Am taking Bumby to Pamplona— Hadley fine too—went up to Paris to see her and Bum—

Write me for <u>anything</u> you want—

We live here damn well on 3$\frac{00}{}$ a day the two of us. Now is the time to buy anything if anybody had money—

Were you ever in Sierra de Gredos? Barco de Avila is wonderful town— Killed a wolf there while we were there— Bear paw nailed to door of Church— Good trout— River Tormes that flows down to Salamanca—wild goats— Eat better than Botins—same dishes— Swell big <u>clean</u> rooms— no chinchas—[7] all people nice— damned intelligent— old banner of Garibaldi from 1st Republic at Verbena of San Juan—[8] All for 8 pesetas a day—

You are the great writer of Spain—if you would naturalize Katy could be Mrs. Ambassador—to any court you name— They all think I am bullshitting because I claim to be a friend of yours— Nobody has read Manhattan less than 4 times— In spite of descriptive introduction you are supposed to be an old man about Unamunos age— Otherwise how did you have time to know the Bajo fundos so well and have so much experience—[9]

I swear to god they think I am one of these Guys who claims to know the toreros when I say we are old pals— Send me a book inscribed to me in warm terms or I will be lynchiado-ed as an impostor— They have taken to lynchiaring considerably—

Write the dope— Love to Katy from Pauline and me—

Yrs always
Hem—

Arm crooked but serviceable.

UVA, ALS

1 EH refers to popular classifications of the many Republican parties, those on the left being dubbed Red, the centrist or conservative groups being called White, and the more extreme right-wing parties, often only nominally attached to the Republic as they pursued local aims, referred to as Black Republicans.

2 Alejandro Lerroux García (1864–1949), Spanish lawyer, journalist, and politician, exiled to Argentina in 1907 for his extreme Republican views. Elected in 1931 as the Spanish Republic's first foreign minister, he began to moderate his extreme leftist stance in favor of pragmatic political alliances.

3 Alfonso XIII and a small entourage drove from Madrid to Cartagena where they boarded a boat for Marseilles on the night of 14 April 1931; his wife and children left Madrid the next day. He would die in exile.

4 Ramón Franco (1896–1938), Spanish aviator who conspired against the dictatorship of Primo de Rivera and the monarchy of Alfonso XIII, most famously by participating in the 1930 seizure of aircraft from the Cuatro Vientos (Four Winds) Air Base outside Madrid in an unsuccessful attempt to drop bombs on Madrid's Royal Palace. In spite of such leftist activities, Ramón would join his brother General Francisco Franco (1892–1975), who would lead the Nationalist military uprising against the elected Republic that sparked the Spanish Civil War in 1936.

5 *La Libertad* (*Liberty*): socialist, antimonarchical, and anticlerical Madrid daily that criticized some of the newly installed Republican officials it had formerly praised. *Le Temps* (*The Times*): mainstream French newspaper. EH would write in *DIA*: "*La Libertad* I find is getting like *Le Temps*. It is no longer the paper where you could put a notice and know the pickpocket would see it now that Republicans are all respectable" (Chapter 20).

6 *Ganaderos*: proprietors or managers of bull-breeding operations (Spanish).

7 Restaurante Botín (Antigua casa sobrino de Botín) on Calle Cuchilleros in Madrid, established in 1725. In Chapter 19 of *SAR*, Jake Barnes and Brett Ashley order the house specialty, roast suckling pig. *Chinches*: bedbugs (Spanish).

8 Giuseppe Garibaldi (1807–1882), Italian revolutionary leader who favored the republican form of government rather than the constitutional monarchy that was eventually adopted for the recently unified Italy. His views made him a popular figure among supporters of Spain's First and Second Republics. Verbena (or Fiesta) de San Juan: a festival that conflates the summer solstice (21 June) and the birth of Saint John (24 June).

9 Dos Passos's novel *Manhattan Transfer* (1925) retained its original title in the Spanish translation. Miguel de Unamuno y Jugo (1864–1936), Spanish writer, intellectual, and academic who was exiled in 1924 and returned to Spain in 1930. The Spanish phrase, *los bajos fondos* ("the lower depths"), refers to poor neighborhoods where society's outcasts, criminals, and homeless gather; hence, the outcasts themselves. It was the title of the Spanish translation of the 1902 play by Russian dramatist Maxim Gorky (né Aleksey Maksimovich Peshkov, 1868–1936), which portrayed the sufferings of the lower classes in czarist Russia and was popular among Republicans in Spain.

To George Marton, 29 June [1931]

Vienna—Austria

Martonplay[1]

Gladly consent Reinhardt Zuckmayer production But must have 500 dollar advance on 4 percent of gross or same percentage gross as Zuckmayer Wire

Hotel Bearritz Madrid if accept these conditions stating percent Make Contract through Reynolds[2] Hemingway

June 29

JFK, ACDS

1 Cable address of George Marton Plays, a literary agency with offices in Berlin and Vienna, established in Vienna by Hungarian-born literary agent George Marton in the mid-1920s.
2 In a letter to EH of 25 June 1931 Marton wrote that he had enlisted the cooperation of Austrian-born director Max Reinhardt (1873–1943) and German playwright Carl Zuckmayer (1896–1977) for a German dramatization of *FTA* to be presented at the Deutsches Theater in Berlin. In his letter Marton asked whether EH or his agent, Reynolds, should negotiate the terms (JFK).

To Archibald MacLeish, 29 June [1931]

June 29th

Dear Archy:—

Pauline brought the swell telegram you sent us when I met her at San Sebastian.

How are you both?

I've been lousy about writing because when get through work am too pooped— Then it's been hot too—really hot—42° and one day 46° in shade— Try that on your fahrenheit thermometer— When it gets that hot I think of you merchants at Conway and what a smart fellow MacLeish is—

Today it is hot again after a fine cool spell so am writing you instead of starting work—

Old Bumby is in fine shape— I went up to Paris to see them (came here direct on 2 days notice because a fast boat (sic) was calling Havana enroute to Vigo and Rotterdam—) Went, also, to see Caresse [Crosby] but was in Paris less than 24 hrs and missed her. Will see her there in September—

Have seen most of whats happened here—very interesting— Very fine to follow politics and the revolution very closely and not have to write a word about it—

Can live here on the least have ever lived well without everybody being bastardized as in Germany— Fine room and 3 <u>damned</u> good meals a day in this hotel cost 3$\frac{00}{}$ a day for us both— No sniveling pensione economies— Excellent food— Vino Tinto at 7¢ the liter—[1] Every thing in proportion— If had money could buy some wonderful things—

We got that old house—in Key West— You remember the white one with the iron gratings and the big yard— Down the street where we lived when you were there? So now youse have a winter home in Florida— Bra says people live to be 350 years old in the Bahamas—where gin is 30¢ a bottle— We must make a cruise there—

I wish Gerald would sail that boat they are building to Key West and we could all go out and live at Dry Tortugas on her—

Did he send you a picture of her deck plan?[2]

We had a letter from Sarah about coming to Austria—will go there to see them— They all sound in excellent shape—[3]

This is a punk letter Archie— There is something about writing becoming not a physically painful but merely an uncomfortable act that buggers up the writing of letters— If you were here I would tell you a lot of funny things but it is too damned physically uncomfortable to start writeing anything— This no complaint—just an explanantion—

I wish I was at Conway working in the cool— Have heard nothing about the Belles Lettres racket for a long time— What do you know?

Georgio Joyce married Mrs. Fleischmann who was keeping him— Lucia has had her eyes straightened and the Joyces are in London where she can meet some nice young men—[4]

Sylvia [Beach] has had bad headaches but is as damned sweet as ever—[5] Adrienne [Monnier] looked well—

Am taking Bumby to Pamplona—for the fireworks and to take Papa home at night—

Max Reinhart has hired a cast to put on Farewell etc arms at Theater Guild in Berlin with German dramatization by Zuckmayer—entirely new dramatization— Zuckmayers last 2 plays ran 5000 nights in Germany— Probably one of them was Abies Irish Rose —[6] They offer $400 and 2% of gross—(letter just received) have just wired holding out for $500 and 4% or will accept equal terms with Zuckmayer—once on a basis of equality with Zuckmayer I'll probably cut you dead in the street, Mac— If

we <u>have</u> to stay here this fall I'm going shooting in Ireland or in Hungary—
(Probably end up by only shooting my lunch in Lipps—)

Well old Zuckmayer I wish the hell you were here— But we will get our feet under the same table soon I hope to God and anyway we will go to Africa together— How are you shooting? Shoot a lot of any kind of shooting— Thing to do is get easy with guns— My god but I hope the times pick up and your divedends start again. Please write to Pappy even though he writes a punk letter— Oh yes—a letter from Dick Meyers saying he had been doing his best for a long time and the Curtis Pub. Company were now ready to take my stuff But that he wanted to have a chat with me first to explain their likes and dislikes— It seems there are things you mustnt write— Good old Dick—[7] I knew he'd make a writer of me—

A funny thing happened on the boat too—

One night I passed <u>12</u> times at craps— If there had been any real money could have made a fortune— (made all bar bills, tips etc) and finally they wouldnt fade me. So I showed them that bump on the palm of my hand from the pressure sore— It is sort of a little calloused pyramid—and told them would tell them a secret—never shoot dice with a man with one of those—a dice callous— The mark of the proffessional crap shooter—all great Crap shooters have them—from the long years of practice— Nothing dishonest about it— Just pure skill—

The only professional mark I have is callouses on my ass from sitting at a table trying to write—

What marks have you, Mac?

Well So long Kid and much love from Pauline and Pappy

LOC, ALS; postmark: [*illegible*] / 31, HENDAYE / B[SES]PYRENEES

1 *Vino tinto*: red wine (Spanish).
2 Gerald Murphy and his studio assistant Vladimir Orloff, longtime manager of his boats, had been designing the *Weatherbird*, a 100-foot wooden racing schooner, since January 1931. The boat would be completed in early 1933.
3 The Murphy family spent the summer of 1931 in Bad Aussee, Austria. Sara's letter remains unlocated.

4 James Joyce's son, Giorgio Joyce (1905–1976), married American Helen Fleischman (née Kastor, 1894–1963) on 10 December 1930, soon after her divorce from journalist and former Boni & Liveright agent Leon Fleischman (1889–1946) was granted. Joyce's daughter, Lucia Joyce (1907–1982), had an operation in 1931 in Paris to correct strabismus (crossed eyes). She had had several brief affairs with artists and writers before the Joyces moved from Paris to London in the spring of 1931.

5 Sylvia Beach had suffered from chronic migraine headaches since childhood and developed painful bouts of facial neuralgia in the late 1920s.

6 The cast of *Kat* would include Käthe Dorsch as Catherine Barkley, Gustav Fröhlich as Frederic Henry, and Paul Hörbiger as Rinaldi. Zuckmayer's earlier work includes the 1925 comedy *Der Fröhliche Weinberg* (*The Merry Vineyard*), a popular and critical success that earned him the prestigious Kleist Prize, and the satirical 1931 comedy *Der Hauptmann von Köpenic* (*The Captain of Köpenick*). *Kat* would be the last of Zuckmayer's plays staged in Germany, as his work, like Reinhardt's, would be proscribed by the Nazis in 1933. *Abie's Irish Rose*, popular comedy about the love affair and marriage of a Jewish man (Abraham Levy) and an Irish Catholic woman (Rose Mary Murphy) by American playwright Anne Nichols (1891–1966). The play established a Broadway record, running for more than 2,000 performances between 1922 and 1927, and was followed by a touring production and film (1928).

7 Richard Edwin Myers (1887–1958), European associate editor (1929–1932) of the *Ladies' Home Journal*, owned by the Curtis Publishing Company. The Philadelphia firm, founded by Cyrus H. K. Curtis (1850–1933), established *Ladies' Home Journal* in 1883 and took over the *Saturday Evening Post* in 1897. American expatriates during the 1920s, Myers and his wife, Alice Lee Herrick Myers (1890–1986), were friends of Gerald and Sara Murphy. The letter from Myers to EH has not been located.

To Edward Saunders, 29 June 1931

Dear Bra: We are all well and hope you and your wife and Annie are the same.[1] Things are very interesting here now. Also everything very cheap. Good wine only 7 <u>cents</u> a quart. The kind Pena sells for 3.00 a bottle costs 25¢ here.[2]

It has been very hot but I have been working hard. Lately it has been too hot to do anything but drink beer in the shade and eat shrimps.

Plenty of bull fights but they haven't been very good.

I will send you the money in September so count on it. Look— I wonder if you would grease that outboard engine of mine all over and oil it around plugs so it won't rust? Charles will know where it is.

Hope you have had good luck if you went spongeing. I won a little money at the cockfights in Havana and playing poker and dice on the boat.[3] Didn't get seasick any on the trip—took 12 days from Havana to Vigo—pretty rough the last six.

Met Pauline at the French–Spanish border. Went up to Paris to see Bumby. They are all in fine shape.

There is no chance of the King coming back here but they have plenty of trouble of their own on their hands.

I certainly wish you were here so we could go to the bullfight this afternoon—and show you around afterwards.

Give my best to your wife Julia and to Annie and best luck to you always.

Ernest Hemingway

Pauline sends her love to all. Tell Charles the reason I haven't written is because have been working so bloody hard.

phPUL, Typewritten transcription of EH letter

This transcription is preserved in the Carlos Baker Collection at PUL and is reproduced here verbatim. The transcription is headed with the typewritten notation, "TO CAPTAIN EDDIE SAUNDERS, MADRID, JUNE 29, 1931."

1 Annie Marie Saunders (1916–1975), daughter of Bra and Julia Lois Saunders (1874–1955).
2 Albino Pena Morales (1888–1976), Spanish-born owner of Pena's Garden of Roses Night Club in Key West, was arrested several times in the 1920s and 1930s for violating prohibition laws.
3 A ticket for a cockfight in Havana, dated 3 May 1932, survives in the Bruce Family Archive.

To Maxwell Perkins, 2 July 1931

Hotel Biarritz
Calle Victoria, 2
Madrid—Spain
July 2—1931

Dear Max:—

We are all fine so dont worry about us, of your friends,—[1]

Got in a damned good month of work—then it got so bloody hot that couldnt write my name even— 42° and 46° Centigrade in shade—going to some beach somewhere now where it is cool and bite on the nail again—

I left Key West in a hurry to catch Volendam that touched in Havana and Vigo on way to Rotterdam— Figured I would get a solid month of work in Madrid with no interruption—which I did— Pauline went Direct to Paris and then down here— Patrick and Henriette are at Hendaye— We go up to see them day after tomorrow— Then am going to take Bumby to Pamplona if he is well enough after having his tonsils out 3 days ago— He and Hadley are fine and we are all in best shape so dont worry about us—

The Republic is swinging from left to right fairly smoothly although there may be plenty of trouble in Navarra when they come to separate Church and State and sure to be trouble in Andalucia if the peasants are dissatisfied with the land distribution the Cortes will tackle in July— I dont believe the Catalonian business will break up the Republic— They may compromise verbally on a Federated Republic or some such nonsense—[2] I have been following it all damned closely

About business—

What about that Grosset and Dunlop money? When is it due?

The income tax people have written wanting to know at what times in the year of 1929 I was paid my money as it seems I have no tax to pay on earned income while I was residing in Europe— But as I spent 3 months of 1929 in U.S. the money received then was taxable— I paid tax on all of it— This is a question of adjustment and possible refund—

So will you please send me a statement of money paid me in 1929 with dates—and indicate whether it was royalties—for serial—or advance on Farewell— As I recall I got at least half of the money before I left to return to Europe— But maybe not— Is money received when you get the check or when you <u>cash</u> it? You wouldnt know when I cashed those checks would you? It probably was before I left the country—

I wish to hell I was in Wyoming now instead of here— Dont give a damn about Europe anymore and feel a summer Spring and fall gone out of my life for the sake of this bloody book— Could be waist deep in a trout stream now and instead am sweating, fat in the heat from no exercise and from so much cold beer, the beer is good but I'd rather have a bottle of home brew on the porch of the cabin after having worked well all morning and fished well all afternoon— Jesus Christ and then people worry and talk about your being an expatriate—

Thanks for depositing the 500 and for the wire about it— Was overdrawn at the bank—

When I think that I had to pay 6675$\underline{^{00}}$ income tax last year because I was in the country and wouldnt have had to pay <u>any</u> if I had been in Canada—or Europe under Section 116A— It is funny luck all that money should have come in the one of the two years out of ten—[3] I could have bought a ranch in the mts in Canada and lived on it all year for that amount— Certainly the law is a strange business—

Please have them send me the year 1929 information and let me know about the Grosset and Dunlop—when it is due—

And good luck to you Max— I hope the hay fever isnt too bad—

Pauline sends her best wishes— When I went up to Paris to see Bumby and Hadley ran into the Colums— M had hurt her foot quite badly but it was getting better— They talked about you—[4] Chub riding alone over the mountains from Red Lodge to the L-T ranch had his horse fall with him—in the Clarks Fork Canon and broke his collar bone and 3 ribs and had to ride all that day and the next alone before getting to a doctor in Red Lodge— It must have hurt like hell—

What do you hear from Johnny Herrmann?

Best always—

Ernest—

PUL, ALS

1 EH is responding to Perkins's long letter of 11 June 1931 which contained news of Waldo Peirce and Henry Strater, explained how reprint publishing houses diminish the income of authors, and repeatedly asked for reassurance that "you are going safely through revolutionary Spain" (PUL).

2. The Catalans, like the Basques, insisted upon a degree of autonomy within the larger entity of Spain. The Pact of San Sebastian, signed in August 1930, had enlisted the Catalans in the Republican antimonarchical movement in return for a guarantee of Catalan autonomy under the hoped-for Republic.

3 Section 116 (a) (1) of the U.S. tax code established that an American citizen who has lived abroad for "an uninterrupted period which includes an entire taxable year" need not pay U.S. taxes on income earned outside the United States during that year.

4 Molly and Padraic Colum were neighbors and friends of Perkins.

To Guy Hickok, 15 July [1931]

Hotel Barron
Hendaye-Plage
(B.P.)
France
July 15—

Dear Guy:—

What about Pamplona you big stiff? After I wrote thought we would hear from you every day. Finally went with Bumby and your fellow Brooklinite S. Franklin— Everyone asked for you—the popular Monsieur Tripas. Swimming out above Aoiz as good as ever. It seems you did something with a two sou piece in your eye that all remember as irresistable— Ce bon Monsieur Tripas— The girl still has the picture—[1]

Write me at the above will you? Hope you didnt stay away just because of what I read in Steff's book[2] and because of the Meet The Hickocks Campaign—

We will be here for a week or 10 days— Then back to Spain— Tarragona probably—

Look—or rather listen— Pauline is going to have a baby about Nov 15— This is for your information— Not the Eagles nor any Eagle visitors— The problem is probability of Caeserian— We know that can be done by Dr. who has been in there before at KC. But Pauline says trip Paris to K.C. to K. W. not shortest distance between two points. As a matter of fact it is a bitch of a trip— Also if she goes to Piggott beforehand (2nd child sometimes early) if anything starts impossible to get to KC.

So she wants to know about Paris. What do you know about having Caeserian in Paris?— Who is best Doc? What about Bauffe de Sainte Blaise? How much cost? How much Hospital cost? American Hospital?[3] How soon could travel across ocean to N.Y. to get Havana Special to Key West after baby born?

Do you think it would be gambling for her to have the baby in Paris?

You see Piggott is 60 mile auto-ride and 12 hrs. on train from any civilized point—

I came up to Paris to ask you these questions but figured when I had to leave would see you surely in Madrid or Pamplona— Wrote you from Madrid about Pamplona soon as got your letter about our missing connections in Paris—

This is all of this because must get this off to you—

What else do you know?—

Yours always

Ernest

Am having a hell of a time to write and couldnt go worse—

Dont make some hearty crack about millions of babies born safely in France— I want to know what you would do in our place.

I cant write for shit nor little green apples— If you know of any odd jobs for one armed ex-service man around Eagle office let me know— Do you want a left handed greeter to help people to Meet The Hickocks?

Original plan was for Pauline to go back to U.S. in August— But she has gotten spooked on being caught in Piggott at mercy of Doc Cone—Ex German army pharmacist 2nd class— No hospital in Key West—[4] Damn if we could only have it in K.W. Catholic church if it insists on production of more Catholics by all Catholics ought to make some provision for rolling hospital kitchens for members who have to risk death to conform to Papal encyclicals—

I wish they'd have <u>one</u> married <u>Pape</u>—you'd see how long he'd put out those encyclicals—

phPUL, ALS

1 Aoiz, a village about 17 miles east of Pamplona on the Irati River. After returning to Paris from Pamplona two years earlier, Hickok had reminisced fondly about the fiesta, during which they had gone swimming in the Irati. However, he commented, he "almost fainted" when he later saw himself in a mirror in "that bathing suit" (Hickok to EH, 23 July 1929, JFK). "Monsieur Tripas" may be a joking reference to Hickok's girth, his writing, or both. *Tripas*: "intestines," can also mean "paunch" or "big belly" (Spanish); Hickok's nickname in correspondence with EH is "Gros" (French for "fat"). In the same July 1929 letter, Hickok also wrote, "Seven days in Pamplona produced fourteen columns of Eagle tripas" (referring to his series of articles for the *Brooklyn Daily Eagle*), and he concluded the letter, "Now back to the Eagle tripe."

2 In *The Autobiography of Lincoln Steffens* (New York: Harcourt, Brace, 1931), Steffens quoted a remark by Hickok about EH: "'Oh,' Guy said, 'Hem was sitting by the window in my office (at the *Brooklyn Eagle*) while a visitor and I were talking about

birth control, and all of a sudden Hem up and grumbled, "There is no sure preventative.'" A little later Mrs. Hem bore, laughing, their great, big Bumbi Hem" (835).

3 The American Hospital in Paris, located in the northwestern suburb of Neuilly-sur-Seine.

4 German-born chemist and pharmacist George Cone (1877–1936) moved to the United States in 1901, earned a medical degree in Chicago in 1909, and settled in Piggott in 1918, becoming a city and county health officer. In 1931 Key West had three medical facilities: the Public Health Services' Marine Hospital (established in 1845 to serve seamen but also open to civilians), the small privately owned Louise Maloney Hospital (established 1908), and the Mercedes Hospital (established 1911).

To Henry Strater, 15 July [1931]

July 15
Hendaye Plage
(B.P.)
address
Guaranty Trust Co. of NY
4 Place de la Concorde
Paris—

Dear Mike:—

Thanks for the letter enclosing the White Hunters information. Look I would appreciate it if you would find out all you can about these different guys— Their rates, ratings what time they advise as best etc. Might answer any ads you see that you have time for. Then when I come through in fall or winter we can go over all the dope.[1]

I'm trying to get this bastardly book done and cant go into it or my mind will start to work on that— Imagine your mind also working on something but painters are supposed to be practical coves—able to do two things at once— Have children and shows at same time say— How is Maggie and all the snuff heirs of the ages?

From this guy you sent me it seems Sept–Oct–Nov—better months than either July–Aug Sept or May–June–July— Let's really find out— Starting from U.S. in September would be better for me— Imagine just as good for Charles and Archie— How about you?

Let's find out—

We're here for a little while seeing the kids— All fine— Damned hard to write— Spain very interesting— Write me will you to Guaranty Trust—4 Place de la Concorde— Good luck with the Tuna— Kept all Tuna articles for you put away so carefully could never find them—

[*EH insertion, written in left, bottom, and right margins of page:* Just here from Spain and going back— Sick as a bastard of Europe— But Spain the best of it— Wish the hell we were out on the ranch— Pauline is fine— Took Bumby to Pamplona—]

The main point though was they wouldnt hit it after clear daylight and bit like tarpon in the dark before daylight— They went out till they hit the mackerel fishing fleet—off Scarborough— Caught them over 700 lbs on Hardy tackle—

[*EH thoroughly blacked out with pencil a paragraph-length section*]

Well So Long Governor— Hope you have your Tuna by now—

Love to Maggie—

Hem

[*EH drew arrow to blacked out material:*]

The above was about something decided not worth bothering you to look up— Crumpled letter up to throw it away— Then didn't have pep to copy it— Let it go as new view of Dark Continent—

PUL, ALS

1 In a letter of 30 April 1931, Strater had enclosed a three-page letter of recommendations for arranging their trip to Africa supplied by a knowledgeable acquaintance who advised that they hire a first-rate "white hunter" to organize and lead their party. He recommended J. A. Hunter of Nairobi (JKF).

To Caresse Crosby, 22 July [1931]

Hotel Barron
Hendaye—Plage—
(B.P.)
July 22—

Dear Caresse Crosby:—

I am terribly sorry to have made you so much trouble and I hope you will let me know what you have spent in cables etc. so that I may reimbourse it. The thing has been complicated by various accidents (including sailing in a hurry and leaving the MSS. in Key West) but the real difficulty since I got to Europe [*EH insertion*: and started writing again, and have the Mss.] has been that I do not know whether to have A Natural History of the Dead come out separately or in this book I am finishing. Until the book is finished I cant really tell but I must apologize for having been so much trouble to you.[1]

As for being in Paris— I came up for one day—with an appointment in Madrid the day after—to see about an operation for one of the boys— Did none of the things I needed to do in Paris—there was no time—and left with no one seen and nothing arranged but the operation and some family business which took all my time—[2]

I should have called you up to let you know I couldn't decide—but have been hoping every day that I'd know what to do about it so I could write you— ~~If I had seen you~~

It isnt that I do not want very much to give you something to publish— I do and will—if you're not disgusted with waiting— But have been about bughouse with working and with everything having piled up during the six or seven months I couldnt write— I owe letters to everyone— correspondance business and otherwise completely gone to hell— If I had seen you I would most certainly have promised you the Mss. at once— But as soon as was alone again with the work I would have had the same doubts and have had to write you that—[*EH insertion*: I couldnt tell yet—] I cant tell if I need it until this thing is done— Anyway we will be in Paris in September and can go into it then if all this has not worn out your patience— I sailed the 2nd of May from Havana direct to Spain and have been there ever since except for the day in Paris and a visit here to establish the children for the summer—

You have been very good about this and I have treated both you and MacLeish very badly—

Mrs. Hemingway sends her best greetings— I my shame at not having answered your letters and cables— Please at least let me pay for the cables—

Yours always—

Ernest Hemingway.

I wish you very good luck with the press— Hope things are going well.

SIU, ALS

1 In Crosby's January 1931 cable to EH, she agreed with MacLeish's "magnificent" suggestion that the Black Sun Press publish what she mistitled "Natural History of Death," and she asked EH to name terms (SIU). MacLeish acted as an intermediary in the negotiations. In a 3 April 1931 cable to MacLeish, Crosby offered EH $1,000; MacLeish forwarded her cable to EH, adding a note of his own on the verso saying he had wired Crosby saying that $1,500 would be a minimum (Stanford). On 7 May 1931 she cabled EH offering $1,500 "at once rest paid in royalty to be agreed on later" (SIU). Here EH responds to Crosby's letter from Paris dated 17 July 1931, in which she asked him for a decision, mentioning "the numerous telegrams from MacLeish" regarding this publication (SIU).
2 Crosby wrote that she had heard EH had been in Paris and was sorry not to have seen him. Bumby had a tonsillectomy around 30 June.

To Maurice Speiser, 22 July [1931]

July 22

Dear Mr. Speiser:—

Here are the three tickets and a couple of books. Hope you had a good trip.

Yours

Ernest Hemingway.

USCar, ALS

To Archibald MacLeish, 28 July [1931]

July 28

Dear Archie:—

Look—the first thing I've written Uncle Gus saying we wont be going until the fall of 1932 instead of the Spring— That will give your business that much more time— Then if you are still being bastardized by those guys in Chicago we can stall again—[1] We'll figure on Sept 1932 now instead of June— So dont give up anything— We will probably see you 1st part of Oct wherever you are—

Pat Morgan I figure could only have had a limited capacity for bed sports or he would have gotten into trouble at earlier age like the rest of us and Maude has an infinite capacity and desire for I imagine—hence his whiteness— He showed just a little of La Coté du Chez Shit at Key West this last time— Just a little— It was a tough trip to Tortugas but he didnt light up any under the difficulty—on the other hand—if your other hand isnt busy— Mac—he is a very nice kid— But a little spoiled by something— Shooting old women on the sit and a vague tendency toward feathered gestures or something—

Glad Stewart is a preacher— All he lacks for it is education— He has the eloquence— He ought to take a trip to the Holy Land— I'll bet he'd think people, by Christ, had never thought of these things as they are before—[2] The guy had a great and fine talent for kidding—if he had been equipped with taste, intelligence and honor he could have been an artist instead of having to hate them all— Well to hell with Stewart— I like Pat Morgan for instance even though he was a nuisance at Key West— But I'm damned if I like Stewart anymore— Though like Italy and other hysterical businesses it is nice enough when you are with it—

Like Horace who?

I am damned glad you are going well on the poem— If I was or were as much of a citizen as you can write a poem it would be a cinch for monuments at all the railway stations— But Iam a shit Mac and you a ~~swell~~ great poet— If they paid off on ability with the shotgun might get somewhere but Jesus Christ almighty writing has been difficult lately—

Spain still very interesting— Have good pictures— This crap nearly finished— Feel the summer gone because were not out west but what the hell— We'll see you in October—will you be at Conway or N.Y?

Bumby wants to be a bull fighter— Took him to Spain to see some and he met everybody and had lessons and shows talent— Will do him no harm to learn with the calves anyway— They wanted him to stay on a ranch at Salamanca and learn— He may be able to sell bonds to some of his friends there later—like college— All I want him to do is never meet Ames Stewart—[3]

Love to Ada and yourself from us both—

Pappy—

My german publisher gone broke owing me 4–5 thousand bucks.[4]

LOC, ALS

1 Neither EH's letter to Gus Pfeiffer nor the MacLeish letter that EH is answering has been located. The stock market crash had considerably reduced the value of MacLeish's shares in the Chicago department store Carson Pirie Scott, founded and managed by his father, Andrew MacLeish (1838–1928). Beset by family and financial pressures, MacLeish doubted he could afford a long absence from work.
2 EH might be referring to Donald Ogden Stewart's screenplay for the Paramount film *Tarnished Lady*, based on his unpublished play "New York Lady" and released in May 1931. A melodramatic love story that ends on a note of reconciliation and forgiveness, the movie was directed by George Cukor and starred Tallulah Bankhead.
3 Stewart's son Ames Ogden Stewart (1928–2007).
4 Rowohlt announced bankruptcy and began negotiations with creditors in June 1931.

To Maxwell Perkins, 1 August [1931]

August 1—

Address care Guaranty Trust Co. of N.Y.

4 Place de la Concorde

Paris

Dear Max:—

Thanks very much for your prompt answer about the 1929 money.[1] Hope things are going well with you and that you are getting some vacation and that the hay fever isnt too bad. Have been working like hell last two weeks and am getting much done—work every day until my eyes poop out— Also think will have some swell pictures. Certainly will be damned glad when this is done and I can start a novel. Hear Ray Long has left Cosmopolitan so that lets me out of that bloody promise and I'll be able to sell a few stories—[2]

My German publisher has gone broke I just hear owing me for a 40,000 sale of Farewell— I only took 500 marks advance this last time because he told me times were hard and I wanted to help him out. Believe he is an honest bird and may get more backing—conditions have been pretty frightful in Germany and I suppose nobody can be blamed for going broke—[3] Still had figured pretty strongly on the money—

Look I havent my papers with me and forget what the last (before I left U.S.) royalty statement showed as due me— I have drawn 1000 and 500 since— Could you let me know what I still stand to the good so I will know what I can draw? Have to figure pretty close— We were overdrawn when I wired you to deposit that 500—

This is really getting to be a hell of a good solid book I think— I'll finish the dictionary the end of next week—then have only 2 chapters to write—[4] Have been all over the rest—

Bumby, Pat and Pauline all well—we will probably hit U.S.A. in Oct barring accidents— If you know how to Bar them let me know the secret— You'll be glad to know Carol got A in all her studies and lead her class in spite of getting back late from Tortugas that time—think she is going to get a scholarship this next year—

Max Reinhardt is staging Farewell this fall with dramatization by Zückmayer—not using any of the Stallings—[5] I get $500 advance less Reynolds and 3% of gross— Reynolds had closed for 400 and 2%—on that percent even cant make much booming sales of bankrupt publisher in depreciated currency— But what the hell—

Good luck to you Max— What do you hear from Scott? I hear nothing—

Ernest—

Wish there was some market for what I know about present Spanish Situation— Have followed it as closely as though I were working for a paper— Damned hard to break habits—

PUL, ALS

1 In his letter of 22 July 1931, Perkins listed the payments made by Scribner's to EH in 1929 and reported that payments for the two reprint editions of *FTA* by Grosset & Dunlap and by the Modern Library would not be due until 1932 (PUL).
2 Long had extended an offer to EH in 1927 for the rights to serialize *FTA* in *Cosmopolitan*, which EH rejected. While negotiating with Perkins over the book's serialization rights in *Scribner's Magazine*, EH wrote, "I quite gratuitously promised Ray Long I would let him have the first look at my next book if I decided to serialize it" (*Letters* vol. 3, 457). Long's retirement, effective 1 October 1931, was announced in the *New York Times* ("Ray Long to Quit Hearst Magazines," 21 July 1931, 23).
3 Undermined by WWI reparations payments, the Great Depression, and high unemployment, the German mark, as well as many of Germany's banks, collapsed in the summer of 1931.
4 EH refers to the 84-page glossary, the end of Chapter 19, and Chapter 20 of *DIA*.
5 Approaching EH about a German dramatization, literary agent George Marton had written that he admired *FTA* but had not liked Laurence Stallings's dramatization (Marton to EH, 25 June 1931, JFK).

To Caresse Crosby, [9 August 1931]

9 pm Sunday—

Dear Caresse:—

Pauline left her bag in the back of your car with our three passports in it. We found it out as soon as we were in the hotel and I took a taxi after you but couldnt catch up or else missed you if you stopped—[*EH insertion*: at Pasajes—].[1] Left taxi at Spanish border crossed French frontier and came here to hotel but you not arrived.

Could you telephone us tonight at <u>Hotel Avenida</u> San Sebastian that you are sending the 3 passports by Express—registered mail to that hotel—

Imagine it would be too much trouble to bring them— Regret terribly making you this trouble—

Ernest Hemingway

SIU, ALS; letterhead: G^D. HOTEL ESKUALDUNA / HENDAYE (BP)

The conjectured letter date is based on Caresse Crosby's December 1931 letter to EH in which she would mention the corrida they had seen together in San Sebastian "last August" at which comic actor and filmmaker Charlie Chaplin was also present. Afterwards she had departed for Biarritz, "with all the Hemingway passports" (Crosby, 294). The presence of Chaplin, noted in various newspapers, dates the corrida to Sunday, 9 August 1931, in San Sebastian. A facsimile of this letter is reproduced as an appendix to Crosby's memoir.

1 Pasajes, Spanish name for the Basque port town of Pasaia, about 5 miles east of San Sebastian and 14 miles from the French border.

To Maxwell Perkins, 14 August 1931

Dear Max:—

Could you ask the retail department to forward a copy of "In Our Time" "Men without Women" and The Torrents to

Earl Shelton

    Box 43656

    San Quentin, California

    He is serving, he claims, 5 yrs. to Life—[1]

Everything fine here—going to Madrid again the 17th—then wont be long before on way home—

Best always—
Ernest
Aug 14—1931
Hendaye—Plage—

PUL, ALS

1 In a letter of 16 May 1931, addressed to EH c/o Scribner's, Shelton reported having read two of EH's works and asked him to send *IOT* and *MWW* (JFK).

To Maurice Speiser, [c. 14–15 August 1931]

Dear Speiser:—

See you Monday— You can keep this great work of art —[1]

Hemingway.

Rec'd registered letter

Have fixed up every thing

Will return your 1500 Monday.

USCar, ALS

EH penciled this note on the verso of a letter he received from F. M. Clouter dated 21 July 1931, written on letterhead stationery of the Boston publishers Little, Brown & Company. Clouter asked EH to comment on "a rather extraordinary book" that he was sending, *The Cross of Carl: An Allegory* by Walter Owen (1884–1953) with a foreword by General Ian Hamilton, scheduled for publication on 14 August 1931. Clouter's letter was sent to New York City c/o Scribner's and apparently forwarded to EH, catching up with him in Hendaye. The conjectured date of EH's note takes into account his arrival in Hendaye 14 August (Friday), his plan to meet Speiser on Monday, and his return to San Sebastian by 18 August (Tuesday).

1 EH's note presumably accompanied the pre-publication copy of the book Clouter had sent to him.

To Henry Strater, [c. 14–15 August 1931]

Dear Mike:—

Thanks for the letter. Certainly hope you butcher the tuna— You ought to get them this summer— Sure the great advantage of Scarborough is its virgin fishing and the gt. advt of Ogunquit is it's in the front yard—[1]

But look the gt advantage and necessity if your hunting out west is to be in camp on the grounds the day the season opens—which is Sept. 15th— Lawrence Nordquist writes me there will be big extra big heads this fall as last seasons open winter kept the game in wonderful shape—

Once you've hunted in mts you'll know what I mean about the first of season— Those animals are really wild—ordinarily there is no one in the country where the range the entire summer—when someone moves in they are on their usual range—using certain wallows in the timber—feeding certain places—as soon as someone comes in they move to more inaccessible places—show only rarely in the open—keep in the heavy timber— They are not like the Eastern deer etc that are used to living among civilization— When they get spooked they pull completely out of the country—an old bull rounds up his cows and pulls out—travelling at night—you see the country is a succession of high mountain valleys— God it's beautiful country.

But to be there at the start is wonderful hunting— You hear the bulls bugle—have to stalk them <u>against</u> the wind— If they catch your scent you never see them—they're gone like ghosts— If you stalk them right you see the whole band feeding— But you cant believe the wildness and constant caution and cunning they have— It is wonderful hunting— Especially Timber Creek where we hunted last year— You ought to get a Grizzly— They broke up the cabins and kept the trappers from working—

We know the only way to get in there— If you are out before the 15th you have the pick of the country— You ought to get a Mt. Sheep ram, a good bull elk and a bear— I saw two splendid bull moose—one with over a 60 inch head—

Lawrence and Ivan Wallace are both <u>great</u> hunters— Do what they tell you because they know the game and the country—

I wish to hell I could go out— This will be the last season that will be virgin hunting because they are building a govt. motor road in over the mts from Red Lodge Montana— Cant possibly make it—we are stone broke— and with complications—

So wont sail from here until Oct 1st—

Take plenty of 220 grain 30–06's— You may not need them but if you start missing you will—

Wish the hell Charles [Thompson] could go to get the experience—

If you go in to camp the 15th and hunt two weeks you will have a swell time—

Write to Lawrence Nordquist at L-T ranch—Cooke City— Montana—tell him you are friend of mine— He will give you all dope—ask him lowest rate he can give you for 2 week hunt— For two of you it should be $25 a day a head — That sounds like lots of money but it takes a 12 horse pack outfit, a cook, reserving her—and guide— He will do it for you the cheapest he can—

I'd write to him as soon as you get this if you havent already— The hunting is in Wyo. altho the ranch address is Montana—

I'm so damned glad you're going because it is like going myself—

Well must get this off— Good luck to you and Weare[2] and love to Maggie—

Hem

Glad September is O.K. for Africa. Thanks for getting dope. Did you write Charles or should I?

PUL, ALS

The conjectured letter date reflects the fact that Strater's incoming letter, dated 24 July 1931 and addressed to EH c/o Guaranty Trust Co. of N.Y., 4, Place de la Concorde, Paris, was postmarked in Maine on 27 July 1931. From Paris it was forwarded to EH at "Villa Goiseko Izarra / Hendaye / Plage B.P" (JFK). It was probably waiting for EH when he arrived in Hendaye c. 14 August.

1 In his letter Strater reported on fishing and hunting in his home town of Ogunquit, Maine, and commented that his friend George Peabody had praised the tuna fishing in Scarborough, England (JFK).
2 Ogunquit resident George Dunlap Weare (1896–1991), whom Strater had invited on a fishing and hunting trip to Montana in October.

To Earl Shelton, 15 August [1931]

Hendaye—
(B. P.)
France.
Aug 15

Dear Mr. Shelton:—

I've written to Scribners to send you In Our Time, Men without Women and Torrents of Spring. Hope they help you kill some time. Thanks for your letter and good luck to you—

Yours always—
Ernest Hemingway.

Charles Hamilton catalog, New York, 5 August 1971, Lot 191, (illustrated), ALS; reproduced in Bruccoli and Clark *Auction*, 163

To Maurice Speiser, [c. 18 August 1931]

Dear Dr. Speiser:—

Thanks very much for the francs—

If I promised to give you any books last night please let me know—

Yours

Ernest Hemingway.

USCar, ALS

To Hadley Hemingway, [18 August 1931]

Fine absinthe here![1] Go to Madrid tomorrow— Will make grand trip in car from Madrid to Segovia-Avila and over Mts. to Barco de Avila— When we were there before they killed a wolf right outside the gate— Bear paw nailed to church door— 12 storks nest on old castle—[2]

Bumby is crazy to go— Wish you were going—

E.

Forgive him for not writing— Hes not much of a writer yet! But wait for his Diary!

JFK, A Postcard S; verso: photograph of bulling with people on wide exterior stairway; caption on recto: "San Sebastian. / Subida a la Plaza de Toros." [Stairway to the Bullring]; postmark: [EST]ACIO[N] / SAN SEBA[STIAN], 18 AGO 3[1]

EH addressed the postcard to "Madame H. R. Hemingway / 98[B.D.] Auguste Blanque / Paris XIII / France."

1 Absinthe had been banned in France in 1915 but not in Spain, where the characters in *SAR* drink it.
2 The storks in Barco de Avila would figure in Chapter 20 of *DIA*.

To Grace Hall Hemingway, 23 August 1931

August 23 Madrid

Dear Mother:—

Started a letter to Carol and found it got into Financial matters—since it was about her college—whether able to go or not— So outlined the family situation and asked her to show it to you— Thought with all this depression talk it might be good to outline the family situation.

My financial situation is that I am writing a book on which I received an advance which was <u>entirely used</u> to pay taxes on money received and put into Trust funds etc. Book must make $6500 which publisher advanced me before I get anything. It should make that and more—also it is not the last book I will write— But returns from books come slowly— So Sterlings sad losses do not impress me—[1] Counted on profits of the Sale of 40,000 copies of Farewell to Arms in Germany was due this Spring— Publisher went bankrupt— So got nothing— Not even promises. We have been living here on less money than your monthly income—

With this book finished will be out of the woods by next winter— not this one— We have enough to get along all right but are not in position to make donations— What did the sum total of Marces and Sterlings contributions amount to? I would be curious to know its relation to capital— I'll bet it didnt total $5,000— But am certainly glad they did what they did <u>anyway</u>.

I have outlined the families situation in the letter to Carol and must say it is as good or better than most— You should have nearly or better than $3000 or $3100 a year—depending on how much of the 25,000 Dad left was spent on that last tax business in Florida— Carol has 50 a month clear toward her schooling—

I appreciate your hard work, struggles and economies— These are <u>hard</u> times and you have a regular income— So you are luckier than most— Know you have a hard time[.] But no one has money this year— Know many people whose income is from common stocks who are <u>absolutely</u> without income—

The only one who seems not to be pulling his weight in the boat is Leicester— As far as I know he has never had any sort of a money producing part time job— I know he broke his arm which put this summer out— But what was last job he had? He must be 15 by now—[2]

When I was in Holmes School delivered Oak Leaves—a regular route— worked at different jobs in Xmas vacations— Worked in Lunch room at high School—[3] It was no fun and I <u>hated</u> it— But did it— <u>Worked</u> on

Longfield—odd jobs—[4] Sold vegetables— Worked <u>all</u> summer every summer I was in High School— I know that Les probably does not like to work any more than I did— But if he has any pride he will get some out of school job that will contribute something—or at least pay his own expenses. Being the youngest in the family it may never occurr to him that people have to work— But I will know what to think of him if he doesnt try.

Anyway <u>Dont worry</u> — Your regular income <u>cant</u> go wrong— With what Sunny contributes—and what you can make you are all right— If you have pressing taxes which are <u>accumulating interest</u>—on 600 N. Kenilworth write me what they are and how much. What are the taxes and how much do you owe? It may be best to pay <u>these</u> <u>dwelling house</u> taxes up out of the money Dad left to avoid ruinous interest— But <u>do not do this without consulting me first</u>— That is the source of your income and must be preserved— If you had the Money you poured and got me to pour down the rat hole of that Florida land—now more hopelessly worthless than ever with this national slump and their tax situation—(with taxes so high no one will ever buy any land there— It is economically impossible to make money out of it) you would be in excellent financial shape—as it is you are in good financial shape— Am very glad that got you safely provided for before everything slumped so badly— You[r] dollars are worth <u>more</u> in buying power each week.

Anyway good luck to you all— We will soon be in U.S. Am working hard— all well— Bumby here now— Pauline, Bumby and Patrick send their best—

Love to Sun and Les and you all—

Ernie

Dont worry about us— My financial situation is O.K. Simply told you we need to watch money so you will realize how well off you are yourself—

Please let me know

① What money you owe on 600 N. Kenilworth Taxes—<u>complete</u>—when due and amount due—

② Exact amount remaining in Securities and cash of the Securities bought with money Dad left—

③ What you owe on car—if any—

I take it for granted you have paid no more money in Florida taxes— No Florida lots can be given away— The taxes eat up the value, if there were any value, of land in ten years— Hence no one sane can or will buy—

IndU, ALS

1 In her letter to EH of 23 August 1931, Grace reported that Marcelline's husband, Sterling Sanford, was struggling financially and could no longer afford to help her with her mortgage (JFK).
2 Born on 1 April 1915, EH's brother was sixteen years old.
3 EH attended the Oliver Wendell Holmes Elementary School in Oak Park (1905–1913) and the Oak Park and River Forest High School (1913–1917). *Oak Leaves*: local Oak Park newspaper.
4 Longfield Farm, a 40-acre property across Walloon Lake from Windemere Cottage, was purchased by Clarence and Grace in 1905 and leased to tenant farmers. As a teenager, EH worked on the farm during the summer and early fall, haying and harvesting the apple and potato crops (*Letters* vol. 1, lxi–lxii, 17).

To Grace Hall Hemingway, 24 August [1931]

August 24$^{\text{th.}}$

Calle Victoria, 2

Madrid.

Dear Mother:— I wrote you and Carol last night and today have your good letter of August 10—[1]

About Carols school—

She is very studious and I know would not waste her time staying out for a term— I could send her enough French books etc to keep her busy— Things she should read and wouldnt have time to in college— Later can probably get credit on them—

However do <u>not</u> want her to stay out if it will mean delaying or losing her degree or losing her standing— Staying out one term may be a good enough idea— But if it is in any way a sacrifice of her prospects she should not be allowed to make it— I can cable her the necessary money—

Tell her anyway to count on spending Xmas with us in Key West whether in college then or not— If not in college she can come down and go up to college after Xmas. vacation when her term starts—

As for Leicester the situation as you outline it seems just what I had imagined.

It is up to him to <u>earn all his spending money and expenses</u>— I didnt realize he is 16— It is enough for you to feed, lodge and clothe him reasonably— If he doesnt learn to work now he never will work— Tell him for me that the fact that he doesnt want to work is no reason to believe he is not adapted to it—

It is within my ability to give him some times that he would never be able to have otherwise— He must have imagination to know that— But if he doesnt pull his weight in the boat I promise I will never lift a finger to help him or give him fun— Also if he wants to travel, explore etc in what capacity does he plan to do this if he is without education, training or experience. Does he think someone will take him on an expedition because he is 6 feet tall? Tell him to read the article in Sat Eve Post of Aug 22 by <u>Roy Chapman Andrews</u>[2]

If you want me to write and bawl him out tell me so—or tell him you will do so— Tell him he's not too old to be spanked until he can whip me— If he needs a whipping and there is no man in the house will be glad to make a jump to Chicago to administer it—

Keep cheerful and remember anytime you need disciplining action that the family is not without a head

Love to all—

Ernie—

Dont worry about 600 N. Kenilworth not selling. I do not expect any possibility of sale for several years— It does give Les Schooling— Sunny and you and he a home and you a studio—

IndU, ALS

1 Grace's 10 August 1931 letter remains unlocated, as does EH's 23 August 1931 letter to Carol.
2 "Explorers and Their Work" by American naturalist and explorer Roy Chapman Andrews (1884–1960) advised young people attracted by the romance of exploration to stay in school "until you have some special knowledge that will make you useful" (*Saturday Evening Post*, 22 August 1931, 6).

To Caresse Crosby, 25 August [1931]

Hotel Biarritz
Calle Victoria, 2
Madrid.
August 25—

Dear Caresse:—

Thanks for the Anthology letter—hope can see him in Paris in September—He sounds very hard working—[1]

We left Hendaye Aug 15 for here or I would be raising hell for your dress in the Eskualduna now—could you write if you havent received it to me at Villa Goiseka Izarra[2]—where I will be depositing Bumby in first days of September and I will go over and try to get it—

Pauline and Bumby send you their love— Pauline feels very badly about the dress—

Give my best to Jacques—[3]

Yours always
Ernest Hemingway—

Send this to Paris in case you are travelling—

SIU, ALS

1 In a 31 May 1931 letter to EH, Romanian-born American author and editor Peter Neagoe (1881–1960) requested a contribution for an anthology "of significant American artists abroad, covering roughly the after-war decade," saying he was leaving his letter with Caresse Crosby to give to EH (Syracuse). Not having received a reply, Neagoe repeated his request in another letter to EH of 9 July 1931 (JFK). Neagoe's *Americans Abroad: An Anthology* (The Hague: Servire Press; London: Faber & Faber, 1932) would include EH's "Big Two-Hearted River" as well as selected poems by Caresse Crosby.

2 EH had recently received mail at the Villa Goiseko Izarra in Hendaye Plage (see EH to Henry Strater, [c. 14–15 August 1931]). *Goizeko Izarra*: Morning Star (Basque).

3 French writer Jacques Porel (1893–1982) was Caresse Crosby's partner in Crosby Continental Editions, a publishing venture they conceived together in the fall of 1930. Crosby and Porel had been staying at the Grand Hôtel Eskualduna in Hendaye when they attended a bullfight with the Hemingways in San Sebastian on 9 August.

To Archibald MacLeish, 31 August [1931]

Madrid

~~Sept~~ Aug 31—

Dear Archie:—

I'm so damned sorry you've been laid up Kid— It's damned rotten when youre working— Im so sorry— What kind of a bowel racket was it? Remember your back experience and keep away from Specialists or they will ruin your gut— Hope to Christ it was only some summer bowell business— Anyway it is a hell of a thing to be laid up like that—

I wrote Uncle Gus about postponing the trip and offering to call it off since he had proposed it during comparative prosperous times and they being so bad now— He answered that any time we wanted to make it was fine and that he was prosperous as ever—business O.K. and to have <u>no thought</u> of cancelling it— To absolutely count on it—

Not much news— We'll be seeing you early in Oct.— My eyes went haywire about 2 weeks ago—cant read nor write—or [rather ?]—nor shouldnt write— Worked too hard in July and Aug I guess—but they have been buggared up before and come right again with a lay off— Havent read for 10 days—

Have been to some fine places—

Cant wait to see you and Ada—

Best love to you both and I hope you are all right inside of you—

Pappy

LOC, ALS

To Paul and Mary Pfeiffer, 31 August 1931

Madrid

August 31—1931

Dear Family:—

It is very shameful to have been so long without writing— But have either been laid up or working very hard to make up time lost laid up— We got the fine birthday presents the day of my birthday— Thank you very much— It is wonderful how you have presents arrive on the exact day—and such fine presents!

[*EH insertion*: News here less gloomy than a month ago although] All Europe except France in very bad way— When bad times come people who practice thrift and are ordinarily sneered at by the promotors and gamblers are in luck. So the French are having their turn—

Spain is in fair shape— Separation of Church and State inevitable— Believe that is only logical condition in modern world— Believe the Pope would be glad now if he had never decided to go in with Mussolini— Church is necessarily at odds with aspirations of any modern state and much better to be in opposition than to try to have a Co-alition—[1]

May go to Berlin for a day or so— German publisher went bankrupt owing 40,000 (reported) sale of Farewell to Arms! Max Rhinehart brings out a German Dramatization of same book first week in September in 42 scenes— using the new revolving stage— Would be good luck if it were a success— But believe 42 scenes a good many for an audience to take—[2]

Pauline has been very well— Patrick fine— Bumby has been taking bullfight lessons from Sydney Franklin— May support us all yet— He says if he is very good he will make papa lots of money and if he is bad papa can collect the bottles they throw at him and sell them. So it is good business any way.

Pauline decided finally on Kansas City for the so called blessed eventing— She had a hunch this child would be born early and did not want to be far from hospital center— After all Dr. Guffy in K.C. is familiar with the case—and it is best to be on the ground with minimum of exhausting travel— If we can find a suitable nurse for Patrick so he will not be an unmitigated nuisance— He can come down to Piggott with nurse from St. Louis or K.C. We can pick him up on the train at Jonesboro when we leave K.C. direct for K. West— Plan to have Pauline stay in hospital until she is really fit to travel— Learned from that last Billings business that a person should stay in hospital until really fit to leave it— or they are no good for themselves or others— We had both counted on a visit to you in Piggott this fall— But believe best thing for Pauline and child is to go direct to K.C. and direct from K.C. to Florida— Not to mention what is best for yourselves. I inflicted enough trouble on you last winter— Anyway if it were a question of seeing Patrick or his mother or his father believe Patrick would get the vote— But wont send him without someone to take all care of him so he'll be as little nuisance as possible—

Of course all plans liable to smash—but that is how we plan at present—

We must line up someone to see that K.W. house is cleaned and ordered and our Paris furniture installed before we arrive— Will be fine to have a home again all right— Pauline wont be in shape to look after that— We hope to get to K.W. by Christmas— If all goes well— Jinny might feel like stopping in K. West on her way back from Mexico in late Nov. or early December— Pauline was going to write her but felt she had been asked to do so much for Karl's family we had no right to ask her—[3] I said she could refuse if she wanted not to do it— Might even be interested in installing the furniture— Be glad to hire her as Interior Decorator and highly paid installer— Have to hire someone and she has more talent than any—and knows where the things were in Paris as well—

Glad there is a good cotton and corn crop— Very sorry about low prices—[4]

Pauline has been extraordinarily well and very cheerful— We have had a fine time and much work accomplished—

Sorry to write such a dull letter but it is after mid-night and news much easier to find when you write oftener—as I am very ashamed not to have done—and will do in the future—

Arm is useful but quite crooked— However it will hold a pen, a gun or a fishing rod and is a useful alibi to avoid lifting trunks or any distasteful forms of manual labor—

Dont worry about Pauline, Mother— Everything is being played on an absolutely safety first, regardless of anything else, basis—

Love to all

Ernest

PUL, ALS

1 The Lateran Treaty would be signed on 9 December 1931 by Italian dictator Benito Mussolini and Cardinal Pietro Gasparri, on behalf of Pope Pius XI (Ambrogio Damiano Achille Ratti, 1857–1939; reigned 1922–1939), proclaiming Roman Catholicism the sole state religion of Italy and granting the Vatican the status of an independent state. In a letter of 18 September 1931, Paul Pfeiffer would agree that "Church and state should be separate" and that this necessarily drew the church into politics (PUL).

2 *Kat* would premiere on 1 September 1931 at the Deutsches Theater in Berlin. The performance involved twenty-two scenes and sixteen sets, played on a revolving stage Max Reinhardt had introduced to that theater. The son of Ernst Rowohlt, EH's German publisher, Heinrich Maria Ledig-Rowohlt (1908–1992) later recalled meeting EH for the first time when EH came to Berlin for the opening of the play: "After the first act, he spent this premiere of his in the theatre bar" (Ledig-Rowohlt, 34). In a letter to Ezra Pound of 2 February 1932, EH would report that he left Spain in September and returned to the United States "via Paris–Berlin–NY" (Yale).

3 In his 18 September 1931 letter, Paul Pfeiffer would report that Jinny and a friend, then in Mexico, planned to return to Piggott around 1 October (PUL). While Karl and Matilda Pfeiffer toured Europe (January–April 1931), Jinny had taken care of their children.

4 In his letter of 18 June 1931, Pfeiffer wrote that crops were good and prices were "at the lowest in thirty years" (JFK).

To Maurice Speiser, 31 August [1931]

Madrid—

Monday—~~Sep~~ Aug 31

Dear Moe:—

Thanks for the two photostats and your letters—

The Fox answer looks very suspicious— To me at least— They got away with the Men Without Women and it looks as though they were going to try this other—the phrase "So far as I have been able to ascertain etc.)[1]

If they are not planning to use the title they may be planning to steal the story—changing it just enough [*EH insertion*: or no] to get by—

If as they say "claim must be based on vogue and celebrity given by him to the title"—as far as I know no other book was ever so entitled— The title was made famous or notorious by that particular book— It should be able to prove damage to me by the use of a title made famous or notorious by me and which to anybody reading it or seeing it would imply that it was made from the novel so entitled which is my saleable property—

Of course I know that what is right or wrong has nothing to do with it— What we had better do is sell the book and title to some company before some other bastards steal it— If the Farewell to Arms was worth 75,000— This should be worth 50,000—

It should have additional selling value now since the enclosed which I hear is a hit— This clipping came just now from Franklins brother in N.Y.[2]

Film is made from the stories by John Monk Saunders which appeared last year in "Liberty"—[3] They were, shall we say, Inspired by Sun Also—at least readers kept writing to the magazine and asking why they paid J. M. S. to rewrite the Sun Also—

This not my testimony— See files of Liberty— Oh well what the hell—

I read a little of it and would call it Inspired—no more than that—

If the Barthelmess[4] Post war Sun derived picture is a hit they will all be making them—chizelling a little here—a little there— So better sell it before it is all chizelled off—

Tell me what you think—

Best to you and to Mrs. Speiser— Hope you have a good crossing—[5] We had damned good luck to meet you in Hendaye!

Seys picture was very good—[6] Not what I like but certainly at the <u>very top</u> of his racket— He's such a good egg I see how you get to like his pictures— So damned capable—

Well good by and good luck—address Guaranty Trust—Paris—cable address <u>Garritus</u> until Sept 17th— Care Scribners—597 Fifth Avenue will get me in N.Y.

Yours always—and damned gratefully—
Ernest—

Pauline and kids all fine—

USCar, ALS

1 The letter from which EH quotes has not been located.
2 EH enclosed a review of the movie *The Last Flight*, released in August 1931 (William Boehnel, "'The Last Flight' Gives Another View of War's Effect on Daredevils," *New York World Telegram*, 20 August 1931, 16). The clipping bears a note addressed to Sidney Franklin and signed "Mike": "Sidney— Not to recognize an EH—I believe it is the 'Sun Also Rises'—in the Last Flight one would have to be blind— I haven't read the Single Lady which is given credit but it would have to be almost identical with E. H. story to agree with the picture. Show it to EH and ask him— By the way—they show the [stands]—entrance and first part of a real bullfight—and a small part of the second showing a goring. In the small part of the second part this bull has a few darts in him" (USCar).
3 The script for *The Last Flight* was written by American journalist John Monk Saunders (1897–1940), based on his novel *Single Lady* (New York: Brewer & Warren, 1930), which one reviewer described as "a rather tame and emasculated imitation of Hemingway" ("The Hemingway Trail," *New York Times*, 12 April 1931, BR4). The novel was based on Saunders's short-story series known as "Nikki and Her War Birds," published in ten consecutive issues of *Liberty* (November 1930–January 1931). The stories also inspired the short-lived Broadway musical *Nikki*, which would run from 29 September to 31 October 1931 and star Canadian-born actress Fay Wray (1907–2004), who was then married to Saunders.

4 American actor Richard Barthelmess starred in *The Last Flight*.
5 On 31 August 1931 Maurice and Martha Speiser (née Glazer, 1885–1968) sailed from Cherbourg on the *Bremen*, arriving in New York City on 5 September.
6 American painter Leopold Gould Seyffert (1887–1956), known for portraits of American politicians and businessmen. He appears in a photograph with EH and the Speisers, taken in Hendaye, France, 1931 (USCar).

To Charles Thompson, [c. 31 August 1931]

Hope Lorine is in fine shape and Hobo Thompson[1] also well— Give Lorine my love—

Hope keeping the guns in shape hasnt been too damned much bother—

Havent heard from John [Herrmann]— Archie has been laid up [*EH insertion*: Something wrong with his gut] and they have been having money trouble—

Mike hasnt written that he has caught any tuna yet— Like Uncle Gus his profits havent been hit by depression—

Give my very best to Sully [J. B. Sullivan] will you please?

So long Dr.

If you write to Guaranty Trust Co. of N. Y.

    4 Place de la Concorde

    Paris

when you get this I'd probably get it before we sail—

I'm ashamed not to have written before— You were damned fine about getting us all shipped off—

Best to Bra— Suppose Burge regards me as another of those who have betrayed and gypped him— But give him my best if you see him—

Yours always—

Ernest

DiSilvestro, ALFragS

This is written on a single page bearing the circled number 3 in EH's hand; the first two pages of the letter remain unlocated. An auction catalog description of this item reads: "Third and final page only of an autograph letter signed ("Ernest") to [Charles Thompson]" (Christie's catalog, New York, 17 May 1989, Lot 76).

1 Hobo was the Thompsons' dog, according to the recollections of Patrick Hemingway (interview with Sandra Spanier, Bozeman, Montana, 10 October 2016).

To Guy Hickok, [7] September 1931

Monday Sept

31

Dear Guy:—

The Franklin film item is bullshit—[1] I offered to let Bumby appear in
a newsreel shot torear-ing under Sidneys direction to help Sidney to a few
$s— It fell through— That's all there is to the story— I never held out any
news on you—

However Sidney may fight here this Thursday or Sunday— He is seeing
the promoters now—[2] If he signs to fight I'll stay to see it—otherwise will
be in Paris by end of week— Pauline left last night for Paris— We are
going to play the overture in Kansas City— Leaving around last of Sept.
Do you want me to wire you when Franklin fights— (Too late for
afternoon papers—could catch them possibly direct if he were gored and
scoop A.P. though)

Will give you some Spanish politics when come up— You can slug any
locality on it you want and get expenses for trip to Spain—or maybe balled
out— will find out about Catalan taxes—

Havent seen Dosch's book— What about it?[3]

Dont believe it about Ferdy altho depression might do anything—[4]

They say now that Don Jaime $\left(\begin{matrix} \text{Legitimist} \\ \text{pretender} \end{matrix} \right)$ and Alfonso held family
council and will <u>both</u> abdicate as well as Prince of Asturias (bleeder)
and Afonso 2nd Son also named Jaime (Deaf mute) in favor of 3rd
son of King Don Juan only normal and pretty smart and healthy
one— He to be combined monarquist and legitimist Candidate for
throne starting with Navarre and hoping to Spread—[5] (You've
probably had this)

Govt has been disarming Navarre and the Basque provinces all this last
10 days—

Still that is where (Eibar in Guipuzcoa) they make all the arms—and
have been arming steadily since the Republic so it's quite a job—

See you soon—

Ernest

Pauline is at Hotel Paris Dinan
Rue Cassette[6]
for <u>your</u> not general info—
Thanks for the damn good Dr. information—[7]
Waited to answer until we knew what we were going to do—

phPUL, ALS

1 Hickok may have enclosed a short unsigned news article titled "Sidney Franklin Prepares Bull Fight Shorts" in his letter to EH of 28 August 1931 (PUL). The article reported that Franklin and EH were collaborating on six short movies collectively titled "Bull Fighting and Other Spanish Sports," and that EH, "a first-rate amateur matador," would act as Franklin's assistant in the bullfighting scenes (*Brooklyn Daily Eagle*, 12 August 1931, 19).

2 Because of the aftereffects of his goring in March 1930, Franklin did not perform in Spain in 1931.

3 *Through War to Revolution: Being the Experiences of a Newspaper Correspondent in War and Revolution, 1914–1920* (London: John Lane, 1931), by American journalist Arno Dosch-Fleurot (1879–1951), European correspondent for the *New York World* until it closed in 1931. Hickok praised the book in his review (*Brooklyn Daily Eagle*, 20 August 1931, 17) and asked EH about it in his 28 August letter.

4 Hickok wrote in his letter, "Ferdy Tuihy has apparently come back." English journalist James Ferdinand Tuohy (1891–1953), an officer in the British Military Intelligence Service and an expert on codebreaking, espionage, and counterespionage, had written two books (*The Secret Corps: A Tale of "Intelligence" on All Fronts* [1920] and *The Cockpit of Peace* [1926]) and then fallen silent until the late 1920s, when he published *The Crater of Mars: Reminiscence of the European War* (1929), *The Battle of Brains* (1930), and *Occupied, 1918–1930: A Postscript to the Western Front* (1931).

5 The exiled king, Alfonso XIII, and the Carlist (legitimist) claimant, Don Jaime de Borbón y Borbón-Parma, were planning a joint strategy in case the Republic permitted a royal figurehead. As this did not happen, the alliances and abdications EH mentions did not occur, and Alfonso XIII insisted on his right to the throne until shortly before his death in 1941. EH refers to three of Alfonso XIII's sons: Alfonso de Borbón y Battenberg (1907–1938), who held the title Prince of Asturias (traditional title of the Spanish crown prince) and was a hemophiliac; Jaime (1908–1975), who had been rendered deaf by a botched operation for mastoiditis at age four; and Juan (1913–1993). None of Alfonso XIII's sons would rule Spain, but Juan's son, Juan Carlos (b. 1938), would assume the throne upon the death of Spanish dictator Francisco Franco in 1975.

6 Probably the Hôtel Paris-Dinard at 29, rue Cassette, two blocks from the Luxembourg Gardens. Pauline, first with Jinny and later with Ernest, would stay there in October and November 1933 before going to Africa.

7 In his letter of 17 July 1931 Hickok wrote, "Caesereans. . . . Ouf," discussing obstetricians and praising the doctor who had treated his mother in her last days (PUL). Not having received a response from EH, Hickok asked in his 28 August letter, "And what did you think of me as a medical adviser?"

To Maxwell Perkins, 14 September 1931

ER3. FP308

PARIS 43 14TH.

NLT MAXWELL PERKINS CHARLES SCRIBNERS SONS NEWYORK
PLEASE DEPOSIT FIVEHUNDRED DOLLARS ROYALTY MY
ACCOUNT CITIBANK FARMERS TRUST FORTYTHREE
EXCHANGEPLC BEEN UNABLE WRITE SPANISH ARTICLE DUE
SEVERE EYETROUBLE HOPED ABLE DO DAILY BEST NOT COUNT
ON IT NOW STOP[1] ALL ILLUSTRATIONS BOOK COMPLETED
HEMINGWAY

PUL, Cable; Commercial Cables destination receipt stamp: SEP 14 1931

1 Perkins would reply by cable on 15 September 1931: "Deposit made" (PUL). EH's interest in reporting on Spain, which Perkins had encouraged (Perkins to EH, 20 August 1931, PUL), did not result in a publication.

To Caresse Crosby, 23 September [1931]

Hotel Crystal

Sept 23rd

Dear Caresse:—

If you will return me the Mss. to N.Y. I will be very glad to send you a check for 700 dollars from New York on October First. Am very sorry to have cashed your checks or would return them with this letter.[1]

The Story is over 3,000 words long as I stated to you—it is not fragmentary but is quite complete in its-self—

You may remember I was quite reluctant about the entire business and agreed to it at your solicitation—not mine— The terms, (except for size of edition which I stipulated as 125 when we first talked and later raised to 150 to please you) were entirely yours— I doubt if you could consider that I sought publication—

I consider the entire thing off and will be glad to return you your contract at once if you wish, as well as releasing you from the Sun and Torrents options.

Yours always

Ernest Hemingway

(written in haste)

Having just had to pay $350 for a 1st edition of a book of mine of 58 pages brought out in 350 copies (I got this one for the doctor) containing nothing as good as what I gave you[2] I cant feel tragic about anyone paying $700 to publish an edition of 150 copies with 5 hors de commerce for the editor[3]—of a story I could have sold in N.Y. for a minimum of $1500

I'm not a bit angry but truly cannot dicker on such things—nor be in a position of defending or peddling what I write— So please absolutely and finally consider it off—

Best luck to you—

SIU, ALS

1 In a letter to EH of 10 September 1931, Crosby had asked if she could bring out "Three Short Stories" as the first Crosby Continental Edition, noting that she could publish stories he had been unable to publish in America because of censorship. The Crosby Continental Editions venture was dedicated to publishing inexpensive paperback reprints of avant-garde literature.

2 The first and only edition of EH's *TSTP* had 58 pages of text and was printed in a limited edition of 300 copies. EH apparently purchased the book for Dr. Don Carlos Guffey (see EH's inscriptions of *TSTP* to Guffey [c. late 1931] in the "Undated Inscriptions" section of this volume).

3 *Hors de commerce*: copies of a limited edition designated "out of trade" or not for sale.

To Caresse Crosby, [23 September 1931]

on boat train to Le Havre

Dear Caresse:—

Thanks so much for your letter but I would <u>really</u> rather not have you publish something of the value of which, shall we say, "commercially" or anyway the suitability you are in doubt or the least bit uneasy over— So I will send you a check and you will send me the Mss. and it will perfectly all right—

If my note was brusque it was due to being really in a great hurry and being, perhaps, surprized—

If you wish to publish the Sun Also or The Torrents or both or either you can send me a contract and if you decide on the amount of the advance or advances and want me to deduct them from the check when I send it you may let me know care Scribners—597 Fifth Avenue—N.Y.C.

Anyway good luck— I have not mentioned the matter of our not agreeing to any one and am glad to do anything I can to help you with the Continental Editions—

Give my best to Jacques [Porel]—he came around and was very nice—

Yours always—

Ernest Hemingway.

SIU, ALS

To Sylvia Beach, [23 September 1931]

on the train—

enroute to Havre[1]

Dearest Sylvia:—

Pauline and I both feel terribly not to have seen you again and to say goodbye to Adrienne too— Pauline got a rotten cold sunday and was in bed since and I was around like a chicken with head off doing business and such nonsense and couldnt come— You can tell how little time I had to do what I wanted by the small amount of time I had to come to Shakespeare and Co. because, if I were free I would be in every day—

I do hope your headaches are better and Thank you and Adrienne for the wonderful dinner and the fine presents to the Children—

Best love to you always from Pauline and me—

Let me know care Scribners—597 Fifth Avenue—N.YC. anything you wish done for Joyce—

Ernest

PUL, ALS

1 EH, Pauline, and Patrick sailed for the United States from Le Havre on 23 September aboard the *Île de France.*

To Edward Saunders, 2 October 1931

October 2—1931

~~Conway,~~

~~Massachusetts~~

address—

c/o Charles Scribners Sons

597 Fifth Avenue

New York City—

Dear Bra:—

Well Dr. we are finally back in this country and I hurry to send you the 150\underline{^{00}}$ to put in the new bottom. In the boat. Not in you, Bra—

Jerry Trevor will cash this for you at the bank.[1] I would have sent it sooner but didnt have it. But you said you didnt need it until after hurricane season.

Pauline Pat and Bumby are all fine. We expect a new baby in about a month.

We had a fine summer in Spain and a good trip back. Nobody sick. Won a little shooting pigeons.

England and Germany are in bad shape. US. in bad shape too but will be plenty worse.

Cash this check as soon as you get it.

I praised up Key West in the Paris and New York papers. Hope it will send some strangers down for you merchants to work on.[2]

We will come down as soon after the baby is born as Pauline can travel. Hope to be there before Christmas.

Everybody in N.Y. is broke—really broke—money is very hard to get hold of and will be worse— But as long as the galdings, grunts, grits and conchs hold out we wont worry—[3]

Pauline sends her love to Julia and to Annie—and to you— My very best to you all—

Ernest Hemingway.

KWAHS, ALS; letterhead (cancelled by EH): ~~ADA H MACLEISH / Cricket Hill Farm / Conway, Mass.~~

1 Jeremiah Joseph (Jerry) Trevor (1898–1958), Key West native, WWI veteran, and 1920 graduate of the University of Pennsylvania, worked at the First National Bank in Key West, becoming the bank's president in the 1950s. He owned the house at 907 Whitehead Street before it was deeded to EH on 29 April 1931. The First National Bank would appear in EH's 1937 novel *THHN* as the First State Trust and Savings.
2 Although any EH comments in the Paris and New York newspapers remain unlocated, the Oak Park newspaper had earlier reported his description of Key West as a beacon for painters and writers (*Oak Leaves*, 8 May 1931, 95).
3 Galdings, or gauldings: West Indian term for a type of heron that was commonly eaten.

To Waldo Peirce, 5 October 1931

BC26 12=CONWAY MASS 5 830A

WALDO PIERCE=

BANGOR ME=

SWELL TO SEE YOU WILL BE NEWYORK UNTIL SATURDAY LOVE TO ALL=

ERNEST AND PAULINE.

Colby, Cable; Western Union destination receipt stamp: 1931 OCT 5 AM 8 37

To Richard Simon, [c. 5 October 1931]

Ogden Nash gives me
a pain in my ash.
E.H.

Swann Galleries catalog, New York, 2 February 1995, Lot 106 (illustrated), ANS

EH wrote this couplet directly on a 3 October 1931 letter that Simon sent to him c/o Scribner's, which EH may have received on 5 October when he met with Max Perkins in New York to deliver pictures for *DIA*. In the letter Simon asked EH to provide "a two-line comment" to appear on the wrapper for Ogden Nash's forthcoming book, *Free Wheeling* (New York: Simon & Schuster). Simon likely enclosed a proof copy of Nash's book that EH gave away, inscribing on the front flyleaf, "Love to Helen / from Ernest" (dated "New York City, 1931" in the Swann Galleries auction catalogue, Lot 105). EH's couplet was not printed on the jacket of Nash's book, which was released on 15 October.

To Eric Knight, [10 October 1931]

Saturday

Dear Mr. Knight:—

It is around 4 A.M. and have just waked up with the jeebies.

You see I've never talked for publication—truly—<u>never</u>— Because I know from having interviewed them for years that when a writer talks 9 times out of 10 he makes a horses ass of himself. If you never talk you never have to and you double cross nobody by not talking— They know if you say you dont talk that you dont—

Then I get drunk with Moe [Speiser] and yourself[1] and have diorrhea (misspelled) of the mouth about myself and if you write the story then I've lied to everybody I say I dont talk to and been a lousy faker.

If you want to do me the best favor any one man can do another you wont write any interview. You see it is awfully damned important to me because I believe so Completely in not talking because it destroys all pleasure in the work and in <u>everything</u> if you talk about it—and once you start you cant stop—and then any pride or pleasure or satisfaction is gone.

This may sound like a lot of horseshit but truly it is more important to me than I can write you.

If you'll do me this favor of not writing any interview it will be really a hell of a great favor—more important than I can possibly repay. But will be glad to do absolutely anything you say in return.

Not just going to bat for your stuff with publishers—which I am damned happy to do anyway— But any damned thing—

All right that is that—

If on the other hand you say why should I do this bastard a favor—he said I could write a piece and now he takes it back— In that case will you not have me make any cracks against other writers, Nor say anything about my own life nor about the war.

You were an infantryman and paid for your knowlege and have a right to talk and write about war— and I look forward to reading it when you write it— The Cambrai story should be swell.[2] I was a lousy ambulance driver and have no right to open my pan about the late war—and know it—

So if you want to write a kidding piece about our getting tight together as I said, I'll stand for it—but please dont make me make any cracks about [*EH insertion*: i.e. against] other writers.— Nor about my own life or about the war.

But if you want to do me a hell of a swell favor dont write any piece at all—

Am sending over the book Her Privates We—[3] Mrs. Hemingway and I both enjoyed meeting you very much—and I wish you a lot of luck.

Yours always
Ernest Hemingway.

USCar, ALS; letterhead: HOTEL BREVOORT / Fifth Avenue / AT EIGHTH STREET / New York; postmark: NEW YORK / G.P.O., OCT 10 / 830AM

EH addressed the envelope to "Eric M. Knight Esq. / Philadelphia Public Ledger / Philadelphia / Pa." with the notation "Personal / Important."

1 Maurice Speiser had arranged a meeting to introduce EH to Knight, a newspaperman. Knight and Speiser's son, Raymond Arthur Speiser (1908–1959), were then dating sisters Ruth Frances "Jere" Brylawski (1907–1996) and Jeanne Brylawski (1910–2007).

2 British-born Knight enlisted in Princess Patricia's Canadian Light Infantry regiment in 1917 and was a signal corpsman in France from 31 May 1918 through 20 March 1919. The Battle of Cambrai, in northern France, began on 20 November 1917 when British tanks penetrated German defenses in a surprise attack. The German counterattack (30 November–5 December 1917) drove the British back nearly to their original position. The battle, among the first to involve significant tank warfare, resulted in an estimated 40,000 casualties on each side.

3 *Her Privates We* (London: Peter Davies, 1930; New York: G. P. Putnam's Sons, 1930), a realistic novel about life on the Western Front, is the expurgated version of *The Middle Parts of Fortune: Somme & Ancre, 1916* (London: Piazza Press, 1929), a two-volume work published in a limited edition of 520 numbered copies "issued to subscribers by Peter Davies." Authorship was attributed to "Private 19022," pseudonym for Frederic Manning (1882–1935), Australian novelist, poet, and WWI veteran. EH owned copies of both works (Brasch and Sigman, items 4218 and 4219).

To Maurice Speiser, [12 October 1931]

Monday—

Dear Moe:—

A play broker and agent named Leland Hayward just tells me he had an offer of 25,000 for Motion Picture rights to the Sun Also from Fox last Spring— This offer was never transmitted to me. Hayward said he was told by Scribners that an Ann Watkins—also agent—was handling the book and that she turned down the offer. I asked him if he would communicate with you and give you the dope. He said he would write you today. His address is 43 W. 42nd Street.[1]

I have never had any dealings with Ann Watkins nor ever authorized her to act as my agent.[2]

The Sun Also Rises I gave to Bumby's mother—Hadley R. Hemingway—care Guaranty Trust Co. of N.Y—cable address Garritus—at the time of Publication and have had Scribners pay all royalties always direct to her. I however have handled all the business such as sale of right to reprint to Grossett and Dunlop and The Modern Library but have had the Checks sent direct to her. Nobody knows she owns it except Scribners. One reason I have been particularly anxious about protecting and selling this property is because it is hers.

The only possible explanation of this Ann Watkins angle would be if she had spoken to Hadley about picture rights. But I told Hadley I was trying to sell the Sun Also for her last June and again this summer

(September) and she was very pleased and made no reference to Watkins and I believe Watkins is either an Alibi of Haywards or just another chiseler.

If Watkins has any authority (which should be easily ascertainable) I will have Hadley revoke it by cable.

About the book Captain— I was just overly suspicious (my private life being an open sewer am sometimes a little touchy) Capt. Cohn holding so many of my 1st editions couldnt afford to make me out a shite in print—it would decrease the value of his stock— But I hate a curious man—

Our very best to you and to Martha— I hope it wont be long before we are together again— Thanks very much for the liquor, the party and for being so damned nice—

This written in some haste—

Ernest

USCar, ALS; letterhead: HOTEL BREVOORT / Fifth Avenue / AT EIGHTH STREET / New York; postmark: PHILA.PA. / NORTHPHILA.STA., OCT 12 / 6 P M / 1931

1 In his 15 October 1931 reply, Speiser would write that he had not heard from Hayward and was "dropping him a note today" (USCar).
2 Literary agent Ann Watkins (née Angeline Whiton, 1885–1967) had spoken with Perkins on 13 February 1931 and written him a letter dated 14 February 1931 indicating Universal's interest in producing a film version of *SAR* and asking Perkins to secure EH's authorization for her agency to pursue the project (PUL). As Perkins explained to Watkins in a letter of 26 February 1931, he did not write to EH about her motion picture offer in order not to arouse EH's hopes unnecessarily (PUL). .

To Maxwell Perkins, 14 October 1931

St. Louis

Oct 14

Dear Max:—

Leland Hayward the play broker and agent tells me he went to you with an offer of $25,000 from Fox for The Sun Also Rises last Spring and that you told him Ann Watkins controlled the movie rights of that book. Anyway I never heard of the offer (now withdrawn) and Hadley is 25,000 short on that account!—[1]

I have always handled all business on The Sun Also even though ~~sending the~~ having the money sent direct to Hadley— I saw Hadley in June and September and She was under the impression I was still handling it—

What about this Watkins business— How accurate is Haywards statement?— He said Watkins turned down the offer—on what authority?[2]

If true it cost Hadley 25,000 as I would have sold the picture rights instantly for that sum—

It is possible Hayward is full of ball room bananas but it didnt sound that way—

John Monk Saunders and others have been chizeling steadily off that book—[3]

Anyway I told Hayward I would write you to put him in touch with me direct if he had any such offers—

I've received [only? every?] piddling stinking $500-$150 offer at elaborate extent and when I have a chance to get something really fine for Hadley it isnt put through—

Had something else to write about but this has knocked it out of my head—oh yes—that Living authors racket—[4]

Can you write them as follows—

Mr Ernest Hemingway requests us to write you stating that the biographical sketch of him published in your volumne is unauthorized by him and was never submitted to him; that it is altogether inaccurate and contains extravagant statements too ridiculous to be worth denying in detail. He requests that this sketch ~~either~~ be entirely eliminated. ~~or a statement appended embodying the above statement~~

I havent it here and am damned if I'll buy it to deny it. If they refuse to eliminate it they must either print a denial or I'll get an injunction stopping the sale of the book. To hell with these bastards getting out biographical sketches which have obviously been written by ½ the people in question and never ever submitting them to you yourself to cut out the crap—

This is one of the worst, smuggest, most hick, most depressing dammed towns in the world— Thank God we pull out of it tomorrow—

Patricks nurse very satisfactory—[5]

Best always

Ernest

Capt. Cohn is the owner of the corrected type script (complete including part later eliminated) of The Sun Also Rises which he got from Scribners—it having been thrown away with other worthless matter—

The only thing is that I could have given it (had it been returned to me) to someone like John H. [Herrmann] or Evan [Shipman] who could have sold it and got 2 or 3 hundred dollars which would have been damned useful to them to live on while engaged in the practice of letters—

or I might have donated to some worthy charity such as Patrick or Bumby—

PUL, ALS; letterhead: HOTEL STATLER ST.LOUIS / Washington Avenue at Ninth and Saint Charles

1 In his 16 October 1931 reply, Perkins would explain that Watkins had contacted him in February 1931, that Hayward had also expressed interest, and that neither had produced an offer solid enough for Perkins to transmit to EH. Perkins added that he had just telephoned both Watkins and Hayward, neither of whom could document an offer for $25,000 earlier in the year or make one now (PUL).

2 According to Perkins's 16 October 1931 letter, Watkins told him Hayward had telephoned her in late spring and proposed splitting an offer of $12,500, which she had rejected as "ridiculously low"; Hayward had also called Perkins then but did not extend an offer. Perkins reassured EH that he would relay him any legitimate offer, adding, "there is no use fooling with all these nibbles ... there is often trickery back of it and it is best to say nothing except that any offer will be considered, and not to give the impression that the rights will go cheap."

3 Perkins would reply that Watkins told him the Saunders film, *The Last Flight*, which also featured bullfighting, had dampened other producers' interest in the subject and that they also feared censorship "on that other element" in *SAR*.

4 *Living Authors: A Book of Biographies* (New York: H. W. Wilson, 1931), edited by "Dilly Tante," a pseudonym for Stanley Kunitz (1905–2006), contained a sketch of EH that gave the wrong birth date, misreported his army service, inaccurately recounted taurine adventures, and claimed that during a middleweight championship boxing match in Paris, EH jumped into the ring and knocked out the champion, who he thought was delivering illegal blows. In a note dated 21 October 1931, Scribner's would transmit EH's message verbatim to Kunitz's publishing house (PUL).

5 Gabrielle Jacquot (b. 1892), the French nanny recently hired to replace Henriette.

To Charles MacGregor, [14 October 1931]

Dear Mac:—

If you have not received the camera it is because it was packed in the trunk Monday morning in my absence and shipped direct for Kansas City by Gabrielle (Gaby) Jaquot Patrick's new nurse. She also packed and shipped all my clean shirts, my slippers etc. If they cant fix it in Kansas City maybe I'll send it to you.

Owing to the depression the only size 17 plain white shirts with attached collars on sale here are those that have been on sale in the windows.

It has not been considered smart business to stock clean shirts until these slightly soiled shirts have been sold at reduced prices. You can get a pretty nice soiled shirt now for around $1.79.

If you ever become dissatisfied with your life with Benchley and that whole gin crazed Saturnalia[1] and want to lead a cleaner life bring your Shortwave set down to Key West and we could try to turn an honest penny running chinamen.

The goddamned chinamen are still crazy to get into this country and we could bring them in and then have a hearty laugh at their expense.[2]

Ernie

Fritch, ALS; letterhead: HOTEL STATLER ST.LOUIS / Washington Avenue at Ninth and Saint Charles; postmark: SAINT LOUIS / MO., OCT14 / 430PM / 1931

EH addressed the envelope to "Mr MacGregor / care Mr. R. Benchley / Hotel Royalton / W. 44th Street / New York City."

1 As Robert Benchley's secretary, MacGregor would have been well acquainted with the members of the Algonquin Round Table.
2 Until it outlawed slavery in 1886, Cuba imported large numbers of free and indentured Chinese laborers for the sugar and tobacco industries, railroad construction, and other manual labor. Anxious for a better life, many sought illegal entry to the United States. The often deadly business of smuggling Cuban Chinese would be depicted in EH's 1937 novel, *THHN*.

To Maxwell Perkins, 16 October 1931

NBM51 14=KANSASCITY MO 16 945A
MAXWELL PERKINS, CARE CHARLES SCRIBNERS SONS=
597 FIFTH AVE=
SEND MAIL CARE MALCOM LOWRY SIX FOUR THREE FIVE
INDIAN LENE KANSASCITY MISSOURI REGARDS=
    ERNEST.

PUL, Cable; Western Union destination receipt stamp: 1931 OCT 16 AM 10 54

EH and Pauline stayed in Kansas City with Malcolm and Ruth Lowry before the births of
Patrick in 1928 and Gregory in 1931.

To John Herrmann and Josephine Herbst, [18 October 1931]

Kansas City

MO.

Care

Malcom Lowry

6435 Indian Lane

K.C.

Mo.

Dear John and Jo:—

I've felt a lousy bastard every time I remembered not having sent that
manuscript but what happened was this— I beat it off to Spain in a hell of a
hurry to see the Revolution (not much to see but heard a lot) and left all
those Mss. for Pauline to have copied. She did but filed the originals at K.W.
So when I get down In December will send you something—[1]

The enclosed is good if you cash it quick enough— Dont let it stay around
the house the way the finance kings are acting— Please cash it right away so
I wont feel as lousy about forgetting the Mss.

~~We are~~ Pauline is going to have a baby here next month— We Just
got out here— Go to K.W. when P. is all right again— My ~~goddam~~

arm is OK for writing etc. but no strength—probably will get all right with time—

Hope you merchants are in good condition—am awfully sorry I was crabby on that trip—maybe we can lay it to lay off from being able to work and general spleen— Do you remember the size of the Kingfish that kept striking Josey that last night?

Spain is in good shape—nice sensible little revolution so far— Bumby learned bull fighting all summer—may support us all yet—

I hope you have both been going good— Pauline sends her love— Patrick She and Bumby are all well—

Best to you always—

Hem—

Yale, ALS; postmark: KANSAS CITY / MO., OCT 18 / 6 PM / 1931; forwarding postmark: IRWIN / PA., OCT20 / 12 PM / 19[31]

EH addressed the envelope to "Mr. and Mrs. John Herrman / Erwinna / Pennsylvania," but the envelope bears the stamp "Missent to IRWIN PA" and was readdressed to "218 Washington Ave / Lansing, Mich."

1 EH had sent Herrmann the manuscript of "Bullfighting, Sport and Industry" with his letter of [13 June 1930]. He may have intended to send Herrmann some or all parts of the manuscript of *DIA*, although that manuscript would later become the property of Don Carlos Guffey.

To Maxwell Perkins, [19 October 1931]

Monday—

Dear Max:—

Thanks very much for the explanation of the Watkins–Hayward business— The Saunders story in question was a dead steal from mine (at least according to critics etc.) So we were royally buggered all the way around.[1]

Have been going damned well here—quiet—fine sharp fall weather—country very beautiful— Re-writing going excellently and whipping it into shape and cutting out the crap—

Dont worry about the Cohn typescript— I was implying no criticism of the excellent Capt.— His explanation of how he came by it was perfectly

O.K. and no one had done anything dirty—[2] I was sore at not having it back with the galleys— Remember being upset at the time—had to correct from galleys with no original—but had troubles that summer that made that seem such a damned small inconvenience that it made no impression— I had a carbon in Paris—but did the galleys at Cap D'Antibes— What the hell— Forget about it—

Must get back to work— Let me know when you hear from the Living Author pimps— If they say they cant withdraw it entirely— If I'm sent a copy I'll cut the worst crap out of it—

But there is no law that requires me to write an autobiography for them— nor furnish them any facts about my life— I can however protest against printing a lot of untrue swill—

I'm awfully glad you have all that money business settled—it must be a tremendous relief—

Pauline sends her best—

Yours always
Ernest—

Oh yes— In the Captains bibliography—he says that at the time I wrote My Old Man I had never read any thing by Anderson— This is crazy—wait a minute and I'll find what he says—

11. It has been said that My Old Man stemmed from Sherwood Andersons' Story <u>Im A Fool</u>. The story was written before Hemingway had ever read any thing by Anderson—[3]

Could the Publicity Dept. send this out—

Ernest Hemingway writes to his publishers asking them to correct this statement which appears in a recent bibliography of his writings published by Random House. (give statement) Mr. Hemingway asks his publishers to state that he had not only read Mr. Andersons writings at that time but admired them greatly.[4]

Jesus Christ people should take it on themselves to protect me from charges of Copying, stemming from etc— I never copy and whatever I stem from I stem a long way from—

Ernest Hemingway.

Corrected copy

Max:—

P.S. When they finish with it will you have them please return it debiting me with the 2.$\frac{00}{}$ it cost? I'm sick of seeing these things sold at fancy prices and buying back my own letters to take them out of circulation. The Mss. of A Farewell never came back with the galleys from the magazine nor did the Mss. of Wine of Wyoming— I've never sold one but would rather give them away to some citizen thats broke than see them turn up at some fancy price. I know nobody you know in the office would peddle them but somebody picks them up. Its gotten to be a racket like stamp collecting.

Or if its too much bother to send it back give it to Capt. Cohn with my compliments for his birthday.

PUL, ALS; letterhead: 6435 INDIAN LANE / KANSAS CITY, MISSOURI

1 See EH's 14 October 1931 letter to Perkins.
2 In his letter to EH of 16 October 1931, Perkins wrote that when *SAR* was in press "we were not on to the value of typescripts," and they were customarily destroyed after a certain length of time. He offered to find out how Louis Henry Cohn acquired the *SAR* typescript and to buy it back (PUL).
3 EH quotes accurately from the "Compiler's Notebook" section of Cohn's bibliography (Cohn, 113).
4 This paragraph alone is typewritten. The remainder of the letter is handwritten.

To Maurice Speiser, [19] October [1931]

Monday (Oct ?)

Dear Moe:—

Your air mail of Oct 17 just received— Also the enclosed—Which is self explanatory— The Capt. C. thing is of no importance— I merely do not clip it off so you wont think I am holding anything out on my lawyer— It refers to Scribners throwing away a corrected typescript of Sun Also containing all stuff eliminated from galleys and which should have been returned to me with the galleys— I could have given it to any friend who was broke and they could have got $500 or so for it— Cohn got it quite legitimately with a mass of thrown away galley proofs— Will you return me the letter when through? I should file it—[1]

It is a lousy break that the sale should have been impeded by Mr. Saunders book which was an afterbirth if I ever saw one—

Had a fine letter from Eric Knight today—he is a hell of a nice fellow—[2]

Hope you and Martha and your family are all well— Patrick has gone to Piggott with Paulines family— Pauline is in excellent shape— Dr. expects baby Nov 10–15— Am working very hard and going damned well—will make this mass of crap into a good book yet——

Yours always—
Ernest—

USCar, ALS; letterhead: 6435 INDIAN LANE / KANSAS CITY, MISSOURI; postmark: KANSAS CITY / MO., OCT19 / 730PM / 1931

1 EH enclosed Perkins's letter of 16 October 1931, in which Perkins had explained the situation involving Leland Hayward and Ann Watkins and said he would look into how Cohn had acquired the *SAR* typescript (PUL). A typewritten copy of Perkins's letter, probably made by Speiser or his staff before returning Perkins's letter to EH, includes this inserted comment about Saunders: "(Evidently our old friend John Monk) E.H. Goddam his eyes" (USCar).
2 Although Knight's letter to EH remains unlocated, Speiser referred to it in his letter to EH of 15 October 1931, saying Knight had told him he had already written to EH saying "that he would not write any article as per your request" (USCar).

To Caresse Crosby, [c. 19 October 1931]

Blacksun
Paris
~~Glad exchange~~[+]
~~Certainly~~
Answering ~~wire~~ cable October Twelfth Quotes Certainly
Hemingway

RR Auction online catalog, Boston, 15 August 2012, Item 604 (illustrated), ACDS

1 EH is responding to Crosby's 12 October cable, which reads: "MIGHT I HAVE CONTINENTAL RIGTS IN OUR TIME INSTEAD SON ALSO RISES PLEASE CABLE ANSWER BLACKSUN PARIS" (JFK).

To Caresse Crosby, 19 October 1931

[On flap of folded telegram form:] LCO BLACKSUN
RHS973
KANSASCITY
MISSOURI 10 19 18H2
ANSWERING CABLE OCTOBER TWELFTH QUOTE[1] CERTAINLY
HEMINGWAY

SIU, Cable; postmark: PARIS 110 / R. DE RENNES, 7 [20] 20 X / 1931

1 In EH's handwritten draft (immediately preceding in this volume), this word is "quotes." This cable, printed on a form headed "TÉLÉGRAMME / VIA WESTERN UNION," survives among Crosby's papers at SIU.

To Eric Knight, [c. 19 October 1931]

Care M. L owr y
6435 Indi an Lane
K. C..MO.

Dear Mr. Knight ;

It was damned nice to hear from you and you were damned sporting about the inte rviewing .

This bitch of a typewriter is a R emington noiseless presented by the company and it skips letters and makes typeing bloody impossible . What are you supposed to write them in a case like that .

D id you get the Her Privates We ? That is the expurgated version -the original was called T he Middle Parts of Fortune — you remember the quotation fortunes cap not the very butt on something som ething faith her privates we .- Christ the citizen who wrote it has a fine eye for his shakespere .[1]

Send me the Cambrai when you get it done -[2] I look forward to it . The hell of prose is that you have a swell idea but then you have to write it a word at a time — getting to the point you had the big feeling about long after the feeling is gone .

About the books — wd be very happy to sign them . The doing of a doubtful honor to them .- Send anything anytime you want me to write about the mechanics of it .- critic ize or whatever or send it to editor or whatever you say .

Am working like a bastard against time on this book — going well — seeing how much I can get done before the next bloody accident , sickness or whatever they are sending this fall . Maybe have a run on the red now for a while , not in the red, on the red , and be over accidents etc. for a while .

Best to you always[3] and to your girl[4] from Mrs. Hemingway and me— Maybe we can get together in Philadelphia sometime—

Hope so—

Ernest Hemingway—

USCar, TL/ALS

The irregular spacing caused by EH's malfunctioning typewriter has been reproduced in this transcription but regularized in subsequent letters he typed on the same machine: to Harry Marks, 26 October 1931; to Waldo Peirce, [c. late October–early November 1931]; to Guy Hickok, 12 December [1931]; and to Archibald MacLeish, 23 December [1931].

1 The titles of Frederic Manning's two-volume novel *The Middle Parts of Fortune* (1929) and the expurgated version, *Her Privates We* (1930), are drawn from *Hamlet*. The title page of the first volume of the 1929 novel features this epigraph, spoken by Guildenstern to Rosencrantz and Hamlet (2.2.247–52): "On fortune's cap we are not the very button ... Then you live about her waist, or in the middle of her favours? ... 'Faith, her privates we. - - - - SHAKESPEARE." In both versions of the novel, every chapter is prefaced by a quotation from a Shakespearean play.
2 See EH to Knight, [10 October 1931].
3 The remainder of the letter is handwritten.

4 Knight would marry American writer and editor Jere Brylawski on 2 December 1932, thus becoming the brother-in-law of Speiser's son Raymond, who would marry Ruth's younger sister, Jeanne, the same year.

To Eric Knight, [c. late October 1931]

For Eric Knight remembering a fine evening we spent listening to Mr. Dashiell Hammett tell us not to be mugs— get the money—that's all that means any thing— Get the money— That tall white haired drink of contented cowpiss— The talented cheap bastard—

Why dont you get the money Eric Knight? You're too good a guy—that was the trouble—

Ernest Hemingway.

Christie's catalog, New York, 11 October 2002, Lot 151 (illustrated), Inscription

EH wrote this inscription in a first-edition copy of *MWW* (Hanneman A7a). The dates of this inscription and of the one that follows in this volume are conjectured relative to EH's offer in his letter to Knight of [c. 19 October 1931] to sign books and to Knight's 28 December 1931 reply to EH, thanking him for signing the books and apologizing for not having thanked him sooner (JFK).

To Eric Knight, [c. late October 1931]

To Eric Knight

this account of life and travels in Northern Italy during 1917 and 18 with a short excursion on the Italian lakes and an account of part of a winter spent in French Switzerland above Lake Leman—

with best wishes from the author—
Ernest Hemingway

[*On the following page:*]

Because this book is dear to me I send it to you

Christie's catalog, New York, 11 October 2002, Lot 152 (illustrated), Inscription

EH wrote this inscription in a first-edition copy of *FTA* (Hanneman A10a).

To Harry Marks, 26 October 1931

October 26, 1931

Dear Mr. Marks;

Mrs. Crosby is not publishing any book by me except, possibly, reprints in English of In Our Time and The Torrents of Spring in a continental edition. I have had two cables from Mrs. Crosby and am awaiting a letter from her about these two books which I have written and cabled her she may reprint in her projected Continental Editions series.[1] The project of publishing a story of part of a book by me in a Black Sun Press edition has been definitely abandoned.[2]

Yours very truly,

Ernest Hemingway

Stanford, TLS; letterhead: 6435 INDIAN LANE / KANSAS CITY, MISSOURI

1 Crosby would publish *TOS* in January 1932 and *IOT* in June 1932.
2 In a letter to EH dated 15 October 1931 and sent from Paris, Crosby wrote that she had hoped EH would change his mind but was returning his manuscript "very reluctantly" and asked him to send back his copy of the contract (JFK).

To Waldo Peirce, [c. late October–early November 1931]

Querido Valdito mio;

?Que tal hombre? lo siento un barbaridad not to see you anymore you bearded twin begetting bum. Now that you know you have twinmaking cojones for gods sake layoff of domestic life and come down to Key West this winter so we can make a trip out to Tortugas again.[1] We will go there from here as soon as Pauline and the offspring can travel. Sometime before Christmas if the child is timed for No. 15. Will stay until May anyway. Come on down in March anyway for the Tortugas trip. You've never been there since we found those damned big kings.— It was a shame we didnt get together in N.Y.

The Drs. all say this is another boy so you better hedge in the sweeps. I want a girl very much but so far have never had a legitimate nor illegit daughter so dont know how to go about it. Maybe Max can tell.

You sound in swell shape down to 195. With my damned finn paralysed 8 months or so and not able to get any bloody exercise picked up weight like a hog on cervezeria Alvarez product.[2] Ran it up to 218 with clothes on. Now down to 211 clothed. Imagine around 200 even sttripped. Once we have this baby and get down to K.W. am going to really get in shape again. Working like a bastard now on this book and must knock off and get back to it. Thats why I haven't written

Best love to Alzira from us both and to you you louzy pere de famille—[3] If you don't leave your damned domestic layout in March once you get things organized and come down for a little of the old life youre a twirp—

Anyway in the meantime best to you both—this damned typer skips like a stammering flannel mouthed nigger—

Spain was damned nice with the revolution. Had a fine time all spring and summer—hated like hell to leave the percebes[4] and come back—

Sent Bra some jack to put a new bottom in the old boat. They are all damned fond of you down there. You wouldn't have had any twins if the tarpon that jumped into the boat and hit me in the middle of the back would have hit Alzira in the lap.— Well so long Chico—if I don't write it is because I 'm so bloody pooped after working all day on this bloody book—

Love from us all

Ernesto

Colby, TLS

1 *¿Qué tal, hombre? lo siento una barbaridad*: How are things, old fellow? I'm tremendously sorry (Spanish). In the *DIA* glossary, which he was working on at about this time, EH would play on the expression *¿Qué tal?* offering a series of translations and variants ("An Explanatory Glossary," s.v. *Tal*). *Cojones*: testicles (Spanish).
2 *Cervecería*: brewery, or a place where beer is sold or consumed (Spanish). Cervecería (or Casa) Álvarez, a bar-café on Calle Victoria in Madrid, established and sequentially owned by Joaquín and Antonio Álvarez. In *DIA*'s "Explanatory Glossary," EH would praise its draft beer as the best in the city (s.v. *Cerveza*).
3 *Père de famille*: father; male head of a family; family man (French).
4 *Percebes*: goose barnacles that grow along the rocks of the Atlantic coast of Spain where they are served as tapas to accompany beer (Spanish). In *DIA*, EH would praise this delicacy ("An Explanatory Glossary," s.v. *Mariscos*).

To Charles MacGregor, 3 November [1931]

Care R. W. Lowry—
6435 Indian Lane
K.C. Mo.
November 3—

Dear Mr. MacGregor:—

You would do me a fine favor, Mac, if you would call up Mr. Howard E. Reinheimer or Rheinheimer or possibly Rinehymer—altho I doubt that last—and believe it to be Reinheimer—[1] Anyway Stallings lawyer and say you are speaking for Mr. Hemingway—Mr Ernest Hemingway who hasnt Mr. R—h—rs address—nor Miss Landis address— And wants Mr. Rinyheimy to please present Mr. Hemingsteins compliments to Miss Landi and Mr. and Mrs. Hemingway feel very badly about it but they wont be in Kansas City—when Miss Landi is going through—very sorry— Have had to leave (Am going Duckshooting [*EH insertion*: but you dont need to say that]) Illness in the family— So it wont be necessary for Mr. Rheineheimer to get a reservation on the Chief with stop over at Kansas City—for Miss Landi—[2]

Make it plain enough Mac but very polite—

You know—the old MacGregor tact—

For its always fair weather when Mr. MacGregor pulls Mr. Benchley together—[3]

Let me know that youve got this and done this will you?

Ernie

You may remember Miss Landi—Mr McGregor— She was the English Speaking Icebox we got a little drunk that afternoon and invited her to K. City with, of all things, her Mother—

Book is going damned well— Dr. says baby not due maybe until toward end of month— Best to Robert [Benchley]— Thanks ever so much, kid.

Fritch, ALS

1 Howard E. Reinheimer (1899–1970), American attorney specializing in contract, copyright, and theater law who represented Stallings in brokering the dramatic rights for *FTA*.
2 Elissa Landi played Catherine Barkley in Stallings's Broadway adaptation of *FTA*. The Chief, an "extra-fare" train on the Santa Fe Line offering sleeping cars, meals, showers, and other services, ran between Chicago and Los Angeles.
3 EH plays on lines from "A Stein Song," lyrics by Richard Hovey (1864–1900) and music by Frederic Field Bullard (1864–1904): "For it's always fair weather / When good fellows get together, / With a stein on the table and a good song ringing clear."

To Paul Pfeiffer, 12 November 1931

LR AY 27 VD Kansas City Mo. 1020AM Nov. 12th..-31.
P M Pfeiffer,
Piggott, Ark.

Gregory Hancock born eight AM weight nine pounds perfect child caeserian after twelve hours labor Pauline and baby fine will call you telephone one thirty best love.

Ernest . . . . . . 1034AM.

PUL, Cable

EH and Pauline's second son, Gregory Hancock Hemingway (1931–2001), was born at Research Hospital, Kansas City.

To Grace Hall Hemingway, 12 November 1931

C37 9=UD KANSASCITY MO 12 1032A
MRS C E HEMINGWAY AND FAMILY=
600 NORTH KENILWORTH AVE OAKPARK ILL=
GREGORY HANCOCK 9 POUNDS AFTER CAESERIAN ALL WELL LOVE=
ERNIE.

JFK, Cable; Western Union destination receipt stamp: 1931 NOV 12 AM 10 44

591

To Mary Pfeiffer, 12 November [1931]

Nov. 12—

6.35 a.m.—

Dear Mother:—

Pauline's pains started at 6 pm. armistice night.[1] She commenced active labor about 10 o'clock and now at 25 to seven the next morning in spite of very heavy labor and terrible suffering the child has not come down at all— Dr. Guffey wanted to try the natural labour to see if the child would come down— Pauline suffers much worse than before, even, and has no sort of normal labor at all since the child does not descend in spite of the most terrific pains—after the first 4 hours— her nerves were pretty well gone and the next seven hours she suffered terribly with no result— Pains, contractions and spasms which would ordinarily bring the childs head to the mouth of the womb did not move the child at all—at 10 minutes to Seven Dr. Guffey decided a caeserian was the only thing as 7 hours of labour had not moved it down a half an inch even— By the time the anesthetician and the other Dr. arrived and things were gotten ready Pauline was in pretty bad shape— She suffered much more than with Patrick although she was not as prostrated physically—

The operation was performed at 20 minutes to 8— Dr. Guffey did the operation <u>very</u> well— It took a long time to get the baby to breathe—around 20 minutes of working— But when he did he was in fine shape— Weighed nearly nine pounds— Very lean and long of limb— Much like Patrick in the face but better looking perhaps— Physically perfect— All organs in proper place— Wide shoulders and big head—

Pauline slept until 9.$^{\underline{30}}$ woke with quite a lot of pain but very happy—then with a hypodermic slept soundly and peacefully until 12$^{\underline{00}}$ when I left while she was still sleeping— In meantime wired relatives etc.—

Gregory is a good saints name and Hancock is my grandmothers name— John Hancock etc.—[2] We would have called him Max but it seemed bad luck maybe— you can call him Max if you want and we can put it in the names—[3] But Greg is a fine name too—

We had just moved from Ruth's [Lowry's] to this very nice apt. building—
Riviera Apartments—229 Ward Parkway—
when Pauline's pains started—

She really had a very terrible time—there are pains and pains you know— You hear of people having 24–48 hours of labor—but normal labor is its own cure—when the child is descending it eases the pain and makes it more natural— Dr. Guffey examining inside said Paulines pelvis was so shaped that it was impossible for the baby's head to descend—otherwise with the violence of her labor the baby would have come in the 1st 5 hours— He wanted to be sure a normal labor was impossible since the caeserian is dangerous of course and only justifiable if altogether necessary— He is sure enough now—

If the Church insists that I must put Pauline through what I have just seen her through am afraid must consider myself an outlyer from now on—"a lesser breed without the law" If a sovereign Pontiff bore children when not built for it he might write a bull of exceptions—[4]

Oh well—

Pauline is fine—resting well— I go down now to see her— The baby is fine and I hope will support us all— He is built like Battling Siki—[5] I'll call you up now—then mail this— then go down to the hospital again—

Best love to you all— I have written in detail so you will know that you know all about it— Pauline suffered more but seems in better shape physically than last time. If you dont hear from me everything is going finely— I will wire or telephone you about everything so dont worry!

Please excuse rotten penmanship— Jinny can read it perhaps—

Love
Ernest

Excuse me not having written before the event—have been working each day as long as eyes would work—
[*On envelope verso:*]
Pauline resting comfortably at 6.30 pm

PUL, ALS; postmark: KANSAS CITY / MO., NOV 12 / 10 PM / 1931

EH addressed the envelope to "Mr. and Mrs. P.M. Pfeiffer / Piggott / Arkansas" but the letter itself is directed to Mary Pfeiffer.

1 The Armistice agreement, signed by the Allied forces and the Germans to cease fighting on the Western Front, went into effect at 11 a.m. (Paris time) on 11 November 1918, effectively ending World War I. In 1931, Armistice Day was recognized in the United States by lowering the flag to half-mast at 11 a.m., followed by two minutes of radio silence, after which President Herbert Hoover addressed the nation.
2 EH refers to his maternal grandmother, Caroline Hancock Hall, and American statesman John Hancock.
3 Gus and Louise Pfeiffer's son Max was born and died (at the age of two months) in 1897; Paul and Mary's son Paul Mark Pfeiffer (1907–1918), who died during the influenza pandemic, had been called Max, both "to distinguish him from his father and to honor the memory of his cousin" (Hawkins, 13, 19, 136).
4 The line "lesser breeds without the law" is from Rudyard Kipling's poem "Recessional" (1897). After the Lambeth Conference of Anglican Bishops passed a resolution in August 1930 allowing the use of contraception within a marriage, Pope Pius XI issued the encyclical *Casti Connubii* (On Christian Marriage) in December 1930, reaffirming the Catholic Church's opposition to birth control.
5 Senegalese boxer Louis Fall (also known as Amadou M'Barick Fall; né Baye Phal, 1897–1925), who held the light heavyweight title from 24 September 1922 to 17 March 1923. EH had seen him fight several times in Paris in 1923 (*Letters* vol. 2, 23–24).

To Maurice and Martha Speiser, 13 November 1931

GA120 26 DL=PL KANSASCITY MO 13 1043A
MR AND MRS MAURICE E SPEISER=
NORTH AMERICAN BLDG PHILADELPHIA PENN=
GREGORY HANCOCK NINE POUND BUILT LIKE LATE BATTLING
SIKI BUT WHITE OR SAY RED PAULINE FINE RESTING
COMFORTABLY AFTER CAESERIAN AM HOLDING GREEN
STRIPED CELEBRATION LOVE=
    ERNEST.

USCar, Cable; Western Union destination receipt stamp: 1931 NOV 13 PM 12 12

To Louis Henry Cohn, [13 November 1931]

Friday.

Dear Captain Cohn:—

You were damned nice to send the wire. Dr. Guffey told me he was wiring you when we were sitting, me watching him and the anaesthetist eat breakfast, after the operation.[1] The baby is very strongly and longly built— Somewhat on the lines of the late Battling Siki— Usual eskimo face of the new born— Mrs Hemingway is quite comfortable and rested well last night and today.

Thank you very much for your letter. When you let me know how much The Middle Parts of Fortune is will send the money— Unless, of course, he wants too much. Then I'll send the books—

I think Dr. Guffey would like the bastard sheet—[2] Also—have you a French <u>Kiki</u>—[3] I would like to give him one and translate a little of it to show him that part was really good— He is a great Collector and a hell of a fine obstretrician— You can send me a bill with it if you have one—

I hope Mrs Cohn is well and that things are going well— Thanks again for the wire—

Best wishes—

Ernest Hemingway.

The childs name is Gregory Hancock— Hancock for my grandmother etc.

Greg for any of numerous Popes for Gregorian chant and for Greg Clark of Toronto.[4]

UDel, ALS; postmark: KANSAS CITY / MO., NOV 16 / 1230PM / 1931

1 In a letter dated 2 November 1931, Cohn had asked Guffey to wire him collect when the baby was born (UTulsa). Guffey cabled Cohn on 12 November at 9:15 a.m, and Cohn apparently wired his congratulations to EH right away. Although the letter is postmarked 16 November (a Monday), EH dated it "Friday," suggesting he wrote it on 13 November.

2 In December 1931 Cohn would issue in a limited edition a facsimile proof sheet of the legal disclaimer that appeared in the second printing of *FTA*. The disclaimer was printed on the

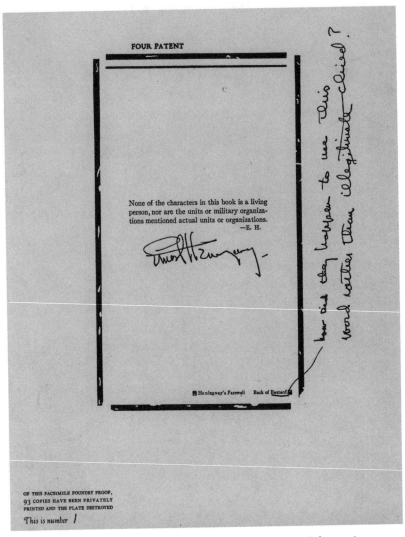

This print of the facsimile "bastard sheet" issued by Louis Henry Cohn survives among his papers. The legend in the lower left corner reads: "OF THIS FACSIMILE FOUNDRY PROOF, / 93 COPIES HAVE BEEN PRIVATELY / PRINTED AND THE PLATE DESTROYED / *This is number* 1" (MSS 100, Louis Henry and Marguerite Cohn Collection, Special Collections, University of Delaware Library, Newark, Delaware).

verso of the "bastard title" page (which bears the book's abbreviated title and precedes the full title page in the front matter). At the bottom right side of the proof sheet, a printed legend reads "Hemingway's Farewell   Back of Bastard." EH underlined "Bastard" and wrote, "how did they happen to use this word rather than illegitimate child?" (Hanneman F150).

3 *Les Souvenirs de Kiki* (Paris: Editions Broca, 1929).
4 Gregory Clark (1892–1977), Canadian WWI veteran and journalist who worked for the *Toronto Star* from 1911 to 1947. Clark was features editor for the *Star* when EH began working for the newspaper in 1920, and the two became good friends.

To Paul Pfeiffer, 14 November [1931]

LR AY 18 Kansas City Mo. 1118 AM Nov. 14th.
Paul M Pfeiffer,
Piggott, Ark.
Pauline and baby both fine very comfortable no fever wants to hear from you address research Hospital love.

Ernest . . . . . . 1133AM.

PUL, Cable

To Charles MacGregor, [c. 16 November 1931]

Address
Riviera Apartments
229 Ward Parkway
K.C.
Mo.

It's a boy at the Ernest (one F-) Hemingways.

Dear Mac— Thanks for the letter and for calling up Rheiny [Howard E. Reinheimer]— This makes three boys—a matador—a banderillero and a sword handler—or one for Devils Island—one for Wormwood Scrubs and the balance for Sing Sing—[1] Let Mr. Benchley know I miss him very much and our old club life— There is a Mc Gregor Beauty College here on Main between 2 pawn Shops and we are thinking of having a photo made, enlarged and framed for the Royalton—[2] In time these things become as valuable as Currier and Ives Prints—[3]

Was off shooting and came back on a hunch the night before—

Pauline is swell— She took one of these Joe Grimm beatings— once I went out to take a drink of water and thought to console with the old one about anyway He who dies this year is quit for the next—[4] But it turned out all night and she is comfortable today—

Baby named Gregory Hancock—

Gregory for any 3rd Pope you name and Greg Clark of Toronto— Hancock for my Grandfather's wife Miss Hancock— And all her forebears— weight 9 lbs — Caeserian — Signs of life in Greg 20 minutes after birth— O.K. now— Craps, peas—in fact the works— Had a good sound erection as soon as life appeared—

W'd appreciate your informing Mrs. Parker—

Tell Mr. Stewart too if you run into him preferably with a second hand car—

Tell Mr. Stewart I broke 21 out of 25 in the same afternoon sixteen yard rise[5]—not having had my shoes off since the morning of the day before— It was evidently taking my shoes off that buggared my shooting on the boat— On the other hand no one can say what might have broken with my shoes off— These things are hard to figure—

Best to you kid—

Hemingstein

Killed eleven live birds straight at the 30 yard rise same aft.— Only three states you can shoot them in— Here, Kentucky and Pennsylvania—[6] Here every Thursday—Sat—Sunday— Big Shoot tomorrow— Might write a piece on Live Bird shooting for the N. Yorker— I'll give you the dope if you want— Big Shoot here is for $2000 first money—$120 entry— Glad to see the banks arent broke— My best to the citizens

Ernie

Fritch, ALS; postmark: KANSAS CITY / MO., NOV16 / 1230PM / 1931

EH addressed the envelope to "Charles Mac Gregor, Esq. / c/o Mr. R. Benchley / Hotel Royalton / 44 W. 44th / New York City."

1 Three prisons: Devil's Island, penal colony in the Atlantic Ocean, off the coast of French Guiana; Wormwood Scrubs, in London; and Sing Sing, in Ossining, New York.
2 The 1931 edition of Polk's Kansas City (Missouri) Directory shows the MacGregor College of Beauty Culture, operated by Clara B. MacGregor, at 1314½ Main Street; Joseph Shaftan, pawnbroker, at 1316 Main Street; and the Gateway Loan Company at 1330 Main Street. The Royalton (44 West 44th Street), exclusive hotel where Benchley lived in New York City, on the same block as the Algonquin Hotel (59 West 44th Street).
3 Nathaniel Currier (1813–1888), American printer and lithographer, and James Merritt Ives (1824–1895), accountant and general manager, were partners in the lithography firm Currier & Ives, established in New York City in 1857. Their hand-colored prints depicting American life were advertised as "Cheap and Popular Pictures."
4 Joe Grim (né Saverio Giannone, 1881–1939), Italian American boxer variously known as the "Iron Man" (for his iron will and heart) and "The Human Punching Bag" (because of the punishment he endured as he lost fight after fight). EH quotes Shakespeare's character Feeble in *Henry IV, Part Two*: "By my troth, I care not. A man can die but once. We owe God a death. I'll ne'er bear a base mind. An't be my destiny, so; an't it be not so, so. No man's too good to serve's prince. And let it go which way it will, he that dies this year is quit for the next" (3.2.216–20).
5 A round of trapshooting consists of 25 attempts to break clay pigeons from a standard 16–yard distance from the trap house, where the targets are launched.
6 Live bird shoots were prohibited in most states around 1900.

To Mary Pfeiffer, [16 November 1931]

Monday

Dear Mother:—

Pauline got your good letter today and yesterday her Fathers fine letter with the big check for Gregory— Call him Greg for short— I got the letter today at Lowrys that you wrote when you got the wire and appreciated it very much— You ask for a daily written report and am sorry I havent made one but the news has all been so good that there has practically been none— Pauline is practically out of pain and, in fact, had ~~almost none~~ very little after the operation— She never had over °100 temperature and <u>no</u> gas pains—

Also no milk—

Wound healing well— Bowells now moving—temperature normal— She looks fine—

Baby gained 1½ ounces today after usual loss for first few days—

(Hospital pen)

He is very dark—blue black hair—Pauline's forehead—eskimo nose—my ears—no lobes—all testicles descended—no apparent physical defects— only cries when hungry—

We had a fine letter from Gabrielle— Tell her the soup will be very welcome— Send direct to Research Hospital—

We will work out details of going to Key West later—

All our furniture has arrived in N.Y and will be shipped by boat to K.W. Dec 2—arriving Dec 6—

Everything from France came duty free— Have not heard about Spanish shipment yet—as to duty—

Pauline says to tell you there is no comparison between how well she feels now and how she felt after Patrick—

Sorry not to have written more— Am trying awfully hard to finish my book and work at that each day as long as I can see— Eyes plenty bad even with the glasses— Then want to write you but eyes on the bum—

Patrick looks grand in the pictures— Wonder if Jinny would send some and a note to Henriette— Jinny writes the best French of any of us— Poor Henriette misses P. very much—

Think this is really a fine baby—at his age looks better than either Bumby or Pat did.

If all goes well we should be leaving here about December 11 or 12— If Jinny is in Florida a week before we get there that should give her time enough. Bumby has very good report card at school—

Am going to work very hard on my book this week and then will plan about coming down to shoot toward end of month— For Thanksgiving maybe— Though that is perhaps a little too early— Might come right after Thanksgiving. Jinny might want to come up for a day or two to see Pauline and I could drive down with her from here— Have a car I use here and could use for that trip if Jinny came up on train— Then I could drive back bringing Gabrielle if we should decide to bring her up here—

There is a fine shooting school with live birds on Thursday—Sat. and Sunday—and if Jinny came to spend a Thursday or a Sat or Sunday here

I could really teach her to shoot on live birds so she would get much more fun out of her hunting—[1] Well anyway love to you all—

from Pauline Greg and Ernest

Am not being more exact about dates because want to work like the devil the next ten days—

Please excuse bad penmanship!

PUL, ALS; postmark: KANSAS CITY / MO., NOV 16 / 9 PM / 1931

1 Probably the Elliott Shooting Park, established in 1887 at 7500 Independence Avenue, near the Blue River, east of downtown Kansas City.

To Waldo Peirce, 17 November 1931

NA173 19 DL=KANSASCITY MO 17 354P
WALDO PEIRCE=
BANGOR ME=
YOU LOSE GREGORY HANCOCK HOWS THAT FOR NAME NINE POUNDS PAULINE AND BABY FINE LOVE TO YOU AND ALZIRA=
ERNEST.

Colby, Cable; Western Union destination receipt stamp: 1931 NOV 17 PM 5 10

To Maxwell Perkins, [c. 20 November 1931]

Dear Max:—

Pauline had a bad time but is O.K. now— Baby is well, very dark, long arms and legs and wide shoulders— They took nearly ½ an hour to start him to breathing— Hope he never regrets the decision but then as soon as he started he had a very healthy erection—

I'd been with Pauline and hadnt been to bed for 24 hrs so when went down to Station to send the wires asked Mike to let you know— Thanks very much for the wire— If you let me know the secret of having daughters I'll tell you how you have sons—[1]

About the book— Except for the two days interruption of Greg have never been going better— Have been going so swell I hate to end it— Am getting everything in that I knew I had to get in to make it come off completely—all the grand stuff— You'll like it—

As to the estimate of length— I have cut the body of the text in the rewriting to approximately 75,000 words— It may go more— There are, so far 5 appendixes—all to be set in same type except possibly one—The 13,000 word one

(1) of 1,300 words— (1) of 13,000 words— (1) of about 4 pages of the book (a calendar of dates etc.) (1) of about 4 pages (1) of about 6 pages. And a descriptive glossary approximately 20,000 words in Length— It takes up 129 pages of long foolscap in my writing. So may take more space since sentences and paragraphs irregular in length as in Dialogue—

Does this give you enough of an idea of length?[2]

About the insurance on pictures— The Juan Gris is worth $7500 cash— Will be worth an amount impossible to estimate.— The others are worth about $300 between them—[3]

How much will the Treasurer have to pay in insurance on $7800 valuation—

Excuse my not having written—have been working every day until my eyes give out and then cant write letters—

Everything is completed except this swell last chapter that I am still writing on and the translation of the 13,000 words of reglamento.[4] May get some one to rough out the translation to save me time and work— Then I will correct it and fix it up— My damned eyes will only do so much even with the glasses and would rather do writing than hack work—

This is a hell of a fine book, Max— I've never gone better than lately—

You know that while you have published plenty books with grand illustrations and swell plates most of that stuff has been imported from England— What about the processes that Fortune uses? Do you have to have all illustrations made in the firm or is that stuff let out to be done? Have you done anything about reproducing the photographs yet—any tries? I'd like to see them— I want the photographs back as soon as possible to have for marking where they go on the galleys—

The Roberto Domingo drawings and pictures I ordered are in N.Y. customs and I am having them sent here as soon as cleared so I can see them—[5]

I can have the Mss. ready for delivery before Xmas—the one appendix might not be in shape but can give you the exact length by counting the words—

What about the new magazine format—when does it come out?[6] Do you want a story to inaugurate with and what can you pay? What about running a few chapters from the Death In The Afternoon just before it comes out— Do you think that would be good for it— The book I mean?—

Will you write me and ask them to send my mail to—Riviera Apartments—229 Ward Parkway—K.C. Mo— My cousins have gone to California—

Pauline did wonderfully after the operation—very little pain— She sits up today and can get up a little while tomorrow—

Are the firm going to be able to pay the royalty money announced in Aug as Due in Dec? Do you know when that goes out to the orthors?

My correspondents in Paris inform me that with the Laval-Hoover agreement the $ is OK for a while and that no new crisis in Banking world until February— Damned glad they pulled things out—[7] What a nonsense business in Kentucky—[8] I would give $50 toward keeping Dreiser out of Pen any time I had it—even though he is a twirp and a punk writer— All this is just excitement imitating Zola in his declining years l'homme politique—il ne manque que ca—[9] But would sell every damned thing I own and work the rest of my life to keep Dos out— But hope they wont be mugs enough to go back there to stand trial—

Thanks for telling me about the check sent to Hadley for Sun royalties— The movies really did make an offer—but I never heard of it—would certainly have accepted it— Then J. M. Saunders swiped all he could of the book— It having now been stolen they dont want it any more— Result Hadley out a minimum of $15,000— Had it looked up— May sell it of course later— But not much chance now—

Not much news here—only the people who played the market are broke— unemployment lowest anywhere in country— Down in Arkansas Paulines father has made 2600 bales of cotton— They all would be prosperous as hell in Ark. this year if cotton had any price—as it is he may let 50,000 acres go for taxes—[10]

Hows the book racket? How much longer are they going to let Galsworthy write those things[11]—or does he do it for a worthy charity!

Best to you always—

Ernest

PUL, ALS

Conjectured date is based on EH's mention of Pauline's sitting up for the first time, which EH had not mentioned previously and which he would note in the next letter, to Pauline's parents.

1 Perkins had cabled, "Mighty glad to get news about Pauline and boy stop Envious Congratulations" (12 November 1931, PUL). Perkins had five daughters.

2 In a letter of 29 October 1931, Perkins had asked EH for an estimate of the length of the new book (PUL).

3 In the same letter, Perkins wrote that insurance for the artwork would be expensive and suggested insuring only the frontispiece, a reference to Juan Gris's *Le Torero*, which EH had purchased earlier that year and brought back with him from Europe in September.

4 *Reglamento*: Spanish legal code governing the bullfight, adopted in 1923, revised and applied in 1924, gradually modified by a series of addenda. EH intended to include a translation of it in *DIA*, but by the time of publication knew that a new edition would be published soon, so he decided against it, as he explains in the glossary of *DIA* (s.v. *Reglamento*).

5 EH owned two oil paintings (*Toros* and *Suerte de Varas*) and two gouaches by Roberto Domingo Fallola (1883–1956), a Spanish painter whose depictions of bullfighting were often reproduced on posters. EH met Domingo in the 1920s and probably acquired these works, as well as signed photos of several other Domingo works, when he visited the painter's studio in Madrid. EH's large Domingo oil, *Toros* (1923), would be reproduced on the dust jacket of *DIA*.

6 Beginning with the January 1932 issue, *Scribner's Magazine* would appear in a new format, with fewer but larger pages (about an inch longer and wider) and a greater focus on "free discussion" about "American civilization and new forces to direct its course" while continuing to publish fiction ("An Editorial Announcement," 1).

7 French Premier Pierre Jean Marie Laval (1883–1945) and President Hoover met in Washington, D.C., 22–25 October 1931, to discuss disarmament, the gold standard, the possibility of extending the moratorium on France's war debts and Germany's reparation payments, and other financial issues. Laval and Hoover agreed to preserve the gold standard, which Great Britain had abandoned, but were unable to establish firm policies in other areas.

8 The National Committee for the Defense of Political Prisoners (NCDPP), founded in June 1931 and sponsored by the American Communist Party, was chaired by Theodore Dreiser. On 5 November 1931, Dreiser, Dos Passos, and other committee members traveled to Harlan County, Kentucky, to investigate the conditions in coalmining camps where workers were on strike. On 16 November they were indicted on charges of violating Kentucky's criminal syndicalism law, which carried maximum penalties of imprisonment of twenty-one years and $10,000 fines. In conjunction with further

interviews conducted in February 1932, the group's findings would be published as *Harlan Miners Speak: Report on Terrorism in the Kentucky Coal Fields* (1932). The criminal charges would be dropped in March 1933.

9 Émile-Édouard-Charles-Antoine Zola (1840–1902), French novelist and political activist whose 1885 novel *Germinal* portrayed a community of miners who strike in protest over reduced wages. Zola's 1898 open letter "J'accuse!" denounced the French Army and defended Jewish French Army officer Alfred Dreyfus, who had been wrongfully convicted of treason in 1894. *L'homme politique—il ne manque que ça*: the politician—that's all that's missing (French).

10 In a letter of 18 September 1931, Paul Pfeiffer wrote to EH and Pauline that Piggott was enjoying a strong cotton harvest but that the price had fallen to 6 cents per pound, "the lowest price in thirty years" (PUL).

11 John Galsworthy's popular Forsyte Chronicles was a series of novels alternating with short stories or "interludes," chronicling the lives of a large English upper-middle-class family, starting with *The Man of Property* (1906) and most recently including *On Forsyte 'Change* (1930) and *Maid in Waiting* (1931). The final two novels would appear in 1932 (the year he would win the Nobel Prize) and 1933. Scribner's had begun publishing Galsworthy's work in 1910; his English publisher was Heinemann.

To Paul and Mary Pfeiffer, [22 November 1931]

Sunday 10. a.m
Riviera Apts.
229 Ward Parkway
K.C. Mo

Dear Family:—

Pauline is fine; can sit up, wound well healed; most stitches out; no pain. Can laugh without danger. Had to be careful first few days not to make her laugh. We are going to eat wild ducks today that I shot down on Mo. river a little way out from here the other morning early.

The baby is a fine kid—very well behaved—gained back all the weight he lost first few days.

Book has been going wonderfully well— am Batching here with the radio and a little prescription whiskey— Have prescriptions for Pauline— Greg and myself in rotation as needed.

Dont believe we will need Gabrielle up here to get away— Will pick her and Pat up on same train at Jonesboro about Dec 11–10 or 12— Everything is packed here— Pauline will come out of hospital three or four days before we leave and rest here at Apartment— (There is elevator etc.) with me.

Will leave Greg at hospital with the nurse until we go— Take him from hospital to train—

If Jin wants to come up to see Pauline—who'd love to see her—and they could talk over the house etc— Maybe she could leave Piggott Thankgiving night and get here Friday morning— She and I could come back to Jonesboro-Piggott leaving here Sunday night—or Monday— You might write Karl to come for shooting whenever he wanted that week—week Dec 1–7— I'll stay that week out— We might all go down to Stuttgart toward the end of the week and shoot some ducks—[1]

Pauline is really in grand shape— We feel very badly that Aunt Kate is laid up and Mother has such a sad trip to make—[2]

Ink run out and no knife to sharpen this pencil— Regular Hoover management—

So will close—

Love to all—

Ernest

PUL, ALS; postmark: KANSAS CITY / MO., NOV23 / 2[30] PM / 1931

The envelope bears the printed return address: Research Hospital / TWENTY THIRD AND HOLMES STREET / KANSAS CITY, MISSOURI.

1 Stuttgart, Arkansas: approximately 160 miles southwest of Piggott. The area's rice farms attracted large numbers of migratory ducks.
2 Pauline's maternal aunt, Katherine Louise Downey (1862–1938), who married Charles A. Coffin (1857–1936) in 1891.

To Maurice Speiser, [23 November 1931]

Riviera Apartments
229 Ward Parkway
K.C. Mo.

Dear Moe:—

Thank you very much for the damned fine Scotch and the old Shenley— and the picture—[1] It is a damned nice picture and you were both very sweet to us to send it— Thank you again very much.

My cousins have gone out to the coast—am batching it here with the
Ushers Striped product and Prescription Bourbon but can drink a pint of
that any time before ~~meals~~ supper.

Pauline is in wonderful shape—no pain now—wound healed beautifully—
Baby is damned good—looks more like Bumby than Patrick—same build and
pan—but very black hair—forehead like Paulines— The old man's lobeless
ears—

Pauline took a regular Joe Grimm beating—more than you can imagine
but got a break on no gas pains nor anything afterwards— She feels
splendidly now—

This book is getting pretty damned good— You will like it I think—

Will be all through and in Scribners hands before Xmas—

Then the play—or what?

Have a radio up here but no matter where you turn the bastard it plays
Alice Blue Gown—[2]

It's Sunday morning and have to go to church and down to the hospital—

Best to you and Martha— Forgive me not writing sooner— Have been
working every day until my damned eyes would poop out on this book—
Then too shot to write a letter—

Thank you again for the liquor and the picture—

Yours always—

Ernest

Did you see where they gave that squirt Monk Saunders a prize in
Hollywood for Best original story when he was being sued for plagiarizing
it—[3] Next they'll give him the Pulitzer Prize for the Last Flight— When I am
going as good as I am now I can afford to let the chizelers steal even my
B.V.D's—[4] Plenty of Juice in the old Factory—

We go to Key West for Christmas or a little before—until May—
Delighted to see you!

USCar, ALS; postmark: KANSAS CITY / MO., NOV23 / 230PM / 1931

1 To celebrate the birth of Gregory Hemingway, Speiser had sent EH a bottle of Usher's
Green Stripe Scotch, a bottle of Schenley bourbon, and a painting by American modernist
Morton Livingston Schamberg (1881–1918), who had died in the influenza pandemic.

2 This waltz, originally sung by soprano Edith Day (1896–1971), was a hit song from the musical comedy *Irene*, written by James Montgomery (1878–1966) with music by Harry Tierney (1890–1965) and lyrics by Joseph McCarthy (1885–1943). *Irene* opened on Broadway on 18 November 1919 and ran for eighteen seasons. Day's orchestra-backed rendition of "Alice Blue Gown" was recorded by RCA Victor in 1920, and the song was quickly assimilated into the repertoire of contemporary dance bands.

3 On 10 November 1931, at the Fourth Academy Awards honoring movies released between 1 August 1930 and 31 July 1931, Saunders won the Oscar for Writing (Original Story) for *The Dawn Patrol* (1930). When the movie came out, its director, Howard Hawks, was sued by Howard Hughes for plagiarizing from Hughes's film *Hell's Angels* (1930). The suit was dropped.

4 B.V.D.s: Slang for men's underwear; derived from the trademark name of Bradley, Voorhees, and Day, the company that began manufacturing the popular brand in the 1870s.

To Paul and Mary Pfeiffer, 25 November 1931

11–25 [19]31
PAUL M. PFEiFFERS
PiggOTT
ARKANSAS
BEST THANKSGiViNg LOVE DELigHTED
JiNNY COMiNg TELL HER BRiNg HER SHOTGUN AND WiRE TiME
ARRiVAL EVERYTHiNg SPLENDiD HERE
PAULiNE and ERNEST
    Ernest Hemingway— Research Hospital—

UT, ACDS; letterhead: WESTERN UNION

In the transciptions of this handwritten cable draft and the two that follow in this volume, EH's mixture of capital and lower case letters has been preserved.

To Paul and Mary Pfeiffer, 30 November 1931

11–30 [19]31
PaUL PFEiFFERS
PiggOTT
ARKANSAS

ARRiViNg BUS TUESDAY MORNiNg
ALL FiNE HERE ERNEST JiNNY
    Ernest Hemingway Research Hospital

UT, ACDS; letterhead: WESTERN UNION

To Karl Pfeiffer, [c. late November 1931]

KARL PFEiFFER
249 HeYWOOD AVENUE
ORANGE NeWJERSEY
REgRET CANT CHANgE DATES SiNCE LEAViNG KANSAS CiTY FOR
KEYWEST DECEMBER ELEVENTH BUT CAN SHOOT WiTH YOU
PiggOTT SEVENTH AND EiGHTH UNLESS ThAT MEANS MiSSINg
UNCLE GUS iN KANSAS CiTY STOP HAD pLANNED BE KANSAS
CiTY EihHTh WHEN PAULINE LEAVES HOSPiTAL ERNEST
    Ernest Hemingway—Research Hospital—

UT, ACDS; letterhead: WESTERN UNION

To Jonathan Cape, [c. 3–4 December 1931]

Address Key West
Florida
until May—

My Dear Cape:—

    I was sorry to miss you in Paris— And that your letter should have gone to Paris and back so this may miss you in N.Y.—

    About the book— It is for next fall but I hope to have a completed Mss with Scribners by the first of the year— Have finished all but some detail in an appendix— If we make a satisfactory agreement wouldnt you rather have corrected galleys than Mss. since they will be in your hands in plenty of time and since they will save us both trouble and expense on correcting Galleys after it has been set from Mss—

About making the illustrations— I will mark on the galleys where they are to go— If Max Perkins cant get the proper plates made in N.Y. perhaps you and he can get together on them— The format will be something about the size of the T. E. Lawrence Book—[1]
The Illustrations I have are 9¼ × 7 inches and I want them without borders—with the explanation or caption to be ~~opposite~~ on the opposite page like this

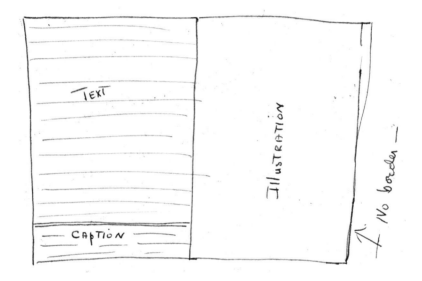

This was the way the paintings etc were reproduced in Men of Art by Thomas Craven—[2] except his captions were on the back— Having the captions on flimsy paper is very ineffective— In the way I have indicated the captions come just opposite the text and they will be marked as inserts on the Galleys— Then when page proofs are made up they will be put in their proper place— Some will be a good deal longer than others—

Max might be able to save money by having the plates for the illustrations made in England— At any rate you might discuss that— It is none of my businessess—

With best regards to yourself and to Mrs. Cape—

Yours always

Ernest Hemingway—

URead, ALS

1 In his letter to EH of 10 November 1931, Cape mentioned the English edition of *Revolt in the Desert* (London: Jonathan Cape, 1927) by English military officer, archeologist, and writer Thomas Edward (T. E.) Lawrence (1888–1935), known as Lawrence of Arabia. Cape had suggested that the format of that book might be appropriate for EH's bullfighting book (URead). The English edition of Lawrence's book featured nineteen plates, some in color, and a folding map.

2 *Men of Art* (New York: Simon & Schuster, 1931), by American art critic and historian Thomas Craven (1888–1969).

To Archibald MacLeish, 9 December [1931]

Dec 9

Riviera Apartments

229 Ward Parkway

K.C.

Mo.

Dear Archie:—

I'm so glad the poem is finished. Max wrote me to tell me how great he thought it was and how you thought you might have to stay with H.M. He wrote me in great detail putting me on my honor not to write you as he felt you must make your own decision—[1] I was pretty sore at being put on my honor about something I <u>would</u> have advised about but as the Spinnish admiral said when the fleet was sunk—<u>mas vale honor sin buques que buques sin honor</u>"— And I suppose you can call buques books as well as warships—[2] Had he told me by word of mouth would have refused to accept the honor racket— Anyway I went to Piggott for a week—great shooting every day—and am back and find your letter and Maxs that you decided to stay with H.M. so that lets me out of the honor racket (it being decided) and can tell you he said the Poem was one of the grandest he'd ever read and that it made publishing books seem worth doing and that he wanted to publish it more than any thing in the world.[3]

I'd have been glad to pay Mssers Houghtons and Mifflins fees myself and would have considered it money well invested—

Anyway as the other, military this time, authority said never discuss casualties—and the publisher is the smallest part of writing—except Max is so white to deal with and I had promised you to him as a great gift to make up for how tough I've been with him very often—

You are a great poet—having become one slowly, gradually and as solid as the earth—and it makes no damned difference who publishes you except in the pleasantness or unpleasantness of your relations—

Pauline had a lovely letter from Ada— Glad you have a fine place to live—[4]

You're going to come to K.W pretty soon for a while arent you? Jinny is there opening up now before she goes over to ski in January—with luck we should get there a week before Christmas—

This book is done except for about 20,000 words of translation from Spanish in an appendix I think I can dictate and then correct— That is just hack work and think am justified in dictating—

Believe made the god damned miracle we have to always make happen at the end happen again—although may disillusion on it when see it in type— But if anything should happen to me it would be all right to publish as it is— and doesnt need illustrations— The boys get those free—

Sorry about Geralds father— The trouble for him and the freezing— I never liked him—always thought him plenty mean and I hate an after dinner speaker—[5] Gerald maybe didnt love him much either— If he gets spooked about death that (having hated him) will make him feel worse— The Irish pay for their charm in many ways—

Faulkner is a smart fellow to read you and me and live in Mississippi—the combination should get him a long way— Fortunately he's read Mr. Joyce and Mr Doestoevsky and lived in Mississippi with them too— An advantage

the Messers Joyce and Dusty never enjoyed— Joyce has read everything—
What did Dostoevsky read? What did Shakespeare read? You tell us, Mac—
    Mike [Strater] is at 115 East 86th—

    About the enclosed—was delayed getting it because of working so hard—
Pauline is hospital etc. With it you can open box and get me out some
money if I need some which may be pretty soon— If not too much trouble—
Bank moratorium successfully postponed but possible again whenever next
german crisis comes— or has prosperity returned—[6] He asks you—

    Well you must feel pretty good with your poem done and your two fine
sons and a beautiful daughter and your wife Ada and if you dont come to
Key West pretty soon your a lousy bastard— you have to learn to shoot for
one thing— Did you see where the lion killed the citizen?[7] Do you want to
be killed and eaten by wild beasts or do you want to be able to address the
waiter in French—

    Give Ada our love— Pauline will be writing— Ada sent a swell present to
Greg—also my underwear—very welcome underwear—

Pappy—

    Best to Dotty [Dorothy Parker] when you see her—

    The fact H.M. have allowed your books to go out of print would be reason
enough to leave— They could not hold you— I have ordered New Found
Land 3 times—always out of print— No edition obtainable—[8] If you are
staying with them give the bastards hell. They sell all they print of you—

LOC, ALS

1 In his letter to EH of 25 November 1931, Perkins called MacLeish's *Conquistador* "a
   magnificent poem" (PUL). Although interested in publishing it, Perkins wrote that the
   matter was complicated by MacLeish's friendship with his editor at Houghton Mifflin,
   Robert Linscott (1886–1964), and that Houghton Mifflin was "putting up a terrible fight" to
   keep MacLeish.
2 *Más vale honra sin buques que buques sin honra*: Better to have honor without ships than
   ships without honor (Spanish). The phrase is attributed to Casto Méndez Núñez
   (1824–1869), admiral of the Spanish Armada, who in 1866, in defiance of massive local,
   British, and American armed opposition, attacked several South American cities as part of
   Spain's attempt to retain its colonies.
3 Perkins reported to EH in a letter of 30 November 1931 that MacLeish could not bring
   himself to break away from Houghton Mifflin "and I could not bring myself to try to force
   him to do it" (PUL). MacLeish's letter informing EH of his decision remains unlocated.

4 Ada MacLeish's letter remains unlocated. Archibald MacLeish's work for *Fortune* magazine required him to be in New York, where he rented a small apartment at 182 Sullivan Street in Greenwich Village. Owing to the family's straitened circumstances, Ada and the children alternated between their home in Conway, Massachusetts, and Ada's father's house in Farmington, Connecticut.

5 Patrick Francis Murphy (1858–1931), owner of the Mark Cross Company, which produced luxury leather goods, was a well-known after-dinner speaker. Refusing to wear overcoats, he had caught a chill, developed pneumonia, and died on 23 November 1931.

6 The Hoover Moratorium, proposed by President Hoover in June 1931 but not approved by Congress until December 1931, offered Germany a one-year suspension of its debts and an easier schedule for subsequent payments in an attempt to ease the failing German economy and prevent the collapse of Germany's banking system.

7 American construction magnate and hunter William Henry Herren (1885–1931) was killed by a lion on 25 October while on safari in East Africa. Herren's hunting companions filmed the attack.

8 Houghton Mifflin had published *New Found Land* in an edition of only 500 copies, followed by a limited edition of 135 copies.

To Maxwell Perkins, 9 December [1931]

Dec 9

Dear Max:—

After I finished the book went down to Piggott for a week—back yesterday—intended to write you there but got up at seven every morning and hunted quail until dark—one drink—Supper—bed—out again with the dog— Best quail shooting ever— The way it was when I was a boy—country lovely in the fall—

When I got back there was your letter about Archie gone to H.M. and one from him about how bad he felt at being forced to do it— I've just written him how you wrote me and put me on my honor not to write him what you'd written telling him about it now that there's no longer any need not to—

Your point of honor in not wanting me to write him made me feel badly because I could have out-urged Linscott and it is silly to stay with H.M. after what happened— But couldnt write him after the way you put it— Well I dont have much luck getting you writers do I? On the other hand how many good writers are there? At least I've never gotten you any punks nor flashes in the pan nor imitators— No need to get any more second string Hemingsteins because I am going awfully damned good—

When we get to Key West—the 15th or 16th unless present possible complications hold us up—which god forbid—I'll get the bulk of the book re-typed and send it to you—following with the appendixes as ready— If it's to be out in Early fall we might run some pieces at irregular intervals—will talk about that later—

Cape wrote something about having the illustration plates made in England—[1] nothing Jonathan and I have ever done together turned out right so am suspicious—on other hand plates might be made economically and well in England with falling pound— But the financial end of that is your hard luck to figure out—

I feel damned bad about Archie—

About the story—will think it over— I always remember the 750 they paid Anderson for that lousy story—and the 250 I got offered for Fifty Grand if I'd get 1500 words out of it—[2] Still as you say— Times are hard— but they dont feel hard to me when I have been going as well as I have gone on the last three Chapters of that book— Christ— When you can write well and get it as you want it nothing seems important and when you cant—silly things seem so bloody important— All I want now is to get the bloody thing out of my way so I can go on—

Thanks for the royalty money—and for the Winston Churchill book— Good old Winston— What a place he would have in history if he were an honest man or if he'd had luck at the Dardanelles—[3]

Max Eastmans book is pretentious rubbish—cheap whoreing articles for the magazines pooping on the things he does not understand—my what a disappointed mans book it is—[4] The humorless writer on humor—the poet who had only the looks and couldnt write the poetry—the virgins dream of how a writer should be—the fondler of the arts and unable to fornicate with them—the respectable radical—the revolutionary who never missed a meal—once the friend of every man and holds no mans respect— What shit what shit the boys write and get it published— What about Joseph Wood Krutch[5] or Gorham B. Munson[6] those other two impotent nose pickers of the arts— Cant we get more books by them?

No news from Scott except an alcoholic telegram urging me to take some local Hollywood chizeller as my agent— What the devil is he doing out there? I thought he was going to Alabama to work— Write me what you hear— What about Zelda?—[7]

That is tough about the retroactive tax—[8]

I'm so damned sorry you have had such a hell of a year of it—[9]

Best to you always—

Ernest

PUL, ALS

1 In his 10 November 1931 letter, Jonathan Cape suggested to EH that the plates for *DIA* could be made in England (URead).

2 In a letter of 25 November 1931, Perkins wrote, "we always want your stories" but explained that Scribner's could only offer $500 per story (PUL). In 1926 former *Scribner's Magazine* editor Robert Bridges paid Sherwood Anderson $750 for his story "Another Wife," which later appeared in the December 1929 issue of the magazine. In 1926, EH had refused Perkins's offer of $250 for a shortened version of "Fifty Grand" (*Letters* vol. 3, 31 n. 7).

3 *A Roving Commission: My Early Life* (London: Butterworth; New York: Scribner's, 1930), the autobiography of English statesman Winston Churchill (1874–1965), spanning the years from his birth to his early years in Parliament, which he first joined in 1900. As First Lord of the Admiralty, Churchill believed that control of the Dardanelles was essential to an Allied victory in WWI. Under his lead, repeated military attempts between February 1915 and January 1916 to control the Dardanelles were thwarted in one of the war's most significant campaign defeats. Churchill was demoted and would remain associated with this loss for the remainder of his life.

4 Max Forrester Eastman (1883–1969), American poet, critic, magazine writer, and editor of leftist journals including the *Masses* (1912–1917) and the *Liberator* (1918–1924). In *The Literary Mind: Its Place in an Age of Science* (New York: Scribner's, 1931), Eastman argued that the precision of measurement and evidence offered by the physical, natural, and social sciences were diminishing the status of the vague, subjective arguments offered by writers and literary critics.

5 Joseph Wood Krutch (1893–1970), American teacher; political and cultural commentator; and editor, drama critic, and book reviewer for the *Nation* (1924 to 1952). In his bestseller *The Modern Temper: A Study and a Confession* (1929), Krutch argued that although science had displaced the beauty and optimism offered by poetry and myth, it could not offer a satisfactory alternative. His recent books included *Five Masters: A Study of the Mutation of the Novel* (1930) and *Living Philosophies* (1931).

6 Gorham B. Munson (1896–1969), American teacher of writing, literary critic, and editor. In *Style and Form in American Prose* (1929) and *The Dilemma of the Liberated: An Interpretation of Twentieth Century Humanism* (1930), he argued that the rejection of the New Humanism was an international philosophical tendency.

7 Fitzgerald's telegram remains unlocated. Early in November 1931, Fitzgerald had gone to Hollywood to work on a film adaptation of the 1931 novel *Red-Headed Woman* by Katherine Bush, but his screenplay would be rejected. By late December he had rejoined Zelda in Montgomery, Alabama, where the Fitzgeralds had gone after she was released from the hospital in Switzerland.

8 A new tax program recommended by the U.S. Treasury to balance the budget and to maintain the credit of the country would be adopted early in January 1932 but would not be made retroactive to 1931.

9 In a letter of 30 November 1931, Perkins wrote, "Everything is pretty bad around here, including even the weather" (PUL). In addition to Depression-related business worries, Perkins had lost his beloved brother-in-law Archibald Cox (b. 1874) in March 1931 and was concerned about the health of his daughter Bertha and of his wife, Louise.

To Paul Romaine, 9 December [1931]

Dec. 9

Rivera Apartments

229 Ward Parkway

KC.

Mo.

Dear Mr. Romaine:—

I cannot recall the poem in question so cant consent— But if you will mail me a copy of it air mail to this address will wire you yes or no after reading it—provided of course if it is reprinted that mention is made of its place and date of publication— If it is too lousy I will wire no and you will understand my motives—[1]

With best wishes—

Ernest Hemingway

USCar, ALS; postmark: KANSAS CITY / MO., DEC 9 / 10 PM / 1931

1 In his 11 December 1931 reply, Romaine would offer to send a copy of EH's four-line poem, "Ultimately," which had appeared in the June 1922 issue of the New Orleans literary magazine *Double Dealer* on the same page as William Faulkner's poem "Portrait" (JFK). EH's poem would be reprinted on the back cover of Faulkner's *Salmagundi* (Milwaukee: The Casanova Press, 1932), which Romaine published in a limited edition of 525 copies.

To Israel Bram, 9 December [1931]

Kansas City—Mo
Dec 9

Dear Dr. Bram—

Answering your questions in order

(1) – 9 hours for maximum—

2 – Dont know

3 – Worry causes me sleeplessness—also lack of exercise—overcome by stopping worry and taking exercise—

4 – Never work at night because of difficulty of getting to sleep afterwards— Coffee keeps awake if strong—wine and beer make sleep well — Drink light red wine or beer with supper— Brandy keeps me awake— rarely drink after eating at night except continuing beer and wine drunk with meal—

5 – Dream every night—all sorts—very enjoyable and detailed— occassional nightmares—

6 – Dont know—varied—

7 – Enjoy sleep and dreams very much— Have gone with very little sleep for long periods due pain of wounds, infections, broken bones etc—very hard on nerves— Have often heard clock strike every hour and half hour from midnight to daylight—would like to sleep 9 hrs. every night—

Yours very truly
Ernest Hemingway.

CPP, ALS

Bram, who was medical director of the Bram Goiter Institute of Upland, Pennsylvania, had sent a one-page letter to a number of persons listed in *Who's Who in America* in order to gather data for a study of the relationship between sleep and the endocrine and nervous systems (copies survive at the Library of the College of Physicians of Philadelphia). Bram had asked these questions:

1. How many hours do you find it necessary to devote to sound sleep in order to enjoy maximum physical and mental efficiency?
2. In your opinion, how much sleep should the average man and woman take in order to enjoy the maximum of health and efficiency?
3. Do you have any difficulty in falling asleep? If so, what is the probable cause and what measures, if any, do you employ to overcome it?

4. What effect, if any, do tea, coffee, or other beverages, food, and physical and mental activity, close to bedtime, have upon your sleep?
5. Are you subject to dreams? If so, will you comment upon them?
6. What effect, if any, do the events of the day have upon your sleep or dreams?
7. What comments, personal or abstract, would you make on sleep and dreams?

To Mr. Turner, 9 December [1931]

Kansas City—

Dec 9

Dear Mr. Turner:—

Thank you very much for your letter.[1] I am glad you liked the books and am sorry that I have no photo. Charles Scribners Sons publish the other books you mention—also one called The Torrents of Spring—you might like them—but no one can tell!—

With best wishes—

Yours very truly

Ernest Hemingway—

PUL, ALS

1 The letter to which EH is responding has not been located. EH's handwriting is unclear; the recipient's name could be "Tuner."

To Ray Long, [c. 9 December 1931]

[*Excerpt as quoted in book*:]

Have you done any shooting this fall? I've just had a week of quail in Arkansas, after finishing my book. If I could write as well as I can shoot sometimes—boy! what literature we'd have. One double in thick brush—followed them out of a cornfield—the one ahead and to the left, the other all the way back and over my <u>right</u> shoulder, shooting the gun with no chance to get it to the shoulder, and swinging it as you would swing a pitchfork. Boy!

From Ray Long, ed., *20 Best Short Stories in Ray Long's 20 Years as an Editor*
(New York: Ray Long & Richard R. Smith, 1932), 3, Published excerpt of letter

This section of EH's letter is quoted by Ray Long in "Why Editors Go Wrong," his introduction to *20 Best Short Stories in Ray Long's 20 Years as an Editor*, which included EH's "Fifty
Grand." EH's original letter has not been located. The conjectured letter date is based on EH's
reference to hunting quail in Arkansas.

To Henry Strater, 10 December [1931]

> Riviera Apartments
> 229 Ward Parkway
> KC. Mo.
> Dec 10—

Dear Mike:—

Glad you had such a fine trip and I hope Maggie is all right so you can get
down to K.W. soon. If everything goes well here we should be there a week
or 10 days before Xmas—

Finished my book except some hack work on the Appendix— Think
you'll like it— Will get it copied in K.W. and send to Max—will have a copy
for you to read—

Greg weighs 10½ lbs at a month—no fat—all build—solemn bastard—

Have just been to Piggott shooting quail for a week—swell
shooting—killed 3 straight three times—four straight once—the four in
the woods—followed them in out of a corn field—got a double in thick
brush—briars and hanging vines from the trees— First one went straight
away—couldn't see him fall—turned and swung with second over <u>right</u>
shoulder—swinging the gun like a pitchfork—butt down opposite my
belly— Dog brought in the first one while I was picking up the second—
Paulines brother for a witness—both shots the brush too thick to get the gun
to the shoulder even for a snap— Damn but they are fun to shoot— Coveys
bother me—believe you kill more birds if you only kill one out of a covey—
mark him and then mark down all the others— If you shoot more than
twice at a covey in high corn or any sort of cover you cant see where
they go—

We must hunt there together some fall— You could hunt a new place every day for two months— Lots of peas and beans in the corn for feed— Two years of drought been hard on birds—on account of that I never shot over the limit—12—one day found 7 big coveys—could have killed plenty— Shot my 16 ga Browning—

Listen what did you suffer so getting the buck out for? Why not butcher where you kill—hang up meat and pack out what you can take— That's what we do— Bring in head and scalp and liver and go back for the rest— Why carry a whole buck around? a good bull elk will weigh 1200 lbs. How would you like to tote him to camp?

What about a Spring bear hunt in first two weeks of June out at Lawrence's? Bears grow swell hides all winter—come out and shit that plug out and then are fine to hunt— You could try your big gun— Hall Smith[1] has loaned me a 10.5 Mauser that he claims is great Buffalo gun—he killed elephants with it but says it is a little small for that—

Duck season here—30 days—they guessed wrong—it was all over before we got any cold weather—killed 3 one time—8 another— Day after it closed came the first cold and ducks flying all day and all night—lots of geese—

Uncle Gus is back from buying furniture for their new apartment at 770 Park—[2] They are moved in there— Why dont you go to see him?

Archie is down on Sullivan Street— Get him through time—[3]

Caesars form of childbirth dangerous, expensive and difficult— Tough on Pauline to have to go through that every time—

Have been shooting live pigeons out here— Shoot from 30 yards—pigeon spring from one of 5 traps 12 yards apart on a line— Fly like hell—you have to hit them ~~with~~ always shoot both barrells and kill them before they get outside distance—will send you copy of rules— Big shoot here $120 entrance—$2500 sweep— Dec 12–13—

Best I've shot is 21 × 25— Dead inside enclosure—other four I killed one coming on too late so it fell at my feet and three flew on with shot and went down outside— I average about 20 × 30—

Took Jinny out to try them— She killed 3 quail one day when we hunted but missed 30 live blue rocks[4] straight—from 27 yards— The lead is 6 to 12

feet on the ones that go off fast to either side— Only 3 states where you still
have it—Penn— Ky. and Mo. Going out this afternoon—

   Well hope Maggie is fine and that we'll see you soon!

Best always—

Hem

PUL, ALS

1 Walton Hall Smith (1898–1955), boxing and hunting acquaintance whom EH had met in
  Kansas City, probably in the early 1920s (*Letters* vol. 3, 465).
2 Gus and Louise Pfeiffer's apartment at 770 Park Avenue in New York City, one of several
  luxurious residential buildings designed by Sicilian-born American architect Rosario
  Candela (1890–1953) and built between 1929 and 1931.
3 *Time* magazine, like *Fortune*, was a Henry Luce publication. MacLeish had served as
  education editor for *Time* in 1923.
4 Blue Rock pigeons, traditionally considered the most desirable type for live bird trapshooting.

To Guy Hickok, 12 December [1931]

Dec 12

Address

Key West

Dear Guy:—

   Well here we are leaving Kansas City and the whole racket over and you
not yet written to. But we did send you a wire to the Eagle when you were
supposed to be over with Laval and the Eagle answered almost instantly
Hickock did not accompany laval.[1] So I thought what the hell it's not worth
writing to a guy who didnt even accompany Laval and plunged back ijto the
joys of obstetricity. It certainly [w]ould have been a break for an old surgical
fan like you to have seen Pauline opened up like a picadors horse but it wasnt
worth a nickel to me because I have written that story two or three times
already. Anyway the baby is named Gregory Hancock after any number of
bad popes and my grandmothers family. Is built like the late Battling Siki—
all shoulders—length and legs—long arms—big feet—weighed 9 lbs when
born—or removed rather—and now weighs 10 and 10 ounces four weeks
after and isn't fat. Pauline is fine and sends her love to Mary and you. She

had a hell of a time before they decided on a caeserian as the dr. wanted to make sure normal delivery was impossible but a good time afterwards.
No gas pains and suffered practically not at all. Today is the 12th
of December and day after tomorrow we leave for Key West picking up Gabrielle, french speaking-English speaking 210lb Parigotte who expertizes in care of children, veterinary surgery, cooking and brewing and who has her 2nd papers so you won't have to get her in and out of the country,[2]
and Patrick at Jonesboro at 6.20 a.m. Reports from Piggott on Gabrielle is that she is a glutton for work and a good cook. We picked her u[p] in N.Y. and left her in Piggott when we came to N.Y. My bloody book is finished except for[3]

This Dr. Logan Clendenning that lives out here is a hell of a fine guy. You would like him.[4]

Most Drug Store prescription whiskey is phoney the druggists cutting it with grain alcohol and distilled water. Only two good brands I've drunk are Briargate and Golden Wedding.[5] Well what else do you want to know?

Saw old Haskell.[6] He spoke very highly of you. I of course told him you were the best newspaper man in Europe. Alsways use that one whenever you or Paul Mowrer are mentioned. Do something for me sometime.
The star is probably making the most money of any paper in the country. No morning opposition at all. Their morning paper carried 16 full pages ads beside six pages classifides. They have their payments set aside for 6 years ahead already on buying the paperand are all dragging down plenty. Roy Roberts not so happy as managing editor. Dislikes respectability of sheet and misses Washington.[7] He's a good fellow.

Well Gros maybe better knock off now— Pauline sends her best love—
I'm sorry didn't write sooner. Have never been working harder and then would go to hospital and then eyes too pooped to write. Wearing glasses to read and write but eyes get damned pooped. Need a long layoff. Well so long Guy

Ernest

Haven't heard Frank on the radio— He was innocuous on the boat. Very mysterious about his job and very pleased with piece in Time about him that came out while we were on the boat.[8] Tell Mary we had a wonderful trip and were treated fine. When we got off she can tell the French line that I had a column in all the papers from the shipnews and that at the end of the column it said also aboard were Grand Duchess Marie of Russia and Grace Moore.[9] Tell her that so they won't think they were gypped. She better tell them because having had a taste of that boat would like to cross cheap again!

phPUL, TLS

1 In a letter to EH of 28 September 1931, Hickok had written that he might be in New York around 18 October if he were assigned to cover French Premier Pierre Laval, who was scheduled to meet with President Hoover on 22–25 October 1931 (PUL). EH's wire to the Brooklyn *Eagle* remains unlocated.
2 *Parigote*: Parisienne (colloquial French). The Basic Naturalization Act of 1906 stipulated two primary steps: a declaration of intent to naturalize (first papers), which could be filed after the applicant had lived in the United States for two years, and a petition for citizenship (second papers) after five years' residency.
3 The first page of the letter ends here. The unfinished sentence may have continued on a page that is now missing.
4 Logan Clendening (1884–1945), well-known Kansas City physician, professor of medicine at the University of Kansas, syndicated columnist, and author of the bestseller *The Human Body* (1927) and *The Care and Feeding of Adults, With Doubts About Children* (1931).
5 Old Briargate Kentucky Straight Bourbon and Golden Wedding whiskey, also known as Finch's Golden Wedding. During Prohibition such alcoholic products carried the label "For Medicinal Purpose Only / Sale or Use for Other Purpose Will Cause Heavy Penalties To Be Inflicted."
6 Henry Joseph Haskell (1874–1952), chief editorial writer of the *Kansas City Star* who had hired EH as a reporter in 1917.
7 Roy Allison Roberts (1887–1967) had joined the *Kansas City Star* in 1909 and was assigned to the newspaper's Washington bureau before being named managing editor in 1928. He would be its president, editor, and general manager from the 1950s until he retired in 1963.
8 Frank Mason had become president of the International News Service in 1928 but in 1931 left the Hearst organization to become vice president of NBC, a position he would hold until 1945. The 14 September 1931 issue of *Time* ran a piece about Mason's resignation from the Hearst company. Mason and EH both sailed to New York City aboard the *Île de France*, EH boarding at Le Havre on 23 September and Mason at Plymouth, England, the next day.
9 After the Russian Revolution of 1917, Grand Duchess Maria Pavlovna Romanova (1890–1958) settled in Paris, where she opened an embroidery workshop that supplied the couture house of Chanel. Mary Willie Grace Moore (1898–1947), American Broadway performer, opera singer, and Hollywood star who brought opera to the movies. She starred in pictures such as *Lady's Morals* (1930) and *New Moon* (1931).

To Eric Knight, 13 December [1931]

229 Ward Parkway

K.C.

Mo.

Dec 13

Dear E.M.K.;

I think the story is <u>damned</u> good— and would have written you before if I hadnt gone down to Arkansas to shoot a week and celebrate the end of this book. Pauline liked it too very much.

I can send it with a letter to either Scribners or the Cosmopolitan— they are where I have most drag— Can guaranty nothing but that they will read it— But would be delighted to send it—[1]

Would you write me to Key West what to do about it— We are just leaving— Everything in a hell of a stew

Dont ever think you cant write!—

Yours always—

E.H.

USCar, ALS; postmark: KANSAS CITY / MO., DEC 14 / 8 PM / 1931

1 In his reply to EH of 28 December 1931, Knight would describe his unnamed story as "pretty soggy" and gratefully decline EH's offer to help find it a publisher (JFK).

To Grace Hall, Madelaine, and Leicester Hemingway, 20 December [1931]

Dec 20

Dear Mother, Sunny and ~~Caro~~ Les:—

Hope this letter reaches you by Christmas. Am sending it Special Delivery.

Carol should be here tomorrow. As soon as we were in K.C. wrote her telling her we expected her for Christmas and to Come as soon as school closed. She wrote she was going on a houseparty but would be down some of the time. Later houseparty was cancelled. We had written her again sending her money for trip a couple of [day]s before received your appeal to write her.[1]

Pauline was in plenty bad shape and me working 18 hrs or so a day on book until completed. That was why didnt write. Then you may recall joys of travelling with new born babies; nurses who get sick etc. In the midst of all this a man is supposed to write books.

Fine weather here—practically no mosquitoes— No northers yet this season— New house will be fine when fixed up—

These Christmas checks are small on account no money— Send me a list of your birthdays and will see what can do about them—[2]

Greg weighs 11 lbs 6 oz— Patrick very well— Pauline fine now— Bumby doing excellently in school— Hadley well— They probably going Switzerland for Christmas—

Weather has been very warm here—all November and December— Have a citizen typing on my book manuscript— Hope you all have a fine Chistmas

Best love from us all— And very merry Xmas—

Yours

Ernie

Pauline appreciated your letters and gifts to hospital very much— She was delayed answering by being not able to sit up to write.[3]

HSOPRF, ALS; postmark: KEY WEST / FLA., DEC22 / 11 AM / 1931

EH addressed the envelope to "Mrs. C. E. Hemingway / and Family / 600 N. Kenilworth Avenue / Oak Park / Illinois" and wrote on it "Special Delivery."

1 In a letter to EH dated 'Tuesday,' Carol wrote, "The house party was called off, and we have vacation from December 18th to January fourth, which probably sounds hellishly long to you" adding, "When do you want me down?" The letter is addressed "Dear Oinbones" and signed "love Beefy" (JFK). The letters to Carol that EH mentions here remain unlocated.
2 In her reply of 27 December 1931, Grace would write that EH's letter arrived Christmas morning and "All shouted for joy, at your generous checks." Sunny would use her money for travel, Leicester would buy a new suit, and Grace herself had already bought two new dresses with his gift. Her letter also included a list of family birthdays, including EH's and her own, noting she would turn sixty in June (JFK).
3 Pauline had previously written a letter to Sunny dated 10 December 1931, thanking her for "showering us with telegrams, letters, and presents" (IndU).

To Marcelline Hemingway Sanford, 20 December [1931]

Dec 20

Box 406

Key West—

Dear Marce:—

Merry Xmas to you and Sterling and all your outfit! You were very sweet to write Pauline in hospital and send presents and she would have answered if she could— But was on her back— She will write you and is very grateful. I should have written but was finishing book and between that and hospital no could do— Then the joys of travelling with new born child etc— You probably know them—

Hope every thing goes well with you— Splendid weather here— Greg weighs 11 lbs 6 oz—not fat just big— Pat well— Pauline now too— Carol expected here today or tomorrow—

Best to you and Sterling and <u>your children</u> from Pauline and me and all of us

Always

Ernie

James Sanford, ALS; postmark: KEY WEST / FLA., DEC 22 / 11 AM / 1931

EH marked the envelope "Special Delivery" and enclosed a check. In an undated reply, Marcelline would write, "Dear Ernie, The special, with its simply grand enclosure, arrived at 11 o'clock Christmas eve and was much appreciated" (Sanford, 339).

To Archibald MacLeish, 22 [December 1931]

NBF48 26 DL=KEY WEST FLO / 22 1120A

ARCHIBALD MACLEISH=

=205 EAST 42 ST=

ITS A VERY GREAT POEM AND YOU OUGHT TO FEEL PRETTY FINE[1] STOP WRITING STOP LOVE AND MERRY CHRISTMAS TO YOU AND ADA AND THE CHILDREN=

    PAPPY AND PAULINE.

LOC, Cable

1 With a letter to EH of 12 December 1931, Robert Linscott, MacLeish's editor at Houghton Mifflin, had enclosed a hand-corrected 97-page carbon typescript of *Conquistador* requesting a short blurb for its publicity. Linscott addressed the letter to EH in Kansas City and signed it "Honest Abe" (JFK).

To Archibald MacLeish, 23 December [1931]

Dec. 23

Box 406 Key West

Dear Archie,

Before the poem came I wrote you something like this—but then did not send it because I thought you might think I was preparing an alibi in case I didn't like the poem. I wrote there was probably no one who was fonder of you or believed more in your work than I do and for that reason it might be questionable policy to have a quotation from me to advertize it since my affection, loyalty and admiration for you being known some Kirstein, Galantiere, Wilson or other shit might take that opportunity to avoid facing the value of the poem by saying here was one friend writing about another.

Having seen these gentlemen perform in the past you can only expect worse than the worst from them.

I believe completely in the poem, in the NewFound Land in the Hamlet[1] and in you and I have said it very many times and would be happy to be identified in any way or glad to make any public statement of belief but the wisdom of having a blurb written by me does not seem ~~very~~ wholly wise. [*EH autograph marginal insertion*: Later— Believe two sent are O.K.][2] This is not John Brown's Body by Stephen St. Vixen Benet or Laughing Boy by Oliver Onions LaFarge[3] and Linscott's letter asking me "would you be willing to lead the cheering by giving a brief preliminary yip for the book which can be quoted in our advance publicity?

"I wouldn't ask this for anything except "Conquistador" and not even then unless you agree with me that it is so absolutely swell as to over-rule all ordinary considerations of policy or reticence. If you prefer not to be quoted, don't for Pete's sake, hesitate to say so. Otherwise something short and hot and <u>soon</u>. I do want to give Archie all the breaks."[4]

When we both have the English language in common wouldn't you think R.N.Linscott would not feel it necessary to write in a special language that he feels I will understand? Or don't you play contract Mr. MacLeish.

It is a wonderful poem, Archie. Who publishes or how many it sells or what the crickets write about it is of no importance. I don't know exactly what you want in writing but believe it is the same as I want, to be a great goddamned writer, always competeing therefore with the dead, not your bloody contemporaries, and knowing that the greatness will be in the writing and not in what people say about it. In so far as they praise you they will turn against you and the less they fawn on this poem the more they will have to pay for it later. You are going wonderfully and you ought to be damned happy and damned proud and go some more.

Do you think you would be any happier if you got the Pulitzer Prize? You are not responsible to anyone any more. What does Linscott want you to do? Make Good? Mr. MacLeish you are in the part now that is very lonesome and prizes don't help, they only complicate, and it didn't aid Mr. Valery to get in the academy[5] and I am very happy to have you for a friend because there are very few friends in this racket and if you say you are gladto have me for a friend I understand what you mean.

MR. Faulkner's best friend is his wheelbarrow.[6] Mr. Hemingways ~~best~~ only other friend is his faithful old wastebasket and his severest critic is alcohol. Mrs. Parkers best little pal is the unrealized sorrow of others. Mr. Stewrts best friends are the Whitneys but Mr. Stewart is not their best friend. A girls best friend is her mother and a bulls best friend is his balls. Set them up in the next alley men the master's not himself today.[7]

All right—now what about the blurb? It is you it will hurt—not me. I believe in the stuff and can praise it honestly. I happen to have no felicity for doing it— I don't mean facility—could overcome that by certain amount of work but you can't beat out felicity.

~~How about these—you can use any or all of them~~

~~He has the skill of Eliot without his sterility~~

[*EH autograph insertion*:

(Interval of work)

After writing all that now have two that I think solve the problem— Either one seems ~~good~~—OK.]

Enclosed are two ~~blurbs~~ you can send to Linscott—or send either one— believe they solve the problem of writing something which cannot be criticized on grounds of friendship— Hope they are all right. If not write me and will write something else. Think they are both all right. [*EH autograph insertion*: Truly—]

Must send this so you'll get it.

Merry Christmas to you all and much love from us. Wish you would come down as soon as you can.

Tell Linscott to excuse me not writing him direct as I am pretty occupied on book, new house, travelling with 5 week child, etc.

I truly think both these blurbs [*EH autograph insertion*: as written—] over-ride the objection there might be, ethically and tactically, for me writing about your book.

Pappy

You know how truly happy I am to write something about it— I only wanted to get the problem straight before trying to solve it—

[*Enclosures: two autograph blurbs in EH's hand, which MacLeish later forwarded to Houghton Mifflin editor Robert Linscott. The blurbs are housed at the University of Virginia Library.*]

[*On letterhead*: Carling Hotel / Jacksonville / Florida]

Because I am fond of him I do not want to write about his book since I do not believe in friends writing about each others work but even those who do not like him nor what he writes must see by now that he is a great poet.

Ernest Hemingway[8]

[*On separate half-sheet of paper, the top portion torn away*:]

No 2

"If it is of any interest to you to read great poetry as it is published before it becomes classic and compulsory I advise you to read Conquistador" and New Found Land—

Ernest Hemingway

LOC/UVA, TLS with autograph postscript and enclosures

1 *Conquistador* (forthcoming in March 1932), *New Found Land: Fourteen Poems* (1930), and *The Hamlet of A. MacLeish* (1928), all published by Houghton Mifflin.

2 EH enclosed the two blurbs with this letter.

3 EH puns on the names of two contemporary American writers: Stephen Vincent Benét (1898–1943), whose epic poem about the American Civil War, *John Brown's Body* (Garden City, New York: Doubleday, 1928), won the 1929 Pulitzer Prize for Poetry; and Oliver Hazard Perry La Farge (1901–1963), whose novel *Laughing Boy* (Boston: Houghton Mifflin, 1929) won the 1929 Pulitzer Prize for Fiction. *Conquistador* would earn MacLeish the Pulitzer Prize for Poetry in 1933.

4 EH quotes from the 12 December 1931 letter he received from Linscott (JFK).

5 Paul Valéry was elected to the Académie Française in 1925 without having been awarded France's prestigious Prix Goncourt and prior to receiving a number of later Nobel Prize nominations.

6 Faulkner claimed that during his nightshift in a heating plant he turned over the wheelbarrow in which he transported coal and used it as a table on which he wrote *As I Lay Dying* (1930) in six weeks.

7 "Set 'em Up in the Other Alley," a humorous song by American lyricists Ren Shields (1868–1915) and Andrew B. Sterling (1874–1955) with music by J. Fred Helf (1870–1915), was recorded c. 1909.

8 This page bears MacLeish's autograph note to Linscott in the upper left corner: "Bob: This, of course, is written as an excerpt (in quotes) from a letter to H.M. Co from E.H.. He sends it to me with apologies for not writing you direct as he is very busy. A." The shorter second blurb that follows was used on the book band and front dust-jacket flap of *Conquistador*.

To Maxwell Perkins, 26 December [1931]

Key West

Dec 26

Dear Max:—

We've been here a week—in the new house—plumbers, carpenters, nurse sick, and a citizen in the front room typing all day on this manuscript— Hoped to have it done to send you for Xmas but he will certainly have it done for the first of the year— I hate like hell to end it—could write on for another year easily enough—[1] or is it well enough; or maybe just write on for another year handles it.

Started this in bed—bad throat back—this is really going to be the hell of a fine house; the lawn is coming well, figs on the fig tree, coconuts on the trees and plenty of limes. Will plant more limes and coconuts. Wish you could plant a gin tree. Young Patrick filled the mosquito sprayer yesterday with mosquito dope, tooth powder, talcum powder while he was supposed to be taking his nap and sprayed his little brother thoroughly— he woke up and cried loud enough to attract attention before it killed him—Patrick spraying manfully the harder he cried the more spray he received. "Did you want to hurt your little brother?"

"Y e s," said Patrick, very scared.

This rotten throat has filled my head so full of pus that the brain won't work, so enough of this letter. Hope things are going well with you.

Would you ask them ie. retail department to send one of those monumental quail books to Karl Pfeiffer 249 Heywood Avenue, Orange, NJ. and one to me here and the last two Will James books Sun Up and Big Enough I think they are to Bumby,[2]

> John H.N. Hemingway
> Ecole de Montcel
> Chateau de Montcel
> Jouy en Josas
> France

Charles and Lorine [Thompson] are fine; both in good shape. There has been no cold weather yet at all. Warm as when we made that trip over to the Cape. Not a Norther yet this season. Steady south east breezes all day and all night.

Bra has a new bottom in his boat and otherwised fixed up that I financed. He is in good shape. Burge hasn't been drinking but came here plenty drunk Christmas eve to tell me how I was his best friend in the world and how it was all John's [Herrmann's] fault they didn't get back to Tortugas that time. John's story is different. Neither of them were too good about that trip but I told Burge if he'd stay sober and prove it by not getting drunk would trust him again. It was as bad as a revival meeting. Of course I can't trust him again but he is a hell of a good man in a boat.

What about Scott?

Write me if you get time. You will be crazy about this place when you see it. I haven't heard anything lately from Europe. February is supposed to be the next big wallop.

What did you really think about M. Eastman's book?[3] Don't be so bloody careful in discussing these great writers. When is your World Genius going to publish again? Or is he so worried about living up to his press notices that he'll never be able to put it out? I hope he has a damned fine book.—[4] I feel like hell about Archies poem going to those buzzards.

I have a fine theory about the reason syphylis always speeds up production so with a writer who also likes his bed sports. It isn't that the spiros stimulate the brain so much as that it makes the writer stop his sporting life and that gives him so damned much energy inspite of the old disease that he turns them out with all the over-energy of a Wolfe who's never stood at stud for any length of time. Or am I wrong. And what's become of Bunny Wilson?[5]

Dos has left Harper's for Harcourt Brace or out of the frying pan into the cook's apron because they wouldn't print something about J.P. MOrgan the elder—next he says Harcourt will probably refuse to print something about Henry Ford in the next volumne and he will end up being published only in lithuanian. Shall I send him to you? The first I heard abut him having trouble was when he wrote he had switched over. He says this new book is a hell of a lot better than the 42nd parrallel.[6]

Well so long Max and good luck—we have enough cases that our furniture came in to build on Tortugas.— there are some drawings and some other stuff by Roberto to come still.

Ernest

Has Morley whelped yet? and what? Wish him luck for me.[7]

PUL, AL/TLS

1 The remainder of the letter is typewritten.
2 In 1931, Scribner's published *The Bobwhite Quail: Its Habits, Preservation, and Increase*, a 559-page study by American conservationist Herbert Lee Stoddard (1889–1970), as well as *Sun Up: Tales of the Cow Camps* and *Big-Enough*, both by Will James.
3 Max Eastman's *The Literary Mind* was published by Scribner's on 13 November 1931.
4 Perkins would reply on 14 January 1932 that Thomas Wolfe, who had not published anything since *Look Homeward, Angel* (1929), "has accomplished a great volume of work, and what I have seen of it, not much, is as good as it could be" (PUL). Wolfe's next book, *Of Time and the River*, would be published by Scribner's in January 1935.
5 Perkins did not respond to EH's question in his 14 January reply, but Edmund Wilson's life during this period was marked by alcoholism, mood swings, shock treatments, adultery, divorce, remarriage, and drunken disputes with his second wife, Margaret Canby. Despite these difficulties, Wilson published *Axel's Castle: A Study in the Imaginative Literature of 1870–1930* (1931) and *The American Jitters: A Year of the Slump* (1932), both with Scribner's.
6 *The 42nd Parallel* (1930), the first volume of Dos Passos's *U.S.A.* trilogy. The second volume, *1919*, contained unflattering portraits of American financier James Pierpont (J. P.) Morgan (1837–1913), who had saved Harper & Brothers from insolvency in 1896 and assumed its management in 1899, and of Ford Motor Company founder Henry Ford (1863–1947). In 1931 Dos Passos moved to Harcourt, Brace, which would publish *1919* (1932) and *The Big Money* (1936), the third installment in the trilogy.
7 Loretto and Morley Callaghan's first child, Michael, was born on 20 November 1931.

Undated Inscriptions

Undated inscriptions that most likely fall within the period of the volume are presented in this section, arranged alphabetically by recipient. If EH inscribed more than one book to a given person, the titles are presented in chronological order of publication.

To Logan Clendening, [c. November 1931]

this bull as originally conceived by Scribners artist had neither balls nor anything else and looked rather like a Lesbian Cow— Under Papa's protests they hung him a little heavier but what the hell— It's all literature one week and shit the next E.H.

Sotheby's catalog, Maurice Neville Collection of Modern Literature (Part III), New York, 24 April 2017, Lot 51 (illustrated), Inscription

EH wrote this inscription on the front free endpaper of a first edition, first reprint (1928) copy of *MWW* (Hanneman A7). The endpapers are yellow with three deeper yellow horizontal bands at the top, center, and bottom of the pages. In a yellow circle centered in the middle band is the silhouette of a charging bull. EH drew an arrow pointing from the words "this bull" in his inscription toward the image just above it. EH had objected to Scribner's first draft rendering of the bull for the dust jacket and endpaper design, telling Maxwell Perkins "he has a faintly lesbian look which might be very attractive in a cow but would never get a bull anywhere" (10 June [1927], *Letters* vol. 3, 247). After seeing a second draft rendering of the bull, EH wrote Perkins, "I'm sorry I ever interfered with him because what he has gained in masculinity he seems to have lost in energy and horns" (17 August [1927], *Letters* vol. 3, 265). The conjectured dating of the inscription is based on EH and Clendening's having first met each other in Kansas City around the time of Gregory Hemingway's birth in November 1931.

To Louis Henry Cohn, [c. late 1931]

And what to write in this copy of Capt. Cohns monumental work except to wish he had confined his zeal and go-get-icity to classing Mr. Galsworthys output[1] and let me alone—

Ernest Hemingway—

RR Auction online catalog, Boston, 18 February 2016, Lot 4057 (illustrated), Inscription

EH wrote this inscription on the front free endpaper of Cohn's *A Bibliography of the Works of Ernest Hemingway*, published in August 1931 in a limited edition of 500 copies (New York: Random House). This copy is numbered 321/500.

1 A collector of Galsworthy's letters and manuscripts, Cohn had helped English editor and bibliographer Harold Vincent Marrot (1898–1954) compile *A Bibliography of the Works of John Galsworthy* (New York: Scribner's; London: Elkin Mathews & Marrot, 1928).

To Don Carlos Guffey, [c. late 1931]

Dear Dr. Guffey:—

This book was published by a citizen named Robert McAlmon at his request in his publishing house which he had founded to publish his own writings which he was too hanged (hung) over to spell, punctuate and put in acceptable shape for a commercial publishing house to take. [*EH insertion*: Some of them were pretty damned good if he would clean them up and put them in shape.] He had married a Miss Ellerman—bastard—at the time of marriage daughter of Sir John Ellerman a British Steamship, brewing and Ellerman's liniment magnate.[1] His wife was living with H.D. (Hilda Doolittle) the poet and MacAlmon was merely a well paid convenience—[2] He was given enough money to publish his books and all I received from the publication of this one was the enmity of MacAlmon because it sold out while his own volumes remained in Stock—

Ernest

Sotheby Parke Bernet catalog, Collection of Jonathan Goodwin Sale (Part Two), New York, 25 October 1977, Lot 398 (illustrated), Inscription

EH wrote this inscription in a copy of *TSTP* (Hanneman A1A). According to the catalog description, "laid in and tipped in are 2 letters (1930 & 1931) from Ben Ray Redman to a Mr. Wallace discussing obtaining copies of 'Three Stories & Ten Poems.'"

1 McAlmon was married from 1921 to 1927 to the poet Bryher (née Annie Winifred Ellerman, 1894–1983), daughter of English shipping and brewing magnate Sir John Reeves Ellerman (1862–1933) and Hannah Glover (d. 1939), who married in 1909. Bryher's father provided the funding for McAlmon's Paris-based Contact Press, which published EH's first book, *TSTP*. EH makes joking reference to Elliman's Universal and Royal Embrocation, a British brand of liniment marketed since the late 1800s for human and veterinary use.

2 Bryher had been involved since 1918 in a lesbian relationship with American poet H.D. (Hilda Doolittle, 1886–1961). McAlmon later described his marriage to Bryher as "legal only, unromantic and strictly an agreement" because as an unmarried woman she could not be away from home and travel freely (Robert McAlmon and Kay Boyle, *Being Geniuses Together 1920–1930*, rev. edn. With supplementary chapters and an afterword by Kay Boyle [San Francisco: North Point Press, 1984], 45).

To Don Carlos Guffey, [c. late 1931]

To Dr. Don Carlos Guffey
   this book purchased at great expense by him hoping if he is to sell it he will not wait for the market to reach top—

Ernest Hemingway

Printers Row Fine and Rare Books online listing, Chicago, Inventory #4587 (illustrated), Inscription

EH wrote this in a copy of *TSTP* (Hanneman A1A).

To Don Carlos Guffey, [c. late 1931]

[Description as published in Parke-Bernet catalog:]
"The book is inscribed on the front endpaper 'To Dr. Don Carlos Guffey with great admiration Ernest Hemingway.' A second inscription, reading only 'Dr. Don Carlos Guffey,' appears in the upper right corner of the dust jacket. Laid in at the front of the book is a small blank card, *carte de visite* size, with the following three lines in pencil in the author's hand: 'Hoping to see you within two weeks—Ernest Hemingway.'"

Parke-Bernet Galleries catalog, The Library of Dr. Don Carlos Guffey, New York, 14 October 1958, Lot 151, Inscriptions; reproduced in Bruccoli and Clark *Auction*, 29

EH inscribed a copy of *TSTP*, with "original printed wrappers, uncut and unopened, MINT," according to the catalog description. The catalog entry also states: "The book is very rare in this state and the dust jacket, thus authenticated in the author's hand, may be unique. Although it is large enough to go around the book in the usual manner, in this instance it has obviously been wrapped completely around and sealed along one edge as a protective open-end envelope rather than a conventional dust jacket . . . . This may be the retained copy to which Hemingway refers in the two autograph letters offered as Lot No. 147" (EH's letters to Guffey of 12 and 27 April 1931).

To Don Carlos Guffey, [c. late 1931]

Dear Dr. Guffey:—

This book was printed and published by Bill Bird who had bought an old hand press and set it up on the Isle Saint Louis in Paris. It came out about a year after it should because I introduced Bill to Ezra Pound and Ezra suggested a series of books— "There'll be me and old Ford and Bill Williams and Eliot and Lewis (Wyndham)" and some others Ezra said "and we'll call it an inquest into the state of English prose. Eliot didnt include—nor did Lewis and finally Ezra had five titles— Bill said, "What about Hem?"

"Hem's will come Sixth," Ezra said.[1] So when they were all printed and this one finally gotten out it was later than the Three Stories and 10 poems although Bill had the manuscript long before McAlmon had the other set up—

Ernest

Parke-Bernet Galleries catalog, The Library of Dr. Don Carlos Guffey, New York, 14 October 1958, Lot 152 (illustrated), Inscription; reproduced in Bruccoli and Clark *Auction*, 39

EH wrote this inscription in a copy of *iot*.

1 The first five volumes of Pound's Inquest series, printed by Bill Bird's Three Mountains Press, were published in 1923: *Indiscretions* by Pound; *Women and Men* by Ford Madox Ford; *Elimus* by Bernard Cyril Windeler (b. c. 1886); *The Great American Novel* by William Carlos Williams (1883–1963); and *England* by B. M. G.-Adams (pen name of Bride Scratton, née Evelyn St. Bride Mary Goold-Adams, 1882–1964). EH's *iot* was published in April 1924. Neither T. S. Eliot nor Wyndham Lewis would have works published as part of the series.

To Don Carlos Guffey, [c. late 1931]

To Dr. Don Carlos Guffey—

Dear Dr. Guffey:— Since you are a collector, marks, mis-spelled words and other evidences of seniority in a volumne are probably more important than how it was written but if it is of any interest to you the first draft of this book was commenced on my birthday—July 21 in Madrid and it was finished September 6 of the same year—in Paris—

It was written at Madrid, Valencia, Madrid, San Sebastian, Hendaye and Paris. After it was finished I wrote The Torrents of Spring in the week preceding Thanksgiving of that year.—

In November we went to Schruns in the Voralberg in Austria and there I re-wrote the 1st part of this book—went to N.Y. and came back and re-wrote the rest—

Ernest Hemingway

The portrait on the jacket was by a twirp who said he was making drawings for Vanity Fair and then <u>sold</u> this, which he got me to sign—To Scribners—[1]

[*Written on dedication page, which is printed*: "This book is for Hadley and for John Hadley Nicanor":]

only child of any sort of E.H. not born through Caesarian section[2]

Sotheby's catalog, Maurice F. Neville Collection of Modern Literature (Part I), New York, 13 April 2004, Lot 93 (illustrated), Inscription

EH wrote this inscription on the front free endpaper of a first edition, first issue copy of *SAR* (Hanneman A6a).

1 This sentence appears to have been squeezed into the space above and below EH's signature. The back of the dust jacket features a drawing of EH by American artist John Blomshield (1895–1953). The portrait, dated Paris 1925, was also used in Scribner's advertising and as an illustration for a number of published reviews of *SAR*.
2 This inscription was apparently written after the birth of Gregory Hemingway on 12 November 1931, the second of EH's sons to be delivered surgically by Dr. Guffey.

To Don Carlos Guffey, [c. late September 1929 or after]

[*Inscription on flyleaf.*]

Dear Dr. Guffey:— I don't know what the retail price of this book was but it is my idea of a lousy limited edition— Scribner's printed it from the same plates as the regular edition and I like a fool signed the detached sheets they sent over— The only possible excuse for a limited edition was if they would publish the text un-deleted which they, of course did not have the guts maybe to do. I receive the same royalty percentage on it as on the regular edition—if I'd known what I know now about the racket [I] would have insisted that they publish it unexpurgated—before I was fool enough to sign the sheets.

Ernest.

[Inscription on final page of the novel:]

This book was started in Paris in January—written on in Key West in April— May— Piggott— Ark— early in June— K.C. June— July— Finished in Wyoming in August and 1st week in September

EH.

My father shot himself Dec 16 when I was half way through re-writing it and I finished re-writing it in Dec and January—

Sotheby Parke Bernet catalog, New York, 21 January 1975, Lot 214 (partially illustrated), Inscription

This transcription derives from the auction catalog description, and partial illustration of the inscription. EH inscribed a presentation copy of the limited edition of *FTA*, produced in 510 numbered and signed copies and issued by Scribner's simultaneously with the first regular edition of the novel on 27 September 1929 (Hanneman A8b). According to the catalog description, throughout the novel (in three different colors of ink), EH "has systematically supplied the words expurgated by Scribner's, and substituted his original monosyllables for the editors' euphemisms." EH also presented Dr. Guffey with a copy of the first printing of the first regular edition of *FTA* (Hanneman A8a), inscribed "To Dr. Guffey from his friend Ernest Hemingway" (Sotheby Parke Bernet catalog, Collection of Jonathan Goodwin Sale [Part Two], New York, 25 October 1977, lot 403).

To Joan Whitney, [c. late October 1930 or after]

To Miss Mouse[1]
from one who reads a little French

Ernest Hemingway

William Doyle Galleries catalog, New York, 17 May 1984 (illustrated), Inscription

1 EH wrote this inscription on the front free endpaper of a copy of the 1930 Scribner's edition of *IOT*, drawing a line pointing to the Whitney bookplate, which pictures a mouse.

ROSTER OF CORRESPONDENTS

The recipients of letters and inscriptions included in this volume are identified here, rather than in endnotes, which provide additional information as deemed necessary in the context of a particular letter. When Hemingway's letter is directed to a publication, business, or other institutional recipient rather than a named individual, any editorial commentary will appear in an annotation to that letter. We provide birth and death dates for recipients whenever possible. When we have been unable to confirm both dates, we have supplied whatever partial dating information we have been able to establish.

George Sumner Albee (1905–1964). American fiction writer who traveled widely, including visits to Paris, after his graduation from the University of California in 1927. His short story "Fame Takes the J Car" would appear in *Story* (December 1932) and in Edward O'Brien's *The Best Short Stories of 1933*. His first novel, *Not in a Day*, would be published in 1935.

James Benjamin Aswell, Jr. (1906–1955). American journalist, novelist, and critic whose enthusiastic review of *A Farewell to Arms* for the *Richmond Times-Dispatch* (6 October 1929) prompted EH to write him a letter of appreciation. Aswell's three novels, published in the 1940s and 1950s, would be set in his native Natchitoches, Louisiana. He was the son of James B. Aswell (1869–1931), prominent Louisiana educator and U.S. Congressman (1913–1931).

Milford J. Baker (1895–1970). An advertising executive for Young & Rubicam and a collector of first edition works by EH. Baker served with EH in the American Red Cross Ambulance Service in Italy and received both the Croix de Guerre and the commemorative Italian WWI cross commissioned by the Duke of Aosta, commander of the Italian Army. Baker and EH renewed their friendship after crossing paths in New York City in 1929, and in a series of detailed letters Baker advised EH on guns and ammunition needed for African game hunting.

Otto Raymond Barnett (1868–1945) Chicago patent attorney, a graduate of Northwestern University Law School (1888). Barnett was president of the Glencoe [Illinois] Library Board from 1905 to 1933. Among his civic activities was the establishment of achievement awards to local high school students for their competitive essays on birds. Otto's son Lawrence T. Barnett served with EH in Italy during WWI in the American Red Cross Ambulance Service.

Sylvia Beach (1887–1962). Owner of the Left Bank Paris bookstore Shakespeare and Company at 12, rue de l'Odéon, which also served as a lending library and permanent address for expatriate writers and artists. Beach was the publisher of James Joyce's *Ulysses* (1922) and in 1929 published a collection of essays about Joyce, *Our exagmination round his Factification for incamination of Work in progress*. In 1930–1931 she was embroiled in legal battles against the pirating of *Ulysses* in the United States. In 1932, at Joyce's insistence, she relinquished her rights as publisher of *Ulysses* so that he could obtain a U.S. copyright and be paid royalties. EH met Beach when he and Hadley first came to Paris, and her shop carried the first copies of his *Three Stories and Ten Poems* (1923) and *in our time* (1924). He would later write of her: "No one I ever knew was nicer to me" (*MF*).

R. P. (Richard Palmer) Blackmur (1904–1965). American literary critic, poet, and playwright. An autodidact who attended lectures at Harvard but never enrolled, Blackmur contributed reviews and critical essays, largely focused on modernist poetry, to the literary quarterly *Hound & Horn* (1927–1934), serving as its first managing editor (1928–1930). He would later come to be associated with the New Criticism. His first publication, a satirical pamphlet protesting censorship, *Dirty Hands: or, The true-born censor* (1930), would be followed by six volumes of criticism, four of poetry, and honors including election to the National Institute of Arts and Letters (1956) and the American Academy of Arts and Sciences (1964).

Charles William Brackett (1892–1969). American lawyer (Harvard Law School, class of 1920), drama critic for the *New Yorker* (1925–1929), and author of short stories and novels, including *American Colony* (1929), about American expatriates on the French Riviera. In the late 1920s several of his short stories were made into movies, and in 1932 he went to Hollywood, where he would become a successful scriptwriter and producer. He would later collaborate with Billy Wilder on such films as *The Lost Weekend* (1945) and *Sunset Boulevard* (1950), become president of the Academy of Motion Pictures and Sciences (1949–1955), and garner four Oscars.

Israel Bram (1883–1955). American endocrinologist, textbook author, and director of the Bram Institute in Pennsylvania. His investigation of the theory that modern stress leads to endocrine disorders such as Graves' disease prompted him to develop a questionnaire about sleep habits that was sent to 150 *Who's Who* personalities (including Clarence Darrow, Dorothea Dix, John Dos Passos, Albert Einstein, Fannie Hurst, H. L. Mencken, Henry Morgenthau, and EH) to gather statistics relevant to "the relationship of sleep and dream phenomena to the endocrine glands and the involuntary nervous system." In 1936 Bram would publish the results of his research in the *Journal of American Psychiatry*, reporting that while many with a genetic predisposition never develop the disease, "psychic trauma (imminent danger to life and limb)" can precipitate its advent.

Robert Bridges (1858–1941). American editor, 1879 graduate of Princeton University. Bridges was a literary critic for the humor magazine *Life* and worked on the staff of the *New York Evening Post* from 1881 to 1887, when he joined the newly established *Scribner's Magazine* as assistant to the editor in chief, Edward Burlingame. Bridges succeeded Burlingame in 1914 and served as the magazine's editor in chief until 1930.

Jefferson Beale Browne (1857–1937). Key West attorney, politician, and author. Browne had served as Key West postmaster (1885–1890), Florida state senator (1891–1895), Key West customs collector (1893–1897), Florida Supreme Court justice (1917–1925), and chief justice (1917–1923), before becoming a circuit court judge (1925–1937). His 1896 *National Geographic* article "Across the Gulf by Rail to Key West" proposed what would become the railroad route along the Florida Keys. While chairman of the Florida Railroad Commission (1903–1907), Browne was instrumental in promoting the construction of the Florida East Coast Railway and its extension, the Florida Over Sea Railroad, linking the mainland to the Keys and reaching Key West in 1912. His book *Key West: The Old and the New* (1912) praised the determination of Henry M. Flagler (1830–1913), heir to the Standard Oil fortune, who built the railroad.

Maxwell Struthers Burt (1882–1954). American poet, novelist, and nonfiction writer. A 1904 Princeton graduate, Burt moved to Wyoming in 1908, establishing the Bar B C Ranch near Moose in 1912 and the Three Rivers ranch (later part of Grand Teton National Park) in 1929. A frequent contributor to *Scribner's Magazine, Collier's,* and the *Saturday Evening Post,* Burt became a Scribner's author with his second book, *John O'May and Other Stories* (1918). Subsequent Scribner's titles included *When I Grew Up to Middle Age* (1925), *The Other Side* (1928), and *Festival* (1931). EH had visited the Burts at the Bar B C Ranch during the summer of 1928.

Manuel Caberas. Spanish official in the city of Pontevedra to whom EH wrote in August 1929 regarding fishing licenses for himself and Pauline.

Maud Cabot (1903–1999). American abstract expressionist painter born into an aristocratic New York family. Cabot moved abroad to paint, settling in Paris, where she often worked at the apartment of Ivy Troutman, Waldo Peirce's estranged wife. Cabot married Patrick Morgan in 1931.

Morley Callaghan (1903–1990). Canadian writer, 1925 graduate of the University of Toronto. EH encouraged Callaghan, a cub reporter at the *Toronto Daily Star* when they met in 1923, to write fiction. Callaghan's first published story, "A Girl With Ambition," appeared in *This Quarter* (Autumn–Winter 1925–1926) alongside EH's "The Undefeated." His collection of short stories, *A Native Argosy* (1929), was followed by the novels *It's Never Over* (1930) and *A Broken Journey* (1932). Callaghan gained fame when he was reported to have knocked down EH in a 1929 boxing match in Paris that was refereed by F. Scott Fitzgerald, who, as timekeeper, allowed the round to run on too long. Callaghan would chronicle the event in his memoir, *That Summer in Paris* (1963).

Jonathan Cape (1879–1960). British publisher whose firm, established in 1921 with his junior partner, George Wren Howard, featured the works of many American writers, including Sinclair Lewis, Eugene O'Neill, Sherwood Anderson, Louis Bromfield, Carl Sandburg, and Edna St. Vincent Millay. Cape's British edition of *In Our Time* (1926) included unauthorized revisions that angered EH. Nevertheless, EH agreed to let Cape publish British editions of *The Sun Also Rises* (as *Fiesta,* 1927), *Men Without Women* (1928), *A Farewell to Arms* (1929), and *Death in the Afternoon* (1932).

Bennett Alfred Cerf (1898–1971). American journalist, publisher, and author. Cerf joined the publishing house of Boni & Liveright in 1923. Two years later he and business partner Donald S. Klopfer (1902–1986) acquired the Modern

643

Library imprint and expanded the enterprise by adding popular contemporary authors. In 1927 they launched Random House, aimed at publishing general interest titles "at random." They added *The Sun Also Rises* to their Modern Library list in 1930 and *A Farewell to Arms* in 1932.

Cyril Coniston Clemens (1902–1999). Third cousin, twice removed of American writer Mark Twain (né Samuel Langhorne Clemens, 1835–1910), who founded the International Mark Twain Society and the *Mark Twain Quarterly* (later *Mark Twain Journal*), which he edited from 1936 to 1982. In 1930 Clemens offered EH the honorary vice presidency of the Mark Twain Society, which EH accepted. Clemens published numerous articles, pamphlets, and books about Twain. Beginning in 1932, he would become embroiled in copyright disputes with the Samuel Clemens estate.

Logan Clendening (1884–1945). American physician, professor, and author whom EH befriended in Kansas City after the birth of his son Gregory in November 1931. Clendening earned his medical degree in 1907 at the University of Kansas, where he taught for many years. He was also the author of the widely syndicated medical advice column "Diet and Health." In early 1932, Clendening would give to EH copies of six letters he had received from readers with medical inquiries. One letter served as the model for EH's "One Reader Writes," a story in which a woman writes to a doctor-columnist about her husband's contracting "sifilus." The story would appear in the 1933 collection *Winner Take Nothing*.

Louis Henry Cohn (1889–1953). New York City book collector and seller. Cohn married Marguerite Arnold (1887–1984) in 1930, and the two opened their bookshop, House of Books. Cohn collected EH's manuscripts, typescripts, and first editions. That same year he sent EH a lengthy questionnaire about the publication of his work for the purpose of preparing *A Bibliography of the Works of Ernest Hemingway*, published in 1931 in a limited edition of 500 copies. House of Books would publish EH's short story "God Rest You Merry, Gentlemen" (1933) in a limited edition series called the Crown Octavos (1932–1969). Cohn's military sobriquet "Captain Cohn" derives from his distinguished service with the French Army and the Foreign Legion before and during WWI.

Maurice-Edgar Coindreau (1892–1990). French translator of North and South American literature, Princeton professor of Romance languages (1922–1961). Coindreau's translations of contemporary writers such as John Dos Passos,

William Faulkner, John Steinbeck, Truman Capote, William Styron, Juan Goytisolo, and Ramón del Valle-Inclán (all published under the Éditions Gallimard imprint) introduced these writers to the French public. After seeing Coindreau's 1928 translation of Dos Passos's *Manhattan Transfer*, EH requested him as translator for *A Farewell to Arms* (*L'adieu aux Armes*, 1931) and *The Sun Also Rises* (*Le Soleil Se Lève Aussi*, 1933).

Dorothy M. Connable (1893–1975). Daughter of Harriet Gridley Connable and Ralph Connable, Sr., and a 1916 graduate of Wellesley College. Dorothy ran an American Red Cross canteen in France during WWI. She and EH met in 1920 when he moved into the Connable family home in Toronto as a short-term hired companion for her brother, Ralph (1900–1957), and renewed their friendship when EH and Hadley moved to Toronto in 1923. Connable attended the Clarence White School of Photography in New York and began working in 1926 as a professional photographer, spending winters in New York and summering at Walloon Lake and in Petoskey, Michigan.

Caresse Crosby (née Mary "Polly" Phelps Jacob, 1892–1970). American writer and publisher, who married Richard Peabody (1892–1936) in 1915 and in 1921 divorced him to marry Harry Crosby (1898–1929) in 1922. Known in Paris for their eccentricities and their open marriage, the Crosbys established the Black Sun Press in 1925, publishing excerpts from James Joyce's *Finnegans Wake* (1929), *Short Stories* by Kay Boyle (1929), Hart Crane's *The Bridge* (1930), and Archibald MacLeish's *New Found Land* (1930). After her husband's death in 1929 in an apparent murder-suicide pact with a lover, Caresse ran the press single-handedly. In addition to publishing her late husband's work, she launched Crosby Continental Editions, offering inexpensive paperback copies of expatriate and avant-garde literature including EH's *The Torrents of Spring* and *In Our Time: Stories* in 1932. She would discontinue the unprofitable series in 1933.

Alfred Sheppard Dashiell (1901–1970). American writer and editor, a 1923 graduate of Princeton University who contributed to the *Saturday Review*, *New Republic*, and other literary magazines. In 1923 Dashiell joined the staff of *Scribner's Magazine* as an associate editor and succeeded Robert Bridges as editor in chief from 1930 until 1936, when he left to join *Reader's Digest*.

Otto R. Dempewolf (1898–1979). Resident of Brooklyn, New York, and American WWI veteran who worked as shipping clerk for a wholesale hardware company and for Brooklyn Edison's Waterside gas station. In 1929 he wrote to EH asking him to autograph a copy of *The Sun Also Rises*.

Alan Taylor Devoe (1909–1955). American editor, author, and naturalist, who inscribed a copy of his first publication, *The Naturalist's Christmas* (privately printed in 1925), to EH. Devoe would write prolifically about birds in the 1930s and 1940s, his articles appearing in *Reader's Digest, American Mercury*, and *Nature*. His books included *The Portrait of Mr. Oscar Wilde* (1930).

John Dos Passos (1896–1970). American novelist whose works include his WWI novel *Three Soldiers* (1921) and his experimental fiction, including *Manhattan Transfer* (1925) and the panoramic trilogy *U.S.A.*, comprising *The 42nd Parallel* (1930), *1919* (1932), and *The Big Money* (1936). Dos Passos served as director of the experimental New Playwrights Theatre until 1929, when it produced his play *Airways* before ceasing operation. He served with the American Red Cross Ambulance Service in Italy during WWI, and became friends with EH in Paris around 1924. Dos Passos is credited with introducing EH to Key West, where they were often together. He was a passenger in the car EH was driving at the time of the November 1930 accident near Billings, Montana, that shattered EH's arm. Dos Passos and EH's longtime friend Katharine Foster (Kate) Smith (1894–1947) were married in August 1929.

Lawrence Drake (né Samuel Pessin, 1900–1984). Russian-born American editor and author. He edited the short-lived *Milwaukee Arts Monthly* (renamed *Prairie*, 1922–1923) which featured writers such as Jean Toomer, Waldo Frank, and Conrad Aiken. His only novel, *Don't Call Me Clever* (1929), traces the relationship between two Jewish brothers living in Milwaukee.

Mr. Feldheym. In his October 1929 response to this reader's letter, EH thanked him for his admiration and expressed regret that he could not satisfy Feldheym's request for a picture, hoping that his signature would suffice as an autograph.

F. Scott Fitzgerald (1896–1940). American author who gained early success with his novels *This Side of Paradise* (1920), *The Beautiful and Damned* (1922), and *The Great Gatsby* (1925), and with his short stories collected in *Flappers and Philosophers* (1920), *Tales of the Jazz Age* (1922), and *All the Sad Young Men* (1926). He married Zelda Sayre (1900–1948) in 1920, met EH in Paris in 1925, and was instrumental in helping EH move from Boni & Liveright to Charles Scribner's Sons in 1926. The *Saturday Evening Post* paid top prices for some nineteen Fitzgerald stories published between 1929 and 1931. Fitzgerald would not publish his next novel, *Tender Is the Night*, until 1934.

Ford Madox Ford (né Ford Hermann Hueffer, 1873–1939). English novelist, critic, and founding editor of the literary journal *English Review* (1908–1937) and the short-lived *Transatlantic Review* (1924). EH published three stories in the *Transatlantic Review* and worked as its subeditor from February 1924 until the magazine folded that December. Ford's WWI experiences served as the foundation for his best-known novels, *The Good Soldier* (1915) and the tetralogy *Parade's End* (1924–1928). His subsequent works included *The English Novel: From the Earliest Days to the Death of Joseph Conrad* (1929) and the autobiographical books *No Enemy: A Tale of Reconstruction* (1929) and *Return to Yesterday: Reminiscences 1894–1914* (1931). During a 1927 lecture tour in the United States, Ford met Grace Hall Hemingway in Oak Park, Illinois. EH's disenchantment with Ford is evident in the chapter titled "Ford Madox Ford and the Devil's Disciple" in *A Moveable Feast*.

Nino Frank (né Jacques-Henri Frank, 1904–1988). Italian-born Swiss film critic, writer, and editor. Accused of anti-Fascism and exiled from Italy for publishing left-wing writers in his magazine *900*, Frank lived in France after 1928. In addition to writing for the cinema magazine *Pour Vous*, he was a founding editor of the avant-garde Paris-based magazine *Bifur* (1929–1931), which published translations of contemporary international authors including James Joyce, Blaise Cendrars, Tristan Tzara, and Isaac Babel. Joyce suggested EH's work to *Bifur*, and a translation of "Hills Like White Elephants" ("Les Collines Sont Comme des Éléphants Blancs") appeared in the magazine's third issue (30 September 1929).

David Garnett (1892–1981). English bookseller, novelist, biographer, editor, and critic. A member of the Bloomsbury group, he ran a London bookshop in the 1920s and cofounded the private Nonesuch Press, which would continue to publish until the mid-1960s. Garnett wrote more than a dozen novels, including *Lady into Fox* (1922), *The Sailor's Return* (1925), and *No Love* (1929), as well as a collection of short stories (*The Old Dovecote and Other Stories*, 1928) and the first of four volumes of his memoirs, *Never Be a Bookseller* (1929). In 1933 he would write an introduction to the Jonathan Cape edition of *The Torrents of Spring*. He was the son of Edward Garnett (1868–1937), literary advisor to Cape, and Constance Garnett (1861–1946), the renowned translator of Russian writers.

Christian Gauss (1878–1951). Professor of Modern Languages (1907–1946), department chairman (1912–1936), and Dean of the College (1925–1946) at Princeton University, where his students included such major literary figures as John Peale Bishop, Edmund Wilson, and F. Scott Fitzgerald. Gauss's articles appeared in a variety of venues, including the *New York Times*, *Saturday Review*, *Saturday Evening Post*, and *New Republic*. In 1930 he published *Life in College* and an English translation of Gustave Flaubert's *Madame Bovary*.

Mildred Durst Giraud (1886–1970). A fan whom EH met aboard *La Bourdonnais* in January 1930 while sailing from Bordeaux to Havana via New York City. Widow of successful Houston, Texas, businessman James Arthur Giraud (1875–1923), she traveled frequently. EH autographed a copy of *The Sun Also Rises* for her as a souvenir of the twenty-one-day voyage.

Isabelle Simmons Godolphin (1901–1964). A next-door neighbor of the Hemingway family while she and EH were growing up in Oak Park, Illinois, Simmons was a 1920 graduate of Oak Park and River Forest High School and attended the University of Chicago. In 1923 she visited EH and Hadley in Switzerland and Italy. In 1925 she married Francis R. B. "Frisco" Godolphin (1903–1974), a 1924 Princeton graduate who began teaching classics at his alma mater in 1927. The couple had two children, Katherine Jeanne (b. 1927) and Thomas (1931–1962).

Ivan Goll (né Isaac Lang, 1891–1950; pseudonyms Tristan Torso and John Lasang). Artist, playwright, and translator, born in France, and bilingual in French and German, Goll moved to Switzerland to escape conscription during WWI and lived in Paris after the war. His works include *Die Chapliniade* (a cine-poem illustrated by Fernand Léger, 1920), the play *Mathusalem* (1922), and the surrealist opera libretto for *Royal Palace* (1927). He was influential in the surrealist movement, which he defined and defended in a manifesto published in the sole issue of his magazine *Surréalisme* (October 1924). Goll was the Paris agent for the Swiss publishing house Rhein Verlag, which published Georg Goyert's German translation of *Ulysses* in 1927. Together, with Samuel Beckett, Eugene Jolas, and others, Goll assisted Joyce with the French translation of *Anna Livia Plurabelle*, published in *La Nouvelle Revue Française* on 1 May 1931.

Giles Pollard Greene (1888–1941). Architect, graduate of Yale (1911) and Columbia (1915), WWI veteran. Greene designed granite, marble, and bronze memorials for the Presbrey-Leland Company in New York City before starting his own company in 1932. In May 1930 Greene wrote to ask if EH would autograph his copy of *A Farewell to Arms*.

Anton Gud (né Anthony Gudaitis, 1908–1993). American author and bookseller known for ghostwriting the pulp romance *Lady Chatterley's Husbands* (1931). In October 1929 EH responded to a letter from Gud, thanking him for his praise of EH's work.

Don Carlos Guffey (1878–1966). American gynecologist, obstetrician, and book collector; he joined the faculty of the newly established University of Kansas in 1905, becoming the founder and first chairman of the Department of Obstetrics and Gynecology in 1911. EH and Pauline chose him to deliver their sons Patrick (1928) and Gregory (1931) at Research Hospital in Kansas City. Guffey's library included over 4,000 first editions, the original manuscript of *Death in the Afternoon*, and inscribed copies of *In Our Time, The Torrents of Spring, The Sun Also Rises*, and *A Farewell to Arms*.

Arthur Hawkins, Jr. (1903–1985). New York City artist associated with the Art Students League (a syndicate run by and for artists, established in 1875), serving as one of its directors. Hawkins's work, which included drypoint caricatures of notable contemporary authors including EH, was exhibited at the G. R. D. Studio in New York in October 1928 and 1930. From 1927 onward Hawkins designed magazine and book jackets, quickly gaining popularity as a modernist cover artist for books such as Samuel Putnam's *Francois Rabelais, Man of the Renaissance* (1929) and William Faulkner's *Sanctuary* (1931).

Carol Hemingway (1911–2002). EH's sister and fifth of the six Hemingway children. Though twelve years apart in age, EH and Carol were fond of each other, and EH took over financial responsibility for her in 1928 after their father's death. While a student at Oak Park and River Forest High School, Carol was on the staff of *Tabula*, the yearbook and literary magazine to which EH had contributed as a student. Carol enrolled at Rollins College in Winter Park, Florida, in the fall of 1930, holding a writing scholarship. While a student in Florida, Carol frequently visited EH in Key West, but a rift would develop between them over her relationship with fellow Rollins student John Fentress Gardner (1912–1988), whom she would marry in 1933 against EH's wishes.

Grace Hall Hemingway (1872–1951). EH's mother, a singer, voice teacher, and artist. Grace began to study painting in 1925, became active in the Oak Park Art

League, and exhibited and sold her paintings in several Chicago area shows during the 1920s and early 1930s. Following the suicide of his father, Clarence Hemingway (1871–1928), EH assumed financial responsibility for Grace and his two youngest siblings, Carol and Leicester, setting up a trust fund that would supply Grace with a regular income starting in April 1930. Although they corresponded regularly, EH and his mother did not see each other for more than two years after his father's death, until she made a two-day visit to Key West in January 1931.

Hadley Richardson Hemingway (née Elizabeth Hadley Richardson, 1891–1979). EH's first wife. A native of St. Louis, she met EH in the fall of 1920, and they married in Horton Bay, Michigan, in September 1921 before moving to Paris that December. Their son, John Hadley Nicanor "Bumby" Hemingway, was born in Toronto in October 1923. After EH and Hadley divorced in March 1927, Bumby spent the school year with his mother in Paris and summers and vacations with EH and Pauline. EH granted Hadley all royalty rights to *The Sun Also Rises*. In 1933, Hadley would marry Paris-based journalist and poet Paul Scott Mowrer (1887–1971), who worked for the *Chicago Daily News* from 1910 to 1944 and was awarded a Pulitzer Prize in 1929.

John Hadley Nicanor Hemingway (1923–2000). EH's first son, named for both his mother (Hadley Richardson Hemingway) and the bullfighter Nicanor Villalta. After EH and Hadley divorced in early 1927, Bumby lived with Hadley in Paris, coming to the United States and staying with EH and Pauline for vacations and travel. He was with EH and Pauline in late March and most of April 1929 (sailing with them from Havana to Boulogne), from July to September 1930 (accompanying them to Wyoming), and, in the summer of 1931 (accompanying EH in Pamplona in July and staying with EH and Pauline in Madrid in August). [Bumby]

Leicester Hemingway (1915–1982). EH's brother and youngest of the six Hemingway children. Between May and September of 1929, Leicester underwent both an appendectomy and tonsillectomy, was involved in a minor car accident, and traveled to Honolulu to spend a year living with his paternal aunt, Grace Livingston. Growing up to become a journalist and author, he would publish a biography titled *My Brother, Ernest Hemingway* (1962) shortly after EH's death. [Les]

Madelaine Hemingway (1904–1995). EH's sister and fourth of the six Hemingway children. In the 1920s she worked as a dental assistant in Oak Park but left that job to stay with EH and Pauline in Key West from late 1928 until April 1929, babysitting for Patrick and helping to type the manuscript of *A Farewell to Arms*. In April 1929 she sailed with EH and his family to Europe, spending a month in Paris and then travelling to France, Italy, and Switzerland with a friend. After returning to Oak Park in August 1929, Sunny lived with her mother and younger siblings and worked in a doctor's office. She later would publish *Ernie: Hemingway's Sister "Sunny" Remembers* (1975), a series of recollections accompanied by photographs, artifacts, and letters. [Nunbones, Sunny, Sun]

Pauline Pfeiffer Hemingway (1895–1951). EH's second wife, the daughter of Paul and Mary Pfeiffer, a wealthy Roman Catholic family of Piggott, Arkansas. After receiving a degree in journalism from the University of Missouri in 1918, she worked as a writer for *Vanity Fair* and *Vogue* in New York and in Paris, where she met EH and Hadley in 1925. EH and Pauline were married in Paris on 10 May 1927 and had two sons, Patrick (b. 1928) and Gregory (1931–2001). They came to Key West in 1928, buying a home at 907 Whitehead Street in 1931.

Barklie McKee Henry (1902–1966). American writer, banker, and philanthropist. In 1924 Henry graduated from Harvard, published his only novel, *Deceit*, and married Barbara Whitney (1903–1982), an heiress to the Vanderbilt, Whitney, and Payne family fortunes. Henry then became assistant to the editor of the *Boston American* and, in 1926, managing editor for the *Youth's Companion*. From 1928 to 1930 he worked in the bond department of the Guaranty Trust Company; in 1931 he quit his job at the bank to manage the family's wealth and engage in philanthropic work.

Josephine Herbst (1892–1969). American journalist and novelist whose work addressed Midwestern, proletarian, feminist, and autobiographical topics. After graduating in 1918 from the University of California, she worked in New York City as editorial reader for H. L. Mencken's *Smart Set* and other magazines, and her first publications appeared under the pseudonym Carlotta Greet in *Smart Set* in 1923. In 1926 she married fellow writer John Herrmann, and in 1928 they moved into the Erwinna, Pennsylvania, farmhouse where Herbst would live until her death. There she would write her most successful novels, including *Nothing Is Sacred* (1928) and *Money for Love* (1929), as well as the trilogy *Pity Is Not Enough* (1933), *The Executioner Waits* (1934), and *Rope of Gold* (1939). [Jo]

Matthew Gering Herold (1894–1960). American lawyer, a graduate of the University of Nebraska (1916) and Harvard Law School (1921). Herold was a second cousin of Pauline Pfeiffer and worked for the Pfeiffer pharmaceutical enterprises in New York City. He and Pauline were briefly engaged before his marriage to Constance Degnan (1899–1973) in early 1925. Herold acted as EH's attorney in matters regarding the Laurence Stallings 1930 stage adaptation of *FTA*.

John Theodore Herrmann (1900–1959). Michigan-born writer, expatriate, and political novelist. Herrmann and EH met in 1924 in Paris, where Herrmann also met writer Josephine Herbst, whom he married in 1926. After the couple returned to the United States in 1924, Herrmann continued to publish in expatriate avant-garde periodicals, including *transition* and *This Quarter*. His first novel, *What Happens* (1926), published in Paris by Robert McAlmon's Contact Editions, was denied entry to the United States by customs and officially banned as "obscene." He attended the 1930 International Congress of Revolutionary Writers in Kharkov, Ukraine, and subsequently joined the American Communist Party. Herrmann's later novels would draw on his youth in the Midwest (*Summer Is Ended*, 1932) and his stint as a traveling seed salesman (*The Salesman*, 1939). He and Herbst would separate in 1934 and divorce in 1940.

Guy Hickok (1888–1951). American newspaper reporter, he joined the *Brooklyn Daily Eagle* in 1914 and became the head of its Paris bureau in 1918. EH met Hickok soon after arriving in Paris in 1921, and the two took a road trip to Italy in March 1927. In July 1929 Hickok joined EH for the annual fiesta in Pamplona. As Paris correspondent, Hickok reported on European and expatriate culture for readers in the United States, including the rise of fascism in Italy and of Hitler in Germany. He would return to the United States in 1933. [Gros]

Lansing Colton Holden, Jr. (1896–1938). A 1919 Princeton graduate, decorated WWI flying ace, archeologist, architect, and Technicolor expert who worked for RKO and MGM studios. Holden interrupted his Princeton studies to join the American Air Force; he later joined the French effort to subdue the Rif uprising in Morocco (1924–1926) and is considered a prototype for Tommy Barban in Fitzgerald's 1934 novel *Tender Is the Night*. In 1924 Holden married Edith Harrold Gillingham (1896–1970), an American nurse with the Allied Armies who was decorated by the French government for her volunteer war work. The couple visited EH in Key West with Mike and Maggie Strater in February 1929. [Denny]

Frances Horne (née Thorne, 1904–1991). Granddaughter of George R. Thorne (1837–1918), co-founder with his brother-in-law, Aaron Montgomery Ward, of the successful mail order firm Montgomery Ward & Company, established in 1872. Socialite, community volunteer, and philanthropist, she was associated with several Chicago area bookshops. She and EH's longtime friend Bill Horne were married in August 1929, and the couple vacationed with EH and Pauline in Wyoming in August 1930. [Bunny]

William Dodge Horne, Jr. (1892–1986). A 1913 graduate of Princeton, Horne met EH in the American Red Cross Ambulance Service in Italy during WWI, and they later shared living quarters in Chicago in 1920. Horne married Frances Thorne in August 1929. He worked for the Chicago advertising company of Green, Fulton, Cunningham from 1923 until the outbreak of World War II. Horne would be a pallbearer at EH's funeral in 1961.

Cyril Hume (1900–1966). American fiction writer whose novels include *Wife of the Centaur* (1923), *Cruel Fellowship* (1925), and *My Sister My Bride* (1932). His short stories appeared in *Harper's Magazine* and were collected in *Street of the Malcontents and Other Stories* (1927) and *Myself and the Young Bowman and Other Fantasies* (1932). In 1930, Hume began writing for MGM films, concentrating on adaptations and screenplays for the rest of his career.

Mrs. Jamar. A reader who wrote to EH to praise his work (probably *A Farewell to Arms*) and request an autograph, which EH supplied in a signed letter to her in October 1929.

Richard Johns (né Johnson, 1904–1970). Affluent littérateur who started a literary magazine, *Pagany: A Native Quarterly*, which ran from January 1930 to December 1932 (the last issue actually printed in February 1933). Focusing on American writers, *Pagany* published excerpts from work by William Carlos Williams, Gertrude Stein, Ezra Pound, Erskine Caldwell, Conrad Aiken, E. E. Cummings, and John Dos Passos, among others. EH responded in June 1929 to an unlocated letter from Johns soliciting a manuscript; EH's work never appeared in the magazine.

Paul Johnston (1899–1987). American printer, founder of several small presses, and editor and designer of books. Working with Random House, he designed, illustrated, and printed a collection of twelve brochures, each presenting a new poem by a well-known American poet, in a limited edition of 475 copies. This collection, *The Poetry Quartos* (1929), was followed by *The Prose Quartos* (1930), to which EH was invited to contribute; he declined. Johnston wrote the standard book on typography, *Biblio-Typographica: A Survey of Contemporary Fine Printing Style* (1930).

James Joyce (1882–1941). Irish author of *Dubliners* (1914), *A Portrait of the Artist as a Young Man* (1916), and *Ulysses* (1922), which was banned on obscenity charges in both the United States and England after portions were serialized in the *Little Review* beginning in 1918. Like *Ulysses,* Joyce's volume of poetry, *Pomes Penyeach* (1927), was published in Paris by Sylvia Beach's Shakespeare and Company. Sections of his novel-in-progress appeared in magazines for almost two decades before its publication as *Finnegans Wake* in 1939. EH inscribed a copy of his 1929 novel, *A Farewell to Arms,* to Joyce.

Eric Mowbray Knight (also known as Richard Hallas, 1897–1943). English journalist and author who moved to Philadelphia in 1912, saw action in WWI, and served as drama and film critic for the *Philadelphia Public Ledger* from 1928 to 1934. He sold his first story, "The Two-Fifty Hat," to *Liberty* magazine in 1930, and thereafter published short stories, mostly dealing with English village life, in *Cosmopolitan,* the *Saturday Evening Post,* and other magazines. Knight would achieve popular success with *Lassie Come Home,* a short story published in 1938 in the *Saturday Evening Post* and expanded into a novel in 1940.

H. Lawrence Lack, Jr. A resident of New Brunswick, New Jersey, who in a September 1929 letter to EH expressed his desire "to enter the field of authorship." In late October EH drafted but did not mail a sarcastic reply.

Louise Lafitte (b. c. 1893). Russian-born resident of Brooklyn, New York. Lafitte was author of "The Russian Experiment," a critique of Soviet policy toward its citizens dated 22 May 1929 and published in *The Commonweal: A Weekly Review of Literature, the Arts and Public Affairs.* In an October 1929 letter Lafitte asked EH to help her find a publisher for her first novel, "Leah."

Megan Laird (1908–1981). American graduate of Barnard College (1929) who wrote to EH about having seen bullfights in Spain in November 1930. She was a linguist who became a professor at Southern Methodist University, where she would teach from the 1950s until her retirement.

Milton Seligman Leidner (1904–1994). American criminal lawyer, graduate of the University of Pennsylvania (1926) and its law school (1930), who lived and practiced in Philadelphia. Leidner wrote to EH in 1930 asking about the availability of first editions of his works.

William Charles Lengel (1888–1965). Editor and writer, a Kansas City (Missouri) Law School graduate. After briefly practicing law in Missouri, he worked under Theodore Dreiser on the staff of the women's magazine *The Delineator*. He began work at the International Magazine Company in 1920, which led to editorial positions within the Hearst media empire at *Hearst's International Magazine, Smart Set*, and *Cosmopolitan*. While working for Ray Long at *Cosmopolitan*, Lengel recommended the publication of EH's "Fifty Grand," but the magazine turned down the story, which was later published in *Atlantic Monthly* in 1927. Lengel's first novel, *Forever and Ever* (1932), was published under the pseudonym Warren Spencer. In 1933 he would leave Hearst's to become associate editor of *Liberty* magazine.

Georgia Lingafelt (1898–1957). American writer, editor, teacher, and bookstore owner. Upon graduating from the University of Chicago, Lingafelt worked for a trade magazine publisher in the Chicago area before moving to Yellow Springs, Ohio, where she taught journalism at Antioch College and served as the college's publicity director. She returned to Chicago in 1928 and began working at Walden Books. From 1933 to 1950 she would operate her own bookstore, Georgia Lingafelt Books, in the Wrigley Building on Michigan Avenue, specializing in rare books, first editions, and imported foreign-language books for children.

Jeanette Mills Littell (1892–1986). A resident of Gloversville, New York, who wrote an admiring letter to EH shortly after publication of *A Farewell to Arms*, to which he responded in October 1929.

Ray Long (1878–1935). American journalist, magazine editor, and publisher. After serving as editor of *Red Book* magazine (1911–1918), Long assumed editorship of *Cosmopolitan* (1918–1931) and served as editor in chief (1918–1931) and president (1926–1931) of Hearst's International Magazine Company, publishers of *Cosmopolitan, Good Housekeeping, Harper's Bazaar, Smart Set*, and other magazines. Long also published a series of magazine articles and edited anthologies of short stories. In 1931 he resigned from the Hearst corporation to go into book publishing in partnership with Richard

R. Smith. That business would fail, and Long would move to Hollywood to write and edit movies. He committed suicide in 1935.

E. V. (Edward Verrall) Lucas (1868–1938). English essayist, humorist, journalist, novelist, biographer, and travel writer. Lucas was apprenticed to a bookseller at the age of sixteen and because of family financial strains, he never completed a university degree, but he made up for his lack of formal education by reading voraciously, attending lectures, and visiting museums and galleries. A popular London literary figure, Lucas wrote more than one hundred books, many published in both London and New York, including *Vermeer the Magical* (1929), *Windfall's Eve* (1929), *Turning Things Over* (1929), *If Dogs Could Write* (1929), *Down the Sky* (1930), *Traveller's Luck* (1930), *French Leaves* (1931), *Visibility Good* (1931), *The Barber's Clock* (1931), and *No-Nose at the Show* (1931). Scribner's published one book by Lucas, *The Colvins and Their Friends* (1928).

Henry R. Luce (1898–1967). China-born American editor and publisher and a 1920 Yale graduate who co-founded and edited the weekly news magazine *Time* (1923) and founded *Fortune* (1930), which published EH's article "Bullfighting, Sport and Industry" in its second issue. While serving as editor in chief of Time Inc. (1929–1964), Luce would solidify his position as a magazine magnate by founding *Life* (1936), *House and Home* (1952), and *Sports Illustrated* (1954).

Charles Walter MacGregor (1888–1934). American writer who published stories in *America's Humor* magazine and the *New Yorker*. He was secretary to Robert Benchley and appeared as a character in several of Benchley's stories.

Archibald MacLeish (1892–1982). American poet and playwright. A 1915 Yale graduate, WWI military veteran, and a 1919 graduate of Harvard Law School, MacLeish left his career as a Boston trial lawyer in 1923 to write poetry in Paris, where he lived with his wife, Ada (née Ada Taylor Hitchcock, 1892–1984), until 1928. EH and MacLeish met in Paris in 1924, and they remained good if sometimes uneasy friends for decades. His books of poetry include *Streets in the Moon* (1926), *The Hamlet of A. MacLeish* (1928), *New Found Land: Fourteen Poems* (1930), and *Conquistador* (1932; Pulitzer Prize, 1933). MacLeish wrote essays for Henry Luce's *Fortune* magazine (1929–1938), as well as occasional pieces for the *Saturday Review of Literature*, *Nation*, and *New Republic*. He would serve as Librarian of Congress from 1939 to 1944. His *Collected Poems 1917–1952* (1952) and the play *J.B.* (1958) would also win Pulitzer Prizes.

Harry F. Marks (1882–1958). London-born, New York-based bookseller specializing in limited edition sporting books and erotica in fine bindings. Marks collected works by Charles Dickens and the letters of Abraham Lincoln, and in the 1920s became the distributor of Black Sun Press books in the United States.

George Marton (1899–1979). Hungarian-born literary agent. Educated at the University of Berlin and at the Sorbonne in Paris, he established a well-known literary agency in Vienna in the mid-1920s. To escape Nazism, Marton moved to Paris in 1937 and immigrated to the United States in 1939.

Frank Ross McCoy (1874–1954). An 1897 West Point graduate, McCoy began his military career in the Spanish-American War and served as an aide to presidents William Howard Taft and Theodore Roosevelt. He commanded New York's "Fighting 69th" regiment in the Champagne–Marne defensive and the Aisne–Marne offensive during WWI. From 1929 to 1932, as a newly appointed major general, McCoy commanded the Fourth Corps Area, which included Florida and the Atlantic coast, and visited Key West in March 1931, where he met EH.

Patrick Morgan (1904–1982). American abstract painter and son of the wealthy financier James Hewitt Morgan. He studied at Harvard before moving to Paris in the late 1920s with his friend Whitney Cromwell. Morgan enrolled at the École des Beaux-Arts, maintained a studio, and met EH around 1927. In 1931 he married Maud Cabot.

Alzira Peirce (née Alzira Handforth Boehm, 1908–2010). American painter, third wife of Waldo Peirce, whom she married on 16 December 1930. The couple had twin sons, Mellen Chamberlain (Bill) and Michael, born in France on 3 October 1930, and a daughter, Anna Gabrielle (1934–1991). They would divorce c. 1945.

Waldo Peirce (1884–1970). American painter, Harvard class of 1909, WWI veteran born and based in Bangor, Maine, where his family owned large tracts of timberland. Peirce and EH met in Paris in 1927 and became lifelong friends, sharing a passion for bullfighting, fishing, and the outdoor life. Peirce separated from his second wife, the actress and painter Ivy Troutman (1883–1979), in 1927. After their divorce became final on 10 October 1930, he married Alzira Handforth Boehm, who had given birth to their twin sons a week earlier. Peirce painted an oil portrait of EH in spring 1928 and another in winter 1929. His painting *Katie's Boys* (early 1930s) shows EH, Dos Passos, and the artist in the Dry Tortugas; his *Death in the Gulf Stream* (1932) humorously depicts EH shooting a shark; and *The Silver Slipper* (1932) depicts the dance hall of Sloppy Joe's Bar in Key West, featuring EH, Pauline, and the artist along with many locals. His painting of EH holding a fishing pole would appear on the cover of *Time* magazine's 18 October 1937 issue.

Maxwell Evarts Perkins (1884–1947). Editor at Charles Scribner's Sons from 1914 until his death. One of the most influential literary editors of the twentieth century, he was instrumental in the acquisition and promotion of such authors as F. Scott Fitzgerald, Ring Lardner, Marjorie Kinnan Rawlings, and Thomas Wolfe, as well as EH, who left his first American publisher, Boni & Liveright, to become a lifelong Scribner's author in early 1926. Perkins's expertise and cordial interaction with EH smoothed the way for the publication of EH's stories in *Scribner's Magazine* and for the publication of *The Torrents of Spring* and *The Sun Also Rises* in 1926, *Men Without Women* in 1927, and *A Farewell to Arms*, serialized in *Scribner's Magazine* and then published in book form, in 1929. Perkins advised EH on the several offers generated by the success of *A Farewell to Arms* (dramatizations, syndication, translation), advice that EH usually took. Perkins joined EH in Key West for fishing expeditions during the winters of 1930 and 1931.

Gustavus Adolphus Pfeiffer (1872–1953). Paternal uncle of Pauline Pfeiffer Hemingway. A German American businessman (dealing mostly in pharmaceuticals, with branches in several countries), Gus married Louise Foote (1872–1948) in 1896, and the couple, whose only child died in infancy, were generous to their nieces and nephews. They established a trust fund that provided Pauline with monthly payments of $250, and extended their generosity to her husband, regularly providing cars, trips, and other gifts, which inspired EH to dedicate *A Farewell to Arms* "To G. A. Pfeiffer." In 1929, Gus helped EH create a trust fund for the benefit of EH's mother and his younger siblings, which came into effect in April 1930. In 1931 Gus financed the purchase of EH and Pauline's house at 907 Whitehead Street, Key West. Gus rejoiced in EH's success, joined him on fishing trips, and assisted with research for *Death in the Afternoon* by requesting books on bullfighting from a Spanish business contact.

Karl Gustavus Pfeiffer (1900–1981). Brother of Pauline, married Matilda C. Schmidt (1904–2002) in 1922. Pfeiffer worked for the Pfeiffer family-owned Richard Hudnut Perfume Company in New York and would become president of the Piggott Land Company upon his father's death in 1944. Karl and Matilda had three children, Margaret Pfeiffer (1923–1927), Barbara Pfeiffer (1925–1961), and Paul Mark Pfeiffer (1928–1962).

Mary Alice Pfeiffer (née Downey, 1867–1950). Mother of Pauline Pfeiffer Hemingway. A devout Irish American Catholic, she married Paul Pfeiffer in Parkersburg, Iowa, in 1894 and was active in their business and philanthropic life in Piggott, Arkansas, holding office at the Piggott State Bank and the Piggott Land Company, operating a soup kitchen, and supporting local churches. The Hemingways usually spent Christmas with the Pfeiffers, and during EH and Pauline's frequent and lengthy travels, Mary often took care of one or both of their children. In addition to her first born, Pauline Marie Pfeiffer, Mary was mother to Karl Gustavus Pfeiffer, Virginia Ruth Pfeiffer, and Paul (Max) Pfeiffer.

Paul Mark Pfeiffer (1867–1944). Father of Pauline. A successful German American businessman involved in real estate and farming, he married Mary Alice Downey with whom he had four children. In the early 1900s Paul began to invest in land in Piggott, Arkansas, moving his family there from St. Louis in 1913 and developing a successful farmstead-leasing enterprise. As founder of the Piggott Cotton Gin Company in 1923 and of the Piggott Land Company (jointly with his brother Gus) in 1929, he became the area's largest landowner and leading citizen. In 1930, Pfeiffer was elected president of the Piggott State Bank and kept it afloat during the Great Depression.

Virginia Ruth Pfeiffer (1902–1973). Sister of Pauline, with whom she had a close relationship. Jinny, who traveled frequently with friends and relatives, met several of EH's friends at Pamplona in July 1929 and joined EH, Pauline, and Gerald and Sara Murphy, and other friends in Switzerland for Christmas in 1929. She accompanied Bumby, EH's son from his marriage to Hadley Richardson, on the transatlantic voyage when Bumby visited EH in the summer of 1930. In 1931, Jinny designed and supervised the transformation of the Pfeiffer family's barn in Piggott for EH to use as a guest apartment and writing studio. Frequently called on to assist during a family crisis, she helped her mother care for the Hemingway children when they were left in Piggott. When EH and Pauline were in Kansas City in November 1931 for the birth of Gregory, she helped unpack and set up the furniture they had shipped from Paris to Key West. [Jinny]

Laurence Edward Pollinger (1898–1976). English literary agent for Curtis Brown Ltd., whose clients included Ezra Pound, D. H. Lawrence, and James Joyce. Pollinger mediated between EH and Jonathan Cape as early as 1926, when he negotiated the publication of the British edition of *IOT* on behalf of EH and secured an advance of £50, which Cape had been unwilling to pay. In 1935 he and two colleagues would leave Curtis Brown to open their own agency, Pearn, Pollinger, and Highham.

Dorothy Shakespear Pound (1886–1973). English artist who married Ezra Pound in 1914. Influenced by the Vorticist movement in the 1920s, she designed notices and book covers for Vorticist artists and poets, including covers and illustrations for Pound's *Cantos*. When Dorothy was ready to give birth to her son, Omar Shakespear Pound (1926–2010), it was EH who drove her to the American Hospital in Paris.

Ezra Loomis Pound (1885–1972). American poet, author of the *Cantos* (1917–1969), translator, mentor, and advisor to modernist writers. Pound met EH in Paris in 1922, encouraged his writing, and became one of EH's earliest and strongest advocates, including publishing EH's *in our time* (1924) in the series Pound edited for the Three Mountains Press, "An Inquest into the State of Contemporary English Prose." After winning the $2,000 *Dial* prize in 1927, Pound founded the short-lived literary review *The Exile* (1927–1928). He then published *A Draft of XXX Cantos* (1930), *Imaginary Letters* (1930), and *How to Read* (1931) and edited the fourth volume of *The Collected Poems of Harry Crosby* (1931). Pound's prose writing began taking on an increasingly political focus in the early 1930s, reflecting his increasing support for Italian dictator Benito Mussolini.

Samuel Putnam (1892–1950). American writer, translator, and editor. Putnam was a reporter and writer for several Chicago newspapers, including the *Tribune, Herald and Examiner*, and *Evening Post*, and a writer and editor for magazines including *Modern Review, Chicago Literary Times*, and the *Dill Pickler*. He also translated selections from French writers for several periodicals and was comissioned by publisher Pascal Covici for more translation work. Putnam had met Ford Madox Ford in Chicago; they renewed their friendship in 1927 when Putnam moved to Paris, where Ford introduced him to Allen Tate, Sylvia Beach, Gertrude Stein, and EH. In 1929 Edward Titus hired Putnam to translate Alice Prin's book *Les Souvenirs de Kiki* (1929) for the Black Manikin Press, and EH wrote an introductory note to the volume, published as *Kiki's Memoirs* (1930). Putnam edited *The European Caravan: An Anthology of the New Spirit in European Literature* (1931) and launched the short-lived *New Review* in January 1931 with the editorial support of Ezra Pound.

Cranston Dunlop Raymond (1896–1991). A salesman for Scribner's living in Seattle, Washington, whom EH met in Billings, Montana while he was hospitalized for injuries suffered in a November 1930 car crash. Raymond would later work at the Scribner's office in San Francisco and eventually become a dealer in art and rare books.

Frieda Inescort Redman (nee Wightman, 1901–1976). Scottish-born actress known professionally as Frieda Inescort, whose career began on Broadway in 1922. She performed in the 1923 show *You and I*, which helped launch the career of dramatist Phillip Barry, and in 1931 she performed in two Broadway comedies, *Napi* and *Company's Coming*. She married American writer and literary critic Ben Ray Redman (1896–1961) in 1926. In the 1930s the Redmans moved to Hollywood, where Frieda would pursue a film career.

Paul Romaine (1906–1984). American independent bookseller from Chicago, who prepared and published *Salmagundi* for the Casanova Press of Milwaukee, Wisconsin, in 1932. The collection included some of William Faulkner's early writings as well as EH's four-line poem "Ultimately," which had appeared in *The Double Dealer* in 1922.

Ernst Rowohlt (1887–1960). German publisher. His first Leipzig-based publishing house, Ernst Rowohlt Verlag (1908–1912), was succeeded in 1919 by Rowohlt Verlag in Berlin, which became one of Germany's leading publishing houses during the 1920s. Its list expanded to include foreign as well as German writers, publishing translations of William Faulkner, Sinclair Lewis, Thomas Wolfe, and EH. As EH's German publisher, Rowohlt published *Fiesta* (*The Sun Also Rises*) in 1928, *Männer* (*Men Without Women*) in 1929, *In Einem Andern Land* (*A Farewell to Arms*) in 1930, and *In Unserer Zeit* (*In Our Time*) in 1932, all translated by Annemarie Horschitz. The financial crisis of the early 1930s forced Rowohlt into bankruptcy, causing him to renege on royalty payment commitments to his authors—EH among them. When the firm was reconstituted after WWII, Rowohlt Verlag would continue to act as EH's German publishers throughout his life, also translating and publishing some of his posthumous work.

Robert de Saint Jean (1901–1987). French journalist and author, foreign correspondent for the leading French newspaper *Paris-Soir* (1923–1944), and editor in chief of the literary review *La Revue Hebdomadaire* from 1927 to 1934. His books include *La Jeunesse Littéraire Devant la Politique* (1928), *La Vraie Révolution de Roosevelt* (1934), and *Le Feu Sacré* (1936) as well as several works co-authored with Anne Green (1891–1979) and her brother Julian (1900–1998), whose parents emigrated from the United States to France in 1893. Julian Green, Saint Jean's longtime companion, would become the first non-French national elected to the French Academy (in 1971).

Marcelline Hemingway Sanford (1898–1963). The eldest of EH's siblings. She and EH graduated together from Oak Park and River Forest High School in 1917, and she married Sterling Skillman Sanford in 1923. Marcelline and Sterling lived in Detroit and had three children: Carol Hemingway Sanford (1924–2013), James Sterling Sanford (b. 1929), and John Edmonds Sanford (1930–2016). She would publish a memoir in 1962, *At the Hemingways: A Family Portrait.*

Edward Saunders (1876–1949). Key West charter boat captain and fishing guide; half-brother to Birchland "Berge" Saunders (1897–1970), also a fishing guide in Key West. He and EH became friends in 1928 and often fished together in the Keys and nearby waters. EH based his 1932 story "After the Storm" on Saunders's account of his exploration of the *Valbanera*, a Spanish passenger steamship sunk by a hurricane in 1919, whose valuable cargo he had been unable to retrieve. [Bra]

Bernard C. Schoenfeld (1907–1990). American playwright and screenwriter, graduate of Harvard University (1928) and the Yale School of Drama (1930). The Yale University Experimental Theatre presented his one-act play *Solo Flight* in May 1929. While still a student, Schoenfeld wrote to EH in 1929, asking permission to dramatize *The Sun Also Rises*; permission was denied. Schoenfeld would go on to write several Broadway hits in the 1930s before moving to Hollywood as a scriptwriter.

Gilbert Vivian Seldes (1893–1970). American journalist, writer, translator, and literary and cultural critic. Seldes served as managing editor of the *Dial* (1921–1922) and as its drama critic (1920–1929). His best-known book was *The Seven Lively Arts* (1924), a celebration of popular entertainment. Other works include the novel *The Wings of the Eagle* (1929) and *The Future of Drinking* (1930), a study of the effects of Prohibition.

Earl Shelton (1907–1974). Inmate at the California State Prison in San Quentin who wrote to EH in 1931 requesting copies of EH's work. He would later work for a photographic and modeling studio in San Francisco.

Evan Biddle Shipman (1904–1957). American poet and horse-racing expert whose poetry and journalism appeared in magazines such as *transition, Scribner's, Nation,* and *Esquire.* Shipman and EH met in Paris in late 1924 and maintained a lifelong friendship. While in Paris, Shipman lived predominantly on the proceeds from an inheritance, with occasional help from EH. After dedicating *Men Without Women* to Shipman in 1927, EH would later write about Shipman in his memoirs ("Evan Shipman at the Lilas," *A Moveable Feast*). Shipman returned to the United States in 1930 and continued to write prose and poetry, particularly about horse racing.

Richard Leo Simon (1899–1960). American publisher and co-founder with Max Lincoln Schuster of the Simon & Schuster publishing firm, established in 1924.

George Edward Slocombe (1894–1963). English journalist whose first assignment at the *London Daily Herald* was to report on the sinking of the *Titanic* in 1912; he was chief foreign correspondent for the newspaper from 1919 to 1931. In 1923 EH interviewed Slocombe for an insider's view of Georgy Vasilyevich Tchicherin, commissar of foreign affairs for the Soviet Union, as he reported in "A Russian Toy Soldier" (*Toronto Daily Star*, 10 February 1923). Slocombe headed the Anglo-American Press Association of Paris in 1927. His books include the illustrated guide *Paris in Profile* (1929), which he hoped EH would endorse.

Mr. Small. A reader whose flattering letter, most likely about *A Farewell to Arms*, EH replied to in December 1930.

Martha Speiser (née Glazer, 1885–1968). American art collector and bibliophile. She served as a member of the Pennsylvania House of Representatives (1923–1924) and spent much of the rest of her life encouraging and promoting modern artists.

Maurice Joseph Speiser (1880–1948). American lawyer, patron of music and theatre, bibliophile, and art collector. Speiser was appointed assistant district attorney of Philadelphia in 1911 and served in the Pennsylvania State House of Representatives 1913–1914. In 1926 he opened his own general law practice. In 1928 his successful pro bono defense of sculptor Constantin Brancusi, whose *Bird in Space* was deemed subject to high taxation as a "manufactured metal object or machine part" rather than as a tax-free work of art, established Speiser as a champion of modern artists. Speiser met EH in Paris in the 1920s and would serve as his lawyer from 1929 until 1948. [Moe]

Laurence Tucker Stallings, Jr. (1894–1968). American playwright, screenwriter, drama critic, journalist, magazine editor, and member of the Algonquin Round Table. A 1916 graduate of Wake Forest College in North Carolina, Stallings served in WWI and received the Croix de Guerre for his wounding at the Battle of Belleau Wood (1918). He is best known for his semi-autobiographical writing about the war, especially the play he wrote with Maxwell Anderson, *What Price Glory* (1924), which ran on Broadway for 435 performances and was adapted into a film in 1926; his bestselling novel *Plumes* (1924); and his 1924 short story "The Big Parade," which was also adapted into a hit silent film (1925). Stallings wrote the Broadway stage adaptation of EH's *A Farewell to Arms*, which ran for twenty-four performances starting 22 September 1930. His 1931 wartime hospital story, "Vale of Tears," would be anthologized in EH's collection *Men At War* (1942).

Edgar Stanton (1884–1943). Wealthy Chicago businessman, educated at Harvard. Stanton's father, George Edgar Stanton, Jr., was a U.S. Consul in Russia when Edgar was born; George moved the family back to Chicago in the early 1890s and joined Stanton & Company, his family's lucrative imports and grocery business. Edgar succeeded his father as company president in 1910. He helped establish a successful candy store chain (Mrs. Snyder's Home Made Candies) and served as a director of a local manufacturing company. He and his wife, Harriet Rew Stanton, married in 1908 and had two sons, Edgar Jr. and Francis Rew Stanton. An avid sportsman, Edgar was a member of the Indian Hill Golf Club in Winnetka and a member of the Coleman Lake Club, a private hunting and fishing preserve in Wisconsin. Stanton visited EH in Key West in the spring of 1931, and the two men practiced target shooting.

Jewell Flavel Stevens (1890–1966). Advertising executive, history buff, and book collector for whom EH autographed a bookplate for *A Farewell to Arms* in 1929. Stevens's collection of Lincolniana would be acquired by the Michigan State University Library in 1959; his collection of American and British manuscripts as well as first and rare book editions would be acquired by the Southern Illinois University Library that same year.

Donald Ogden Stewart (1894–1980). American humorist, novelist, and screenwriter. A 1916 graduate of Yale, Stewart wrote a series of satires in the 1920s, including *A Parody Outline of History* (1921), *Mr. and Mrs. Haddock Abroad* (1924), and *The Crazy Fool* (1925), a bestseller. He was a member of the Algonquin Round Table and an actor on Broadway in the 1928 production of Philip Barry's *Holiday*. Stewart and Beatrice Ames (1902–1981) were married in 1926 and had two sons, Ames Ogden Stewart (1928–2007) and Donald Ogden Stewart, Jr. (1932–2015). EH and Stewart met in Paris in 1924, and Stewart was among EH's companions at the 1924 Fiesta of San Fermín in Pamplona. EH's comic short story "My Life in the Bull Ring with Donald Ogden Stewart" was rejected by *Vanity Fair* in 1924 and remained unpublished until 2015, when it appeared for the first time in *Letters* vol. 2. Stewart also served as a model for the character Bill Gorton in *SAR*. In 1930 Stewart moved with his family to Hollywood, where he launched his screenwriting career with *Laughter* (1930), *Tarnished Lady* (1931), *Rebound* (1931), and *Finn and Hattie* (1931). He would win an Academy Award for his screenplay of *The Philadelphia Story* (1940).

Henry Hyacinth Strater (1896–1987). American painter, illustrator, and printmaker. Strater and EH met in Paris in 1922 and became friends. Strater painted two portraits of EH in Paris (1922 and 1923) and a third in Key West (February 1930). Strater visited EH in Key West in February 1929, in February 1930, and in March 1931. In January 1930 EH visited Strater in New York City. [Mike]

Allen Tate (né John Orley Allen Tate, 1899–1979). Southern American poet, biographer, and literary critic. A 1923 graduate of Vanderbilt University, Tate was a founding editor of the poetry journal the *Fugitive*, along with Robert Penn Warren and Ridley Wills. He moved to New York City in 1924 and met author Caroline Gordon (1895–1981), whom he married in 1925. Tate wrote for the *Nation* and *New Republic* and in 1928 published his first volume of poetry, *Mr. Pope, and Other Poems*, and his biography *Stonewall Jackson: The Good Soldier*. Tate came to Europe on a Guggenheim Fellowship, and he met EH in Paris in October 1929. His subsequent publications include *Jefferson Davis: His Rise and Fall* (1929), *Three Poems: Ode to the Confederate Dead, Message from Abroad, The Cross* (1930), and *Poems, 1928–1931* (1932).

Charles Philip Thompson (1898–1978). A Key West native who ran his family's successful marine hardware store business and shared EH's love of fishing and hunting. EH had met Thompson when he first came to Key West in 1928. He played a major role in introducing EH to big game sport fishing, and he and his wife, Lorine, became close friends of EH and Pauline. Charles would accompany EH and Pauline on the African safari of 1933–1934, serving as the model for Karl in *Green Hills of Africa* (1935).

Lorine Thompson (née Louise Epsy Carter, 1898–1985). A native of Richmond, Georgia, and a 1919 graduate of Agnes Scott College in Decatur, Georgia, Lorine came to Key West to teach at Key West High School in 1921 and married Charles Thompson in 1923. The Thompsons became close friends of the Hemingways; Lorine would remain a lifelong friend of Pauline. She found the house on Whitehead Street in Key West that the Hemingways bought in 1931.

Edward William Titus (1870–1952). Polish-born American journalist, editor, and expatriate, who had married cosmetics magnate Helena Rubenstein (1872–1965) in 1908. His Paris bookstore, At the Sign of the Black Manikin, opened in 1924. In 1926 he founded At the Sign of the Black Manikin Press, which published limited editions, including the second edition of D. H. Lawrence's *Lady Chatterley's Lover* (1929) and the English translation of *Kiki's Memoirs* (1930), for which EH wrote the introduction. In 1929 Titus took over as owner and editor of *This Quarter*. Both the press and the magazine folded in 1932.

Mr. Turner. A reader who wrote to EH in December 1931 praising his work and requesting a photo.

Hugh Seymour Walpole (1884–1941). New Zealand-born English author of some three dozen novels in addition to plays, memoirs, and volumes of short stories. In 1927 Walpole had called EH "the most interesting figure in American letters in the last ten years" and described "The Killers" as "one of the best short stories in the American language." He admired *A Farewell to Arms*, which he read in manuscript, and his enthusiastic praise was quoted in Scribner's advertisements for the novel.

Joan Whitney (1903–1975). American heiress, philanthropist, art collector, and racehorse owner, sister of John Hay (Jock) Whitney. After attending Miss Chapin's School in Manhattan, she studied briefly at both Barnard College and at Brown University. In 1924 she married lawyer and businessman Charles Shipman Payson (1898–1985), and the couple would have five children. In 1929 Whitney helped open a children's bookstore, Young Books, on Madison Avenue; it would run for more than a decade.

Thornton Wilder (1897–1975). American novelist and playwright, a Yale graduate (class of 1920) whose bestselling novel *The Bridge of San Luis Rey* (1927) won a Pulitzer Prize. Wilder's works also included the novel *The Woman of Andros* (1930) and *The Long Christmas Dinner and Other Plays in One Act* (1931). From 1930 to 1936 he taught literature and creative writing at the University of Chicago; his plays *Our Town* (1938) and *The Skin of Our Teeth* (1942) would win him two more Pulitzer Prizes.

Irma Rosalind Sompayrac Willard (1897–1991). American artist, graduate of Newcomb College, New Orleans (1920), and co-founder (with Gladys Breazeale) of the Natchitoches Art Colony in Louisiana (1921–1937). Recognized as the first art colony in the South, it was supported by local patronage and, drawing on faculty from Newcomb College, encouraged local artists and promoted Southern landscape painting.

George Frederick Wilson. A resident of New York City, Wilson had written to EH expressing admiration for *A Farewell to Arms*. EH responded with a letter of thanks in October 1929.

Owen Wister (1860–1938). American lawyer, writer, and Harvard graduate (1882), author of the celebrated novel *The Virginian* (1902) and biographies of Ulysses S. Grant (1901), George Washington (1907), and his friend Theodore Roosevelt (1930), whom he had met at Harvard. EH and Wister met in Shell, Wyoming, in 1928, and Wister's admiration for *A Farewell to Arms* (and his reservations about its ending) led to a lively correspondence among EH, Wister, and Perkins in 1929.

Mrs. Wolfenstein. A reader whose admiring letter, presumably about *A Farewell to Arms*, EH answered in December 1929.

George M. Yohalem (1893–1968). American screenwriter and movie producer. Yohalem worked for the Lasky Corporation in the 1920s (renamed Paramount Famous Lasky Corporation in 1927) and then for Universal Studios and Monogram Pictures. He wrote the scripts for such silent movies as *Lotus Blossom* and *No Woman Knows* (both 1921). In the 1930s he helped to produce talking pictures, including *The Past of Mary Holmes* and *After Tonight* (both 1933).

CALENDAR OF LETTERS

Date of Correspondence	Recipient	Form	Location of Source Text	Previous Publication*
[c. 7–20 April 1929]	Henry Strater and Lansing Holden, Jr.	AN with enclosed ALS	JFK	unpublished
21 April [1929]	Charles and Lorine Thompson	ALS	RR Auction catalog	unpublished
[22 April 1929]	Grace Hall Hemingway	ANS on ALS by Madelaine Hemingway	JFK	unpublished
[23 April 1929]	Maxwell Perkins	ALS	PUL	unpublished
[c. April 1929]	Alfred Dashiell	AL	PUL	unpublished
[c. late April 1929]	John Dos Passos	ALFrag	UVA	unpublished
10 May 1929	Grace Hall Hemingway	ALS	IndU	unpublished
12 May [1929]	Owen Wister	ALS	LOC	unpublished
13 May 1929	Maxwell Perkins	Cable	PUL	unpublished
[c. mid-May 1929]	Jonathan Cape	ALS	Christie's catalog	unpublished
18 May [1929]	Robert Bridges	ALS	PUL	unpublished
26[–27] May [1929]	Thornton Wilder	TL/ALS	Yale	unpublished
1 June 1929	Madelaine Hemingway	Cable	PSU	unpublished
2 June [1929]	Madelaine Hemingway	ALS	PSU	unpublished
[c. 3 June 1929]	Grace Hall Hemingway	AL	JFK	unpublished

---

* Listed are known full-text English-language publications of EH letters, excluding dealer or sale catalog listings and newspaper articles

Date of Correspondence	Recipient	Form	Location of Source Text	Previous Publication
7 June 1929	Maxwell Perkins	ALS	PUL	*SL*, Trogdon *Reference*, *TOTTC*
7 June [1929]	Maxwell Perkins	ALS	PUL	*TOTTC*
[c. 7 June 1929]	Gustavus A. Pfeiffer	TCD with typewritten signature	JFK	unpublished
[15 June 1929]	Owen Wister	ALS	LOC	unpublished
[c. mid-June 1929]	Mary Pfeiffer	TL	JFK	unpublished
[23] June [1929]	Waldo Peirce	TL with typewritten signature	Colby	unpublished
[23] June [1929]	Owen Wister	ALS	LOC	unpublished
[23] June [1929]	Maxwell Perkins	TL with typewritten signature	PUL	*SL*, *TOTTC*
24 June 1929	Grace Hall Hemingway	ALS	IndU	unpublished
24 June [1929]	William Lengel	ALS	Profiles in History catalog	unpublished
24 June [1929]	Richard Johns	ALS	UDel	unpublished
24 June [1929]	Otto Dempewolf	ALS	Stanford	unpublished
[c. 6–14 July 1929]	[Unknown]	ALD	JFK	unpublished
14 July [1929]	Charles Thompson	A Postcard S	Profiles in History catalog	unpublished
14 July [1929]	Edward Saunders	Postcard [transcription]	PUL	unpublished
18 July [1929]	Thornton Wilder	ALS	Yale	unpublished
18 July [1929]	Archibald MacLeish	ALS	LOC	*SL*
21 July [1929]	Henry Strater	ALS	PUL	unpublished
22 July 1929	Nino Frank	ALS	UTulsa	unpublished
[23 July 1929]	F. Scott Fitzgerald	ALSFrag	PUL	Bruccoli *Fitz–Hem*
26 July [1929]	Maxwell Perkins	ALS	PUL	*TOTTC*
26 July [1929]	Owen Wister	ALS	LOC	*SL*

Date of Correspondence	Recipient	Form	Location of Source Text	Previous Publication
27 July [1929]	Grace Hall Hemingway and Family	ALS	PSU	unpublished
[28] July [1929]	Waldo Peirce	ALS	LOC	unpublished
30 July [1929]	Guy Hickok	ALS	phPUL	unpublished
[c. 30 July 1929]	Guy Hickok	ALS	phPUL	unpublished
31 July [1929]	Maxwell Perkins	ALS	PUL	*TOTTC*
8 August 1929	Manuel Caberas	ALS	JFK	unpublished
18 August [1929]	Sylvia Beach	ALS	PUL	unpublished
[22 August 1929]	Paul and Mary Pfeiffer	ALS	PUL	unpublished
24 August [1929]	Evan Shipman	ALS	Channick	unpublished
24 August [1929]	Charles Brackett	ALS	JFK	unpublished
28 August [1929]	Maxwell Perkins	AL	PUL	*SL, TOTTC*
[c. late August 1929]	Maxwell Perkins	ALFragS	PUL	*TOTTC*, Bruccoli *Sons*
29 August [1929]	Waldo Peirce	ALS	Colby	unpublished
4 September 1929	F. Scott Fitzgerald	ALS	PUL	*SL*, Bruccoli *Fitz–Hem*
4 September [1929]	John Dos Passos	ALS	UVA	*SL*
[c. 4 September 1929]	Charles Thompson	ALS	USCar	unpublished
7 September 1929	Maxwell Perkins	Cable	PUL	*TOTTC*
9 September [1929]	Maxwell Perkins	ALS	PUL	unpublished
9 September [1929]	William D. and Frances Horne	ALS	PUL	unpublished
13 September [1929]	F. Scott Fitzgerald	ALS	PUL	*SL*, Bruccoli *Fitz–Hem*
14 September [1929]	Paul Johnston	ALS	JFK	unpublished
14 and 15 September [1929]	Madelaine Hemingway	ALS	PSU	unpublished
15 September [1929]	Madelaine Hemingway	ALS	PSU	unpublished
[c. 16 September 1929]	Virginia Pfeiffer	ALS	JFK	unpublished

Date of Correspondence	Recipient	Form	Location of Source Text	Previous Publication
27 September [1929]	Maxwell Perkins	TL/ALS	PUL	unpublished
27 September [1929]	Maxwell Perkins	TLS	PUL	unpublished
[c. late September 1929]	James Joyce	Inscription	SUNYB	unpublished
[c. late September 1929]	Guy Hickok	Inscription	Sotheby's catalog	unpublished
[1 October 1929]	Arthur Hawkins	LS [excerpt]	University Archives catalog	unpublished
3 October [1929]	Maxwell Perkins	ALS	JFK	*TOTTC*
4 October 1929	Maxwell Perkins	ALS	PUL	unpublished
4 October 1929	Mr. Feldheym	ALS	William Doyle Galleries catalog	unpublished
[c. early October 1929]	Carol Hemingway	ALS	JFK	*SL*
5 October 1929	Maxwell Perkins	ALS	PUL	unpublished
12 October [1929]	Grace Hall Hemingway	ALS	PSU	unpublished
15 October 1929	Maxwell Perkins	Cable	PUL	unpublished
16 October 1929	Hugh Walpole	ALS	NYPL–Berg	unpublished
19 October 1929	Cyril Hume	ALS [excerpt]	Christie's catalog	unpublished
19 October 1929	Mrs. Jamar	ALS	UMD	unpublished
20–21 October 1929	Maxwell Perkins	ALS	PUL	unpublished
[21] October [1929]	Maxwell Perkins	TLS	PUL	unpublished
[c. 21 October 1929]	Maxwell Perkins	Cable	PUL	unpublished
21 October 1929	James Aswell	ALS	NWSU	unpublished
[c. 21 October 1929]	Ivan Goll	ACD	JFK	unpublished
[c. 22 October 1929]	Charles and Lorine Thompson	ALS	Profiles in History catalog	unpublished
25 October [1929]	Maxwell Perkins	ALS	PUL	unpublished
25 October 1929	Laurence Pollinger	ALS	PUL	unpublished

Date of Correspondence	Recipient	Form	Location of Source Text	Previous Publication
[25 October 1929]	Ernst Rowohlt	TCD with typewritten signature	JFK	unpublished
28 October 1929	R. P. Blackmur	ALS	PUL	unpublished
28 October 1929	Anton Gud	ALS	phPUL	unpublished
28 October 1929	Jeanette Mills Littell	ALS	Smith	unpublished
28 October 1929	George Frederick Wilson	ALS	Knox	unpublished
31 October 1929	Robert Bridges	ALS	PUL	unpublished
31 October 1929	Maxwell Perkins	ALS	PUL	*SL*
31 October [1929]	Owen Wister	AL	JFK	unpublished
[c. 31 October 1929]	Isabelle Simmons Godolphin	ALS	phPUL	unpublished
[c. late October 1929]	H. Lawrence Lack, Jr.	AL	JFK	unpublished
[c. late October 1929]	Gustavus A. Pfeiffer	ACDS	JFK	unpublished
5 November 1929	Bernard C. Schoenfeld	ALS	Knox	*SL*
8 November 1929	Maxwell Perkins	Cable	PUL	unpublished
10 November [1929]	Maxwell Perkins	ALS	JFK	*TOTTC*
16 November 1929	Maxwell Perkins	Cable	PUL	unpublished
[c. 16 November 1929]	F. Scott Fitzgerald	ALS	PUL	Bruccoli *Fitz–Hem*
[c. 17 November 1929]	Waldo Peirce	ALS	Colby	unpublished
17 November [1929]	Maxwell Perkins	AL	JFK	*TOTTC*
19 November [1929]	Maxwell Perkins	ALS	PUL	*TOTTC*
19 November [1929]	Grace Hall Hemingway	ALS	IndU	unpublished
19 November [1929]	Madelaine Hemingway	ALS	PSU	unpublished
[19 November 1929]	Charles Thompson	ALS [excerpt]	Christie's catalog	unpublished

Date of Correspondence	Recipient	Form	Location of Source Text	Previous Publication
20 November [1929]	Maxwell Perkins	ALS	PUL	*TOTTC*
21 November [1929]	Lawrence Drake	ALS	Stanford	unpublished
[c. 24 November 1929]	F. Scott Fitzgerald	ALS	PUL	*SL*, Bruccoli *Fitz-Hem*
26 November [1929]	George Slocombe	ALS	PUL	unpublished
[c. 28 November 1929]	F. Scott Fitzgerald	ALS	PUL	*SL*, Bruccoli *Fitz-Hem*
30 November [1929]	Maxwell Perkins	ALS	PUL	unpublished
30 November [1929]	Maxwell Perkins	ALS	PUL	*TOTTC*, Bruccoli *Sons*
30 November [1929]	Louise Lafitte	AL	JFK	unpublished
30 November [1929]	Struthers Burt	ALS	Penn	unpublished
1 December 1929	Archibald MacLeish	ALS	LOC	unpublished
1 December 1929	Jewell Stevens	ALS with enclosed inscription	SIU	unpublished
[1 December 1929]	Mrs. Wolfenstein	ALS	University Archives catalog	unpublished
1 December 1929	Irma Sompayrac Willard	ALS	NWSU	unpublished
2 December [1929]	Barklie McKee Henry	ALS	PUL	unpublished
2 December [1929]	George Yohalem	ALS	Mills	unpublished
[3 December 1929]	Christian Gauss	ALS	PUL	unpublished
[8–10 December 1929]	Maxwell Perkins	ALDS Frags	JFK	*TOTTC*
[8]-10 December [1929]	Maxwell Perkins	ALS	PUL	*TOTTC*, Bruccoli *Sons*
10 December [1929]	Hugh Walpole	ALS	NYPL–Berg	unpublished
10 December [1929]	David Garnett	ALS	UT	unpublished
10 December [1929]	Grace Hall Hemingway	ALS	PSU	unpublished
10 December 1929	Edward Verrall Lucas	ALS	UT	unpublished

Date of Correspondence	Recipient	Form	Location of Source Text	Previous Publication
11 December 1929	Maxwell Perkins	Cable	PUL	unpublished
[12 December 1929]	F. Scott Fitzgerald	ALS	PUL	*SL*, Bruccoli *Fitz–Hem*
15 December [1929]	Maxwell Perkins	ALS	PUL	*SL, TOTTC*
19 December 1929	Maxwell Perkins	Cable	PUL	unpublished
30 December [1929]	Gilbert Seldes	ALS	phPUL	*SL*
30 December 1929	Alan Devoe	ALS	PSU	unpublished
31 December [1929]	Archibald MacLeish	ALS	LOC	unpublished
[c. 3 January 1930]	F. Scott Fitzgerald	ALS	PUL	*SL*, Bruccoli *Fitz–Hem*
4 January [1930]	Morley Callaghan	ALScc	PUL	*SL*, Bruccoli *Fitz–Hem*
4 January [1930]	Maxwell Perkins	ALS	PUL	unpublished
4 January 1930	Bennett Cerf	ALS	Columbia	unpublished
4 January [1930]	Edward Titus	ALS	UT	unpublished
[6 January 1930]	Grace Hall Hemingway	ALS	DPL	unpublished
8 January 1930	Maxwell Perkins	Cable	PUL	unpublished
[c. 8 January 1930]	Guy Hickok	ALS	phPUL	unpublished
10 January [1930]	Maxwell Perkins	ALS	PUL	*TOTTC*
27 January [1930]	Grace Hall Hemingway	ALS	PSU	unpublished
[c. 28 January 1930]	Maxwell Perkins	ALS	PUL	unpublished
30 January 1930	Mildred D. Giraud	Inscription	Bookbid listing	unpublished
[4 February 1930]	Robert de Saint Jean	ALS	RR Auction catalog	unpublished
7 February [1930]	Waldo Peirce	ALS	Colby	unpublished
[7] February [1930]	Maxwell Perkins	ALS	PUL	unpublished
8 February 1930	Jonathan Cape	ALS	URead	unpublished
[10 February 1930]	Milford Baker	ALS	PUL	unpublished
[12 February 1930]	Archibald MacLeish	ALS	LOC	unpublished
[12 February 1930]	Milton Leidner	ALS	Karpeles	unpublished

Date of Correspondence	Recipient	Form	Location of Source Text	Previous Publication
18 February 1930	Ernst Rowohlt	TLS	phDLA	Ledig-Rowohlt
18 February [1930]	Henry Strater	ALS	PUL	unpublished
18 February 1930	William D. and Frances Horne	ALS	Newberry	unpublished
19 February 1930	Grace Hall Hemingway	AL/TLS with autograph postscript	PSU	unpublished
21 February [1930]	Morley Callaghan	TLS	phMason	unpublished
28 February [1930]	Maxwell Perkins	ALS	PUL	unpublished
28 February [1930]	Ezra Pound	ALS	Yale	unpublished
10 March [1930]	Grace Hall Hemingway	TLS	PSU	unpublished
[10 March 1930]	Carol Hemingway	TLS [excerpt]	Herman Darvick catalog	unpublished
10 March 1930	Henry Luce	TLS	Weinberg	unpublished
10 March [1930]	Maxwell Perkins	TLS	PUL	unpublished
14 March 1930	Milford Baker	TLS	PUL	unpublished
16 March [1930]	Otto Barnett	ALS	JFK	unpublished
17 March [1930]	Gustavus A. Pfeiffer	ALS	JFK	unpublished
17 March [1930]	Grace Hall Hemingway	ALS	PSU	unpublished
30 March 1930	Pauline Pfeiffer Hemingway	Cable	JFK	unpublished
5 April 1930	Milford Baker	TLS	PUL	unpublished
6 April 1930	Georgia Lingafelt	ALS	Private Collection	unpublished
6 April 1930	Laurence Stallings	ALS	Wake Forest	unpublished
6 April [1930]	Waldo Peirce	ALS	Colby	unpublished
6 April 1930	Cyril Clemens	ALS	MHM	*Mark Twain Journal* (Summer 1962)
8 April 1930	Milford Baker	ALS	PUL	unpublished

Date of Correspondence	Recipient	Form	Location of Source Text	Previous Publication
[c. 11 April 1930]	Maxwell Perkins	ALS	PUL	*SL, TOTTC*
15 April [1930]	Milford Baker	ALS	PUL	unpublished
15 April [1930]	Henry Strater	ALS	PUL	unpublished
23 April [1930]	Louis Henry Cohn	ALS	UDel	unpublished
23 April [1930]	Paul and Mary Pfeiffer	ALS	PUL	unpublished
23 April [1930]	Laurence Stallings	ALS	Wake Forest	unpublished
[c. 24 April 1930]	Maxwell Perkins	ALS	PUL	unpublished
[c. 25 April 1930]	Guy Hickok	TLS with autograph postscript	phPUL	unpublished
[c. 25 April 1930]	Editor of the *New York World*	TLS	JFK	unpublished
April 1930	Jefferson B. Browne	Inscription	PBA Galleries catalog	unpublished
5 May [1930]	Milford Baker	ALS	PUL	unpublished
7 May [1930]	Maurice-Edgar Coindreau	Letter [transcription]	PUL	unpublished
9 May [1930]	Waldo Peirce	TLS	Colby	unpublished
[c. 10 May 1930]	Maxwell Perkins	ALS	PUL	unpublished
12 May 1930	Maurice-Edgar Coindreau	Letter [transcription]	PUL	unpublished
[c. 12–17 May 1930]	John Herrmann	ALS	UT	unpublished
16 May [1930]	Waldo Peirce	ALS	Colby	unpublished
17 May [1930]	Milford Baker	TLS	PUL	unpublished
[c. mid-May 1930]	Guy Hickok	ALS	phPUL	unpublished
20 May [1930]	Henry Strater	TLS	PUL	*SL*
22 May [1930]	Maxwell Perkins	ALS	PUL	unpublished
27 May [1930]	Maxwell Perkins	ALS	PUL	unpublished
31 May [1930]	Maxwell Perkins	ALS	PUL	*SL*
[c. late May-early June 1930]	John Herrmann	ALS	UT	unpublished

Date of Correspondence	Recipient	Form	Location of Source Text	Previous Publication
1 June [1930]	William D. Horne, Jr.	ALS	PUL	unpublished
[2] June 1930	Waldo Peirce	ALS	Colby	unpublished
2 June [1930]	Maxwell Perkins	ALS	PUL	unpublished
2 June 1930	Giles P. Greene	ALS	USCar	unpublished
[3 June 1930]	Evan Shipman	ALS	Channick	unpublished
8 June [1930]	Archibald MacLeish	ALS	LOC	unpublished
[c. 8 June 1930]	Allen Tate	ALS	PUL	unpublished
[8 June 1930]	Guy Hickok	ALS	phPUL	unpublished
[c. 12 June 1930]	Henry Strater	ALS	PUL	*SL*
[13 June 1930]	John Herrmann	ALS	PUL	unpublished
[14 June 1930]	Charles Thompson	ALS [excerpt]	Christie's catalog	unpublished
20 June 1930	Milford Baker	Cable	PUL	unpublished
24 June [1930]	Louis Henry Cohn	ALS with AN and TN questionnaire responses	UDel	unpublished
[30 June 1930]	Milford Baker	ALS	PUL	unpublished
30 June [1930]	Archibald MacLeish	ALS	LOC	*SL*
1 July 1930	Jonathan Cape	ALS	URead	unpublished
10 July 1930	Maxwell Perkins	Cable	PUL	unpublished
14 July 1930	Maxwell Perkins	Cable	PUL	unpublished
[21 July 1930]	Milford Baker	ALS	PUL	unpublished
24 July [1930]	Maxwell Perkins	ALS	PUL	unpublished
29 July [1930]	Louis Henry Cohn	ALS and TN questionnaire responses	UDel	unpublished
[c. late July 1930]	Waldo Peirce	ALS	Colby	unpublished
31 July 1930	Maxwell Perkins	ALS	PUL	unpublished
31 July [1930]	Frieda Inescort Redman	Letter [transcription]	PUL	unpublished
6 August 1930	Maxwell Perkins	Cable	PUL	unpublished

Date of Correspondence	Recipient	Form	Location of Source Text	Previous Publication
[early to mid-August 1930]	Hemingway Family	ALS	PSU	unpublished
12 August [1930]	Maxwell Perkins	ALS	PUL	*SL, TOTTC*
12 August [1930]	Milford Baker	ALS	PUL	unpublished
[c. early to mid-August 1930]	Archibald MacLeish	ALS	LOC	unpublished
[25 August 1930]	Henry Strater	A Postcard S	PUL	unpublished
[c. 31 August 1930]	John Herrmann	ALS	UT	unpublished
[c. 31 August 1930]	Archibald MacLeish	ALS	LOC	unpublished
3 September [1930]	Maxwell Perkins	ALS	PUL	*TOTTC*
[3] September [1930]	Louis Henry Cohn	ALS	UDel	unpublished
[c. 3–4 September 1930]	Henry Strater	ALS	PUL	*SL*
10 September 1930	Milford Baker	Cable	PUL	unpublished
12 September [1930]	Jonathan Cape	ALS	URead	unpublished
12 September [1930]	Milford Baker	ALS	PUL	unpublished
12 September [1930]	William D. and Frances Horne	ALS	Newberry	unpublished
28 September [1930]	John Herrmann	ALS	UT	unpublished
28 September [1930]	Maxwell Perkins	ALS	PUL	unpublished
29 September 1930	Maxwell Perkins	Cable	PUL	unpublished
[c. early October 1930]	John Hemingway	ANS	JFK	unpublished
2 October [1930]	Milford Baker	ALS	PUL	unpublished
2 October [1930]	Grace Hall Hemingway	ALS	PSU	unpublished
3 October 1930	Maxwell Perkins	Cable	PUL	unpublished
6 October [1930]	Archibald MacLeish	ALS	LOC	unpublished
6 October [1930]	Madelaine Hemingway	ALS	PSU	unpublished
6 October [1930]	Grace Hall Hemingway	ALS	PSU	unpublished

Date of Correspondence	Recipient	Form	Location of Source Text	Previous Publication
10 October 1930	Matthew Herold	ALS	OPPL	unpublished
[12 October 1930]	Maurice-Edgar Coindreau	Letter [transcription]	PUL	unpublished
12 October [1930]	Archibald MacLeish	ALS	LOC	unpublished
28 October [1930]	Maxwell Perkins	ALS	PUL	unpublished
28 October [1930]	Ford Madox Ford	ALS	Cornell	unpublished
28 October [1930]	Caresse Crosby	ALS	SIU	unpublished
[c. 28 October 1930]	Samuel Putnam	ALS	PUL	unpublished
28 October [1930]	Dorothy Connable	ALS	phPUL	unpublished
29 October 1930	Ray Long	ALS	SIU	unpublished
3 November 1930	Maxwell Perkins	Cable	PUL	unpublished
14 November 1930	Maxwell Perkins	Cable	PUL	unpublished
[c. mid-November 1930]	Henry Strater	TL [dictated] with ANS from Pauline	PUL	unpublished
17 November [1930]	Maxwell Perkins	TL with typewritten signature [dictated]	PUL	unpublished
20 November 1930	Maxwell Perkins	Cable	PUL	unpublished
[22 November 1930]	Archibald MacLeish	TL with typewritten signature [dictated]	LOC	*SL*
[22 November 1930]	Grace Hall Hemingway	TL with typewritten signature [dictated]	PSU	unpublished
23 November [1930]	William D. Horne, Jr.	TL with typewritten signature [dictated]	phPUL	unpublished
23 November 1930	Maxwell Perkins	Cable	PUL	unpublished

Date of Correspondence	Recipient	Form	Location of Source Text	Previous Publication
[c. 23 November 1930]	Henry Strater	TL with typewritten signature [dictated]	PUL	unpublished
[c. 27 November 1930]	Waldo Peirce	TL with typewritten signature [dictated] with ANS from Pauline	Colby	unpublished
30 November 1930	Ernst Rowohlt	TLS [dictated]	phDLA	Ledig-Rowohlt
1 December 1930	Maxwell Perkins	ALS [dictated] with AN from Pauline	PUL	*TOTTC*
[c. 2 December 1930]	Henry Strater	TL with typewritten signature [dictated] with ANS from Pauline	PUL	*SL*
[c. 4 December 1930]	Archibald MacLeish	TL with typewritten signature [dictated] with AN from Pauline	LOC	unpublished
5 December [1930]	Guy Hickok	TL with typewritten signature [dictated]	phPUL	*SL*
8 December 1930	Maxwell Perkins	Cable	PUL	*TOTTC*
8 December 1930	Louis Henry Cohn	Cable	UDel	unpublished
18 December 1930	Maxwell Perkins	Cable	PUL	unpublished
[19 December 1930]	Louis Henry Cohn	TL [dictated]	UDel	unpublished

Date of Correspondence	Recipient	Form	Location of Source Text	Previous Publication
26 December [1930]	Bennett Cerf	TL with typewritten signature [dictated]	Columbia	unpublished
26 December [1930]	William D. Horne, Jr.	TL with typewritten signature [dictated]	phPUL	unpublished
28 December [1930]	Maxwell Perkins	TL with typewritten signature [dictated]	PUL	*SL*
28 December [1930]	Archibald MacLeish	TL with typewritten signature [dictated]	LOC	unpublished
28 December [1930]	Donald Ogden Stewart	TL with typewritten signature [dictated]	Yale	unpublished
31 December [1930]	Maurice-Edgar Coindreau	Letter [transcription]	PUL	unpublished
31 December 1930	Mr. Small	TLS with autograph postscript	Clean Sweep Auctions catalog	unpublished
[c. late December 1930–January 1931]	Don Carlos Guffey	Inscription	UMKC	unpublished
1 January 1931	Maurice-Edgar Coindreau	Inscription [transcription] and typewritten notes	PUL	unpublished
1 January [1931]	Karl Pfeiffer	TLcc with typewritten signature [dictated]	Stanford	unpublished
1 January [1931]	Megan Laird	TL with typewritten signature	Comini	unpublished

Date of Correspondence	Recipient	Form	Location of Source Text	Previous Publication
[2 January 1931]	Louis Henry Cohn	TL with typewritten signature	UDel	unpublished
2 January [1931]	Henry Strater	TL with typewritten signature	PUL	unpublished
14 January [1931]	Archibald MacLeish	ALS	LOC	unpublished
15 January [1931]	Maxwell Perkins	TL with typewritten signature	PUL	unpublished
17 January [1931]	Waldo Peirce	TL with typewritten signature	Colby	unpublished
21 January [1931]	William Lengel	ALS	SIU	unpublished
21 January 1931	Ezra and Dorothy Pound	ALS	Yale	unpublished
28 January [1931]	Paul and Mary Pfeiffer	TL with typewritten signature	PUL	unpublished
26 December [1930]– [31 January 1931]	Owen Wister	TL [dictated] / ALS	LOC	unpublished
[31 January 1931]	Louis Henry Cohn	ALS	UDel	unpublished
5 February [1931]	Maxwell Perkins	TL with typewritten signature	PUL	unpublished
[c. 5 February 1931]	John Dos Passos	TL with typewritten signature	UVA	unpublished
[7 February 1931]	Donald Ogden Stewart	TL/ALS	Yale	unpublished
[c. 7 February 1931]	Patrick Morgan and Maud Cabot	Published copy of cable	Cabot	Cabot
[9 February 1931]	Evan Shipman	TL with typewritten signature [dictated]	Channick	unpublished

Date of Correspondence	Recipient	Form	Location of Source Text	Previous Publication
[c. 14 February 1931]	Henry Strater	TL with typewritten signature	PUL	unpublished
16 February [1931]	Evan Shipman	ALS	Channick	unpublished
[mid- to late February 1931]	Edward Titus	ALS	Karpeles	unpublished
21 February [1931]	Maxwell Perkins	Cable	PUL	unpublished
[26 February 1931]	Edgar Stanton	ALS [excerpt]	David Schulson Autographs listing	unpublished
12 March 1931	Maxwell Perkins	Cable	PUL	unpublished
14 March [1931]	Archibald MacLeish	ALS	LOC	*SL*
16 March [1931]	Maurice-Edgar Coindreau	Letter [transcription]	PUL	unpublished
16 March [1931]	Laurence Stallings	ALS	Wake Forest	unpublished
[20 March 1931]	Edward Titus	ALS [excerpt]	Christie's catalog	unpublished
[c. 25 March 1931]	Archibald MacLeish	ALS	LOC	unpublished
[26] March [1931]	William D. Horne, Jr.	ALS	PUL	unpublished
10 April [1931]	Laurence Stallings	TL/ALS	Wake Forest	unpublished
11 April [1931]	Evan Shipman	ALS	Channick	unpublished
12 April 1931	F. Scott Fitzgerald	ALS	PUL	*SL*, Bruccoli *Fitz-Hem*
12 April 1931	Don Carlos Guffey	ALS	phJFK	unpublished
12 April [1931]	Maxwell Perkins	ALS	PUL	unpublished
19 April [1931]	Archibald MacLeish	ALS	LOC	unpublished
27 April [1931]	Don Carlos Guffey	ALS	phJFK	unpublished

Date of Correspondence	Recipient	Form	Location of Source Text	Previous Publication
27 April [1931]	Maxwell Perkins	ALS	PUL	*TOTTC*
30 April 1931	Waldo and Alzira Peirce	Cable	Colby	unpublished
[1 May 1931]	Maxwell Perkins	ALS	PUL	unpublished
[c. 1 May 1931]	Henry Strater	ALS	PUL	unpublished
1 May [1931]	George Albee	ALS	UCalB	unpublished
4 May 1931	Ezra and Dorothy Pound	A Postcard S	Yale	unpublished
4 May [1931]	Waldo Peirce	ALS	Colby	*SL*
4 May 1931	Charles Thompson	ALS	Yoken	unpublished
4 May 1931	Frank McCoy	ALS	LOC	unpublished
6 May [1931]	Thornton Wilder	ALS	Yale	unpublished
7 May 1931	George Albee	ALS	UCalB	unpublished
7 May [1931]	Guy Hickok	ALS	Sotheby's catalog / Kotte Autographs catalog	unpublished
8 May [1931]	Cranston D. Raymond	ALS	Stanford	unpublished
13 May 1931	Mary Pfeiffer	ALS	PUL	unpublished
14 May [1931]	Waldo Peirce	ALS	Colby	unpublished
[c. 18 May 1931]	Pauline Pfeiffer Hemingway	ACDS	JFK	unpublished
15 June 1931	Maxwell Perkins	Cable	PUL	unpublished
16 June [1931]	Ezra Pound	ALS	Yale	unpublished
[17] June [1931]	Guy Hickok	ALS	phPUL	unpublished
26 June [1931]	John Dos Passos	ALS	UVA	*SL*
29 June [1931]	George Marton	ACDS	JFK	unpublished
29 June [1931]	Archibald MacLeish	ALS	LOC	unpublished
29 June 1931	Edward Saunders	Letter [transcription]	phPUL	*SL*
2 July 1931	Maxwell Perkins	ALS	PUL	unpublished
15 July [1931]	Guy Hickok	ALS	phPUL	unpublished

Date of Correspondence	Recipient	Form	Location of Source Text	Previous Publication
15 July [1931]	Henry Strater	ALS	PUL	unpublished
22 July [1931]	Caresse Crosby	ALS	SIU	unpublished
22 July [1931]	Maurice Speiser	ALS	USCar	unpublished
28 July [1931]	Archibald MacLeish	ALS	LOC	unpublished
1 August [1931]	Maxwell Perkins	ALS	PUL	unpublished
[9 August 1931]	Caresse Crosby	ALS	SIU	Crosby
14 August 1931	Maxwell Perkins	ALS	PUL	unpublished
[c. 14–15 August 1931]	Maurice Speiser	ALS	USCar	unpublished
[c. 14–15 August 1931]	Henry Strater	ALS	PUL	unpublished
15 August [1931]	Earl Shelton	ALS	Charles Hamilton catalog	Bruccoli and Clark *Auction*
[c. 18 August 1931]	Maurice Speiser	ALS	USCar	unpublished
[18 August 1931]	Hadley Hemingway	A Postcard S	JFK	unpublished
23 August 1931	Grace Hall Hemingway	ALS	IndU	unpublished
24 August [1931]	Grace Hall Hemingway	ALS	IndU	unpublished
25 August [1931]	Caresse Crosby	ALS	SIU	unpublished
31 August [1931]	Archibald MacLeish	ALS	LOC	unpublished
31 August 1931	Paul and Mary Pfeiffer	ALS	PUL	unpublished
31 August [1931]	Maurice Speiser	ALS	USCar	unpublished
[c. 31 August 1931]	Charles Thompson	ALFragS	Di Silvestro	unpublished
[7] September 1931	Guy Hickok	ALS	phPUL	unpublished
14 September 1931	Maxwell Perkins	Cable	PUL	unpublished
23 September [1931]	Caresse Crosby	ALS	SIU	unpublished
[23 September 1931]	Caresse Crosby	ALS	SIU	unpublished
[23 September 1931]	Sylvia Beach	ALS	PUL	unpublished

Date of Correspondence	Recipient	Form	Location of Source Text	Previous Publication
2 October 1931	Edward Saunders	ALS	KWAHS	unpublished
5 October 1931	Waldo Peirce	Cable	Colby	unpublished
[c. 5 October 1931]	Richard Simon	ANS	Swann Galleries catalog	unpublished
[10 October 1931]	Eric Knight	ALS	USCar	unpublished
[12 October 1931]	Maurice Speiser	ALS	USCar	unpublished
14 October 1931	Maxwell Perkins	ALS	PUL	unpublished
[14 October 1931]	Charles MacGregor	ALS	Fritch	unpublished
16 October 1931	Maxwell Perkins	Cable	PUL	unpublished
[18 October 1931]	John Herrmann and Josephine Herbst	ALS	Yale	unpublished
[19 October 1931]	Maxwell Perkins	ALS	PUL	unpublished
[19] October [1931]	Maurice Speiser	ALS	USCar	unpublished
[c. 19 October 1931]	Caresse Crosby	ACDS	RR Auction catalog	unpublished
19 October 1931	Caresse Crosby	Cable	SIU	unpublished
[c. 19 October 1931]	Eric Knight	TL/ALS	USCar	unpublished
[c. late October 1931]	Eric Knight	Inscription	Christie's catalog	unpublished
[c. late October 1931]	Eric Knight	Inscription	Christie's catalog	unpublished
26 October 1931	Harry Marks	TLS	Stanford	unpublished
[c. late October–early November 1931]	Waldo Peirce	TLS	Colby	*SL*
3 November [1931]	Charles MacGregor	ALS	Fritch	unpublished
12 November 1931	Paul Pfeiffer	Cable	PUL	unpublished
12 November 1931	Grace Hall Hemingway	Cable	JFK	unpublished
12 November [1931]	Mary Pfeiffer	ALS	PUL	unpublished
13 November 1931	Maurice and Martha Speiser	Cable	USCar	unpublished

Date of Correspondence	Recipient	Form	Location of Source Text	Previous Publication
[13 November 1931]	Louis Henry Cohn	ALS	UDel	unpublished
14 November [1931]	Paul Pfeiffer	Cable	PUL	unpublished
[c. 16 November 1931]	Charles MacGregor	ALS	Fritch	unpublished
[16 November 1931]	Mary Pfeiffer	ALS	PUL	unpublished
17 November 1931	Waldo Peirce	Cable	Colby	unpublished
[c. 20 November 1931]	Maxwell Perkins	ALS	PUL	unpublished
[22 November 1931]	Paul and Mary Pfeiffer	ALS	PUL	unpublished
[23 November 1931]	Maurice Speiser	ALS	USCar	unpublished
25 November 1931	Paul and Mary Pfeiffer	ACDS	UT	unpublished
30 November 1931	Paul and Mary Pfeiffer	ACDS	UT	unpublished
[c. late November 1931]	Karl Pfeiffer	ACDS	UT	unpublished
[c. 3–4 December 1931]	Jonathan Cape	ALS	URead	unpublished
9 December [1931]	Archibald MacLeish	ALS	LOC	unpublished
9 December [1931]	Maxwell Perkins	ALS	PUL	unpublished
9 December [1931]	Paul Romaine	ALS	USCar	*SL*
9 December [1931]	Israel Bram	ALS	CPP	unpublished
9 December [1931]	Mr. Turner	ALS	PUL	unpublished
[c. 9 December 1931]	Ray Long	Published excerpt of letter	Long	Long
10 December [1931]	Henry Strater	ALS	PUL	*SL*
12 December [1931]	Guy Hickok	TLS	phPUL	unpublished
13 December [1931]	Eric Knight	ALS	USCar	unpublished
20 December [1931]	Grace Hall, Madelaine, and Leicester Hemingway	ALS	HSOPRF	Elder, Vetch, and Cirino

Date of Correspondence	Recipient	Form	Location of Source Text	Previous Publication
20 December [1931]	Marcelline Hemingway Sanford	ALS	James Sanford	Sanford
22 [December 1931]	Archibald MacLeish	Cable	LOC	unpublished
23 December [1931]	Archibald MacLeish	TLS with autograph postscript and enclosures	LOC/UVA	unpublished
26 December [1931]	Maxwell Perkins	AL/TLS	PUL	*SL*
[c. November 1931]	Logan Clendening	Inscription	Sotheby's catalog	unpublished
[c. late 1931]	Louis Henry Cohn	Inscription	RR Auction catalog	unpublished
[c. late 1931]	Don Carlos Guffey	Inscription	Sotheby Parke Bernet catalog	Trogdon *Reference*
[c. late 1931]	Don Carlos Guffey	Inscription	Printers Row listing	unpublished
[c. late 1931]	Don Carlos Guffey	*Inscription*	Parke-Bernet Galleries	Bruccoli and Clark *Auction*
[c. late 1931]	Don Carlos Guffey	Inscription	Parke-Bernet Galleries catalog	Bruccoli and Clark *Auction*, Trogdon *Reference, SL*, Norman
[c. late 1931]	Don Carlos Guffey	Inscription	Sotheby's catalog	unpublished
[c. late September 1929 or after]	Don Carlos Guffey	Inscription	Sotheby Parke Bernet catalog	Trogdon *Reference*
[late October 1930 or after]	Joan Whitney	Inscription	William Doyle Galleries catalog	unpublished

INDEX OF RECIPIENTS

In this index of recipients, only the first page of each letter is cited. Letters to more than one person are indexed under each name and marked †.

GENERAL INDEX

References to works by Ernest Hemingway appear under his name. Literary and theatrical works by others appear alphabetically by the title of the work, as well as under the author's name. Paintings and musical works appear under the artist's name only. Newspapers, magazines, and films are alphabetized by title. Indexed references to automobiles (owned by EH), boxers, bullfighters, guns (brands, manufacturers, and sellers), racehorses, ships (including boats and shipping companies), and trains and railroads are consolidated under those categorical headings. All biblical references are gathered under "Bible." References to localities within a particular city (hotels, restaurants, bars, bookstores, churches, schools, museums, monuments, and other sites) appear as final subentries under the name of the city.

Persons are listed according to the names by which they are primarily known in the context of this volume, including married names, professional names, and pseudonyms. When necessary for clarity, maiden names and nicknames are indexed alphabetically with a *See* reference to the name under which page references to that person appear. Spanish names are alphabetized by the paternal surname, which generally appears next to last in the sequence of a full formal name and is followed by the maternal surname (which is often dropped in common usage); for example, the matador Rafael Gómez Ortega is listed under "bullfighters" as "Gómez Ortega, Rafael."

In addition to appearing in the "Index of Recipients," the letters in this volume are indexed here as well, listed under the recipient's name and the subentry "EH letters to." Only the first page of each letter is cited.